T0135250

Lecture Notes in Computer Science   13184

More information about this series at https://link.springer.com/bookseries/558

Jong-Hoon Kim · Madhusudan Singh ·
Javed Khan · Uma Shanker Tiwary ·
Marigankar Sur · Dhananjay Singh (Eds.)

Intelligent Human Computer Interaction

13th International Conference, IHCI 2021
Kent, OH, USA, December 20–22, 2021
Revised Selected Papers

Springer

Editors
Jong-Hoon Kim 🆔
Kent State University
Kent, OH, USA

Javed Khan
Kent State University
Kent, OH, USA

Marigankar Sur 🆔
Massachusetts Institute of Technology
Cambridge, MA, USA

Madhusudan Singh 🆔
University of Tartu
Tartu, Estonia

Uma Shanker Tiwary 🆔
Indian Institute of Information Technology
Allahabad, India

Dhananjay Singh 🆔
Hankuk University of Foreign Studies
Seoul, Korea (Republic of)

ISSN 0302-9743   ISSN 1611-3349 (electronic)
Lecture Notes in Computer Science
ISBN 978-3-030-98403-8   ISBN 978-3-030-98404-5 (eBook)
https://doi.org/10.1007/978-3-030-98404-5

This Springer imprint is published by the registered company Springer Nature Switzerland AG
The registered company address is: Gewerbestrasse 11, 6330 Cham, Switzerland

Preface

The science and technology of Human Computer Interaction (HCI) has taken a giant leap forward in the last few years. This has given impetus to two opposing trends. One divergent trend is to organize separate conferences on focused topics such as 'Interaction Design and User-Centered Design', etc., which earlier would have been covered under HCI. The other convergent trend is to assimilate new areas into HCI conferences, such as 'Computing with Words', 'Prosocial Agents Development', and 'Attention-based Applications', etc. IHCI is one of the rare conferences focusing on issues of 'Intelligence' and 'Human Computer Interaction' which exist at the crossroads of the above-mentioned trends.

It is a privilege to present the proceedings of the 13th International Conference on Intelligent Human Computer Interaction (IHCI 2021) organized by Kent State University and held during December 20–22, 2021, at the Design Innovation Hub at Kent State University, Ohio, USA. IHCI is an annual international conference in the Human Computer Interaction field where we explore research challenges emerging in the complex interaction between machine intelligence and human intelligence. This year's event had a theme of "Intelligent Interaction beyond Physical Limits", having 12 special tracks related to the main theme of the conference as well as general topics in the IHCI fields.

Out of 142 submitted papers, 68 papers were accepted for oral presentation and publication by the Technical Program Committee (TPC) based on the recommendations of at least three expert reviewers per paper. The proceedings are organized in nine sections corresponding to each track of the conference. The 13th IHCI conference included five keynote speakers and ten invited talks with 29 powerful expert session chairs and six forum organizers, who have worked in both industry and academia, to attract more than 200 participants, emerging as the foremost worldwide (more than 22 countries) gathering of academic researchers, graduate students, top research think tanks, and industry technology developers in this area. Therefore, we do believe that the biggest benefit to participants is the actualization of their goals in the field of HCI. This will ultimately lead to greater success in business, which is ultimately beneficial to society.

Our warm gratitude goes to all the authors who submitted their work to IHCI 2021. During the submission, review, and editing stages, the EasyChair conference system proved very helpful. We are grateful to the TPC and local organizing committee for their immeasurable efforts to ensure the success of this conference. Finally, we would like to thank our speakers, authors, and participants for their contribution in making IHCI 2021 a stimulating and productive conference. This IHCI conference series cannot achieve yearly milestones without their continued support in future.

December 2021

Jong-Hoon Kim
Dhananjay Singh
Madhusudan Singh
Javed Khan
Uma Shanker Tiwary

Organization

General Chairs

Javed Khan	Kent State University, USA
Marigankar Sur	Massachusetts Institute of Technology, USA

Technical Program Chairs

Jong-Hoon Kim	Kent State University, USA
Madhusudan Singh	Woosong University, South Korea
Javed Khan	Kent State University, USA
Uma Shanker Tiwary	IIIT Allahabad, India
Marigankar Sur	Massachusetts Institute of Technology, USA
Dhananjay Singh	Hankuk University of Foreign Studies, South Korea

Steering Committee

Uma Shanker Tiwary	IIIT Allahabad, India
Santanu Chaudhury	IIT Jodhpur, India
Tom D. Gedeon	Australian National University, Australia
Debasis Samanta	IIT Kharagpur, India
Atanendu Sekhar Mandal	CSIR-CEERI, Pilani, India
Tanveer Siddiqui	University of Allahabad, India
Jaroslav Pokorny	Charles University, Czech Republic
Sukhendu Das	IIT Madras, India
Samit Bhattacharya	IIT Guwahati, India
Wan-Young Chung	Pukyong National University, South Korea
Dhananjay Singh	Hankuk University of Foreign Studies, South Korea

Session Chairs

Uma Shanker Tiwary	IIIT Allahabad, India
Madhusudan Singh	Woosong University, South Korea
Suzana Brown	State University of New York, South Korea
Mark D. Whitaker	State University of New York, South Korea
Arvind W. Kiwelekar	Dr. Babasaheb Ambedkar Technological University, India

Julio Ariel Hurtado Alegria   University of Cauca, Colombia
Roopak Tamboli   Saarland University, Germany
Mohd Helmy Abd Wahab   Universiti Tun Hussein Onn, Malaysia
Masoud Mohammadian   University of Canberra, Australia
Eui-Chul Lee   Sangmyung University, Korea
Jee Hang Lee   Sangmyung University, Korea
Hakimjon Zaynidinov   Tashkent University of IT, Uzbekistan
Elmira Nazirova   Tashkent University of IT, Uzbekistan
Ibrohimbek Yusupov   Tashkent University of IT, Uzbekistan
Sarvarbek Makhmudjanov   Tashkent University of IT, Uzbekistan
Jong-Ha Lee   Keimyung University, South Korea
Byoung Chul Ko   Keimyung University, South Korea
Shyam Perugu   NIT Warangal, India
Preethi Ananthachari   Woosong University, South Korea
Gaurav Tripathi   Bharat Electronics Limited, India
Irish Singh   Ajou University, South Korea
Surya Kanth V. Gangasetty   KL University, India
Nagamani Molakatala   University of Hyderabad, India
David (Bong Jun) Choi   Soongsil University, South Korea
Hanumant Singh Shekhawat   IIT Guwahati, India
Dhananjay Singh   Hankuk University of Foreign Studies, South Korea

Nagarajan Prabakar   Florida International University, USA
Elena Novak   Kent State University, USA
Jong-Hoon Kim   Kent State University, USA

Publicity Chair

Wan Young Chung   Pukyoung National University, South Korea

Local Chair

Gokarna Sharma   Kent State University, USA

Event Chair

J. R. Campbell   Kent State University, USA

Industry Forum Chairs

Austin Melton   Kent State University, USA
Gokarna Sharma   Kent State University, USA

Student Forum Chairs

Jonathan I. Maletic	Kent State University, USA
Micheal Collard	University of Akron, USA

Organizing Chair

Jong-Hoon Kim	Kent State University, USA

Local Arrangement Committee

Jong-Hoon Kim	Kent State University, USA
Gokarna Sharma	Kent State University, USA
J. R. Campbell	Kent State University, USA
Xiang Lian	Kent State University, USA
Qiang Guan	Kent State University, USA
Jungyoon Kim	Kent State University, USA
Younghun Chae	Kent State University, USA
Jakyung Seo	Kent State University, USA
Angela Guercio	Kent State University, USA
Lauren Copeland	Kent State University, USA
Jonathan Maletic	Kent State University, USA
Seon Jeong "Ally" Lee	Kent State University, USA
Rui Liu	Kent State University, USA

Technical Program Committee

Azizuddin Khan	IIT Bombay, India
Dae-Ki Kang	Dongseo University, South Korea
Dhananjay Singh	Hankuk University of Foreign Studies, South Korea
Gokarna Sharma	Kent State University, USA
Young Jin Jung	Dongseo University, South Korea
Srivathsan Srinivasagopalan	AT&T, USA
Yongseok Chi	Dongseo University, South Korea
Rajesh Sankaran	Argonne National Laboratory, USA
Jungyoon Kim	Kent State University, USA
Younghoon Chae	Kent State University, USA
Ayan Dutta	University of North Florida, USA
Jangwoon Park	Texas A&M University, USA
Slim Rekhis	University of Carthage, Tunisia
Noureddine Boudriga	University of Carthage, Tunisia
Kambiz Ghaginour	State University of New York, USA

Neeraj Parolia	Towson University, USA
Stella Tomasi	Towson University, USA
Marcelo Marciszack	National University of Technology, Argentina
Andres Adolfo Navarro Newball	Pontificia Universidad Javeriana, Colombia
Indranath Chatterjee	Tongmyong University, South Korea
Gaurav Tripathi	Bharat Electronics Limited, India
Bernardo Nugroho Yahya	Hankuk University of Foreign Studies, South Korea
Carlene Campbell	University of Wales Trinity Saint David, UK
Himanshu Chaudhary	University of Gothenburg, Sweden
Rajiv Mishra	iOligos Technologies, India
Rakesh Pandey	Banaras Hindu University, India
Anwar Alluwari	Stevens Institute of Technology, USA
Sayed Chhattan Shah	Hankuk University of Foreign Studies, South Korea
Rajesh Mishra	Gautam Buddha University, India
Akshay Bhardwaj	IIT Guwahati, India
Mario Divan	National University of La Pampa Santa Rosa, Argentina
Mina Choi	Kent State University, USA
Lauren Copeland	Kent State University, USA
Jaehyun Park	Incheon National University, South Korea
Hyun K. Kim	Kwangwoon University, South Korea

Keynote Speakers

Jonathan Lazar	University of Maryland, USA
Rajiv Jain	Adobe Research, USA
Brygg Ullmer	Clemson University, USA
Youngjin Yoo	Case Western Reserve University, USA
S. S. Iyengar	Florida International University, USA

Invited Speakers

D. V. K. Vasudcvan	University of Hyderabad, India
Rajesh Sankaran	Argonne National Laboratory, USA
Rodrigo da Rosa Righi	University of Vale do Rio dos Sinos (Unisinos), Brazil
Garima Bajpai	DevOps Institute, Canada
Ujwal Gadiraju	Delft University of Technology, The Netherlands
Prasad Onkar	IIT Hyderabad, India
Chakravarthy Bhagvati	University of Hyderabad, India
Jan-Willem van't Klooster	University of Twente, The Netherlands

Jay (Ju Yup) Lee   Youngstown State University, USA
Dimple Kaur   Applied Natya Therapy, USA

Contents

Intelligent Interaction and Cognitive Computing

Immersive and Tangible Interface

AI-Inspired Solutions

Human Centered AI

Machine Learning Techniques for Grading of PowerPoint Slides

Jyoti G. Borade[✉] and Laxman D. Netak

Dr. Babasaheb Ambedkar Technological University,
Lonere 402103, Raigad (MS), India
jyoti.borade81@gmail.com, ldnetak@dbatu.ac.in

Abstract. This paper describes the design and implementation of automated techniques for grading students' PowerPoint slides. Preparing PowerPoint slides for seminars, workshops, and conferences is one of the crucial activity of graduate and undergraduate students. Educational institutes use rubrics to assess the PowerPoint slides' quality on different grounds, such as the use of diagrams, text highlighting techniques, and animations. The proposed system describes a method and dataset designed to automate the task of grading students' PowerPoint slides. The system aims to evaluate students' knowledge about various functionalities provided by presentation software. Multiple machine learning techniques are used to grade presentations. Decision Tree classifiers gives 100% accuracy while predicting grade of PowerPoint presentation.

Keywords: Feature extraction · Automated grading · Decision Tree · Logistic regression · Support vector machine · K-means clustering · Naive Bayes classifier · Multi-layer perceptron

1 Introduction

Developing computer-based automated techniques for assessment is referred by multiple terms in the existing literature such as Automated Grading of Essays [1], Computer Automated Scoring [2], and simply Automated Scoring [3]. The use of machine learning [4] and NLP techniques [5] for this purpose is continuously increasing. These automated scoring techniques assess various skills such as essay writing, physician's patient management skills, dentistry assessment skills, and architects registration process [2]. Teachers spend a significant amount of time assessing students' performance in descriptive writings such as research papers [6], articles, thesis, reports, and PowerPoint presentations. Grading such kinds of essay work is challenging because it is time-intensive and susceptible to inconsistencies and inaccuracies on account of evaluators.

Creating and delivering a convincing presentation is an indispensable soft skill that is to be imparted during graduate programs. However, evaluating presentations is a challenging task because it is often a subjective assessment, needs to comply with institute-specific rubrics, and is a time-consuming mechanical

© Springer Nature Switzerland AG 2022
J.-H. Kim et al. (Eds.): IHCI 2021, LNCS 13184, pp. 3–15, 2022.
https://doi.org/10.1007/978-3-030-98404-5_1

activity. To overcome these challenges, we present the design of a data-driven approach to grade students' presentations. This approach is based on extracting the features that contribute in enhancing the quality of the presentation and grading it on presentation quality parameters and not on the content covered in the presentation. The task of grading a presentation based on content can be delegated to a human expert. The presentations are graded on two different parameters to simplify the grading. The first is based on presentation quality, and the second is on the accuracy and authenticity of the topics covered in the presentation. Our main objective is to focus and evaluate the efforts put by the students for preparing PowerPoint presentations.

Many researchers have developed techniques for automated grading of explanatory answers for various languages [7–11], programming codes, and research papers. These approaches use a combination of technologies to grade descriptive assignments. Automatic Grading of Essays (AGE) relies on Natural Language Processing (NLP) and Machine Learning (ML). The adoption of NLP [12–15] for AGE is driven by the motivation to handle linguistic issues such as multiple meanings of words in different contexts [16]. While machine learning techniques are employed to extract features and perform grading tasks. For example, one of the earliest approaches called Project Essay Grader(PEG) extracts a set of language-based features using NLP and uses multiple regression techniques to grade essays. Linguistic features can also be extracted using NLP and Deep learning approaches [17–20].

2   Challenges in Grading Students' Presentations

Grading students' PowerPoint presentations against a set of quality parameters involve checking the PowerPoint slides prepared by students with the norms set by an institute or criteria as expected in a professional presentation. With this view, when a teacher starts assessing the quality of presentations, the challenges faced by a teacher are numerous. Some of these are listed below.

1. **Lack of Systematic Assessment Methodology:** As observed in [21,22] assessment is usually subjective, driven by knowledge and experience of evaluators, and the mindset of evaluators (e.g., harsh vs lenient raters). The use of rubrics is often suggested to overcome this subjectivity in the assessment. However, many evaluators rely on their experience to grade the students' presentations instead of using predefined rubrics.
2. **Absence of Automated Approaches:** Creating and delivering the students' presentation is a compulsory activity included in most undergraduate post-graduate programs. Many educators think that judging the presentation quality is a time-consuming and routine activity. But, very few researchers have employed the advances in machine learning to automate the task of grading students' presentations.
3. **Absence of Standardized Dataset:** The development of data-driven and machine learning-based automated techniques depends on the availability of quality datasets.

4. **No Universal File Format for Presentation File:** Students create presentations using different sets of presentation software. This presentation software supports various file formats such as *ppt*, *pptx*, *odp*, *pdf*, which makes the development of automated techniques difficult, to extract features.
5. **Evolving functionalities in Presentation Software:** The presentation software such as $MicrosoftOffice$, $LibreOffice$, and $GoogleDocuments$ continuously add new functionalities and features. The students' presentations may be power-packed with graphical images, info-graphics, videos, hyperlinks, and more appropriated templates. Hence defining a comprehensive feature set becomes difficult.

One way to address these challenges is to define quality assessment criteria and adopt automated techniques to reduce the assessment process's subjectivity.

3 Methodology

A machine learning model is a mapping function f that transforms input data X into output data Y.

$$Y = f(X)$$

where X is an n-dimensional vector holding input data and is also known as input features. Building a machine learning model includes the following steps.

1. **Identification of Features and Data Collection:** This is a preparatory step that aims to collect the input data necessary to build the model. Further, it identifies input features and also aims to develop techniques to automatically extract features from the collected observations. Sometimes data needs to be normalized or re-scaled to bring all input features within the same range.
2. **Feature Selection:** The performance of machine learning-based models depends on the set of input features used and the correlation among them. Feature selection aims to identify the minimal number of features required for optimal performance. The Linear Discriminant Analysis (LDA) and Principal Component Analysis (PCA) techniques are typically used to determine the optimal set of features needed to build the machine learning models [23].
3. **Model Development:** The model development involves two steps. In the first stage, a model is built using any one of the machine learning techniques discussed in the following section. The data set which is used to develop the model is typically referred to as training data set. In the testing phase, the performance is checked against the unobserved or unknown data.
4. **Model Evaluation:** This step aims at evaluating the performance of the developed model against parameters such as f1-score, accuracy, recall and precision. This step gives us an idea about how exactly the model responds to unobserved data points.

3.1   System Architecture

Figure 1 shows the architecture of our system designed to carry out automated grading of PowerPoint presentation slides. Solid lines show the training process of the model. Dotted lines show the testing process of our model. We have PowerPoint presentation samples in the dataset which are already graded manually by the experts. Dataset contains input feature vector of 24 features representing the quality of a PowerPoint presentation and output is the grade of a PowerPoint presentation. After training and testing model is ready to evaluate grade of the ungraded PowerPoint presentations. Ungraded PowerPoint presentation feature vector is directly given as input to the trained machine learning model, which will predict its grade.

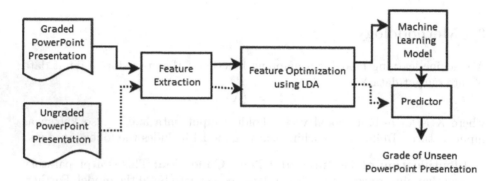

Fig. 1. Grading of PowerPoint presentations

4   Data Collection

We have collected the presentation slides prepared by students to deliver a course seminar. Delivering a course seminar is a compulsory activity included in the undergraduate curricula of all Engineering programs offered by all the Indian Universities. The course Seminar is included in the curricula to develop the communication and presentation skills of students. No formal training is provided to the students on developing PowerPoint slides using any presentation software (e.g., MS Office). Students learn using this software on their own as a part of the course Seminar activity. Students select a topic on emerging technology and deliver a talk of about 20 min using PowerPoint slides.

The course seminar is typically evaluated against the efforts put by a student to prepare PowerPoint slides, coverage of the topic selected by a student, and communication skills of a student. We aim to check the PowerPoint slides prepared by students for presentation quality and not for the topic and communication skills. We have collected about twenty six PowerPoint presentations. The collected slides are used to extract the features required to build the machine learning model. PowerPoint slides as well as dataset generated after features extraction have been made available on GitHub (https://github.com/jyotiborade/Presentation_grading/).

5   Feature Identification and Selection

In grading students' presentations, the goal of feature engineering is to identify attributes or input variables that can help us evaluate the quality of the presentation. For automatic grading of essays, many researchers have either used linguistic features that may be lexical, syntactic, semantic or they used automated techniques based on Deep Learning to extract relevant features. We have identified the following set of features to assess the quality of slides included in a presentation. These features include:

1. **Bullet Features:** These features capture information about the number and types of bullets used by a student in a presentation.
2. **Text Appearance:** These features mainly capture the information about the appearance of text on the slide. We presume that a diverse presentation in terms of text color, font size, and font type. Usually, these features aim to attract the audience's attention.
3. **Image and Animation:** This set of features captures the information about the use of images and animation. A presentation that includes images, diagrams, graphs, and charts usually conveys information effectively.
4. **Text Formatting:** These features capture information about the formatting of the text such as whether there are lengthy paragraphs included in the presentation and whether hyper-links and inter navigational links are provided to smoothly move across the presentation.
5. **Output Features:** We have included two different types of output variables. The first variable indicates whether the presentation is of an acceptable standard or not. The second output variable further grades an acceptable presentation in grades such as *Excellent, Very Good, Good*, and *Fair*.

Many programming languages such as Java, JavaScript, and Python provide programming language libraries to process PowerPoint presentations created in *PPT* format. For example, Apache POI is the Java API for handling Microsoft documents. While $Python - pptx$ and $nodejs - pptx$ are programming interfaces to handle *PPT* files in Python and Javascript, respectively. Features can be extracted from PowerPoint slides using $Python - pptx$ library [24]. Deep neural network-based approaches such as AutoEncoders can also be developed for automatic feature extraction; these approaches are preferred for feature engineering. In contrast to the linguistic features extracted for automatic grading of essays, the features mentioned above focus on the non-technical aspect of PowerPoint presentations. As shown in Table 1 and 2, we have used features about bullets, image, font, colours, hyperlinks, header footer, animation, etc., which captures various aspects that enhance the quality of PowerPoint presentations. The output features capture a teacher's evaluation of PPT slides with or without knowledge of features, which we are using to develop automated techniques.

Table 1. Features for bulleting and text appearance

Feature group	Features	Remark
1	No of Bullets per slides	It shows the number of bullets per slide
	Are different bullet types used for a topic and sub-topic	It represents the organization of a topic in sub-topic
	Types of bullets used	It represents different types of bullets used
2	Use of contrast effect	It indicates whether text color contrasts with background color or not
	Use of different colors for the title and main content	It represents the use of different colors for title of the slide and main content
	Number of colors used to display content	It indicates the use of a different number of colors used in the main body of the slide
	Empty space around the text	It checks text window used is large enough
	Is the font readable?	It checks whether font size is large enough
	The font size used for the title is same across?	It shows the use of the same font size across all the slides
	Use of italic fonts?	It checks whether a text is emphasized by use of the italic font
	Number of font types	It indicates the different number of fonts used in the presentation

6 Model Development

This section briefly reviews the various algorithms used to build classifier models and the implementation of our approach.

6.1 Classifier Algorithms

The grading of PowerPoint presentations can be treated as a classification problem. Binary classification can be used to differentiate PowerPoint presentations into two broad categories labeled as *acceptable* and *non-acceptable* satisfying presentation norms. Further, the technique of multi-class classification can be used to grade the PowerPoint presentations among grades such as *Excellent, Very*

Table 2. Features for images, animations, and text formatting

Feature group	Features	Remark
3	Image quality	It checks that image of sufficient resolution is used
	Space around an image	It shows that the image is displayed with a frame of sufficient size leaving enough space around the image
	Number of images	It indicates the number of images used
	Patterned background	It Checks whether the patterned background is used or not
	Are Transitions Present?	It shows the use of transitions in the presentation
4	Text Sentence	It represents whether text includes complete sentences or not
	Capital Words	It checks conventions regarding capital words
	Abbreviations or Acronyms	It shows the presence of abbreviations
	Paragraph	It represents the presence of lengthy paragraphs
	Special Characters	It checks the presence of special characters
	Header and footer	It checks the presence of headers and footers
	Hyperlinks	It checks the presence of hyperlinks to external sources
	Non-linear navigation	It checks the presence of navigational links to internal slides

Good, *Good*, and *Fair*. Following machine learning algorithms are used in our work to assess grade of PowerPoint presentations.

1. **Decision Tree (DT):** It is a popular classifier modeling technique, representing classification problem in the form of a decision tree. The tree has two types of nodes viz, decision nodes and leaf nodes. The leaf nodes indicate predicted value of the class for a label in our case these are: *Excellent*, *Very Good*, *Good*, and *Fair* for multi class classification. Decision nodes test fea-

tures for some specific criteria useful to designate the class labels. Here we have used *Gini Index* for the construction of decision tree.

2. **Logistic Regression (LR):** The logistic regression technique is derived from Linear regression. In linear regression, the relationship between input and output variables is modeled as a linear function described below.

$$Y = \beta_0 + \beta_1 x_1 + \beta_2 x_2 + \ldots + \beta_n x_n + \epsilon$$

In logistic regression, a sigmoid function is used to transform the output values in the range between 0 to 1. The class label 0 is assigned when the output value is less than 0.5 and class label 1 is assigned when the output value of a sigmoid function is above or equal to 0.5. The sigmoid function is:

$$g(z) = \frac{1}{1 + e^{-z}}$$

where

$$z = h_\beta(x) = \sum_{i=0}^{n} \beta_i x_i$$

We have used a *'liblinear'* solver for fitting the model, the maxiter is 100, a penalty is 12 that decides whether there is regularization or not. It uses L1 Regularization.

3. **Multi-Layer Perceptron (MLP):** It is typically used when input and output variables are related through nonlinear function. Our training data is small, hence We have used a *'lbfgs'* solver. We have used regularization parameter alpha with value *'1e − 5'*, the number of hidden layers with hidden neurons is (18,8).

4. **Support Vector Machine (SVM):** It builds a classifier that maximizes the separation between data points and decision boundaries. For the implementation of SVM, we have the penalty term C with value 180 to avoid misclassification. We have used a *'linear'* kernel to classify data points.

5. **K-Means Clustering (KM):** It groups set of objects such a way that objects in the same group are more similar to each other than other groups. We have used this classifier for binary classification. Hence the number of cluster parameter is set to 2.

6. **Naive Bayes Classifier (NB):** It assumes that input features are independent of each other, and they are numeric or continuous data types. It uses Bayes theorem to assign class labels C_k given a data observation x. We have applied default parameters for this classifier.

$$p(C_k|x) = \frac{p(C_k)p(x|C_k))}{p(x)}$$

6.2   Implementation

We have implemented a proof of concept classifier model. A data set of 26 PowerPoint presentations has been collected. We have manually extracted all the features mentioned in Tables 1 and 2. Two teachers have separately validated the correctness of extracted features. The PowerPoint presentation slides have been graded separately by two different evaluators to whom we have not disclosed the machine learning models' features. They were agreed upon grade has been recorded in the data set as output label. To reduce the similar correlated features, we have used linear discriminant analysis (LDA), a feature reduction technique. We have implemented a machine learning model using the Scikit-learn library provided by python. From the dataset of PowerPoint presentations, 70% presentations are used for training and 30% presentations are used for testing.

7   Model Evaluation

Quantitative metrics such as *F1-score*, *Precision*, *Recall*, and *Accuracy* are used to evaluate classifier systems. To define these evaluation metrics, *true values* and *predicted values* play an important role. In our case, a *true value* is a value of the class labels assigned to the output variables *acceptable* and *grade*. These values are assigned by a human evaluator. A *predicted value* is the class label assigned by a particular classifier. The first step to evaluate any classifier's performance is to prepare a table called *confusion matrix*. It represents the number of true values and predicted values in the form of a matrix as shown in Table 3. Due to lack of space, it is not possible to present the confusion matrix of each classifier. As shown in Fig. 2, we have tried to explain a general format of a confusion matrix for the Decision Tree classifier's confusion matrix.

Table 3. A general format for confusion matrix of binary classifier

Predicated Value			
Actual Value		Positive (1)	Negative(0)
	Positive (1)	True Positive(TP)	False Negative (FN)
	Negative(0)	False Positive (FP)	True Negative (TN)

The output of a classifier model can be divided into the following four types which can also be mapped into 4 cells of a confusion matrix as shown in Table 3. These are:

1. **True Positive (TP):** These are the total number of correctly predicted positive values. In our classifier value of TP is 10.
2. **True Negatives (TN):** These are the total number of correctly predicted negative values. In our classifier value of TN is 20.
3. **False Positives (FP):** When actual class is 0 and predicted class is 1. In our classifier value of FP is 0.
4. **False Negatives (FN):** When actual class is 1 but predicted class is 0. In our classifier value of FN is 0.

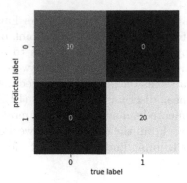

Fig. 2. Decision Tree binary classification confusion matrix

Table 4. Precision, recall, F1-score for multiclass classification

Machine Learning Model	Precision				Recall				F1-score			
	Excellent	Very Good	Good	Fair	Excellent	VeryGood	Good	Fair	Excellent	Very Good	Good	Fair
DT	1.00	1.00	1.00	1.00	1.00	1.00	1.00	1.00	1.00	1.00	1.00	1.00
SVM	0.56	0.00	0.92	1.00	0.00	1.00	0.80	0.82	0.00	0.82	0.76	0.90
MLP	0.62	1.00	0.92	1.00	1.00	0.20	1.00	1.00	0.77	0.33	0.96	1.00
NB	0.00	0.70	0.73	1.00	0.83	0.00	1.00	1.00	0.67	0.00	0.96	1.00

Table 5. Precision, Recall, F1-score for Binaryclass classification

Machine Learning Model	Precision		Recall		F1-score	
	Acceptable	Not Acceptable	Acceptable	Not Acceptable	Acceptable	Not Acceptable
DT	1.00	1.00	1.00	1.00	1.00	1.00
LR	0.90	1.00	1.00	0.83	0.95	0.91
SVM	0.87	0.93	0.93	0.88	0.90	0.90
MLP	0.95	0.89	0.95	0.89	0.95	0.89
NB	1.00	0.86	0.89	1.00	0.94	0.92
Kmeans	0.69	0.71	0.73	0.67	0.71	0.69

$$Precision = \frac{TP}{TP+FP} = \frac{10}{10+0} = 1$$

$$Recall = \frac{TP}{TP+FN} = \frac{10}{10+0} = 1$$

$$F1 - Score = 2 \times \frac{Recall \times Precision}{Recall + Precision} = 2 \times \frac{1 \times 1}{1+1} = 1$$

$$Accuracy = 100 \times \frac{TP+TN}{TP+FP+FN+TN} = 100 \times \frac{10+20}{10+0+0+20} = 100$$

Precision, Recall and F1-Score metrics for all the classifiers are shown in Table 4 and Table 5. Decision Tree is having highest value i.e. 1 for all these metrics.

The bar charts in Fig. 3 show the accuracy of various machine learning classifiers. Logistic regression, Naive Bayes, Decision Tree, and Support Vector Machine show good performance while predicting the class labels of presentations. The Decision Tree-based classifier predicts output class with 100%

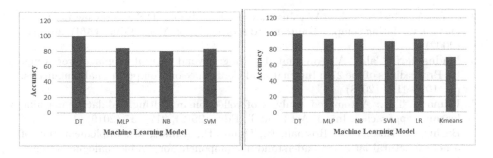

Fig. 3. Accuracy for Multiclass and Binaryclass classification

accuracy in both types of classification. The MLP, SVM, Naive Bayes classifier gives an accuracy of more than 80% in both multiclass and binary class classification. It shows that the features we have considered for grading students' presentations are appropriate and give an acceptable level of performance in the classification. Also, grade of PowerPoint presentation predicted by Decision Tree is more relevant compared to other classifiers. We have used Kmeans only for binary classification and it shows poor performance in comparison with others while predicting class. This may be due to the use of a small-sized dataset.

8   Conclusion and Future Work

In this paper, we have offered an approach to assess the students' presentation skills. Students demonstrate their presentation skills by preparing and delivering a PowerPoint presentation. To simplify developing an automated technique of evaluating such presentations, we separate technical content included in the PowerPoint presentation from the presentation quality manifested through various functionalities supported by presentation software. To demonstrate the approach, we have identified a set of useful features to determine the presentation quality. We have developed a small data set to enable the development of machine learning techniques. A data-driven approach to assess the presentation skill is demonstrated through various prototype classifiers. Decision tree predicts grade of the PowerPoint presentation with 100% accuracy.

In the future, we are going to take technical aspects like speaker's volume, communication skill, time and content management, topic selection etc., into consideration for automatic grading. Also, the performance of various classifiers needs to be fine-tuned.

References

1. Hearst, M.A.: The debate on automated essay grading. IEEE Intell. Syst. Appl. **15**, 22–37 (2000)

2. Yang, Y., Buckendahl, C.W., Juszkiewicz, P.J., Bhola, D.S.: A review of strategies for validating computer-automated scoring. Appl. Meas. Educ. **15**(4), 391–412 (2002)
3. Madnani, N., Cahill, A.: Automated scoring: beyond natural language processing. In: Proceedings of the 27th International Conference on Computational Linguistics, pp. 1099–1109 (2018)
4. Ullmann, T.D.: Automated analysis of reflection in writing: validating machine learning approaches. Int. J. Artif. Intell. Educ. **29**(2), 217–257 (2019)
5. Bashir, A., Hassan, A., Rosman, B., Duma, D., Ahmed, M.: Implementation of a neural natural language understanding component for Arabic dialogue systems. Proc. Comput. Sci. **142**, 222–229 (2018)
6. Leng, Y., Yu, L., Xiong, J.: DeepReviewer: collaborative grammar and innovation neural network for automatic paper review, pp. 395–403 (2019)
7. Peng, X., Ke, D., Chen, Z., Xu, B.: Automated Chinese essay scoring using vector space models. In: 2010 4th International Universal Communication Symposium, Beijing, pp. 149–153 (2010)
8. Al-Jouie, M., Azmi, A.M.: Automated evaluation of school children essays in Arabic. Proc. Comput. Sci. **117**, 19–22 (2017)
9. Azmi Aqil M., Al-Jouie M.F. and Hussain M., AAEE-Automated evaluation of students' essays in Arabic language, Information Processing & Management, 56(5), pp. 1736–1752
10. Walia, T., Josan, G., Singh, A.: An efficient automated answer scoring system for the Punjabi language. Egypt. Inform. J. **20**, 89–96 (2018)
11. Anak, R., Putri, A., Dyah, L., Ihsan, I., Diyanatul, H., Purnamasari, P.: Automatic essay grading system for Japanese language examination using winnowing algorithm. In: International Seminar on Application for Technology of Information and Communication (iSemantic), pp. 565–569 (2018)
12. Ramalingam, V.V., Pandian, A., Chetry, P., Nigam, H.: Automated essay grading using machine learning algorithm. J. Phys.: Conf. Ser. (2018)
13. Haendchen Filho, A., Prado, H., Ferneda, E., Nau, J.: An approach to evaluate adherence to the theme and the argumentative structure of essays. Proc. Comput. Sci. **12**, 788–797 (2018)
14. Fazal, A., Hussain, F., Dillon, T.: An innovative approach for automatically grading spelling in essays using rubric-based scoring. J. Comput. Syst. Sci. **79**, 1040–1056 (2013)
15. Olowolayemo, A., Nawi, S., Mantoro, T.: Short answer scoring in English grammar using text similarity measurement. In: International Conference on Computing, Engineering, and Design (ICCED), pp. 131–136 (2018)
16. Janda, H.K., Pawar, A., Du, S., Mago, V.: Syntactic, semantic and sentiment analysis: the joint effect on automated essay evaluation. IEEE Access **7**, 108486–108503 (2019)
17. George, N., Sijimol, P.J., Varghese, S.M.: Grading descriptive answer scripts using deep learning. Int. J. Innov. Technol. Explor. Eng. (IJITEE) **8**(5) (2019)
18. Jin, C., He, B., Hui, K., Sun, L.: TDNN: a two-stage deep neural network for prompt-independent automated essay scoring. In: ACL, Melbourne, Australia (2018)
19. Surya, K., Gayakwad, E., Nallakaruppan, M.: Deep learning for short answer scoring. Int. J. Recent Technol. Eng. **7**, 1712–1715 (2019)
20. Rodriguez, P., Jafari, A., Ormerod, C.: Language Models and Automated Essay Scoring (2019)

21. Bauer, C.: Grading rubrics for engineering presentations and reports. In: ASME International Mechanical Engineering Congress and Exposition (2008)
22. Peeters, M.J., Sahloff, E.G., Stone, G.E.: A standardized rubric to evaluate student presentations. Am. J. Pharm. Educ. (2010)
23. Borade, J.G., Netak, L.D.: Automated grading of essays: a review. In: Singh, M., Kang, D.-K., Lee, J.-H., Tiwary, U.S., Singh, D., Chung, W.-Y. (eds.) IHCI 2020. LNCS, vol. 12615, pp. 238–249. Springer, Cham (2021). https://doi.org/10.1007/978-3-030-68449-5_25
24. Borade, J.G., Kiwelekar, A.W., Netak, L.D.: Feature extraction for automatic grading of students' presentations. In: Tuba, M., Akashe, S., Joshi, A. (eds.) ICT Systems and Sustainability. LNCS, vol. 321, pp. 293–301. Springer, Singapore (2022). https://doi.org/10.1007/978-981-16-5987-4_30

Textual Description Generation for Visual Content Using Neural Networks

Komal Garg$^{(\boxtimes)}$, Varsha Singh, and Uma Shanker Tiwary

Indian Institute of Information Technology, Allahabad, Allahabad, India
komalgarg.iiita@gmail.com, {rsi2018002,ust}@iiita.ac.in

Abstract. Various methods in machine learning have noticeable use in generating descriptive text for images and video frames and processing them. This area has attracted the immense interest of researchers in past years. For text generation, various models contain CNN and RNN combined approaches. RNN works well in language modeling; it lacks in maintaining information for a long time. An LSTM language model can overcome this drawback because of its long-term dependency handling. Here, the proposed methodology is an Encoder-Decoder approach where VGG19 Convolution Neural Network is working as Encoder; LSTM language model is working as Decoder to generate the sentence. The model is trained and tested on the Flickr8K dataset and can generate textual descriptions on a larger dataset Flickr30K with the slightest modifications. The results are generated using BLEU scores (Bilingual Evaluation Understudy Score). A GUI tool is developed to help in the field of child education. This tool generates audio for the generated textual description for images and helps to search for similar content on the internet.

Keywords: Convolutional Neural Network · Long Short-Term Memory · Bilingual Evaluation Understudy Score

1 Introduction

1.1 Overview

Here we are combining two different neural networks to get the most suitable sentence for the input image. The convolutional neural network is used to get the encoding of the input image. It takes an image as input and creates its feature vector for processing. For this purpose, the VGG19 CNN model is being used. Many other architectures are also available to get encodings of images but they are time-consuming while training the model. In [1], ResNet50 is used as CNN which generates descriptive sentence with moderate efficiency. In this proposed model, we are using VGG19 which is comparatively slightly efficient in terms of time and space used for training. The input image is first converted into a $224 \times 224 \times 3$ dimensional image which is then fed to VGG19. The encoded image is passed to the LSTM (long short-term memory) network which

© Springer Nature Switzerland AG 2022
J.-H. Kim et al. (Eds.): IHCI 2021, LNCS 13184, pp. 16–26, 2022.
https://doi.org/10.1007/978-3-030-98404-5_2

is kind of similar in patterns to machine translation. Using LSTM in place of RNN generates better sentences as it can handle information for a long time. Paper [2] lacked in this prospect which was improved using LSTM network in our approach. This LSTM generates a suitable text description for the input image with the help of Beam-search. Paper [6] helps the idea that VGG19 and LSTM model can give efficient results using local small dataset. We separately preprocess the sentences in the training set to create the dictionary. Flickr8k dataset is being used for training the model. This model is called the encoder-decoder model. A big part of this task is image classification which is itself a complicated one to perform. It involves not only identifying the objects and content of the image but also finding relationships between those objects to generate the meaning of the image.

The task is to generate a natural language sentence that can describe the image significantly. The sentence should be in an understandable language like - English. This can only be performed with the help of a language model. We are using LSTM for this purpose. This model is a combination of an encoder - CNN and decoder - LSTM.

1.2 Motivation

Text generation for an image has many applications in the physical world like image editing applications, image indexing, virtual assistants in mobile phones and computers, etc. In social media, when a user posts an image, this tool can help in predicting the description for the posted image and suggests emoticons according to the sentiment of the sentence. For visually incapable persons, this text generation tool can generate descriptions in audio to help them in daily activities. Also, it can be used for video summarising by taking video frames as image input and creating a sentence for that frame. After that, all the generated sentences create a summary for the video in the form of paragraphs. In the child education field, text generation for visual content can have a very useful application; children are known to be more attentive towards images or visuals. A tool can help teach children about various things using images and their description in audio forms. Google search and image search with this tool can provide more relevant knowledge to the given image. These all applications happen to be the motivation behind choosing this topic for the proposed model.

1.3 Related Work

There has been a lot of active research, with many papers using CNN (Convolutional Neural Network) and RNN (Recurrent Neural Network) combined approach to solving this problem. As a substitute to RNN, other similar models can be used as LSTM (Long Short-term Memory), GRU (Gated Recurrent Unit), or TNN (Temporal Neural Network), etc. As of CNN, there is a lot of CNN model are available to use for the encoding purpose like VGG16, VGG19, ResNet50, Xception, AlexNet, etc. For Dataset, a large number of datasets are being used - Flickr8K, Flickr30K, MSCOCO, SUN dataset, etc.

As various researches support Convolutional Neural Network along With the LSTM approach, this literature review majorly focuses on this technique for model generation. Aung, San Pa, Win nwe, tin [6] compared two most used and widely popular models for feature extraction Visual geometry group(VGG) OxfordNet 16-layer model - **VGG16** and 19-layer model - **VGG19**. According to them, VGG-19 performs better than VGG-16 in terms of accuracy but takes little more space in memory. Chu, Yan Yue et al. [1] supports the use of ResNet50 and LSTM with a soft attention layer incorporated. ResNet, short form for Residual Networks is an exemplary neural network utilized as a spine for some Computer vision assignments. This ResNet model was the champion of the ImageNet challenge in 2015 for feature collection. The main part about the breakthrough with ResNet was it permitted us to prepare a very profound neural Network with 150+layers effectively. The main problem behind the occasional failure of ResNet was Vanishing Gradient.

Long Short-term Memory got attention recently among Computer vision enthusiasts. This LSTM model consists of Contextual cell states which behave like long-term memory cells or short-term memory cells depending on the requirements. A Karpathy [8] researches the probability of sentence generation in natural understandable language using LSTM. Their methodology utilizes image datasets and their depiction in normal language and looks for a multi-purpose correspondence between words from the depiction and visual information. There is a various paper explaining the CNN along with RNN technique to generate model explaining the encoder-decoder approach of this problem. CNN works efficiently in creating a feature vector which is used in the model as raw data of an image. LSTM performs words connectivity using the contextual cells to generate a sentence and with the help of beam-search, a proper sentence is selected.

- In paper [1], one joint model AICRL is presented, which can conduct the automatic text generation for an image based on ResNet50 and LSTM. The whole model is fully trainable by using the stochastic gradient descent that makes the training process easier.
- In paper [2], presented a multi-level policy and reward reinforcement learning framework for image description that can be integrated with RNN-based captioning models, language metrics, or visual-semantic functions for optimization.
- In paper [3], an integrated model using CNN and LSTM has been developed to automatically view an image and generate a reasonable description in plain English. It uses Flickr8k, MSCOCO, and pascal dataset to train and test this model. CNN used is VGG16 to preprocess the images to generate the feature vectors.
- Research paper [6] uses a generative merge model based on Convolutional Neural Network (CNN) and Long-Short Term Memory (LSTM) which uses VGG19 for feature extraction from Myanmar dataset and single hidden layer LSTM for sentence generation. This dataset is a smaller part of Flickr's data.

This proposed methodology focuses mainly on creating a description for the input image in natural language with help of efficient models for feature extraction and also an LSTM decoder to generate a sentence. In addition, a tool was also generated to help kids in education using the audio form of generated sentence and google query and image search.

1.4 Problem Statement

To generate human like textual description for visual content by using a combination of encoder decoder.

2 Methodology

We are proposing an encode-decoder architecture for generating text for given image where the encoder part is performed by the VGG19 CNN model and we use LSTM for decoding. The encoder performs the task of creating image encoding in the form of feature vectors and these encodings are taken as input to the main model architecture where LSTM generates sentences with the help of beam-search. For this work, we are using Flickr8K [15] dataset which consists of around 8k images and respectively 5 sentences for each image in the dataset. The pictures were chosen from six diverse Flickr groups and tend not to contain any notable individuals or areas, however were manually chosen to portray an assortment of scenes and circumstances. This dataset contains two folders separately for images and respective descriptive sentences. Each image has a unique id given to it and its corresponding sentence. All the images are in RGB format and preprocessed using VGG19 before passing to the model. Figure 4 shows the way images are kept in the dataset. Dataset is divided into 6k, 1k, 1k respectively in the train set, validation set, and test set (Figs. 1 and 2).

2.1 Model Architecture

The input image is passed through VGG19 to extract its feature vector. We take image in $224 \times 224 \times 3$ dimensions and retrieve the output features in 4096×1. To get the desired output shape, the last layer of VGG19 is removed. This process generates a feature vector in 4096×1 size. All the feature vectors are then saved into a file separately. This file is used in training, testing, and validation to extract features for each image. Now we preprocess the text part of the dataset by removing punctuation, single-letter words, and words that have numbers within. After cleaning these sentences, vocabulary is generated and we get the max length of the sentence in the dataset. In this step, Word embeddings are also generated. Then it is passed to the model along with feature vectors. Using LSTM and Beam-search with beam width $= 5$, the model generates 5 sentences for each image, and the final sentence is selected at the final time-stamp because this sentence is the most improved of all. For language modeling, LSTM is given preference over RNNs because LSTM has the capability of forgetting, remembering, and updating information in long-term dependencies. In LSTM

36422830_55c84
4bc2d.jpg

41999070_83808
9137e.jpg

42637986_135a9
786a6.jpg

42637987_86663
5edf6.jpg

50030244_02cd4
de372.jpg

53043785_c468d
6f931.jpg

54501196_a9ac9
d66f2.jpg

54723805_bcf7af
3f16.jpg

Fig. 1. This illustrates the images in the Flickr8K dataset

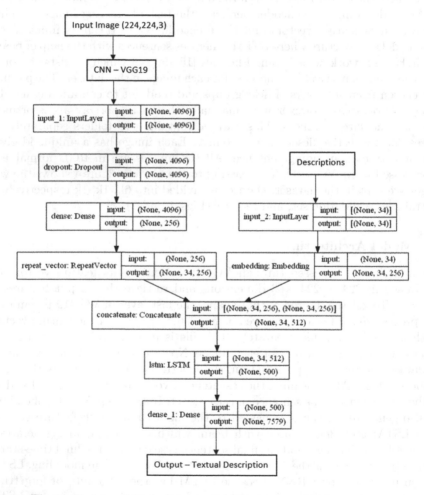

Fig. 2. Model architecture to perform text generation for an image

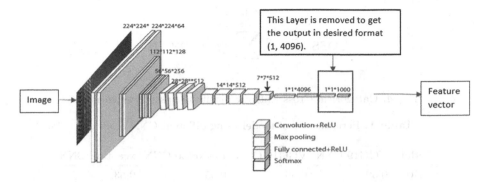

Fig. 3. Encoder Description: VGG19 is used as an encoder to extract feature vector from images. From VGG19 architecture, last fully-connected layer is removed to get desired output format.

architecture, we are using embedding dimension = 256 and lstm layers = 2 with dropout rate of 0.2.

For the Automatic text generation task, model is trained for 20 epochs on a training set consisting of 6000 images. The fewer number of epochs is sufficient to train the model efficiently while using stochastic gradient descent in model regularization. Categorical Cross-Entropy Loss is used for the classification purpose as multi-class classification is required. This loss function uses an optimizer that tunes the learning rate for all the parameters. The parameter learning rate helps the optimizer in updating weights in the opposite direction of the gradient. Here learning rate = 0.02 is used. In Fig. 4, the formula to calculate loss shows the details. The model with the lowest validation loss is saved and used for testing purposes. Intel(R) Xeon(R) CPU @ 2.30 GHz and 12 GB NVIDIA Tesla K80 GPU is used for training purposes.

3 Experimental Results

The BLEU-score (Bilingual Evaluation Understudy) metric is used to determine the accuracy of this model to generate textual description for an image. BLEU is an N-gram comparison of referenced sentence and model-generated sentence. N-gram can be in the size of 1 to 4. Therefore BLEU-1, BLEU-2, BLEU-3, and BLEU-4 are used for determining the accuracy of the generated sentence. Here the testing data has 1000 images. There are 1000 sentences generated for the test dataset and the model calculates the BLEU score using their already generated sentences present in the dataset. After evaluation, the results are shown in Table 1 with their comparison to results achieved while using different CNN models.

$$\text{Loss} = -\sum_{i=1}^{\substack{\text{output} \\ \text{size}}} y_i \cdot \log \hat{y}_i$$

Fig. 4. Categorical Cross Entropy for multi-class classification

Table 1. Performance of model using different CNN models

Model	VGG19 CNN	VGG16 CNN	ResNet50 CNN	xception CNN
BLEU-1	0.59	0.58	0.55	0.53
BLEU-2	0.35	0.34	0.31	0.29
BLEU-3	0.25	0.25	0.23	0.21
BLEU-4	0.13	0.14	0.12	0.11

VGG19 is 19 layers deep convolutional neural network. The pre-trained VGG19 model has been trained over a very large dataset 'ImageNet' which contains over a million images with 1000 object classes and learned a rich feature vector representation. We trained this model for our Flikr8k training dataset. Because of its deeper network, this model creates better feature vectors than VGG16. These features are used by LSTM in descriptive sentence creation, so using VGG19 instead of VGG16 also improves the generated sentence.

Table 2. Comparison of results of different approaches on Flickr8K Dataset using evaluation metric BLEU-1

Approaches	Model	BLEU-1 score
Junhua Mao [16]	AlexNet + m-RNN	0.565
Karpathy [8]	CNN + m-RNN	0.579
Yin Cui [17]	Show N Tell	0.56
Our Approach	**VGG19 + LSTM**	**0.59**

In the Table 2, we can conclude that VGG19 along with LSTM gives better results than other implemented approaches in the Flickr8K dataset. By using larger datasets like MSCOCO, Flickr30K, the model can perform more significantly.

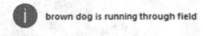
brown dog is running through field

white dog is running through the water

4 Application

Image to text generation has various real-world applications like aid for visually impaired people, image editing tools, child education, in video summarising. In this work, we implemented a tool with GUI which is helpful in child education as it can provide more information about the content of the image and also pronounces the generated sentence in audio form. This tool asks the user for the input image and then generates description in text form as well as audio form and later on asks the user for google query search or image search using GUI buttons. This can be an interesting and easy-to-use tool for children. This tool works better than other such existing tools because it considers not only foreground details but also the background to describe the input image which helps in generating a sentence containing all the details about the image.

young boy is playing on the edge of pool

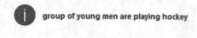
group of young men are playing hockey

5 Conclusion

This model is an encoder-decoder framework that gives a natural language sentence as output when an image is given as input. This combines two neural networks for this purpose. The convolutional neural network to identify objects in the image and finding relationships between them, therefore creating a feature vector for the input image; and LSTM neural network is used for generating meaningful sentences describing the input image. We are using Flickr8K dataset and the model can be used with other datasets like Flickr30K and MSCOCO also with some slight modifications in preprocessing part.

The model implemented here is successfully generating the text description for the input image along with its audio caption. In most of the cases, it is generating a good caption but in some cases, it is getting confused and identifying the wrong object because of dense features which is leading to mismatched caption. Overall it is generating a sufficiently good description which can be further used in several applications. We implemented an application in child education using text generation for image.

6 Future Work

In this model, the main problem was to decrease the time taken while generating a description for the input image which has been improved by fine-tuning the model. Along with this issue, the model is developed to work as a real-world application that can be helpful for other people. Here, an application for child education is developed that can be easily used to teach children with the help of image search and query search of google. Further, this can be improved in terms of accuracy if the model is trained on larger datasets like MSCOCO, Flickr30k, etc. This way the model would be more generic for new images and new surroundings. Apart from it, there can be more applications such as making a tool for blind people which can help them while walking; also it can be used in a video summarizing that can narrate an ongoing scene to the listeners and also for movie summarizing.

References

1. Chu, Y., Yue, X., Yu, L., Sergei, M., Wang, Z.: Automatic image captioning based on ResNet50 and LSTM with soft attention. Wirel. Commun. Mob. Comput. **2020**, 1–7 (2020)
2. Xu, N., et al.: Multi-level policy and reward-based deep reinforcement learning framework for image captioning. IEEE Trans. Multimed. **22**(5), 1372–1383 (2020)
3. Xu, K., et al.: Show, attend and tell: neural image caption generation with visual attention. In: International Conference on Machine Learning. PMLR (2015)
4. You, Q., Jin, H., Wang, Z., Fang, C., Luo, J.: Proceedings of the IEEE Conference on Computer Vision and Pattern Recognition (CVPR), pp. 4651–4659 (2016)
5. Wang, C., Yang, H., Bartz, C., Meinel, C.: Image captioning with deep bidirectional LSTMs. In: Proceedings of the 24th ACM International Conference on Multimedia (MM 2016), pp. 988–997. Association for Computing Machinery, New York (2016)
6. Aung, S., Pa, W., Nwe, T.: Automatic Myanmar image captioning using CNN and LSTM-based language model. In: 1st Joint SLTU and CCURL Workshop (SLTU-CCURL 2020), Marseille, France (2020)
7. Hewage, R.: Extract Features, Visualize Filters and Feature Maps in VGG16 and VGG19 CNN Models (2020). https://towardsdatascience.com/extract-features-visualize-filters-and-feature-maps-in-vgg16-and-vgg19-cnn-models-d2da6333edd0?. Accessed 29 June 2021
8. Karpathy, A., Fei-Fei, L.: Deep visual-semantic alignments for generating image descriptions. Stanford University (2017)
9. Papineni, K., Roukos, S., Ward, T., Zhu, W.J.: BLEU: a method for automatic evaluation of machine translation. In: Proceedings of the 40th Annual Meeting of the Association for Computational Linguistics, Philadelphia, pp. 311–318 (2002)
10. Wang, J., Yang, Y., Mao, J., Huang, Z., Huang, C., Xu, W.: CNN RNN: a unified frame-work for multi-label image classification. In: The IEEE Conference on Computer Vision and Pattern Recognition (CVPR), pp. 2285–2294 (2016)
11. You, Q., Jin, H., Wang, Z., Fang, C., Luo, J.: Image captioning with semantic attention. In: CVPR, 4651–4659 (2016)
12. Kulkarni, G., et al.: Baby talk: understanding and generating simple image descriptions. In: CVPR, 1601–1608 (2011)
13. Alzubi, J.A., Jain, R., Nagrath, P., Satapathy, S., Taneja, S., Gupta, P.: Deep image captioning using an ensemble of CNN and LSTM based deep neural networks. J. Intell. Fuzzy Syst. **40**(4), 5761–5769 (2021). https://doi.org/10.3233/jifs-189415
14. Hossain, M.D.Z., Sohel, F., Shiratuddin, M.F., Laga, H.: A comprehensive survey of deep learning for image captioning. ACM Comput. Surv. **51**(6), 1–36 (2018)
15. Rashtchian, C., Young, P., Hodosh, M., Hockenmaier, J.: Collecting image annotations using Amazon's mechanical Turk. In: NAACL-HLT Workshop 2010, pp. 139–147 (2010)
16. Mao, J., Xu, W., Yang, Y., Wang, J., Huang, Z., Yuille, A.: Deep Captioning with Multimodal Recurrent Neural Networks (m-RNN). In: ICLR 2015. arXiv:1412.6632
17. Cui, Y., Yang, G., Veit, A., Huang, X., Belongie, S.: Proceedings of the IEEE Conference on Computer Vision and Pattern Recognition (CVPR), pp. 5804–5812 (2018)
18. Yao, T., Pan, Y., Li, Y., Qiu, Z., Mei, T.: Proceedings of the IEEE International Conference on Computer Vision (ICCV), pp. 4894–4902 (2017)
19. Aneja, J., Deshpande, A., Schwing, A.G.: Proceedings of the IEEE Conference on Computer Vision and Pattern Recognition (CVPR), pp. 5561–5570 (2018)

20. Feng, Y., Ma, L., Liu, W., Luo, J.: Proceedings of the IEEE/CVF Conference on Computer Vision and Pattern Recognition (CVPR), pp. 4125–4134 (2019)
21. Rennie, S.J., Marcheret, E., Mroueh, Y., Ross, J., Goel, V.: Proceedings of the IEEE Conference on Computer Vision and Pattern Recognition (CVPR), pp. 7008–7024 (2017)
22. Zhou, Y., Sun, Y., Honavar, V.: Improving image captioning by leveraging knowledge graphs. In: IEEE Winter Conference on Applications of Computer Vision (WACV) 2019, pp. 283–293 (2019). https://doi.org/10.1109/WACV.2019.00036
23. Tran, K., et al.: Proceedings of the IEEE Conference on Computer Vision and Pattern Recognition (CVPR) Workshops, pp. 49–56 (2016)
24. Sun, B., et al.: Supercaptioning: image captioning using two-dimensional word embedding. arXiv preprint arXiv:1905.10515 (2019)
25. Amirian, S., Rasheed, K., Taha, T.R., Arabnia, H.R.: Automatic image and video caption generation with deep learning: a concise review and algorithmic overlap. IEEE Access **8**, 218386–218400 (2020). https://doi.org/10.1109/ACCESS.2020.3042484
26. Sharma, P., Ding, N., Goodman, S., Soricut, R.: Conceptual captions: a cleaned, hypernymed, image alt-text dataset for automatic image captioning. In: Proceedings of the 56th Annual Meeting of the Association for Computational Linguistics (Volume 1: Long Papers), pp. 2556–2565, July 2018
27. Bai, S., An, S.: A survey on automatic image caption generation. Neurocomputing **311**, 291–304 (2018)

Using LSTM Models on Accelerometer Data to Improve Accuracy of Tap Strap 2 Wearable Keyboard

Kristian Mrazek and Tauheed Khan Mohd[✉]

Augustana College, Rock Island, IL 61201, USA
tauheedkhanmohd@augustana.edu

Abstract. This paper proposes the implementation of three different long short-term memory (LSTM) recurrent neural network (RNN) models to improve the accuracy of the input readings of the Tap Strap 2, a Bluetooth wearable keyboard device. The Tap Strap 2 was found in the previous study to have an undesirably low level of accuracy when it came to outputting the correct characters upon interpreting data from the built-in sensors. In response to this, raw accelerometer data was obtained from the device and used to train an LSTM model. This model would be used to not only determine which features correspond to which characters, but also would use contextual information from past characters to determine which character was most likely pressed whenever the input seems ambiguous. This paper first provides an description of the LSTM RNN used in this experiment. It then evaluates the effectiveness of the models in reducing the accuracy problems of the Tap Strap 2.

Keywords: RNN · LSTM · Keyboard · Wearable · Accelerometer

1 Introduction

Human-computer interaction (HCI) is a rapidly growing field of computer science. Innovators are constantly looking for new ways for users to interact with their devices, and preferably these ways will be more practical and efficient than current ones. A particularly burgeoning area of HCI is that of wearable computing, which concerns electronic devices that can be worn on one's own body. Arguably the most famous of these is the smartwatch, but there is a wide variety of other forms that wearable computing can assume; for example, the Tap Strap 2 that is the focus of this paper acts as a wearable keyboard and mouse. Devices such as the standard QWERTY keyboard and physical computer mouse have long been the main means of HCI, and they remain that way since they are readily available and generally fairly straightforward to use. However, they are often bulky and not particularly portable. Additionally, electronic QWERTY keyboards such as those on phones and smartwatches are small, which can easily lead to typing errors. The fact that such keyboards are entirely flat by nature also makes them inaccessible to blind users.

© Springer Nature Switzerland AG 2022
J.-H. Kim et al. (Eds.): IHCI 2021, LNCS 13184, pp. 27–38, 2022.
https://doi.org/10.1007/978-3-030-98404-5_3

One major advantage of wearable keyboards and mice (as well as other wearable devices) is that they are a form of ubiquitous computing: computing embedded in practical everyday objects such as watches and wristbands. This makes them highly portable in contrast to physical keyboards and mice. The Tap Strap 2, a wearable keyboard device designed by the international company Tap Systems, Inc., is worn in a similar fashion to a glove, with five rings that go around each of the user's five digits on either of their hands. The user can tap different combinations of fingers to type different characters; for example, tapping the index finger alone inputs an "e". Each of the rings has a built-in accelerometer that measures the acceleration of the finger it is attached to, and the readings from these accelerometers are used to determine whether or not each finger was tapped. There is also an inertial measurement unit (IMU) built into the thumb ring that controls the Tap Strap 2's mouse functions. The fact that the device can be worn and uses accelerometer data to determine input means that the user can tap on their chair when seated, or even their own leg. This eliminates the issue of physical keyboards being bulky and obstructive when used on one's lap.

Additionally, as most of these keyboards are Bluetooth powered by nature, they can be used with mobile devices in addition to normal computers and laptops. The Tap Strap 2 has such functionality, and can be used with a mobile device instead of the onscreen keyboards. This is also particularly important for blind users, since the onscreen keys are impalpable, yet the Tap Strap 2 functions by touch and incorporates a system of touch patterns comparable in many way to the Braille alphabet.

There is a key problem with these devices in general, however. The use of accelerometer-based collision detection to determine the key being pressed is a double-edged sword since it is more error-prone than a normal key depression. Errors in input readings are common. For example, one will sometimes attempt to type an "i" (which corresponds to the middle finger only) and get an "l" (middle and ring fingers) instead if the ring finger moves at all. In the preceding publication "The Tap Strap 2: Evaluating Performance of One-Handed Wearable Keyboard and Mouse", it was found that when every letter of the alphabet was typed 100 times on a hard surface, the average accuracy was only 84.7%. The accuracy was particularly poor for characters such as "j" and "w", which require the user to tap both the middle and small fingers while keeping the ring finger raised. Additionally, the Tap Strap 2 has many special characters and commands, which generally require more complicated combinations than the letters.

To resolve these issues, a recurrent neural network (RNN) model was initially proposed. This model would function as a spell checker, using context information from the series of words leading up to the current word in order to determine whether the word actually typed was what the user intended. However, while this would possibly improve the word accuracy level, it would do nothing to help make sure the correct characters are always typed to begin with, and would only perform the correction when the user decided to end the word through a space or some other special character. Furthermore, it would lead to the possibility of correctly-typed words being incorrectly changed, as is frequently the problem with auto-correct features. Therefore, a different type of model will be implemented in this paper, one that will use contextual information to resolve issues on a character basis using both sensors data and contextual information.

A recurrent neural network is a type of neural network that is designed to deal with sequences of values. This could be a sequence of characters, such as a sentence, paragraph, or entire text. An RNN accomplishes this through feedback loops, which allow each layer of the network to "remember" their output values. "Normal" feed-forward neural networks, by contrast, are entirely one-way, so there is no way to establish memory of earlier values. This makes RNNs powerful, since they can use contextual information from previous values in the sequence to determine what value comes next.

One of the most useful varieties of RNN is the Long Short Term Memory (LSTM) network. Standard RNNs are useful in that they can "remember" recent values, which is all that is necessary in many cases; however, they are often rather poor at recalling much older information. LSTM networks combat this issue by being able to relate values over much longer intervals in the sequence. These RNNs are perhaps most frequently used in language translation and auto-complete features due to their ability to form long-term connections between values. However, they can also be used for a variety of other purposes. These include combining sensors data with the context of the situation to recognize different types of human activity, as will be detailed in the rest of this paper.

In the next section, an overview of recent projects of this particular nature will be given. Multiple different LSTM RNN models, trained on raw sensors data from the Tap Strap 2, will then be proposed in Sect. 3 to improve the accuracy of the device. Finally, in Sect. 4, the level of accuracy improvement will be quantified to judge the effectiveness of the model.

2   Related Work

The application of LSTM RNNs to human activity recognition is a small field, but one that carries significant implications. Generally, another type of network called the convolution neural network (CNN) is used to improve accuracy of device readings from sensors data. This is because the application of CNNs is more straightforward: CNNs seek out features in large data sets by grouping nearby data points together. This allows them to easily detect features such as the eyes and ears of a cat in an image, or in the case of time series sensors data, a spike in the measured acceleration indicating a finger tap (or some similar event). In contrast, RNNs are more well-known for their usefulness in word prediction and "auto-complete" features. However, RNNs pose a potential advantage over CNNs in their ability to consider contextual information.

2.1   Recurrent Neural Networks in Sequence to Sequence Mapping and Spelling Correction

Importantly, RNNs, including LSTM RNNs, are useful for their reliability in dealing with sequences. A common variant of this is statistical machine translation (SMT), which maps a sentence (sequence of words) in one language to a sentence in another language: for example, English to French. This is relevant since "normal" deep neural networks (DNNs) have trouble dealing with sequences of values, due to the fact that they are feed-forward; they have no way of considering past information. It also shows that RNNs are capable of both predicting the next value in a sequence and finding and resolving errors in sequences of values.

Cho et al. [1] performed a study using an RNN-based model to translate between English and French in 2014. The model in question, referred to as an encoder-decoder, would encode a sentence in one language by transforming it into a vector before decoding this vector into a sentence in the other language. The model overall outperformed a more traditional phrase-based SMT model in terms of BLEU scores, a means through which accuracy in sequence-to-sequence mapping is quantified.

Sutskever et al. [2] similarly used an RNN for English-French translation. Unlike the model used by Cho et al., an LSTM RNN was used in this experiment due to its ability to handle long-term dependencies. This network was found to significantly outperform the phrase-based SMT model as well as the one designed by Cho et al., having a higher BLEU score than either of them and performing better than Cho et al. when it came to translating long sentences.

RNNs have also been applied to spell checking by Li et al. [3] in 2018. In this case, a type of RNN similar to LSTM called a gated recurrent unit (GRU) was used, and this considered context at both the word level and the character level. This RNN was found to outperform both Python's built-in "enchant" spell checker and two other neural network-based spell checkers by a considerable margin. Importantly, the ability of the RNN to consider context allowed mistakes to be corrected even when the mistake involved a real word: for example, typing "though" when one actually intended to type "thought".

2.2   Recurrent Neural Networks in Human Activity Recognition

While LSTM RNNs have proven to be incredibly useful in dealing with the syntax and semantics of sentences, they have also been prominent in human activity recognition (HAR), though perhaps not as much as CNNs. HAR involving neural networks involves the use of sensors data as training data. Several projects in HAR using RNNs have been conducted over the past decade, and these have various methods and purposes.

In 2015, Lebefre et al. [4] performed an experiment using a bidirectional long short-term memory RNN (BLSTM-RNN) in gesture recognition for smartphones. Bidirectional networks feature two layers ("forward" and "backward") are able to consider context from both past and future data in a sequence. It was found that the BLSTM-RNN was more effective when trained on data from both the device's accelerometer and gyrometer, as opposed to just one of them.

In 2018, Shakya et al. [5] performed an inquiry into the use of various forms of machine learning and deep learning architectures, including RNNs, to recognize human activity. This experiment used the Wireless Sensor Data Mining Dataset

(WISDM), which contained sensors data from a smartphone suspended from the waist, along with a second data set for five accelerometers located on different parts of the body. These datasets were considered "unbalanced" and "balanced" respectively, since the latter monitored acceleration at multiple locations on the body while the former only measured it at the waist. They also covered a variety of day-to-day activities, such as sitting, standing, and walking, to be recognized by the neural network models. It was found that both the CNN and RNN model were significantly more accurate when they used the "balanced" dataset with five sensors. This is important, as it suggests that a wider distribution of sensors leads to better results, and therefore this experiment should make use of all the sensors the device leverages.

In 2019, Soselia et al. [6] used an RNN with two LSTM layers and two dense layers to recognize and predict written characters. In this experiment, the device used consisted of a accelerometer and gyroscope attached to a pen. The RNN system used the transmitted accelerometer and gyroscope data to determine which character was being written by the user. This model obtained an accuracy rate above 88% [6]. The project is especially significant due to the similarities it bears to this one, particularly in terms of mapping features in sensors data to alphabetical characters.

The purpose of this experiment is to combine both approaches to significantly improve the accuracy of the Tap Strap 2, as well as the quality of the user's experience with it. The network here will prove able to decide which character was typed based on both the raw accelerometer values and the characters that were typed before it. Section 3 will discuss the implementation details of this network as well as the methods used to evaluate its effectiveness.

3   Experimental Setup

3.1   Obtaining and Processing the Sensors Data

The first step in the experiment was to obtain the raw sensors data used to train the model. This was done using the Python Tap Software Development Kit (SDK) available on the TapWithUs GitHub [7]. This is a Python file that allows a user to get input reads and sensors data, among other features. Notably, it is impossible to obtain the input reads and the sensors data simultaneously, meaning there is no way to tell how a certain tap combination was interpreted. This may seem problematic since this experiment incorporates a supervised machine learning algorithm, in which the labels in the training data must be known. However, the proper plan of action is to manually label the inputs instead. This is because the model will be able to recognize the intended input regardless of whether it was actually recognized correctly by the Tap Strap 2.

The data collection procedure was conducted as follows. With the SDK opened in the Spyder IDE and the Tap Strap 2 worn on the right hand, the Tap was connected to a laptop via Bluetooth. The SDK was then run in "raw sensors" mode, initiating accelerometer and IMU data collection as soon as the device was recognized. The letter "a" was then typed 60 times while the program was running. When this was complete, the program was terminated, and the sensors data produced was copied and pasted into a text file. This process was repeated two more times for the letter "a", with the only differences being that the letter was typed 70 times during the second time and 80 times during the third. The entire procedure was then repeated for every letter up to "z", resulting in a total of 78 text files.

Now that the data was collected, it was important to get it into a usable format that can be processed by the RNN. In addition to the data, the raw output from the SDK had was full of commas, parentheses, and unwanted words, all of which had to be cleaned. For each text file, the data was imported into an Excel sheet. Spaces were used as separators so that all columns containing only parentheses or words could be easily removed. The only unwanted features that remained after this were commas, which were easily removed by replacing them with empty strings (""). This left only the data for the accelerometers and the IMU. The accelerometer data have 15 columns, since there are five accelerometers and three axes of measurement for each. In contrast, the IMU data only have six columns, corresponding to the six measurement axes of the IMU. Both types of data were left together in the same columns, since they had different structures and therefore could be easily distinguished.

Furthermore, there were no labels in the data indicating which quantity each value was referring to. It was determined from the data-cleaning process that repeating the same procedure for 78 Excel sheets is very tedious and time-consuming, so it was important to automate the process in order to save time. This was done using an Excel Macro, an program that can automatically repeat the same procedure for many files in the same folder. This Macro was designed so that it would attach the appropriate label to each column ("acc_1_x/IMU_1", "acc_1_y/IMU_2", etc.). Additionally, row labels were added to further distinguish accelerometer and IMU data, and these labels were decided by determining whether or not the seventh column was blank with an IF statement. The Macro was then run on all 78 Excel files in the folder to label them. This could be done since the format was identical for all the sheets.

In the final step of the data preparation process was to indicate the locations of the peaks in acceleration corresponding to the inputs. This could potentially be complicated since the input combinations are different for each letter. Fortunately, it is easy to generalize, since only one (known) letter is typed in each file, so there is no need to distinguish between different types of inputs in one file. That is, the only conditions are "input" and "no input". The method used to determine the locations of the inputs involved finding where the x-acceleration for any of the accelerometers deviated from the mean value for that accelerometer by more than 600. Deviation from the mean was used as opposed to a raw value threshold since each of the accelerometers had their acceleration values "centered" around a different mean. The reason for the use of the value of 600 was because this value was small enough to pick up inputs of low acceleration without accidentally interpreting normal fluctuations in acceleration as character inputs. The x-acceleration was used because it responded more strongly to the taps than the y- and z-accelerations.

3.2   Standard LSTM-RNN Model

The first model used in this experiment was an "ordinary" one-dimensional LSTM-RNN derived from a template at Machine Learning Mastery [8]. The original model from the link is designed for HAR from time series sensors data. The architecture of this model consists of one LSTM layer, a dropout layer, and two dense (entirely connected) layers. The dropout layer, which sets input values to zero at random while increasing the other input values, primarily serves the purpose of keeping the network from overfitting. Overfitting is a phenomenon where a machine learning model becomes so familiar with a particular training data set that it becomes unable to intelligently assign labels in other data sets.

In this experiment, the architecture of the network itself was mostly left unchanged. The plan was for significant changes to be made only if the accuracy turned out to be poor. The primary difference is the way in which the data is fed into the neural network, since the structure of the Tap accelerometer data is quite different from that of the data set used in the original HAR study. In the HAR study that the template was originally utilized for, the data was already split into testing and training data sets, with 9 different files for each containing information from different sensors. In this experiment, by contrast, the data set is split into three files for each letter of the alphabet, and each file has x-, y-, and z-acceleration data in different columns for every sensor. Evidently, this data will need to be entered into the neural network model in a different manner.

The data set was split up and fed into the model as follows. The files for each letter containing 70 and 80 inputs were combined into the training data set, while the files containing 60 inputs went to the testing data. This is because the training data set should optimally be large, presenting as many possible situations to the model so that the model can successfully recognize any input regardless of the context. For both of the data sets, the files were loaded in and the data was stacked vertically in an array so that there is effectively a very long time series of data. This may seem problematic, since the timer resets at the end of each file in the array, but the experiment will not consider the time values themselves, as they originate from the Tap Strap 2's internal clock and are therefore somewhat arbitrary. The main purpose of them is to be able to chronologically sort the data within the Excel files, and the order of the data is what matters here.

For both the training and testing data sets, the labels column (which contains either the character being typed or a blank space) was separated off from the features (sensors data). The next step was to one-hot encode the labels. In data categorization algorithms such as this one, one-hot encoding is when each category (or label) is represented by a number. This is necessary because the experiment involves non-numerical data, and the model only recognizes numerical data. Since is possible to type 26 letters of the alphabet, as well as no input at all, there are 27 numbered categories in this experiment that each time step can fall into.

The final step was to feed the data into the network and fit the model. The parameters of the model were mostly left unchanged, using 15 epochs per run and a batch size of 64 data points. It is also important to evaluate the model multiple times before the accuracy of the model can be quantified, so the model was evaluated a total of 10 times with the accuracy being averaged. The next step will be to move on and explore two other variations of the LSTM that will be compared to this model accuracy-wise.

3.3   CNN-LSTM Model

Recurrent neural networks such as the LSTM have an advantage over convolutional neural networks due to their ability to use contextual information when predicting a value. In spite of this, CNNs are more commonly used to analyze time series sensors data due to their feature extraction capabilities. There is some reasoning behind this, as CNN-based models have been shown to outperform LSTM-based ones for fall detection [9]. As it is clear that both of these types of neural networks hold different advantages over one another, it is not surprising that some experiments have attempted to combine the functionality of CNNs and RNNs together for greater accuracy. The result of using both convolutional and LSTM layers in a model is a CNN-LSTM model. The CNN-LSTM has been used on accelerometer data in experiments that focus on human activity recognition [10,11] and fall detection [12].

The idea of using a CNN-LSTM and comparing its accuracy to that of the normal LSTM originated from the fact that the Machine Learning Mastery site also had an example of a CNN-LSTM. This model consists of two one-dimensional CNN layers, a one-dimensional max pooling layer, a flatten layer, the LSTM layer, and two dense layers. In this experiment, the model was largely left unchanged except for the shape of the input data. To fit the input data into the model, much of the same processing was done as for the normal LSTM. The same training and testing data sets were used, and the labels were separated off from the features and one-hot encoded. For the CNN-LSTM, 25 epochs were used with the same batch size of 64. Again, the model was evaluated a total of 10 times and the accuracy was averaged.

3.4   Convolutional LSTM Model

The third neural network model proposed by this experiment is a convolutional LSTM (ConvLSTM) model. A convolutional LSTM differs from a CNN-LSTM in that, as opposed to the model simply having both convolutional and LSTM layers working alongside each other, the CNN and LSTM are integrated together as one layer. Much like CNN-LSTMs, they can be of great use for human activity [13] and gesture [14] recognition, which this experiment entails. When compared to CNN-LSTM models in their ability to analyze sensors data, ConvLSTM models have been shown to be capable of outperforming CNN-LSTM ones [15].

As with the previous two models, the ConvLSTM model used in this experiment was based off an example from the Machine Learning Mastery site. This model is structured very similarly to the normal LSTM except for the fact that the LSTM layer is replaced with a two-dimensional ConvLSTM layer. The data was processed in the same way as for the previous two models. As with the CNN-LSTM, the model was trained with 25 epochs and a batch size of 64, and it was evaluated 10 times with the accuracy being averaged. From background research, it was expected for the ConvLSTM to have the best accuracy of the models, followed by the CNN-LSTM.

4   Experimental Results

Table 1 summarizes the accuracy results of the each of the evaluation runs for the LSTM, CNN-LSTM, and ConvLSTM, as well as the average accuracy for each model. The average accuracy was 97.470% for the regular LSTM, 96.684% for the CNN-LSTM, and 96.658% for the ConvLSTM. These results are actually highly surprising, as they are opposite to what was expected. The normal LSTM actually boasts the highest accuracy of the three models, followed by the CNN-LSTM, while the ConvLSTM has the worst accuracy of the three, although the results for all three models are reasonably similar. It is also surprising that the difference in accuracy between the LSTM and CNN-LSTM is greater than that between the CNN-LSTM and ConvLSTM. The LSTM outperforms both the CNN-LSTM and ConvLSTM by a significant amount: nearly an entire percent. By contrast, the difference in accuracy between the CNN-LSTM and ConvLSTM is marginal, with some runs of the ConvLSTM outperforming certain runs of the CNN-LSTM.

Table 1. Accuracy rates of LSTM model evaluation

Evaluation	LSTM	CNN-LSTM	ConvLSTM
1	97.452%	96.691%	96.658%
2	97.518%	96.682%	96.658%
3	97.482%	96.726%	96.655%
4	97.496%	96.647%	96.657%
5	97.471%	96.659%	96.659%
6	97.445%	96.656%	96.660%
7	97.532%	96.745%	96.658%
8	97.407%	96.705%	96.656%
9	97.522%	96.659%	96.659%
10	97.427%	96.673%	96.659%
Average	97.470%	96.684%	96.658%

From the fact that all accuracy values are above 95%, it is quite evident that all three models were very effective in fitting the data. Figure 1 plots the training and validation (test) accuracy and loss for each epoch on the 10th and final run of the LSTM model. For both the CNN-LSTM and ConvLSTM, the trends observed were very similar, as is shown by Figs. 2 and 3. There does appear to be some degree of overfitting, which is evident from the fact that the validation loss increases and the validation accuracy remains relatively unchanging near 96.8%. This is not too alarming, as the validation accuracy does not appear to be negatively impacted. It is also not very surprising, since the task that the neural network is instructed to perform is relatively simple. Because the inputs are labeled based on the x-accelerometer values, there is very high separability in the data set, meaning it is easy for an algorithm to distinguish between different character inputs based on the corresponding sensors information. It is likely that the neural network already achieved very high accuracy on the testing data set during the first epoch, and therefore there were few adjustments to be made in the first place.

A possible improvement that could be made to this model is the addition of a spatial attention mechanism. Attention mechanisms identify areas in the data that are expectionally influential to the output while placing less weight on less important ones since they can lead to complications in the results. Zhang et al. performed an inquiry into attention mechanisms in ConvLSTMs in particular [16]. In this study, it was found that certain variants of the ConvLSTM with attention mechanisms outperformed a "standard" ConvLSTM when it came to video-based gesture recognition. While this often means putting emphasis on certain regions of an image in the context of CNNs, it can also be applied to human activity recognition from sensors data. Such a study using normal CNNs with attention to analyze the UCI HAR Dataset was performed by Wang et al. [17]. This could prove beneficial by allowing the ConvLSTM model to obtain higher accuracy.

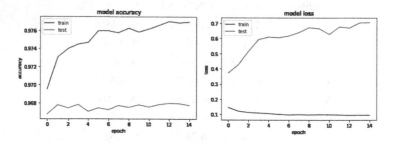

Fig. 1. Training and validation accuracy and loss for 10th run of LSTM.

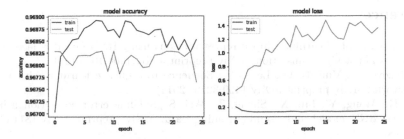

Fig. 2. Training and validation accuracy and loss for 10th run of CNN-LSTM.

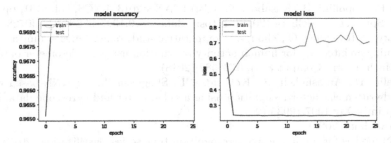

Fig. 3. Training and validation accuracy and loss for 10th run of ConvLSTM.

5   Conclusions and Future Work

This experiment proposed three LSTM models to interpret Tap Strap 2 inputs from raw accelerometer data. These were a standard LSTM model, a model with both CNN and LSTM layers, and a convolutional LSTM. The LSTM was found to have had the highest accuracy at an average of 97.470%, followed by the CNN-LSTM with an accuracy of 96.684% and the ConvLSTM with an accuracy of 96.658%. While the model did overfit, it did not appear to have any impact of the accuracy, which remained high.

Further work on this project would focus on implementing an algorithm similar to this one into the device itself. While this experiment involved collecting raw sensors data from the device and using it to train and test the model with solid results, the model is not particularly useful without being integrated with the device's software. Therefore, the main goal of future experiments would be to allow the model to decide on inputs the moment they are typed, likely working in tandem with the software on-board the Tap Strap 2. Additional work can also be done to probe into why the CNN-LSTM and ConvLSTM actually perform slightly worse than the normal LSTM model. Finally, a spatial attention mechanism similar to the one described in the previous section could be implemented with the goal of improving the validation accuracy of the model.

References

1. Cho, K., et al.: Learning phrase representations using RNN encoder-decoder for statistical machine translation. arXiv preprint arXiv:1406.1078 (2014)
2. Sutskever, I., Vinyals, O., Le, Q.V.: Sequence to sequence learning with neural networks. arXiv preprint arXiv:1409.3215 (2014)
3. Li, H., Wang, Y., Liu, X., Sheng, Z., Wei, S.: Spelling error correction using a nested RNN model and pseudo training data. arXiv preprint arXiv:1811.00238 (2018)
4. Lefebvre, G., Berlemont, S., Mamalet, F., Garcia, C.: BLSTM-RNN Based 3D gesture classification. In: Mladenov, V., Koprinkova-Hristova, P., Palm, G., Villa, A.E.P., Appollini, B., Kasabov, N. (eds.) ICANN 2013. LNCS, vol. 8131, pp. 381–388. Springer, Heidelberg (2013). https://doi.org/10.1007/978-3-642-40728-4_48
5. Shakya, S.R., Zhang, C., Zhou, Z.: Comparative study of machine learning and deep learning architecture for human activity recognition using accelerometer data. Int. J. Mach. Learn. Comput 8(6), 577–582 (2018)
6. Soselia, D., Amashukeli, S., Koberidze, I., Shugliashvili, L.: RNN-based online handwritten character recognition using accelerometer and gyroscope data. arXiv preprint arXiv:1907.12935 (2019)
7. Tap with us (2020)
8. RNN models for human activity recognition time series classification (2020)
9. Santos, G.L., Endo, P.T., Monteiro, K.H.D.C., Rocha, E.D.S., Silva, I., Lynn, T.: Accelerometer-based human fall detection using convolutional neural networks. Sensors 19(7), 1644 (2019)
10. Deep, S., Zheng, X.: Hybrid model featuring CNN and LSTM architecture for human activity recognition on smartphone sensor data. In: 2019 20th International Conference on Parallel and Distributed Computing, Applications and Technologies (PDCAT), pp. 259–264. IEEE (2019)
11. Xia, K., Huang, J., Wang, H.: LSTM-CNN architecture for human activity recognition. IEEE Access 8, 56855–56866 (2020)
12. Xu, J., He, Z., Zhang, Y.: CNN-LSTM combined network for IoT enabled fall detection applications. J. Phys.: Conf. Ser. 1267, 012044 (2019)
13. Zhang, Z., Lv, Z., Gan, C., Zhu, Q.: Human action recognition using convolutional LSTM and fully-connected LSTM with different attentions. Neurocomputing 410, 304–316 (2020)
14. Zhang, L., Zhu, G., Shen, P., Song, J., Afaq Shah, S., Bennamoun, M.: Learning spatiotemporal features using 3DCNN and convolutional LSTM for gesture recognition. In: Proceedings of the IEEE International Conference on Computer Vision Workshops, pp. 3120–3128 (2017)
15. Çiçek, E., Gören, S.: Smartphone power management based on ConvLSTM model. Neural Comput. Appl. 33, 8017–8029 (2021). https://doi.org/10.1007/s00521-020-05544-9
16. Zhang, L., Zhu, G., Mei, L., Shen, P., Shah, S.A.A., Bennamoun, M.: Attention in convolutional LSTM for gesture recognition. In: Proceedings of the 32nd International Conference on Neural Information Processing Systems, pp. 1957–1966 (2018)
17. Wang, K., He, J., Zhang, L.: Attention-based convolutional neural network for weakly labeled human activities' recognition with wearable sensors. IEEE Sens. J. 19(17), 7598–7604 (2019)

Electronic Dictionary and Translator of Bilingual Turkish Languages

E. Sh. Nazirova[1]([⊠]), Sh. B. Abidova[2], and Sh. Sh. Yuldasheva[1]

[1] Department of Multimedia Technologies, DSc, Tashkent University of Information Technologies named after Muhammad al-Khwarizmi, Tashkent, Uzbekistan
shaxnoza23@mail.ru
[2] Tashkent University of Information Technologies named after Muhammad al-Khwarizmi, Tashkent, Uzbekistan

Abstract. The article presents the IDEF0 model, functional module for the implementation of electronic translation in Uzbek and Karakalpak languages, which belong to the family of Turkic languages, as well as software for electronic translation based on these models and modules.

Keywords: Electronic translator · Uzbek and Karakalpak language · IDEF0 model · Software

1 Introduction

Since the development of electronic translators today is based on the formalization of information about linguistic objects in applied linguistics, the successful formation and functioning of electronic translators will need to be studied in terms of the ability to translate linguistic information into machine language.

Analyzing the work done on machine translators [1], the idea of the TurkLang-7 project is to create a data set for Russian-Turkish sources for low-language pairs and a system for translating neural machines. In this paper, a semi-automatic process for creating parallel corpora has been developed.

[2, 10] In this article, a database of phraseological verbs, morphological lexicon, affixes in Uzbek and English, and their morphological and syntactic models are created. The agreement of simple sentence models for automatic translation has been determined. recommendations for combining paradigmatic approaches to the creation of electronic dictionary and software principles for a linguistic database have been developed.

Based on the foregoing, among the urgent tasks are the comparative study of the Turkic languages, the linguistic support of machine translation systems and the development of other special lexicographic resources.

J.-H. Kim et al. (Eds.): IHCI 2021, LNCS 13184, pp. 39–49, 2022.
https://doi.org/10.1007/978-3-030-98404-5_4

Accordingly, this article describes the principle of operation of a software package that provides electronic translation into Uzbek and Karakalpak languages, which belong to the family of Turkic languages.

Before implementing the electronic translator, we will build a mathematical model of sentence construction in Uzbek and Karakalpak languages.

Uzbek and Karakalpak languages belong to the group of agglutinative languages of the Turkic language family. That is, the formation of words in these languages is done by adding word-forming suffixes to the root word.

It is known that in Uzbek language there is a normal order of words. According to this order, the possessive is placed before the possessive, and the participle is placed after it, the definite article and the complement are placed before the participle, which means that the participle usually comes at the end of the sentence.

However, in order to express a particular methodological meaning, the usual order of words in a sentence can be changed, such a changed word order is also called inversion.

In scientific and formal styles, the usual order of words in a sentence is largely maintained. But in conversational, artistic, and journalistic styles, this order change, i.e., inversion order, can be applied.

The Karakalpak language uses the same sentence structure as the Uzbek language.

Mathematical models of simple and complex sentences in Uzbek and Karakalpak languages were developed on the basis of the scheme of simple and complex sentences formation in two languages.

$$G_{\text{сод}} = A(x_i, \ldots, x_n) \cup B(x_i, \ldots, x_n)$$
$$G_{\text{мур}} = A(x_i, \ldots, x_n) \cup D(x_i, \ldots, x_n) \cup S(x_i, \ldots, x_n) \cup K(x_i, \ldots, x_n) \cup B(x_i, \ldots, x_n)$$

Here $G_{\text{сод}}$ – simple sentence, $G_{\text{мур}}$ – complex sentence, $A(x_i, \ldots, x_n)$ – possessive, $D(x_i, \ldots, x_n)$ – complement, $S(x_i, \ldots, x_n)$ – case, $K(x_i, \ldots, x_n)$ – determiner, $B(x_i, \ldots, x_n)$ – cut.

Using this model, we can see 8 different ways of creating simple and complex sentences in Uzbek and Karakalpak:

For the Uzbek language

$$G_1 = \begin{cases} A(x_i, \dots, x_n) \\ B(x_i, \dots, x_n) \rightarrow f_{k(\phi)} \oplus P_{r(\text{от})} \oplus f_{k(\phi)} \oplus a_{j(\text{от})} \oplus P_{r(\phi)} \oplus f_{k(\phi)} \end{cases}$$

$$G_2 = \begin{cases} A(x_i, \dots, x_n) \\ K(x_i, \dots, x_n) \rightarrow a_{j(\text{от})} \oplus P_{r(\text{сиф})} \oplus P_{r(\phi)} \\ B(x_i, \dots, x_n) \rightarrow f_{k(\phi)} \oplus P_{r(\text{от})} \oplus f_{k(\phi)} \oplus a_{j(\text{от})} \oplus P_{r(\phi)} \oplus f_{k(\phi)} \end{cases}$$

$$G_3 = \begin{cases} A(x_i, \dots, x_n) \\ S(x_i, \dots, x_n) \rightarrow P_{r(\text{от})} \oplus P_{r(\text{рав})} \oplus P_{r(\phi)} \\ B(x_i, \dots, x_n) \rightarrow f_{k(\phi)} \oplus P_{r(\text{от})} \oplus f_{k(\phi)} \oplus a_{j(\text{от})} \oplus P_{r(\phi)} \oplus f_{k(\phi)} \end{cases}$$

$$G_4 = \begin{cases} A(x_i, \dots, x_n) \\ K(x_i, \dots, x_n) \rightarrow a_{j(\text{от})} \oplus P_{r(\text{сиф})} \oplus P_{r(\phi)} \\ D(x_i, \dots, x_n) \rightarrow f_{k(\text{рав})} \oplus P_{r(\text{от})} \oplus P_{r(\phi)} \oplus P_{r(\text{рав})} \\ B(x_i, \dots, x_n) \rightarrow f_{k(\phi)} \oplus P_{r(\text{от})} \oplus f_{k(\phi)} \oplus a_{j(\text{от})} \oplus P_{r(\phi)} \oplus f_{k(\phi)} \end{cases}$$

$$G_5 = \begin{cases} A(x_i, \dots, x_n) \\ D(x_i, \dots, x_n) \rightarrow f_{k(\text{рав})} \oplus P_{r(\text{от})} \oplus P_{r(\phi)} \oplus P_{r(\text{рав})} \\ S(x_i, \dots, x_n) \rightarrow P_{r(\text{от})} \oplus P_{r(\text{рав})} \oplus P_{r(\phi)} \\ B(x_i, \dots, x_n) \rightarrow f_{k(\phi)} \oplus P_{r(\text{от})} \oplus f_{k(\phi)} \oplus a_{j(\text{от})} \oplus P_{r(\phi)} \oplus f_{k(\phi)} \end{cases}$$

$$G_6 = \begin{cases} K(x_i, \dots, x_n) \rightarrow a_{j(\text{от})} \oplus P_{r(\text{сиф})} \oplus P_{r(\phi)} \\ A(x_i, \dots, x_n) \\ D(x_i, \dots, x_n) \rightarrow f_{k(\text{рав})} \oplus P_{r(\text{от})} \oplus P_{r(\phi)} \oplus P_{r(\text{рав})} \\ B(x_i, \dots, x_n) \rightarrow f_{k(\phi)} \oplus P_{r(\text{от})} \oplus f_{k(\phi)} \oplus a_{j(\text{от})} \oplus P_{r(\phi)} \oplus f_{k(\phi)} \end{cases}$$

$$G_7 = \begin{cases} D(x_i, \dots, x_n) \rightarrow f_{k(\text{рав})} \oplus P_{r(\text{от})} \oplus P_{r(\phi)} \oplus P_{r(\text{рав})} \\ B(x_i, \dots, x_n) \rightarrow f_{k(\phi)} \oplus P_{r(\text{от})} \oplus f_{k(\phi)} \oplus a_{j(\text{от})} \oplus P_{r(\phi)} \oplus f_{k(\phi)} \end{cases}$$

$$G_8 = \{ B(x_i, \dots, x_n) \rightarrow f_{k(\phi)} \oplus P_{r(\text{от})} \oplus f_{k(\phi)} \oplus a_{j(\text{от})} \oplus P_{r(\phi)} \oplus f_{k(\phi)}$$

For the Karakalpak language

$$G_1 = \begin{cases} A(x_i, ..., x_n) \\ B(x_i, ..., x_n) \rightarrow f_{k(\text{от})} \oplus a_{j(\text{от})} \oplus f_{k(\phi)} \end{cases}$$

$$G_2 = \begin{cases} A(x_i, ..., x_n) \\ K(x_i, ..., x_n) \rightarrow a_{j(\text{от})} \oplus f_{k(\text{сиф})} \oplus f_{k(\phi)} \\ B(x_i, ..., x_n) \rightarrow f_{k(\text{от})} \oplus a_{j(\text{от})} \oplus f_{k(\phi)} \end{cases}$$

$$G_3 = \begin{cases} A(x_i, ..., x_n) \\ S(x_i, ..., x_n) \rightarrow f_{k(\text{от})} \oplus f_{k(\text{рав})} \oplus f_{k(\phi)} \\ B(x_i, ..., x_n) \rightarrow f_{k(\text{от})} \oplus a_{j(\text{от})} \oplus f_{k(\phi)} \end{cases}$$

$$G_4 = \begin{cases} A(x_i, ..., x_n) \\ K(x_i, ..., x_n) \rightarrow a_{j(\text{от})} \oplus f_{k(\text{сиф})} \oplus f_{k(\phi)} \\ D(x_i, ..., x_n) \rightarrow f_{k(\text{от})} \oplus f_{k(\phi)} \oplus f_{k(\text{рав})} \\ B(x_i, ..., x_n) \rightarrow f_{k(\text{от})} \oplus a_{j(\text{от})} \oplus f_{k(\phi)} \end{cases}$$

$$G_5 = \begin{cases} A(x_i, ..., x_n) \\ D(x_i, ..., x_n) \rightarrow f_{k(\text{от})} \oplus f_{k(\phi)} \oplus f_{k(\text{рав})} \\ S(x_i, ..., x_n) \rightarrow f_{k(\text{от})} \oplus f_{k(\text{рав})} \oplus f_{k(\phi)} \\ B(x_i, ..., x_n) \rightarrow f_{k(\text{от})} \oplus a_{j(\text{от})} \oplus f_{k(\phi)} \end{cases}$$

$$G_6 = \begin{cases} K(x_i, ..., x_n) \rightarrow a_{j(\text{от})} \oplus f_{k(\text{сиф})} \oplus f_{k(\phi)} \\ A(x_i, ..., x_n) \\ D(x_i, ..., x_n) \rightarrow f_{k(\text{от})} \oplus f_{k(\phi)} \oplus f_{k(\text{рав})} \\ B(x_i, ..., x_n) \rightarrow f_{k(\text{от})} \oplus a_{j(\text{от})} \oplus f_{k(\phi)} \end{cases}$$

$$G_7 = \begin{cases} D(x_i, ..., x_n) \rightarrow f_{k(\text{от})} \oplus f_{k(\phi)} \oplus f_{k(\text{рав})} \\ B(x_i, ..., x_n) \rightarrow f_{k(\text{от})} \oplus a_{j(\text{от})} \oplus f_{k(\phi)} \end{cases}$$

$$G_8 = \{ B(x_i, ..., x_n) \rightarrow f_{k(\text{от})} \oplus a_{j(\text{от})} \oplus f_{k(\phi)}$$

The process of translation in electronic translation is carried out on the basis of the following sequence:

- in the first place, each word in a given sentence is singled out;
- the anterior and posterior suffixes and stems of each word are checked and separated;
- the extracted pieces are first checked conditionally, then searched from the database;
- The appropriate translation of the allocated piece in the database is taken and the piece is replaced.

Thus, all the pieces are combined and the result is achieved (Fig. 1).

First, we check and prefix each element of the selected array.

If word have a prefix, it is assimilated as an element of the prefix [j] array. Then the suffix is checked and separated in the same way.

If a suffix exists, it is assimilated as an element of the suffix [j] array. In some cases, a suffix can be multiple words. The rest remains in place as an element of the array.

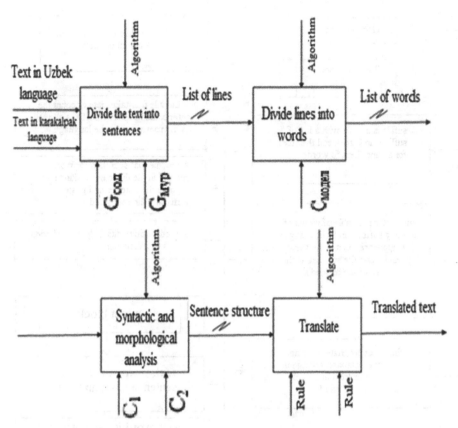

Fig. 1. IDEF0 drawing of electronic translator

The extracted prefix, stem, and suffix are checked from the database (Table 1-2-3), respectively. After verification, a new word is created and printed. If no word is found in the table, it is printed as translated text [3–6].

Based on the above models and algorithms, electronic translator software has been developed. The figure below shows the functional modules of software performance (Fig. 2).

The developed interface of the software "Bilingual electronic translator" has the following appearance.

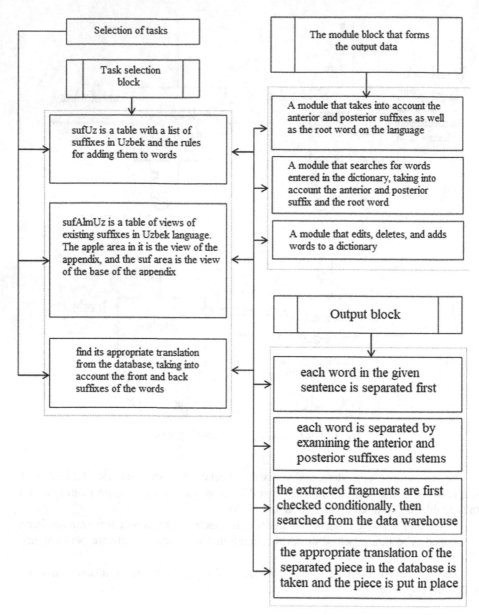

Fig. 2. Functional diagram of software performance

Figure 3 shows a view of the homepage of the program.

The main page consists of the main part of the program performing electronic translation, a translation window, an electronic dictionary, an annotated dictionary, a link, adding a new word, a button to download a file and copying sections.

Fig. 3. Home page

In Fig. 4, in the language selection section, the menu for selecting the Uzbek-Karakalpak (Karakalpak-Uzbek) language is shown. The user can translate by selecting the desired language (Fig. 5).

Enter the word in Uzbek and Karakalpak. The meaning of the entered word is indicated in the section "Word Meaning" (Fig. 6).

In the section of the annotated dictionary, the word in Uzbek is entered in the "Enter a word" field, and in the section "Meaning of a word" it is given with comments on word groups.

In the "Add word" section you can add new words to the database in Uzbek and Karakalpak languages. In this case, the word is entered in the "Enter a new word" section, and in the "Select language" section, the language in which the word is entered is selected, and the "Add" button is used to add a new word to the database (Figs. 7 and 8).

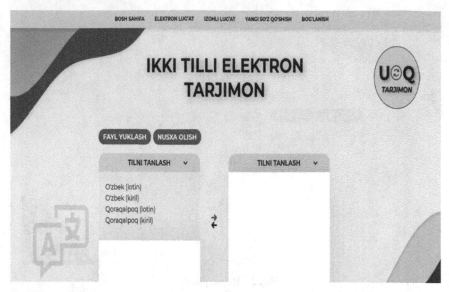

Fig. 4. Language selection department when performing electronic translation

In the links section, the user can enter the first name, last name and postal address and leave a message to the developer in the "Message" section.

In the file upload section, the user can upload a.doc file and translate the full text.

In the "Copy" section, the user can make a copy of the translated text and paste it into the desired file [7–9].

Fig. 5. Electronic dictionary department

Fig. 6. Annotated dictionary section

Fig. 7. Add a new word section

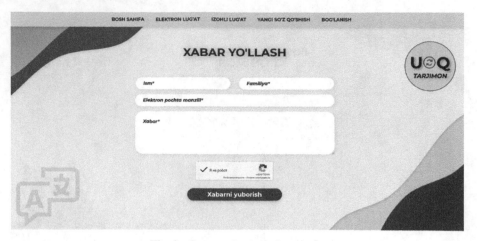

Fig. 8. Communications department

Conclusion. In conclusion, it can be said that the electronic translator was implemented using the mentioned IDEF0 model and the functional module of the software. This model and functional module can be used in languages belonging to the family of Turkic languages and agglutinative languages.

References

1. Khusainov, A., Suleymanov, D., Gilmullin, R., Minsafina, A., Kubedinova, L., Abdurakhmonova, N.: First Results of the TurkLang-7 project: creating Russian-Turkic parallel corpora and MT systems, pp. 90–101 (2020)
2. Abdurakhmonova, N.Z., Teshabayev, A.G.: Modeling IT of discourse analysis and the ussues machine translation, pp. 101–107 (2019)
3. Абидова, Ш.Б.: Электрон таржимон яратишда ўзбек тилининг морфологик таҳлилини амалга оширишнинг инфологик модели. Мухаммад ал-Хоразмий авлодлари **3**(13), 131–136 (2020). (05.00.00; №10)
4. Нуралиев, Ф.М., Абидова, Ш.Б.: Икки тилнинг семантик таҳлили. ТАТУ хабарлари журнали. **3**(40), 113–117 (2017). (05.00.00; №31)
5. Nazirova, E.Sh., Abidova, Sh.B.: Mathematical model and algorithm for calculating complex words in the Karakalpak language. Bull. TUIT Manage. Commun. Technol. **1**(44), 1–7 (2019). (30.07.2020; №283/7.1)
6. Nazirova, E., Abidova, S.: Mathematical model and algorithm for calculating complex words int Uzbek language. Solid State Technol. **64**(2), 4347–4359 (2021)
7. Абидова, Ш.Б.: Лингвистическая схема трансферной системы двуязычного перевода. In: Тезисы международной конференции "Актуальные проблемы прикладной математики и информационных технологий". Тошкент, 2019 г., 14–15 ноябр, pp. 283–284 (2019)
8. Абидова, Ш.Б.: Туркий тиллар учун электрон луғат яратиш муаммолари. In: Иқтисодиётнинг реал тармоқларини инновацион ривожланишида ахборот-коммуникация технологияларининг аҳамияти. Республика илмий-техник анжумани. Тошкент 2017 й. 6–7 апрел, pp. 267–269 (2017)

9. Абидова, Ш.Б.: Особенности морфологии узбекского языка создании электронного узбекско-каракалпакского словаря-переводчика. In: «Актуальные проблемы математики и механики – CAWMA-2018» тезисы докладов республиканской научно-практической конференции с участием зарубежных женщин-ученых. Хива, 25–26 октябр 2018, pp. 4–5 (2018)
10. Абдурахманова, Н., Хакимов, М.: Логико-лингвистические модели слов и предложений английского языка для многоязычных ситуаций компьютернеого перевода. Компьютерная обработка тюркских языков. Латинизация письменности. 1-я Международная конференция. Астана, pp. 297–302 (2013)

Facial Recognition Technologies: A Survey and Comparison of Systems and Practical Applications

Nicholas Muskopf-Stone, Georgia Votta, Joshua Van Essen, Aira Peregrino, and Tauheed Khan Mohd[✉]

Augustana College, Rock Island, IL 61201, USA
tauheedkhanmohd@augustana.edu

Abstract. Through recent years, facial recognition technology has become increasingly relevant in a widespread area of applications. There are numerous approaches to facial recognition technology, each best-suited for different types of practices. A survey which compares the infrared, thermal, and deep learning methods is performed in this study. Each method is evaluated based on its speed, accuracy, and efficiency and is given a overall percentage of reliability. Further, we examine the advantages and disadvantages of each method and assess what common usage of each method would be in a practical setting. We find a point of commonality between each method type where accuracy and efficiency must strike a balance, further compounded by the practical applications of each method. Our findings show that while there is an ideal method of facial recognition for each individual application, there is no ideal method that applies to every application.

Keywords: Facial recognition · Infrared · Eigenface · Biometrics · Neural network · Convolution

1 Introduction

Facial recognition is not a new concept. Manual facial recognition, or the process of physically comparing a human's face to a potentially matching image, has been in use for decades. For example, facial recognition is used as a means of identifying suspects and perpetrators in law enforcement agencies. Over the past few decades, facial recognition algorithms have been recognized not only for their benefits in identifying suspects, but also for potential applications in security and surveillance. With the emergence of digitized facial recognition technology, facial recognition has become increasingly accessible and it has been utilized for broader properties outside of law enforcement. As opposed to manual facial recognition practices, digitized facial recognition technology is quicker, less strenuous, and more adaptable to a wide group of individuals. With these benefits, it makes sense that facial recognition is one of the most prominent areas of Human-Computer Interaction (HCI) emerging in the field of computer science.

© Springer Nature Switzerland AG 2022
J.-H. Kim et al. (Eds.): IHCI 2021, LNCS 13184, pp. 50–61, 2022.
https://doi.org/10.1007/978-3-030-98404-5_5

Because of newfound focus on this technology, the architecture of digitized facial recognition has been tested and experimented with by professionals in computer science. As a result, different improvements and variations of the technology have emerged.

Applicable facial recognition technology was first rooted in biometrics, or the study of converting physical features into mathematical structures using measurements and geometry. In the late 20th century, the concept of the eigenface was introduced which pioneered this approach to facial recognition [1]. Translating the features of the face into mathematics was pivotal to facial recognition technology as it allowed for an image's subject to be digitized, stored and compared through computer software. The architecture behind the eigenface method is found in many other forms of facial recognition, most prominently the Viola-Jones algorithm in the early 21st century [2]. Nevertheless, as this technology advances, other approaches have been formed. Infrared technology has been introduced which, theoretically, maps out the vessels in a human's face in order to create a distinct, fingerprint-like template [3]. Similarly, thermal approaches that detect particular unique heated areas of the face have been used as another method of mapping out the human face [4]. Outside of the pioneered feature-based approach, the development of AI and deep learning have permitted new holistic methods of facial recognition [5].

As facial technology continues to advance, so too do it's applications outside of computer science. Currently, it holds relevance in medicine [6], criminal justice [7], sociology [8], pure mathematics [9], and has even sparked discussion of the ethics of privacy. The face is a critical part of an individual's identity that humans are trained from birth to recognize and interpret information from. Now, technology is catching up to humans' ability to distinguish faces and identities through image or video [6]. Facial recognition technology has been used for generalized surveillance, but its overall complexity makes it hard to use consistently for more critical and reliable work. In a study done in 2019, facial recognition technology was able to identify minor criminals that had been observed at public events, but it was later revealed that the cameras led to multiple false positives, and the system at the time was scrapped [10]. While it may seem that each method is an extension of the previous one, every approach should be examined for both its benefits as well as its drawbacks. That is the goal of this paper. By studying a variety of techniques in digitized facial recognition, a comparison will be drawn of the advantages and disadvantages of each one. Specifically, factors such as speed, accuracy, efficiency, and general applicability in the real world will be examined through aforementioned recognition methods like eigenfaces, infrared, and thermal detection.

2 Related Work

In the field of facial recognition systems, there are already a significant amount of surveys relating to different facial recognition methods. In their 2009 survey, Jafri and Arabnia examined different biometric approaches in their attempt to compare their effectiveness in spite of both intrinsic and extrinsic factors. The survey explores a geometric feature-based approach that uses 35 geometric shapes to map the face as well as a template-based approach that holds greater accuracy than the first method [3]. To make improvements on the feature-based method, a Gabor filter was introduced that takes into account textural analysis [3]. Although accurate, the added step of textual analysis proved difficult due to the manual input of a facial structure to be repeated a multitude of times before garnering a dependable system for comparison [3]. Jafri and Arabnia then considered Kaufman and Breeding's facial profile approach in which vectors along distinctive portions from the side of the face are used instead of a typical front-facing method [3]. The survey additionally looked at one of the most relevant facial recognition systems, the Eigenface method. This method proved to be accurate, but when different extrinsic factors were introduced, the quality declined.

As opposed to pure biometrics in which the face is converted into geometric components, You et al. explores other methods that incorporate artificial intelligence as a means of improving accuracy. You et al. discuss the use of deep convolutional neural networking (DCNNs) as a form of facial recognition in which a program implores deep learning to modify its facial recognition in real-time [5]. The survey finds that deep learning's reliance on a loss function, or a function that modifies a program if the model produced differs too far from the real results, improves facial recognition software accuracy tremendously [5]. In comparing four different deep learning techniques (VGG-16, GoogLe-Net, Face-ResNet, ResNet-50) with different network changes applied to each one, each system was examined with and without batch normalization as well as feature normalization to great results [5]. The overall study concluded the benefits of deep neural networking as well as vertical expansion over horizontal.

Furthermore, Kortli et al.'s Facial Recognition Systems: A Survey (2020) combines similar research from Jafri and Arabnia and You et al. to compare both feature-based facial recognition as well as more holistic, AI-related approaches. Kortli et al. splits their analysis into three different categories: local approaches, holistic approaches, and hybrid approaches. In local approaches, the survey looks at specific examples of both key-point face strategies that map out the face in geometric terms (LBP, KNN, HOG, etc.) and local appearance-based strategies that map out the face using specific facial features (SIFT, SURF, and BRIEF) [2]. Holistic approaches process the face as a whole instead of focusing on particular parts like local methods, with approaches including the eigenface, the Fisherface, FDDL, and other methods of extracting information from an entire face rather than individual facial features [2]. Lastly, hybrid approaches provide the benefit of multiple layers of comparison for improved accuracy. This includes the incorporation of techniques like PCA, Fisher's linear discriminant (FLD), and Gabor filters as mentioned in Jafri and Arabnia's survey [2]. The survey concludes with realistic advantages and disadvantages to each of the three categories of facial recognition, with hybrid solutions proving to be the most accurate of the three but at the cost of difficult implementation, cost, and efficiency [2].

Kortli et al.'s expansion on previous surveys combines both feature-based and holistic approaches as well as a mixture of both to give a thorough, well-rounded comparison on over 30 different techniques to facial recognition.

The discrepancy that our team faced when trying to compare the data from different tests that were done, was that the tests were not identical. This would prove to be an obstacle in our research. Jafri and Arabnia as well as You et al. never mention the use of thermal or infrared approaches despite them becoming more popular uses in the field of facial recognition: Every person with an iPhone X or newer generation uses infrared facial recognition on a daily basis. Kortli et al. mentions these approaches during their introduction in the discussion of different sensors, but they fail to go into further depth in the analysis of local, holistic, and hybrid approaches [2]. It would be beneficial to see a comparison and real-life analysis of different facial recognition techniques in these un-discussed fields, compared with each other as well as the techniques that have already been touched on. In this way, a survey on infrared and thermal approaches with an incorporation of popular feature-based and holistic approaches could be beneficial to the discussion of facial recognition methods and applications. For this reason, thermal facial recognition will be included in this survey, as it is not generally included in other surveys.

As stated above, the popularity of thermal (infrared) facial recognition is rising significantly. Thermal facial recognition is yet another biometric approach, which focuses on the features of the face and converts those features into vector objects. There are four main methods of thermal facial recognition: fusion [11], Deep Neural Networks [12], Viola Jones Algorithm [13], and the Gabor Filter method [13]. Both Neural Networking and the Gabor Filter have been discussed in this survey, as they perform similarly in infrared light frequencies as they do in visible light ranges. Thus, the focus will be shifted to the Fusion method and the Viola Jones Algorithm.

One of the most significant drawbacks to thermal facial recognition alone is identifying those who wear glasses [12]. Since light in the infrared range cannot pass through glass, the features of the eyes are blocked out from infrared sensors. This results in a drastic reduction in accuracy. To compensate for this, the fusion method was developed in order to reap the benefits of both infrared and visible light for facial recognition use. Fusion is a fairly straightforward method, as the fused image is obtained by taking an inverse multiscale transform [12]. A specific ellipse fitting method is used to determine the region in which the eyeglasses are located, and then replaces the darkened eyeglasses with the visible version of that region [11]. This way, the benefits of both the infrared and visible light are being used here.

The Viola Jones Algorithm has become more well-known as a method for object detection, including face detection, in recent years. Both Viola and Jones had proposed this algorithm as a machine learning approach for rapidly identifying certain objects with great accuracy. It has since been adjusted to be used in the thermal range for facial recognition. There are three different aspects of the Viola Jones Algorithm that make it as quick and reliable as it is today - integral images, the Adaboost algorithm, and cascading classifiers [13]. These pieces of the algorithm are essential to making it work, and will be discussed further in the Analysis.

3 Analysis of Technologies

3.1 Overview

Through our related work, a common theme has emerged that Jafri and Arabnia mention quite succinctly in their research: "The difficulty of [facial recognition] stems from the fact that in their most common form (i.e., the frontal view) faces appear to be roughly alike and the differences between them are quite subtle" [3]. They argue that there are two categories of variation when it comes to facial recognition: intrinsic, which are physical features of the face, and extrinsic, which involve outside factors such as sunlight and orientation of the face. Intrinsic variation can be further broken down into two separate types: intrapersonal, which involves physical variations on one person's face over time, and interpersonal, which concerns facial variations between different people. Different hardware corresponds to different ways of capturing one's face, and each type of hardware has favorable and unfavorable conditions of operation.

Facial recognition technology can be divided into two distinct methods and three distinct technologies, each having their distinct benefits and shortcomings depending on the application it is used for. Jafri and Arabnia classify facial recognition methods into two primary categories: "feature-based and holistic" [3]. Feature-based facial recognition uses image input and machine learning (ML) to identify facial features, reducing the images to a vector of geometric features. On the other hand, holistic facial recognition classifies faces based on global representation instead of local facial features, utilizing either statistical methods of artificial intelligence (AI). The primary three technologies used for facial recognition are video-based, infrared, and thermal technologies. Video-based technologies consist of three modules, one to detect a face, one to track a face throughout the video, and another that recognizes a face in relation to a database. Infrared technologies can detect the vein and tissue structure of a human face, a type of identification analogous to fingerprints. Thermal technologies involve the creation of a heat map of one's face and finding specific heat zones that would differentiate one face from another.

3.2 Facial Geometry and Eigenfaces

Early work on facial recognition technology involved feature-based methods, identifying, extracting, and measuring distinctive facial features such as one's eyes, nose, mouth, and other reference points, reducing the facial image to a vector of geographic features [3]. These images are represented as a two-dimensional array of intensity values where recognition is a matter of direct comparisons between one 2D array against another. This approach works under limited circumstances, however; it assumes equal illumination, scale, and pose, and is computationally expensive. Schemes have been proposed that attempt to "counter this curse of dimensionality" [3], one of which is the rise of eigenfaces. Eigenfaces are an economic solution to the computational issues of direct matching algorithms for facial recognition, relying on a grouping of eigenvectors which aim to capture the variation of a collection of facial images [1].

In their survey, Jafri and Arabnia analyzed face profiles from research performed by Kaufman and Breeding [possible citation needed]. In their analysis, they found that the accuracy of a basic geometric feature-based approach using 35 geometric shapes to map the face was 90%. They deemed this was less effective than that of a similar template-based approach that garnered a 100% accuracy result from the same database of facial images [3]. To improve the accuracy of geometric face mapping, the survey introduced a Gabor filters method incorporating textual analysis of the face. Over two trials, the analysis resulted in a 98% accuracy rate in one trial and a 99% rate in the other [3]. When considering the simplest version of holistic approaches, Jeri and Arabnia found the reliability of eigenfaces on their own to be remarkably lower compared to the accuracy of feature-based methods. "Recognition rates of 96%, 85% and 64% were reported for lighting, orientation and scale variation. Though the method appears to be fairly robust to lighting variations, its performance degrades with scale changes" [3]. Their analysis of a "multiple observer" method involving a set of M separate eigenspaces, one for each of the N views, yields better accuracy than with eigenfaces alone.

3.3   Neural Networks

You et al. surveyed facial recognition technology as it relates to the advent of the deep convolutional neural networks (DCNNs), noting that the "bottlenecks in performance [of early facial recognition methods] due to the limitations of computing power and model capability have been rapidly eliminated" [5]. The four deep learning techniques analyzed by You et al. provide insight into the benefits of neural networks in facial recognition technology. An analysis of the DeepID network, whose authors "trained 60 relatively shallow networks that shared the same architecture [and] processed different face regions with different sizes. Features extracted by these subnetworks were then combined as the final embedding" [5]. DeepID3, the third generation of the DeepID neural network, has achieved recognition accuracy near 99.5%. Other neural networks evaluated include the VGG-16, GoogLe-Net, Face-ResNet, and ResNet-50 networks. Using each of these networks as-is after two training sessions, You et al. find that the ResNet-50 network achieved the highest accuracy in all validation sets with a maximum accuracy of 98.52%, and GoogLe-Net obtained the lowest accuracy with a minimum accuracy of 87.36% [5]. You et al. attributes Face-ResNet's varying rank in accuracy to the structural incompleteness of the neural network, coming to the conclusion that "vertical expansion of a network can be more efficient that horizontal expansion for facial feature extraction" [5].

You et al. continued their research by finding ways to optimize the training of these neural networks. They made great strides in two types of data normalization: batch normalization (BN) and feature normalization (FN). The effect that BN had on the final accuracy was positive, especially for ResNet-50. You et al. focused on the location of the BN layer in their data and found that the location of this layer was critical to the training process of these algorithms: "For GoogLeNet and VGG-16, an incorrect location makes the training process unable to converge, and for Face-ResNet, an incorrect location leads to a decline in the accuracy" [5]. The researchers also found that FN led to a clear increase in accuracy for all four networks, most notable for the Face-ResNet network. The VGG-16 network experienced a peak accuracy of 98.94% with the BN layer placed before the activation function, and the Face-ResNet network achieved a peak accuracy of 99.37% when FN was used on the network architecture [5].

3.4 Thermal

As stated earlier, there are four main methods used in the infrared light range for facial detection. Two of these methods are also used in the visible light range, and the results they show are similar. The Deep Neural Networks (DNN) method is a similar type of strategy used to learn and recognize faces. In particular Convolutional Neural Networks (CNN) are used most often for this type of application. In particular, Deep Perceptual Mapping (DPM) was used in a Notre Dame study. The non-linear mapping from thermal to visible are learned while maintaining the identity of the face being analyzed. The newly mapped descriptors of the visible images are concatenated together to create a long feature vector, whose values are then normalized and matched with the vector that comes from the thermal image. Using this method with the Notre Dame Data yielded an overall reliability of 83.33% [12].

The second of the previously mentioned methods is the Gabor filter method. This operates the same was as it does in the visible range – providing a feature-based analysis of the face. While this method did perform quite well at a reliability of 86.13% [13], it is not as reliable in the infrared light range as it is in the visible range. This is because a lot of facial features that are used in textural analysis are more difficult to define in the infrared spectrum. This could be due to a lack of temperature gradient on the face, or some external factor that causes the face's heat profile to change drastically.

The fusion method of facial recognition takes into account some of the set-backs of purely infrared imaging, which is extremely helpful when recognizing people who wear glasses. The fusion method is implemented by a special algorithm which first searches for the area on the image where the glasses are likely to be located. The method then creates a feature map for both thermal and visible images in order to highlight common features between the two images. This is where a geometrical transformation is then placed over the eyeglass area to place the information from the visible light range onto the thermal image. This method, used with eyeglasses, yields a reliability of 85% [11].

The Viola Jones Algorithm is able to both work accurately and quickly, which provides many benefits to users. In order to work so well, this algorithm uses three specific methods – integral images, the Adaboost algorithm, and cascading classifiers. Integral images calculate features on the face by summing the pixels within several rectangular areas. The Aadaboost Algorithm is a learning algorithm. Of course, when used to do facial recognition this algorithm learns features present in the image. Eventually, this facilitates the process of distinguishing a face from the background. The cascading classifiers method is used to greatly speed up the facial recognition process. This method avoids areas that are unlikely to contain a face in a cascading fashion, where the avoided areas are rejected completely. This helps greatly to save time, but also risks throwing away valuable data. Thankfully, the Adaboost Algorithm helps prevent this type of error. With all three of these methods working together, the Viola Jones algorithm is able to provide a reliability of 89.98% [13].

Table 1 condenses our findings into tabular format, organized by method type, name, and reliability.

Table 1. Reliability of methodology in related work

Method type	Method name	Reliability
Facial Geometry [3]	Geometric Shape Mapping	98.5%
	Facial Profile Vectors	90%
	Eigenface Method (best)	96%
	Eigenface Method (worst)	64%
Template mapping [3]	Template-Based Approach	>99%
Facial Geometry + Textual Analysis [3]	Gabor Filters Method	90%
Neural Networking [5]	DeepID2	99.15%
	DeepID3	>99.5 %
	ResNet-50 (training only)	98.52%
	GoogLe-Net (training only)	87.36%
	VGG-16 (with BN before AF)	98.94%
	Face-ResNet (with FN)	99.37%
Thermal [12,14]	Fusion (visible and IR)	85%
	Deep Neural Networks	83.73%
	Viola Jones Algorithm	89.98%
	Gabor Filter Method	86.13%

4   Results

4.1   Facial Geometry and Neural Networks

After examining each of the aforementioned facial recognition methods and techniques, this paper aims to take such information and interpret both the advantages and disadvantages as well as the subsequent applications these methods have. Arguably the most common problem that each facial recognition method encounters is the prominence of extrinsic factors when examining one's face. When it comes to the feature-based methods, a base reliance on geometric shapes and points on the face can be problematic because of these extrinsic factors: The calculation of geometric shapes can be skewed with different positionings of the face as well as light exposure. Additionally, feature-based methods like facial profile vectors or geometric shape mapping are deemed "computationally expensive" by Jafri and Arabnia, implying that there are a significant number of steps to feature-based methods that can require more programming, storage, and computational power. Efficiency comes at the cost of reliability for eigenfaces, with accuracy declining in comparison to the other feature-based methods. Because of feature-based methods' accuracy and higher computational requirements, the methods are more applicable to larger systems like police databases while smaller systems such as smartphones or laptops would be less appropriate for these kinds of methods. Since eigenfaces are less computationally intensive yet are susceptible to extrinsic factors like light, the eigenface approach would be applicable to any system where conditions can be stabilized.

The problem of external factors is not exclusive to the feature-based sector of facial recognition: Certain types of neural network systems are also susceptible to changes in the examinee's environment. As mentioned previously, Face-ResNet declined in quality when the location of the face was different from the location in the comparison image used, while an incorrect location caused GoogLeNet and VGG-16 to function improperly. Again, the large influence of outside factors to the facial scan would imply systems should be used in stable environments where extrinsic elements can be controlled; for example, security within a building since factors like lighting can be controlled in these environments. Adding layers to the programming, like batch normalization or feature normalization, can help improve the problems listed above while increasing accuracy.

4.2   Layered and Non-layered Filtering Systems

As with any program in computer science, the more steps and code that is used, the longer it takes the system to run the program. On the scale of facial recognition, it is critical for a large portion of techniques to use multiple layers in order to reduce influence of outside sources as well as improve accuracy. Additional layers, such as Gabor filters, can be beneficial in this sense but lend themselves to reducing the efficiency and speed of their appropriate programs. Because of this, facial recognition systems can be split into two different categories: layered (improved accuracy, reduced efficiency) and non-layered (reduced accuracy, improved efficiency). For layered systems, the most appropriate applications are related to security purposes such as accessing a smartphone, laptop, or highly protected possessions like a bank account. Facial recognition in security requires extreme accuracy because there is no margin for error when it comes to protecting one's assets; it is critical that an imposter cannot be recognized as the person they impersonate. On the other hand, non-layered methods are more appropriate for criminal databases like police systems. These systems require scanning a significant number of facial images in a short period of time, meaning that a system that is highly efficient is more appropriate here than one that takes more time. Furthermore, a criminal scanning system has a larger margin for error because the recognition system is double checked by human eyes. While criminal scanning systems can be checked by a non-computer, security typically cannot do the same which is why accuracy is vital to facial recognition for security purposes.

4.3   Applications of Advanced Filtering Systems

Facial recognition systems that utilize facial geometry in conjunction with template mapping, such as Gabor filters, tend to be more accurate than other methods but come at the cost of computational power and processing time. Layered facial recognition systems utilize the geometry of the face, similar in nature to the eigenface method and combine it with the comprehensive analysis that Gabor filters provide. The ability to combine these layers together and analyze the face in greater detail allow for variations of facial types to be analyzed and recognized by a computer program, such as facial expressions. Research from Lyons et al. explain how the recognition of facial expressions "make use of more natural communication modes in human-computer interaction and ultimately computer facilitated human interaction" [15].

One of the major advantages to a neural networking system, such as DeepID2 and DeepID3, are that as they analyze more data and build off of past analysis, these neural networking models continuously adapt to reach convergence. Despite this, they are subject to the same restrictions as basic facial geometry and template-based approaches. Neural networks require stable conditions, such as lighting and a consistent angle of the face, to be effective in facial recognition. Furthermore, neural networks benefit from data correction techniques such as batch normalization and feature normalization for a greater chance of reaching convergence. Neural networks have been consistent in accuracy and are making improvements in recognition time, which are making neural networks more suited for many applications. Practical applications for facial recognition based on neural networking include wearable computing and augmented reality, which Mitchell's Scouter system utilizes to create "a light and powerful wearable computing system platform for real-time augmented reality and near-real-time facial processing [and] facial localization" [16].

4.4   Thermal

Facial recognition in the visible light range is not always the most reliable. There are a lot of external factors that could affect the performance of a facial recognition algorithm in visible light that would not cause a change in how a face looks in the infrared spectrum. There are two methods of thermal facial recognition that are also used in the visible light range, the Gabor Filter Method and Deep Neural Networks. Unfortunately, the benefits of infrared over visible light do not outweigh the disadvantages. This is due to the fact that there are more external factors that could affect the thermal profile of a person's face. This could be due to drinking alcohol [4], or even something as simple as being exposed to too much wind. Another setback is that finer details of the human face are more difficult to identify in the infrared range than in the visible range, which presents issues in the Gabor Filter Method, which relies on the texture and finer features of the face. One of the biggest benefits of infrared facial recognition is that it can be used in low light situations, and always performs better than visible light in a completely or mostly dark environment [12]. This may seem like a great application for security purposes, however infrared facial recognition is only accurate within a short range of distance. Table 2 below condenses the advantages and disadvantages of each facial recognition technology.

Table 2. Advantages and disadvantages of facial recognition technologies

Method type	Advantages	Disadvantages
Facial Geometry	Less expensive than feature-based methods	More susceptible to external factors
Template Mapping	Faster than other methods	Less accurate than other methods
Facial Geometry + Textual Analysis [15]	More accurate than other methods	More expensive from time and fiscal perspectives
Neural Networking [16]	Continuously adapting to reach convergence	Requires stable conditions and techniques to effectively converge
Thermal [12,14]	Most accurate in low light scenarios	Only accurate within short range of distance.

5   Conclusion

From our results, we can conclude that the neural networking type ResNet-50 is the most reliable method for identifying faces consistently (98.52% accuracy), using two individual training sessions, with geometric shape mapping being the second most accurate (98.5% accuracy).

The most prominent obstruction to the development of facial recognition technology now comes from not lack of computational power but the ability to optimize how neural networks are trained.

As mentioned before, every method types has its own advantages and disadvantages, and depending on the intended use of the technology, the most viable method type may differ from case to case. Our previously stated "most reliable method" necessitates a very controlled environment to work well, even though it is undeniably powerful when properly trained.

References

1. Lata, Y.V., Tungathurthi, C.K.B., Rao, H.R.M., Govardhan, A., Reddy, L.: Facial recognition using eigenfaces by PCA. Int. J. Recent Trends Eng. 1(1), 587 (2009)
2. Kortli, Y., Jridi, M., Al Falou, A., Atri, M.: Face recognition systems: a survey. Sensors 20(2), 342 (2020)
3. Jafri, R., Arabnia, H.R.: A survey of face recognition techniques. J. Inf. Process. Syst. 5(2), 41–68 (2009)
4. Sancen-Plaza, A., Contreras-Medina, L.M., Barranco-Gutiérrez, A.I., Villaseñor-Mora, C., Martínez-Nolasco, J.J., Padilla-Medina, J.A.: Facial recognition for drunk people using thermal imaging. Math. Probl. Eng. 2020, 1–9 (2020)
5. You, M., Han, X., Xu, Y., Li, L.: Systematic evaluation of deep face recognition methods. Neurocomputing 388, 144–156 (2020)
6. Zuo, K.J., Saun, T.J., Forrest, C.R.: Facial recognition technology: a primer for plastic surgeons. Plastic Reconstr. Surg. 143(6), 1298e–1306e (2019)
7. Fadillah, D., Nuryana, Z., et al.: Public opinion of the facial recognition policy in China by Indonesian student in Nanjing city (2020)
8. Zeng, Y., Lu, E., Sun, Y., Tian, R.: Responsible facial recognition and beyond. arXiv preprint arXiv:1909.12935 (2019)
9. Tajudeen, M.N.: Optimizing Computational Time of Face Recognition System Using Chinese Remainder Theorem. Ph.D. thesis, Kwara State University (Nigeria), 2020
10. Hamann, K., Smith, R.: Facial recognition technology. Crim. Justice 34(1), 9–13 (2019)
11. Kong, S.G., et al.: Multiscale fusion of visible and thermal IR images for illumination-invariant face recognition. Int. J. Comput. Vis. 71(2), 215–233 (2007)
12. Kakkirala, K.R., Chalamala, S.R., Jami, S.K.: Thermal infrared face recognition: a review. In: 2017 UKSim-AMSS 19th International Conference on Computer Modelling & Simulation (UKSim), pp. 55–60. IEEE (2017)
13. Reese, K., Zheng, Y., Elmaghraby, A.: A comparison of face detection algorithms in visible and thermal spectrums. In: International Conference on Advances in Computer Science and Application. CiteSeer (2012)
14. Krišto, M., Ivasic-Kos, M.: An overview of thermal face recognition methods. In: 2018 41st International Convention on Information and Communication Technology, Electronics and Microelectronics (MIPRO), pp. 1098–1103. IEEE (2018)
15. Lyons, M., Akamatsu, S., Kamachi, M., Gyoba, J.: Coding facial expressions with Gabor wavelets. In: Proceedings, Third IEEE International Conference on Automatic Face and Gesture Recognition, Nara, Japan, pp. 200–205. IEEE Computer Society, April 1998. A database of facial expressions collected for the research accompanies the article and is available for use by other researchers. JAFFE Facial Expression Image Database. https://doi.org/10.5281/zenodo.3451524
16. Mitchell, C.: Applications of convolutional neural networks to facial detection and recognition for augmented reality and wearable computing. Ph.D. thesis, Cooper Union for the Advancement of Science and Art, Albert Nerken School of Engineering (2010)

Technological Evaluation of Virtual and Augmented Reality to Impart Social Skills

Vinayak V. Mukkawar$^{(\boxtimes)}$ (iD) and Laxman D. Netak$^{(\boxtimes)}$ (iD)

Department of Computer Engineering, Dr. Babasaheb Ambedkar
Technological University, Lonere 402103, Raigad, India
{mukkawar.vv,ldnetak}@dbatu.ac.in

Abstract. The global spread of COVID-19 has disrupted education in recent times. Imparting social skills necessary to survive in professional life is becoming increasingly challenging in the post-COVID-19 new normal. The existing online learning platforms which have been primarily developed as a technology for content delivery need to be augmented with additional features required to impart social skills and provide better learning experiences. In this paper, we provide a technical evaluation of two emerging technologies called augmented and virtual reality from the point of view of imparting social skills such as working as a team member, group-based learning, participating in real-life physical events (e.g., seminars and conferences, group discussion), and carrying out physical experiments in the laboratories. This paper describes the approaches to impart social skills through AR and VR based platforms.

Keywords: Augmented Reality · Virtual Reality · Social skills · Competencies · Education

1 Introduction

Virtual Reality (VR) and Augmented Reality (AR) techniques have amazingly changed how we explore our physical world. These techniques provide you with a simulated experience of things similar to or completely different from that thing's physical existence. Virtual Reality, Augmented Reality has received the attention of common people, particularly in the gaming industry. In addition to gaming, these techniques cover different application fields like data and architectural visualization [5], scientific visualization [6], Medicine and Surgery [12], Training [24], Telepresence [4], and Entertainment [19], are some of the examples. The accessibility of VR and AR on mobile devices makes them very popular among common people [11].

This paper explores one of the application areas for AR and VR, i.e. using AR and VR for educational purposes. We suppose that the use of AR and VR will have far-reaching consequences in the field of Education. Coronavirus Disease (COVID-19) is having a significant impact on social relationships, and

© Springer Nature Switzerland AG 2022
J.-H. Kim et al. (Eds.): IHCI 2021, LNCS 13184, pp. 62–73, 2022.
https://doi.org/10.1007/978-3-030-98404-5_6

radical changes have occurred in people's social habits and ways of social inter-action. The global spread of COVID-19 has disrupted Education in recent times [16]. Imparting social skills necessary to survive in professional life is becom-ing increasingly challenging in the post-COVID-19 new normal. The existing online learning platforms which have been primarily developed as a technology for content delivery need to be augmented with additional features required to impart social skills and provide better learning experiences. The adverse effect of COVID-19 on social-skill motivates us to explore the option using these immer-sive technologies called AR and VR to train students on social skills.

Attending school and college is the primary way of enhancing social skills. School-time has been fun memorable, and thus it improves social skills and social awareness among students [22]. The recommendations from education stakehold-ers given in [1] insist a lot to enhance social skills among learners.

Many institutes around the world have moved teaching and assessments online due to the pandemic situation. The conventional teaching-learning methodologies have become irrelevant during this period. Teachers have started using an open meeting platform such as Google Meet and Zoom to interact with students and deliver the lectures. These tools fail to assure that all students have actively participated or engaged in an online class. Educators find it diffi-cult to impart social skills through these platforms because these platforms fail to establish an eye-to-eye contact necessary for effective two-way communication.

The adoption of AR and VR technologies in Education can improve student-teacher interaction and satisfaction levels. Use of such technology may result in the development of communication and interpersonal skill [21]. An eye to eye contact is possible to establish through such technologies absent in conventional mode of online. With these technologies, we can fix the black-holes of the online education model. Further, AR and VR technologies make it possible to have personal attention like a physical classroom. The AR and VR technologies can supplement most of the conventional and modern teaching methodologies such as teacher-centric, learner-centric, flipped-classroom, activity-based and experi-ential learning.

2   Social Skills Expected from Engineers

This section briefly review the social skills, cognitive-social skills and abilities that are expected to become a profession engineer.

2.1   Social Skills

Social skills are the skills how we communicate and interact with others in var-ious situations. The interaction may be either verbal through face-to-face, or non-verbal through gestures and body language [3]. A person having impres-sive socials skills can easily face the demands and challenges of day-to-day life. Social skills not only improve personal relationships but also act as a critical fac-tor to success. It also has an impact on health, wealth, education, and profession.

Table 1. Desired abilities to become professional engineers

Ability	Definition
Empathy	It is an ability to understand other's emotions
Coping with stress	It is an ability to deal with and minimize stress
Managing Emotions	It is an ability to understand and manage one's own emotion
Adaptability	Adaptability is the ability to push and change ourselves according to needs continuously. This enables the one to work positively in any condition. Adaptability improves the change management skill of an individual
Optimism	Even though it is not a social skill, it is a good attribute that every team member shall possess. Persons with high optimistic attitude create an enthusiastic surrounding at the workplace to work as a team
Diligence	Diligence is the ability to work continuously. A Person can achieve diligence by competing continuously with oneself
Resilience	A person can recover quickly from a difficult situation. An engineer has to face failure many times in his profession, considering the failure as a stepping stone of success an individual has to bounce back every time

Social skills are responsible for building essential characters in a human being like respectfulness, responsibility, trustworthiness, and fairness. All these actual characters are required to enhance social competence. With all these social skills and social competence, the person can effectively communicate with others [13].

World Health Organization (WHO) identified certain life skills that everyone should acquire. Acquisition of these skills results in the overall growth of an individual. The life skills identified by WHO are:

1. *Self Awareness:* It is a skill to take an honest look of oneself and check how one acts, thinks, and how one is emotionally connected with each other.
2. *Interpersonal Skills:* It is a skill to interact with others through listening, speaking, and questioning.
3. *Communication Skills:* Like that of Interpersonal skill, it is a skill to send and receive information from colleagues.
4. *Collaboration:* Collaboration is a skill to work with peoples from different domains or disciplines. For example, delivering the software product is not possible by single or multiple people, many teams like product creation, system innovation, service execution, and maintenance are working behind. It is an essential skill for an engineer to work with many teams.
5. *Leadership:* Leadership is a skill to lead a team and it is different from the management. Leadership skill focuses on defining vision, setting direction to get the required task, motivate people, and align people to work in a team to achieve success. A leader is a mentor or a model person for workers and employees in an organization. A leader has the vision to inspire individuals,

challenge them, offer them new growth opportunities, enable the team members to engage in a meaningful act, and set exemplary leadership practices.

6. *Teamwork:* Teamwork is a skill of a person to be a part of a work-group. Most of the engineers work with a team to complete the temporary endeavour within a given time. A good team member is a person who has good interpersonal skills. In an organization, team-based culture motivates the people to accomplish the challenging task.

These are pure social skills in the sense that they get developed through social interaction. Every individual especially professional engineers need to acquire them in order to succeed in the profession.

2.2 Cognitive-Social Skills

Engineering being a professional program, students enrolled in an engineering program need to acquire following cognitive skills which either complements to the social skills mentioned above or get developed through social interaction.

1. *Critical Thinking:* It is an ability to analyze, synthesize, apply, and evaluate the information obtained different means such as through communication and observation.
2. *Creative Thinking:* It is an ability to provide novel solutions to pressing problems.
3. *Problem Solving:* It is an ability to deal with problems by understanding the root causes and providing them an effective solution.
4. *Decision Making:* It is an ability to make a decision based on information and alternatives available.
5. *Technical Skills:* One needs to continuously update knowledge to work in the rapidly changing engineering industry. Education, experience, and domain knowledge makes the person able to work on the high-end application. The widespread adoption of information communication technologies requires various training programs to acquire emerging technologies.

To acquire these social-skills and cognitive social skills, an engineer need to possess certain abilities and attitude as described in Table 1.

3   Augmented Reality and Virtual Reality

Augmented Reality is a technique that consists of superimposing virtual elements in the real world [17]. The term Augmented Reality was coined in 1990 by Thomas Caudell [7]. Augmented Reality (AR) is a term for a live direct or indirect view of the physical or real-world environment whose elements are augmented by virtual computer-generated imagery and information. It is related to a more general concept called *mediated reality* in which a view of reality is modified, possibly even diminished rather than augmented, by a computer. As a result, technology plays the role of enhancing one's current perception of reality.

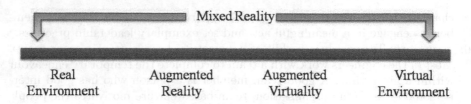

Fig. 1. Milgram's reality-virtuality continnum [18]

In Augmented Reality, the augmentation is conventionally in real-time and in semantic context with environmental elements. For example, they are adding sports scores while the match is going on and steamed on television. With the help of advanced AR technologies, one can add features like computer vision and object recognition about the objects surrounding the real world to become interactive and digitally immersed in the environment. Artificial information about the environment and its objects can be stored and retrieved as an information layer on top of the real world view.

There are two commonly accepted definitions of Augmented Reality. Ronald Azuma gives the first in [2] which says that, Augmented Reality combines the real and virtual world in three-dimensional space through interactive and real-time mode.

The second definition is given by Paul Milgram and Fumio Kishin, which describes Reality-Virtuality Continuum in 1994 [18] as shown in Fig. 1. They represent a continuum that spans from the real environment to a purely virtual environment. Figure 1 shows Milgram's Reality-Virtuality Continuum, which identifies various parts of the generic idea called Mixed Reality. The mixed Reality includes (i) Augmented Reality, (ii) Augmented Virtuality, and (iii) Virtual Environment beside real environment. As shown in Fig. 1, Augmented Reality is near to the Real Environment. So it must have a large amount of real environment and less amount of virtual environment.

Another definition of AR based on the Mixed Reality continuum says that AR is a technology having an interactive virtual object in the real world. There are mainly two categories of AR as per this definition, i.e. (i) Marker-less, and (ii) Marker-based.

Depending on the application scenario, various kinds of hardware and software elements are utilized to have the full-fledged Augmented Reality experience [9]. The interaction between these various components is shown in Fig. 2.

Virtual Reality is a simulation-based environment of the physical world or a completely new imaginary world. With its characteristic of immersion, conception, and interactivity, the virtual reality provides a way to simulate a real and imaginary world. The virtual or imaginary world is created by rendering visual elements with the help of computer graphics.

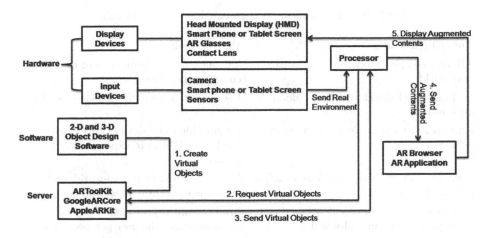

Fig. 2. Interaction of AR components

An immersion specifies the insertion of an user in the virtual world by means of a VR headset known as Head Mounted Display (HMD). To make a real feel of the virtual world, HMD may possess an element with which the user can interact virtual environment.

A VR-based system is a collection of displays, connectors, and IO devices. Such systems have an interactive system with high computer graphics through which a user enters in an imaginary world. Formally VR is defined as *the technology that focuses on spatial multi-sensory representation, interaction, and presence, combined with real-time simulation technique and high-level management of the handled virtual environments* [10].

In the augmented reality, the virtual object is inserted in the real environment, while in virtual reality, the user is inserted in a completely new imaginary world. The level of user penetration in the virtual world is known as *immersion*. The user with VR may present in a state of mental immersion (deep engagement) or physical immersion based on a deep engagement of mindset or physical engagement mindset. Examples of mental immersion are video games where our mind believes that we are in another world. Examples of physical immersion are the VR games where users feel that they entered into a synthetic world. Based on the level of immersion VR has three categories:

1. *Non-immersive VR:* Non-immersive VR accesses 3-D content via monitor or display. It is the low-level implementation of VR. An example of such VR is architecture demonstrating the 3-D building plan and elevation design to the customer using a projector or monitor.
2. *Semi-immersive VR:* The user is partially immersed in the virtual world. The virtual world may be created by a high-end computer system and can have multiple projections. Flight simulation technique, fire safety training techniques falls into this category.

Table 2. A comparison of Augmented and Virtual Reality

Augmented Reality	Virtual Reality
AR lays computer generated object in real world	VR does mental immersion of user in computer generated world
Enhances real-world view with added information	User experiences entire digitized world
Run on AR compatible low-end smart devices	Require high-end devices and extra hardware (HMD) to experience full immersion
User stays in real-world while interacting with virtual objects	User is isolated from real-world while experiencing synthetic world
Behaviour of virtual object is based on users perspective in real-world	Position and size of virtual object changes as per the user perspective in computer generated world
AR allows the user to interact with both real and virtual worlds at the same time and allow user to distinguish between the two	In VR it is difficult to distinguish between what is real and what is not, users feel inability while trying to pick virtual objects
As suitable for low-end devices, implementation cost is low	Costly hardware requirement increases the cost of implementation

3. *(Fully) Immersive VR:* User can feel their complete presence in the synthetic world by stimulating their senses. Stimulation of sense done by using a tracking device, motion detection tool, Head-mounted display is used. It is a high-end VR experience. The VR application like Star War game that using HMD falls into this category.

   The Table 2 compares virtual and augmented reality. Also there exist a mixed reality which is a combination of VR, AR, and physical reality.

4 Existing Approaches to Impart Social Skills

Social skills are essential to becoming successful in life. The teacher can teach you how to get knowledge from the book and earn bread butter, however social skills bear good moral conduct throughout life. Social competencies can be learned through experience. In addition to knowledge, social skills are an important factor to become a credible and reputable expert in any domain. Achieving goals is not a complete definition of success, the goal achieved by maintaining the relationship handling emotional intelligence truly defines success. Social competencies can learn through rigorous training and practice.

   The training model available for enhancing the social skills of a user follows steps of instruction, modeling, role-playing, feedback, and homework. Instruction based training model firstly choose particular skills to develop and then elaborate on the benefits of skill. Instruction regarding the skill is narrative and can be given using storytelling. In the modeling, the trainer will act as a model and shows the required skills using playing video created by them in front of users. Role-play activities are done by the user on demand of the trainer. Emotions may learn by analyzing facial expressions while playing an act. Feedback from colleagues, family, and friends is collected for a social skill that you want to enhance. Homework includes practicing social behavior by the user. Reading personality development books also enhances social skills. Focus on one social skill at a time instead of improving several social skills at once.

Various Social Skill Training (SST) like PROLIDER and PRODIP are available to enhance social skills [23]. Kagan suggested cooperative learning structures [15] to improve the social skills of students. Famous Kagan cooperative learning structure includes Think-Pair-Share, Mix-Pair-Share, Mix-Freeze-Pair, Mix-N-Match, RoundRobin, RallyTable, RallyCoach, RoundTable, Showdown, Quiz-Quiz-Trade, and StandUp-HandUp-PairUp. All these strategies are used in education to practice social skills. In addition to these strategies in general an individual may enhance the social skills by asking open-ended questions, creating short-term and long-term goals, providing compliments to others, and identifying and replacing negative thoughts.

5   AR and VR Based Approaches to Impart Social Skills

Imparting social skills is the key to success. Immersion and experience property of Augmented and Virtual Reality makes it a powerful tool to improve constructivism, experiential learning, and social learning. By immersing the user in a computer-generated 3-D world, the user feels a strong sense of presence. The user is engaged completely to interact with the virtual world leads to improvement in cognition. Virtual worlds are more constructive where participants can create the objects, modify them, and interact with objects will help the participant to enhance problem-solving social competence. Two or more virtual worlds are connected to form a network to provide a shared environment for communication and collaboration. The basic techniques like instruction, role-play, and modeling to impart social are also used interestingly in Virtual and Augmented Reality applications.

Let's consider a person, who is shy and hesitant to talk in public may wear HMD and practice public speaking with virtual members in the virtual world [25]. The same technique may be applied for giving interviews confidently. Decision making is an important skill for quarterback player in football they have to make the decision in a fraction of a second to win the game. Instruction from expertise may help to improve play but at a time of the match, it is very difficult to get instructions. Better way player is immersed in the virtual world and can do the practice of decision making based on various conditions. In the virtual environment, the play can be practiced across many settings, a player can make many time decision and observe the result.

Collaboration is the ability to work with people, the most commonly used skill in an industry where people from different domains work together to provide better solutions. Before a pandemic, meetings and communication between various stakeholders are responsible for collaboration among the people. Due to pandemics, face-to-face meetings and communication are highly impossible. The video meeting through different platforms does not guarantee the full immersion of the stakeholder remotely. The use of VR technology makes it possible to immerse the stakeholders in an ongoing meeting through their Avatar (Virtual Representer). Full immersion of stakeholders results in better collaboration. The applications like Breakrooms, SpatialWeb are used to achieve collaboration amongst participants remotely.

The person or child who suffered from Autism Spectrum Disorder is very poor in social interaction and communication. They were not too practical with their verbal and non-verbal communication. Virtual Reality helps such patients to improve their social skills and social competence [8,14,26]. Many approaches are there explaining the use of VR to treat Autism Spectrum Disorder one of them is discussed later in the section. Let's have a look at some approaches to enhance social skill through Augmented Reality and Virtual Reality;

1. *Bridge Building:* Prerequisite required to build the bridge taught to students and some live bridge examples are explained. Now the students are grouped and asked to build the bridge using material available in the virtual environment. In this case, as we have the groups of students, they work cooperatively to decide the architecture of the bridge. Once it is decided, students will build the bridge from the virtual structure provided by the software. The software then checks the construction according to the physics and gravitational laws. It is ok if the construction is as per the rules otherwise software falls the construction and students have to work again to find a successful solution. Such software increases the active participation of students, cooperative learning, and improves team-building skills.

2. *Kinful:* This application enhances social-emotional learning, it has more numbers of SEL hands-on to experience. Kinful addresses five core skills Self-awareness, Self-management, Social Awareness, Relationship Skills, and Decision-making. Kinful divided into two categories, one category uses VR based film, and another category is SEL activity.

3. *InMind 2 VR:* It is an adventure game that working on human emotions. This game works on the principle Lovheim's theory of emotions, which consist of an interaction between monoamine neurotransmitter and human emotions. The game uses the character John whose future will be decided by a decision made by the player. In the game, John was surrounded by several precious moments, and answers to these moments result in new interest. It is a scientific game providing information on stimuli of the brain and their impact on human emotions.

4. *Virtual Orator:* This software improves public speaking skill by creating a sensation in user treating he/she presenting in front of the audience [20]. This application provides a manual setting for the type of audience (kind/unkind,

interested/uninterested) and the number of audiences. Also, it provides various situations of public speaking like group meetings in office (a small number of people), society meeting (moderate number of people), and in function or rallies (more number of people). The audience provided by the software feels realistic and can ask questions also.

5. *Augmented CaRer:* It is therapeutic technology for patients suffered from Autism. The children with Autism lack communication and conceptualization. This Augmented Reality based platform superimposes images and videos to demonstrate daily routine to autism patients, make them understand things, and act accordingly. To elaborate on the daily routine and grasp the concepts quickly Augment CaRer provides more than 30,000 pictograms. It uses alternative and augmentative communication (AAC) techniques to help children reach speech development as well as achieve desired lifestyle skills and behaviors.

6. *Autism Glass Project:* A powerful tool to recognize facial expression through wearable glasses and provides real-time social cues. It uses machine learning and artificial intelligence for recognition. This application helps the children to better understand facial expressions.

7. *Charisma - Youth Virtual Social Training:* It is a virtual social training platform used to teach social strategies that enhance the way an individual think, work, and thrive socially. Under the observation of the trainer, the practice of social scenarios is done by an individual in the virtual world. The trainer will provide real-time feedback, which helps the individual to improve their communication, confidence, and resilience.

6 Conclusion

The paper describes the relevance of augmented and virtual reality applications to improve learning and teaching experiences for enhancing social abilities of students.

The augmented reality aims to enhance the quality of perception about the physical objects through additional sensory information. The extrasensory information includes visual, auditory and tactile information. Several hardware platforms and software systems have been developed in recent times for this purpose.

The virtual reality builds entirely new imagined reality. A user of VR-based system can experience this imagined reality through special-purpose devices such as head-mounted displays.

Both technologies have created new avenues of designing education applications based on their strengths. One of the everyday use of these AR technologies is to enrich existing educational content with additional sensory information. In contrast, the VR is commonly used for the feeling of immersion in the learning environment.

Another strength of the AR and VR technologies is that they can recognize real-time objects. Developers can effectively leverage this strength to impart social skills required for interacting between human-to-human and human-to-machine. The paper describes a few such applications.

References

1. Akat, M., Karataş, K.: Psychological effects of COVID-19 pandemic on society and its reflections on education **15**, 1–13 (2020)
2. Azuma, R.T.: A survey of augmented reality. Presence: Teleoper. Virtual Environ. **6**(4), 355–385 (1997)
3. Beauchamp, M., Anderson, V.: Social: an integrative framework for the development of social skills. Psychol. Bull. **136**, 39–64 (2010)
4. Bolas, M.T., Fisher, S.S.: Head-coupled remote stereoscopic camera system for telepresence applications. In: Fisher, S.S., Merritt, J.O. (eds.) Stereoscopic Displays and Applications, Volume 1256 of Society of Photo-Optical Instrumentation Engineers (SPIE) Conference Series, pp. 113–123, September 1990
5. Brooks, F.P.: Walkthrough-a dynamic graphics system for simulating virtual buildings. In: Proceedings of the 1986 Workshop on Interactive 3D Graphics, I3D 1986, New York, NY, USA, pp. 9–21. Association for Computing Machinery (1987)
6. Bryson, S., Levit, C.: The virtual wind tunnel. IEEE Comput. Graph. Appl. **12**(4), 25–34 (1992)
7. Caudell, T.P.: Introduction to augmented and virtual reality. In: Das, H. (ed.) Telemanipulator and Telepresence Technologies, vol. 2351, pp. 272–281. International Society for Optics and Photonics, SPIE, Bellingham (1995)
8. Chan, S., Cai, Y., Lu, A., Tun, N.Z., Huang, L., Chandrasekaran, I.: Virtual reality enhanced pink dolphin game for children with ASD. In: Proceedings of the 3rd Asia-Europe Symposium on Simulation & Serious Gaming, VRCAI 2016, New York, NY, USA, pp. 215–218. Association for Computing Machinery (2016)
9. Craig, A.B.: Augmented reality applications (chap. 8). In: Craig, A.B. (eds.) Understanding Augmented Reality, pp. 221–254. Morgan Kaufmann, Boston (2013)
10. Cruz-Neira, C., Sandin, D.J., DeFanti, T.A., Kenyon, R.V., Hart, J.C.: The CAVE: audio visual experience automatic virtual environment. Commun. ACM **35**(6), 64–72 (1992)
11. Herskovitz, J., et al.: Making mobile augmented reality applications accessible. In: The 22nd International ACM SIGACCESS Conference on Computers and Accessibility, ASSETS 2020, New York, NY, USA. Association for Computing Machinery (2020)
12. Hunter, I.W., et al.: A teleoperated microsurgical robot and associated virtual environment for eye surgery. Presence Teleoper. Virtual Environ. **2**(4), 265–280 (1993)
13. Jurevičienė, M., Kaffemaniene, I., Ruškus, J.: Concept and structural components of social skills. Baltic J. Sport Health Sci. **3**, 10 (2018)
14. Jyoti, V., Lahiri, U.: Virtual reality based joint attention task platform for children with Autism. IEEE Trans. Learn. Technol. **13**(1), 198–210 (2020)
15. Kagan, S., Kagan, S.: Cooperative Learning, vol. 2. Kagan Cooperative Learning, San Juan Capistrano (1994)
16. Mambo, S.M., Omusilibwa, F.M.: Effects of coronavirus pandemic spread on science, technology, engineering and mathematics education in higher learning institutions. In: 2020 IFEES World Engineering Education Forum - Global Engineering Deans Council (WEEF-GEDC), pp. 1–4 (2020)
17. Mann, S.: Phenomenal augmented reality: advancing technology for the future of humanity. IEEE Consum. Electron. Mag. **4**(4), 92–97 (2015)
18. Milgram, P., Takemura, H., Utsumi, A., Kishino, F.: Augmented reality: a class of displays on the reality-virtuality continuum. Telemanipulator Telepresence Technol. **2351**, 282–292 (1994)

19. Onyesolu, M.O., et al.: Virtual reality: an emerging computer technology of the 21st century. Electrosc. J. **1**(1), 36–40 (2016)
20. Pellett, K., Zaidi, S.F.M.: A framework for virtual reality training to improve public speaking. In: 25th ACM Symposium on Virtual Reality Software and Technology, VRST 2019, New York, NY, USA. Association for Computing Machinery (2019)
21. Requena-Carrión, J., Alonso-Atienza, F., Guerrero-Curieses, A., Rodríguez-González, A.B.: A student-centered collaborative learning environment for developing communication skills in engineering education. In: IEEE EDUCON 2010 Conference, pp. 783–786 (2010)
22. Sievertsen, H.H., Burgess, S.: Schools, skills, and learning: the impact of COVID-19 on education. https://voxeu.org/article/impact-covid-19-education. Accessed 24 December 2020
23. Slovák, P., Fitzpatrick, G.: Teaching and developing social and emotional skills with technology. ACM Trans. Comput.-Hum. Interact. **22**(4), 1–34 (2015)
24. Vince, J.: Virtual reality techniques in flight simulation. In: Virtual Reality Systems (1993)
25. Yan, S., Yan, X., Shen, X.: Exploring social interactions for live performance in virtual reality. In: SIGGRAPH Asia 2020 Posters, SA 2020. Association for Computing Machinery (2020)
26. Zhao, H., Swanson, A.R., Weitlauf, A.S., Warren, Z.E., Sarkar, N.: Hand-in-hand: a communication-enhancement collaborative virtual reality system for promoting social interaction in children with autism spectrum disorders. IEEE Trans. Hum.-Mach. Syst. **48**(2), 136–148 (2018)

Deep Convolutional Neural Network Approach for Classification of Poems

Rushali Deshmukh[1]([✉]) and Arvind W. Kiwelekar[2]

[1] Department of Computer Engineering, JSPM's Rajarshi Shahu College
of Engineering, Pune 411033, India
radeshmukh_comp@jspmrscoe.edu.in
[2] Department of Computer Engineering, Dr. Babasaheb Ambedkar
Technological University, Lonere 402103, Raigad (M. S.), India
awk@dbatu.ac.in

Abstract. In this paper, we proposed an automatic convolutional neural network (CNN)-based method to classify poems written in Marathi, one of the popular Indian languages. Using this classification, a person unaware of Marathi Language can come to know what kind of emotion the given poem indicates. To the best of our knowledge, this is probably the first attempt of deep learning strategy in the field of Marathi poem classification. We conducted experiments with different models of CNN, considering different batch sizes, filter sizes, regularization methods like dropout, early stopping. Experimental results witness that our proposed approach outperforms both in effectiveness and efficiency. Our proposed CNN architecture for the classification of poems produces an impressive accuracy of 73%.

Keywords: Classification · Convolution · Convolutional neural network · Poem classification

1 Classification

Classification is the task of assigning one of the predefined classes to given data. It can be binary or multiclass classification. We aim to build a model for the automatic classification of poems. Traditional machine learning algorithms don't perform well with massive data. Gu et al. [1] surveyed recent advances in convolutional neural networks (CNN) and introduced applications of CNN in speech, computer vision, and natural language processing. In our approach, we considered around 3000 poems of 9 classes. We explored various CNN models considering the number of filters, their sizes, and batch size as a hyperparameter for the classification of poems. To avoid overfitting, 'dropout' and 'early stopping' regularization techniques are used. First, we did a survey of classification using deep learning. We also surveyed classification techniques for the Marathi language. The rest of the paper is organized as follows, Sect. 1 contains the introduction

© Springer Nature Switzerland AG 2022
J.-H. Kim et al. (Eds.): IHCI 2021, LNCS 13184, pp. 74–88, 2022.
https://doi.org/10.1007/978-3-030-98404-5_7

of classification, Sect. 2 contains the related work of classification using CNN, Sect. 3 presents different models using CNN for Marathi poem classification, Sect. 4 concludes with the conclusion and future scope.

2 Literature Survey

Kowsari et al. [2] surveyed various classification algorithms such as Naive Bayes, Decision tree, Random forest, Support vector machines, K nearest neighbor, Deep learning etc. and reported advantages and limitations of each of it. Minaee et al. [3] discussed more than 150 deep learning models like feed forward neural network, RNN-Based models, CNN-Based models, Capsule neural networks, Models with attention mechanism, Memory augmented networks, Graph neural networks, Siamese neural networks, Hybrid models, Transformers and Pretrained language models and their strengths for classification of text. Kamath et al. [4] classified Health Dataset from an insurance company with 13500 documents into 18 classes and Tobacco-3482 dataset of images related to tobacco with 2800 documents into nine classes. Maximum accuracy of 73% was achieved on raw data and 67% on processed data for the tobacco dataset among all traditional machine learning algorithms for Health data. For Tobacco data, maximum accuracy of 81% and 77% accuracy was achieved on raw and processed data respectively using machine learning algorithms. CNN gave 82% accuracy on raw data and 96% on processed Health data. For Tobacco data, 84% and 89% accuracy was achieved on processed and raw data respectively. Georgakopoulos et al. [5] classified Toxic Comment using three convolutional layers with a filter size width of 128 and a height of 3,4 and 5 respectively. After each convolutional layer, the max-pooling layer was used. The last pooling layer's output concatenates to a fully connected layer, which was connected to the output layer, which uses a softmax function. The accuracy obtained was around 91%, while for traditional machine learning algorithms, it was in the range of 65% to 85%. Cano and M. Morisio [6] implemented Ngram CNN architecture with the following layers, 1) Embedding layer 2) Convolution layer with a filter of 1-gram, 2-gram, ..., Ngram with Relu activation function 3) Max pooling layer/4, which pools max value from four values 4) Convolution layer with a filter of 1-gram, 2-gram, ..., Ngram with Relu activation function 5) Max pooling layer/4 6) Dense layer of 100 units and L2 regularization with 0.09 weight 7) Dropout layer with 0.5 dropout rate 8) Output layer. MLPN dataset 2,500 positive and 2,500 negative song lyrics, and IMDB Movie review dataset of 50K size with two classes positive and negative and Mobile Phone reviews of size 232 k with positive and negative classes used for experimentation. 1) For the MLPN dataset, the accuracy achieved was 75.6%. 2) IMDB Movie review dataset accuracy achieved was 91.2%. 3) Mobile Phone review accuracy achieved was 95.9%. Hughes [7] classified Medical documents each of 50 words with a vector of size 100. The model consists of the following layers. 1) Embedding layer 2) Convolution layer of filter size 5 and 256 filters ReLU activation 3) Max pooling 4) Convolution layer of filter size 5 and 256 filters and ReLU activation 5) Max pooling 6) Dropout layer with a rate 0.5 7) Fully connected layer of size 128 and ReLU 8) Dropout layer with rate 0.5 9) Output layer of size 26 with softmax activation. Twenty-six categories were used with 4000 sentences of each category of clinical text. For validation, 1000 sentences from each category were used. The accuracy achieved was 0.68%. Hsu and Tzuhan [8] did Petroleum Engineering Data Text Classification Using Convolutional Neural Network Based Classifier. They used the Raw dataset of 400,000 texts with six classes. The accuracy achieved with CNN was 85.83%. Kalchbrenner et al. [9] did Binary and Multiclass classification of Twitter sentiment prediction and TREC question dataset. Dynamic Convolutional Neural Network was implemented for a seven-word input sentence with word embedding of 4. Following layers were used: 1) Convolutional layer with two feature maps and width of filter was 3, 2) Dynamic k max-pooling with k = 5, 3) Convolutional layer with two feature maps and width of filter was 2, 4) folding, 5) Dynamic k max-pooling with k = 3, 6) Fully connected layer. For Movie reviews dataset with binary and multiclass classification accuracy obtained was in the range of 86.8%, for Twitter sentiment accuracy achieved was 87.4%, and for Question classification accuracy was 93%. Kim [10] implemented the CNN-rand model in which all words are randomly initialized, CNN-static model with pre-trained vectors from word2vec, CNN-nonstatic with fine-tuned pre-trained vectors and CNN-multichannel using two sets of word vectors. For MR dataset among existing models using CNN-nonstatic highest accuracy of 81.5% was obtained. For SST-2 dataset accuracy of 88.1%, for CR dataset 85.0% of accuracy was obtained using CNN-multichannel. For the MPQA dataset using CNN-static 89.6% accuracy was achieved. For sentence classification, Zhang and Wallace [11] fine-tuned parameters like the effect of filter region size, number of feature maps for each filter region size, number of feature maps for each filter region size, multiple region size, activation functions, pooling strategy, the effect of regularization. For datasets MR, SST-1, SST-2, Subj, TREC, CR, MPQA, Opi, Irony, they provided guidelines for finding the best configuration of a model for a given dataset. De Sousa Pereira Amorim [12] implemented Logistic Regression and Deep Learning for 13,651 tweets in Portuguese with 6851 of the political class and 6800 of non-political class. With Logistic Regression accuracy achieved Severyn and Moschitti implemented message and phrase was 90.5%, and Deep learning accuracy obtained was 83.8%. Severyn and Moschitti [13] implemented message and phrase-level twitter sentiment classification using three approaches 1) Randomly initialized parameters 2) an unsupervised neural language model to initialize word embeddings, which are further tuned. Baker et al. [14] used Convolutional Neural Networks for Biomedical text classification of cancer domain dataset. After the embedding layer, they used convolutions of different filter sizes and 1-max pooling and finally fully connected layer. They achieved an F-score of 81.0%.

An earlier study for classification of Indian languages like Urdu, Punjabi, and Tamil was mainly focused using machine learning techniques like Naive Bayes, SVM, Artificial neural network [15–17]. For Marathi language, fourth spoken language in India Label Induction Grouping (LINGO) algorithm was used to categirize 200 documents into 20 categories by patil and Bogiri [18]. For 1170

Marathi poems of 5 categories, Support vector machine was used in the approach of Deshmukh et al. [19].

The above literature survey shows that text classification for Indian languages is mainly focused on using traditional machine learning algorithms. Classification using attention CNN+LSTM deep learning for 9142 poems in the English language was done in the approach of Ahmed et al. [20] and acheived accuracy of 88%. Our approach is focused on the classification of around 3000 poems of 9 categories using a convolutional neural network.

3   Classification of Poems Using Deep Learning

Here we gathered Marathi poems from https://marathikavita.co.in/. Details are as shown in Table 1. 80% of the dataset is used for training, and 20% is used for testing. Out of 2803 poems, 561 poems are used for testing, and 2242 poems are used for training. A stratified train/test split is used. It makes split so that the same proportion of values from each class of dataset appears in train and test data.

Table 1. Category wise poem count.

Sr. no.	Type of poem	No. of poems
1	Badbad	207
2	Bhakti	465
3	Gambhir	330
4	Maitri	211
5	Motivation	286
6	Prem	372
7	Shrungar	316
8	Vidamban	345
9	Vinodi	271
Total		**2803**

From training data, 20% is used for validation purpose. We experimented with CNN models with the following approaches.

- Effect of region size,
- Effect of multiple regions,
- Effect of batch size.

3.1   Convolutional Neural Network Approach

In earlier days, CNN's were mainly used for Image processing. Nowadays, it has been successful in text classification tasks. There are three types of layers in CNN namely convolutional layers, pooling layers, and fully connected layers [21]. Convolution operation reduces the number of free parameters. The pooling layer also reduces the number of parameters by reducing the spatial size of the representation. It operates on each feature map independently. The common approach used is max pooling. Max pooling partitions input into nonoverlapping regions and from each region partition outputs maximum. Another approach is average pooling or L2-norm pooling outputs average from each region. After several convolutional and pooling layers at the end of CNN, a fully connected layer of neurons is used that have full connections to all activation's in the previous layer. Figure 1 shows that the sentence of size seven words is represented using a vector of the dimension of 5. Convolution is done using the region sizes of 2, 3, 4 with six filters, 2 for each region.

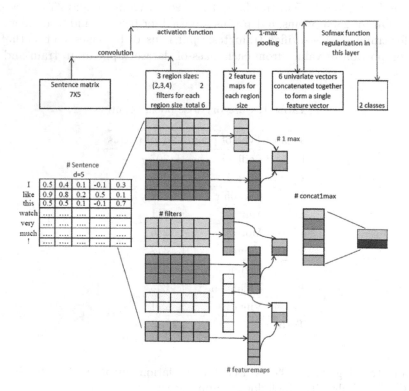

Fig. 1. CNN for classification example.

Let us consider how CNN performs convolutions. Some numbers are filled out for clarity in the matrix of the sentence and the filter matrix. Figure 2 shows the action of a 2-word filter on the sentence matrix using convolution as a matrix product [22]. A filter is of size 2*5, where 2 is region size. First, it performs convolution on the first two words 'I' and 'Like'.

It performs an element-wise product with a filter, then sums to obtain the final value.

$$(0.6*0.2+0.5*0.1+0.2*0.2.........+0.1*0.1 = 0.51).$$

The first value in the output is computed. The next filter moves one word down and overlays with 'like' and 'this' words. Output O has a shape of $(S-R+1*1)$, where S is sentence size, and R is region size. Next, we add bias term to it, then activation function ReLU is applied to obtain a feature map of the same size $(S-R+1*1)$ after that 1-max pooling is applied to obtain max value from each feature map. After that, obtained six univariate vectors are concatenated to obtain a single feature vector. Finally, the softmax activation function in the output layer classifies input into two classes.

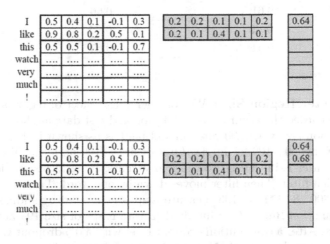

Fig. 2. Convolution example.

In our case, vocabulary size is 2000. Maximum words for each document is 200. If a document word size is less than 200, post padding is done. Using the embedding layer of Keras for each word, a word vector of size 100 is generated.

The output of the embedding layer is given to the convolution layer for filtering of different region sizes of 2, 3, 4, 6, 8, 10. After filtering, feature maps are generated using activation function ReLU. The next layer is a dropout layer with a 0.5 dropout value. Then Max-pooling layer pools 50% max values. The next flatten layer generates a 1-D vector, which is given as input to a dense layer of 256 size with the ReLU activation function. The final output layer generates probabilities for nine poem classes using a softmax function. As it is a multiclass classification, 'categorical_crossentropy' is the loss function used, and 'adam' is the optimizer used. Adam optimizer is computationally efficient with little memory requirements and suitable for problems of large data and/or parameters [23].

Dropout is used to avoid the overfitting of neural networks. During training, dropout regularization randomly drops units from the neural network [24].

For regularization, 'early stopping' is used, which monitors the value of loss for test data and immediately stops training of model if performance on test data becomes worst. The batch size is 32 with ten epochs or iterations. We have also explored the effect of different batch sizes, the effect of region sizes, the effect of multichannel with different region sizes.

Table 2. Effect of filter region size.

Region size	Accuracy on validation data	Accuracy on test data
1	0.66	0.65
2	0.68	0.65
4	0.64	0.68
6	0.61	0.66
8	**0.69**	**0.71**
10	0.64	0.65

Effect of Filter Region Size: We considered the effect of region sizes of 1, 2, 4, 6, 8 and recorded the accuracy of validation and test data as shown in Table 2. For eight region size with 100 filter model built is as shown in Fig. 3. For each document of size 200*100, eight size filter of size 8*100 performs filtering of size 8*100. Each filter is initialized to random weights. It performs an element-wise product with a filter. Then filter moves down by one word. The output of it has a shape of $(200-8+1*1) = 193$. Feature map is generated by adding bias, then activation function ReLU. One hundred feature maps of size 193 are generated for 100 filters. After a convolution dropout layer with a 0.5 dropout value is used. Then max-pooling layer pools 50% max values from each feature map. Output after Maxpooling is 100 feature maps with 96 values. Next Flatten layer generates a 1-D vector of size $96*100 = 9600$ values, which is connected to a dense layer of 256 neurons. The final output layer applies a softmax function and generates probabilities for nine classes. Figure 4 shows that as no. of epochs increases loss decreases for training data, but for validation data after six epochs, loss increases. As we have used early stopping, it will stop the training of the model after seven epochs. Figure 5 shows epochwise accuracy for train and validation data.

Classwise precision, recall, f1-score is shown in Table 3.

The average precision score, micro-averaged over all classes for model of Fig. 3 is 0.72. Table 3 shows that the maximum F1-score of 0.83 is obtained for 'Bhakti' type of poems. Confusion matrix in Fig. 6 shows that 13 poems from the 'gambhir' category are classified in the 'vidamban' category. For 'motivation' class 11 poems are classified in the 'vidamban' class. Because of that, precision for 'vidamban' is 0.48. Recall for motivation is 0.54. Figure 7 shows class wise ROC curves. The area for ROC curves is in the range of 0.80 to 0.89, except for the 'motivation' class is 0.75. The micro-average of the ROC curve is 0.84, and the macro-average of the ROC curve is 0.83.

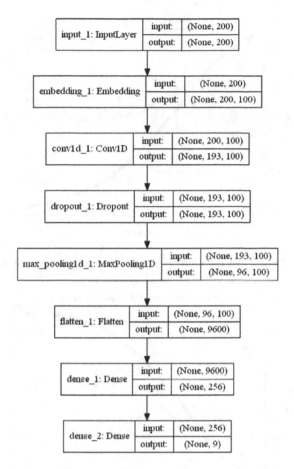

Fig. 3. A model with 100 filters and eight region size

Effect of Multiple Region Size: Here we considered the effect of 2, 3, and 4 regions.

1. **Effect of 2 regions with different size**

   Here we used 50 filters for each region, and experimentation is done for two regions of different sizes. We experimented with two regions of different sizes, as shown in Table 4. Accuracy on validation data is 0.67 for (3,5) region size. Two channels are built one for each region size, same as that of 1 region model. The output from two channels is concatenated before it is given to a dense layer.

   Table 5 shows classwise precision, recall, f1-measure for (3,5) region model. It shows that a maximum f1-score of 0.79 is obtained for 'Bhakti' type of classes. The average precision score, micro-averaged over all classes for 2 regions (3,5): 0.70.

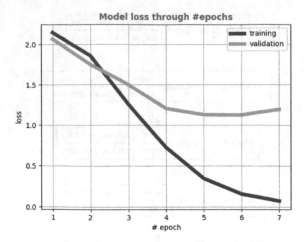

Fig. 4. Model loss through epochs for the model shown in Fig. 3

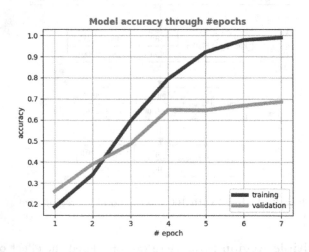

Fig. 5. Model accuracy through epochs for the model shown in Fig. 3

Figure 8 shows the confusion matrix for (3,5) region. It shows that maximum poems of 'vidamban' type of category get misclassified into 'gambhir' and 'vinodi' type of category. Also, maximum of 'Shrungar' types of poems gets misclassified into 'prem' category. Micro-average ROC curve is 0.83, and the macro-average ROC curve is 0.82 for the (3,5) model.

2. **Effect of 3 regions with different size**

   Here we experimented with 3 regions of different sizes with 32 filters for each region. For three regions, three channels are created, which are then concatenated. The model for each channel is the same as the model for one region, except 32 filters are used for each region. Convolutions are performed using 32 filters for three words for the region of size 3. Similarly, for four

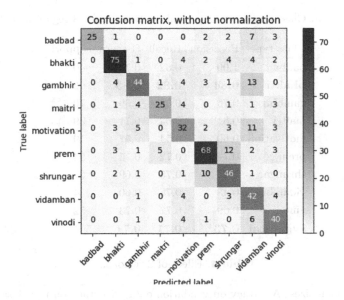

Fig. 6. Confusion matrix for the model shown in Fig. 3

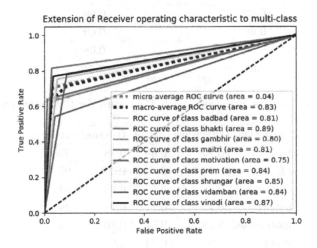

Fig. 7. ROC curve for the model shown in Fig. 3

regions, four words and for five regions, five words filtering is done. The highest accuracy of 69% is achieved for the three regions as shown in Table 6.

3. **Effect of 4 regions with different size**

We experimented with four regions of different sizes with 32 filters for each region. Table 7 shows that maximum accuracy of 0.71 on validation data and 0.73 on test data is obtained for four regions (4, 5, 6, 7). Table 8 shows

Table 3. Classwise precision, recall, f1-measure for 8 region model.

Class type	Precision	Recall	f1-score	support
badbad	1.00	0.62	0.77	40
bhakti	**0.84**	**0.82**	**0.83**	92
gambhir	0.76	0.63	0.69	70
maitri	0.81	0.64	0.71	39
motivation	0.60	0.54	0.57	59
prem	0.77	0.72	0.75	94
shrungar	0.64	0.75	0.69	61
vidamban	0.48	0.78	0.60	54
vinodi	0.69	0.77	0.73	52
avg/total	**0.73**	**0.71**	**0.71**	561

Table 4. Effect of 2 regions.

Region sizes	Accuracy on validation data	Accuracy on test data
(2,4)	0.66	**0.70**
(3,5)	**0.67**	0.69
(4,6)	0.66	0.69
(5,7)	0.66	0.68
(6,8)	0.66	**0.70**

Table 5. Classwise precision, recall, f1-measure for (3,5) region model.

Class type	Precision	Recall	f1-score	support
badbad	**0.89**	0.69	0.78	45
bhakti	0.76	**0.82**	**0.79**	97
gambhir	0.74	0.55	0.63	64
maitri	0.71	0.77	0.74	39
motivation	0.38	0.57	0.46	49
prem	0.60	0.72	0.66	80
shrungar	0.85	0.59	0.69	56
vidamban	0.73	0.62	0.67	77
vinodi	0.72	0.76	0.74	54
avg/total	**0.71**	**0.68**	**0.69**	561

classwise precision, recall, f1-measure for four regions model of size (4, 5, 6, 7). Figure 9 shows the confusion matrix for the model with four regions of size (4,5,6,7).

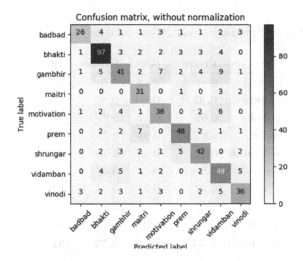

Fig. 8. Confusion matrix for the (3,5) region model

Table 6. Effect of 3 regions.

Region sizes	Accuracy on validation data	Accuracy on test data
(2,3,4)	0.66	0.68
(2,4,6)	0.69	**0.69**
(3,4,5)	0.68	0.68
(4,5,6)	0.67	0.68
(4,6,8)	0.67	**0.69**
(5,6,7)	0.68	**0.69**
(6,7,8)	**0.71**	0.68

Table 7. Effect of 4 regions.

Region sizes	Accuracy on validation data	Accuracy on test data
(2,3,4,5)	0.69	0.65
(3,4,5,6)	0.69	0.71
(4,5,6,7)	**0.71**	**0.72**
(5,6,7,8)	0.68	0.71

Effect of Different Batch Sizes: Here we experimented with different batch sizes of 16, 32, 64 and 128, considering three regions 4, 6 and 8 with 32 filters for each region. Table 9 shows the results for different batch sizes.

Table 8. Classwise precision, recall, f1-measure for (4, 5, 6, 7) regions model.

Class type	Precision	Recall	f1-score	support
badbad	0.81	0.62	0.70	42
bhakti	**0.82**	**0.84**	**0.83**	**115**
gambhir	0.66	0.57	0.61	72
maitri	0.65	0.84	0.73	37
motivation	0.67	0.69	0.68	52
prem	0.80	0.76	0.78	63
shrungar	0.72	0.74	0.73	57
vidamban	0.62	0.72	0.67	68
vinodi	0.72	0.65	0.69	55
avg/total	**0.73**	**0.72**	**0.72**	**561**

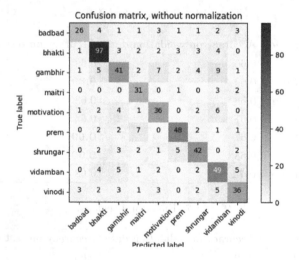

Fig. 9. Confusion matrix for the model shown in model of 4, 5, 6, 7 regions

Table 9. Effect of different batch size.

Batch size	Accuracy on validation data	Accuracy on test data
16	0.67	0.70
32	0.69	0.71
64	**0.66**	**0.73**
128	0.70	0.69

4   Conclusion

Here we used CNN based deep learning models for the classification of Marathi poems. In this approach, we experimented with one region, 2, 3, 4 regions for filtering. For 1-region size filter, maximum accuracy 0.69 on validation, and 0.71 for test data is obtained for 8-region size. For 2-regions, filter maximum accuracy 0.66 on validation and 0.70 for test data is obtained for (2,4) and (6,8) regions. For 3-regions, filter maximum accuracy 0.69 on validation and 0.69 for test data is obtained for (2, 4, 6) regions. For 4-regions filter maximum accuracy 0.71 on validation and 0.72 for test data is obtained for (4, 5, 6, 7) regions. For different regions, results show that maximum accuracy achieved is 0.72. In CNN, we also experimented for different batch sizes for three regions (4, 6, 8), each with 32 filters. Results show that for a batch of 64, the maximum accuracy on test data achieved is 0.73. All the above models show that a maximum accuracy of 0.73 is achieved for the classification of 2803 poems into nine categories. Our models can be used for essay classification, news classification, story classification, etc. In the future, we can increase the dataset, tune different parameters like batch size, activation function, optimizers, etc. Future work can be focused on the use of Recurrent neural network, Long short-term memory, auto encoder-decoder models, pretrained models, attention based models for Marathi text classification.

References

1. Gu, J., et al.: Recent advances in convolutional neural networks. Pattern Recogn. **77**, 354–377 (2018)
2. Kowsari, K., Jafari Meimandi, K., Heidarysafa, M., Mendu, S., Barnes, L., Brown, D.: Text classification algorithms: a survey. Information **10**(4), 150 (2019)
3. Minaee, S., Kalchbrenner, N., Cambria, E., Nikzad, N., Chenaghlu, M., Gao, J.: Deep learning-based text classification: a comprehensive review. ACM Comput. Surv. (CSUR) **54**(3), 1–40 (2021)
4. Kamath, C.N., Bukhari, S.S., Dengel, A.: Comparative study between traditional machine learning and deep learning approaches for text classification. In: Proceedings of the ACM Symposium on Document Engineering, p. 14 (2018)
5. Georgakopoulos, S.V., Tasoulis, S.K., Vrahatis, A.G.: Convolutional neural networks for toxic comment classification. In: Proceedings of the 10th Hellenic Conference on Artificial Intelligence, p. 35. ACM (2018)
6. Cano, E., Morisio, M.: A deep learning architecture for sentiment analysis. In: Proceedings of the International Conference on Geoinformatics and Data Analysis, pp. 122–126. ACM (2018)
7. Hughes, M., Li, I., Kotoulas, S., Suzumura, T.: Medical text classification using convolutional neural networks. Stud. Health Technol. Inform. **235**, 246–250 (2017)
8. Hsu, T., Tzuhan, Y.: Petroleum engineering data text classification using convolutional neural network based classifier. In: Proceedings of the 2018 International Conference on Machine Learning Technologies, pp. 63–68. ACM (2018)
9. Kalchbrenner, N., Grefenstette, E., Blunsom, P.: A convolutional neural network for modelling sentences. arXiv preprint arXiv:1404.2188 (2014)

10. Kim, Y.: Convolutional neural networks for sentence classification. arXiv preprint arXiv:1408.5882 (2014)
11. Zhang, Y., Wallace, B.: A sensitivity analysis of (and practitioners' guide to) convolutional neural networks for sentence classification. arXiv preprint arXiv:1510.03820 (2015)
12. de Sousa Pereira Amorim, B., Alves, A.L.F., de Oliveira, M.G., de Souza Baptista, C.: Using supervised classification to detect political tweets with political content. In: Proceedings of the 24th Brazilian Symposium on Multimedia and the Web, pp. 245–252. ACM (2018)
13. Severyn, A., Moschitti, A.: UNITN: training deep convolutional neural network for twitter sentiment classification. In: Proceedings of the 9th International Workshop on Semantic Evaluation (SemEval 2015), pp. 464–469 (2015)
14. Baker, S., Korhonen, A., Pyysalo, S.: Cancer hallmark text classification using convolutional neural networks. In: Proceedings of the Fifth Workshop on Building and Evaluating Resources for Biomedical Text Mining (BioTxtM 2016), pp. 1–9 (2016)
15. Ali, A.R., Ijaz, M.: Urdu text classification. In: Proceedings of the 7th International Conference on Frontiers of Information Technology, p. 21. ACM, December 2009
16. Krail, N., Gupta, V.: Domain based classification of Punjabi text documents using ontology and hybrid based approach. In: Proceedings of the 3rd Workshop on South and Southeast Asian Natural Language Processing, pp. 109–122 (2012)
17. Rajan, K., Ramalingam, V., Ganesan, M., Palanivel, S., Palaniappan, B.: Automatic classification of Tamil documents using vector space model and artificial neural network. Expert Syst. Appl. **36**(8), 10914–10918 (2009)
18. Patil, J.J., Bogiri, N.: Automatic text categorization: Marathi documents. In: 2015 International Conference on Energy Systems and Applications, pp. 689–694. IEEE (2015)
19. Deshmukh, R.A., Kore, S., Chavan, N., Gole, S., Kumar, A.: Marathi poem classification using machine learning. Int. J. Recent Technol. Eng. (IJRTE) 2723–2727 (2019). ISSN 2277–3878
20. Ahmad, S., Asghar, M.Z., Alotaibi, F.M., Khan, S.: Classification of poetry text into the emotional states using deep learning technique. IEEE Access **8**, 73865–73878 (2020)
21. O'Shea, K., Nash, R.: An introduction to convolutional neural networks. arXiv preprint arXiv:1511.08458 (2015)
22. Wu, J.: Introduction to convolutional neural networks, vol. 5, no. 23, p. 495. National Key Lab for Novel Software Technology. Nanjing University, China (2017)
23. Kingma, D.P., Ba, J.: Adam: a method for stochastic optimization. arXiv preprint arXiv:1412.6980 (2014)
24. Srivastava, N., Hinton, G., Krizhevsky, A., Sutskever, I., Salakhutdinov, R.: Dropout: a simple way to prevent neural networks from overfitting. J. Mach. Learn. Res. **15**(1), 1929–1958 (2014)

Three Decision Points Vetting a More Ideal Online Technical Platform for Monitoring and Treating Mental Health Problems like Depression and Schizophrenia

Mark D. Whitaker[1]([✉]), Nara Hwang[1], Durdonakhon Usmonova[1], Kangrim Cho[2], and Nara Park[1]

[1] Department of Technology and Society, Stony Brook University, State University of New York, Korea (SUNY Korea), Incheon, Songdo, South Korea
mark.whitaker@sunykorea.ac.kr, narahwangg@gmail.com,
diana.usmonova.94@gmail.com, nara.park@stonybrook.edu
[2] Cognitive Science Department, Yonsei University, Seoul, Sinchon, South Korea
whrkdfla@yonsei.ac.kr

Abstract. To improve Information Communication Technology for Development (ICT4D) in e-health applications means getting the maximum advantage at the minimum cost to purveyors and consumers. This is a conceptual and empirical paper arguing three informed decision points, taken in order, should happen whenever maximizing advantages of health diagnostics and/or treatment facilitation via online platforms. Three kinds of data are important to know beforehand to create informed decisions to maximize beneficial uses of online technology to aid mental health: (1) how do you define the etiology of mental health problems; (2) how do you define who should be helped as a priority, and (3) how do you make decisions technically to fit the former two points? Since serving patients is more important than technical profiteering, these three critical decision points mean primary medical choices of diagnosis and secondary social demographic research should guide a more conditioned tertiary technical use, instead of vice versa that regularly leads to cutting patients to fit a pre-determined and thus misaligned technological investment. Due to limitations of space, only the third vetting point is analyzed in detail. The current state of the art for how to reach patients best via Internet-connected technologies for monitoring and treating depression and schizophrenia is analyzed. Policy advice on platform design is given from this vetting procedure that might later be scaled worldwide.

Keywords: ICT4D · Mental health · e-health · Depression · Schizophrenia · Monitoring · Diagnosis · Treatment · Demographics · Technology policy · Online platform · SaMD · EMA · EMI

1 Introduction

This paper explores the current state of the art in Internet-connected technologies for diagnosing and treating depression and schizophrenia to improve technology investment

© Springer Nature Switzerland AG 2022
J.-H. Kim et al. (Eds.): IHCI 2021, LNCS 13184, pp. 89–105, 2022.
https://doi.org/10.1007/978-3-030-98404-5_8

and design policies in such online tools[1] Some of what follows is similar to other literature reviewing anxiety mobile apps [1, 2]. However, the novel aspects of this research are more holistic in two ways. First, the analysis asked would be the best and widest social levels of access via certain communication infrastructures that should influence platform design, instead of being only an analysis of the platform design itself. Second, analysis documents for the first time all various strategic goals and technical means designed so far across the most popular online platforms monitoring and treating these two mental problems, with an aim to make better and more holistic recommendations on platform design. To elaborate, this is a review of over fifty total instances of (1) the hardware of small, portable, or wearable data-gathering or bio/neuro-treatment technologies involved in monitoring and treating mental problems, (2) the hardware for which personal information communication technology (ICT) is the best option for widespread use to maximize access and thus how to design such hardware access into online platforms, and (3) software design of the most popular (measured by highest number of downloads) online platforms for depression and for schizophrenia by comparing their different characteristics and purposes.

This study comes out of a wider international project team that wants to make more rational e-health decisions on national mental health policies to minimize depression, schizophrenia, and suicide. The question was how 'e-health' services can facilitate monitoring and/or treatment of large numbers of people with these problems more cheaply. E-health tactics can treat populations more cheaply in the millions that were historically or economically unreachable in the past.

As background to this project, this interdisciplinary research is funded by a grant from the Korean National Research Foundation in the category of a "Joint Program of Cooperation in Science and Technology." Established in 2020 and continuing through 2023, this Joint Program is tasked to create a "Group Center for Depression Diagnosis and Medication Adherence" between the skill sets of many universities and institutes across the Republic of Korea (South Korea) and the Republic of India. Both the Korean National Research Foundation and the Indian State together fund a team of eleven professors in nine universities and institutes in Korea and India, respectively, to work on one common project. This team includes personnel or professors from both national mental health institutes of the two countries involved. In Korea, this is the National Center for Mental Health in the Ministry of Health and Welfare. In India, this is the Institute of Mental Health and Neurosciences (NIMHANS). Around these two nations' funding agencies and these two national mental health centers, five universities in Korea and four universities in India join this international team. The research that follows summarizes research production in the team hired by Dr. Whitaker of the Department of Technology and Society at the State University of New York, Korea (SUNY Korea), one of the Korean universities in this project.

Despite focusing on a short technical review, we argue that three critical decisions, taken in order, are required to make rational and vetted decisions for using online technology to aid mental health that maximize patient access and minimize technical costs:

---
[1] This research was supported under the National Research Foundation (NRF) Korea (2020K1A3A1A68093469) funded by the Ministry of Science and ICT (MSIT) Korea and by the Department of Biotechnology (India) (DBT/IC-12031(22)-ICD-DBT).

(1) how do you define the etiology or causes of mental health problems; (2) how do you define who should be helped first as a priority, and only then (3) how do you make decisions technically on how you can help via your chosen treatment interventions that maximize your target audience(s)? These three critical variables mean medical episte- mological choices of diagnosis and treatment have to be thought about seriously first in a more holistic manner even before finding treatment audiences and before investing in technology blindly. For the first point, there are at least three options to consider here: are mental health problems caused primarily by biophysical, individually psychological, or sociological factors? [3–6] The literature indicates all do matter instead of only one of these, so treatment should proceed in e-health with this in mind. Second, that first etiological choice then is exercised on select target audiences in particular countries after inductive research of what are the social demographic priorities of mental problems. This is in contrast to thinking mental health is only an individualized or globalized problem. Why are national demographics important to know? First, it is documented that national economic inequalities greatly increase prevalence of all kinds of inequalities in health problems, particularly higher among marginalized ethnic minorities, marginalized occu- pations, and marginalized genders [7]. Second, national hegemonic cultures can worsen instead of help equitable health outcomes in minorities of various kinds by coding lower ascribed national statuses and stigmas on such groups that greatly demote their aggre- gate life chances, increase their stresses, and demote their mental health [8]. Therefore, unique *national* demographics of mental health and the ascribed national social status of the patients in question in those national demographics have to be understood together when treating individuals with mental problems. Third, only after the first two points are researched and are clear, can a rational vetted decision on technology policy in e-health be made that fits a nation's priorities by finding the largest numbers of patients and/or the most extreme demographics with mental problems. In other words, it is important to avoid falling either in love first with a particular target audience or with a particular technological artifact without reexamining preconceptions about how mental problems get treated. Only then can we get around treatment biases that can rig the treatment game from the start.

In conclusion, the goal of this research is to focus on the third level of vetting to push forward debate on how technology policy can maximize interventions socially and economically in a virtual/online space. We review and advise on monitoring/treatment peripherals, communication access by noting the most socially distributed personal com- munication devices, and online platform design and software techniques—while being cognizant of limitations of an exclusively technical online space of monitoring and treatment. In short, what kind of technology policies and design would be needed for a smooth and equitable implementation to help millions of people previously unreachable via online platforms in their mental problems?

2 How Should We Help Them? Analysis of the Current Market of Mobile Applications in Mental Health

This section's analysis from the raw data in the Appendices (unnecessary to this review summary and so available online [9]) catalogue many technical choices. Thus the fol- lowing information is readable without the appendices. The data is based on six months of our research team's analysis of what applications exist already in the technical side of monitoring and treating mental problems of depression and schizophrenia as well as telecommunication access capacities. The team reviewed three areas: (1) general personal ICT access choices, (2) 20 instances of small, portable, or wearable data-gathering or bio/neuro-treatment technologies involved in monitoring and treating mental problems, and (3) online platforms for depression (n = 15) and for schizophrenia (n = 9) by comparing their different characteristics and purposes. In the final section on Recommendations we summarize policy ideas for either better access or better design of online platforms for mental problems, along with current obstacles to improving either of these technologies or access to these technologies. To monitor or to treat mental problems digitally requires these three research questions about available communication technology. Therefore in the following analysis the research team asked these three interrelated questions about which choices of information communication technology (ICT) for e-health would be the best options for how it would particularly fit well into the two countries of interest, South Korea and India. However, recommendations were made based on the ultimate desire to use these two countries as prototypes to go beyond them into a global online application for monitoring and treating mental problems.

The first question is *what are the best choices of ICT hardware communications infrastructure for access,* for aiding particular national demographics of mental problems in both countries? Online accessibility depends upon hardware: (1) what kinds of communication hardware nationally is already owned, shared, or generally distributed in these two countries that would grant prioritized target audiences the greatest equality of access to potential e-health online platforms? This analysis identified two main options upon which access to online platforms for mental problems should be optimized for because these are the cheapest and most distributed kinds of ICT hardware in these countries and indeed in the world: smartphones and smartwatches.

The second question is *what are the best choices of ICT hardware communications infrastructure for digital monitoring or for treatment options of a particular person?* This is answered with Appendices 3 and 4. This means (2) what kinds of technologies of monitoring or biofeedback have the most widespread utility and cost effectiveness? This analysis catalogued what we call general "strategic" goals or purposes of such technologies for mental problems and many "tactics" through which those strategic goals are attempted to be achieved either by monitoring and/or treatment. The use of these terms strategy and tactics are meant in the following way. By analogy, if the ultimate strategy or goal is to win a war, then issues of tactics would be how and in what specific or plural actions or materials you try to achieve that general strategy: like tactics of spies, tanks, airplanes, troops, submarines/missiles, or civilian militias. This analysis identified nine strategic goals of technical solutions for monitoring or treating mental problems and nine kinds of tactics for how to do such data gathering. The nine technical strategies as platforms are (1) mobile smartphones/apps, (2) smart watches, (3) wearable patches, (4) headset monitors, (5) headphones, (6) earbuds, (7) e-rings, (8) limited smartwatch wearables like FitBits, and (9) head cap monitoring. The nine strategies (of those nine different technologies) are to have small portable versions of: (1) EEG: Electroencephalogram (voltage fluctuations from ionic current within neurons of the brain); (2) ECG: Electrocardiogram (voltage of heart over time);

(3) BLAST: Bilateral Alternating Stimulation Tactiles; (4) HRV: Heart Rate Variability (measuring ongoing variations in the beat-to-beat interval of the heart rate); (4) CES: Cranial electrotherapy stimulation (pulsed low alternating current via electrodes on the head); (5) PPG: Photoplethysmogram (detect blood volume changes in microvascular tissue with a LED light acting as a pulse oximeter to illuminate skin then measure changes in light absorption); (6) tDCS: transcranial direct current stimulation (constant low direct current via electrodes on the head); (7) TMS: transcranial magnetic stimulation (pulsed low magnetic fields to stimulate nerve cells in the brain); (8) Light Therapy (or known as phototherapy or heliotherapy), and (9) Sound Therapy. Some platforms reviewed employ multiple tactics simultaneously. Some strategies and tactics can be more quickly expanded than others. Those are noted with asterisks in Appendix 3 and 4. Particularly of interest are three: (2.1) health-monitoring mobile apps that utilize existing smartphone internal or peripheral hardware (which we call using the smartphone as a temporarily "placed wearable" on the body for a short while), (2.2) wearable health-monitoring 'limited smartwatches' like FitBit's, (2.3) and even smaller "e-rings" that have yet to develop a large market yet are more of an unobtrusive monitoring tool with greater promise than even FitBits.

The third question is about software instead of hardware: *what kind of software strategies and tactics of monitoring and treatment do the world's already popular platforms exhibit in their attempts to aid patients' mental problems*? This is answered with Appendices 5 through 7. This question asks how people have programmed software for mental problems in the past, and how can we do this better in the future while keeping in mind of course the first two hardware questions of digital communications accessibility and digital monitoring/treatment accessibility via the most widely distributed ICT hardware already available? We identify nine strategies of such online platforms that might be merged, as well as identified nine tactics of such online platforms that might be merged. As noted in Appendices 5 through 7, we find all nine basic strategic purposes of online platforms for mental health share a goal of giving users portable tools to help themselves via: 1. a changed mental state (CBT: cognitive behavioral therapy); 2. a virtual community for sharing; 3. self-tracking of mood changes; 4. access to professional counseling; 5. increase awareness of common treatment means (informational/reference service); 6. calendar; 7. mood boost; 8. ways to track depression level; and 9. 'S.O.S' instant assistance. There are anther nine basic software tactics for how online platforms attempt to achieve the nine basic strategic goals. They use: 1. chatbots/machine learning; 2. live chat; 3. games/goals; 4. social media platforms; 5. mood/progress tracker; 6. daily diary/journal; 7. videos/articles/audio; 8. meditation/breathing techniques; and 9. clinically approved tests.

In short, which choices are strategically best for reaching the widest treatment audiences at the lowest costs? A wealth of technological strategies and tactics already use mobile/portable data monitoring or portable biofeedback treatments. The following analysis and recommendations below on how to design better mental health treatments in league with online platforms are based on assembled raw data in appendices offered in interests of transparency yet unrequired for the summary below.

2.1 Three Important Concepts for Planning Online Platforms in Monitoring and Treatment of Mental Problems: SaMD, EMA, and EMI

"SaMD" (Software as Medical Device) means acceleration of diagnosis, management, and treatment of a wide spectrum of medical conditions and diseases by automating aspects of care. This is done via hardware like smartphones, tablets, or wearable devices. Second, software itself for medical purposes can perform tasks without being part of a hardware device [10]. The US Food and Drug Administration (FDA) has a three-part definition of SaMD: Software as a Medical Device is capable of running on general purpose (non-medical purpose) computing platforms; Software as a medical device running on these general purpose computing platforms could be located in a hardware medical device; Software connected to a hardware medical device but is not needed by that hardware medical device to achieve its intended medical purpose is Software as a Medical Device and not accessory to the hardware medical device [11].

Ecological momentary assessment (EMA) methods collect data on repeated occasions in real time and in the context of daily life. If phenomena get measured as they arise and evolve over time, they can be measured more accurately, and they can depict dynamic relationships between variables. EMA takes advantage of several digital technologies to provide automated delivery and recording of data. This can be a prompted or desired recording on demand, or it can be a passive capture of ongoing data like waking/sleeping patterns or ambulatory/physiological data via actigraphy, heart rate, motion sense, and skin conductance. Up to nine different kinds of data gathering are now possible in small portable or wearable devices that employ EMA, listed in Appendix 3. Plus, a benefit is how 'ecological' or context-sensitive 'momentary' data can be captured based on ongoing place or social/environmental conditions to investigate associated external triggers and other catalysts of mental problems [12].

Ecological momentary intervention (EMI) is an extension or derivative of EMA. EMI extends a one-way methodology of data gathering and monitoring of remote patients into an ongoing two-way immediate yet remote clinical intervention based either on user requests or on automatic algorithmic triggering based on the EMA data itself. EMI was defined first by Heron and Smyth as "digital interventions" that provide treatment via telecommunication to people anywhere they are in current settings in real time. EMIs use digital technology similar to EMA like smartphone apps and SMS text messages yet EMI delivers statements or instructions to promote positive behaviors and coping when needed in daily life [12]. There are many working examples of EMA in mobile health care for mental problems particularly for management or intervention with schizophrenia as mentioned in Appendix 5.

Both EMA and EMI have potential applications to psychosis management, capitalizing on a number of key capabilities of mobile technologies to provide a means of accurate assessment; they can also be used to remind people of intervention strategies in the moment they are needed. Such assessments and reminders may be especially beneficial in psychotic disorders, because difficulties with memory and executive functioning can limit accurate recall of past events and motivational difficulties can impede generalization of intervention strategies outside the consulting room. Overall, these applications seem potentially valuable in empowering people in more effective self-management... [12].

2.2 Surveyed List of Tactics on Online Platforms for Mental Problems of Depression and Schizophrenia

Next, what about a review of software for mental problems around depression? After reviewing the world's most popular fifteen mobile applications related to this judged by the highest number of downloads, nine different strategies and nine different tactics of such online platforms were identified and assessed. The fifteen platforms are: 1. Headspace; 2. Breathwrk; 3. Doctot; 4. Woebot; 5. AntiStress; 6. Happify; 7. Bloom; 8. GDS; 9. InnerHour; 10. Wysa; 11. Moodpress; 12. AlbaMind; 13. ThinkLadder; 14. Cove; and 15. TalkLife. By analyzing these, it was possible to list and to quantify the most common online tools for mental problems designed into software platforms. This helped to get a sense of the currently most used features on the most popular mobile app platforms, as well as their least used and presumably least desirable tools. These total nine tactics found are: 1. chatbots/machine learning; 2. live chat; 3. games/goals/gamification; 4. social platform; 5. mood tracker/progress tracker; 6. daily diary/journal; 7. videos/articles/audio; 8. meditation/breathing techniques; and 9. clinically approved tests. Review the raw data in Appendix 6 and 7 to browse what 'the market' has made successful in these various strategies and tactics of online platforms. Some tactics used are popular and well represented across all current mobile apps for mental health, while other tactics are very poorly represented. Equally, nine popular mobile apps for monitoring or treating schizophrenia were reviewed: 1. Coping with Voices (pilot project, USA); 2. Temstem (Reframing Studio, Amsterdam, Netherlands); 3. MHASC (France); 4. MindFrame (Monsenso, Denmark); 5. CrossCheck (USA); 6. PRIME (USA); 7. ReMind Care (Spain); 8. FOCUS (U. of Washington, BRiTE Center, Seattle, USA); and 9. AVATAR Therapy (proof-of-concept study, UK univ. group). The reviews of two other tactics of EMI and EMA dealing with schizophrenia are discussed in the wider Recommendations. Below, the nine software tactics are reviewed in the depression mobile apps framed in terms of more improvements or recommendations to these.

1. Using chatbots and machine learning in chatbots, yet equally a way to contact a real 'digital practitioner' as well. The use of a chatbot feature is uneven within the top fifteen mobile applications, but the main objective is to design software to act as if the user were communicating with a friend or therapist. As users are aware that it is an AI instead of a person, the chatbot can act as a friendly and approachable method for users to open up and to talk about subjects that they would have difficulty discussing in real life even with an anonymous person. This adds a 'double level' of anonymity with the first level of anonymity being conversations with anonymous persons and the second level being conversations with anonymous AIs. It is conjectured that a chatbot (instead of a chat function with real people) helps users be more honest about their emotions (ironically, to a machine) and helps them to expose issues related to their mental problems in perfect anonymity. For the Apple Store's reviews of WoeBot which has such a chatbot: "It eliminates any anxiety (that) comes with human interaction."; "I love that it's AI and not going to judge me. It's only there to help." Anonymity is very important to integrate into a future ideal mobile app for mental health in other words, even to the level of this 'double level' anonymity since people seem to prefer to talk to machines instead of people for preliminary advice to avoid stigmas.

2. *Live chat.* Chat appears in two ways: chat with *digital practitioners and/or user peer groups.* However, there is a seen potential in some of these existing platforms of a way to 'escalate' contact via the mobile app/platform that can be useful. So a requested instant chat with "digital practitioners" may be another way of medical and techno-logical cooperation for mental health treatment. First, they know that the person they are chatting with is a professional. Second, security regarding the personal information will/must be provided. Third, if digital practitioners are available like customer service representatives, patients will be able to reach out for professional help anonymously almost any time they want help. On the one hand, chat functions with other peer users on online platforms can remove social dislocation from participants. This could be a key social feature of some mental health apps so chat should be taken seriously as a means toward a patient's social-psychological reintegration. Even if hardly everyone on a platform will use the chat, there will be a self-selection into the platform by those who desire it as part of their treatment and happiness on the platform. However, on the other hand, as you can see from Appendix 6, chat functions are not highly popular in the app domain now if we trust the vague idea that the world's already most popular current online tools for mental problems show the popularity of the discrete nine tactics they are currently using. Chat just appears only once, in the app TalkLife. Though this is a popular app worldwide, TalkLife seems a more specialized chat service function for mental problems. However on the whole the other top fourteen mobile apps for mental problems do fail to feature chat at all. Our interpretation is that a combined high level of stigma about mental problems and the 'troll-based' internet world of intentionally harmful comments for fun by anonymous people loving to wreck conversations might render chat as having a low popularity as a tactic except for people who seek it in a specialized app environment like TalkLife.

3. *Using games/goal/gamification.* Some of the applications reviewed included easy games/exercises targeted to help reduce anxiety and change one's thought process. For example, Happify claims that their "science-based activities and games can help you overcome negative thoughts, stress, and life's challenges." These game- and goal-based strategies add competitive aspects to push users to keep making progress. The Apple Store's review of Happify states: "It has the perfect balance of a little information accom-panying activities that actually really do boost my mood. And the activities that encourage you to connect with other people make it impact my mood and well-being past just when I am in the app."

4. *Using social platform.* Four applications include a feature where peer users can communicate with each other to remove their dislocation in life somewhat. For example, TalkLife is specifically a social media platform for people suffering from a mental illness. On the platform, users can share as much or as little about their experience as they want. The pseudo-anonymity on demand allows users to open up voluntarily, and they can also see that they are not alone in their illness. Users can share tips, and stories from their personal experience, as well as offer messages to support each other in a safe and

supportive environment. It creates a sense of community. There are positive and negative comments to relay here. First, for positive comments, three of the Apple Store's reviews of TalkLife state very positive comments: "The people on here are so understanding, they don't judge you, they give advice, they support you, etc. Getting help from people with feelings/thoughts/experiences similar to mine really gives me a sense of comfort…." "I was able to say the things I was feeling and I was able to share things I wouldn't share with others."…."I was looking for an app where I could express my feelings without being judged, and this app is full of people feeling the same things you do. It really does help to know you're actually not alone in what's going on with your life and other people are there to help you".

On the other hand, negative comments come after viewing the TalkLife interface as confusing and after viewing an actual chat online that appears to be full of 'trolls' (anonymous people who intentionally disrupt a service or conversation, simply for their own destructive fun). Thus, anonymous chat has potential of being as much harmful as useful. Negativity may cause users to remain in a present bad mental state without progress. Thus a vetted chat that can be publicly anonymous yet with registered users only may be a solution, yet even that may hardly remove insistent trolls.

5. *Using mood tracker/progress tracker.* The tracking feature allows users to look back on their achievements and growths. They can also remember the hard times that they overcame and give themselves further confidence in their mental health journey. From viewing Appendix 6, there are a massive number of popular apps with this tactic, so it is a highly recommended tactic. We suggest any future successful app for mental help should include a mood tracker and progress tracker.

6. *Using diary/journal.* Similar to the mood tracker tactic, having a diary implemented into the application allows users to 'write' down their thoughts and emotions without any limitations in time or location. For example, the mobile app called Bloom uses guided journaling exercises for a hyper-personalized digital therapy experience. These sessions are aimed to improve personal well-being, to manage stress and anxiety, and to increase emotional health. The Apple Store has one review for Bloom that reads: "The writing exercises have helped me realize my thought patterns and how I can make small adjustments in many areas." In viewing Appendix 6, given a massive number of popular apps with this tactic, it is highly recommended that any future successful app for mental help include a daily journal as well.

7. *Using videos/articles/audio.* For an example of this, InnerHour provides 'guided imagery' sessions which are relaxation techniques to help visualize a calm and serene setting. Such sessions can help a user release negative thoughts and can reduce stress. These sessions are provided via listening to audio recordings which helps add a personal touch. This was the third most popular tactic.

8. *Using meditation/breathing techniques to manage anxiety.* Meditation and breathing exercises are seen in the majority of these fifteen popular applications. Obviously the market for online mental health wants to see meditation guides to help users practice more mindfulness and relaxation. Meditation is a useful technique helping people feel more grounded when experiencing severe stress or anxiety. Depression is now seen as "depression/anxiety" admixed [13, 14]. Therefore to cure depression, it helps to start laterally by treating anxiety. Meditation techniques regularly are a subsection within

these popular mobile apps for depression management and even within specialized anti-anxiety apps not reviewed here [1]. For meditation, many customizable features exist for every experience level and lifestyle like length of time, specific topic, and sounds. The Apple Store review of one of these apps named Headspace (which features meditation coaching and customization) reads: "I....have a tendency to get bored with things including meditation, so the variety of approaches, techniques, and goals provided keep it fresh."....[and keeps them coming back like good gamification should.]...."I travel quite a bit, and I love that I'm able to pick my environment of choice to meditate."....
"Headspace takes a different approach than most other meditation/mindfulness apps by not only teaching you the techniques, but also teaching you how to apply mindfulness with everything that you do."

9. *Using clinically approved tests.* Five applications reviewed integrated clinically approved tests for depression (and Appendix 1 has a list of these) to improve accuracy of the diagnosed illness and to measure ongoing improvement or change by recognized tests. It serves to indicate progress through the period of use of the applications. This is the only way to test if the platforms are doing what they say they are doing: helping people improve management of their mental problems. This is a crucial feature. However, this feature is missing in fully 10 of 15 of the most popular apps, so regardless of their popularity, no one really can know if many mobile apps clinically are helping people without having parallel tests for the same people in the same app.

In conclusion, what are the most popular tactics observed if you want to make a future better 'killer app' in this mental health field? The mood tracker/progress tracker and the daily journal are the most widely used tactics in the most popular mobile applications for managing mental problems. The third post popular was using multimedia video and audio in information received instead of only via text. It is safe to assume these three are a crucial 'selling' point: consumers want a mobile app/platform for mental health that they can use to track their progress over time (long term or short term) and want a visual representation of progress or change for effort that they put in to give accurate data in the app over weeks or even months, and they want an easy way of learning visually or with audio. This allows more sensory participation, since simply reading text can become dull and lack interest. It is the least a programmer can do to create sensory experiences that entice people to come back so they avoid easy excuses of avoiding apps they downloaded or websites they visited to try to change their mental states for the better.

3   Overall Recommendations

Five kinds of recommendations are made for ideal online platforms for monitoring and treating depression. Ideas drawn from the review of applications of schizophrenia are applied to this, though we feel schizophrenia deserves to have separate application solutions. For lack of space, that schizophrenia application review is not included. So what follows is only for managing, monitoring, or treating depression/anxiety yet ideas are drawn from analysis of 15 depression and 9 schizophrenia platforms.

First, what are best choices of *ICT hardware infrastructure* for aiding communication access to mental health in most countries in the world at present? We recommend a combination of three access points: smartphones, smartwatches, and various health tracker/limited smartwatches like FitBits. Pre-existing mobile phone networks of smartphones and smartwatches should be taken advantage of as the basic platform tools however. This is because of the two-way use of such an infrastructure for both access as well as potentially for EMA and EMI. Such platforms if designed to work with smartphones and smartwatches (which connect smartphones; and smartphones might be a hub that connect to many other biofeedback/monitoring peripherals if desired by users) have a good multiplier effects for users providing and uploading ongoing updates to the platform from other self-monitoring tools that they own.

While smartphones and smartwatches themselves can conduct a great many EMA data poolings already now (with raw data in Appendix 3 and 4), rolling out a modular online platform can be linked to many other mobile-accessible separate apps as mentioned with asterisks in Appendix 4 to add more data gathering and monitoring capabilities if users desire. We suggest future mobile health platforms should examine potentials for partnership-based data gathering from any other kind of Bluetooth-linked EMA monitoring from other peripherals. It could be an option on a future mobile platform for mental health to link all the various peripherals for data uploading and user-desired analysis of their own data. *We note that this has yet to be done in any popular platforms yet,* however there are already mobile apps linked to monitoring peripherals that allow a user to sync other devices like those mentioned in Appendix 3 and 4 to their own online mobile app/health platform connected to that machine.

It should be easy to do strategic partnerships with corporations that already make peripherals with mobile functionality, to see if they are interested in collaborating in a larger national project to aid mental health using their equipment while allowing that data to be equally linked to a national platform or other 'superapp' designed for such a purpose of being a hub of data gathering as well. There are nine data tools involved here as mentioned earlier (and in Appendix 3). We suggest prototyping such a plural synching. This would mean merging all nine various data-gathering strategies already in existence plus showing how to do free or cheap biofeedback monitoring. This future integrated platform could be given to the world.

Cheap access to mental health services via synched peripherals is our global plan for marginalized regions or underclasses. Such places and peoples universally are the ones in which the majority of mental problems exist worldwide [7], yet they are the very people without access to treatment in many countries. It would be ideal once online platforms are synched to various smartwatches and other EMA-monitoring peripherals particularly if machine learning could then analyze the data for the user as well as abstract 'big data' analysis for scientific work for others as well. However, while smartwatches and FitBits may not be as available in rural marginalized areas, smartphone applications do have better chances to assist patients with mental health issues and/or raise awareness about the importance of popular education and destigmatization of mental problems to make treatment more culturally accessible.

Second, of these various peripherals, *which of the nine basic hardware peripherals* are better so that the widest treatment audiences could be reached? Of the nine mentioned, these are: (1) mobile smartphones/apps, (2) smart watches, (3) wearable patches, (4) headset monitors, (5) headphones, (6) earbuds, (7) e-rings, (8) limited smartwatch wearables like FitBits, and (9) head cap monitoring. We recommend once more the dual use of smartphones/apps and smartwatches yet we keep in mind great potentials of limited-smartphone 'wearables' of health monitoring like FitBits connected to such online platforms as well as 'e-rings', earbuds, or headphones. We consider a distributed use of head cap monitoring as overly expensive and unlikely yet there are mobile apps to learn from that can be clearing houses of such data gathered like the mobile apps created by the T2 center in the USA (featured in the first two rows of Appendix 4 like BioZen and the T2 MoodTracker). It is recommended to create strategic partnerships with the T2 organization for online platforms that have functionality as a hub for much biodata.

There are nine strategic goals of these nine different technologies for what kind of data they are actually gathering. The nine strategic goals are to have small portable versions of these, mentioned in the earlier paragraph. We recommend embeddedness within a smartphone environment, so we recommend beginning with built-in possibilities of Light Therapy and Sound Therapy, and with measurements of HRV and PPG. All four of these might be used via the daily smartphone infrastructure for monitoring or collecting body data live, if desired to be integrated into a platform or for biofeedback treatments. We note nine basic techniques already in the market in mobile/portable devices listed in Appendix 3. These nine techniques are EEG, ECG*, BLAST, HRV*, CES, PPG*, tDCS, TMS, Light Therapy*, and Sound Therapy.* Five of these (with asterisks) already are bundled into software or hardware of many smartphones or wearables like FitBits or Smartwatches for e-health already. We suggest connecting data synching/gathering potentials of at least these free data gathering tools to a future online platform for mental health. That has yet to be done.

Third, what kind of *ICT software tactics* do we suggest as improvements to existing online platforms for addressing mental problems? Other suggestions are to merge all nine tactics together on one 'superapp' or online platform, which has yet to be done yet. Plus, second, we recommend more focus on more ideal technology of EMA or EMI for mental health disorders. We would like to emphasize that medical professionals' participation in such EMA/EMI platforms is a new field open to new opportunities in mental health treatment with technology. It is currently only used in schizophrenia applications, though can be more widely applied to depression. Third, we observed gaps or lacks in the fifteen mobile apps reviewed. These lacks that can be fixed for more ideal future mobile platforms for monitoring or treating mental problems and are summarized as: 1. Lack of initial guidance; 2. Lack of emphasis on the importance of discipline and continuous use of the apps. 3. Little or no consideration towards people with disabilities (ex., hearing disability); 4. Little gamification, 5. Some apps were not available for Android users so at least we recommend Apple iOS and Android should be dual common languages of access; 6. Lack of use of the certified clinical tests for the evaluation or scaling of depression; 7. Apps that include social platforms need better control, guidance, or intervention possibility from systems administrators to avoid intentional negativity or trolling that could make depression or anxiety worse; and 8. Lack of emphasis on "S.O.S situations" of panic in terms of mental problems or expedited suicide prevention.

For solving point #4, the promise of gamification to bring discipline of users to such online mental health apps is a technique used irregularly if at all so far. Only six total examples of gamification in mental monitoring and treatment were found in a quite exhaustive research survey. This was only a minority of two out of nine online platforms using gamification for treating or monitoring schizophrenia. This was Temstem (a mobile app for language games to interrupt the vividness or emotionality of auditory verbal hallucinations (AVH), and "MHASC" (Multisensory Hallucinations Scale for Children (allowing children to discuss and document hallucinatory experiences via videogame-based aesthetics to increase engagement and motivation of children during assessment)). Equally, only a minority of 4 of 15 popular mobile apps for other kinds of mental health monitoring were found to use games and gamification to treat depression: Headspace, Happify, InnerHour, and Cove. We recommend more efforts to brainstorm how to use gamification in mental health in online situations.

For solving point #6, it is critically important to have existing clinical tests (somehow potentially 'gamified'?) on online platforms. Without this, studies of the validity of such online platforms for improving mental health are unable to be justified and to be improved themselves. Without putting up existing clinical tests, there is no way to compare 'new online platforms' validity or effects with older surveys' ways of measuring depression. We encourage software designers to encourage their users on such platforms to take existing peer-reviewed measurement tests regularly as part of how they interface on the 'new online platforms.' Therefore, we recommend a few surveys mentioned in Appendix 1 should always be integrated on any fresh online platforms particularly for depression management.

Fourth, what kind of improvement on strategic goals of such platforms can be made? We find nine basic strategic goals of such online platforms for mental health aiming to give users portable tools to help themselves. These were mentioned in a paragraph above. Our recommendation is to use all of these simultaneously.

Fifth, there are another nine basic tactics in software design for how online platforms attempt to achieve those nine basic strategic goals. (Review these in Sect. 2.2). All the tactics should be used as well. As seen in Appendix 6 and 7, there is a very uneven use of the nine techniques. Conceptualizing nine techniques as the full universe of tactics online in mental health facilitation is one gift of this analysis. This is the first synthesis to do so. Plus, there might be wider tactics beyond this review, as discussed by the larger team in this project: like a platform to sample pauses between words to give a rating for depression, or which monitor slowness or quickness of body movements via wearables to measure depression. These are a presumed 'tenth and eleventh tactic' that are the specialties of other researchers in this wider team.

Sixth, which is the best method to gather data for mental disease diagnosis? We can first discuss about how data gathered from devices or apps reviewed include the concept of EMA and EMI. Data gathering tactics are mostly so far about the active data provision of patients like answering questions that the app provides, or solving tasks while wearing devices linked to the app. EMA and EMI definitely depend on patients' ongoing data. For precise diagnosis, we should extend data gathering from patients. A 'Digital Phenotype' solution can be used. This includes not just active data that a patient provides but also passive data automatically generated and aggregated by digital devices like smartphones or smartwatches that we have recommended to use as hardware infrastructure. Although there are privacy issues, there can be much research to diagnose one's mental state or general health state by such passive data. This can solve a difficulty of how we found a lack of a way to gather accurate or timely data in many current mobile app tools [15].

In summary, why is it important to provide accessible technology for patients with mental health diseases? First, this research on technology (apps and devices) shows that it is already possible to receive continuous, accessible, and non-traditional (non-face-to-face therapy) treatment with positive results and at low-cost. Second, it is important that patients understand as early as possible their state of mental health and the purpose of taking any medical aid. This early self-diagnosis or treatment of mental illnesses can prevent worsening crises leading to consequences that are less likely to be cured. Mobile applications can help facilitate this early treatment and self-awareness. That is why it is important to make for the first time a 'mental health superapp' with all nine strategic goals of such platforms with all nine different tactics to do it. This would additionally synch to many other EMA-data gathering peripherals as said above that have their own nine strategic goals of data provisioning and monitoring. However, to make this socially palatable instead of a frightening breach of privacy, we recommend anonymous data entry is respectful and ethical given normal privacy desires and insecurities of users with such sensitive data. Therefore, any data collecting of such data should be based on providing free personalized analysis assistance to users yet should promise anonymity of such services to particular accounts. This might be a hard kind of judgment how to design anonymity of data with ongoing accounts on mobile apps along with data sharing though it could be done with an encrypted PKI (public key infrastructure) arrangement where only the user would have the key to encrypt/decrypt their own data. We note none of these apps offer encrypted data, yet we argue the first online 'mental health superapp' platform to offer such data securities would soon set a good standard for the world.

Plus, in such a 'superapp,' since each person has a different preference for what helps them, it is more feasible to allow users to select features they deem are the most needed, as a 'machine learning' app will work to provide necessary further tactics to users. On the other hand, design has to be cautious. There is a 'paradox of plenty' phenomenon where 'too many choices' if immediately visible hamper choosing any options themselves. From the research team's time on such platforms, the feeling is having 'too many' visible features has been as confusing or off-putting as 'too few.' Therefore, the suggestion is to identify a few key features crucial in the beginning that are useful to novice users. Over time, via machine learning prompting or by a neutral and regular introduction of other areas on the platform at subsequent visits, users would be prompted to see and to choose a wider selection of all features later.

The goal of such a 'superapp' would be, if the user desired, sharing results and suggesting specific challenges or even advice on specific medications that may work (of course, with the consultation from a mental health professional). The above extended goal of such a platform is feasible with the assistance of (fairly new) Ecological momentary assessment (EMA) and Ecological momentary intervention (EMI) technology. As mentioned by Thomas et al. (2019), it would be ideal to combine wearables with EMA/EMI technology to collect real-time data to improve precision and accuracy of data to treat not only psychotic disorders but also other mental health diseases [16]. As mental health diseases are complex regardless of their level of seriousness (minor to critical), real-time data collection and assessment with technology intervention can assist patients in avoiding dependence on medications and improve their personal skills in a more effective self-management.

What are barriers to taking early action in treating mental health diseases? The social stigmatization of depression and anxiety disorders is one of the main reasons people avoid social help in treating such mental problems. Plus, second, specialization in medical treatments themselves can ignore the hybrid basis of treatments discussed above that should take into account potential interactions of biophysical, individually psychological, or sociological factors. Therefore, we feel online platforms can avoid both the moralized stigmas with mental problems and can avoid professional overspecialization in mental health treatment. Mobile apps can give information about how to connect or to use a more medicalized analysis on oneself via free or inexpensive mental data-gathering peripherals, and even encourage potential virtual communities to avoid social dislocation. Raising awareness and improving social support of people with mental health diseases can prevent critical outcomes such as suicide. This is why we recommend assuring strict anonymity even while building online platforms for EMA and EMI in order to get around national stigmas to provide a self-help community with a platform to help bring on their own improvement. This is useful for underclasses or marginalized regions with little social services to access mental health treatments beyond a virtual access online first. This promise of a 'mobile revolution' in mental health diagnosis, self-help, and treatment interventions is possible now.

As said by a wise man long ago, you can take a horse to water, though you can't make it drink. It is hardly enough to build a large 'superapp' edifice for mental health and self-evaluation if patients are unaware how their own medical treatment is really based on a personal effort to improve their mental state. That is more possible with technological tools such as mental health supporting mobile apps, yet some people will want some kind of coach to keep them going. That is where a gamification solution may be useful to encourage people to keep returning. As said above, gamification was used so far in only a minority of these mobile applications for mental health. Another kind of gamification would be user's ability to connect their already pre-existing kinds of EMA data gathering machines to the online platform. Linking up other ICT hardware peripherals to an online platform could be a great analysis service for such a 'superapp' that would keep people coming back to such a platform.

The ideal future mobile app for mental health does not eliminate clinical medical intervention. It is simply first trying to catalyze greater mental health with technological intervention as well as prompt proper clinical intervention, like a good online catalyst should. Thus, it is important to have locations in the ideal mobile app for how to further contact clinical guidance, as well as to understand mental health diseases are treatable and can have useful intervention just like other diseases.

4 Conclusion

In conclusion, this review had three purposes. First, it is a suggestion to vet medical technological purchases and investments always through a three-part series of social choices of treatment, actual national demographic research, and only then tertiary technological decisions that fit these two earlier social choices. Doing the reverse by only focusing on the technology first is argued to be responsible for much misaligned and wasted technological investment.

Appendices

By the editor's recommendation, appendices are at an external link or by contacting the authors since the appendices are not crucial for describing results of this study, though are raw data in the interests of transparency demonstrating empirical points already summarized in this paper: https://mega.nz/file/kwZBhIib#lnhIwRs34NcK86KpR34_C AOXycopLOUUgvCQMF3wxiE.

References

1. Hammond, T., Lampe, L., Campbell, A., Perisic, S., Brakoulias, V.: Psychoeducational social anxiety mobile apps: systematic search in app stores, content analysis, and evaluation. JMIR Mhealth Uhealth 9(9), e26603 (2021). https://mhealth.jmir.org/2021/9/e26603. https://doi.org/10.2196/26603
2. Stoyanov, S., Hides, L., Kavanagh, D., Zelenko, O., Tjondronegoro, D., Mani, M.: Mobile app rating scale: a new tool for assessing the quality of health mobile apps. JMIR Mhealth Uhealth 3(1), e27 (2015). https://mhealth.jmir.org/2015/1/e27. https://doi.org/10.2196/mhealth.3422
3. Alexander, B.: The Globalisation of Addiction: A Study in Poverty of the Spirit. Oxford University Press, Oxford (2008)
4. Szasz, T.: Ceremonial Chemistry: The Ritual Persecution of Drugs, Addicts, and Pushers. Syracuse University Press, Syracuse, New York. Reprint. (2003/1974)
5. Whitaker, M.D., Brown, S.: Is mobile addiction a unique addiction: findings from an international sample of university students. Int. J. Ment. Health Addict. 18(5), 1360–1388 (2019). https://doi.org/10.1007/s11469-019-00155-5
6. Brown, E.R.: Rockefeller Medicine Men: Medicine and Capitalism in America. University of California Press, Berkeley (1980)
7. Wilkinson, R., Pickett, K.: The Spirit Level: Why Greater Equality Makes Societies Stronger. Bloomsbury Publishing. Revised and Updated Edition (2011)
8. Pellow, D.N.: Environmental racism: inequality in a toxic world (chap. 7). In: Romero, M., Margolis, E. (eds.) The Blackwell Companion to Social Inequalities, pp. 147–164. Blackwell Publishing, Ltd., (2005)
9. By editor's recommendation, raw data in appendices are at an external link: http://mega.nz/file/kwZBhIib#lnhIwRs34NcK86KpR34_CAOXycopLOUUgvCQMF3wxiE
10. International Medical Device Regulators Forum SaMD Working Group: Software as a Medical Device (SaMD): Key Definitions, International Medical Device Regulators Forum (IMDRF), p. 6 (2013). http://www.imdrf.org/docs/imdrf/final/technical/imdrf-tech-131209-samd-key-definitions-140901.pdf
11. US Food and Drug Administration (US FDA): FDA Definition on SaMD. https://www.fda.gov/medical-devices/digital-health-center-excellence/software-medical-device-samd. (Unk.)
12. Bell, I.H., Lim, M.H., Rossell, S.L., Thomas, N.: Ecological momentary assessment and intervention in the treatment of psychotic disorders: a systematic review. Psychiatric Serv. 68(11), 1172–1181 (2017). https://ps.psychiatryonline.org/doi/10.1176/appi.ps.201600523
13. Baldwin, D.S., Birsistle, J.: An Atlas of Depression (The Encyclopedia of Visual Medicine Series), p. 7. The Parthenon Publishing Group, A CRC Press Company, London, U.K. (2002)
14. Baldwin, D.S., Birsistle, J.: An Atlas of Depression (The Encyclopedia of Visual Medicine Series), p. 60. The Parthenon Publishing Group, A CRC Press Company, London, U.K. (Chart Adapted from The functioning and well-being of depressed patients. Results from the Medical Outcomes Study. JAMA 262, 914–919 (2002)

15. Huckvale, K., Venkatesh, S., Christensen, H.: Toward clinical digital phenotyping: a timely opportunity to consider purpose, quality, and safety. NPJ Digit. Med. **2**(1) (2019). https://doi.org/10.1038/s41746-019-0166-1
16. Thomas, N., et al.: Potential applications of digital technology in assessment, treatment, and self-help for hallucinations. Schizophr. Bull. **45**(1), S32–S42, (2019), https://academic.oup.com/schizophreniabulletin/article/45/Supplement_1/S32/5305655#130300402. https://doi.org/10.1093/schbul/sby103

Touching Minds: Deep Generative Models Composing the Digital Contents to Practice Mindfulness

So Hyeon Kim[1] (ID), Ji Hun Kim[2] (ID), Jung Ahn Yang[2] (ID), Jung Yeon Lee[2],
and Jee Hang Lee[2(✉)] (ID)

[1] Department of AI and Informatics, Sangmyung University, Seoul, Republic of Korea
[2] Department of Human-Centered AI, Sangmyung University, Seoul, Republic of Korea
jeehang@smu.ac.kr

Abstract. Interest in the proper treatment of mental health has been rapidly growing under the steep changes in society, family structure and lifestyle. COVID-19 pandemic in addition drastically accelerates this necessity worldwide, which brings about a huge demand on digital therapeutics for this purpose. One of the key ingredients to this attempt is the appropriately designed practice contents for the prevention and treatment of mental illness. In this paper, we present novel deep generative models to construct the mental training contents based upon mindfulness approach, with a particular focus on providing Acceptance and Commitment Therapy (ACT) on the self-talk techniques. To this end, we first introduce ACT script generator for mindfulness meditation. With over one-thousand sentences collected from the various sources for ACT training practices, we develop a text generative model through fine-tuning on the variant of GPT-2. Next, we introduce a voice generator to implement the self-talk technique, a text-to-speech application using the ACT training script generated above. Computational and human evaluation results demonstrate the high quality of generated training scripts and self-talk contents. To the best of our knowledge, this is the first approach to generate the meditation contents using artificial intelligence techniques, which is able to deeply touch the human mind to care and cure the mental health of individuals. Applications would be main treatment contents for digital therapeutics and meditation curriculum design.

Keywords: Generative model · Deep learning · Mindfulness meditation · Self-talk

1 Introduction

The rapid increase in one-person households ranging from early 20's to the elderly has given rise to the serious social problems, a crisis in mental health in recent decades. There are growing numbers of people suffering from a serious mental illness such as depression, or anxiety disorder. As COVID-19 pandemic prolonged, these social phenomena would be drastically accelerated worldwide [1]. According to statistics surveyed by Korean

J.-H. Kim et al. (Eds.): IHCI 2021, LNCS 13184, pp. 106–116, 2022.
https://doi.org/10.1007/978-3-030-98404-5_9

government in 2021, approximately 30% of young generations between 20's and 30's is seen as a group suffered from depression, and even worse is that one-fourth of those can be potentially seen as a group of people suicidally depressed [2].

The use of digital therapeutics (DTx) has been paid much attention to resolve such tension in preventing and monitoring of mental health. With a special guideline "Pre-Cert-Working Model v1.0" published by FDA in, the US government emphasised the importance of timely provision of DTx to relieve the mental health problem, and actively supported both academia and industry to this end. The UK government also has joined this policy as "NHS Long Term Plan" announced in 2019 [3].

Mindfulness and meditation have a long tradition as a means to treat and relieve the mental states of individuals based upon cognitive behaviour therapy [1, 4]. Thanks to the recent advances in mobile technologies, these approaches are actively adopted in the form of mobile apps, and rapidly spread out to individuals' living. For example, experiments using a mobile Mindfulness Meditation application showed the efficient treatment of mental illness [5]. The study confirmed that not only a short-term use of the mobile application could improve the negative aspect of mental states, but also a long-term, regular use of it significantly strengthened the positive aspect of mental states.

One of the key ingredients that can amplify the efficacy of those DTx is the appropriately designed practice contents for the prevention and treatment of mental illness. To this end, we present novel deep generative models to construct the mental training contents based upon mindfulness approach, with a particular focus on providing Acceptance and Commitment Therapy (ACT) on the self-talk techniques.

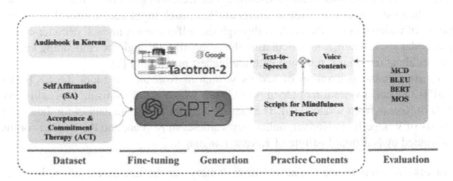

Fig. 1. System overview

As shown in Fig. 1, we first introduce ACT script generator for mindfulness meditation. With over one-thousand sentences collected from the various sources for ACT training practices, we develop a text generative model through fine-tuning on the variant of GPT-2. Next, we present a voice generator to implement the self-talk technique [6, 10], a text-to-speech application using the ACT training script generated above. After the computational and human evaluation, we demonstrate the high-quality of generated training scripts and self-talk contents.

To the best of our knowledge, this is the first approach to generate the contents of meditation using artificial intelligence techniques, which is able to have a high potential to deeply touch the human mind to care and cure the mental health of individuals.

This paper is organized as follows. After a brief introduction in Sect. 1, we describe the computational framework implementing the generative models for both script and voice in Sect. 2. It is followed by the experiment results and their computational and human evaluation in Sect. 3. With discussions on the results in Sect. 4, we conclude the paper in Sect. 5 with addressing the future works.

2 Experimental Settings

2.1 The Deep Generative Model for Building Mindfulness Scripts

Baseline Model. We used a family of the Transformer model, Generative Pre-trained Transformer version 2 (GPT-2), a self-attention-based language model, as a baseline model to set up the deep generative model for the script generations [7]. Unlike BERT [8], which is a widely known natural language understanding model, GPT-2 uses both encoder and decoder, in which the previous output value becomes the next input value using masked self-attention through Transformer's decoder stack. As BERT is specialised sentence understanding by employing the encoder stack solely, GPT-2 is mainly used to generate sentences through the utilisation of encoder and decoder at the same time.

In GPT-2, the model divides the characters into tokens through Byte Pair Encoding (BPE), converts these tokens into embedding matrices, and gives them into the decoder stack when the sentence is given as an input. Here, each input vector goes through the process of understanding the context through the self-attention in each decoder cell in the decoder stack. Then, after calculating the probability through the embedding vector, it brings about the output sentence with the highest probability [9].

To support the generation of scripts written in Korean, we adopt the SKT-AI's KoGPT-2 model, a variation of Open AI's GPT-2, which is trained using approximately 20GB of Korean from scratch [10]. The main source of the Korean dataset for the model consists of Wikipedia in Korean, online news articles in Korean, and the Korean corpus constructed by National Institute of Korean Language.

Datasets. We constructed the new dataset to carry out the fine-tuning of the baseline GPT-2. The newly constructed dataset is a set of approximately one thousand scripts for mindfulness meditation referred from sentences specifically dedicated to cognitive behaviour therapy.

The dataset has three categories – sentences aiming to practice self-affirmation (SA) [11], acceptance and commitment therapy (ACT) [12], and neutral (Fig. 2). The main function of SA is well known for a treatment of affirming one's moral and adaptive adequacy. ACT is a mental or psychological therapy ensuring to help patients accepting the (mental/physical) pain they faced. The neutral is literally a set of normal sentences describing factual information. We employed it to a control condition used in the assessment on the capacity of the generative model.

Dataset	Examples
Self Affirmation (SA)	(SA) 나는 나의 기분을 스스로 다스릴 수 있다. (EN: I am confident in my ability to manage my temper.)
Acceptance & Commitment Therapy (ACT)	(ACT) 분노와 미워하는 마음 모두 멀리 구름과 함께 날려 보낸다. (EN: Imagine that an emotion of anger and hatred is blown away with the cloud.)
Neutral (N)	(N) 제품이 무거우니 옮길 때 주의하시기 바랍니다. (EN: Be careful when moving due to its heavy weight.)

Fig. 2. An overview on the dataset for training a generative model. Three types of sentences in the dataset (Left). Example sentences for each type (Right). All sentences are composed in Korean. For convenience, we here provide an English version of each example sentence.

Model Training. Following a concept of fine-tuning, we trained the base model using the dataset described above. The input of KoGPT2 model is composed of three elements – weight, genre and a pure text. In our setting, we only used a pure text as an input, the others, weight and genre elements were not used. Perhaps we may use the weight and the genre elements to specify one's mental- or emotional states in order to convey more adaptive mindfulness practice to individuals. In the training process, we used a cross-entropy for a loss function, *Adam* for an optimizer. We approximately iterate the training process with the epoch size 200.

2.2 The Voice Synthesis Model for Building Self-talk

Baseline Model. We employed Tacotron-2 [13, 14] to build a voice synthesis model in order to facilitate self-talk. In Tacotron-2, a network consists of an encoder, a decoder, and an attention. The overall architecture is shown in Fig. 3.

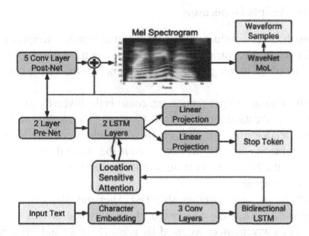

Fig. 3. Architectural overview of tacotron2 [13] (copyright © Shen *et al.*)

Since the original version of Tacotron 2 implemented here [15] only supported a single speaker model, we adopted the Multi-Speaker version of Tacotron 2. On top of this, we extended it from English speaking to Korean speaking Tacotron-2 [16].

Datasets. We used two datasets to train the baseline model in order to build the voice synthesizer for self-talk. Each dataset consists of a pair of one sentence-long voice and its associated sentence in a textual form. The one is the KSS dataset [17] containing approximately 12 h-long voice recordings of a Korean single speaker. It is recorded by a professional female voice actor, which was sampled at 3–6 s. The other is a newly constructed dataset by us sampled from a proprietary audiobook, which is an hour-long Korean single male voice recording. To construct the dataset in a form of one sentence-long voices, we split the whole audio file into one-sentence length using silence-period as a delimiter. Afterwards, we converted each voice file into the text using Google Speech-to-Text API to have the voice-sentence pairs [18].

Model Training. The main objective of building a voice synthesizer is a generation of individual's own voice to compose the self-talk contents. One big challenge lies in this is the size of data to train – it is very hard to collect sufficient amounts of voice data from individuals. Thus, we carried out the fine-tuning based upon the Multi Speaker model proposed by DeepVoice2 [19]. Multi Speaker model enables to improve the quality (e.g., speaker similarity, naturalness) of unseen speakers' synthesized voice although trained only with a limited amount of data [20].

In the training stage, we used the sample rate 24000, the fft size 2048, and the minimum token size 30 that is heuristically optimal in Korean datasets. The loss was the mean squared error (MSE) between the mel-spectrogram of the ground truth and the generated mel-spectrogram.

3   Results

3.1   Mindfulness Scripts Generator

Experiment Results. We conducted the generation of mindful scripts after 400 epochs training. In order to acquire various sets of scripts, we used two hyper-parameters to set the degree of freedom in the generation of sentences – the one is *Creativity*, and the other is *N-gram*.

Creativity, a float valued hyper-parameter, controls the diversity of a generated script. The default value is 1. We used three levels of *Creativity* – Low, Mid and High. The Low option sets the model deterministic and repetitive, which effectively intends to conform the vocabularies and sentence structures appeared in the original sentences of the training dataset. In contrast, the High option results in the generated scripts following the way in more random completion.

N-gram stands for the number of words given to generate the scripts. As an example, we use only one word to start the generation of the sentence, which we call a unigram that sets N = 1. For convenience, we used Bi-gram (N = 2) and Tri-gram (N = 3) in this experiment. Table 1 shows the generated samples in relation to different settings of hyper-parameters.

Evaluations. We conducted the evaluation for each generated script in two ways – computational and human evaluations.

Table 1. Examples of generated mindfulness scripts. All sentences are generated in Korean. For convenience, we here provide an English version of each example sentence.

		Reference sentence
		나는 어려운 상황일수록 긍정적으로 생각하려고 노력한다 (EN: I try to have a positive thought whenever under the humble circumstances.)
N-gram	Creativity	Generated sentence
2	High	나는 어려운 일을 하더라도 차분하게 진행한다 (EN: I can resolve the problem smoothly despite it being very difficult.)
3	High	나는 어려운 상황일수록 침착하게 일을 현명하게 마무리하려고 한다 (EN: I can resolve the problem thoughtfully and carefully as it is getting more difficult.)

For the former, we tested each generated sentence using BLEU and BERT score. BLEU score refers to the Bilingual Evaluation Understudy Score, which is widely used to evaluate the quality of natural language generation (NLG) tasks [21]. It computes the likelihood of joint probability between two N-gram sentences. The value is ranging from 0 to 1 – the higher the BLEU score is, the better quality the generated sentence shows.

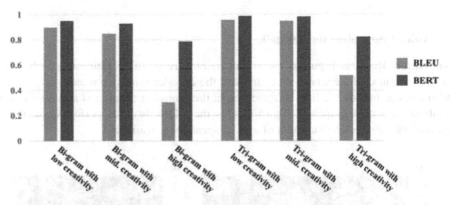

Fig. 4. Evaluation results by BLEU, BERT score

In addition, we adopted another evaluation metric to ensure the validity of the evaluation. BERT score stands for Bidirectional Encoder Representations [8], which appeared in Transformers. Compared to the BLEU score, the BERT score exhibits superior capacity, particularly to understand the context of the generated sentence more naturally, with bidirectionality. In this paper, we used the Ko-BERT score pre-trained by a Korean dataset [22]. Figure 4 shows the results depending upon the settings of the Creativity and N-gram hyper-parameters.

For the latter, we conducted the survey on the Mean-Opinion-Score (MOS) to demonstrate the quality of generated script as shown in Table 2. We adopted the Likert scale proposed in [23]. A 5-point scale was used to evaluate Readability, Grammatically, Naturalness, Overall Quality and Writing Style. All 22 subjects participated in the survey constructed with randomly chosen six scripts from generated sentences.

Table 2. Mean Opinion Score (MOS) via human evaluation (N = 22).

	Mean	Std. Dev	Question
Readability	3.98	1.089	How easy is the sentence to understand?
Grammatically	4.70	0.553	How do you judge the Grammatical Correctness?
Naturalness	2.48	1.089	How fluent is the sentence?
Overall quality	1.89	1.039	Overall, this is a good sentence for meditation practices
Writing style	3.34	1.256	How do you judge the writing style for meditation practices?

Table 3. MCD score

Gender	Sentences	MCD
Female	78	6.416188
Male	80	6.386884
Overall		**6.401536**

3.2 Voice Synthesizer for Self-talk

Experiment Results. Figure 5 shows the training results illustrating the probability that the output of the encoder time step and the decoder time step match. The clearer and more continuous the line is in the graph, the more the training is successful. The attention alignment graphs in Fig. 5 depicts the relatively good performance of our proposal although a small amount of unseen speakers is available.

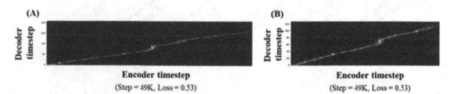

Fig. 5. Attention alignment graph. (A) Original version of Tacotron-2. (B) Proposed version

Evaluations. Like the previous section, computational- and human evaluations were conducted to ensure the quality of the voice synthesizer.

In order to compare the reference (i.e., original) and the synthesized utterance for the same text, 78 (KSS dataset)/80 (proprietary dataset) sentences were randomly selected from the training datasets. Afterwards, we computed the degree of Mel Cepstral Distortion (MCD) representing the distortion rate of the synthesized voices in comparison to that of reference voices. In detail, MCD calculates the distance between the original and synthesized Mel-cepstral coefficients (MCEPs), which is defined in Eq. 1 [24]:

$$MCD = \frac{10}{\ln 10} \sqrt{2 \sum_{i=0}^{34} \left(mcc - mcc^{converted}\right)^2},$$ (1)

where mcc and $mcc^{converted}$ denote the target and converted MCEPs, respectively.

To do so, we converted wav files of each pair of an original voice recording and a synthesized voice to MCEP features to calculate MCD, extracting 34 MCEPs. The smaller the MCD value is, the more similar the original and synthesized MCEPs are. Figure 10 shows the mean MCD score of all pairs in the dataset (Table 3).

Here, the human evaluation using MOS was also conducted. A mean opinion scale (MOS) is a well established measure of text-to-speech quality [25]. It represents an established and widely used method for subjective quality assessment [26]. We performed the test with 26 Korean native participants. Each of them listened to three synthesized voices per female and male dataset, which in total six voices randomly sampled. Then participants evaluated the quality of synthesized voices using a 5-point scale [26]. The result is shown in Table 4.

Table 4. Mean Opinion Score (MOS) via human evaluation for synthesized voices (N = 26).

	Mean	Std Dev.	Question
Overall impression	3.83	1.224	Please rate the sound quality of the voice you heard
Listening effort	3.38	1.182	Please rate the degree of effort you had to make to understand the message
Pronunciation	3.85	1.090	Did you notice any problems in the naturalness of sentence pronunciation?
Speaking rate	4.31	.800	Was the speed of delivery of the message appropriate?
Voice pleasantness	3.21	.873	Was the voice you heard pleasant to listen to?
Voice naturalness	3.22	1.030	Did the voice sound natural?
Ease of listening	2.82	1.013	Would it be easy to listen to this voice for long periods of time?
Comprehension	4.35	.914	Were single words hard to understand?

4 Discussion

In the case of the Mindfulness scripts generator, the quality of generated scripts is moderately good. According to the BLEU and BERT scores, the sentences showed a high naturalness and contained a good level of semantics in relation to original sentences. However, due to the relatively small amount of training data, the generated scripts showed some shortcomings with regards to the overfitting issue, particularly in the context of the low *Creativity* setting.

In the subsequent human evaluation, the scale on the naturalness and the overall quality is lower than that on others. We assumed that this is caused by the overfitting issue, ultimately originate from the small dataset. This brought about additional concerns in the high *Creativity* setting – a lot of unrelated vocabularies were appeared while the syntactic and semantic structures were seriously degraded. Therefore, it is necessary to deal with them more carefully with taking into account the appropriate control of *Creativity* setting in future works. Of course more training datasets should be constructed to avoid the overfitting issue as well as to enhance the quality of the sentences generated with more hyper-parameter settings.

In the voice generator part, it presented good results in both computational and human evaluations. In the computational evaluation, our model exhibited a lower MCD score, 6.4, than that, 6.69, in [27]. The MOS score, 3.57, was similar to that, 3.52, in state-of-the-art MOS in Lim, Dan et al. [28] in which the same female database was used. Looking at the scores by item in Table 4, 'Overall impression' scored a good rating of 3.83, higher than the mean MOS (3.57). In other criteria, 'Speaking rate' and 'Comprehension' received very high scores of 4.31 and 4.35 respectively, which can boost the attraction of more attention which is one of the crucial components of meditation practice [29].

However, 'Ease of Listening' received 2.82, which was less than fair (score 3), followed by 'voice pleasantness' (3.21) and 'voice naturalness' (3.22). These low-scored criteria were closely related to questions of whether the voice was comfortable when listening for a long time. Considering the importance of calming the mind in meditation, it will be necessary for future research.

Interestingly, with an hour of voice recordings, both MCD and MOS showed similar levels of those in 12 h recordings. This reflects the superior capacity in data efficiency which is an important ability to synthesize the meditation content in which the small amount of individual voices are available.

5 Conclusion

In this paper, we proposed two deep generative models to produce the digital contents for mindfulness practices that can be used for digital therapeutics and meditation curriculum design.

For the mindfulness script generator, we used the fine-tuned KoGPT-2, and evaluated through computational ways using BLEU and BERT scores and surveys on MOS. Next, in the voice synthesis, we used fine-tuned Tacotron-2. It showed a fairly good performance in both evaluation methods. The mean MCD score (6.4) was lower than MCD 6.69 [27] in the reference model. A higher MOS score (3.57) was also marked than that in the comparative model [28]. For future studies, we suggest using the WaveGlow and few-shot models presented in this paper to induce meditation by providing self-talk techniques suitable for each situation.

Further, it would be possible to expand our study to an experiment to investigate whether subjects using the combination of two deep generative models actually change their emotions or mental states through self-talk techniques.

Acknowledgement. This research was supported by (i) the Samsung Research Funding Center of Samsung Electronics under Project Number No. SRFC-TC1603-52, and (ii) the National Research Foundation of Korea (NRF) grant funded by the Korean government (No. 2020R1G1A1102683).

References

1. Behan, C.: The benefits of meditation and mindfulness practices during times of crisis such as COVID-19. Irish J. Psychol. Med. **37**(4), 256–258 (2020)
2. Results of COVID-19 National mental health survey in the first quarter of 2021 by Ministry of Health and Welfare. http://www.mohw.go.kr/react/al/sal0301vw.jsp?PAR_MENU_ID=04& MENU_ID=0403&CONT_SEQ=365582&page=1. Accessed 15 Nov 2021
3. Alderwick, H., Dixon, J.: The NHS long term plan. BMJ **364**, 184 (2019). https://doi.org/10. 1136/bmj.l84
4. Bunker, L., Williams, J.M., Zinsser, N.: Cognitive techniques for improving performance and building confidence. Appl. Sport Psychol.: Pers. Growth Peak Perform. **2**(1), 225–242 (1993)
5. Flett, J.A.M., et al.: Mobile mindfulness meditation: a randomised controlled trial of the effect of two popular apps on mental health. Mindfulness **10**(5), 863–876 (2019)
6. Van Raalte, J.L., Vincent, A.: Self-talk in sport and performance. In: Oxford Research Encyclopedia of Psychology (2017)
7. Radford, A., et al.: Language models are unsupervised multitask learners. OpenAI Blog **1**(8), 9 (2019)
8. Devlin, J., et al.: BERT: pre-training of deep bidirectional transformers for language understanding. arXiv preprint arXiv:1810.04805 (2018)
9. An, S.H., Jeong, O.R.: A study on the psychological counseling AI Chatbot system based on sentiment analysis. J. Inf. Technol. Serv. **20**(3), 75–86 (2021)
10. SKT-AI KoGPT2. https://github.com/SKT-AI/KoGPT2/tree/589182bc85a0741b8ac20b49 cdd56d9e44b9479c. Accessed 15 Nov 2021
11. Steele, C.M.: The psychology of self-affirmation: sustaining the integrity of the self. In: Advances in Experimental Social Psychology, vol. 21, pp. 261–302. Academic Press (1988)
12. Hayes, S.C., Wilson, K.G.: Acceptance and commitment therapy: altering the verbal support for experiential avoidance. Behav. Analyst **17**(2), 289–303 (1994)
13. Shen, J., et al.: Natural TTS synthesis by conditioning WaveNet on MEL spectrogram predictions. In: 2018 IEEE International Conference on Acoustics, Speech and Signal Processing (ICASSP). IEEE (2018)
14. Wang, Y., et al.: Tacotron: towards end-to-end speech synthesis. arXiv preprint arXiv:1703. 10135 (2017)
15. Tacotron2-original. https://github.com/Rayhane-mamah/Tacotron-2.git. Accessed 15 Nov 2021
16. Tacotron2-multi-speaker-korean.   https://github.com/hccho2/Tacotron2-Wavcnet-Korean- TTS.git. Accessed 15 Nov 2021
17. Park, K.: KSS Dataset: Korean Single speaker Speech Dataset (2018). https://kaggle.com/bry anpark/korean-single-speaker-speech-dataset
18. Google STT API. https://cloud.google.com/speech-to-text?hl=ko. Accessed 15 Nov 2021
19. Arik, S., et al.: Deep voice 2: multi-speaker neural text-to-speech. arXiv preprint arXiv:1705. 08947 (2017)
20. Cooper, E., et al.: Zero-shot multi-speaker text-to-speech with state-of-the-art neural speaker embeddings. In: ICASSP 2020-2020 IEEE International Conference on Acoustics, Speech and Signal Processing (ICASSP). IEEE (2020)

21. Papineni, K., et al.: BLEU: a method for automatic evaluation of machine translation. In: Proceedings of the 40th Annual Meeting of the Association for Computational Linguistics (2002)
22. KoBERT. https://github.com/lovit/KoBERTScore. Accessed 15 Nov 2021
23. Amidei, J., Piwek, P., Willis, A.: The use of rating and Likert scales in Natural Language Generation human evaluation tasks: a review and some recommendations (2019)
24. Kaneko, T., et al.: StarGAN-VC2: rethinking conditional methods for StarGAN-based voice conversion. arXiv preprint arXiv:1907.12279 (2019)
25. ITU-T Recommendation: Telephone transmission quality subjective opinion tests. A method for subjective performance assessment of the quality of speech voice output devices, p. 85 (1994)
26. De Koning, T.C.M., et al.: Of MOS and men: bridging the gap between objective and subjective quality measurements in mobile TV. In: Multimedia on Mobile Devices 2007, vol. 6507. International Society for Optics and Photonics (2007)
27. Weiss, R.J., et al.: Wave-Tacotron: spectrogram-free end-to-end text-to-speech synthesis. In: ICASSP 2021-2021 IEEE International Conference on Acoustics, Speech and Signal Processing (ICASSP). IEEE (2021)
28. Lim, D., et al.: JDI-T: jointly trained duration informed transformer for text-to-speech without explicit alignment. arXiv preprint arXiv:2005.07799 (2020)
29. Tang, Y.-Y., Hölzel, B.K., Posner, M.I.: The neuroscience of mindfulness meditation. Nat. Rev. Neurosci. 16(4), 213–225 (2015)

Remote Monitoring of Disability: A Case Study of Mobility Aid in Rohingya Camp

Suzana Brown[1]([⊠]) [ID], Faheem Hussain[2], Achilles Vairis[3] [ID], Emily Hacker[4], and Maurice Bess[1]

[1] SUNY Korea, Incheon 21985, South Korea
suzana.brown@sunykorea.ac.kr
[2] Arizona State University in Tempe, Tempe, AZ, USA
[3] Hellenic Mediterranean University, Heraklion, Greece
[4] University of Utah, Salt Lake City, Utah, USA

Abstract. Examining disability within the context of displacement is a vital area of study. Additionally, further study of assistive technology devices for refugees with disabilities and those in low-resource settings presents the opportunity to dramatically improve the safety and medical welfare of people with disabilities. Mobility Aid project is a pilot study in a Rohingya refugee camp with refugees who have suffered debilitating injuries and need to use crutches to walk. The goal of the project is to improve remote monitoring of disability in the context of displacement. It could be extended to many other environments where people walk with crutches on uneven and muddy terrain.

Keywords: Disability · Displacement · Mobility

1 Introduction

Current estimates suggest that between seven to ten percent of the world's population lives with some form of disability [1]. When applied to the 2020 UNHCR reports indicating there are approximately 83 million refugees worldwide, between 5.8 million and 8.3 million refugees are living with a disability. While services for people with disabilities are limited among the general population, refugees with disabilities face tremendous challenges in receiving even the most basic support.

Disabilities may exist prior to displacement and armed conflict, or they may be the direct result of such conflict. Some of the primary causes of disability among refugees are injuries and amputations from armed conflict, including lower limb injuries from landmines that are often placed at border crossings [2]. Soldiers from the Myanmar military routinely place landmines near the border with Bangladesh along routes known to be taken by Rohingya refugees. Numerous Rohingya refugees have been killed or severely wounded by these landmines [3].

Refugees with existing disabilities are disproportionately impacted by poor living conditions in many camps and will see an "increase in the causes of impairment through poor nutrition and health conditions" [2].

J.-H. Kim et al. (Eds.): IHCI 2021, LNCS 13184, pp. 117–123, 2022.
https://doi.org/10.1007/978-3-030-98404-5_10

Throughout this paper the term 'disabilities' will be used to encompass a broad range of conditions – psychosocial, intellectual, sensory, and physical disabilities. A case study that is discussed is a project called Mobility Aid, financed by Grand Challenges Canada, which focuses on the needs of persons with physical disabilities that can be ameliorated with modifications to canes or crutches.

The project has been piloted in a Rohingya refugee camp and the refugees who have suffered these debilitating injuries are among those who can most benefit from the services of Mobility Aid.

2   Challenges Within Refugee Camps: Terrain, Safety, and Medical Needs

In recent years, humanitarian actors have begun to consider people with disabilities when developing crisis response plans, constructing refugee camps, and designing services to meet the needs of refugee populations. The delay in these considerations has elicited appropriate criticism from disability advocates.

Of particular interest to our case study, Mobility Aid, are investigations into ways that terrain impacts refugees with disabilities – including soil composition, the slope of hills, camp infrastructure, and the effects of weather on terrain. A UNHCR study of Syrian refugees with disabilities living in refugee camps in Iraq revealed that uneven terrain in camps obstructs movement and these difficulties are "compounded by rains that also damage the often unpaved roads" [4]. Rohingya refugees with disabilities in Cox's Bazar, Bangladesh "struggle to access essential services such as latrines, water points, health centers, and aid distributions because of hilly and flood-prone terrain" [5].

The Jadimura Camp in Bangladesh sees refugees living in "congested, hilly camps prone to landslides and flooding." Refugees without disabilities encounter difficulties when accessing the most basic services in camps and those with physical disabilities, an estimated 15% of the Jadimura Camp population, do not receive the services they need [6]. Researchers with Mobility Aid have identified that "compatibility with the environment is a prerequisite for using certain types of assistive technology." Through modification of traditional rubber shoes/tips of crutches and canes, refugees with disabilities are better able to navigate the terrain of refugee camps in Bangladesh [7]. The typical rubber shoes fitted to crutches are suitable for hard paved surfaces with no mud, abnormalities, or stones on them.

Easier movement across different types of terrain is not the only function of mobility devices for refugees with disabilities. People with disabilities are at increased risk of experiencing violence, abuse, and exploitation. Additionally, refugees with disabilities (depending on the disability) are especially vulnerable to "such safety and security threats because they cannot run for help" [6]. Those will mobility concerns are not able to report security concerns to camp officials or relocate to safer areas within refugee camps. Increasing a person's mobility immediately increases their safety and security.

The provision of medical care in refugee camps is often done through fixed-site locations and depending on available resources, there may only be several locations at which care can be provided. This means patients must walk long distances and wait in lines for extended periods of time to see medical providers – something that may be very difficult for refugees with disabilities.

In Jadimura Camp, Bangladesh for Rohingya refugees, refugees with disabilities were interviewed to gain insight into barriers accessing medical care. The reported barriers were (1) "lack of physically accessible or adapted healthcare facilities," (2) an understaffed mobile medical response, (3) "long distances to service providers," (4) extended wait times, (5) "negative attitudes from services provider," and (6) "low quality/inappropriate services." Additionally, 100% of refugees with disabilities reported that they required family assistance to access health services and 39% reported they needed a mobility assistance device in addition to family help [6].

These barriers represent only a small portion of the obstacles faced by refugees with disabilities, but this study addresses using assistive technology to increase mobility and reduce barriers encountered by people with disabilities in refugee camps.

3 Mobility Aid Project

Mobility Aid project is using 3D printing to manufacture custom crutch shoes on-site in Rohingya refugee camps in Bangladesh. The 3D printers will be used to print molds out of ABS material, which then will be used for the local production of rubber shoes. Rubber material will be poured into these molds using low pressure to produce the crutch shoes, in cycles of a few hours per rubber part. This is a low skilled manual operation to produce small numbers of crutch shoes locally, while allowing for flexible production of different designs of parts as molds can be printed on site, provided the appropriate CAD design files are available. These shoes will be customized for the terrain in the camp and will allow safer movement on the muddy and uneven terrain.

The use of 3D printers in low-resource settings allows for humanitarian agencies to operate independently of logistical supply chains and provide customized assistive technology to patients. Organizations like Field Ready, OxFam, and MyMiniFactory have used 3D printing to produce medical supplies and shelters in areas impacted by both natural disasters and violent conflict [8]. 3D printers operate best in dry, dust-free, and moderate temperature environments – conditions that are frequently unrealistic in refugee camps. These printers also require power sources while requiring limited or no internet connections [9]. Further research into increased durability, portability, and reliability of 3D printers is needed as well as research into independent power sources for these printers, as typical print runs may be over a day long, depending on the complexity and finished quality of the printed part.

Persons with disabilities must be involved in disaster preparedness and emergency management planning as well as the planning for construction and design of refugee camps. Appropriate stakeholder engagement of refugees with disabilities and their family and caregivers is also crucial. This consultation and evaluation must be ongoing with clearly defined and easily measured objectives, goals, and outcomes.

Refugees with disabilities frequently do not have their disability noted during their registration making the identification of future needs difficult. Subsequent data collection efforts on refugees with disabilities were unsuccessful because "data collection staff also lacked the technical expertise to identify and categorize different types of disabilities." Humanitarian actors in refugee settings need improved training on recognition of disability. Ethical data collection and usage and proper data security is imperative to protect refugees with disabilities from targeting, neglect, exclusion, and exploitation.

The IRB approval for this study has been obtained from the organization where the researchers work, and it follows the Declaration of Helsinki and it's set of ethical principles.

4   Remote Monitoring

One of the goals of the Mobility Aid project is to perform remote monitoring of the way disabled people walk using crutches while eliminating expensive setups and simplifying the measurements by using video analysis.

One team member of Mobility Aid was able to enter the refugee camp in Cox Bazar and train field workers on video data collection. In September 2021, they jointly collected video recordings of six disabled participants using simple phone cameras. The cameras were arranged to provide a stereoscopic view of participant's walking pattern with crutches, with one recording the side view of the walk and the second camera, at 90° to the first camera, recording the participant walking towards the camera. The two cameras were calibrated using a large checkerboard pattern to obtain the stereoscopic transformation matrix, which was used to obtain the 3D position data of an object in the covered area. Figure 1 and Fig. 2 show examples of the front-view and the side-view of disabled participants who walk with crutches.

Fig. 1. Participant 1 front-view of camera (calibration checkerboard on bottom right)

This approach is building upon previous work of the Mobility Aid team [10, 11] on evaluating and verifying the approach applied to the gait of disabled people who walk with crutches in the lab environment. During the design stage of the project in South Korea disabled and healthy people were studied using the same camera setup to characterize their gait and assess different crutch shoe designs, among other experimental techniques employed. This non-contact video evaluation has been done using video data,

Fig. 2. Participant 2 side-view camera (calibration checkerboard in bottom center)

which was subsequently used to calculate Signal-to-Noise-Ratio (SNR) of acceleration and jerk, which is the first derivative of acceleration, for the left ankle of the participant.

The two videos of each run for each participant were processed for each video frame to calculate the acceleration (α), as defined by the equation $\alpha = \Delta v/\Delta t$, where v is the velocity and t is the time, and jerk (j), the second derivative of velocity or the first derivative of acceleration, as defined by the equation $j = \Delta a/\Delta t$. The acceleration (a) in the global coordinate system was calculated with Eq. (1), where α_x, α_y, α_z is the acceleration in cartesian coordinates.

$$\alpha = \sqrt{\alpha_x^2 + \alpha_y^2 + \alpha_z^2} \tag{1}$$

In addition, the run was further processed to estimate the Signal-to-Noise-Ratio (SNR) of acceleration and jerk. This parameter is the inverse of the coefficient of variation [12], or it is equal to ratio of the mean of all data (x) divided by the standard deviation of all data (s) as shown in Eq. (2).

$$SNR = x/s \tag{2}$$

The approach assumes that the value of acceleration and jerk are adequate measures of stability. This is justified by the fact that SNR has been used extensively in signal processing [13–15], where there is noise interfering in the signal, and large values of SNR are considered good outcomes since it represents a strong signal with low noise.

The movement analysis of 61 videos of disabled, novice, and experienced crutch users in South Korea showed participants walking in a stable and confident manner with crutches as they followed a clear path in a controlled manner, which the SNR values of acceleration and jerk demonstrate. This observation was noted in the videos. In addition, the experienced temporary user showed an improved value in those parameters compared to the disabled users and the novice users, also evident in the videos taken.

The video analysis approach suggested allows us to identify unstable movement, which is not dependent on the level of disability. Further validation of this approach may help individuals to address gait issues and prevent falls.

The next step of Mobility Aid project will be examining field data to verify if the SNR approach will yield the same insights for the field data as it did for the data collected in the lab environment in South Korea.

5   Conclusions

Examining disability within the context of displacement is a vital area of study. Additionally, further study of assistive technology devices for refugees with disabilities and those in low-resource settings presents the opportunity to dramatically improve the safety and medical welfare of people with disabilities. Mobility Aid project is a pilot study in a Rohingya refugee camp with refugees who have suffered debilitating injuries and need to use crutches to walk. The goal of the project is to improve remote monitoring of disability in the context of displacement. It could be extended to many other environments where people walk with crutches on uneven and muddy terrain.

References

1. Women's Commission for Refugee Women and Children: Disabilities among refugees and conflict-affected populations: resource kit for fieldworkers. International Rescue Committee (2008). https://www.corteidh.or.cr/tablas/25417.pdf
2. Karanja, M.: Disability in contexts of displacement. Disabil. Stud. Q. **29**(4) (2009). https://dsq-sds.org/article/view/969/1177
3. Human Rights Watch: Burma: Landmines deadly for fleeing Rohingya (2017). https://www.hrw.org/news/2017/09/23/burma-landmines-deadly-fleeing-rohingya
4. UNHCR: Syrian refugees living with disabilities in camps in Northern Iraq (2014). https://www.refworld.org/pdfid/5492d0204.pdf
5. ACAPS-NPM: Bangladesh: Considering age and disability in the Rohingya response (2021). https://www.acaps.org/special-report/bangladesh-considering-age-and-disability-rohingya-response?acaps_mode=slow&show_mode=1
6. Department for International Development: Inclusive access to services for persons with disabilities: Barriers and facilitators report, Jadimura camp, Teknaf (2019). https://data.humdata.org/dataset/inclusive-access-to-services-for-persons-with-disabilities/resource/be02365a-4037-4fa5-8269-6e88736030fd
7. Brown, S., Vairis, A., Masoumifar, A., Petousis, M.: Enhancing performance of crutches in challenging environments: proposing an alternative design and assessing the expected impact. In: 2019 IEEE Region 10 Conference (2019). https://www.mobilityaid.org/publications
8. Lipsky, S., Przyjemski, A., Velasquez, M., Gershenson, J.: 3D printing for humanitarian relief: the printer problem. In: 2019 IEEE Global Humanitarian Technology Conference pp. 1–7 (2019). https://doi.org/10.1109/GHTC46095.2019.9033053. https://ieeexplore.ieee.org/document/9033053
9. Mercy Corps: Lessons learned from 3D printing in the world's largest Syrian refugee camp (2020). https://www.mercycorps.org/blog/3d-printing-syrian-refugee-camp
10. Vairis, A., Brown, S., Bess, M., Bae, K.H., Boyack, J.: Assessing stability of crutch users by non-contact methods. Int. J. Environ. Res. Public Health **18**(6), 3001 (2021). https://doi.org/10.3390/ijerph18063001

11. Vairis, A., Boyak, J., Brown, S., Bess, M., Bae, K.: Gait analysis using non-contact method for disabled people in marginalized communities. In: Singh, M., Kang, D.-K., Lee, J.-H., Tiwary, U.S., Singh, D., Chung, W.-Y. (eds.) 12th International Conference, IHCI 2020, Daegu, South Korea, 24–26 November 2020, Proceedings, Part II (2020)

12. Smith, S.W.: The Scientist and Engineer's Guide to Digital Signal Processing, vol. 14, p. 626. Technical Publication, San Diego, CA, USA (1997)

13. Tapiovaara, M.J., Wagner, R.F.: SNR and noise measurements for medical imaging: I. A practical approach based on statistical decision theory. Phys. Med. Biol. **38**(1), 71 (1993)

14. Misaridis, T.X., et al.: Potential of coded excitation in medical ultrasound imaging. Ultrasonics **38**(1–8), 183–189 (2000)

15. Pedersen, M.H., Misaridis, T.X., Jensen, J.A.: Clinical evaluation of chirp-coded excitation in medical ultrasound. Ultrasound Med. Biol. **29**(6), 895–905 (2003)

AI Based Convenient Evaluation Software for Rehabilitation Therapy for Finger Tapping Test

Seung-min Hwang[1](✉), Sunha Park[2](✉), Na-yeon Seo[3](✉), Hae-Yean Park[4](✉), and Young-Jin Jung[1,3](✉) (iD)

[1] Interdisciplinary Program of Biomedical Engineering, Chonnam National University, Yeosu-si, Republic of Korea
{216009,yj}@jnu.ac.kr
[2] Occupational Therapy Graduate School Yonsei University, Won-Ju, Republic of Korea
sunha208@gmail.com
[3] School of Healthcare and Biomedical Engineering, Chonnam National University, Yeosu-si, Republic of Korea
qwaszx3194@naver.com
[4] Department of Occupational, Therapy Yonsei University, Won-Ju, Republic of Korea
haepark@yonsei.ac.kr

Abstract. Among the clinical features of Parkinson's disease, It's important to evaluate Bradykinesia. In order to evaluate Bradykinesia, a Finger Tapping Test included in the kinematic test item on the Unified Parkinson's Disease Rating Scale is employed. For the accuracy of evaluation, there is a need for a tool that can perform a Finger Tapping Test based on quantitative data. In this study, An AI based novel approach to evaluate a human motion function quantitatively was suggested and demonstrated for use of rehabilitation therapy using Mediapipe. For a preliminary experiment, the finger tapping test was employed to evaluate its clinical utilization. The developed software showed results that were very consistent with the expert's evaluation opinion. The AI based developed software showed the high potential for clinical use as a quantitative evaluation tool that is cost-effective & easy to use.

Keywords: Finger tapping test · AI · Rehabilitation therapy · Parkinson's disease · Mediapipe

1 Background

Parkinson's disease is a disease in which symptoms such as tremor, slow action, muscle stiffness, and postural imbalance occur because cells in the substantia nigra region of the brain that secrete the 'dopamine' hormone are unable to control hormone secretion due to damage to tissues or bodies caused by external forces or harmful effects. am [1].

The Parkinson's Disease Rating Scale, which evaluates 4 areas (non-motor, exercise experience, motor test, and motor complications), is mainly used for understanding patients of Parkinson's disease [2].

© Springer Nature Switzerland AG 2022
J.-H. Kim et al. (Eds.): IHCI 2021, LNCS 13184, pp. 124–127, 2022.
https://doi.org/10.1007/978-3-030-98404-5_11

In order to evaluate Parkinson's disease, there is a finger tapping test [3] in which the index and thumb are constantly opened and closed. Through this exercise area test, the speed and standard deviation of movement for each section can be calculated. However, up to now, occupational therapists qualitatively evaluate the exact position and movement speed of the fingers based on experience, with 0, 1, 2, 3, 4, and 5 points. These evaluation methods are not objective or quantitative, so there is a possibility that the reliability of the evaluation may be somewhat lowered.

In this study, we tried to develop software that can digitize these evaluation methods based on artificial intelligence and care for patients based on quantitative evaluation records.

2   Method

2.1   Program Design

The software were designed using MATLAB 2021b (Mathworks, USA). The appdesigner in matlab toolbox was employed to developed graphic user interface (GUI) software (Fig. 1).

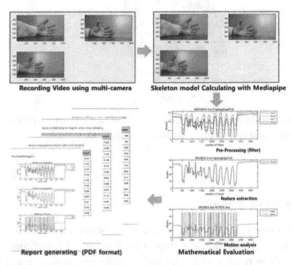

Fig. 1. The AI-motion software flow-chart. The software was designed above processing (recording, motion extraction using AI, pre-processing, feature extraction, motion analysis based on the features)

2.2   Subjects

This study conducted an experiment on 30 normal adult men and women. Subjects selected those who agreed to participant based on a sufficient understanding of the study, and the purpose of this study was explained and conducted after obtaining consent. This study was approved by the Institutional Review Board (IRB) of Yonsei University (IRB: 1041849-202108-BM-133-01).

3   Results

3.1   Developed AI-Motion Software

The AI based motion analysis software (AI-Motion SW) was developed (see Fig. 2). The developed software comprised of 3 parts: 1) Motion capture using multi-webcam, 2) Motion estimation using AI (using mediapipe.com), 3) Quantitative Evaluation for behavior test.

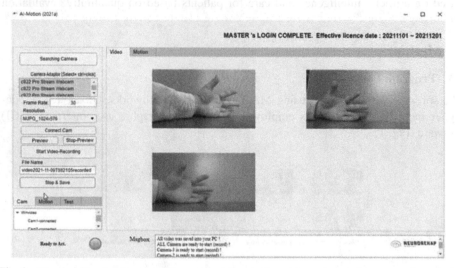

Fig. 2. The developed software that can record the motion video using multi-camera & analysis the measured motion video with proposed evaluation method.

3.2   Preliminary Human Study

The preliminary human test using finger test was conducted with 30 subjects. There is various significant difference that can depict high potential for clinical utilization. The following Table 1 show results which include 5 different motion features.

According to Table 1, there are 4 significant differences between young group and old group. These difference can describe the motion performance of human according to motion ability including position velocity, angle velocity, etc. more detail feature should be studied for enhancing the developed software.

Table 1. Comparison between the elderly and the young group: 5 motion features extracted from the finger-tapping process

Motion feature	Young group: mean (std)	Old group: mean (std)	P-value
Total time	8.49 (0.52)	10.22 (0.93)	0.01*
Open angle	53.82 (6.48)	37.20 (16.26)	0.01*
Close angle	19.21 (6.98)	17.62 (6.56)	0.11
Open distance	0.46 (0.03)	0.37 (0.16)	0.01*
Close distance	0.08 (0.03)	0.14 (0.06)	0.02*

References

1. Son, H.G., Park, H.J., Kim, S.J., Han, A.L.: The lived experience of health management in patients with Parkinson's disease. J. Korean Acad. Soc. Nurs. Educ. **26**(4), 423 (2020)
2. Austin, D., McNames, J., Klein, K., Jimison, H., Pavel, M.: A statistical characterization of the finger tapping test: modeling, estimation, and applications. IEEE J. Biomed. Health Inform. **19**(2), 501–507 (2014)
3. Song, K.H., Lee, T.K., Kwak, J.H., Lim, H.S., Cho, H.Y., Kim, E.: Development of mobile based pre-screening app for Parkinson disease. The HCI Society of Korea, pp. 899–902 (2019)

A Smart Wearable Fall Detection System for Firefighters Using V-RNN

Xiaoqing Chai[1], Boon-Giin Lee[1](✉), Matthew Pike[1], Renjie Wu[1], and Wan-Young Chung[2]

[1] Human-Computer Interaction Laboratory, School of Computer Science, University of Nottingham Ningbo China, Ningbo, China
{xiaoqing.chai,boon-giin.lee,matthew.pike,renjie.wu}@nottingham.edu.cn
[2] Department of Electronic Engineering, Pukyong National University, Busan, Korea
wychung@pknu.ac.kr

Abstract. Falling is one of the leading causes of death among firefighters in China. Fall detection systems (FDS) have yet to be deployed in firefighting applications in China, negatively impacting the safety of firefighters in the fireground. Despite many studies exploring FDSs, few have explored the application of multiple sensors, or applications outside of geriatric healthcare. This study proposes a smart wearable FDS for detecting firefighter falls by incorporating motion sensors in nine different positions on the firefighter's personal protective clothing (PPC). The firefighter's fall activities are detected by a proposed RNN model combined with a Boyer-Moore Voting (BMV) Algorithm (V-RNN) and a fall alert can be issued at an early phase. The results indicated that the proposed FDS with optimized parameters achieves 97.86% and 98.20% in sensitivity and accuracy, respectively.

Keywords: Fall Detection System (FDS) · Personal Protective Clothing (PPC) · Inertial Measurement Unit (IMU) · Recurrent Neural Network (RNN)

1 Introduction

According to the Annual Report of Firefighting in China [2], from 2008 to 2018, there are 625 fatal and nonfatal injuries for firefighters and more than half of them are related to fall activities, including syncope, dropping, and crashed by falling objects like ceiling. The primary reason for this is that the current conventional personal alert safety system (PASS) device used by Chinese firefighters is insufficient to ensure the safety of firefighters [14], which detects immobility in firefighters and emits a loud sound signal after a short period of inactivity (typically half minutes). Moreover, the current PASS device has no data transmission capability, therefore, in most cases, the incident commander (IC) was unaware of

Supported by the Zhejiang Provincial Natural Science Foundation of China under Grant No. LQ21F020024.

the firefighter's falling at fireground and not able to issue rescue in time. Meanwhile, the harsh environment made it more challenging for a firefighter to assess a peer's injury and safety in a timely manner. These difficulties emphasized the importance of smart protection measuring systems that can detect firefighters falling activities in the fireground to guarantee their safety.

FDS has been developed rapidly during the previous decades, particularly in geriatric healthcare. FDS can be classified as: vision-based and sensor-based. As for a vision-based approach, fall detection is modelled on the basis of photos or videos acquired from camera(s) via various sources [4]. Nonetheless, vision-based apporaches have some inherent limitations to be applied in the fireground, including insufficiency in low luminance environment, limited sight of view in smoke-filled environment, low range of field of vision, and view obstructed by objects in fireground [7]. As a result, several research have examined the possibility of using a non-vision-based technique to alleviate the restrictions associated with vision-based approaches. The strengths of this technique include reduced costs for algorithm computing and picture processing, increased privacy, mobility, and resistance to the influences of environment [20].

IMUs integrated in the mobile devices, like smartphones or smartwatches, have been widely used in many researches for fall detection [9–12,17–19]. However, this approach is inapplicable for firefighters since carrying a mobile phone is prohibited in firefighting. Moreover, many reserach have stressed the importance of PASS and personal protective clothing (PPC) in detecting falls among firefighters. Van Thanh ct al. [16] designed a waist-worn device equipped with a triaxial accelerometer and a carbon monoxide sensor as the PASS device. Meanwhile, study by Van Thanh et al. [15] enhanced the PASS device by embedded another barometer for fall detection. However, the activities collected are still insufficient to simulate the falls in realistic way, and the datasets are not publicly available.

The target of our research is to build a smart wearable FDS for firefighters integrated with IMU sensors for various types of fall detection, particularly in harsh environment, and alerts the incident commander for coordinating rescue. Although many studies have proposed FDSs, among the current dataset of fall-detection, most of them directly collected the falling activities started from stand still state and stopped at fallen state. However, such simulation is not as close as realistic falling. Therefore, a new dataset from firefighters with high realistic movements followed by falling had been collected in our previous work [5]. The fall activities collected includes an extra period of walking before and after falling, which collected the whole 3 phases of falling (early fall, impact, and recovery) [3]. Moreover, the majority of previous wearable FDSs only utilized single motion sensor with high sampling rate while the diversity of firefighter's activities makes it more difficult to detect falling based on the motion of one particular place, and higher sampling rate also results in higher power consumption. Our previous work evaluated the performances with various combinations of IMUs, and proved the FDS with 9 IMUs at low sampling rate performs better than those use fewer sensors at high sampling rate. The results revealed that

9-IMU-based system performs better which achieved 92.25%, 94.59%, 94.10% in sensitivity, specificity and accuracy, respectively. Although the results prove to be better than some current studies, there could be room for improvement since the fall detection algorithm is based on a simple RNN model. In this study, we aim at improving the classification performance with the proposed V-RNN model. The performances of the proposed V-RNN with different parameters are evaluated and compared with our previous work and some current studies.

2   Demonstration

2.1   System Overview

The structure of the proposed smart wearable system is shown in Fig. 1. In our previous studies [5], we have designed the prototype of the PPC, which includes a protective garment (PG) and a protective trousers (PT). A total of 9 BNO055 (9-DOF IMU) [1] with a maximum sampling rate of 100 Hz are integrated for capturing motion data from the chest, elbows, wrists, thighs and ankles. The collected motion data is encoded by an MCU, and then transmitted to a terminal PC for further processing. The dataset of the 9 IMUs with 15 Hz transmission rate has been collected in our previous work, which contains the simulated fall activites of 14 firefighters in China [5]. The details of the fall events utilized are summarized in Table 1 with associated figures in Fig. 2.

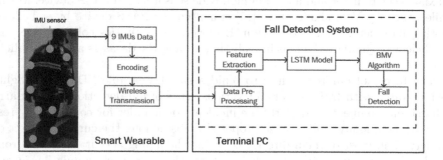

Fig. 1. Flowchart of the proposed smart wearable system.

2.2   Fall Detection Algorithm

The raw motion data of each IMU includes tri-axial gravity acceleration (m/s^2) and tri-axial angular velocity (deg/s^2). In our previous work, quaternion and Euler angles are also computed as the input features [5]. However, in this study, only the raw data are utilized to evaluate if quaternion and Euler angles indeed improve the classification performance. To describe the fluctuation of distinct motions of the firefighter over time, totally 4 metrics are computed as features, including mean (Eq. 1), range (Eq. 2), standard deviation (Eq. 3) and mean

Table 1. Details of activities recorded in the dataset.

Code	Activity	Trials for each subject	Total trials
F1	Forward falls using knees	5	70
F2	Forward falls using hands	5	70
F3	Inclined falls left	4	56
F4	Inclined falls right	4	56
F5	Slow forward falls with crouch first	3	42
F6	Backward falls	3	42

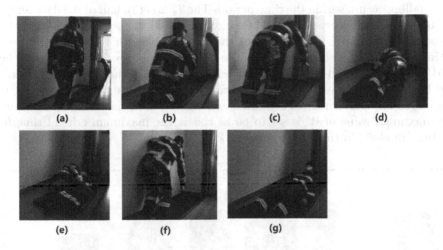

Fig. 2. The falling simulations of a firefighter by wearing the proposed smart wearable PPC which included (a) walking to a mat before falling, (b–g) F1–F6.

absolute deviation (Eq. 4). The window size is set to 0.1 s and the period is 0.5 s. As the result, each IMU generates a 24 vectorized features (6 raw data × 4 metrics), for a total of 216 features (24 features × 9 IMUs) as inputs to fall detection classifier, while in our previous work, the number of input features is 468.

$$\mu = \frac{1}{N}\Sigma x[k] \tag{1}$$

$$R = \max x - \min x \tag{2}$$

$$\sigma = \sqrt{\frac{1}{N}\Sigma(x[k] - \mu)^2} \tag{3}$$

$$MAD = \frac{1}{N}\Sigma|x[k] - \mu| \tag{4}$$

The proposed fall detection algorithm (see Fig. 3) consists of two parts: a front-end with RNN model and a backend with BMV algorithm. The RNN model is based on our previous work, which included three LSTM layers of 128 units, 32 units, and 16 units, followed by a RELU dense layer, and connected to the softmax activation function of 2 units. The output of the RNN model indicated the probability of falling in every 0.1 s. To further evaluate the falling occurrence at t_m moment, a $W/20$ period of fall results before and after this moment are extracted. The fall results of this $W/10$ period with data length of W (0.1 s per result) are stored and added together to get the R_{sum} which represents the overall probability of falling. Since each fall result is either one or zero, if the value is larger than a voting threshold T_v, the result at tm moment would be falling, and vice versa. The threshold T_v is evaluated in the way that larger value will classify the final result as not falling but this may increase the false detection if the falling occurs within the time period. The T_v is set to half of the data length as 50% of falling occurrence, while we also evaluated the performance using the threshold with ±10% (or ±$W/10$) of the half data length $W/2$. The proposed voting algorithm can overcome the false detection by introducing a time delay of $W/20$ as illustrated in Table 2. Therefore, to balance the detection accuracy and the response time of rescue, the parameter of data length W should not be too large. The performances are evaluated with various data length of W and the maximum value of W is set to 60 as this is the maximum critical time for issuing fall alert. (a time delay within 3 s).

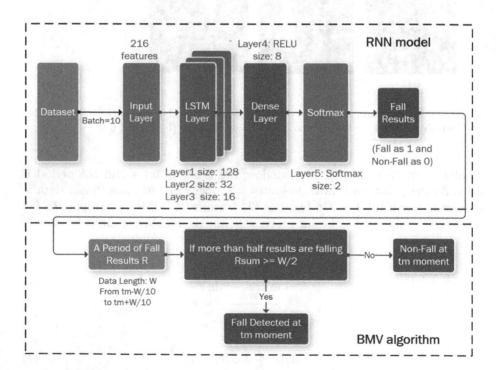

Fig. 3. The structure of the proposed fall detection algorithm.

Table 2. The pseudo code of the proposed BMV.

Boyer-Moore Voting Algorithm
Step 1. Extracting a window size of results with a data length of W
Step 2. Caculate the sum of the period results R_{sum}

Step 3. **if** R_{sum} is larger than the voting threshold T_v
        The result will be 1 as falling
    else
        The result will be 0 as not falling

Step 4. Shift the window with one value (0.1 s) and repeat the Step.1

2.3   Results

Table 3 illustrates the performance of proposed BMV included and excluded in fall detection, where Se, Sp and Ac indicate sensitivity, specificity, and accuracy, respectively. The rank column presents the five best models and the five worst models according to the average value of Se, Sp, and Ac.

The results indicate that the inclusion of BMV algorithm improved the overall fall detection. Based on the performances of M1 and M2-M21, most of the models with the proposed voting algorithm perform better than the M1 that has no voting algorithm in all aspects. It revealed that the BMV algorithm is effective in improving the fall detection results. Moreover, in comparison of the models with the same data length W, the Se (true detection of fall activities) is improved with lower voting threshold whereas Sp (true detection of non-fall activities) is higher with increased voting threshold. The results also stated that the threshold set as half of data length has a better performance according to the rank of these models. In addition, the ranks also indicated that the performances are improved significantly when the data length is increased from 4 to 30 but less significant when increased from 30 to 60. Since a longer data length would result in longer time delay, as a result, M11 with W of 30 and T_v of 15 is the optimal model among others that showed 97.78%, 98.09%, and 98.95% in Se, Sp, and Ac, respectively.

Table 4 showed a results comparison of the proposed M1 and M11 models with existing studies and our previous work. Firstly, the sensors in these studies used sampling rate of 100 Hz whereas the proposed study only used 15 Hz sampling rate. This implied that the proposed study achieved overall better results with lower sampling rate which reduced power consumption and computational cost by more than 50% though the number of IMUs is increased. In comparison of the M1 (raw features) with our previous model (included computed features of quaternion and Euler angles), which have the same RNN model, the results revealed that the raw features are sufficient for fall detection, while the computed quaternion and Euler angles increased the complexity of input features, thus, influences the classification performance. According to Van Thanh et al. studies [15,16], the A1-A4 are the improved algorithms of A5 using a double-

Table 3. The comparison results of the proposed fall detection model.

Group	Models	Se	Sp	Ac	Rank
M1	Without BMV	96.32%	95.63%	95.73%	19 (95.89%)
M2	W* = 4, Tv** = 2	97.04%	95.35%	95.60%	18 (96.00%)
M3	W = 6, Tv = 3	97.09%	95.80%	96.00%	17 (96.30%)
M4	W = 10, Tv = 4	98.58%	94.95%	95.50%	
M5	W = 10, Tv = 5	97.78%	96.43%	96.64%	
M6	W = 10, Tv = 6	95.74%	97.86%	97.54%	
M7	W = 20, Tv = 8	98.92%	96.15%	96.57%	
M8	W = 20, Tv = 10	97.76%	97.81%	97.80%	5 (97.79%)
M9	W = 20, Tv = 12	95.52%	98.89%	98.38%	
M10	W = 30, Tv = 12	99.16%	96.37%	96.79%	
M11	W = 30, Tv = 15	97.78%	98.09%	98.05%	1 (97.97%)
M12	W = 30, Tv = 18	93.67%	99.16%	98.32%	
M13	W = 40, Tv = 16	99.37%	96.14%	96.64%	
M14	W = 40, Tv = 20	97.62%	98.13%	98.05%	2 (97.93%)
M15	W = 40, Tv = 24	91.50%	99.32%	98.13%	
M16	W = 50, Tv = 20	99.54%	95.56%	96.17%	
M17	W = 50, Tv = 25	97.47%	98.16%	98.05%	3 (97.89%)
M18	W = 50, Tv = 30	89.09%	99.46%	97.88%	20 (95.48%)
M19	W = 60, Tv = 24	99.64%	95.10%	95.79%	
M20	W = 60, Tv = 30	97.42%	98.12%	98.01%	4 (97.85%)
M21	W = 60, Tv = 36	86.18%	99.53%	97.49%	21 (94.4%)

* W is the window size (data length);
** Tv is the voting threshold.

check method. The results revealed that A5 performs worse than our 3 models in all aspects, and A2-A4 have a higher sensitivity but the overall accuracy is less efficient. Moreover, A1 showed a 100% accuracy in fall detection, which highlighted the improvement approach of fall detection using multiple types of sensors. Meanwhile, study by Shi et al. [13] showed similar performance with the proposed M1, but less efficient than the proposed M11 with the BMV algorithm. In a summary, the proposed V-RNN apporach showed high sensitivity and accuracy in fall detection, and significantly enhanced the classification performance compared with our previous work.

Table 4. Comparison of fall-detection results with the proposed M1 and M11 models, our previous model, and some previously developed FDSs, where SR, Se, Sp, and Ac represent the sampling rate of IMUs, sensitivity, specificity, and accuracy, respectively.

Reference	Application	Methodology	Algorithm	SR (Hz)	Se (%)	Sp (%)	Ac (%)
Van *et al.* (2018) [16]	Firefighters	1 3-DOF accelerometer	A1	100	100	100	100
Van *et al.* (2018) [15]		and 1 barometer on	A2		100	94.44	95.83
		the thigh pocket, and	A3		100	90.74	93.05
		1 CO sensor on the	A4		100	91.67	93.75
		mask (they raised 4	A5		88.9	94.45	91.67
		algorithms in [16] and					
		1 algorithm in [15])					
Shi *et al.* (2020) [13]	Elderly	1 IMU on waist	/	100	95.54	96.38	95.96
AnkFall (2021) [8]		1 IMU on ankle	/	100	76.8	92.8	/
Kiprijanovska *et al.* (2020) [6]	Ordinary being	2 IMUs in 2 smartwatches	/	100	90.6	86.2	88.9
Previous Work [5]	Firefighters	9 9-DOF IMUs on the	RNN	15	92.25	94.59	94.10
Proposed M1		chest, wrists, elbows,	RNN		96.32	95.63	95.73
Proposed M11		thighs and ankles; [5]	V-RNN		97.78	98.09	98.05
		has extra features of					
		quaternion and Euler					
		angles					

3   Conclusion and Future Work

This paper proposed a novel fall detection algorithm for the wearable FDS with V-RNN that significantly improved the classification performance of our previous work. The study revealed that the proposed V-RNN enhanced the overall fall detection performance with sensitivity and accuracy reached up to 97.86% and 98.20%, respectively. The results showed high sensitivity and accuracy compared with existed studies, though the sampling rate is much lower than others. Future work will aim to improve the design of wearable sensors to meet the criteria of deploying the proposed PPC in actual fireground. Moreover, the study will also consider alternative approach for improving the firefighters' fall detection with different measurements.

Acknowledgement. This research was supported by the Zhejiang Provincial Natural Science Foundation of China under Grant No. LQ21F020024. This research was also funded by a National Research Foundation of Korea (NRF) grant (2019K1A3A1A05088484) funded by the Korean Government (MIST).

References

1. Bno055 inertial measurement unit. https://item.taobao.com/item.htm?spm=a230r.1.14.16.282a69630O3V2r&id=541798409353&ns=1&abbucket=5#detail. Accessed 10 May 2021
2. China Fire Protection Yearbook. Yunnan People's Publishing House (2018). https://books.google.co.jp/books?id=aFnMxQEACAAJ
3. Ahn, S., Kim, J., Koo, B., Kim, Y.: Evaluation of inertial sensor-based pre-impact fall detection algorithms using public dataset. Sensors **19**(4), 774 (2019). https://doi.org/10.3390/s19040774

4. Casilari, E., Santoyo-Ramon, J.A., Cano-Garcia, J.M.: Analysis of public datasets for wearable fall detection systems. Sensors **17**(7), 1513 (2017). https://doi.org/10.3390/s17071513
5. Chai, X., Wu, R., Pike, M., Jin, H., Chung, W.Y., Lee, B.G.: Smart wearables with sensor fusion for fall detection in firefighting. Sensors **21**(20), 6770 (2021). https://doi.org/10.3390/s21206770
6. Kiprijanovska, I., Gjoreski, H., Gams, M.: Detection of gait abnormalities for fall risk assessment using wrist-worn inertial sensors and deep learning. Sensors **20**(18), 5373 (2020). https://doi.org/10.3390/s20185373
7. Lin, C.L., et al.: Innovative head-mounted system based on inertial sensors and magnetometer for detecting falling movements. Sensors **20**(20), 5774 (2020). https://doi.org/10.3390/s20205774
8. Luna-Perejon, F., Munoz-Saavedra, L., Civit-Masot, J., Civit, A., Dominguez-Morales, M.: Ankfall-falls, falling risks and daily-life activities dataset with an ankle-placed accelerometer and training using recurrent neural networks. Sensors **21**(5), 1889 (2021). https://doi.org/10.3390/s21051889
9. Martinez-Villasenor, L., Ponce, H., Brieva, J., Moya-Albor, E., Nunez-Martínez, J., Penafort-Asturiano, C.: Up-fall detection dataset: a multimodal approach. Sensors **19**(9), 1988 (2019). https://doi.org/10.3390/s19091988
10. Medrano, C., Igual, R., Plaza, I., Castro, M.: Detecting falls as novelties in acceleration patterns acquired with smartphones. PloS One **9**, e94811 (2014). https://doi.org/10.1371/journal.pone.0094811
11. Micucci, D., Mobilio, M., Napoletano, P.: Unimib shar: a dataset for human activity recognition using acceleration data from smartphones. Appl. Sci. **7**(10), 1101 (2017). https://doi.org/10.3390/app7101101
12. Santoyo-Ramon, J.A., Casilari-Perez, E., Cano-Garcia, J.: Analysis of a smartphone-based architecture with multiple mobility sensors for fall detection. PLoS One **11**(12), 1–17 (2016). https://doi.org/10.1371/journal.pone.0168069
13. Shi, J., Chen, D., Wang, M.: Pre-impact fall detection with CNN-based class activation mapping method. Sensors **20**(17), 4750 (2020). https://doi.org/10.3390/s20174750
14. Sun, Z.: Research on safety safeguard measures for fire fighting and rescue. China Fire Daily **5**(03), 45–46 (2020)
15. Van Thanh, P., Le, Q.B., Nguyen, D.A., Dang, N.D., Huynh, H.T., Tran, D.T.: Multi-sensor data fusion in a real-time support system for on-duty firefighters. Sensors **19**(21), 4746 (2019). https://doi.org/10.3390/s19214746
16. Van Thanh, P., et al.: Development of a real-time supported system for firefighters in emergency cases. In: Vo Van, T., Nguyen Le, T., Nguyen Duc, T. (eds.) BME 2017. IP, vol. 63, pp. 45–51. Springer, Singapore (2018). https://doi.org/10.1007/978-981-10-4361-1_8
17. Vavoulas, G., Chatzaki, C., Malliotakis, T., Pediaditis, M., Tsiknakis, M.: The MobiAct dataset: recognition of activities of daily living using smartphones, pp. 143–151, January 2016. https://doi.org/10.5220/0005792401430151
18. Vavoulas, G., Pediaditis, M., Spanakis, E.G., Tsiknakis, M.: The MobiFall dataset: an initial evaluation of fall detection algorithms using smartphones. In: 13th IEEE International Conference on BioInformatics and BioEngineering, pp. 1–4 (2013). https://doi.org/10.1109/BIBE.2013.6701629

19. Vilarinho, T., et al.: A combined smartphone and smartwatch fall detection system. In: 2015 IEEE International Conference on Computer and Information Technology; Ubiquitous Computing and Communications; Dependable, Autonomic and Secure Computing; Pervasive Intelligence and Computing, pp. 1443–1448 (2015). https://doi.org/10.1109/CIT/IUCC/DASC/PICOM.2015.216
20. Waheed, M., Afzal, H., Mehmood, K.: NT-FDS-a noise tolerant fall detection system using deep learning on wearable devices. Sensors **21**(6), 2006 (2021). https://doi.org/10.3390/s21062006

CycleGAN Based Motion Artifact Cancellation for Photoplethysmography Wearable Device

Nguyen Mai Hoang Long[1], Jong Jin Kim[2], Boon Giin Lee[3],
and Wan Young Chung[1(✉)]

[1] Department of AI Convergence, Pukyong National University, Busan, South Korea
wychung@pknu.ac.kr
[2] Department of Electronic Engineering, Pukyong National University,
Busan, South Korea
kimjj@pknu.ac.kr
[3] School of Computer Science, University of Nottingham Ningbo China,
Ningbo, China
boon-giin.lee@nottingham.edu.cn

Abstract. Motion artifacts (MA) in photoplethysmography (PPG) signals is a challenging problem in signal processing today although various methods have been researched and developed. Using deep learning techniques recently has demonstrated their performance to overcome many limitations in traditional ones. In this study, we develop a protocol to build the PPG dataset and a cycleGAN-based model which can use to remove MA from PPG signals at the radial artery. We verified that the assumption of noisy PPG signals is a linear combination of clean PPG and accelerator (ACC) signals is not strong enough. Our evaluation of the CycleGAN model for reconstructing PPG signals at the radial artery which consisted of two opposite phases was feasible but the quality of signals needs more further research.

Keywords: Photoplethysmography · GAN Learning · Dataset · Wearable · Motion artifact

1 Introduction

Photoplethysmography (PPG) is an advanced, cost-effective technique for vital signs monitoring which has been integrated into almost all wearable fitness devices. This technique, however, is highly sensitive to motion artifacts (MA). Therefore, extracting health informatics from PPG signals is complicated to gain an accepted accuracy in real life. Recently, a breakthrough in artifact intelligence via deep learning has created a revolutionary wave in computer vision and

This work was supported by an National Research Foundation grant of Korea Government (2019R1A2C1089139).

J.-H. Kim et al. (Eds.): IHCI 2021, LNCS 13184, pp. 138–144, 2022.
https://doi.org/10.1007/978-3-030-98404-5_13

signal processing. To reconstruct noisy/low-resolution images, generative adversarial networks (GAN) can be employed that can provide impressive results [1]. Using CycleGAN method, Hosein et al. [2] has built a deep learning model that allowed removing MA from corrupted PPG signals without using any reference signals. Their results have improved 9.5 times in canceling MA as compared to the state-of-the-art. This approach, however, was limited in the assumption that noisy PPG signals are a linear combination of clean PPG and accelerator signals. In the real world, the shape of PPG will be changed since it depends on the location of attached sensors and types of hand movements. The accelerometer signals are a mixture of object motions and gravity. Thus adding ACC data to generate noisy PPG dataset could be different to the noisy PPG in real life. Moreover, the PPG dataset used for training model was often collected from the finger and posterior side of the wrist. Collecting PPG signals from the locations near to the artery may occur two kinds of PPG phases have opposite polarity [3]. Therefore, machine learning-based MA cancellation needs to consider on specific locations where PPG sensors and accelerators are attached to reduce false.

Based on our previous study, a wearable device named WrisTee for vital signs monitoring was built to measure PPG signals at three locations along the radial artery [4]. Aiming to cancel MA from PPG signals based on GAN learning, this work was conducted to develop a protocol for constructing the PPG dataset that was necessary for training the CycleGan-based model. This work also answers the question of whether feasibility or not to combine ACC into clean PPG signals.

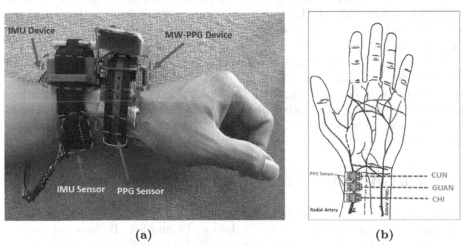

(a)   (b)

Fig. 1. (a) Multi-wavelength PPG (MW-PPG) device and Inertial Measurement Unit (IMU) device, (b) Locations of attached PPG sensors.

2   Experimental Protocol

To build the dataset, 12 volunteers were recruited to collect ACC and PPG signals. In this research, we limited our experiment to a scheme in which subjects

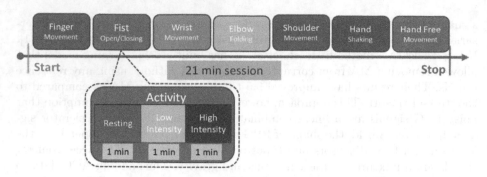

Fig. 2. Experimental protocol with seven activities to gather accelerator (ACC) data and Photoplethysmography (PPG) data.

were in sitting posture. Their right hand was kept unmoving to acquire the reference PPG signals from the index finger via an AFE4900EVM board (Texas Instrument, Dallas, Texas, USA). This board equipped a SFH7072 (Osram, Munich, Germany) sensor and was configured a sampling rate 250 Hz to get three PPG signals at 530, 640, and 940 nm wavelength. The WrisTee was worn on the left hand to measure PPG at four wavelengths 525, 630, 850, and 940 nm, respectively. To check out how different in motions on the anterior and posterior sides, we used another self-developed wearable device which equipped two inertial measurement units (IMU) to measure these motions from both sides of the wrist. Figure 1 shows the devices which were worn on the left hand of a subject for collecting data.

The protocol for acquiring data is illustrated in Fig. 2. Seven activities including micromotions (finger movement, fist open/closing, and shoulder movement), macro motions (elbow folding, wrist movement, and handshaking), and a free movement (combined randomly of hand movements) were conducted in 21 min to investigate the relationship between ACC and PPG signals, and to construct the dataset.

3   CycleGAN Model for Canceling Motion Artifacts

The Cycle Generative Adversarial Network, or CycleGAN, is a deep learning technique to translate images from a dataset to another. It does not require a pair-image dataset for training, thus permitting to build the model from an unexistence dataset. To build the model, two pairs of generators and discriminators were constructed as in Fig. 3. One translating from noisy PPG to clean PPG (G1), and then another one translating from noisy PPG to clean PPG (G2). Two discriminators (D1 and D1) ensured the generated data look similar to the real data. Adversarial loss is used to ensure translated signals look real, sharp, and indistinguishable from the genuine ones. It included the likelihood of real data and the quantity of the Generator can fool the Discriminator as expressed in Eq. (1).

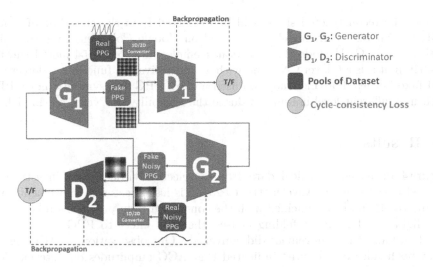

Fig. 3. Cycle Generative Adversarial Network (CycleGAN) to remove motion artifacts.

$$\mathcal{L}_{GAN}(G, D, X, Y) = E_{y \sim p_{data}(y)}[loglog D_Y(y)] +$$
$$E_{x \sim p_{data}(x)}[loglog(1 - D_Y(G(x)))] \quad (1)$$

Because our dataset is in 1-Dimension (1D), to take advantage of some image-to-image translation CycleGAN model, we converted 1D signal to image with size 256×256 where each pixel is given by the equation below:

$$Img_{i,j} = floor((Sig[i] + Sig[j]) \times 128) \quad (2)$$

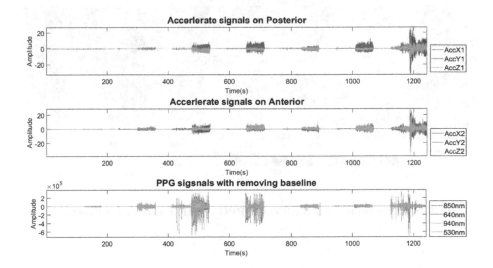

Fig. 4. ACC and PPG signals from a selected subject. (Color figure online)

Hence, the reconstructed signal will be extracted from the cross-line of a generated 2D-image. Our model was trained on Google Colab environment using python 3.7 in GPU mode. The Generator employed a ResNet54 model and the Discriminator is a 6-layer CNN and with a *tanh* activation function to detect real and fake images. For this study, we used a clean PPG and synthetic noisy PPG with five different level noise to evaluate the feasibility of CycleGAN model.

4   Results

Figure 4 displayed a typical data from a selected subject. Our investigation showed that the green wavelength at 525 nm is less affected by movement comparing to others. It is coincided with the conclusion from previous studies about this light [5]. The finger folding caused the least effect to PPG signals while free hand and wrist movement did conversely. Our observation on ACC signals from both sides of the wrist indicated that ACC amplitudes on anterior sides have no significant difference on the posterior side. Noticeably, the scaleogram of the PPG signal from the above subject as shown in Fig. 5 indicates that the heartbeat around 1.5 Hz was almost collapsed under all activities except finger folding. Figure 6 showed a ten samples of PPG signals before and after reconstructed by CycleGAN model after a training with 7500 epochs. The exist of both PPG phases made the shape of signals were not clean except that the baseline were totally removed.

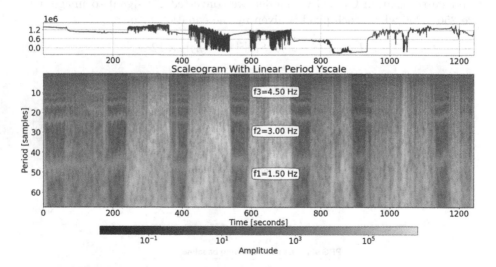

Fig. 5. Scaleogram for the 850-nm-PPG signal of a selected subject.

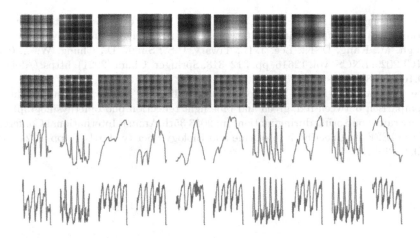

Fig. 6. Ten randomly selected noisy PPG signals before and after were reconstructed by the CycleGAN-based model.

5 Conclusion

In this paper, we investigated the feasibility of linear combining ACC to PPG signals and developed a CycleGAN model to test how well it could reconstruct collapsed PPG signals by MA. Our study showed that except for finger motions, other hand activities totally ruin the original PPG and no evidence supported that a linear combination between ACC and clean PPG to generate noisy PPG is equivalent to a real-life noisy PPG. Therefore, the CycleGAN-based model for MA cancellation need to modify for matching to the specific of PPG data at the radial artery of the wrist. The performance of CycleGAN model for reconstructing noisy PPG with two kinds of PPG phases was not good enough. Therefore, a conditional CycleGAN will be considered in the future to overcome this problem.

References

1. Creswell, A., White, T., Dumoulin, V., Arulkumaran, K., Sengupta, B., Bharath, A.A.: Generative adversarial networks: an overview. IEEE Signal Process. Mag. **35**(1), 53–65 (2018)
2. Zargari, A.H.A., Aqajari, S.A.H., Khodabandeh, H., Rahmani, A.M., Kurdahi, F.: An accurate non-accelerometer-based PPG motion artifact removal technique using CycleGAN. arXiv e-prints (2021). arXiv-2106
3. Kamshilin, A.A., Margaryants, N.B.: Origin of photoplethysmographic waveform at green light. Phys. Procedia **86**, 72–80 (2017)

4. Hoang Long, N.M., Kim, J.-J., Chung, W.-Y.: A prototype wristwatch device for monitoring vital signs using multi-wavelength photoplethysmography sensors. In: Singh, M., Kang, D.-K., Lee, J.-H., Tiwary, U.S., Singh, D., Chung, W.-Y. (eds.) IHCI 2020. LNCS, vol. 12616, pp. 312–318. Springer, Cham (2021). https://doi.org/10.1007/978-3-030-68452-5_32
5. Lee, J., Matsumura, K., Yamakoshi, K.I., Rolfe, P., Tanaka, S., Yamakoshi, T.: Comparison between red, green and blue light reflection photoplethysmography for heart rate monitoring during motion. In: 2013 35th Annual International Conference of the IEEE Engineering in Medicine and Biology Society (EMBC), pp. 1724–1727. IEEE (2013)

Effect of Time Window Size for Converting Frequency Domain in Real-Time Remote Photoplethysmography Extraction

Yu Jin Shin[1] , Woo Jung Han[1] , Kun Ha Suh[2] , and Eui Chul Lee[1(✉)]

[1] Department of Human-Centered Artificial Intelligence, Sangmyung University,
Seoul, South Korea
eclee@smu.ac.kr
[2] R&D Team, Zena Inc., Seoul 04782, Korea

Abstract. Remote-photoplethysmography (rPPG) is an attractive technology that can measure vital signs at a distance without contact. Previous remote-photoplethysmography studies focused mainly on eliminating the artifact such as motion but finding the optimal setup or hyperparameters are also an important factor influencing the performance. As one of them, window size is the length of the signal used to calculate the vital signs once in a spectral method and has not been analyzed in detail in previous works. In general, the use of a long window size increases the re-liability of the estimations, but it cannot reflect continuously changing physiological responses of human. Also, using too short window size increases uncertainty. In this paper, we compare and analyze the pulse rate estimation results according to window sizes from short to long using CHROM, which is one of the popular rPPG algorithms. Results on the PURE dataset showed that the longer the window size, the higher the SNR and the lower the RMSE. At a window size of about 4 s (120 frames), the SNR was switched from negative to positive and an acceptable error rate (RMSE < 5) was observed.

Keywords: Remote PPG · Cardiac pulse · Window size · Pulse rate · Physiological signal

1 Introduction

Remote-photoplethysmography (rPPG) is a promising optical technology that can extract physiological signals to obtain vital information such as a pulse rate in contactless monitoring. The subtle color changes on the skin surface are synchronized with cardiac activities. The fundamental principle of rPPG is to measure blood flow changes by detecting light reflected from the skin tissues by a camera sensor. Unlike conventional contact-based PPG approaches that require additional devices, rPPG has the advantage of being able to remotely measure vital signs using a camera, which is ubiquitous today, under ambient lighting conditions. The rPPG is an emerging technology and can be applied to various fields such as sleep monitoring, home healthcare, elderly care, fitness, entertainment, and forensic science.

© Springer Nature Switzerland AG 2022
J.-H. Kim et al. (Eds.): IHCI 2021, LNCS 13184, pp. 145–149, 2022.
https://doi.org/10.1007/978-3-030-98404-5_14

Studies on the easiness of rPPG extraction for each channel of digital images, noise-resistant component analysis methods, optical/mathematical models of light sources and skin, and performance degradation due to image compression have been conducted [1–5].

On the other hand, most rPPG studies have only estimated a single pulse rate from a long-length input video. However, such measurements cannot reflect a person's active physiological responses which change continuously. Moreover, in practical use, subjects will not want to wait that long for measurements. Therefore, it is necessary to consider short-term measurements for rPPG-based vital sign estimation. The window size refers to the length of the signal for estimating a single estimation and has not been covered in detail in previous studies. In this paper, we aim to contribute to confirming the impact of window size in rPPG-based pulse rate measurement and finding the optimal window size. For rPPG extraction, we used the CHROM method as the default rPPG algorithm from facial skin.

2 Methods

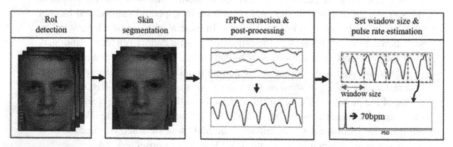

Fig. 1. Overview of the proposed rPPG-based pulse-rate estimation approach

Figure 1 shows the overview of the proposed rPPG-based pulse-rate estimation approach. First, the frontal face is detected by the face detector from OpenCV DNN module [6] at the first frame. Then Kernelized correlation filter (KCF) tracker [7] is used to track the detected face in subsequent frames. This step enables stable facial localization while minimizing the background pixels. Next, since the background has no pulsatile information, a statistical filtering method based on the YCbCr color space [8] is applied to filter out background pixels from the facial rectangle. The range of the skin was determined in a heuristic method. Then the CHROM method [9] is used for rPPG extraction. This algorithm is robust to the subject's motion and is therefore frequently adopted for rPPG extraction. Since the signal still contains noise components, to further improve the signal quality, we apply two post-processing steps. As the first post-processing step, we re-move the breath-like trend from the signal and apply detrending to obtain zero-centered normalized signals. In addition, a Butterworth bandpass filtering [10] with cut-off frequencies of 42 bpm and 240 bpm is applied, which removes components irrelevant to cardiac activities. Finally, to calculate pulse rate from the signal, a spectral method is used. It is considered for rPPG waveforms that are not relatively clean. At this time, to mitigate spectral leakage, we apply the Hann window before the Fourier transform.

The window size determines the interval of the signal to participate in the calculation of a single pulse-rate. In general, the use of a long window size increases the re-liability of the estimation in rPPG-based vital signs estimation, but it cannot reflect continuously changing physiological responses, and if it is too short, an incorrect estimation is obtained. In our experiment, a total of 15 window size candidates (1, 2, 3, 4, 5, 6, 7, 8, 9, 10, 20, 30, 40, 50, and 60 s) were considered. In the PSD-based pulse rate estimation, a low frequency resolution is obtained if short-time signal is provided. When calculating the pulse rate from a signal with the length of 10-s, it means that the frequency resolution is 0.1 Hz in which the interval of each bin indicates 6 bpm. Therefore, to increase the frequency resolution (i.e., calculated with 1 bpm precision), some tricks could be introduced. The zero-padding technique is one of the ways to increase the frequency resolution and was used in our experiment. More specifically, we applied windowing the signal before applying zero-padding. Consecutive pulse rates were obtained by applying sliding window at 1 frame intervals from the signal then the statistical performance was evaluated.

3 Results

The algorithms were validated on PURE dataset [11]. This dataset comprises 10 participants performing different, controlled head motions in front of a camera. It was recorded in 6 different setups such as steady, talking, slow translation, fast translation, small rotation, small rotation, and medium rotation resulting in a total number of 60 sequences of 1 min each. The videos were captured with an eco274CVGE camera by SVS-Vistek GmbH at a frame rate of 30 Hz with a cropped resolution of 640 × 480 pixels and a 4.8 mm lens. Reference data have been captured in parallel using a finger clip pulse oximeter (pulox CMS50E) that delivers pulse rate wave and SpO2 readings with a sampling rate of 60 Hz. The test subjects were placed in front of the camera with an average distance of 1.1 m. Lighting condition was daylight through a large window frontal to the face with clouds changing illumination conditions slightly over time.

Table 1. Result of SNR and RMSE of each window length

Window size (sec)	1	2	3	4	5	6	7	8	9	10	20	30	40	50	60
SNR	−8.92	−5.57	−2.88	−1.00	0.60	4.72	2.93	3.80	4.50	5.01	6.05	6.17	6.26	6.24	5.91
RMSE	22.45	13.19	6.94	4.49	3.16	2.69	2.36	2.23	2.14	1.94	1.60	1.52	1.50	1.45	1.13

We measured SNR values by setting them differently to a total of 15 window sizes. Figure 2 and Table 1 show the SNR and RMSE comparison as a function of window length, respectively. As the window size increases, higher SNR and lower RMSE were obtained. At the window size of about 4 s (120 frames), the SNR is switched from negative to positive and a low error rate (RMSE < 5) was observed. Additionally, it was confirmed that using a window of sufficient length has the effect of reducing the estimation error in moving subject scenarios.

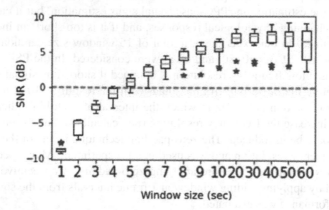

Fig. 2. The SNR comparison as a function of window length on subjects

Figure 2 shows the SNR of the length of the window is a boxplot comparison, the orange line is the mean value of the SNR, the blue star is the outlier, and the dotted line is the reference line when the SNR is zero. A comparison of window sizes by setup according to SNR shows that overall, the larger the window size, the higher the SNR. The larger the window size, the more cardiac information is included. The window size and SNR are proportional because we extract signals based on the most dominant information. As expected, the small window size shows low accuracy due to insufficient information to analyze.

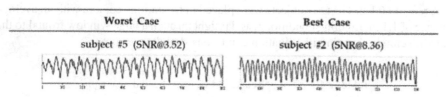

Fig. 3. Best and Worst cases of CHROM waveform when window size is 30

Figure 3 shows the CHROM waveforms for the worst and best cases when window size is 30. The video used is a signal waveform with a total of 900 frames and is 30 s long at 30 fps. Best and worst are extracted based on SNR values, and the values of SNR are written above each waveform. As can be seen from the figure, the best cases show that waveform results are more regular and stable.

4   Conclusion

In this paper, we analyzed how window size affects pulse rate estimation. To extract the rPPG signal and find the most optimal window size for estimating heart rate, we analyzed the accuracy of the estimated pulse-rate according to window size. The pulse-rate was calculated by applying a spectral-based estimation method that multi-plied the maximum power peak by 60 after the FFT was applied. We extracted the pulse signal with varying window-size for the PURE dataset. Each pulse-rate according to different window sizes was compared with SNR and RMSE. Experiments show that the smaller the window size, the less information, the lower the performance, and the longer the window size, the better overall performance. However, it has been observed that long window sizes are not always optimal, and sometimes performance gradually degrades when exceeding a certain size. Consequently, the window size affects the rPPG signal extraction performance, so it is necessary to find the optimal window size according to the application domains.

Acknowledgement. This work was supported by the NRF (National Research Foundation) of Korea funded by the Korea government (Ministry of Science and ICT) (NRF-2019R1A2C4070681).

References

1. de Hann, G., Jeanne, V.: Robust pulse rate from chrominance-based rppg. IEEE Trans. Biomed. Eng. **60**, 2878–2886 (2013)
2. Verkruysse, W., Svaasand, L.O., Nelson, J.S.: Remote plethysmographic imaging using ambient light. Opt. Express **16**(26), 21434 21445 (2008)
3. Lewandowska, M., Rumiński, J., Kocejko, T.: Measuring pulse rate with a webcam – a non-contact method for evaluating cardiac activity. In: IEEE Federated Conference on Computer Science and Information Systems, pp. 405–410 (2011)
4. Ming, P., Daniel, J., McDuff, R., Picard, W.: Non-contact, automated cardiac pulse measurements using video imaging and blind source separation. Opt. Express **18**(10), 10762–10774 (2010)
5. Wang, W., Brinker, A.C., Stuijk, S., de Hann, G.: Algorithmic principles of remote PPG. IEEE Trans. Biomed. Eng. **64**, 1479–1491 (2017)
6. OpenCV deep learning module samples 'OpenCV dnn face detector'. https://github.com/opencv/opencv/tree/master/samples/dnn. Accessed 01 Oct 2021
7. Henriques, J.F., et al.: High-speed tracking with kernelized correlation filters. IEEE Trans. Pattern Anal. Mach. Intell. **37**, 583–596 (2014)
8. Phung, S.L., Bouzerdoum, A., Chai, D.: A novel skin color model in YCbCr color space and its application to human face detection. In: Proceedings. International Conference on Image Processing, vol. 1. IEEE (2002)
9. De Haan, G., Jeanne, V.: Robust pulse rate from chrominance-based rPPG. IEEE Trans. Biomed. Eng. **60**(10), 2878–2886 (2013)
10. Chatterjee, A., Roy, U.K.: PPG based heart rate algorithm improvement with Butterworth IIR filter and Savitzky-Golay FIR filter. In: 2018 2nd International Conference on Electronics, Materials Engineering and Nano-Technology (IEMENTech). IEEE (2018)
11. Stricker, R., Müller, S., Gross, H.M.: Non-contact video-based pulse rate measurement on a mobile service robot. In: IEEE International Symposium on Robot and Human Interactive Communication, pp. 1056–1062 (2014)

Development of Application Usability Evaluation Scale for Seniors

Changhee Seo[1], Jin Suk Lee[2], and Jieun Kwon[1(✉)]

[1] Sangmyung University, Seoul 03016, Republic of Korea
jieun@smu.ac.kr
[2] Dongguk University, Seoul 04620, Republic of Korea

Abstract. **Purpose**: Applications for seniors are emerging because of the increasing number of seniors due to an aging society and popularization of smartphones by the 4th industrial revolution. The purpose of this paper is to establish a usability evaluation scale to develop more convenient and useful applications for seniors. **Research design, data and methodology**: For this study, first, the necessity of developing an application usability evaluation scale for seniors is discussed by examining the definition and context of seniors. Second, the primary usability evaluation factors were derived from collecting the factors of usability evaluation such as applications, seniors and conducting in-depth interviews with experts. Third, the second usability evaluation factors were derived through survey and statistical analysis based on the usability evaluation factors. **Results**: As a result, the usability evaluation scale was established with five factors – Cognition, Navigation, Feedback, Error, Aesthetic - and 20 items. **Conclusions**: This study can be the basis for guidelines of development and design in applications for seniors. Therefore, not only the young generation but also seniors can feel convenience in their daily lives by using customized applications for seniors.

Keywords: Usability · Evaluation scale · Senior · Application

1 Introduction

Recently, due to the decline in fertility rates and the extension of life expectancy, the senior class has increased as entering an aging society at a rapid pace [1]. The senior class is adapting to the era of Digital Transformation, which is emerging with the advent of the Fourth Industrial Revolution. This era is providing a new type of service that applies digital technology to existing analog services. The use of smartphone applications for various services in all areas of life, such as banking, shopping and food ordering etc. is commercialized. According to this, the frequency of using smartphone applications by seniors is increasing rapidly. Therefore, the ability of using applications and web platforms based on the use of smartphones is essential to seniors living in this era. In addition, there is a growing trend of applications that apply intuitive and simple UX designs for customized services targeting the senior class which has increased due to the popularization of smartphone use. Nevertheless, research or standards of usability

© Springer Nature Switzerland AG 2022
J.-H. Kim et al. (Eds.): IHCI 2021, LNCS 13184, pp. 150–162, 2022.
https://doi.org/10.1007/978-3-030-98404-5_15

evaluation testing about applications for seniors are insufficient and specific guidelines are insufficient.

This paper aims to define 1) the characteristics of seniors and the context of seniors in using smartphone applications, and based on this 2) establish application usability evaluation scale for seniors. This is expected to make environment for seniors to easily utilize smartphones and increase the use frequency of smartphone applications widely by providing customized application production guidelines for seniors.

2   Senior User

2.1   Senior User's Definition and Context

The definition of senior can be interpreted from various perspectives. First, in dictionary sense, it refers to the elderly who is over the age of 40 to 50 in the standard Korean Dictionary. Second, from an academic point of view, it refers to a person in a complex form in which physiological, physical, environmental and psychological changes that appear in the human aging process interaction at the International Senior Citizen's Association. Third, in terms of social-cultural aspects, it refers to the elderly over 65 years of retirement age.

Among these diverse and broad-meaning of senior classes, the people who actively strive to learn new digital technologies and try to adapt easily to digital culture in the digitized era have increased recently. These are 'active senior' class, which combines 'active' and 'senior'. The typical difference between existing seniors and active seniors is that active seniors think they are 5 to 10 years younger than their actual age, they want to learn new things actively and continuously in everything and communicate with other generations about various fields.

Active seniors conduct meaningful consumption such as leisure, education, culture and activities for health, continuing social relationship based on time and economic margin. In addition, they intend to take systematic education related to digital technology to develop senior digital utilization capabilities and try to use smartphone applications in various ways. For example, the curriculum has how to use a financial application that allows people to check their balance without going to bank, how to share contents produced by themselves with YouTube or SNS sections.

However, despite these increasing active senior class, very few seniors can use smartphone applications freely. Therefore, application guidelines for all seniors are needed so that not only active seniors who are proficient in digital utilization but also seniors who have not used digital can conveniently and easily use them.

2.2   Usability of Application for Senior

Usability is a qualitative attribute related to the degree of ease of use. In other words, it means convenience and empirical satisfaction of whether a user can conveniently use a product or system [2]. The International Organization for Standards (ISO) defined usability in ISO 9241-11 in terms of 'Effectiveness', 'Efficiency', 'Satisfaction' in a specific context of use to make a product achieve the specific purpose by specific users [3].

Therefore, usability evaluation is a scientific research process that finds problems and discovers ideas to develop or improve a user interface so that consumers can more easily manipulate complex functions of a product [4]. The scope of usability evaluation corresponds to all ranges related to the use of products and services, such as electronic devices, applications and web interfaces and exercise equipment. For accurate usability evaluation, the usability evaluation criteria must be determined according to the characteristics of the medium or system for each product and service [5].

3   Methodology

3.1   Procedure

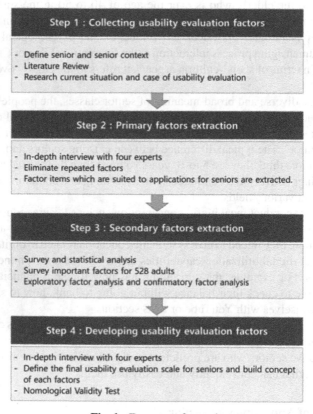

Fig. 1. Four steps for study

In order to develop a usability evaluation scale for senior application, the study proceeded in four steps as shown in Fig. 1.

3.2 Collecting Usability Evaluation Factors

The definition of seniors and their characteristics in physical, psychological and cognition are established. And their conduct and context of using smartphone applications are researched through literature review of papers, journals or books. Based on this, 361 usability evaluation factors were collected related to the subject of this study - smartphone application, seniors, web platforms.

3.3 Primary Factors Extraction

In order to extract the primary usability evaluation factor, the existing usability evaluation factors were first collected for literature review. The factors were collected from ISO (International Organization for Standardization) 9126 software quality evaluation factors, Jakob Nielsen's usability evaluation factors, Peter Morville's Honeycomb evaluation model [8], the Korea Health Industry Development Institute's aging-friendly product usability evaluation factors, Khan's web-related usability evaluation factors, Development of a Usability Evaluation Tool for Web-based Learning Sites by Suh-Young-Suhk, website evaluation items of Lindgaard, etc.

A total of 361 items were collected and duplicate factors were eliminated through in-depth interviews with four experts. It was reorganized through addition and deletion to suit the usability of application for seniors. In addition, a total of 58 items were extracted by adjusting terms and sentences in accordance with this study scope. The experts for the interview consisted of one elderly welfare expert, two design experts and one business administration expert.

3.4 Secondary Factors Extraction

There is a need to identify important factors that seniors consider important when using smartphone application to develop scales to measure the components of applications usability evaluation for seniors. To do this, a survey consisting of 58 features from the primary factors extraction was conducted for secondary factors extraction. The survey was conducted on 528 people in their 50s to 70s via online research. The demographic characteristics of the survey participants were 282 males (53.4%) and 246 females (46.6%). The average age was 60.71 years old (sd = 4.39), 232 in 50s (43.9%), 213 in 60–65 (40.3%), 62 in 65–70 (11.7%), 21 in 70s (4.0%). The education level showed 3 participants were elementary school graduates (0.6%), 9 participants were middle school graduates (1.7%), 141 participants were high school graduates (26.7%), 311 university graduates (58.9%), and 64 graduate school or higher graduates (12.1%). For the use of application or web platform, 23 participants have used for less than 1 year (4.4%) and 18 participants have used for more than 1 year and less than 2 years (3.4%). Also, 15 participants have used for more than 2 years and less than 3 years (2.8%) and 15 participants have used for more than 3 years and less than 4 years (2.8%). Particularly, in the longer period, the number of respondents is increasing. 23 participants have used for more than 4 years and less than 5 years (4.4%) and 434 participants have used for more than 5 years (82.2%). Therefore, the survey found that all of participants have used applications of smartphone.

Survey participants responded to the importance of 58 features extracted from primary factors extraction. The 7 points Likert scale was used ranging from 1-totally disagree to 7-totally agree.

In the analysis, first, in order to figure out the responses of the participants to all items and to confirm whether the systematic measurement errors are, we analyzed the mean and standard deviation of each items. Second, we analyzed exploratory factor analysis (EFA) to identify the sub-factors of application usability evaluation for seniors and tested reliability of items under each factor. Third, we conducted confirmatory factor analysis (CFA) to confirm the construct validity. Lastly, to test nominological validity, we analyzed the correlation between the scale we developed, internet self-efficacy, and innovativeness. SPSS 24.0 was used in analysis.

3.5   Developing Usability Evaluation Factors

Through the result of survey and statistical analysis, the final application usability evaluation scale for seniors is derived. And the concepts and meanings of each factors are defined. A total 5 factors - Cognition, Navigation, Feedback, Error, Aesthetic - and 20 items are established as the standard and guideline for developing applications for seniors. Also, nomological validity test is executed to apply items which are highly related to the derived 5 factors to analyze the correlation. Items are composed of internet self-efficacy and innovativeness to confirm the relation with the application in the stage of verification about established usability evaluation scale.

4   Results

4.1   Means and Standard Deviations of Items

Before conducting factor analysis, means and standard deviations analysis were conducted for examining the variation of responses for the measured items. Means of all items ranged from 4.77 to 5.47 and standard deviations ranged from 1.05 to 1.43. It is acceptable as a measurement of application usability evaluation for seniors in terms of semanticity and discrimination.

4.2   Exploratory Factor Analysis

An EFA of 58 items used in this study was conducted to identify factor structure. The principal component analysis was performed with VARIMAX orthogonal rotation and factor extraction criteria were set to eigenvalue 1 or higher.

As a result, 5 factors were extracted as shown in Table 1. Factor 1 had 29 items and the reliability coefficient was 0.98. Factor 2 had 12 items and reliability coefficient was 0.94. Factor 3 had 8 items and reliability coefficient was 0.94. Factor 4 had 5 items and reliability coefficient was 0.94. Factor 5 had 4 items and reliability coefficient was 0.88. By combining the contents of existing research and items, factor 1 was named 'Cognition', factor 2 'Navigation', factor 3 'Feedback', factor 4 'Error' and factor 5 'Aesthetic'.

Table 1. The results of EFA and reliability test

Factor	Items	Factor					com
		1	2	3	4	5	
Factor 1	The font which is easy to read is applied to the shape of the letter	0.80	0.21	0.15	0.07	0.21	.748
	Spaces between the lines are appropriate to read sentences easy	0.77	0.25	0.12	0.08	0.21	.714
	Terms in a website or application convey their meaning clearly	0.76	0.25	0.19	0.25	0.10	.751
	The user has emotional satisfaction with various senses such as sight, hearing etc. based on provided functions	0.76	0.23	0.17	0.13	0.22	.723
	The font size is appropriately used to increase readability depending on the size and resolution of the screen	0.76	0.24	0.13	0.12	0.19	.699
	It provides various auxiliary functions besides the standard setting function in consideration of the user's physical characteristics and diversity	0.75	0.23	0.22	0.19	0.14	.727
	It is minimizing elements that users should remember for manipulation	0.75	0.22	0.22	0.29	0.10	.749
	Users can use applications or web sites pleasantly enough to have subjective satisfaction	0.74	0.26	0.15	0.11	0.19	.693
	Users can change or reconstruct screen elements	0.74	0.18	0.27	0.14	0.15	.696
	Users can select an automatic function and a manual function	0.74	0.20	0.25	0.20	0.11	.693
	It maintains consistency not to make users confused	0.74	0.27	0.22	0.27	0.12	.750
	Users can have shortcut functions which are used frequently	0.74	0.30	0.22	0.21	0.10	.734
	Appropriate results appear when searching for keywords	0.73	0.30	0.25	0.25	0.14	.764
	Users can use skilfully without having to learn everything again even if the user has not used the applications or websites for a certain period of time	0.73	0.26	0.28	0.28	0.03	.757
	All elements that appear operately and proceed as expected by the user	0.72	0.29	0.21	0.24	0.12	.723

(continued)

Table 1. (*continued*)

Factor	Items	Factor					com
		1	2	3	4	5	
	Users can search with customized conditions	0.70	0.31	0.21	0.27	0.13	.722
	Applications and websites which users use are constantly updating	0.70	0.32	0.23	0.15	0.06	.675
	The information provided in the knowledge space are easy to read and understand	0.69	0.25	0.28	0.35	0.14	.753
	Important information and functions stand out	0.69	0.21	0.28	0.34	0.17	.742
	Items with similar characteristics are collected and placed together	0.68	0.30	0.27	0.18	0.20	.706
	There are no errors that occur when updating	0.68	0.21	0.23	0.37	0.03	.697
	The order is organized according to the importance of information	0.68	0.22	0.22	0.26	0.19	.663
	The screen configuration is arranged effectively to understand contents of the website	0.67	0.29	0.22	0.27	0.26	.722
	Users can intuitively know how to operate the function	0.67	0.23	0.31	0.31	0.17	.721
	It shows that applications or website pages start and end clearly	0.65	0.32	0.18	0.27	0.29	.713
	Users can understand the information required to use an application or web pages easily and accurately	0.64	0.31	0.26	0.35	0.21	.741
	Various choices can be made according to the situation or users' request and preference	0.63	0.26	0.28	0.29	0.23	.687
	Users can understand sufficiently the purpose of using by the name of menu and icon	0.59	0.33	0.22	0.37	0.21	.684
	The screen is comfortable and stable to see	0.58	0.33	0.21	0.25	0.39	.697
Factor 2	Search functions work well on websites or applications	0.26	0.77	0.20	0.17	0.14	.753
	There is a backward function or a cancellation function	0.26	0.75	0.13	0.07	0.19	.693
	Users can play or stop when watching animation or video	0.25	0.73	0.08	0.00	0.11	.616
	Users can search contents as they think	0.22	0.72	0.23	0.27	0.17	.718

(*continued*)

Table 1. (*continued*)

Factor	Items	Factor					com
		1	2	3	4	5	
	It can clearly shows the situation of what kind of work users are currently performing on the website or application they use	0.32	0.70	0.21	0.13	0.13	.662
	There is navigation method to move or visit where users want	0.23	0.69	0.21	0.16	0.11	.606
	There is a link sharing function which is a way to share completed content works	0.25	0.69	0.24	0.09	0.15	.619
	Users can go to the main page from all pages	0.22	0.68	0.09	0.08	0.27	.605
	It clearly shows where users are currently on the website or application they use	0.26	0.68	0.18	0.11	0.06	.573
	It is easy to use the function users want	0.19	0.64	0.26	0.31	0.00	.616
	Users can efficiently manipulate website functions as they want	0.28	0.61	0.34	0.32	0.07	.677
	Users can use the product freely without help or guides	0.21	0.59	0.33	0.37	0.01	.635
Factor 3	It provides appropriate and clear feedback to users	0.38	0.35	0.67	0.21	0.15	.783
	It suggests an appropriate solution when there is a problem	0.34	0.31	0.64	0.39	0.08	.777
	It has hints, directions, instructions and guidance functions by giving messages or alarms to users	0.40	0.35	0.63	0.05	0.18	.713
	Information which is recommended to users is useful	0.39	0.36	0.61	0.06	0.15	.681
	The information content asked is quickly derived	0.33	0.39	0.60	0.29	0.14	.723
	Notifications and warning indictions allow the user to recognize quickly	0.36	0.36	0.59	0.29	0.16	.716
	It accurately informs information on the next screen to be output when users manipulate through an image or symbol	0.40	0.39	0.59	0.23	0.17	.733
	It is convenient to modify stored records	0.33	0.38	0.57	0.25	0.06	.653

(*continued*)

Table 1. (*continued*)

Factor	Items	Factor					com
		1	2	3	4	5	
Factor 4	The error message is clear and easy to understand	0.44	0.24	0.18	0.72	0.10	.806
	There is a means to recover when an error occurs	0.45	0.27	0.20	0.69	0.08	.796
	Helpful usage guides are provided when users can't understand how to use	0.44	0.22	0.27	0.68	0.14	.799
	The menu is configured for users to understand easily	0.48	0.26	0.21	0.65	0.23	.798
	The menu configuration is well arranged at a glance so that users can easily remember	0.47	0.23	0.24	0.64	0.24	.815
Factor 5	Colors are well designed in harmony	0.36	0.27	0.16	0.22	0.69	.757
	Exterior design gives satisfaction to users aesthetically	0.52	0.29	0.19	0.12	0.58	.740
	First impression of screen is good	0.55	0.25	0.16	0.10	0.58	.740
	The volume of the sound is appropriate	0.46	0.26	0.18	0.14	0.55	.635
Eigenvalue		33.69	3.51	1.83	1.18	1.08	–
% of Variance		58.08	6.06	3.15	2.04	1.86	–
Cronbach's α		0.98	0.94	0.94	0.94	0.88	–

※ KMO = .979, Bartlett's $\chi2$ = 18110.704 (p < .001)

4.3 Confirmatory Factor Analysis

CFA was conducted to confirm the factor structure identified by the EFA and to examine the construct validation. Maximum Likelihood Estimation was used for calculation. For CFA, we selected 5 items each for 'Cognition', 4 items each for 'Navigation', 4 items for 'Feedback', 3 items for 'Error' and 4 items for 'Aesthetic' as items representing the meaning of each factor and that do not overlap between items. The reliability coefficients were .93 (cognition), .90 (navigation), .89 (feedback), 92 (error) and .88 (aesthetic). In all cases, they were above .6 securing internal consistency.

The goodness-of-fit of the model for X2 was relatively high as 580.90 (df = 197, p < .001), but the overall model fit were statistically satisfied with acceptable level: GFI = .910, AGFI = .884, CFI = .960, NFI = .941, RMR = .059, and RMSEA = .061. In addition, when comparing the five-factor model with the single-factor model, the five-factor model was more suitable than the single-factor model in all the goodness-of-fit indexes (Table 2).

Table 2. The results of CFA

Model	Fitness							
	x2	NFI	RMR	CFI	RMSEA	GFI	AGFI
5 factor	580.90 (df = 197, p < .001)	.941	.059	.960	.061	.910	.884
1 factor	2255.10 (df = 209, p < .001)	.773	.105	.789	.136	.649	.576

4.4 Nomological Validity Test

In order to verify the nomological validity of the developed scale, a correlation analysis was conducted between 5 factors, innovativeness and internet self-efficacy. According to previous study, the higher the innovativeness and internet self-efficacy, the more knowledge and experience in computer software [7]. These studies suggest that people with high innovation and internet self-efficacy have a better understanding of the detailed factors required for application usability evaluation. Therefore, this study attempted to verify the validity of this scale by analyzing the relationship between individual characteristics and innovation, internet self-efficacy and sub-factors of usability evaluation factors. We measured internet self-efficacy by adopting the 8-items scale from Eastin and LaRosc (2000: 'I can understand terms related to Internet hardware', 'I can understand terms related to Internet software', 'I can explain the functions of Internet hardware', 'I can solve internet problems', 'I can explain why things are not going well on the Internet', 'I can use the Internet to collect data', 'I am confident in learning the latest technology within a particular Internet program', 'I rely on online discussion groups when I need help'). Cronbach's α was .86. To measure individual's innovativeness, we used following 7 items (Parasuraman 2000): 1. Other people come to you for advice on new technologies. 2. It seems your friends are learning more about the newest technologies than you are(r). 3. In general, you are among the first in your circle of friends to acquire new technology when it appears. 4. You can usually figure out new high-tech

Table 3. The results of correlation analysis

	Mean	SD	1	2	3	4	5	6
1 = Cognition	5.11	1.04	1					
2 = Navigation	5.29	1.01	.66**	1				
3 = Feedback	5.09	1.04	.75**	.73**	1			
4 = Error	5.06	1.29	.77**	.62**	.68**	1		
5 = Aesthetic	4.85	0.92	.77**	.62**	.65**	.60**	1	
6 = Internet self-efficacy	4.16	1.11	.37**	.35**	.35**	.33**	.40**	1
7 = Innovativeness	4.54	0.93	.41**	.37**	.40**	.33**	.42**	.71**

**p < .01

Table 4. The usability evaluation scale and items

Factor	Items
Cognition	The font which is easy to read is applied to the shape of the letter
	Terms within a website or application convey their meaning clearly
	It is minimizing the elements that users should remember for manipulation
	Users can intuitively know how to operate the function
	Users can understand sufficiently the purpose of use at the name of menu and icon
Navigation	Search functions work well on websites or applications
	There is a backward function or a cancellation function
	Users can search contents as they think
	It clearly shows the situation of what kind of work users are currently performing on the website or application they use
Feedback	It provides appropriate and clear feedback to users
	It suggests an appropriate solution when there is a problem
	It has hints, directions, instructions and guidance functions by messages or alarms
	Information which is recommended to users is useful
Error	The error message is clear and easy to understand
	There is a means to recover when an error occurs
	Helpful usage guides are provided when users can't understand how to use
Aesthetic	Colors are well designed in harmony
	Exterior design gives satisfaction aesthetically
	First impression of screen is good
	The volume of the sound is appropriate

products and services without help from others. 5. You keep up with the latest technological developments in your areas of interest. 6. You enjoy the challenge of figuring out high-tech gadgets. 7. You find you have fewer problems than other people in making technology work for you. Cronbach's α was .94.

As result of the analysis, as shown in Table 3, the relationship between internet self-efficacy, innovativeness and five factors were found to be positive(+). In particular, the higher internet self-efficacy of applications for seniors, the greater the importance of cognition, navigation, feedback, error, aesthetic considered, The higher the individual's innovativeness, the greater the importance placed on the cognition, navigation, feedback, error, aesthetic. These results indicate that the scale developed in this study proves the nomological validity.

5 Discussion and Conclusion

This paper defined the senior and context about the development of application usability evaluation scale for seniors and established 5 usability evaluation factors and 20 items (Table 4).

Through two times of factor extraction, exploratory factor analysis, confirmatory factor analysis and nomological validity test, five factors - Cognition, Navigation, Feedback, Error and Aesthetic - and 20 items were developed as application usability evaluation factors for seniors. Each factors was defined through the discussion with researchers and four experts. 'Cognition' was defined as evaluation whether seniors can intuitively recognize interface elements of applications such as text, icons and menus. 'Navigation' was defined as an unconstrained movement between functions or screens based on the connected process within an application and determination of user's state. 'Feedback' was defined as effective interaction between a user and an application through performing a reaction to an interaction with messages, alarms and information. 'Error' was defined as matters related to errors such as clarity of error message and evaluation of whether senior users can easily understand and solve errors on their own. 'Aesthetic' was defined as purpose-appropriate design of applications for seniors in terms of color harmony, exterior design related to giving subjective satisfaction to users. The results of usability evaluation scale established from this study emphasize the content of cognition and feedback that recognizes something rather than the criteria for efficiency, learnability and satisfaction of general one. It can be seen that it is more important to use applications intuitively than to learn and know which functions. In particular, in terms of aesthetics, not only visual elements but also auditory content is included. Since it includes the sense of audiovisual, there is also a need to utilize multi-sense. These points make the difference between general application usability evaluation scale for general people and seniors. In addition, it establishes the need to develop customized indicators for seniors.

Therefore, the application usability evaluation scale for seniors established in this study can be used to suggest the correct applications direction and guidelines for seniors. As the development and popularization of applications for seniors are in the early stages, there is a lack of guidelines, standardization, and user experience analysis. The usability evaluation scale developed in this study presents the evaluation of applications guidelines for seniors and will be able to make most of seniors use smartphone applications more freely in many different fields.

For practical verification of usability evaluation for seniors, it is necessary to directly evaluate and verify the usability evaluation scale developed in this study for seniors in the use of specific applications. Through this verification in the future, the guidelines of usability evaluation indicators for seniors are expected to be solidified.

Acknowledgement. This research is supported by Ministry of Culture, Sports and Tourism and Korea Creative Content Agency (Project Number: R2020040068).

References

1. Lee, D., Lee, H.J., Kim, S.I.: Considering about mobile interface for 40, 50 generations - focus on mobile social commerce. KDDA **14**(3), 625–633 (2014)
2. Inition hompage. http://inition.kr/portfolio/senior-uiux-guideline/. Accessed 20 Sep 2021
3. ISO homepage. https://www.iso.org/iso-in-figures.html. Accessed 01 Sep 2021
4. Nielsen, J.: Usability Engineering (Interactive Technologies). Morgan Kaufmann Publishers Inc., Burlington (1994)
5. Lee, J., Kwon, J.: Usability evaluation for life-logging application. KoreaContents **16**(12), 43–49 (2016)
6. KHIDI hompage. https://www.khidi.or.kr. Accessed 18 Sep 2021
7. Sung, K.M., Kim, T.K., Jahng, J.J., Ahn, J.H.: The effect of personal characteristics and user involvement on knowledge sharing in the knowledge-exchange website context. J. Soc. e-Bus. Stud. **24**(4), 229–253 (2009)
8. Morville, P.: Ambient Findability. O'Reilly Media. Inc, Newton (2005)
9. Semantic Studios. https://semanticstudios.com/user_experience_design/. Accessed 03 Sep 2021

Analysis of the Utilization of Telehealth Worldwide and the Requisites for Its Effective Adoption

Yeun Soo Choi, Mingeon Kim, Ahhyun Ryu, Seowon Park[✉], Jason Kim, and Seongbin Lee

Cogito Research, Seoul, Republic of Korea (South Korea)
seowon.park22@gmail.com

Abstract. The popularization of medical devices in households and video calls during the COVID-19 pandemic have set grounds for the necessary conditions for telehealth to thrive. This allowed for patients with chronic diseases to be treated without the need for physical contact with a clinician and to access professional medics regardless of time. However, due to concerns for the safety of sensitive data of patients and both the quality and accuracy of medical treatment provided, telehealth was and is set to become strictly regulated. Finding the necessary technologies to facilitate mobile medical treatment as a viable option for those who struggle with attaining physical presence in hospitals is, therefore, necessary to maintain telehealth. This research aims to conduct user research on how to improve telehealth services to better serve the elderly population.

Keywords: Telehealth · User experience · Digital health

1 Introduction

1.1 A Subsection Sample

The concept of remote medical care referred to as telehealth in the following paper is known to be first implemented in the late 1950s when the Nebraska Psychiatric Institute and Norfolk State Hospital created a closed-circuit television link between the doctor and a patient. Since then, telehealth has been increasingly utilized for stroke care and care for intensive care units [4]. Conventionally, before the advent of SARS-CoV-2 (COVID-19), within the US, telehealth required doctors to obtain licenses through lengthy processes and high costs. However, nowadays, the majority of states alleviated the legal mandate for such requirements in high hopes of mitigating the pandemic. It is becoming increasingly evident that such change was not meant to be permanent; half of the states reverted their law back to strictly regulating practices regarding telehealth [5]. Nevertheless, with the outbreak of COVID-19 as the momentum, the size of the telehealth market has expanded at a compelling speed that compared to 2019, investment in virtual health and revenues of telehealth corporations nearly doubled. Furthermore, digital health service positioned itself as a factor of medical service since its usage rate has largely stabilized ranging

© Springer Nature Switzerland AG 2022
J.-H. Kim et al. (Eds.): IHCI 2021, LNCS 13184, pp. 163–170, 2022.
https://doi.org/10.1007/978-3-030-98404-5_16

from 13 to 17% across all specialties [1]. In April 2021, 84% of medical practitioners offered telehealth services and 57% commented they would continue to provide virtual care. Still, 54% responded not to offer telehealth service yet conduct in-person care at a 15% discount rate. Some barriers such as perceptions of data confidentiality, lack of awareness of virtual medical services, and understanding of insurance coverage remain to be addressed for the wide adaptation of telehealth. As the pandemic wanes, virtual healthcare models need to be evolved. This paper aims to introduce approaches that would assist in generalizing digital care by improving its patient interface dimension (across virtual and in-person) (Fig. 1).

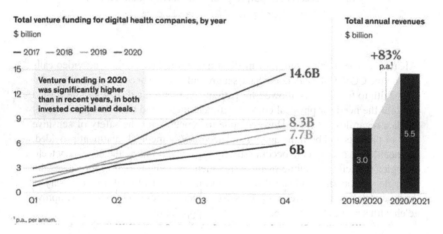

Fig. 1. A shift in digital health and the revenues of telehealth players

2   Previous Work and Existing Studies

Before discussing the necessary requisites for the wide adoption of telehealth as well as addressing the public concern, it is important to analyze the reasoning behind the situational acceptance of telehealth as well as the re-strengthening of regulative policies as the pandemic is starting to abate.

2.1   How Increased Use of Telehealth Benefited Seniors

Simplification of Medical Care. One of the compelling merits of virtual care is the convenience it brings to consumers as it saves time. In the United States, a considerable number of patients often face numerous adversities to meet a doctor immediately when they spot dubious symptoms. Without wasting time on the road or waiting to see a doctor, telehealth enables its users to see one's doctor in a state of comfort while staying in personal accommodation. This direct transaction plays a significant role in saving time, yielding additional surplus that the consumer does not have to modify their schedules. Only two levels of headings should be numbered.

Increased Accessibility to Medical Services. Another compelling benefit of tele-health service is the accessibility of health care to the broader spectrum of individuals, those who reside in the rural area where the access to medical service is limited or have difficulties physically visiting the clinic due to one's severity of symptoms.

Efficient Utilization of Medical Resources. Furthermore, telehealth has enabled effi-cient management of resources during the COVID-19 environment. Specifically, the transition from a physical to a virtual environment eliminated time-consuming processes and reduced in-person meetings [7]. This allowed for a concentration of medical staff on emergency patients, who, during the pandemic, were patients in serious condition due to the COVID-19 virus. Resources other than human resources also experienced bene-fits such as the increased availability of space, most importantly saving the numbers of hospital beds allowing prompt measures towards COVID patients.

2.2 Challenges that Telehealth Services Face

Regardless of virtual health care's ability to conduct consultations transcending the phys-ical limitations of space and time, there remain technical challenges that are challenging to be covered online. Because the entire process of consultation occurs in the digital realm, physicians inevitably confront limitations in physical examinations that would be required in order to conduct a more precise diagnosis. The current system of telehealth has its limitation due to the dearth of medical equipment, thus, it may only provide simple diagnoses or neglect the possibility of severe illness that the patients may have [6]. This assertion is supported by the study conducted by McKinsey, a management consulting firm, revealing that the specialized field utilizing telemedicine the most is psychiatry, mainly offering counseling services, not mandating physical examinations [1]. This aspect arise inquiries among the public whether the service is effective or not (Figs. 2 and 3).

Some researchers concluded that there is no conclusive evidence that telehealth brought meaningful outcomes from a clinical perspective [7]. Telehealth services have the possibility to legitimize ineffective healthcare methods, increasing risks of fragmen-tation in the established national healthcare system. The patient population data of one of the telehealth services based in England shows 89% of the patients are 18 to 39 years old with only 1% of the patients being older than 65 years indicating that the elderly popula-tion with chronic diseases who seek consultation through online means are meager. As such is the case, there are concerns that telehealth services target patients who are not as complex as those who are in dire need of medical attention. The ineffectiveness is alarm-ing not only because there is a low probability that those in need can utilize the benefits of telehealth services to their maximum potential, but also because it implies negative economic consequences for the overall health industry led by health cost inflation [7]. Additionally, such negative effects can lead to wider disparities between populations who are young, relatively healthy, and digitally literate, and the elderly population who find it challenging to utilize online medical services [7].

The shift from physical clinical visits to telehealth has introduced a supplementary obstruction on the table, security of patients' data for the protection of their privacy. Due

Share of telehealth of outpatient and office visit claims by specialty (February 2021)[1], %

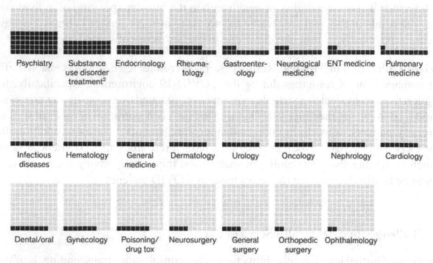

[1] Includes only evaluation and management claims; excludes emergency department, hospital inpatient, and physiatry inpatient claims; excludes certain low-volume specialties.
[2] Also includes addiction medicine and addiction treatment.

Fig. 2. Substantial variation in the share of telehealth across specialties

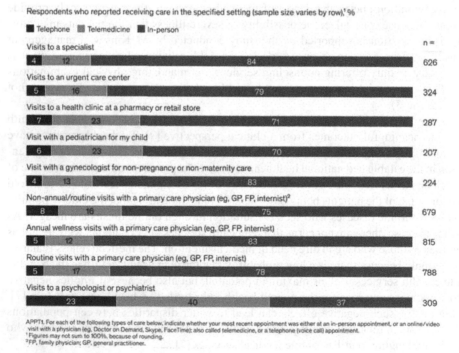

APPT1. For each of the following types of care below, indicate whether your most recent appointment was either at an in-person appointment, or an online/video visit with a physician (eg. Doctor on Demand, Skype, FaceTime); also called telemedicine, or a telephone (voice call) appointment.
[1] Figures may not sum to 100%, because of rounding.
[2] FP, family physician; GP, general practitioner.

Fig. 3. Modality of appointment by setting as of June 14, 2021

to its conflict with the Health Insurance Portability and Accountability Act (HIPAA) which requires secure communication platforms that ensure safe exchanges of sensitive patient data, health clinics have not been able to find technology platforms that comply with HIPAA. Therefore, during COVID-19, when the regulations were loosened; clinicians were not penalized for the platform they utilized "during good faith provision of telehealth [5]." Although such practical changes brought the benefits of telehealth to platforms that are widely used such as Facetime, critics raised concerns about the need to prevent security breaches after the pandemic is under control. Others remarked that revision of the HIPAA is needed to aptly adopt telehealth as a method of diagnosis and treatment by allowing patients to willingly and effectively share information that clinicians require [5].

3 Research Question

How can user experience of telehealth interfaces be enhanced to better serve the elderly population?

3.1 Reason Behind the Research Question

The question was formulated after exploring the literature review on the topic of telehealth; one of the main reasons why telehealth is criticized was that the elderly population does not participate as much as younger generations due to the former's lack of knowledge of digital platforms.

4 Methodology

4.1 Interviews

The first component is the individual interviews held through online video call platforms regarding telehealth services. Participants were either university students from different backgrounds or were the parents of the university students; the former was chosen because they are proficient in using technology while the latter was chosen to directly inquire about the research question. In total, 12 interviews were conducted from September 18 to November 12th between 6 students and 6 adults to collect data on user perceptions on telehealth services (Teladoc Health focus). The following are the questions that were asked to the interviewees:

1. Have you used any telehealth service?
2. Have you heard of Teladoc Health?
3. Would you be comfortable using a remote medical service?
4. Do you think the system will be popularized shortly?
5. How would the application change the medical system that Korea currently has?
6. Do you think it would be easy to apply the same system in Korea?

4.2 Surveys

The second component is the surveys distributed through an online environment to university students and parents. The survey displayed the interface of Teledoc (idk what company) when patients are receiving medical care. The following five questions were asked to 16 students and 14 parents who did not participate in the interview:

1. Is the interface easy to use?
2. Would you find online services to be able to serve as a suitable alternative for physical medical processes?
3. What are the reasons for the answer you provided at question 2?
4. How is the readability and visibility of texts and icons?
5. What are some features and factors that you find to be convenient?
6. What are some factors that you wish were improved?
7. What are some features that you wish were added to the service?

5 Results

5.1 Protection of Patient Privacy and Data Security

During the interview, 4 out of 6 students raised concerns of protection of patient privacy while 5 out of 6 elderly mentioned privacy as a factor of concern. Both the students and elderly were concerned about their personal data such as phone number, address, and name being leaked during the online process. One student was under the process of curing hemorrhoids and was concerned about how such can lead to social stigma if medical sessions are held in non-isolated spaces whether it has to do with family members or friends. 2 students said that they believe in the implementation of necessary technology if telehealth was to be applied in the medical industry. During the survey, 10 students and 12 seniors mentioned that online services may not be suitable because of the higher chance of data leaks. Notably, the survey showed that students have less concern about data protection during telehealth operations when compared to the elderly responders.

5.2 Visibility and Readability of User Interactions

During the interview, 5 elderlies mentioned that they believe they would not be comfortable using telehealth services because of their lack of proficiency with technology; one of the elderly said that since they have difficulties ordering a meal at fast food chain restaurants, which implemented contactless ordering during the COVID-19 pandemic, it does not seem to be ideal to rely on an electronic device to receive clinical advice. Another said that it is frightening to use telehealth because a mistake could lead to unwanted consequences and suggested that there should be preventive measures for certain functions to run in case of mistakes.

During the survey, 13 out of 16 students found that the interface was intuitive and easy to use while 6 out of 14 elders felt the same. While students said that the buttons had clear descriptions, the majority elderly respondents said there should be an option to increase font size or button sizes. In the comment section, one elder respondent suggested that the app should allow for customizable colors for a simpler personalized process.

5.3 Credibility of the Online Environment

Overall, the elderly population was not satisfied with the fact that there is no tangible interaction with the doctor which can lead to delayed observations and treatments; 5 out of 6 elderlies raised concerns about how medical professions would accurately diagnose or treat them when the treatment is being done online. 3 out of 6 students raised similar concerns, where one of them said that it is dubious whether doctors will be able to diagnose accurately through online means when there are many cases of misdiagnosis in offline clinical sessions.

In question 3 of the survey, 4 student respondents said the reliance on electronic devices for medical assessment is not credible while 11 elderly respondents concurred. 12 student respondents said that with the wide availability of smartwatches and the capabilities it has shown in constantly diagnosing irregularities, telehealth should be ready to be expand its services worldwide.

6 Implications

Based on the results of surveys and interviews, it can be concluded that the way telehealth is perceived can be evaluated in three different aspects: data security, interface, and credibility.

6.1 Data Security

As shown in the conclusion, most of the respondents of both the survey and interview were concerned for possible personal data leaks. This means that telehealth companies should strive towards usage of modern technology such as blockchain instead of simple encryptions, and should let patients know what technology they are utilizing to keep patient data secure and only between doctors and patients. This also means that telehealth companies should create their own platforms rather than using existing platforms where other users may approach the patient claiming that they are the doctors. This can become problematic especially for the elderly who are the main targets of voice phishing and are most vulnerable to fraudulent activities.

6.2 Interface

Although the student respondents did not seem to raise much problems about the interface, the elderly wished to have options on increasing font size. This should be applied because the aging of the eye can lower visibility and render it difficult to read small texts that may contain valuable instructions for the patient to proceed with their clinical sessions. As suggested by one respondent, it is also wise to add coloring options for buttons so that it speeds up the cognitive process of receiving online medical advice. This can also help the color-blind population in the future. Additionally, there should be options to resize buttons so that it is larger and more visible rather than focusing on the aesthetics; telehealth should emphasize practicality over aesthetics.

6.3   Credibility

While most medical operations are done successfully, those that don't are covered in media especially if it failed due to human error. In other words, physical clinical sessions and operations are not always successful. This raises the question of whether the online alternative is accurate. To improve these criticisms, telehealth service providers can create tools that are able to monitor without the need for physically visiting hospitals. This can either utilize existing wearable technology such as smartwatches or be created by telehealth providers themselves.

7   Conclusion

The conducted interviews and surveys revealed that despite the positive outlooks for telehealth services, there are fundamental problems that needs to be addressed before telehealth is widely implemented throughout the medical industry. Research also revealed that the recent surge of phone scams and frauds have led to increased concerns for personal privacy. Protecting sensitive information should be the basis of all telehealth services, yet it is similarly important to let patients rest assured that certain measures are taking place.

Additionally, we were able to learn that there is a need to create features that specifically addresses seniors. As suggested, the implementation of customization options for larger icons, larger fonts, and coloring buttons can be helpful for seniors to navigate the telehealth service interface. Telehealth services should further note that it should sacrifice aesthetics when it gets in the way of practicality especially for seniors.

We invite further research to be done in the area as the successful implementation of telehealth may create life-saving changes where patients can get prompt care in cases of emergencies. There are hopes that telehealth was not just a special time-limited feature during the COVID-19 pandemic; the benefits that it has shown in reaching remote places are significant.

References

1. McKinsey & Company, https://www.mckinsey.com/industries/healthcare-systems-and-ser vices/our-insights/telehealth-a-quarter-trillion-dollar-post-covid-19-reality#may29. Accessed 10 Nov 2021
2. Kuziemsky, C.: Ethics in telehealth: comparison between guidelines and practice-based experience -the case for learning health systems. Yearb. Med. Inform. 29(01), 44–50 (2020)
3. Monaghesh, E.: The role of telehealth during COVID-19 outbreak: a systematic review based on current evidence. BMC Public Health 20(1), 1193 (2020). https://doi.org/10.1186/s12889-020-09301-4
4. Nesbitt, T.S.: The evolution of telehealth: where have we been and where are we going? In: The Role of Telehealth in an Evolving Health Care Environment. The Health Resources and the Service Administration (HRSA), 8–9 August 2012, pp. 11–16. The National Academies Press (2012)
5. Shachar, C.: Implications for telehealth in a postpandemic future. JAMA 323(23), 2375 (2020)
6. AAMC.   https://www.aamc.org/news-insights/what-happens-telemedicine-after-covid-19. Accessed 10 Nov 2021
7. Wharton, G.A.: Virtual primary care: fragmentation or integration? Lancet Digit. Health 1(7), 330–331 (2019)

Intelligent Interaction and Cognitive Computing

Cognition Prediction Model for MOOCs Learners Based on ANN

Varsha T. Lokare[1,2]([⊠]), Laxman D. Netak[1], and N. S. Jadhav[1]

[1] Department of Computer Engineering, Dr Babasaheb Ambedkar Technological University, Lonere-Raigad 402103, India
varsha.lokare@ritindia.edu, {ldentak,nsjadhav}@dbatu.ac.in
[2] Rajarambapu Institute of Technology, Sakharale, India

Abstract. Massive Open Online Courses (MOOCs) are becoming increasingly popular in recent years. In a virtual world, examining the cognition processes of the students is a real hassle. The primary goal of this study is to examine the influence of MOOCs on learning. This study presents a Cognitive Model based on brain signals for predicting the most effective MOOCs video lecture. In this work, students' brain signals collected using an Electroencephalogram (EEG) device while watching MOOCs videos are used to classify their level of confusion using a publicly available dataset. The video that causes the least amount of confusion in the majority of students has been chosen as the best. This paper proposes and analyses the Cognitive Model for MOOCs Learning. A Deep Learning-based Artificial Neural Network Model has been created to predict student confusion levels. The methodology has been built using 10K fold cross-validation and shown to be 97% accurate in predicting students' misunderstandings while watching MOOCs videos. The proposed Cognitive Model will aid in the evaluation of MOOCs course performance.

Keywords: Massive Open Online Courses (MOOCs) ·
Electroencephalogram (EEG) · Cognitive model · Confusion level ·
Artificial Neural Network (ANN)

1 Introduction

The efficiency of online courses must be evaluated. The physiological factors that are measured have a direct impact on the learning process. As a result, the quality of MOOCs videos has been measured in this article by recording students' brain waves while they view them. For the purpose of this research, MOOCs in basic algebra, physics, and quantum theory were evaluated. An ANN-based prediction model has been used to forecast the amount of misunderstanding among learners. As shown in Fig. 1, if students display no uncertainty while watching a MOOCs course video, it is expected that the course will aid in the learning process.

Varsha T. Lokare—Presently working as an Assistant Professor, Rajarambapu Institute of Technology, Sakharale, Affiliated to Shivaji University, Kolhapur.

© Springer Nature Switzerland AG 2022
J.-H. Kim et al. (Eds.): IHCI 2021, LNCS 13184, pp. 173–183, 2022.
https://doi.org/10.1007/978-3-030-98404-5_17

A method for measuring the quality of MOOCs videos has been suggested, as illustrated in Fig. 2. It records students' brain waves while they view MOOCs videos. The preprocessed frequency bands, namely Alpha, Beta, Gamma, Delta, and Theta, along with the attention and mediation parameters, were provided as an input to the ANN-based Confusion prediction model. The video with the least amount of confusion has been useful in the learning process based on the value returned by the model.

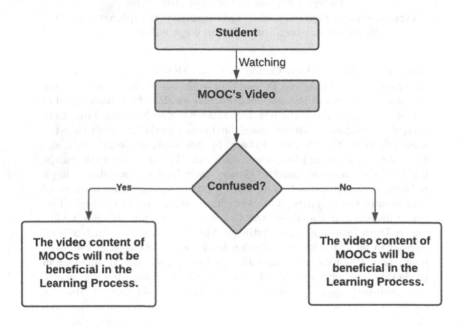

Fig. 1. The impact of misconception on learning through MOOCs

2   Earlier Approach

The assessment of online learning processes using EEG [2,14] has been the subject of many studies. Kahneman's two-systems model had proposed by Arvind W Kiwelekar et al. [8] as a framework for understanding the computational cognitive process. An intelligent learning system based on EEG had created by Aaditya Sharma et al. [16]. It can track the students' attention levels and offer live comments. Haohan Wang et al. [19] proposed an EEG-based algorithm that can predict students' confusion when viewing MOOCs. Amirhessam Tahmassebi et al. [18] created an online system to use EEG signals to improve MOOC performance. For the optimization, they used the Genetic algorithm. S. Kavitha et al. [7] presented a methodology that uses deep learning algorithms to estimate the cognitive capacity of online learners. Rong Gu et al. [3] used EEG to

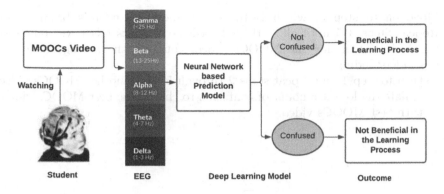

Fig. 2. Proposed Moocs video quality measurement system

analyze MOOC learning, which might assist in rationally designing online courses. Based on EEG, Haoyan Xu et al. [20] suggested arousal of brain detection during MOOC learning. They also offered a plan for adjusting the situation as per the outputs received from the model. With EEG equipment, Furen Lin and Chien-min Kuo [9] proposed a system to record and analyze a user's mental state while watching MOOCs video. Zhaoheng Ni et al. [12] have used EEG to infer the misconception using a Bidirectional LSTM Recurrent Neural Network. Swadha Gupta and Parteek Kumar [5] suggested an EEG-based attention detection system for an online platform. Furthermore, there has been a lot of studies done on quantifying cognitive load while completing various tasks [6,10,11,13,17]. Following this research, we proposed a cognitive model of MOOCs learning in this work.

3   Overview of the Model

A cognitive model and algorithm developed for the prediction of compelling MOOCs videos. The subsections outline the features of the proposed model. To predict the efficiency of MOOCs videos using brain waves acquired during the viewing of the specific video, the cognitive model proposed as shown in Fig. 3. This model includes the stages listed below.

1. Select a video lecture from the Moocs collection.
2. Use EEG equipment to record the student's brain waves while watching the MOOC video.
3. Feed the preprocessed frequency bands to the confusion level prediction model.
4. The ANN-based confusion prediction model returns the confusion value. i.e., if there is no confusion, the value is 0; if there is confusion, the value is 1.

5. Move on to step 2, which is to record another student's brain waves. Repeat Steps 3–5 until all of the selected participants (N) have completed the tasks. Then, for the MOOCs video, compute the average degree of misunderstanding.
6. Return to step 1 and repeat steps 2 through 5 with another MOOCs video. Calculate the lowest amount of confusion to choose the best MOOCs video.
7. Return best MOOCs video.

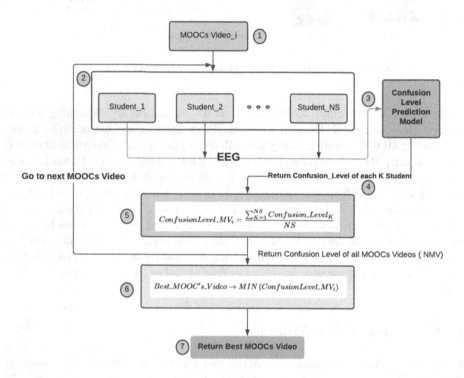

Fig. 3. Proposed cognitive model

3.1 Proposed Algorithm

The proposed algorithm is the cognitive model's algorithmic representation. The model's inputs are the number of students and the number of MOOCs videos. The average of confusion levels does consider to measure the efficiency of each MOOC's video. The amount of uncertainty is determined using an ANN-based confusion prediction model. The cognitive model's result will be the MOOCs video with the least amount of confusion.

INPUT:
NS= Number of Students
NMV= Number of MOOC's Videos

OUTPUT:
Best_MOOC's_Video

ALGORITHM : BEST MOOC's VIDEO Selection(NS, NMV)

Step 1: For each MOOCs Video i to NMV (i = 1 to NMV)
      Confusion_Level_MV_i = 0
          For each Student K to NS (k=1 to NS)
               Confusion_Level_MV_i += Call Confusion_Level(MV_i,K)

Step 2: Calculate Confusion Level of each MOOC's Video

$$ConfusionLevel\_MV_i = \frac{\sum_{K=1}^{NS} Confusion\_Level_K}{NS} \tag{1}$$

Step 3: Compute the MOOC's Video with Minimum Confusion Level

$$Best\_MOOC's\_Video \rightarrow MIN\left(ConfusionLevel\_MV_i\right) \tag{2}$$

Step 4: Return Best_MOOC's_Video

FUNCTION: Confusion_Level(MV_i, K)
{
      Apply Proposed ANN_Model(MV_i, K)
      IF Confusion_Level = 0
          Return 0
      ELSE
          Return 1
}

3.2 ANN-Based Confusion Prediction Model

The brain's biological structure has inspired the Artificial Neural Network (ANN) model, which investigates human cognition. The physical neural network is how a person's nervous system operates and allows complicated actions carried out spontaneously. As a result, the student's cognitive process while watching MOOCs videos was studied using ANN in this article. As shown in Fig. 4, the ANN model predicts the students' state of confusion after viewing the MOOCs video. If there is no uncertainty in the students' minds after seeing a given MOOCs Video, the model returns 0. If there is a misconception, it returns a value of 1.

The following stages had taken when developing a deep ANN model:

1. Create a sequential model.
2. One by one, add many Dense layers. One layer's output becomes the subsequent layer's input. Model sets the weights and biases and links the output of one layer to the input of the next. Only the number of nodes in each layer and the activation function need to be specified.
3. Use an optimizer and a loss function to compile your model.
4. Analyze the dataset and fit the model.

To begin, we have created a layer with 13 input nodes and a relu activation function. Next, used relu activation to add a first hidden layer with eight nodes. Then applied relu activation to build a second hidden layer with eight nodes. Finally, added the last layer, which consists of one node and sigmoid activation.

ANN-Based Model():
```
model = Sequential()
model.add(Dense(13, input_dim=13, activation='relu'))
model.add(Dense(8, activation='relu'))
model.add(Dense(8, activation='relu'))
model.add(Dense(1, activation='sigmoid'))
model.compile(loss='binary_crossentropy', optimizer='adam', metrics=['accuracy'])
```

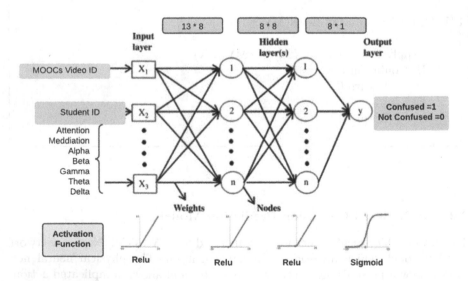

Fig. 4. Neural network based confusion prediction model

4   Model Development

4.1   Dataset Description

The data has gathered by collecting EEG signals from 10 college students as they watched MOOCs videos, as shown in Table 1. Fundamental algebra or geometry introductory videos have looked less perplexing, but Quantum Mechanics and Stem Cell Research videos are pretty confusing. Each video lasted around two minutes. The students wore a single-channel wireless MindSet that monitored frontal brain activity. After each session, the student evaluated their degree of bewilderment on a scale of one to seven, with one being the least confusing and seven indicating the most confusing. These labels are standardized to indicate whether or not the learners are perplexed.

The dataset is publicly available on the link
https://www.kaggle.com/wanghaohan/confused-eeg.

Table 1. Experimental work

Dataset description	EEG signals have been collected from ten college students while they viewed MOOC video snippets.
Number of students	10
Number of MOOCs videos	10
EEG device	Single-channel wireless mindset
MOOCs videos	Algebra and geometry, quantum physics, stem cell research
Input features	Subject ID, video ID, attention, meditation, raw, theta, alpha, beta, gamma, delta
Output features	User defined confusion level and predefined confusion level confused = 1, not confused = 0
Deep learning model	Artificial neural network
Measuring parameters	1. Accuracy 2. Loss
Cross validation	10K fold
Train test split	Random (train split = 70%, test split = 30%)

4.2   Parameters for Measuring Performance

1. Accuracy:
This approach had used to measure the accuracy of a classification model [4]. The number of predictions when the anticipated value matches the real value is known as accuracy. For a specific sample, it's binary (true/false). The proportion of correct predictions to total predictions is known as the correct prediction ratio. The accuracy measure is considered to calculate the proportion of correct predictions delivered out of all forecasts.

2. Loss:

A loss function, sometimes called a cost function, considers the probability or uncertainty of a forecast depending on how far it differs from the actual value [15]. Unlike accuracy, the loss is the total errors produced for each sample in the training or validation sets. A casualty has been frequently utilized in the training process to identify the "best" parameter values (e.g., weights in a neural network). The training procedure aims to reduce this value. The degree of misinterpretation prediction is a binary classification issue, as students will either be confused or not be confused when seeing the MOOCs video. The binary cross-entropy/log loss is an expected loss function for binary classifications like the one we're looking. Confused = 1 and Not confused = 0 are the labels for output(y). For every N inputs, P(y) is the anticipated chance of the point being confused.

$$Loss = -\frac{1}{N} \sum_{i=1}^{N} y_i \cdot log(P(y_i)) + (1 - y_i) \cdot log(P(1 - y_i))) \qquad (3)$$

It is shown from Eq. (3) that for each confused point (y = 1), the loss increased by log(p(y)), which is the log-likelihood of it being confused.

4.3   Results and Observations

Initially, a random Train/Test Split has used to train and test the ANN model. The model was designed using two and three hidden layers, respectively, as illustrated in Figs. 5 and 6. The accuracy of an ANN model with two hidden layers in estimating a student's misunderstanding is 76.32%. In comparison, the accuracy of an ANN model with three hidden layers in predicting a student's misconception is 77.30%. In addition, when comparing two hidden layered ANN models, the loss parameter in the three hidden layered ANN models has a lower score. Another typical approach for assessing the performance of a deep learning algorithm is the k-fold cross-validation procedure. The accuracy increases by about 20% after using cross validation [1] of 10K fold, as seen in Fig. 7. Specifically, an ANN-based model with 10K cross-validation successfully predicts students' misconceptions while viewing MOOC videos with 97% accuracy. The loss value has also decreased significantly from 0.5 to 0.005. It has been observed that re-sampling using cross-validation improves the model's performance since it eliminates overfitting and is based on Monte Carlo techniques (Table 2).

Table 2. Values of accuracy and loss parameters

Performance measuring parameters	ANN with 2 hidden layers	ANN with 3 hidden layers	10K fold cross validation
Accuracy	76.32%	77.30%	97%
Loss	0.503	0.48	0.005

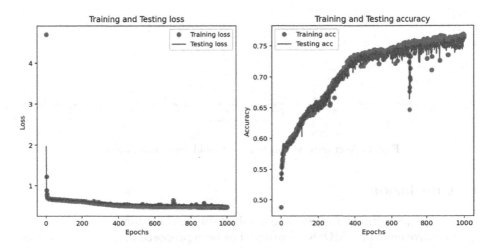

Fig. 5. Accuracy & loss: 2 hidden layer ANN

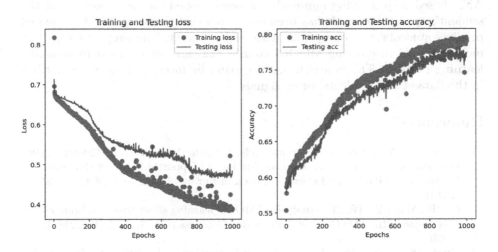

Fig. 6. Accuracy & loss: 3 hidden layer ANN

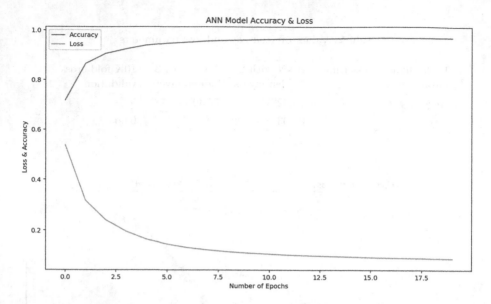

Fig. 7. Accuracy & loss with 10K fold cross validation

5 Conclusion

In an online platform, it isn't easy to monitor students' learning progress. Hence, the cognitive model for MOOCs learning has been proposed and analyzed in this work. The proposed approach will aid in the creation of MOOCs courses that will assist in the learning process. During the viewing of MOOCs videos, the EEG signals of 10 students were recorded and analyzed for research purposes. The ANN-based deep learning approach has been applied for the prediction of the student's misconception. It has been discovered that the suggested ANN model predicts students' misconceptions with 97% accuracy. The proposed cognitive model will aid in creating MOOCs courses that are personalized to students' learning progress. This research might expand by incorporating more MOOCs in the dataset and students' brain signals.

References

1. Browne, M.W.: Cross-validation methods. J. Math. Psychol. **44**(1), 108–132 (2000)
2. Dos Santos, A.I., Punie, Y., Castaño-Muñoz, J.: Opportunities and challenges for the future of MOOCs and open education in Europe. Books to MOOC, pp. 81–91 (2016)
3. Gu, R., Yang, Y., Wu, T.: Analysis of MOOC learning effect based on brain cognition research. In: 2020 Chinese Automation Congress (CAC), pp. 5240–5244. IEEE (2020)
4. Gupta, S., Zhang, W., Wang, F.: Model accuracy and runtime tradeoff in distributed deep learning: a systematic study. In: 2016 IEEE 16th International Conference on Data Mining (ICDM), pp. 171–180. IEEE (2016)

5. Gupta, S., Kumar, P.: Attention recognition system in online learning platform using EEG signals. In: Bora, P.K., Nandi, S., Laskar, S. (eds.) Emerging Technologies for Smart Cities. LNEE, vol. 765, pp. 139–152. Springer, Singapore (2021). https://doi.org/10.1007/978-981-16-1550-4_15
6. Jadhav, N., Manthalkar, R., Joshi, Y.: Analysis of effect of meditation on cognitive load using higher order crossing features. In: International Conference on Communication and Signal Processing 2016 (ICCASP 2016) (2016)
7. Kavitha, S., Mohanavalli, S., Bharathi, B.: Predicting learning behaviour of online course learners' using hybrid deep learning model. In: 2018 IEEE 6th International Conference on MOOCs, Innovation and Technology in Education (MITE), pp. 98–102. IEEE (2018)
8. Kiwelekar, A.W., Navandar, S., Yadav, D.K.: A two-systems perspective for computational thinking. In: Singh, M., Kang, D.-K., Lee, J.-H., Tiwary, U.S., Singh, D., Chung, W.-Y. (eds.) IHCI 2020. LNCS, vol. 12615, pp. 3–11. Springer, Cham (2021). https://doi.org/10.1007/978-3-030-68449-5_1
9. Lin, F.-R., Kao, C.-M.: Mental effort detection using EEG data in e-learning contexts. Comput. Educ. **122**, 63–79 (2018)
10. Lokare, V.T., Netak, L.D.: Concentration level prediction system for the students based on physiological measures using the EEG device. In: Singh, M., Kang, D.-K., Lee, J.-H., Tiwary, U.S., Singh, D., Chung, W.-Y. (eds.) IHCI 2020. LNCS, vol. 12615, pp. 24–33. Springer, Cham (2021). https://doi.org/10.1007/978-3-030-68449-5_3
11. Mayer, R.E., Moreno, R.: Nine ways to reduce cognitive load in multimedia learning. Educ. Psychol. **38**(1), 43–52 (2003)
12. Ni, Z., Yuksel, A.C., Ni, X., Mandel, M.I., Xie, L.: Confused or not confused? Disentangling brain activity from EEG data using bidirectional LSTM recurrent neural networks. In: Proceedings of the 8th ACM International Conference on Bioinformatics, Computational Biology, and Health Informatics, pp. 241–246 (2017)
13. Paas, F., Tuovinen, J.E., Tabbers, H., Van Gerven, P.W.: Cognitive load measurement as a means to advance cognitive load theory. Educ. Psychol. **38**(1), 63–71 (2003)
14. Powell, S., Yuan, L.: MOOCs and open education: implications for higher education (2013)
15. Rolinek, M., Martius, G.: L4: practical loss-based stepsize adaptation for deep learning. arXiv preprint arXiv:1802.05074 (2018)
16. Sharma, A., Gupta, S., Kaur, S., Kumar, P.: Smart learning system based on EEG signals. In: Singh, M., Gupta, P.K., Tyagi, V., Flusser, J., Ören, T., Kashyap, R. (eds.) ICACDS 2019. CCIS, vol. 1046, pp. 465–476. Springer, Singapore (2019). https://doi.org/10.1007/978-981-13-9942-8_44
17. Sweller, J.: Cognitive load theory. In: Psychology of Learning and Motivation, vol. 55, pp. 37–76. Elsevier (2011)
18. Tahmassebi, A., Gandomi, A.H., Meyer-Baese, A.: An evolutionary online framework for MOOC performance using EEG data. In: 2018 IEEE Congress on Evolutionary Computation (CEC), pp. 1–8. IEEE (2018)
19. Wang, H., Li, Y., Hu, X., Yang, Y., Meng, Z., Chang, K.M.: Using EEG to improve massive open online courses feedback interaction. In: AIED Workshops (2013)
20. Xu, H., Xu, X.: Megrez: MOOC-oriented EEG-based arousal of brain detection and adjustment scheme. In: 2019 IEEE Global Engineering Education Conference (EDUCON), pp. 1011–1016. IEEE (2019)

A Novel Methodology for Assessing and Modeling Manufacturing Processes: A Case Study for the Metallurgical Industry

Reschke Jan[1], Gallego-García Diego[2], Gallego-García Sergio[2]([✉]) [ID],
and García-García Manuel[2]

[1] SMS Group GmbH, 41069 Mönchengladbach, Germany
[2] UNED, 28040 Madrid, Spain
gallego101090@gmail.com

Abstract. Historically, researchers and practitioners have often failed to consider all the areas, factors, and implications of a process within an integrated manufacturing model. Thus, the aim of this research was to propose a holistic approach to manufacturing processes to assess their status and performance. Moreover, using the conceptual model, manufacturing systems can be modelled, considering all areas, flows, and factors in the respective areas of production, maintenance, and quality. As a result, the model serves as the basis for the integral management and control of manufacturing systems in digital twin models for the regulation of process stability and quality with maintenance strategies. Thus, a system dynamics simulation model based on the conceptual model is developed for a metallurgical process. The results show how the monitoring of all flows together with the optimal strategies in the quality and maintenance areas enable companies to increase their profitability and customer service level. In conclusion, the conceptual approach and the applied simulation case study allow better decision making, ensuring continuous optimization along the manufacturing asset lifecycle, and providing a unique selling proposition for equipment producers and service engineering suppliers as well as industrial companies.

Keywords: Integrated manufacturing model · Manufacturing process management and control · Quality management · Maintenance management · System dynamics · Simulation · Digital twin · Industry 4.0 · Metallurgical case study

1 Introduction

At present, manufacturing is still a key factor in the global economy [1]. Industrial value chains are evolving rapidly. In this context, companies need to adapt them-selves to allow mass customization and achieve low prices for products with shorter product lifecycles [2, 3]. Furthermore, the level of market uncertainty is higher than ever due to the events resulting from Industry 4.0, the COVID-19 pandemic, and global economic crises. Thus, the adaptability of manufacturing supply chains is a key aspect of companies' success

© Springer Nature Switzerland AG 2022
J.-H. Kim et al. (Eds.): IHCI 2021, LNCS 13184, pp. 184–197, 2022.
https://doi.org/10.1007/978-3-030-98404-5_18

[3]. Therefore, organizations need to rethink their production process with the use of digital technologies [4].

Manufacturing companies are currently dealing with the issue of how to process increasing flows of data [5]. In this regard, digital twins (DT) are a tool that have been proven to be effective in supporting the evaluation and control of manufacturing systems [6] and that help to increase flexibility and robustness to unexpected conditions [7] of the manufacturing system. At the same time, if DTs are combined with computing capabilities, new functionalities can be provided to management processes and support systems [8]. Moreover, the use of a DT model allows us to represent the current status of the manufacturing system and to perform real-time optimizations, decision making, and predictive maintenance according to the actual condition of the system. Research on digital twins is still in its initial stage, and there is a need for future research in this area [7] based on real-time synchronized simulations of production system operations [9].

Although several modeling methodologies have been proposed in the last two decades, so far, no methodology that could serve as a framework to model, design, analyze, and optimize manufacturing systems has been proposed [10]. As a result of this, and despite the evolution of industrial processes, existing manufacturing models do not consider all factors that are relevant to the fourth industrial revolution and do not consider the influence of key indicators of manufacturing quality and performance. Thus, current manufacturing modeling methodologies have not achieved the level of Industry 4.0 [11] and it is therefore necessary to model self-organized manufacturing systems [12] that can address all interactions and interrelationships [13]. Therefore, the new elements, relevant factors, and systems of the third and fourth industrial revolution have not yet been fully integrated in a model to provide a framework for the management and control of a manufacturing process in both present-day and future manufacturing systems. In this regard, the fourth industrial revolution promise to transform the manufacturing process and its management. However, many models of the manufacturing process and quality control are based on hardware quantity and quality and do not pay attention to information flows, money flows, and energy flows; these all have a significant influence on key indicators but have not yet been integrated in a manufacturing model. Thus, the aim of this research is to propose a holistic approach for manufacturing processes that can be used to assess the status of a manufacturing system as well as the impact of changes in the target indicators. The result is an integrated manufacturing model aligned with the fourth industrial revolution that considers all relevant areas and factors influencing the manufacturing process and its output indicators, including product quality and the condition of the manufacturing system or machine. This model enables us to predict the outcomes of the process based on input variables. It is used to increase the planning capability and, therefore, the process stability, as well as providing the continuous optimization of the expected variables based on real data.

2   Theoretical Fundamentals

A manufacturing system is an integration of resources that can carry out one or more production activities [1]; all manufacturing systems have in common the fact that they process material to give it a new functionality [17]. The sustainable market success of products requires an increase in quality level and the definition of quality can be extended to include production factors. Moreover, while current systems are optimized toward a set of target parameters, self-optimizing systems need to be optimized in terms of product quality; expert knowledge is required to achieve this goal [17].

For the conceptual and simulations models, systems theory, and modeling as the representation of a real-world scenario as well as system dynamics simulation are used. The use of simulation for manufacturing system design and analysis is recognized by scientists and industrial managers [18].

3   Conceptual Model Development

The aim of this study is to provide a conceptual model that enables the assessment of manufacturing operations with transparency regarding the areas, flows, and factors involved as well as the predictive, preventive, and corrective measures to deal with potential failure modes of the system. Moreover, the conceptual model seeks to serve as a basis for digital twin models and systems for assessing, managing, monitoring, and for improving decision making in manufacturing systems.

3.1   Delimitation of the Model and Methodological Approach

The conceptual model pursues the goal to provide a "total" conceptual model and "total" simulation to provide a global evaluation and support tool for managers and planning employees addressing the challenges of managing and controlling manufacturing processes with all potential elements of the fourth industrial revolution. The steps performed to develop the model for a generic manufacturing system are as follows:

1. Identification of areas and flows.
2. Breakdown and classification of areas into input, process, output, or other elements.
3. Definition of the factors in each area or flow.
4. Development of the conceptual framework for a generic manufacturing process.
5. Generation of a casual loop diagram (CLD) to represent the interrelationships among relevant factors.
6. Methodology for the application of the conceptual model to assess specific manufacturing processes: manufacturing process case study.

3.2   Identification of Areas and Flows that Have an Influence on the Manufacturing Process

A manufacturing process depends on several flows [15]; without these flows, opera-tions are not possible or will be limited. Furthermore, these flows that enable manufacturing operations to be carried out were developed over the course of different industrial revolutions. Each flow has a set of indicators that determine the effective-ness and efficiency of the flow. Furthermore, if the flow is not working or has operating limitations, the manufacturing process indicators will be influenced and, therefore, its stability and ability to produce products at the required quality level will also be affected. Based on the literature, the following flows are considered in this research: money flow, information flow, material flow, capital equipment flow, energy flow, human resource flow, order flow, maintenance management and control, manufacturing process, and quality management and control.

3.3 Classification of Manufacturing Process Areas

Figure 1 describes the manufacturing process input–output diagram, in which various different areas can be identified:

- Inputs: these include information, material, money, and energy flows.
- Process: factors such as human resources functions, information flows from IT systems, and maintenance functions are relevant during this process.
- Regulation mechanisms: this refers to the functional elements that will ensure the optimization of the process in the future while securing its stability. This includes the maintenance, quality management, and control functions; process design and optimization; and other order flow decisions that influence the current and future system states.
- Finally, the output areas are obtained - i.e., information, material, money, and energy flows. Furthermore, an important output is the quality control of the output according to quality requirements as well as the six goals of logistics [19].

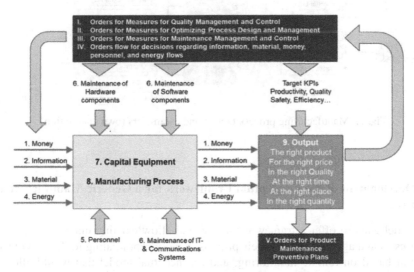

Fig. 1. Diagram of the manufacturing process: areas & flows including decisions/orders (own elaboration).

3.4 Factors and Parameters in Each Area of the Manufacturing Process

After identifying the manufacturing process areas, the identification of parameters and factors that have an impact on the manufacturing process within each of the areas is carried out. For the nine areas, a representative selection of factors related to them is given. Therefore, a representative selection of manufacturing process factors and parameters shown in Fig. 2 that are related to the above-mentioned areas and flows is as follows:

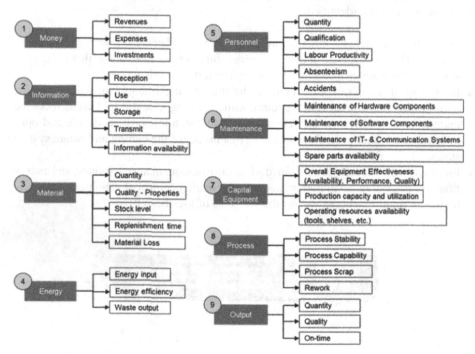

Fig. 2. Manufacturing process factors and parameters (own elaboration).

3.5 Development of the Conceptual Framework for a Generic Manufacturing Process

The model aims to offer a framework that would allow existing manufacturing organizations to manage and control their processes, a concept relating to the servitization potential based on remote monitoring, and a conceptual model that would allow the integration of the real and physical worlds with regulation and self-optimization mechanisms. The model considers all of the flows and areas covered in the previous subchapters. The framework shown in Fig. 3 describes the order in which the different manufacturing process areas are considered in the model. First, the generic process is explained. This consists of five steps: first, whether the company has the necessary means to cover the expenses of the manufacturing operations is deter-mined; second, the preparation and distribution of the planning information needed to specify the required details to plan, monitor, and control the required operations are carried out; third, the required production factors—i.e., material, energy, and hu-man resources—are prepared for the process; fourth, the process is performed, where process stability is key to obtaining the final output product in the fifth step. After describing the generic five steps of the conceptual framework, the differences be-tween the flow of a manufacturing process carried out before the third and fourth industrial revolutions and the flow of current industrial processes can be compared. Due to the fact that many differences exist as a result of the industrial revolutions and the development of production systems, this study focuses on the manufacturing process. Six main differences are syndicated in Fig. 3:

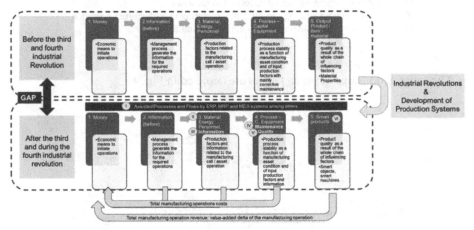

Fig. 3. Conceptual framework for a generic manufacturing process over the industrial revolutions (own elaboration).

From the perspective of the control engineer, the smart factory can be viewed as a closed-loop system [12]. The traditional production line aims to produce a single type of product in an input–output process without a controller or the need for self-regulation. The first-order cybernetic principle introduces an independent controller to the manufacturing process, but there is barely any communication between machines and there is no capability for self-optimization. On the other hand, a manufacturing system within a smart factory aims to produce several products [12] within a self-optimizing production system.

3.6 Interrelationships and Casual Loop Diagrams (CLDs)

Between the areas and factors of any manufacturing process are mutual or direction-al impacts. Table 1 depicts the interrelationships among areas. In this table, the columns are influenced by the lines; that is, the lined areas influence the columns according to the legend below the table.

Table 1. Interrelationships among areas.

No.	Areas	Money	Information	Material	Energy	Personnel	Maintenance	Process	Equipment	Output
1	Money	■	X							
2	Information	[X]	■	X	X	X	X	X	X	X
3	Material		(X)	■				X		X
4	Energy		(X)		■			X		
5	Personnel	(X)				■	X	X		
6	Maintenance		(X)				■	X		
7	Process			(X)	(X)	(X)	(X)	■	(X)	X
8	Capital Equipment	(X)	(X)				(X)	X	■	

[X]: Before manufacturing activities related to the asset.
X: Related to manufacturing activities before/during manufacturing operation.
(X): Feedback of the system related to manufacturing activity.

The interrelationships between factors are depicted in Fig. 4:

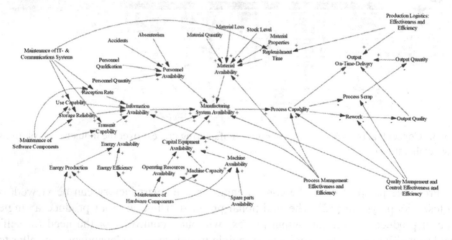

Fig. 4. Casual-loop diagram (CLD) for the manufacturing process factors (own elaboration)

4   Manufacturing Process Case Study

4.1   Design of the Case Study for a Metallurgical Process

The simulation was performed with 250 time periods, each representing one production day. Secondly, the manufacturing system structure was set to apply the conceptual model and to simulate it under certain conditions. The structure consists of a steel-making manufacturer producing shot-peened round bars. The system consists of warehouses of raw materials and finished products in addition to their production facilities. Finally, end-customers are at the end receiving the products shown in Fig. 5:

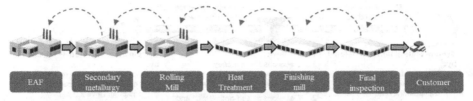

Fig. 5. Manufacturing system of the metallurgical case study (own elaboration).

4.2 Key Performance Indicators (KPIs) for the Case Study

The KPIs for the simulation case study are:

- $\sum$ Demand (tons)
- $\emptyset$ Money availability (%)
- $\emptyset$ Information availability (%)
- $\emptyset$ Material availability (%)
- $\emptyset$ Energy availability (%)
- $\emptyset$ Personnel availability (%)
- $\emptyset$ Capital Equipment availability (%)
- $\emptyset$ OEE (%)
- $\emptyset$ Availability rate (%)
- $\emptyset$ Performance rate (%)
- $\emptyset$ Quality rate (%)
- Labor productivity (tons/empl.*day)
- Process capability (Cpk)
- $\emptyset$ WIP stock (Mio. tons)
- On-time delivery (%)

4.3 Simulation Logic for Assessing the Manufacturing Process

To assess a manufacturing system, first, it is necessary to determine the state of the manufacturing process, i.e., its areas, factors, and parameters, based on real data if possible. Secondly, an organization should understand how the manufacturing system evolves over time. In this regard, Fig. 6 provides how the system develops from a certain system state n to a system state n + 1. As a result, the manufacturing system state, and the output indicators of period n + 1 are determined by the system state at time n and the decisions or order flow related to the levels, self-optimization, or/and goal adjustments determining the output indicators.

After determining how the system evolves over time, the third step is to identify the priorities of the system in which an improvement toward the goals can be achieved to focus on activities with higher impact on the overall manufacturing system. Because of the third step, the conceptual model provides the following statement: "For a manufacturing process to take place, it is needed to secure the money flow; it is fundamental to prepare and provide the necessary information about the management and technical conditions of the process, including the technical parameters, the energy needed, and the

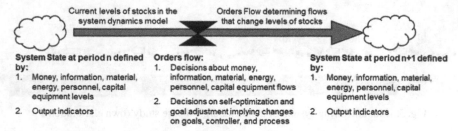

Fig. 6. Manufacturing system state in different periods: decisions from stock and flows (own elaboration)

material input required. Moreover, it is key to describe and coordinate the availability of the required human resources in quantity and qualification as well as to describe and provide the necessary capital equipment, such as machine and tools". The previous conditions first determine whether the resource area is needed; if yes, then it is determined if it is available as required, and if no, then the process regarding this resource is prepared. By conducting this for all resources, it can be determined whether the manufacturing process can initiate and perform its activity with all of the resources needed. Thus, the following formula lead to the manufacturing system availability:

System Availability = Money Availability × Information Availability × Material Availability × Energy Availability × Personnel

Availability × Capital Equipment availability × 100%,

$$(1)$$

4.4 Simulation Models

The three scenarios can be differentiated by the following characteristics:

1. Manufacturing process system modeling:

   a. Input–output process without controller or regulation.
   b. First-order cybernetics.
   c. Second-order cybernetics.

2. Maintenance policy:

   a. Corrective.
   b. Preventive.
   c. Predictive.

3. Quality control:

   a. Without adjustments.
   b. With adjustments.
   c. Predictive adjustments based on self-regulation.

4. Areas in focus:

   a. Only material flow area is in focus.
   b. All areas are in focus.

Based on the previous four characteristics, the simulation models can be described as shown in Fig. 7:

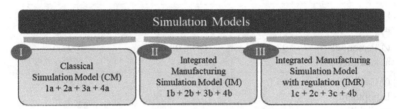

Fig. 7. Simulation models (own elaboration)

4.5 Simulation Results

After a validation with extreme-tests evaluation, scenarios for the simulation case study are generated based on different patterns and values of customer demand over 1 year with 250 periods of working days. Different scenarios with various demand patterns as well as disruptions for the flows were simulated. As a result, all of them show the same trend between the three models. Therefore, the results are shown exemplarily for one scenario for the three simulation models. As shown in Table 2, the third model presents better results than those of the second model, and the second model presents better results for all relevant indicators than those of the classical simulation model. The results show how the IM increases the OTD of the CM by 50% through the improvement of the availability and performance rates by almost 20% and the quality rate by more than 10%, leading to an OEE value that is almost double the OEE of the CM. While the IM enables the manufacturing system to reach acceptable indicator levels, the IMR helps the system to achieve excellence by attaining a 98% quality rate through the use of a more stable process. Moreover, the OEE of the IMR is more than 20% higher than the IM, leading to an OTD of more than 95%.

Table 2. Simulation results.

No.	Key indicator	1. Classical Simulation Model (CM)	2. Integrated Manufacturing Simulation Model (IM)	3. Integrated Manufacturing Simulation Model with Regulation (IMR)
1	$\sum$ Demand (tons)	608,660	608,660	608,660
2	Ø Money availability (%)	100	100	100
3	Ø Information availability (%)	91.0	93.8	95.8
3	Ø Material availability (%)	93.1	96.0	100
4	Ø Energy availability (%)	91.0	93.8	95.8
6	Ø Personnel availability (%)	93.1	98.0	98.0
7	Ø Capital Equipment availability (%)	65.0	84.0	89.0
8	Ø OEE (%)	28.7	53.1	74.1
9	Ø Availability rate (%)	46.6	63.4	80.0
10	Ø Performance rate (%)	74.6	92.3	94.3
11	Ø Quality rate (%)	82.1	92.9	98.0
12	Labor productivity (tons/empl.*day)	0.91	1.86	1.96
13	Process capability (Cpk)	0.83	1.33	2.00
14	Ø WIP stock (Mio. tons)	23.7	37.8	37.9
15	On-time delivery (%)	32.1	84.3	95.4

5 Discussion

Based on the conceptual model developed, an organization must make decisions regarding its manufacturing system while bearing in mind four areas: focus, which takes into account resource areas; scope, which takes into account factors and inter-relationships; organizational structure, which considers how to include the control, assessment, and improvement of the manufacturing process in its functional structure; and development strategy, which considers Industry 4.0 in sequence or in parallel with quality, maintenance, and production logistics improvements.

Finally, the methodological steps to assess and improve manufacturing systems are shown in Fig. 8:

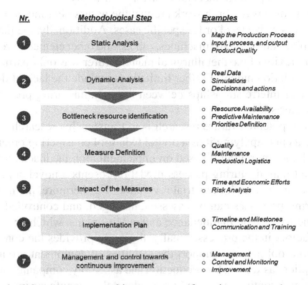

Fig. 8. Methodology to assess and improve manufacturing systems (own elaboration)

This methodology can be applied with sensors and a digital twin model of all are-as, factors, parameters, and interrelationships, enabling a simulation to improve the overall system performance and the managerial decision making. Moreover, this methodology enables condition monitoring to be carried out at the levels of the network, plant, production line, manufacturing cell, and machine. Thus, global transparency can be achieved, enabling the quick identification of the system state, bottlenecks, and risks, as well as potential measures for improvement. On this basis, new business models based on services can be generated to design, manage, control, and improve the manufacturing process and its related areas, flows, and factors.

6 Conclusions and Future Outlook

This paper provides a conceptual model that includes guidelines and steps to follow in order to successfully apply the approach in real manufacturing systems. Moreover, the current challenges faced by manufacturing systems were described and the areas, factors, parameters, and their interrelationships were defined for a generic manufacturing system. In addition, the relevant differences between the industrial revolutions were identified in an attempt to develop strategies for improving manufacturing-related issues. Based on this, a new concept using industrial dynamics was developed and steps used for assessing a manufacturing system were described. Therefore, the application of a conceptual model to digital twin models could become a key strategy in managerial decision making.

Furthermore, to prove the utility of this new concept, a simulation example for a metallurgical manufacturing system was created by applying system dynamics. The benefits of the change from an input–output process to a self-optimizing production system are a global optimization, an increase of the manufacturing system availability, product quality, system performance, and delivery reliability.

The limitations of this research work are that the assessment methodology was not developed for the operative level or for specific cases. Additionally, the individual interactions that take place among staff, machines, robots, and other elements were not considered and the complexity of the metallurgical manufacturer was only partially taken into account in the simulation model. Further limitations include the lack of detail included in the mathematical interrelationships between the manufacturing process parameters and quality characteristics.

As a result, the potential future research is to transfer this research method to real production systems and applying it as a digital twin tool considering organization units within the model and improving it based on implementation feedbacks.

The integrated manufacturing process model represents a novel approach to serve as a guide model for the fourth industrial revolution. Furthermore, the model describes how manufacturing processes can be assessed, managed, and controlled in an integral way allowing one to develop maintenance and quality plans, which enable the prediction of critical factors in the process. Finally, the study provides the conceptual model and the simulation tool that can support the activities of equipment producers, service engineering suppliers as well as for production and assembly companies allowing better decision making and continuous optimization along the manufacturing asset lifecycle. As a result, the proposed methodology represents a useful tool for organizations and managers in order to increase their efficiency, competitiveness and, therefore, viability over time allowing also to develop their traditional business models.

References

1. Qin, J., Liu, Y., Grosvenor, R.: A categorical framework of manufacturing for industry 4.0 and beyond. Procedia Cirp **52**, 173–178 (2016)
2. Schilberg, D., Meisen, T., Reinhard, R.: Virtual production-the connection of the modules through the virtual production intelligence. In: Proceedings of the World Congress on Engineering and Computer Science, vol. 2, pp. 23–25 (2013)
3. Keddis, N., Kainz, G., Buckl, C., Knoll, A.: Towards adaptable manufacturing systems. In: 2013 IEEE International Conference on Industrial Technology (ICIT), pp. 1410–1415. IEEE (2013)
4. Florescu, A., Barabas, S.A.: Modeling and simulation of a flexible manufacturing system—a basic component of industry 4.0. Appl. Sci. **10**, 8300 (2020)

5. Stich, V., Oflazgil, K., Schröter, M., Reschke, J., Jordan, F., Fuhs, G.: Big data implementation for the reaction management in manufacturing systems. In: 2015 XXV International Conference on Information, Communication and Automation Technologies (ICAT), pp. 1–6. IEEE (2015)
6. Magnanini, M.C., Tolio, T.A.: A model-based digital twin to support responsive manufacturing systems. CIRP Ann. **70**, 353–356 (2021)
7. Vaidya, S., Ambad, P., Bhosle, S.: Industry 4.0–a glimpse. Procedia Manuf. **20**, 233–238 (2018)
8. Cortés, C.B.Y., Landeta, J.M.I., Chacón, J.G.B.: El entorno de la industria 4.0: implicaciones y perspectivas futuras. Concienc. Tecnol. **54**, 33–45 (2017)
9. Negri, E., Fumagalli, L., Macchi, M.: A review of the roles of digital twin in CPS-based production systems. Procedia Manuf. **11**, 939–948 (2017)
10. Al-Ahmari, A.M.A., Ridgway, K.: An integrated modeling method to support manufacturing systems analysis and design. Comput. Ind. **38**, 225–238 (1999)
11. Thombansen, U., et al.: Model-based self-optimization for manufacturing systems. In: 2011 17th International Conference on Concurrent Enterprising, pp. 1–9. IEEE (2011)
12. Wang, S., Wan, J., Li, D., Zhang, C.: Implementing smart factory of industrie 4.0: an outlook. Int. J. Distrib. Sensor Netw. **12**, 3159805 (2016)
13. Oztemel, E., Tekez, E.K.: A general framework of a reference model for intelligent integrated manufacturing systems (REMIMS). Eng. Appl. Artif. Intell. **22**, 855–864 (2009)
14. ISO. ISO 9000: 2015 Sistemas de gestión de la calidad-Fundamentos y vocabulario (2015)
15. Hinckeldeyn, J., Dekkers, R., Altfeld, N., Kreutzfeldt, J.: Bottleneck-based synchronisation of engineering and manufacturing. In: Proceedings of the 19th International Conference on Management of Technology, IAMOT 2010, Cairo, Egypt. International Association for Management of Technology (2010)
16. Gutenberg, E.: Grundlagen der Betriebswirtschaftslehre, vol. 22. Springer, Heidelberg (1976). https://doi.org/10.1007/978-3-662-21965-2
17. Permin, E., et al.: Self-optimizing production systems. Procedia Cirp **41**, 417–422 (2016)
18. Habchi, G., Berchet, C.: A model for manufacturing systems simulation with a control dimension. Simul. Model. Pract. Theor. **11**, 21–44 (2003)
19. Schuh, G., Stich, V., Wienholdt, H.: Logistikmanagement. Springer, Heidelberg (2013). https://doi.org/10.1007/978-3-642-28992-7

Research of the Deep Learning Model
for Denoising of ECG Signal and Classification
of Arrhythmias

Ji-Yun Seo[1], Yun-Hong Noh[2], and Do-Un Jeong[1(✉)]

[1] Dongseo University, 47 Jurye-ro, Sasang-gu, Busan 47011, Korea
92sjy02@naver.com, dujeong@gdsu.dongseo.ac.kr
[2] Busan Digital University, 57 Jurye-ro, Sasang-gu, Busan 47011, Korea
yhnoh@bdu.ac.kr

Abstract. In this paper, we propose a DL model that can remove noise signals and classify arrhythmias for effective ECG analysis. The proposed DL model removes noise included in the signal by inputting the ECG signal divided by a specific time into the DAE, and inputs the noise-removed signal to the CNN model to distinguish the normal ECG signal from the arrhythmic ECG signal. The model was trained using the MIT-BIH Arrhythmia DB and the MIT-BIH Noise Stress Test DB, and the performance of the DL model was evaluated with two experiments by constructing a separate evaluation data set that is not used for training. The first experiment compared the noise removal performance of the implemented DAE model and Pan-Tompkins' QRS detection algorithm, and the second experiment performed the classification performance evaluation of the implemented CNN model. As a result of performance evaluation of the proposed DAE model, SNR_imp was 9.8310, RMSE was 0.0446, and PRD was 20.8869. In addition, as a result of classification performance evaluation, the accuracy was 98.50%, the recall rate was 98.0%, the precision was 98.99%, and F1 was 98.50%.

Keywords: ECG Denoise · Arrhythmias classification · Deep learning

1 Introduction

According to the ACC (american college of cardiology), the prevalence of cardiovascular disease has more than doubled over the past 30 years to 523 million people in 2019 [1]. CVD (cardiovascular disease) is the leading cause of death global, so early detection is important. For early detection of CVD, heart monitoring and analysis through ECG (electrocardiogram) signal measurement is essential in daily life [2]. However, the measured ECG signal contains various noises generated by muscle, movement, respiration, environment, and electrical factors. ECG signals containing noise cannot be precisely analyzed. Therefore, in this paper, we propose a DL model that can effectively remove noise and classify arrhythmias by considering the morphological characteristics of ECG signals. Section 2 describes the implemented DL model and data set configuration for

© Springer Nature Switzerland AG 2022
J.-H. Kim et al. (Eds.): IHCI 2021, LNCS 13184, pp. 198–204, 2022.
https://doi.org/10.1007/978-3-030-98404-5_19

model training in detail, and Sect. 3 shows the noise removal and arrhythmia classification performance evaluation experiments. In addition, in the last Sect. 4, the paper ends with a conclusion.

2 Proposed Multiple DL Model Process

The DL model proposed in this paper consists of a DAE (denoising autoencoder) for noise removal and a CNN (convolutional neural network) model for anomaly signal classification. The operation process of the DL model removes noise included in the signal by inputting the ECG signal segmented according to the R peak to the DAE. The R peak has the most distinct characteristic in the ECG signal, and only the interval between the R peaks can determine tachycardia and bradycardia. In general, normal heart rate is 60–100 beats per minute, so if the R-R interval of the ECG signal is greater than 1 s, it is considered bradycardia, and if it is less than 0.6 s, it is considered tachycardia. Therefore, the ECG signal was segmented into 1.5 s to include both tachycardia and bradycardia. After that, the noise-removed ECG signal can be input to the CNN model and classified into normal and abnormal signals.

2.1 Data Set for Model Training

Two training datasets were constructed using MIT-BIH DB (mit-bih arrhythmia data base) [3] and NST DB (mit-bih noise stress test data base) [4] for model training. MIT-BIH DB contains 48 records including 15 types of ECG bits measured from 47 patients, and MIT-BIH NST DB contains BW (baseline wander), EM (electrode motion artifact), and MA (muscle artifact) noise signals. First, the bit type of MIT-BIH was reconstructed into normal class and abnormal class including arrhythmia according to the AAMI EC57 standard. The reconstructed ECG signal was used as a training set by generating noise so that the SNR ratio became -12 to 12, and mixing it with the ECG signal of the MIT-BIH DB. In this case, α is an amplitude coefficient for generating an snr ratio. Example of training data for model training is shown in Table 1.

Table 1. Example of generated training data

2.2 DL Model Configuration and Hyper Parameter Information

The AE (autoencoder) is a neural network composed of an encoder that compresses input data and a decoder that reconstructs and outputs the compressed data to the same size as the input [5]. The DAE adds noise to the input data and learns to reconstruct it into the original noise-free input signal. At this time, adding noise to the input signal prevents the AE from simply copying the input directly to the output, and serves to control it to learn and express more efficiently. The DAE model was implemented with an FCN-based autoencoder to denoise based on the morphological characteristics of the ECG signal. The implemented DAE consists of 11 layers and uses the relu as the activation function of the hidden layer and the sigmoid as the activation function of the output layer. We also implemented a 1D CNN-based learning model for ECG anomaly signal classification. The implemented CNN neural network consists of 9 layers including convolution, polling, dropout, and 3 fully connected layers. The convolutional layer performs the process of extracting features from the input data and uses relu as the activation function. The pooling layer used max pooling. max pooling selects the maximum value from the feature map generated through the convolution layer and reduces the dimension while retaining specific information. Finally, the dense layer connects to the previous layer and serves as the final output. In this case, the softmax function was used as the activation function of the output. The architecture of the implemented DAE and CNN models are shown in Table 2.

Table 2. DL model architecture for ECG noise removal and anomaly classification

No	Layer name	Parameter	Activation function
DAE model			
1	Conv 1D (input)	64 × 16	Relu
2	Conv 1D	32 × 16	Relu
3	Conv 1D	16 × 16	Relu
4	Conv 1D	8 × 16	Relu
5	Conv 1D	1 × 16	Relu
6	Conv 1D	1 × 16	Relu
7	Conv 1D	8 × 16	Relu
8	Conv 1D	16 × 16	Relu
9	Conv 1D	32 × 16	Relu
10	Conv 1D	64 × 16	Relu
11	Conv 1D (output)	1 × 16	Sigmoid
CNN model			
1	Conv 1D (input)	32×16	Relu
2	Max pooling	2	–
3	Dropout	0.5	–
4	Conv 1D	32 × 16	Relu
5	Max pooling	2	–
6	Dropout	0.5	–
7	Conv 1D	32 × 16	Relu
8	Max pooling	2	–
9	Dropout	0.5	–
10	Dense	128	Relu
11	Dense	32	Relu
12	Dense	2	Softmax

3 Experiments and Results

To evaluate the performance of the implemented DL model, two experiments were performed with separate evaluation data sets that were not used for training. The first experiment compared SNR_imp (improved signal to noise ratio), RMSE (root mean square error), and PRD(percent root mean square difference) of the implemented denoising DAE model with the QRS detection algorithm of Pan–Tompkins. SNR is the magnitude of the signal power compared to the noise power, and the relative signal power may be known. The magnitude of the power was calculated as the RMS (root mean square) of the signal, and SNR_imp was calculated through the SNR difference between the filtered

ECG signal and noise ECG signal. The lower the RMSE value means that the higher the similarity to the original. The PRD is an index for measuring distortion between the original signal and the reconstructed signal, and a lower PRD value means that the signal is reconstructed closer to the original. x is the clean ECG signal and $\hat{x}$ is the ECG signal predicted through the model. As a result of performance evaluation of the proposed DAE model, SNR_imp was 9.8310, RMSE was 0.0446, and PRD was 20.8869. The BPF (band pass filter)-based Pantomkins algorithm [6] showed better noise removal performance than the proposed DAE model, but the performance of RMSE and PRD, which means similarity to the original signal, was not good. However, in the case of the proposed DAE model, it was confirmed that the filtered signal was reconstructed similarly to the original ECG signal as well as the denoise performance. Table 3 shows the denoise performance evaluation results.

Table 3. Denoise performance evaluation results

Noise	Algorithm	SNR_imp	RMSE	PRD
BW	Pantomkins	17.2642	0.1953	92.4518
	DAE	9.8350	0.0444	20.8246
EM	Pantomkins	17.2670	0.1953	92.4360
	DAE	9.8180	0.0448	21.0020
MA	Pantomkins	17.2740	0.1952	92.3940
	DAE	9.8400	0.0445	20.8340
Avg	Pantomkins	17.2684	0.1953	92.4273
	DAE	9.8310	0.0446	20.8869

The second experiment performed classification performance evaluation of the implemented CNN model. For classification performance evaluation, TP (positive true), TN (negative true), FP (positive false), and FN (negative false) were calculated for each class classification result through a confusion matrix. And the model's accuracy, recall, precision, and F1 were confirmed through the calculated index. ECG classification model was trained with a total of 40,000 samples of approximately 20,000 normal ECG and abnormal ECG classes. As a result of model training, the loss was 0.0541, acc was 0.9792, val_loss was 0.0731, and val_acc was 0.9761. In addition, as a result of the classification performance evaluation calculated through the confusion matrix, the accuracy of 98.50%, the recall rate of 98.0%, the precision of 98.99%, and the F1 rate of 98.50% were confirmed. In addition, as a result of the classification performance evaluation calculated through confusion matrix, it was confirmed that the accuracy was 98.50%, the recall rate was 98.0%, the precision was 98.99%, and the F1 ratio was 98.50%. Table 4 shows the model training and classification performance evaluation results.

Table 4. Results of model training and classification performance evaluation

Train_acc	Train_loss	Val_acc	Val_loss
0.9792	0.0541	0.9761	0.0731

⬇

TN	TP	FN	FP
0.99	0.98	0.02	0.01

⬇

Accuracy	Recall	Precision	F1
98.50	98.00	98.99	98.50

4 Conclusion

In this paper, we propose DL model for denoising ECG signals and classifying arrhythmias. The proposed DL model removes the noise included in the signal by inputting the ECG signal segmented by the time of 1.5 s based on the R peak to the DAE. Then, the denoised ECG signal is input to the CNN model to classify the normal ECG signal and the arrhythmic ECG signal. For model learning, a training dataset was constructed using MIT-BIH DB and NST DB. The training data is included in two classes, normal and abnormal, and in the case of an ECG signal containing noise, the signal was reconstructed to have an SNR of -12–12dB. To evaluate the performance of the implemented DL model, two experiments were performed with separate evaluation data sets that were not used for training The first experiment compared the noise removal performance of the implemented DAE model and Pan-Tompkins' QRS detection algorithm, and the second experiment performed the classification performance evaluation of the implemented CNN model. As a result of the performance evaluation of the proposed DAE model, SNR_imp was 9.8310, RMSE was 0.0446, and PRD was 20.8869, and as a result of the classification performance evaluation, the accuracy was 98.50%, recall rate was 98.0%, precision rate was 98.99%, and F1 rate was 98.50%. Therefore, we confirmed the excellent performance of the proposed DL model for ECG noise removal and arrhythmia classification, and we intend to conduct research on optimization and weight reduction of models applicable to the cloud in the future.

Acknowledgment. This research was supported by Basic Science Research Program through the National Research Foundation of Korea (NRF) funded by the Ministry of Education (No. 2018R1D1A1B07045337) and MSIT (Ministry of Science, ICT & Future Planning), Korean, under the National Program for Excellence in SW (2019-0-01817) supervised by the IITP (Institute of Information & communications Technology Planning & Evaluation).

References

1. Roth, G.A., et al.: Global burden of cardiovascular diseases and risk factors, 1990–2019: update from the GBD 2019 study. J. Am. Coll. Cardiol. **76**(25), 2982–3021 (2020)

2. Naresh, V., Acharyya, A.: Extraction of ECG significant features for remote CVD monitoring. In: Naik, G. (ed.) Biomedical Signal Processing. SB, pp. 357–386. Springer, Singapore (2020). https://doi.org/10.1007/978-981-13-9097-5_15
3. MIT-BIH Arrhythmia Database. https://physionet.org/content/mitdb/1.0.0/. Accessed 24 Feb 2005
4. MIT-BIH Noise Stress Test Database. https://physionet.org/content/nstdb/1.0.0/. Accessed 03 Aug 1999
5. Nurmaini, S., et al.: Deep learning-based stacked denoising and autoencoder for ECG heartbeat classification. Electronics 9(1), 135 (2020)
6. Pan, J., Tompkins, W.J.: A real-time QRS detection algorithm. IEEE Trans. Biomed. Eng. 3, 230–236 (1985)

XRTI: eXtended Reality Based Telepresence Interface for Multiple Robot Supervision

Naomi Wang and Jong Hoon Kim[✉]

Advanced Telerobotics Research Lab, Computer Science, Kent State University,
Kent, OH, USA
jkim72@kent.edu

Abstract. The XRTI system is an immersive augmented reality (AR) interface proposed to support the supervision of a robot team by providing a highly optimized and accessible method of robot system monitoring. Its design takes advantage of the augmented reality space to enhance the capacity of a single human supervisor to simultaneously monitor multiple telepresence robots. Its 3D data visualization capabilities use extended reality space to display environmental, sensory, and maintenance data provided by the robot over a wrap-around view to prevent data negligence due to human error. By increasing the accessibility of crucial data, the XRTI system aims to reduce cognitive overload of an on-site supervisor. It provides an interactive interface to assist the user's data comprehension and is customizable to a user's preference to prioritize certain data categories. This research can be further optimized to support NASA's exploration extravehicular mobility units (xEMU) in the AARON (Assistive Augmented Reality Operational and Navigation) System. This paper provides proof of concept for the XRTI system.

Keywords: Mixed reality · Augmented reality · Extended reality · Human-Robot Interaction · Human-Computer Interaction · Telepresence · Robot supervision

1 Introduction

Fan out, or the ability of a single operator to control multiple robots, is a metric of human-robot interaction (HRI) which has significant influence on how interaction systems are designed. The increase of fan out (FO) can greatly increase efficiency in an HRI system, but in order for effective management of multiple systems, the comfort of the human operator must be considered. This research proposes an augmented reality (AR) design of an interactive interface to reduce cognitive overload on a robot operator.

Current research in holographic data presentation for robot teleoperation focuses on robot motion integrated into a test environment with a 3D model

This work is supported by the Ohio Space Grant Consortium (OSGC).

© Springer Nature Switzerland AG 2022
J.-H. Kim et al. (Eds.): IHCI 2021, LNCS 13184, pp. 205–217, 2022.
https://doi.org/10.1007/978-3-030-98404-5_20

in extended reality space [1,2]. For example, a robot indicates calculated path and environmental risk through an arrow pointer in 3D space. This model for augmented reality HRI supervision is effective and sufficient for single robot interaction systems, but may have a large overhead on human cognitive capacity when maintaining multiple robots with varying intended paths. We propose a system design which takes advantage of augmented reality extended space to simultaneously observe multiple robots with data including position orientation, 3D data visualization, and camera view. Our hypothesis maintains that given static neglect tolerance, robot supervision can be improved by increasing the accessibility of vital robot data. Although our proposed interface design includes increased interaction effort, the benefit of data availability should reduce memory strain on a robot supervisor and improve user experience. Similar studies are being done by Scholtz [3] and would challenge the accepted model which states that increased interaction effort decreases fan out capability. The proposed design will contribute to the fields of multiple robot supervision, telepresence, and collaboration. The following sections describe the interface design concept and explain the process of developing an augmented reality interface through the support of a literature review.

Design Context: Current implementations of multiple-robot supervision focus primarily on human-robot collaborative performance and provide a similar method of displaying data from multiple robots over the same field of view, as used effectively in [4]. While these displays are sufficient for specialized tasks, they are limited only to the robots' camera data and cannot provide data outside of an individual robot's field of view. Thus, if a robot's component or a task object deviates from the expected functionality outside of the camera's field of view, then the deviation would remain unknown to the supervisor and increase potential hazards in the operation. Other issues arise that the operator may need a field of view from the robot which the camera cannot provide or request data which is outside of visual perception, such as oxygen levels within an environment. Thus, it is necessary to increase the accessibility of non-negligible robot data such as sensory or environmental data in addition to camera view.

2   Literature Review

The works referenced are derived from the fields of HRI and AR. The collaboration between these fields improve and expand on possible applications of these technologies, which is evident in the literature studied.

Human-Robot Interaction: The literature included studies an area of human-robot interaction that specializes in a model of single human, multiple robot interaction. This model has been widely recognized for its effectiveness and efficiency to distribute tasks to robots, reduce physical labor, and alleviate risk to human teams. Enhancing the task output of a single human by offering robot assistance reduces the expense of training multiple operators and increases the availability of human workers for performing higher-level tasks. The literature provides extensive examples of applications of a single human, multiple robot models. One such application is in urban search and rescue [5], which proposes an experiment in which a team of robots navigates a hazardous location to perform a visual search for human disaster victims. Other literature includes surveillance with multiple unmanned air vehicles tasked to perform a delivery [6], and applications in industrial production [7].

In addition to practical applications of multiple robot systems, other work focuses on how these systems are affected by fan out. The research in [8] studies whether multiple robot supervision is more effectively performed in teams or by individuals, and concludes that there is no statistically significant difference. In contrast, [9] also studies multi-operator supervisory control and finds that increasing the number of operators to increase fan out may increase performance if the task does not allow performance to increase as fan-out increases. Additional studies consider the maximum number of robots that a single operator can control [10], examine designs for human-robot teams [11], and provide metrics for supervisory control [12,13].

Augmented Reality: Our work focuses on the application of augmented reality as an assisting technology in HRI. Thus, the included literature relates to the use of augmented reality in human-robot systems. Other than applications in education, service, and emotional robotics [14], AR has been used in HRI interaction systems to collaborate on an augmented reality task [15], increase a robot's ability to perform gestures [16], and execute motion planning [17].

Augmented reality is further gaining recognition for its ability to provide an interface for robot supervision which extends beyond the limitations of usual human perception. It offers a mixed reality experience for robot supervision, such as an extended reality platform where users can see both the physical environment and robot data through see-through augmented reality data visualization [18]. The application of see-through augmented reality allows the user to maintain spacial awareness of natural reality while also receiving assistance from augmented reality. This technology can also be used to manage the tasks of multiple robots at once within the same field of view [4]. These systems allow the human to remained focused on robot supervision without negligence for situational and environmental considerations. Thus, methods for robot supervision in HRI have been improved upon with the use of augmented reality technology.

3 Motivation

With the narrowing gap between human and robot ability within human-robot interactions, human operators may begin to feel overwhelmed when tasked to observe and supervise a complex robot. Advanced robots have many dynamically moving parts and perform complex calculations. To prevent miscalculation or robot damage, the operator may feel the need to monitor required robot data constantly, when constant surveillance is not actually necessary. Interactivity in a human-robot system returns control to the operator, directs them to an area of interest, and allows them the control of prioritizing robot needs. Thus, they can feel at ease and more confident when supervising robot data.

Allowing human judgement to prioritize robot needs is not only beneficial to the human, but also reduces workload on the robot system as well. In a team of multiple robots, it may not yet be possible for robots to be aware of each other and present themselves to the operator in order of greatest priority. Assessing priority has been discussed in [3], which considers the effectiveness of models such as round-robin and automatically computed attention need. Although these selection models may be functional, they may not effective in selecting the robot which is most in need of attention. Thus, human judgement remains a crucial element in human-robot interaction systems in order to assign priority.

A human-robot interaction is a balance between both the human and robot participants. To interact to the best of their ability and deliver the best outcome in a team, the human must consider personal fatigue while robots do not. To accommodate this need and create a more pleasant interaction, we propose holographic interfaces which promote the autonomy for a robot operator and enhance the ability of an operator to manage multiple robots at once.

4   System Design Description

4.1   Design Concept

3D Environments, Apps and UX Elements: We propose a design that allows supervision of multiple robots but provides the advantages of one-on-one interaction. This design involves column shaped information panels which wrap around the user in extended reality space. This interface can be customized to user preference based on their personal priority assessment. Although the data of multiple robots is available through the interface, augmented reality allows a dynamic environment where an operator can either view a single robot or take advantage of multi-view functionality. With a see-through interface design, users can place data of another robot behind the primary interface in order to observe both within the same field of view or compare data between two similar robots. Additional data from other robots can be instantiated within the augmented space. The circular design avoids cognitive overload by allowing the user to focus on specific data by simply turning their back on unnecessary information while it remains behind them, readily available with little effort. To view data from other robots, a user would only need to walk outside of the circular data display and into another which is instantiated in the same environment.

Each column display provides information to the user including camera data streaming from different robot perspectives, robot orientation visualization using a 3D model representation, and numerical data displaying sensory and maintenance data associated with the robot. This data includes temperature, position, and torque data for each of the

Fig. 1. View within the column interface, using an example robot model.

joints maintained by the robot in order to observe workload and prevent overheat or damage of robot components. Sensory data provided by the interface includes numerical values for data which cannot be visualized through camera capability, such as oxygen and gas levels within the robot's environment. This data is also available in graph form for ease of data analysis and understanding data trends. Camera feed is provided through the interface, including a functionality allowing users to toggle the size of the camera display within the interface and view multiple robot cameras at once for convenient supervision.

The overlay capability of concentric circular interface display can be added to an instance of an interface with the plus symbol located on the upper right and can be switched back and forth using the toggle functionality located on the upper left hand side of the display when facing the initially spawned position as shown in Fig. 1.

Interaction and Experience: Our interaction model engages users with point-and-click and drag-and-drop functionality for an effective interaction which requires minimal prior training. The experience also utilizes the user's physical position, primarily rotation.

- Point-and-click, drag-and-drop: *(Point-and-click)* This is a classic implementation of user interaction which remains effective as it allows the user to interact directly with the interface. This method of interaction requires little prior knowledge of the system and little specialized training to adopt the interaction method. This method also permits the communication of clear user intentions by giving full control to the operator.
  (Drag-and-drop) Drag-and-Drop is a widely applied design choice for data driven interfaces such as [19,20] because of its ability to present data dynamically. As an expansion of the Point-and-Click functionality, Drag-and-Drop allows the operator to customize the interface to their preference and priority judgement. This allows for a personalized experience with the interface and keeps the cognitive workload of the operator in mind. The operator can rearrange the information given by the interface in order to prioritize a task which requires certain information to be within the same field of view. The

operator is able to work comfortably according to their own personal preferences. For example, if the operator always places the most important data at the top left corner of their field of view, this increases ease of access and data retrieval efficiency while decreasing cognitive effort.

– Operator position: Because our design takes advantage of extended 3D space, the position of the operator within physical space is a key element within the interface design. This includes both a user's physical position within a space as well as their rotational position.

(Spacial position) When engaging with the interface, the spacial position of the operator can either remain static or be dynamic, depending on the operator's needs. If supervising multiple robots at once, the user can instantiate multiple data interfaces within the same space and can step outside of one interface into another, or they can choose to use only one instance of the interface. The proposed design accommodates interaction with multiple robots, but allows for a one-on-one interaction with each robot within the system.

(Rotational position) In order to change their field of view, the operator uses their rotational position to interact with the interface. This design is intuitive and builds directly onto the natural reality, enclosing the operator within a circular column of data. The circular design allows arrangement of data such that the user can turn away from data which they are not using, but access it easily when it becomes relevant, simply by turning around. This prevents cognitive overload while maintaining important data within the same environment. Rather than requiring the user to manually hide data, this provides a simple and hands-free alternative.

– Content type: We engage the user's attention with the use of 3D visualization and animated streaming data. The ability to interact with 3D data visualization can increase the level of understanding that the user experiences within the human-robot interaction. The benefits of visualizing data within a 3D context has previously been proven with applications in map visualization [21] and educational tasks such as anatomy education [22,23]. Our design also includes streaming data records, such that the operator can better observe data trends within the system.

Coactivity and Collaboration: The collaboration intended by the interface is a observational overview of robot maintenance and sensory data. Through the system, the operator will be able to judge the data provided by the robot and will be able to record the data or decide a plan of action separately from the interface.

4.2   Design Requirements

Operator Status Requirement: The proposed interface will show an overview on the system's current operator, including a name, 3D avatar, and body information. It will also display the operator's current position. The system will also show its power status alongside the operator status and display any error messages associated with the system.

Robot Status Requirement: Data regarding the robot's vitals will be displayed within the interface, including motor, camera, and sensory data. A 3D model of the robot will be included as a reference for the user. *(Robot position motors)* Information related to the motors of the robot, including temperature data to prevent overheat, coordinate position, and torque are all required for observation and maintenance. The motor data display is shown in Fig. 2. If the robot has multiple motors, the user can select

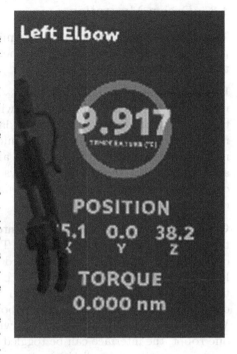

Fig. 2. Joint data detail-view widget

motor whose data will be displayed by hovering the controller over the corresponding joint displayed by the 3D model of the robot. Additional information displayed includes whether or not the motor is in motion, the current speed, power status, and error messages associated with the motor. *(Robot driving motors)* Driving motors will provide data associated with the speed, temperature, power status, and error messages. *(Remote camera view)* The XRTI interface will provide the operator with streaming data from each of the cameras situated on the robot in order to maintain a sufficient understanding of the surrounding environment. The view within the interface includes the ability to toggle the display sizes of the camera data. To view the name of the camera from which the stream originates, the operator should hover their controller over that stream. This is shown in Fig. 3. *(Sensors)* Both internal and external sensor data is accessible through the interface. Internal data includes robot base orientation and scan sensor orientation provided as IMU data, as well as power voltage and power status. External sensory data may include the gas, oxygen, and vibration readings as numerical data, and visible sensory data such as temperature and rust as image data.

Additional Data: The display also includes some additional features, such as a 2D environment map, a chat box to be used if there are multiple remotely-operating users, and the name and status of the robot's current action.

4.3   Design Motivation

The interface design attempts to minimize physical and mental strain on the operator.

Interface Shape: Created with an immersive experience in mind, allowing the user to stand within a column of data maintains focus without creating information overload. The column design also allows for stackable interface displays in concentric circles to observe and compare data from multiple robots with ease.

Color Palette: The colors of the interface are designed to reduce eye strain. The opacity of the interface can be raised or lowered according to the user's needs, particularly when navigating an environment or viewing data from multiple robots. When the user wishes to engage only with one robot, the interface can be toggled to

Fig. 3. Multiple camera data within the same field of view

an opaque setting to eliminate unnecessary distraction. However, if the user needs to compare robot data in the stacked view or monitor the environment, the interface allows a reduction of opacity such that the interface is transparent or semi-transparent to allow the observation of data external to the interface.

5   Concept of Operations (CONOPS)

The proposed XRTI system is intended to be an observation station for managing multiple robots. When used in a human-robot team, it provides a comprehensive overview of each individual robot while also enabling the operator to expand their field of view to include an entire robot team. The interface aims to provide an intuitive display of data provided by a teleoperated robots in order to assist the decision making process regarding a robot's actions. The XRTI system aims to minimize cognitive overload and provide accessible data visuals through its (1) intuitive data display, (2) interactive capabilities, and (3) expanded view for viewing multiple robots.

Interactivity: As described in Sect. 4.1, the system is intended to be customized to user preference via drag-and-drop functionality. Users should interact with the interface to display data. Certain types of data, such as numerical data, is revealed upon request by the user by hovering the controller over the category name. This is intended to prevent confusion and the reduce cognitive workload of viewing multiple types of numerical data at once. The design will engage observational operators to take an active role in human-robot interaction systems by allowing them to select which data to prioritize and keep unnecessary data from cluttering the observational space. Unnecessary interactivity should not hinder the ability of a robot supervisor to work efficiently, so this design will be placed under further scrutiny in order to prove its effectiveness.

Column View: The intuitive data display of the interface uses a column shaped design in order to take advantage of natural human methods of visual data collection (i.e. head turning, body movement to change field of view and gather environmental data). By surrounding the user with a semitransparent display of robot data, the user can maintain natural situational awareness while also expending little effort to maintain observation of robot data. As shown in Fig. 1, The column view uses augmented reality space to provide the user a one-on-one interaction with each robot within a robot team. As described in Sect. 4.3, the system permits comparison of data between two robots with a see-through interface background, allowing another data column to appear behind the primary column.

Expanded View: The system plans to include an expanded view of the robot team in order to provide a big-picture view of operations and allow more informed decision making with consideration for the entire robot team and prevent unintentional negligence of any individual robot. This view will allow users to arrange and plan robot movements in 3D space. In the expanded view, the column interface

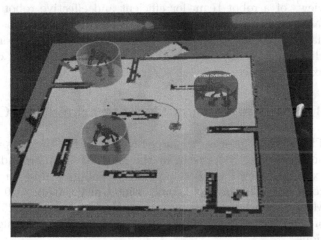

Fig. 4. Possible design for an expanded view of a robot team.

will be minimized to a cylindrical representation with a miniature robot model inside. When using this view, notifications regarding an individual robot status will appear above the cylindrical representation. This is meant to mimic the appearance of game pieces on a board game, in order to improve the understanding of where each robot in a team is within a given environment. The expanded view can include a 2D, 3D, or no environmental representation, based on user preference.

Directive Notification: The notification system as proposed within the interface uses color and animation to capture the user's attention to critical changes in the robot's status. This may include sensory data regarding dangerous environmental components or maintenance situations such as motor overheat. Generally, the interface will present with a blue-green background, but a notification will change the color of the interface to a complementary red hue, as shown in Fig. 4. This visual notification can clearly alert users when working with multiple robots simultaneously, particularly when in expanded view. When working individually with a robot in column view, the system proposes an animated directive component to guide users view to data changes.

However, these methods of notification may be ignored if the operator is inattentive or judges the notification to be negligible. Under hypercritical conditions, the system may also take advantage of a pop-up notification which would warn the user of the situation and strongly suggest observation of that data.

CONOPS Overview: The XRTI interface provides a method for one-way communication of the robot to the operator. It allows the robot to provide data to a human observer which might otherwise be neglected if the human is responsible for multiple robots. Data from multiple robots is made accessible through an interface that focuses on user comfort and allows both one-on-one and big-picture views of a robot team for efficient and effective robot observation. The interface prioritizes user judgement by allowing them to customize and select which data they want to see through interactivity with drag-and-drop and point-and-click functionality, as well as an intuitive arrangement of data displayed within extended space.

6   Implementation Considerations and Constraints

The current process of implementation for the proposed system is focused on solidifying the design of the singular wrap-around column interface. The expanded view for observing multiple robots will be implemented as the project continues. This project is built using Unity version 2020.2.5f1 [24] along with the Magic Leap 1 head-mounted virtual retinal display [25]. The collaborative use of these technologies allows effective development of augmented reality applications.

Design and System Constraints: The current developed system, implemented with Magic Leap 1, has a field of view mentioned in [26], limited to horizontal, vertical, and diagonal view of 40, 30, 50 degrees respectively. Its Near Clipping Plane is set at 37 cm from the device. The column design of the XTRI system is limited by its compatibility with the Magic Leap control system, which could not interact with a curved canvas surface. Our work around for this limitation is to construct the system using flat canvases arranged in an octagonal shape, surrounded by a circular model.

7   Discussion

This paper outlines an overarching goal for our ongoing implementation. We have also kept human-in-loop and system metrics in mind, which will be included in future work. As described, the XRTI interface increases the interaction effort of the operator, so these areas will need extensive testing. If the benefits provided by the system do not outweigh the physical and mental effort enough to reduce strain on the operator, then further design work will be required to improve the current proposal. However, if user supervision of multiple robots improves with use of the system, the result could potentially challenge the understanding that increased interaction effort decreases the capacity for fan out. Considerations must be made in future work to assess the level of interactivity within the system to ensure that it is aligned with our goal of improving the capacity of a supervisor to observe a robot team while minimizing cognitive workload. The current proposal for the interface is limited to observation-only supervisory assistance, but may have future domain expansions into operational assistance.

8 Conclusion and Future Work

This work provides a proof of concept of an augmented reality interface which serves as a visual aid to a robot supervisor. The proposed design keeps the user informed with an intuitive data display and aims to reduce cognitive workload, specifically memory strain, by increasing the accessibility of vital robot data. Reducing the effort expended for data retrieval should increase efficiency and improve the user experience. The system will encourage human participants of human-robot teams by allowing the participants control when they may feel overwhelmed by the task of supervision. As discussed in Sect. 7, future work will include considerations for human-in-loop and metric studies. Implementation of the proposed work is ongoing and will continue to be assessed to make further improvements to the system design. In addition, this work will be optimized for the ATR_Kent Robots [27,28], which are designed for robot-assisted disaster response applications where cognitive workload is critical, and which have been sceptically developed for the World Robot Summit - disaster response robotic challenges [29].

References

1. Reardon, C., Lee, K., Fink, J.: Come see this! Augmented reality to enable human-robot cooperative search. In: 2018 IEEE International Symposium on Safety, Security, and Rescue Robotics (SSRR), pp. 1–7 (2018)
2. Rosen, E., et al.: Communicating robot arm motion intent through mixed reality head-mounted displays. In: Robotics Research, pp. 301–316. Springer, Cham (2020)
3. Olsen, D.R., Goodrich, M.A.: Metrics for evaluating human-robot interactions. In: Proceedings of PERMIS, vol. 2003, p. 4, (2003)
4. DelPreto, J., et al.: Helping robots learn: a human-robot master-apprentice model using demonstrations via virtual reality teleoperation. In: 2020 IEEE International Conference on Robotics and Automation (ICRA), pp. 10226–10233 (2020)
5. Wong, C.Y., Seet, G., Sim, S.K., Pang, W.C.: Single-human multiple-robot systems for urban search and rescue: justifications, design and testing. In: 2010 11th International Conference on Control Automation Robotics Vision, pp. 579–584 (2010)

6. Hayakawa, H., Azumi, T., Sakaguchi, A., Ushio, T.: ROS-based support system for supervision of multiple UAVs by a single operator. In: 2018 ACM/IEEE 9th International Conference on Cyber-Physical Systems (ICCPS), pp. 341–342 (2018)
7. Flordal, H., Spensieri, D., Akesson, K., Fabian, M.: Supervision of multiple industrial robots: optimal and collision free work cycles. In: Proceedings of the 2004 IEEE International Conference on Control Applications, vol. 2, pp. 1404–1409 (2004)
8. Whetten, J.M., Goodrich, M.A.: Specialization, fan-out, and multi-human/multi-robot supervisory control. In: 2010 5th ACM/IEEE International Conference on Human-Robot Interaction (HRI), pp. 147–148 (2010)
9. Whetten, J.M., Goodrich, M.A., Guo, Y.: Beyond robot fan-out: towards multi-operator supervisory control. In: 2010 IEEE International Conference on Systems, Man and Cybernetics, pp. 2008–2015 (2010)
10. Zheng, K., Glas, D.F., Kanda, T., Ishiguro, H., Hagita, N.: How many social robots can one operator control? In: 2011 6th ACM/IEEE International Conference on Human-Robot Interaction (HRI), pp. 379–386 (2011)
11. Zheng, K., Glas, D.F., Kanda, T., Ishiguro, H., Hagita, N.: Designing and implementing a human-robot team for social interactions. IEEE Trans. Syst. Man Cybern. Syst. **43**(4), 843–859 (2013)
12. Olsen, D.R., Wood, S.B., Turner, J.: Metrics for human driving of multiple robots. In: IEEE International Conference on Robotics and Automation, Proceedings, ICRA 2004, vol. 3, pp. 2315–2320 (2004)
13. Crandall, J.W., Cummings, M.L.: Developing performance metrics for the supervisory control of multiple robots. In: 2007 2nd ACM/IEEE International Conference on Human-Robot Interaction (HRI), pp. 33–40 (2007)
14. Zhang, Z., Wang, X.: Machine intelligence matters: rethink human-robot collaboration based on symmetrical reality. In: 2020 IEEE International Symposium on Mixed and Augmented Reality Adjunct (ISMAR-Adjunct), pp. 225–228 (2020)
15. Williams, T., Hirshfield, L., Tran, N., Grant, T., Woodward, N.: Using augmented reality to better study human-robot interaction. In: Chen, J.Y.C., Fragomeni, G. (eds.) HCII 2020. LNCS, vol. 12190, pp. 643–654. Springer, Cham (2020). https://doi.org/10.1007/978-3-030-49695-1_43
16. Williams, T., Bussing, M., Cabrol, S., Boyle, E., Tran, N.: Mixed reality deictic gesture for multi-modal robot communication. In: 2019 14th ACM/IEEE International Conference on Human-Robot Interaction (HRI), pp. 191–201 (2019)
17. Hernández, J.D., Sobti, S., Sciola, A., Moll, M., Kavraki, L.E.: Increasing robot autonomy via motion planning and an augmented reality interface. IEEE Robot. Autom. Lett. **5**(2), 1017–1023 (2020)
18. Huy, D.Q., Vietcheslav, I., Lee, G.S.G.: See-through and spatial augmented reality - a novel framework for human-robot interaction. In: 2017 3rd International Conference on Control, Automation and Robotics (ICCAR), pp. 719–726 (2017)
19. Mirović, M., Miličević, M., Obradović, I.: A framework for dynamic data-driven user interfaces. In: 2018 41st International Convention on Information and Communication Technology, Electronics and Microelectronics (MIPRO), pp. 1421–1426 (2018)
20. Reinhart, G., Vogl, W., Kresse, I.: A projection-based user interface for industrial robots. In: 2007 IEEE Symposium on Virtual Environments, Human-Computer Interfaces and Measurement Systems, pp. 67–71 (2007)
21. Toda, Y., Narita, T., Kubota, N.: Information visualization based on 3D modeling for human-friendly teleoperation. In: 2012 IEEE Congress on Evolutionary Computation, pp. 1–7 (2012)

22. Blum, T., Kleeberger, V., Bichlmeier, C., Navab, N.: mirracle: an augmented reality magic mirror system for anatomy education. In: 2012 IEEE Virtual Reality Workshops (VRW), pp. 115–116 (2012)
23. Trinidad, K.C., Villa, D.L.P., Portillo, I.H.R., Saldaña, F.E.: AR digestive system: 3D visualization of the digestive system with augmented reality. In: 2013 International Conference on Mechatronics, Electronics and Automotive Engineering, pp. 90–95 (2013)
24. Unity engine. https://en.wikipedia.org/wiki/Unity_(game_engine). Accessed 10 June 2021
25. Magic leap. https://en.wikipedia.org/wiki/Magic_Leap. Accessed 10 June 2021
26. Cardenas, I.S., et al.: AARON: assistive augmented reality operations and navigation system for NASA's exploration extravehicular mobility unit (xEMU). In: Singh, M., Kang, D.-K., Lee, J.-H., Tiwary, U.S., Singh, D., Chung, W.-Y. (eds.) IHCI 2020. LNCS, vol. 12616, pp. 406–422. Springer, Cham (2021). https://doi.org/10.1007/978-3-030-68452-5_42
27. Cardenas, I.S., Kim, J.H.: Design of a semi-humanoid telepresence robot for plant disaster response and prevention. In: 2019 IEEE/RSJ International Conference on Intelligent Robots and Systems (IROS), November 2019
28. Cardenas, I.S., et al.: Telesuit: an immersive user-centric telepresence control suit. In: ACM/IEEE International Conference on Human-Robot Interaction HRI (2019)
29. The world robot summit - disaster response category. https://wrs.nedo.go.jp/en/wrs2020/challenge/. Accessed 10 June 2021

Validating Pre-requisite Dependencies Through Student Response Analysis

Manjushree D. Laddha$^{(\boxtimes)}$, Swanand Navandar, and Laxman D. Netak

Department of Computer Engineering, Dr. Babasaheb Ambedkar Technological University Lonere, Raigad 402103, India
{mdladdha,ldnetak}@dbatu.ac.in

Abstract. During examinations, students are unable to solve the problems requiring complex skills because they forget the primary or prerequisite skills or infrequent use of these skills. Also, students have problems with advanced courses due to weakness with prerequisite skills. One of the challenges for an instructor is to find the reason why students are not able to solve complex-skill problems. The reason may be a lack of prerequisite skills or has not mastered the complex skill or combination of both. This paper presents an analysis of the dependencies of prerequisite skills on the post requisite skills. Three assessments are conducted. The assessments are based on the skills required for the computer programming course. Basic assessments are prerequisites to the intermediate skill assessments. Both these assessments are prerequisites to the complex skills assessments. Based on the students' responses, the analysis is carried out. As these variables are the categorical type of variables for that purpose Chi-Squared test is applied. It is observed that there is a statistically significant dependency is present between prerequisite skills and post requisites skills.

Keywords: Prerequisite · Post-requisite · Basic skill · Intermediate skill · Complex skill

1 Introduction

Nowadays, due to COVID-19, all the examinations are conducted online. Instructors are designing multiple-choice questions for assessments. The diverse online platforms are used for course delivery and for conducting examinations. Abundant data of student responses are generated. By in-sighting the data by using statistic and Machine Learning techniques, different problem solved related to students like student performance, understanding related to course, sequence of content studied by students can be predicted, and even placement [8] of students based on technical skills.

Prerequisite skill structures show the ordering of skills in a given knowledge domain. The proper representation of skill structure is essential for several reasons. It informs knowledge domain experts about the proper and best sequencing

© Springer Nature Switzerland AG 2022
J.-H. Kim et al. (Eds.): IHCI 2021, LNCS 13184, pp. 218–228, 2022.
https://doi.org/10.1007/978-3-030-98404-5_21

of instruction to achieve the best learning for students. Additionally, this helps researchers to design and model an intelligent tutorial system that gives accurate student performance. By such an intelligent tutorial system and different teaching approaches [7] learning of introductory programming concepts can benefit students for learning and understanding new skills with optimal sequencing of the prerequisites skills.

Diverse students are present in the first-year programming course. Combinations of students from the different programs take this programming course. Designing such a course with different teaching strategies partially-flipped classroom, pair-programming [11] and on different LMS with animations and games are used to engage students.

Instructors have challenges in designing the paper in such a manner that it should generate a normal distribution curve from the students' responses, but it may or may not always be possible. But to make it possible always, an Instructor can focus much more on the skills. Try to cover every skill from all units of the syllabus. The major challenge is that for each course, the skills are different. There is no standard skills table for courses. Instructors, according to their cognitive thinking, organize the skills for the courses.

Hence in this paper, dependencies between the skills with the help of question items responses for the Computer programming course are explored. This paper is organized into Sect. 2 on the literature survey. Section 3 examines the research problem, and subsections are related to data collection. Section 4 proposed the Skills Table for Computer programming Course(CP) in C Language and shows the dependencies between the skills. Section 5 validates prerequisite dependencies. The paper concludes with a path for future work.

2 Literature Survey

Prerequisite skills are basic concepts, or it is the knowledge required to solve or implement the problem. Sometimes the skills are necessary for the same course, or sometimes skills of the introductory course are needed for an advanced course. This paper [13] differentiates the assessments from two courses as basic skills and advanced skills.

A solution-based intelligent tutoring system [6] is developed for learning programming skills. The intelligent tutorial systems are used to learn the programming skills by drag and drop.

With the help of web technology, an eLearning framework [12] was developed. This framework contains the course material and includes tests, exercises, and an integrated environment to compile the written programming codes. This approach helps in distance education for unlimited participation but accessible through the Internet.

Assessment tools are developed to evaluate students' understanding of skills. To accurately identify these core concepts or skills, experts' advice [5] is required. A concept inventory is developed, which is useful for the instructor to prioritize which skills need to be explained in detail. How much time should be devoted to the major skills? Even Student concentration level prediction model [10] are implements. As concentration also matters while learning.

Statistical and Machine Learning Methods are used as shown in Table 1. The purposes are different for various statistical methods, but all these purposes are related to prerequisite skills and post-requisite skills. The outcome of learning skills is related to the students' performance.

Table 1. Literature survey

Sr. no	Statistical method	Purpose	Source
1	Linear regression	Predicting student performance on post-requisite skills using prerequisite skills data	[1]
2	Correlation	Final exam performance was significantly correlated with prerequisite skills	[15]
3	Q-matrix	To tracking student's post requisite skills from particular knowledge point of view from the exercises	[4]
4	Correlation	To predicting retention performance with prerequisite skill features	[16]
5	Reference distance (RefD)	To measure the prerequisite relation between computer science and math courses	[9]
6	Classification, regression	To predict students' success or failure and final grade in examination	[2]
7	Regression and correlation	To predict prerequisite links between corresponding units of course by using heterogeneous source of content like quizzes data and textual data of course material.	[3]
8	Q-matrix	Discovering prerequisite structure based on variation in student performance on an assessment	[14]

Most research is conducted on the prerequisite and post-requisite skills to predict student performance in this literature survey. Various statistical methods are used based on the nature of the data set and the nature of the problem. Our aim is different from this research work. Our research work is to correlate prerequisite and post-requisite skills.

3 Research Problem

Different skills are required for the Computer programming course, from the *basic skills, intermediate skills to the complex skills*. But for implementing complex skills, knowledge of intermediate and basic skills is mandatory. For this purpose, the skills are organized in the proper sequence. So the skills table for this course is designed.

To validate the skills dependencies the question items are used. In this paper, the question items of basic skills are prerequisites to intermediate skills question items. *Both basic and intermediate skills are prerequisites to complex skills.* So from the student's responses to these question items validates the correlations between the skills.

A research problem is prerequisite skills are associated with post-requisite skills? For this purpose, a hypothesis is formulated.

- **H0:** *There is no association between prerequisite and post-requisite skills.*
- **H1:** *There is an association between prerequisite and post-requisite skills.*

4 Dataset

Data is collected from Google classroom. Computer programming in C exams is conducted for mechanical, civil, chemical and petrochemical courses. A total of 160 students appeared for tests. Total three tests were conducted*Basic skills Assessment, Intermediate skills Assessment, and Complex skills assessment.* Each test carries 10 questions. These assessments are multiple-choice questions. The students' responses are in the dichotomous data. The student who gives the correct answer score one mark, and if the wrong answer, then zero marks. So dataset is consists of a total of students' scores. The sample of assessment questions with skill type and skill is shown in Table 2.

5 Skill Table

In the C programming course, concepts are considered skills. There are many skills, as shown in Table 3 these are arranged from basic skills to complex skills. Each preceding skill is a prerequisite to its successor skill. To implement C programs effectively, it is mandatory to learn all these major skills.

In the C library, keywords are reserved words and used to perform an internal operation. The compiler already knows the working and meaning of these keywords. The SK-id 1, 2, 3, and 4 are required for the variable declarations. The SK-id 5 to SK-id 14 are the different operators which are necessary for the expression. Various operations are performed on the variable for computation purposes. The SK-id 15 manages the input and output operation. The SK-id 16 to SK-id 21 are decision making and branching. The programmer specifies one or more conditions along with a statement or statements for making the decision. If the conditions are determined to be true, then statements are executed. If the condition is determined to be false, then other statements are to be executed.

The SK-id 22 to SK-id 24 are decision-making and looping. A loop is a sequence of instructions that execute again and again until a certain condition hit. The condition may be entry controlled loop or exit controlled loop depends

Table 2. A random sample of assessments questions with skill type and skill

QID	Question text	Skill type	Skill

QI-8	What is output of the following program?
	```#include <stdio.h>```
	```int main()```
	```{```
	```int a = 9, b = 9;```
	```a = b++;```
	```b = a++;```
	```b = ++b;```
	```printf("%d %d", a, b);```
	```return 0;```
	```}```
		Intermediate	Increment operator

QC-3	Predict the output of the following code segment:
	```#include <stdio.h>```
	```int main()```
	```{```
	```int array[10] = {3, 0, 8, 1, 12, 8, 9, 2, 13, 10};```
	```int x, y, z;```
	```x = ++array[2];```
	```y = array[2]++;```
	```z = array[x++];```
	```printf("%d %d %d", x, y, z);```
	```return 0;```
	```}```
		Complex	Array

QB-8	The number of tokens in the following C statement ```printf("%d, %d, %d", x, y, z);```	Basic	Token
QB-9	Identify wrong C keyword	Basic	Keywords

upon which loop is used. After that increment or decrements to counter until it reaches a prescribed number.

SK-id 25 to SK-id 27 is related to the derived data type array, which is fixed-sized with a similar data type. SK-id 28 Function is a block of statement. Rewriting of the logic can be avoided by using functions. A function can be called any number of times. A large C program can be tracked with the help of functions. SK-id 29 and SK-id 30 A structure is a user-defined data type that allows combining data items of different kinds. A union can store different data types in the same memory location.

5.1 Dependencies Between Question Items

In Basic Skills Assessment is based on basic skills like *token, keywords, variables and data types, etc.*

Table 3. Skills table

SK-id	Skill	SK-id	Skill
1	Tokens	2	Keywords
3	Variables	4	Data Types
5	Arithmetic operator	6	Relational operator
7	Logical operator	8	Increment and decrement operator
9	Conditional operator	10	Bitwise operator
11	Assignment operator	12	Special operator
13	Bitwise operator	14	Operator precedence and associativity
15	Managing input and output operations	16	if statement
17	if else statement	18	else if
19	Switch statement	20	?: operator
21	goto statement	22	while statement
23	do while statement	24	for statement
25	Array	26	Multidimensional array
27	String	28	Functions
29	Structures	30	Unions

Intermediate skills Assessment is based on intermediate skills like *Conditional and decision statements, operators, continue and break, etc.*

Complex skills assessment is based on complex skills like *loops, functions array, structure, etc.* all these skills are listed as shown in Table 3. For each question, skills are assigned manually. Skills are the concept that is required for the programming language. The question with the skills is organized in above mention way.

All questions are multiple-choice questions whose incorrect answers correspond to students' common misconceptions. Each assessment carries 10 questions.

6   Validating prerequisite dependencies

For validating prerequisite dependencies with post-requisite students, responses are analyzed. As the dataset consists of *categorical data* for finding correlation *Chi-Square Test* is applied.

As data consists of students' responses that is score. *Categories the students score into poor, good, and excellent.* A score ranging from 0 to 4 is considered a poor score. A score ranging from 5 to 8 is considered a good score. A score ranging from 9 to 10 is considered an excellent score.

Table 4. Contingency table

Students' responses Skills type	Poor	Good	Excellent
Observed frequencies			
Basic	2	119	39
Intermediate	30	98	32
Complex	17	137	6
Expected frequencies			
Basic	16	118	26
Intermediate	16	118	26
Complex	16	118	26

Table 5. Results of Chi-square test

Probability	0.95	Critical value	9.488
Statistic	54.057	p-value	0.000 < 0.05

The Student Responses Categories(X) and Skills Types(Y) are both categorical variables as shown in Table 4. A Chi-square test is performed for finding the association between them.

The hypothesis stated above is validated by performing a Chi-square test.

For the purpose of examining dependencies between the number of student responses in each category and skill types, question items are paired along with different categorical values, and a contingency table as shown in Table 4 is prepared. The graphs show observed frequencies in the dataset and expected frequencies calculated as per the Chi-square test. All questions are multiple-choice questions whose incorrect answers correspond to students' common misconceptions. Each assessment carries 10 questions.

The Python program was implemented for this purpose by using *chi2* module from *Scipy.stat* library to calculate Chi-square. The calculated Chi-square statistic ($x^2 = 54.057$), which is much greater than the predetermined critical value of 9.488 hence the null hypothesis, i.e. (H0) *T*here is no association between prerequisite and post requisite skills. is rejected. Also, the p-value is less than the significance level of 0.05, indicating the results are statistically significant as shown in Table 5. In other words, there is a statistically significant dependency between prerequisite skills and post-requisite skills is observed.

In Fig. 1 the expected frequencies and observed frequencies of basic skill are compared. In the poor score category, the expected is greater than the observed one. The number of poor scores is less as compared to expected.

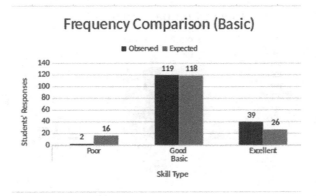

Fig. 1. Observed and expected frequencies are compared in basic skills

For the good score category, both expected and observed are the same. For excellent score category expected is smaller than observed. It proves that the knowledge of students for the basic skills is increased. Basic skills are a prerequisite for intermediate skills.

In Fig. 2 the expected frequencies and observed frequencies of intermediate skills are compared. Though the poor and good score expected frequencies is greater than observed. The excellent score expected frequencies are less than the observed frequency. So overall, the prerequisite means basic skills knowledge improves the post-requisite skills that are intermediate. Intermediate skills are a prerequisite to complex skills.

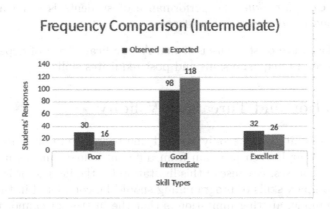

Fig. 2. Observed and expected frequencies are compared in intermediate skills

In Fig. 3 the expected frequencies and observed frequencies of complex skills are compared. In the poor score category, the expected and observed frequencies are near about the same.

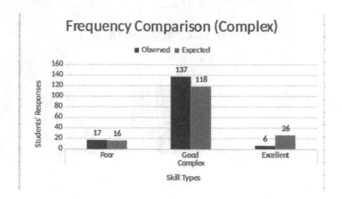

Fig. 3. Observed and expected frequencies are compared in complex skills

The good score category observed is greater than expected frequencies. In the Excellent score category, the observed is less than expected. It may be the excellent assessment is tough.

But the good score category is increased it means that the prerequisites skills knowledge improves the post-requisite skills.

Further, through comparison of expected and observed frequencies, it is observed that

(i) In the *Basic Skills* the performance of students increasing in *poor, good and excellent* scores of students.
(ii) In the *Intermediate Skills* the performance of students increasing in *good and excellent* scores of students.
(iii) In the *Complex Skills* the performance of students is same in *poor* and increasing in *good* scores of students.

Overall performance of students is rising. A significant level of dependencies is present between prerequisite skills and post requisites skills.

7   Limitation and Threats to Validity

This paper is limited as we only studied one-course Computer Programming in C for first Year B.Tech program from different courses means mix students from different courses. Because of this limitation for the instructor is up to what extent the complex skills of programming should be completed in the class.

In online mode, another limitation is that the instructor cannot understand the extent to which students understand the course. The only way to know the understanding of students in the assessments. The Assessments are online without a proctor. So the threat is that students use another tab and run the program using an online compiler to answer the question: What is the program's output? Which is expected to solve manually.

In the complex skills, the excellent score observed frequencies is less than expected. If students do not know the answer, randomly choose options. So the results may be biased for the population of students. This may be one reason. Another reason may be due to the complete syllabus for this complex skill assessment.

8 Conclusion and Future Work

This paper presents the association between prerequisite and post requisites skills for a Computer Programming course. It is observed that the dependency between prerequisite and post requisites skills is statistically significant. The calculated Chi-square statistic ($x^2 = 54.057$) is much greater than the predetermined critical value of 9.488. Also, the p-value is less than the significance level of 0.05. As students who have mastered the prerequisites skills are more likely to solve the post-requisite skills problems.

Moreover, the research can be used to help students to enhance their progress in performance. This research also allows the instructor to determine whether students post requisite skills progress is based on prerequisite skills.

Students' performance improves based on knowledge of prerequisite skills and post-requisite skills. The research reported in this paper is concerned with only one course. The research can be further extended to find whether these results replicate across multiple institutions and across multiple courses for that additional study is needed. However, these results offer a promising glimpse of how prerequisites relate to post requisite for student success.

References

1. Adjei, S.A., Botelho, A.F., Heffernan, N.T.: Predicting student performance on post-requisite skills using prerequisite skill data: an alternative method for refining prerequisite skill structures. In: Proceedings of the Sixth International Conference on Learning Analytics and Knowledge, pp. 469–473 (2016)
2. Bydžovská, H.: A comparative analysis of techniques for predicting student performance. Int. Educ. Data Min. Soc. (2016)
3. Chaplot, D.S., Yang, Y., Carbonell, J., Koedinger, K.R.: Data-driven automated induction of prerequisite structure graphs. Int. Educ. Data Min. Soc. (2016)
4. Chen, Y., et al.: Tracking knowledge proficiency of students with educational priors. In: Proceedings of the 2017 ACM on Conference on Information and Knowledge Management, pp. 989–998 (2017)
5. Goldman, K., et al.: Setting the scope of concept inventories for introductory computing subjects. ACM Trans. Comput. Educ. (TOCE) 10(2), 1–29 (2010)
6. Hooshyar, D., Ahmad, R.B., Yousefi, M., Fathi, M., Horng, S.J., Lim, H.: Sits: a solution-based intelligent tutoring system for students' acquisition of problem-solving skills in computer programming. Innov. Educ. Teach. Int. 55(3), 325–335 (2018)
7. Kunkle, W.M., Allen, R.B.: The impact of different teaching approaches and languages on student learning of introductory programming concepts. ACM Trans. Comput. Educ. (TOCE) 16(1), 1–26 (2016)

8. Laddha, M.D., Lokare, V.T., Kiwelekar, A.W., Netak, L.D.: Performance analysis of the impact of technical skills on employability. Int. J. Performability Eng. **17**(4) (2021)

9. Liang, C., Wu, Z., Huang, W., Giles, C.L.: Measuring prerequisite relations among concepts. In: Proceedings of the 2015 Conference on Empirical Methods in Natural Language Processing, pp. 1668–1674 (2015)

10. Lokare, V.T., Netak, L.D.: Concentration level prediction system for the students based on physiological measures using the EEG device. In: Singh, M., Kang, D.-K., Lee, J.-H., Tiwary, U.S., Singh, D., Chung, W.-Y. (eds.) IHCI 2020. LNCS, vol. 12615, pp. 24–33. Springer, Cham (2021). https://doi.org/10.1007/978-3-030-68449-5_3

11. Mohamed, A.: Designing a CS1 programming course for a mixed-ability class. In: Proceedings of the Western Canadian Conference on Computing Education, pp. 1–6 (2019)

12. Mustakerov, I., Borissova, D.: A framework for development of e-learning system for computer programming: application in the C programming language. J. e-Learning Knowl. Soc. **13**(2) (2017)

13. Nelson, G.L., et al.: Differentiated assessments for advanced courses that reveal issues with prerequisite skills: a design investigation. In: Proceedings of the Working Group Reports on Innovation and Technology in Computer Science Education, pp. 75–129 (2020)

14. Scheines, R., Silver, E., Goldin, I.M.: Discovering prerequisite relationships among knowledge components. In: EDM, pp. 355–356 (2014)

15. Valstar, S., Griswold, W.G., Porter, L.: The relationship between prerequisite proficiency and student performance in an upper-division computing course. In: Proceedings of the 50th ACM Technical Symposium on Computer Science Education, pp. 794–800 (2019)

16. Xiong, X., Adjei, S., Heffernan, N.: Improving retention performance prediction with prerequisite skill features. In: Educational Data Mining 2014. Citeseer (2014)

Pneumonia Classification Using Few-Shot Learning with Visual Explanations

Shipra Madan[1(✉)], Anirudra Diwakar[2], Santanu Chaudhury[1,3],
and Tapan Gandhi[1]

[1] Indian Institute of Technology, Delhi, India
shipra.madan@ee.iitd.ac.in
[2] All India Institute of Medical Sciences, Delhi, India
[3] Indian Institute of Technology, Jodhpur, India

Abstract. Deep learning models have demonstrated state of the art performance in varied domains, however there is still room for improvement when it comes to learning new concepts from little data. Learning relevant features from a few training samples remains a challenge in machine learning applications. In this study, we propose an automated approach for the classification of Viral, Bacterial, and Fungal pneumonia using chest X-rays on a publicly available dataset. We employ distance learning based Siamese Networks with visual explanations for pneumonia detection. Our results demonstrate remarkable improvement in performance over conventional deep convolutional models with just a few training samples. We exhibit the powerful generalization capability of our model which once trained, effectively predicts new unseen data in the test set. Furthermore, we also illustrate the effectiveness of our model by classifying diseases from the same genus like COVID-19 and SARS.

Keywords: COVID-19 · Pneumonia · Chest x-rays · Few-Shot learning · Explainable AI

1 Introduction

Human beings exhibit impeccable learning capability with little supervision and the aptitude to generalize on new concepts quickly is unmatchable. On the contrary, our popular deep learning based methods require thousands of samples to perform optimally, which is generally not the case in the domain of medical image analysis. Machine learning models have recently gained so much attention due to their near-human level accuracy in various tasks such as Computer Vision [1], Natural Language Processing (NLP) [2] and Speech [3]. However, these algorithms fail in prediction scenarios where little supervised information is available. Data augmentation and transfer learning methodologies help ease the burden of large data requirements to some extent but do not fully solve it.

Pneumonia is a type of severe respiratory disease caused by a viral or bacterial or fungal infection. It is life-threatening for people of all ages and is the single

© Springer Nature Switzerland AG 2022
J.-H. Kim et al. (Eds.): IHCI 2021, LNCS 13184, pp. 229–241, 2022.
https://doi.org/10.1007/978-3-030-98404-5_22

largest cause of mortality in children in the World [4]. Pneumonia detection is generally performed by manually examining the chest x-rays by trained physicians and expert radiologists. It typically manifests as an area with increased opacity and appears more opaque on chest x-ray (CXR). Diagnosis is further confirmed by performing additional laboratory tests such as blood tests and tests for causative pathogens. Experts' manual evaluation is a tedious process and often leads to a contradictory interpretation of CXRs by different experts. The key to effective diagnosis and prognosis in pneumonia is to identify the causative pathogens in the etiology of pneumonia. Moreover, automated classification of Viral, Bacterial, and Fungal pneumonia is a very demanding task because of the long-tailed distribution of dataset available, scarcity of annotated images especially in low incidence scenarios, high level of similarity in the infected images. Labeled data is not only a time taking task but often expensive and difficult to acquire as it requires skilled inputs by experts to tag and annotate.

The year 2019 observed the unprecedented chaos due to the outbreak of viral pneumonia called Coronavirus disease 19 (COVID-19) [5]. The current gold standard technique for COVID-19 detection is reverse transcription- polymerase chain reaction (RT-PCR) which takes anywhere around 4 to 24 h for the results to come [6]. Chest Radiography (CXR) can act as an alternate detection tool for rapid COVID-19 detection. CXR remains the preferred imaging modality by healthcare professionals in diagnosing pneumonia for several reasons, such as lower radiation exposure [7], relatively inexpensive than CT scans, thus making radiography a more feasible option economically for patients as well as clinicians.

Our work tries to address the issue of data paucity by incorporating few-shot learning. The proposed model generalizes well on the previously unseen classes without the need for extensive retraining and to make the model visually interpretable, we use explainable AI (XAI) techniques such as Layer Wise Relevance Propagation (LRP) [8] and SmoothGrad [9] to highlight the important regions in support of model's inferencing process.

The main contributions of our paper can be summarized as:

- We demonstrate that the distance-based metric learning [10] works effectively in detecting different types of pneumonia using a small number of training examples.
- Proposed methodology surpasses conventional neural networks in terms of performance as well as training data size.
- We derive visual explanations besides few-shot classification results.

The remaining paper is organized as follows. Section 2 highlights the work carried out on a similar problem area using different techniques. Section 3 discusses the proposed framework with schematic diagrams. Section 4 gives details about the experimentation and evaluation metrics. Section 5 concludes the work proposed.

2 Related Work

In the last couple of years, the availability of a sizeable amount of labeled data in certain realms has facilitated deep learning models to exhibit remarkable performance in myriad domains such as object detection, image classification, medical image analysis, and segmentation [11–15]. However, these models are known to perform effectively where large training data is available, which is usually not the case in the medical domain, especially for rarely occurring diseases. Lately, few-shot learning methods such as meta-learning, metric-learning, transfer learning and semi-supervised models have gained a lot of interest from the research fraternity.

Matching Networks [16] learn a classification model that maps an unlabelled sample image to its label using a small number of labeled examples from the support set. Prototypical Networks [17] work on the idea of generating prototype representations of each class in the metric space and then computing the distances between the query image and the prototype. Their work is based on the fact that there exists a mathematical representation of images, such that the images from similar classes are grouped in clusters as opposed to images from dissimilar classes. In the same vein, Triplet Loss [18] is used for face recognition and verification tasks by learning image feature representations for few-shot learning. Model Agnostic Meta-Learning (MAML) [19] is a gradient-based approach that aims to learn optimal initial weights which quickly adapt to new tasks with only a few training examples. A meta-learning model based on Long Short Term Memory (LSTM) by learning relevant parameter updates is used for quick adaptation on new tasks in [20].

Several computer aided models for pneumonia identification have been proposed in the past, but most of them are either segmentation based or require enormous amount of training data. Jaiswal et al. [21] utilize the Mask R-CNN for pneumonia prediction on dataset released by the Radiological Society of North America (RSNA). A triplet loss based few-shot learning model to detect COVID-19 from CXR is proposed in [22]. Singh et al. [23] evaluates the accuracy of deep learning algorithms for diagnosing abnormalities using regular front view chest radiographs, and monitors the stability or change in findings over radiographs obtained serially. Wang et al. [24] presents a deep learning based model to identify 8 classes of chest diseases related to thorax using a newly created dataset ChestX-ray8 with 108,948 frontal chest radiographs acquired from 32,717 patients. Rajpurkar et al. [25] in their work propose a 121 layer deep convolutional layer network called CheXNet, trained on a large dataset comprising over 100,000 front-view CXR for 14 disease labels.

3 Method

The main aim of this study is to classify different types of pneumonia in a small skewed dataset of chest radiographs. The reason behind this skewness can be attributed to discovery of new mutants everyday and the difficulty of annotating them because of limited expertise. This further restricts the number of labeled samples for infrequent diseases in comparison to commonly occurring diseases. Therefore, our work focuses on automating the detection of Viral, Bacterial and Fungal pneumonia from chest radiographs utilizing few-shot learning method in a low data regime. We now detail on the structure and specifics of Siamese Neural Network used in our work. Figure 1 shows the entire pipeline for pneumonia identification.

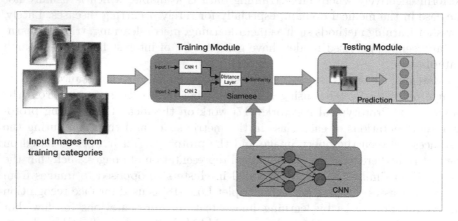

Fig. 1. Figure depicting an overview of the proposed method for pneumonia identification from CXR using Siamese networks.

3.1 Model

Our proposed model is a standard Siamese network [26], comprising two identical convolutional neural networks (CNN) with shared weights. The configuration of the Siamese Net is described as follows. The two images I_1 and I_2 ($I \in R^1, grayscale image$) form the input to the two CNNs with 4 layers each. Image feature representations $R(I_1)$ and $R(I_2)$ of fixed length are generated for the input images by CNNs. The fundamental idea behind this model is based on the premise that - if two images belong to the identical class, then their feature representations would also be similar, while if images are from non-identical classes, then their feature representations would also be different. The network here is not trained to classify an image to its desired output class, rather learns a similarity function for the input images and assigns a similarity score to the images. Two very similar images, should output a high similarity score and similarly two dissimilar images should output a low similarity score. Figure 2 shows the architecture for the proposed model [26].

3.2 Implementation Details

The network used as a backbone feature extractor in our work is a CNN [27] with a stack of 3 convolutional layers and 2×2 MaxPool layers followed by a

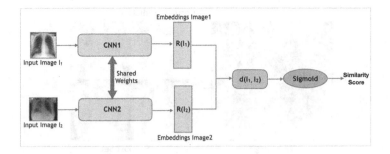

Fig. 2. High level architecture diagram of Siamese networks.

fourth convolutional layer. Convolution blocks are composed of 64, 128, 128 and 256 filters with sizes 10×10, 7×7, 4×4 and 4×4 respectively from input to output. This network reduces an input image into a low dimensional feature vector, which we call an embedding R. A customized layer is added to compute the absolute difference between the feature vectors R generated by the CNN for the two input images I_1 and I_2 as shown in Eq. 1.

$$d = |R(I_1) - R(I_2)| \tag{1}$$

Similarity score is generated by the dense layer with a sigmoid function as shown in Eq. 2.

$$S_{score} = \sigma(d) \tag{2}$$

The model is further validated using N-way one-shot learning, where N refers to the number of image pairs used for prediction. Basically, an image from one class, also referred to as a test set is compared to N other images from different classes called support set and correspondingly N similarity scores are generated. Image pair with the highest similarity score is treated as correct prediction. Correct prediction percentage is calculated by repeating this process 't' times and is given by Eq. 3

$$Prediction\_percentage = (100 * num_{correct})/t \tag{3}$$

where t refers to the number of trials and num_correct are the number of correct predictions made out of t trials. Figure 3 represents the 4-way few-shot learning scenario.

We also perform experiments by incorporating deeper CNN models for generating image embeddings such as the pretrained ResNet50V2 and InceptionV3 trained with the ImageNet weights having an initial learning rate of 1×10^{-4} and Adam as the optimizer. But these deeper architectures have millions of trainable parameters, i.e. the model complexity is very high. Thus, we observe that the pre-trained models tend to easily overfit in the fine-tuning task owing to the increased complexity of a large number of trainable parameters, especially when the amount of training data is exceptionally low, and their distribution

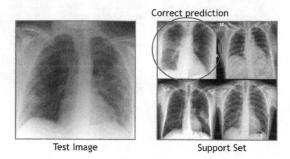

Fig. 3. Sample test image and support set for 4-Way 5-Shot learning

is unbalanced/skewed. Owing to the necessity of generating faithful low dimensional representations of the input images, we decide to incorporate a customized CNN architecture.

4   Experiments and Results

We train our model on covid-chestxray dataset which we first describe and then provide the training details for the techniques proposed.

4.1   Dataset

For this study, we use a publicly available covid-chestxray-dataset [28] comprising of 761 chest x-ray images. Out of which 679 are frontal and 82 are lateral from 412 subjects acquired from various hospitals across countries. Table 1 presents the distribution of chest radiographs based on diagnosis, pneumonia type, and causal microbial agents.

We evaluate our model's performance for 2-way, 3-Way, and 4-Way with 5-shot, 10-shot, and 20-shot settings each, which means that during training 5, 10, and 20 images per class are used for training, sampled randomly from all the classes. For our first set of experiments, referred by Dataset-1 (intra-genus), we use images from COVID-19 and SARS in the training set and COVID-19, MERS-CoV, and SARS in the evaluation set from the viral genus. Similarly, for the second dataset, referred by Dataset-2 (inter-genus), we take images from Streptococcus from the bacterial genus, Pneumocystis from the fungal genus, and COVID-19 and SARS from the Viral genus in the training set. In the evaluation set, we use Pneumocystis from the fungal genus and COVID-19, MERS-CoV, and SARS from the viral genus. We do not consider images from the Lipoid and Aspiration class of disease as the causative pathogens for these diseases are unknown. Table 2 shows the images chosen for various disease categories in training and test set for both Dataset-1 and Dataset-2.

Table 1. Image count of frontal CXR for different types of pneumonia by type and genus or species from covid-chestxray-dataset

Type	Genus/Species	Image count
Viral	COVID-19 (SARSr-CoV-2)	468
	SARS (SARSr-CoV-1)	16
	MERS-CoV	10
	Varicella	5
	Influenza	4
	Herpes	3
Bacterial	Streptococcus spp.	13
	Klebsiella spp.	9
	Escherichia coli	4
	Nocardia spp.	4
	Mycoplasma spp.	5
	Legionella spp.	7
	Unknown	2
	Chlamydophila spp.	1
	Staphylococcus spp.	1
Fungal	Pneumocystis spp.	24
	Aspergillosis spp.	2
Unknown	Lipoid	8
	Aspiration	1

4.2   Parameter Selection

We train our model for 2000 epochs on NVIDIA V100 32 GB GPU which takes approximately 8 h of compute time with a mini-batch size of 4. We compile our model using Adam optimizer [29], the initial learning rate of 0.00006, and binary cross-entropy as the loss function. Validation of the model is done using 2-Way and 4-Way for 5, 10, and 20 shot tasks (no. of classes used in testing), and accuracy is evaluated over 50 trials.

4.3   Comparative Analysis

We compare our method with standard deep convolutional neural networks such as ResNet50 [30] and InceptionV3 [31] and meta-learning algorithm Reptile [32] in a few-shot setting, thereby using a similar amount of data (20 images for each class) as used in our technique. Instead of training the models from scratch, we fine-tune the last layers by augmenting the images using rotation and horizontal flipping. The basic idea behind ResNet architecture is the identity skip connection which helps mitigate the problem of vanishing gradients by allowing the gradients to flow through the alternate shortcut path. The model is composed

Table 2. Disease categories used for various experiments in training and testing set corresponding to type and genus.

Dataset	Training/Testing	Type	Genus
Dataset-1 (intra-genus)	Training	Viral	COVID-19
			SARS
	Testing	Viral	COVID-19
			MERS-CoV
			SARS
Dataset-2 (inter-genus)	Training	Bacterial	Streptococcus
		Fungal	Pneumocystis
		Viral	COVID-19
			SARS
	Testing	Fungal	Pneumocystis
		Viral	COVID-19
			MERS-CoV
			SARS

of 5 phases, each with a convolution and identity skip connection block. Each convolution and identity block further consists of 3 convolution layers with over 23 M trainable parameters.

Inception-v3 is a 48 layers deep convolutional neural network with an inception block as the core idea behind the model. Inception block is an amalgamation of 1×1, 3×3, and 5×5 convolution layers with their output filter banks combined into one output vector acting as the input for the next level.

Reptile is a first order meta-learning algorithm which aims to learn a good initialization of parameters, such that they can be optimized to adapt quickly on the new task using a few examples. Reptile works by sampling a task over and again, training it by performing a few Stochastic Gradient Descent (SGD) steps and then updating the weights thus moving towards the final trained parameters for the task in hand. It can be clearly observed that the proposed method outperforms the ResNet50, Inception-v3 and Reptile for this particular task. Table 3 shows the performance comparison of our model with ResNet50, InceptionV3 and Reptile.

Table 3. Performance comparison of our approach with ResNet50, InceptionV3 and Reptile using a similar amount of data.

Metric/Model	ResNet50	InceptionV3	Reptile	Ours
Precision	0.60	0.50	0.70	0.80
Recall	0.54	0.45	0.60	0.72
Accuracy	0.55	0.45	0.65	0.73

4.4   Results

Table 4 shows the classification accuracy for 2-Way and 3-Way setting and Table 5 shows the classification accuracy for 2-Way, 3-Way and 4-Way setting for 5-shot, 10-shot and 20-shot set-up. It can be observed empirically that the classification accuracy for the 20-shot setting surpasses 10-shot performance, which in turn is more for 5-shot classification in a 2-way mode. The reason behind this trend is intuitive as more training samples lead to better accuracy and vice-versa. Similarly, as the number of ways increases, classification performance decreases because a higher value of 'n' causes more incorrect predictions and a lower value of 'n' leads to more correct predictions.

Table 4. Performance comparison for 2-Way and 3-Way for 5-Shot, 10-Shot and 20-Shot classification tasks for Dataset-1.

Shots/Ways	2-Way	3-Way
5-Shot	64.00	52.00
10-Shot	68.00	52.00
20-Shot	80.00	68.00

Table 5. Performance comparison for 2-Way, 3-Way and 4-Way for 5-Shot, 10-Shot and 20-Shot classification tasks for Dataset-2.

Shots/Ways	2-Way	3-Way	4-Way
5-Shot	62.00	50.00	44.00
10-Shot	70.00	56.00	48.00
20-Shot	73.34	54.16	50.83

4.5   Visual Explanations

In order to make our model more transparent and results visually interpretable, we use explainable AI methods such as Layer Wise Relevance Propagation (LRP) [8] and SmoothGrad [9] to derive few-shot classification explanations. LRP method back propagates a score via the neural network and allocates relevance scores to the neurons in the network. These scores refer to the importance of a particular neuron in the prediction task and red pixels indicate the positive LRP relevance score and blue pixels indicate the negative LRP relevance score. The visualizations in Fig. 4 indicate that our model is not only capable of identifying the disease but also provides accurate localization of the infected regions, as indicated by well-trained radiologists. For a given query image from MERS-CoV class and support images from Pneumocystis, COVID-19, MERS-CoV and SARS in Fig. 4(a.), it can be clearly seen that the query images matches the correct category. Also, the highlighted red pixels in the predicted image over the lung region (positive LRP) validate the model's precise localization of the affected part.

SmoothGrad is based on the premise that the gradients of complex functions change with change in the input. So, it tries to smoothen the bumpiness of gradients by averaging the gradients multiple times with little noise added to the input. Figure 4 (b.) shows the visual explanations for the Pneumocystis query image along with the support set using SmoothGrad method and the red regions in the predicted

Interestingly, in most of the cases, our model correctly classified the query images and highlighted the regions of abnormalities in the CT scans, which are important for the model's decision.

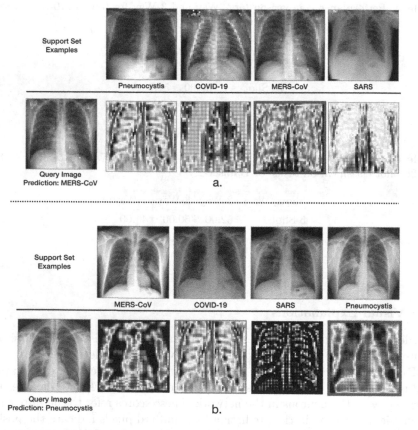

Fig. 4. Visual explanations for the input image with 4 target labels using (a.) LRP (b.) SmoothGrad. The first row illustrates images from the support set and the second row shows the explanation heatmaps for the query image. Predicted image is highlighted with green border.

5   Conclusion and Future Work

We propose an automated pneumonia detection mechanism based on the metric-learning technique in small-sized data scenario. We empirically validate that our methodology outperforms the conventional deep learning methods or transfer learning approaches in a small data regime and demonstrate its visual explainability indicating intuitive interpretation of what our model actually learns. Visual explanations supporting model's decision help provide more confidence and thus encouraging their applicability in risk sensitive areas. We attain an accuracy of 74% in a 2-Way 20-shot classification setup. In addition, we demonstrate that the proposed pneumonia detection framework gives remarkably good results, using as few as 20 samples per class and generalizes well on new test classes in comparison to fully supervised neural networks trained using 10 times large dataset. A further line of research in this domain should focus on extending the meta-learning technique on new mutations of COVID-19 where limited data and expertise is available. We also argue that the meta-learning techniques can be successfully extended on other imaging modalities like CT-scans, MRIs (Magnetic Resonance Imaging), and to other domains, especially in medical image classification.

References

1. Krizhevsky, A., Sutskever, I., Hinton, G.E.: Imagenet classification with deep convolutional neural networks. Adv. Neural. Inf. Process. Syst. **25**, 1097–1105 (2012)
2. Mikolov, T., Karafiát, M., Burget, L., Černocký, J., Khudanpur, S.: Recurrent neural network based language model. In: Eleventh Annual Conference Of The International Speech Communication Association (2010)
3. Hinton, G., et al.: Deep neural networks for acoustic modeling in speech recognition: the shared views of four research groups. IEEE Signal Process. Mag. **29**(6), 82–97 (2012)
4. World health organization. https://www.who.int/health-topics/pneumonia. Accessed 08 June 2021
5. Wu, F., et al.: A new coronavirus associated with human respiratory disease in China. Nature **579**(7798), 265–269 (2020)
6. Clinical management of severe acute respiratory infection when novel coronavirus (2019ncov) infection is suspected: interim guidance, 28 Jan 2020. https://www.who.int/docs/default-source/coronaviruse/clinical-management-of-novel-cov.pdf. Accessed 08 June 2021
7. Mettler, F.A., Jr., Huda, W., Yoshizumi, T.T., Mahesh, M.: Effective doses in radiology and diagnostic nuclear medicine: a catalog. Radiology **248**(1), 254–263 (2008)
8. Bach, S., Binder, A., Montavon, G., Klauschen, F., Müller, K.-R., Samek, W.: On pixel-wise explanations for non-linear classifier decisions by layer-wise relevance propagation. PLoS ONE **10**(7), e0130140 (2015)
9. Smilkov, D., Thorat, N., Kim, B., Viégas, F., Wattenberg, M.: Smoothgrad: removing noise by adding noise, arXiv preprint arXiv:1706.03825 (2017)

10. Suárez, J.L., García, S., Herrera, F.: A tutorial on distance metric learning: mathematical foundations, algorithms, experimental analysis, prospects and challenges. Neurocomputing **425**, 300–322 (2021)
11. LeCun, Y., Bengio, Y., Hinton, G.: Deep learning. Nature **521**(7553), 436–444 (2015)
12. Chen, S., Ma, K., Zheng, Y.: Med3d: transfer learning for 3D medical image analysis, arXiv preprint arXiv:1904.00625 (2019)
13. Eslami, M., Tabarestani, S., Albarqouni, S., Adeli, E., Navab, N., Adjouadi, M.: Image-to-images translation for multi-task organ segmentation and bone suppression in chest x-ray radiography. IEEE Trans. Med. Imaging **39**(7), 2553–2565 (2020)
14. Gessert, N., et al.: Skin lesion classification using CNNs with patch-based attention and diagnosis-guided loss weighting. IEEE Trans. Biomed. Eng. **67**(2), 495–503 (2019)
15. Tang, Y.-B., Tang, Y.-X., Xiao, J., Summers, R.M.: XLSor: a robust and accurate lung segmentor on chest X-rays using Criss-Cross attention and customized radiorealistic abnormalities generation. In: International Conference on Medical Imaging with Deep Learning, PMLR, pp. 457–467 (2019)
16. Vinyals, O., Blundell, C., Lillicrap, T., Kavukcuoglu, K., Wierstra, D.: Matching networks for one shot learning, arXiv preprint arXiv:1606.04080 (2016)
17. Snell, J., Swersky, K., Zemel, R.S.: Prototypical networks for few-shot learning, arXiv preprint arXiv:1703.05175 (2017)
18. Schroff, F., Kalenichenko, D., Philbin, J.: Facenet: a unified embedding for face recognition and clustering. In: Proceedings of the IEEE Conference on Computer Vision and Pattern Recognition, pp. 815–823 (2015)
19. Finn, C., Abbeel, P., Levine, S.: Model-agnostic meta-learning for fast adaptation of deep networks. In: International Conference on Machine Learning, PMLR, pp. 1126–1135 (2017)
20. Ravi, S., Larochelle, H.: Optimization as a model for few-shot learning (2016)
21. Jaiswal, A.K., Tiwari, P., Kumar, S., Gupta, D., Khanna, A., Rodrigues, J.J.: Identifying pneumonia in chest X-rays: a deep learning approach. Measurement **145**, 511–518 (2019)
22. Madan, S., Chaudhury, S., Gandhi, T.K.: Automated detection of COVID-19 on a small dataset of chest CT images using metric learning. In: 2021 International Joint Conference on Neural Networks (IJCNN), pp. 1–8. IEEE (2021)
23. Singh, R., et al.: Deep learning in chest radiography: detection of findings and presence of change. PLoS ONE **13**(10), e0204155 (2018)
24. Wang, X., Peng, Y., Lu, L., Lu, Z., Bagheri, M., Summers, R.M.: ChestX-ray8: hospital-scale chest X-ray database and benchmarks on weakly-supervised classification and localization of common thorax diseases. In: Proceedings of the IEEE Conference on Computer Vision and Pattern Recognition, pp. 2097–2106 (2017)
25. Rajpurkar, P., et al.: Chexnet: radiologist-level pneumonia detection on chest X-rays with deep learning. arXiv preprint arXiv:1711.05225 (2017)
26. Koch, G., Zemel, R., Salakhutdinov, R.: Siamese neural networks for one-shot image recognition. In: ICML Deep Learning Workshop, vol. 2. Lille (2015)
27. Zeiler, M.D., Fergus, R.: Visualizing and understanding convolutional networks. In: Fleet, D., Pajdla, T., Schiele, B., Tuytelaars, T. (eds.) ECCV 2014. LNCS, vol. 8689, pp. 818–833. Springer, Cham (2014). https://doi.org/10.1007/978-3-319-10590-1_53

28. Cohen, J.P., Morrison, P., Dao, L., Roth, K., Duong, T.Q., Ghassemi, M.: Covid-19 image data collection: prospective predictions are the future. arXiv 2006.11988 (2020). https://github.com/ieee8023/covid-chestxray-dataset
29. Kingma, D.P., Ba, J.: Adam: a method for stochastic optimization. arXiv preprint arXiv:1412.6980 (2014)
30. He, K., Zhang, X., Ren, S., Sun, J.: Deep residual learning for image recognition. In: Proceedings of the IEEE Conference on Computer Vision and Pattern Recognition, pp. 770–778 (2016)
31. Szegedy, C., Vanhoucke, V., Ioffe, S., Shlens, J., Wojna, Z.: Rethinking the inception architecture for computer vision. In: Proceedings of the IEEE Conference on Computer Vision and Pattern Recognition, pp. 2818–2826 (2016)
32. Nichol, A., Schulman, J.: Reptile: a scalable meta-learning algorithm. arXiv preprint arXiv:1803.02999 **2**(2) (2018). 1

User Experience Design for Defense Systems with AI

Sunyoung Park[1], Hyun K. Kim[1,2]([✉]), Yuryeon Lee[1], Gyuwon Park[2], and Danbi Lee[2]

[1] Department of Artificial Intelligence Convergence, Kwangwoon University,
20 Kwangwoon-ro, Nowon-gu, Seoul 01897, Korea
hyunkkim@kw.ac.kr
[2] School of Information Convergence, Kwangwoon University,
20 Kwangwoon-ro, Nowon-gu, Seoul 01897, Korea

Abstract. As artificial intelligence (AI) is applied at an increasing frequency in various fields, the number of studies on the user experience (UX) design of human-AI interaction is also increasing. However, the results of these studies on AI UX design principles are insufficient for actual AI systems. In light of this fact, the purpose of this study was to upgrade the UX design of a defense system that uses AI technology to detect land changes and targets. In order to upgrade the UX design of this AI system, a three-step procedure was executed. First, AI UX principles were derived by analyzing literature related to human-AI interaction. Second, ideation was performed to improve the interface. Finally, the results of the ideation were utilized to construct the UX prototype of the AI system with Adobe XD. The results of this study are expected to be used as fundamental data for future research that will develop UX principles and advanced methods for AI systems.

Keywords: Artificial intelligence · User experience · AI UX · AI system design · AI usability · AI system design process

1 Background and Introduction

Artificial intelligence (AI) systems have played significant roles in a variety of fields, including medical area [1], education [2], social media [3], military disciplines [4], and a wide range of other fields [5]. As AI technology spreads, an increasing number of decisions are automatically being processed for human users. Nevertheless, for important decisions, there is a need for AI technology to explain the results of its algorithms because humans prefer to make the final decision for themselves [6]. However, AI technology is difficult to understand, and humans tend not to trust AI because it is characteristic of a black box that does not explain the process through which the results are derived [7]. Accordingly, eXplainable AI (XAI) studies that provide explanations of AI algorithms or convert black box models to glass box models are actively progressing [8]. In addition to these XAI endeavors, numerous guidelines, and recommendations on design methods for human-AI interaction have been proposed over the last 20 years [9], but there is still an insufficient number of studies on how actual users interact with actual systems.

© Springer Nature Switzerland AG 2022
J.-H. Kim et al. (Eds.): IHCI 2021, LNCS 13184, pp. 242–247, 2022.
https://doi.org/10.1007/978-3-030-98404-5_23

In this study, a three-step method involving UX design principles for AI systems was employed to enhance the interface for a defense system that uses AI technology. The goal was to upgrade the UX design of the human-AI interaction by including explainability and transparency. The main functions of the system used in this study include change detection [10] in satellite images of land using the Dense Siamese Network [11] and target detection [12] of planes in satellite images using YOLOv3 [13]. The rest of this paper is organized as follows. Section 2 introduces the procedures performed to enhance the UX design, and Sect. 3 introduces the results of the improved performance. Section 4 discusses the significance of the results and future work.

2   Method

Three steps were performed to upgrade the UX design of the AI system. First, papers related to human-AI interaction were collected, and AI UX principles were developed by selecting and analyzing them in order of relevance. Second, ideas for interface improvement were gathered according to the AI UX principles identified in the previous step. Finally, the ideas were prototyped using Adobe XD.

2.1   Development of AI UX Principles

A total of 120 papers related to human-AI interaction were collected to identify AI UX components and develop the relevant principles. This group of papers included 49 journal articles, 52 conference proceedings, and 19 miscellaneous papers. These papers were filtered in order of relevance to the AI system used in this study: there were 45 papers of high relevance, 34 papers of medium relevance, and 41 papers of low relevance. Using the information in these papers, a list of 49 relevant sub-items were created through component grouping.

2.2   Ideation

In order to advance the AI system, a task hierarchy analysis was initially performed to analyze the essential tasks and understand how to perform them using the UX interface [14]. Then, ideation was conducted for about five minutes to derive functional ideas and improvements. Ideas about the potential inconveniences and improvements for each component group of the principles developed in Sect. 2.1 were written on sticky notes, and the ideas were shared.

2.3   Prototyping

Prototyping was conducted using Adobe XD, a design collaboration tool, to visualize the results derived from the ideation. In addition, aesthetic elements that were difficult to derive in the ideation stage were improved through the prototyping.

3 Results

3.1 AI UX Design Principles

A total of 12 elements can be derived from AI UX design principles: causality, fairness, accountability, explainability, transparency, performance, trust, satisfaction, safety, ease of use, efficiency, and controllability. Table 1 shows examples of AI UX design principles.

Table 1. Examples of AI UX design principles

Explainability	1. The behavior of the algorithm of this AI system is easy to understand
	2. The results of this AI system are interpretable
	3. This AI system is explained sufficiently well for the algorithm and its results to be fully understood
	4. How the results of this AI system were derived is understandable
	5. This AI system provides a description of the errors that may occur
Transparency	1. The criteria for evaluating algorithms used by this AI system are publicly announced and understood by people
	2. All outputs created by this AI system are explained to those affected by them
	3. This AI system describes which algorithms were used

3.2 Ideation

Next, ideation for each AI UX design principle was conducted. Ideas that could be included in multiple principles were duplicated under those principles. The results of two representative design principles, explainability and transparency, are shown in Table 2.

3.3 Prototyping

The interface for the confirmation of the change detection result was the same before (Fig. 1) and after (Fig. 2) the improvement. In the initial program, there was no provision of information in images 1 and 2 and no detailed description (e.g., address, coordinates, change detection rate) of the observed land change. This made it difficult to verify the information. Accordingly, images 1 and 2 and detailed information on the detected land change were provided, and the image of the location of the land change was also included on the right side of the interface. In addition, small text, unused icons, redundant buttons, and unnecessary functions were checked, improved, or removed.

Table 2. Examples of ideation results

Explainability	1. Change detection: description of location of land change detection, changed section, and detection rate 2. Target detection: description of location, number, and detection rate of aircraft 3. Help function 4. Guide function for the first use 5. Change detection: use only one image, click the "Change Detection" icon to indicate that it cannot be executed in Chapter 1, and deactivate the "Change Detection" icon 6. Change detection image selection: after selecting one image, only image coordinates that can be changed are displayed in the map and table 7. Target detection: target detection results are shown by comparing them with the most similar training data (specify the reason for judgment) 8. Provide a preliminary description of the algorithm (image set, learning rate, and epoxy number)
Transparency	1. Target detection: target detection results are shown by comparing them with the most similar training data 2. Provide a preliminary description of the algorithm (image set, learning rate, and epoxy number) 3. Change detection: description of location of land change detection, changed section, and detection rate 4. Target detection: description of location, number, and detection rate of aircraft 5. Help function 6. Guide function for the first use

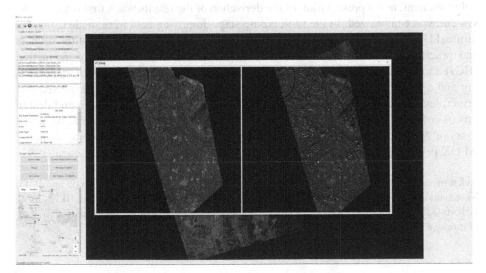

Fig. 1. Interface before the improvement

Fig. 2. Interface after the improvement

4   Conclusion

In this study, a three-step method for enhancing AI system interfaces was proposed. The three steps were: development of AI UX design principles, ideation, and prototyping. The AI UX principles used in this study not only exhibited excellent performance, but they also demonstrated transparency, fairness, and safety in the results. This indicates that user reliability and satisfaction should be considered just as much as performance. In the ideation stage, the importance of explanatory components, such as guide functions, help functions, and a presentation of the derivation of the results when first using the AI system, was emphasized. In the prototyping stage, improvements were made using traditional UX components, such as usability and aesthetics. This suggests that researchers and practitioners interested in the intersection between human-computer interaction (HCI) and AI should develop this field together [15]. As a defense system, generalizing and applying to all AI systems requires more consideration, but it is expected that principles and procedures can be used as reference materials in the design and design process of the system. In future work, usability experiments will be conducted by actual users of AI systems before and after improvement. Furthermore, major components of AI UX principles will be identified, and secondary upgrading will be implemented.

Acknowledgment. This research was supported by the MSIT (Ministry of Science and ICT), Korea, under the ITRC (Information Technology Research Center) support program (IITP-2021-2016-0-00288) supervised by the IITP (Institute for Information & Communications Technology Planning & Evaluation).

References

1. Yu, K.H., Beam, A.L., Kohane, I.S.: Artificial intelligence in healthcare. Nat. Biomed. Eng. **2**(10), 719–731 (2018). https://doi.org/10.1038/s41551-018-0305-z
2. Holmes, W.: Artificial intelligence in education. In: Encyclopedia of Education and Information Technologies, pp. 1–16 (2019). https://doi.org/10.1007/978-3-319-60013-0_107-1
3. Zeng, D., Chen, H., Lusch, R., Li, S.-H.: Social media analytics and intelligence. IEEE Intell. Syst. **25**(6), 13–16 (2010). https://doi.org/10.1109/mis.2010.151
4. Amir, S., Ahmad, F.: Artificial intelligence and its prospective use in armed forces (2019)
5. Nasirian, F., Ahmadian, M., Lee, O.-K.D.: AI-based voice assistant systems: evaluating from the interaction and trust perspectives (2017)
6. Adadi, A., Berrada, M.: Peeking inside the black-box: a survey on explainable artificial intelligence (XAI). IEEE Access **6**, 52138–52160 (2018). https://doi.org/10.1109/access.2018.287 0052
7. Gunning, D., et al.: XAI—explainable artificial intelligence. Sci. Robot. **4**(37) (2019). https://doi.org/10.1126/scirobotics.aay7120
8. Rai, A.: Explainable AI: from black box to glass box. J. Acad. Mark. Sci. **48**(1), 137–141 (2019). https://doi.org/10.1007/s11747-019-00710-5
9. Amershi, S., et al.: Guidelines for human-AI interaction. In: Proceedings of the 2019 CHI Conference on Human Factors in Computing Systems (2019). https://doi.org/10.1145/329 0605.3300233
10. Lu, D., et al.: Change detection techniques. Int. J. Remote Sens. **25**(12), 2365–2401 (2004). https://doi.org/10.1080/0143116031000139863
11. Abdelpakey, M.H., Shehata, M.S., Mohamed, M.M.: DensSiam: end-to-end densely-siamese network with self-attention model for object tracking. In: Bebis, G., et al. (eds.) ISVC 2018. LNCS, vol. 11241, pp. 463–473. Springer, Cham (2018). https://doi.org/10.1007/978-3-030-03801-4_41
12. Li, W., Xiang, S., Wang, H., Pan, C.: Robust airplane detection in satellite images. In: 2011 18th IEEE International Conference on Image Processing (2011). https://doi.org/10.1109/icip.2011.6116259
13. Redmon, J., Farhadi, A.: YOLOv3: an incremental improvement. arXiv preprint arXiv:1804.02767 (2018)
14. Choi, D.K., Lee, C.W., Lee, C.: A graphical user interface design for surveillance and security robot. J. Korea Robot. Soc. **10**(1), 24–32 (2015). https://doi.org/10.7746/jkros.2015.10.1.024
15. Inkpen, K., Chancellor, S., De Choudhury, M., Veale, M., Baumer, E.P.S.: Where is the human? In: Extended Abstracts of the 2019 CHI Conference on Human Factors in Computing Systems (2019). https://doi.org/10.1145/3290607.3299002

Multilayer Tag Extraction for Music Recommendation Systems

Sameeksha Gurrala, M. Naagamani[✉], Sayan Das, Pralhad Kolambkar,
R. P. Yashasvi, Jagjeet Suryawanshi, Pranay Raj, Amarjeet Kumar,
Shankhanil Ghosh, Sri Harsha Navundru, and Rajesh Thalla

School of Computer and Information Sciences, University of Hyderabad,
Hyderabad, India
{nagamanics,20mcmb04}@uohyd.ac.in

Abstract. With hundreds and thousands of songs being added to online music streaming platforms everyday, there is a challenge to recommend songs that the users decide to hear at any given time. Classification of songs plays a vital role in any recommendation system and when it comes to Indian music, there are a lot of parameters to be taken into consideration. The proposed paper takes into account this task and through recent advancement in data processing and signal processing, we have tried to use classification processes on Indian music based on various parameters. These parameters include metadata of music, sentimental values, as well as technical features. India being a diverse country with multiple culture values, is home to variety of local music. At various instances, these various classification parameters play significant roles especially when local music is involved in the process of recommendation. Classifying Indian music based on such parameters will lead to better results and also aid to be an improvement in recommendation system for Indian music.

Keywords: NLP · Root word extraction · Sentiment analysis · Spectrogram · Feature extraction · Emotion analysis tags · KNN · SVM · Naive Bayes

1 Introduction

Music is one of the inherent elements of nature. Discovery of music goes back to pre-historic eras. It is an integral part of social and religious lives. Music is usually defined as an arrangement of sound within a well-defined framework which include the elements like rhythm, tempo, pitch, harmony etc. Over the centuries, music has evolved and has been categorized into many genres and takes different shapes and styles based on different ethnicities, countries, and culture.

Main elements of music of any kind are Pitch, note, rhythm. These elements technically drive music into arranging itself as an art form. Indian music has

© Springer Nature Switzerland AG 2022
J.-H. Kim et al. (Eds.): IHCI 2021, LNCS 13184, pp. 248–259, 2022.
https://doi.org/10.1007/978-3-030-98404-5_24

different names for these elements. Pitch is known as Sruthi/Sur. Note is known as Swara, and Rhythm is known as Tala. Swaras/notes are considered as building blocks of music. They are analogous to the alphabet in English language. There are seven different Swaras - Sa (Shadjama), Ri (Rishabha), Ga (Gaandhara), Ma (Madhyama), Pa (Panchama), Da (Daivatha), Ni (Nishada). These swaras, apart from Sa and Pa, have two variations each. These variations are known as Swarasthanas. These twljust variations combinedly form the basis of any kind of music. These set of twelve Swarasthanas correspond to the twelve-tone chromatic scale, with the note C forming as basis. These twelve Swarasthanas are also considered as Sruthis whose frequencies range from $261.6256\,\mathrm{Hz}$ to $523.2511\,\mathrm{Hz}$. These frequencies are within the range of frequencies audible to human beings whose listening range is $20\,\mathrm{Hz}$ to $20\,\mathrm{KHz}$.

Classification of music based on its technical aspects is a tedious task. However, these technical aspects provide indications for human emotions. For example, a person is able to identify the emotion of a sample of music played without understanding why is that particular emotion relevant to the particular piece of music they listened to. These is because the subconscious human mind makes itself react to different variation of notes, different rhythms, thus producing complex emotions associating to a piece of music. These kinds of association of emotions with technical aspects of music, help us classify music on the basis of emotions. Apart from emotions, music can also be classified based on the context, nature of the song(genre), artists involved, era of music etc.

This classification forms the core of recommendation system proposed in this paper. Recommendation systems are used to provide various options of music to the user which are similar to the music they listened to in the past. This provides a sense of personalisation and a customized experience to the users as the system provides services according to their tastes. These help in satisfying the user needs by providing value to their investment of time and money, and give them a chance to explore new music, while saving costs of computation and resources.

This paper proposes a hybrid recommendation system that classifies songs and recommends them to user based on emotions, artists involved, era of music - taking these parameters into consideration all at once. Given a song, the objective is to collect metadata of the song, extract context and emotions based on sentiment analysis of the song, and also extract and analyse the technical features of song, and provide a set of tags as intermediate output. These tags are further used as input parameters for a recommendation system, which would then recommend songs based on algorithms that use these tags to process further information. The steps involved in the process is shown in Fig. 1.

2 Related Works

In this section, we will be referring to the works done on music recommendation. In the paper published by [2], the authors propose a design of a recommendation system on music that will recommend music on the basis of user's choice. When

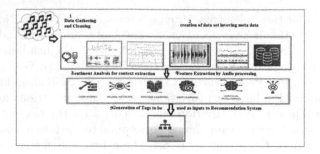

Fig. 1. A flow diagram showing the different steps of the process

a user is playing a song, the recommendation system analyzes the song and extracts the features from it and then recommends next song to the user. It tracks the history of the user and tries to find which type of music does the user hear the most.

In the paper published by [10], the authors propose to recommend music on the basis of context. This recommendation system do not depend thoroughly on user's history or preferences as they could change from time to time. So the authors have tried to explore the fuzzy system in recommending a music. The authors also explore the Bayesian networks and utility theory for recommending music. Fuzzy system is used to associate a degree of membership with the song. The degree of membership for a song is the number of users listening to that song. Songs having higher degree of membership will be recommended to the user. Bayesian network uses the mathematics of Bayes theory to derive the context from the song. Finally comes the utility theory that uses the preferences of the user on the basis of context.

In the paper published by [8], the authors propose to recommend music not only on the basis of user's choice but on the basis of context. The main objective is to recommend similar kind of music in the same context for a specific user. By the term context, the authors define the parameters as location, the identity of the objects around and the chance of those objects. If a person is attending a birthday, then the songs that will be recommended to that user will be birthday songs.

In the paper published by [5], the authors propose to recommend suitable songs that the user used to hear. The main objective of this paper is to recommend songs that are favorite to the users and also new to the them. The authors use a parameter called "Forgetting Curve" to calculate the freshness of the song for a specific user. If there's a song that the user used to hear but hasn't heard for a long time, it will be recommended to the user. The songs that will be recommended are from the user's history.

In the paper published by [11], the authors propose a recommendation system on music based on sentiment analysis. People use social media to express their emotions through text. These texts are classified as positive, negative or neutral. The authors use this sentiment intensity metric that is associated with lexicon based sentiment metric that is extracted from the user's profile. The sentiment of a specific user is calculated by extracting the posts from the user's profile on social media. Then this value is used to recommend song to that specific user.

3   Proposed System

Any music related file consists of various details with respect to its manual data, lyrics and background score. Here, each of these details can act as an input for generating tags which could be helpful in recommending pertinent music to a user. Following architecture shows the flow of process Fig. 2.

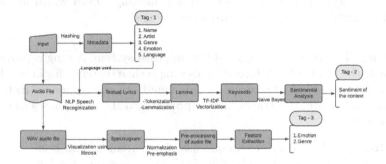

Fig. 2. Architecture depicting flow for Tag Generation System

3.1   Data Preprocessing Phase

Data Gathering. We gather data from YouTube as it is the primary source for various kinds of audio available to public. We then convert the video data to required audio format (WAV - Waveform Audio File Format) using python libraries. This format is used in order to obtain lossless output of audio files from the conversion tools, and it helps in further stages of processing. We gather metadata of the audio files - Name of the song, Singer name, Language, Release date, Genre, Emotion, Music Director, Type of origin (Movie/private album) etc. from Wikipedia and official music streaming sites.

1. **Extracting data from YouTube:-** This process can be carried out in two steps - Downloading videos from YouTube, and converting videos to preferable audio format. The first step is done using the python library **PyTube**. Once the video is downloaded, it is saved in local storage to a specified destination path in mp4 format. Once the video is downloaded, another python library **Moviepy** is used to convert the video into audio of required format.

Dataset Creation. The data gathered is present in multiple formats and is largely unorganised. We then build a tabular data structure to store the gathered information in an organised and structured manner, and index the data with its corresponding attributes. This results in formation of a dataset, which will be stored in excel (XLSX) file format. This is further converted into Comma Separated Variable (CSV) format for processing.

Data Cleaning and Pre-processing. Once the dataset is created and before it is converted to CSV format, it is checked for redundancy and incorrectness, and such data is corrected with proper values, and redundant information is removed. Inconsistencies in data is checked against proper references and corrected to suit the provided format. If an example contains missing values which are by any means irretrievable, it is removed from the dataset.

Searching. This is the first phase of the proposed system. A song is provided as an input in the form of WAV format. This song is then searched for in the dataset using hashing technique. Once the song is found, its corresponding metadata - Language and Genre, is retrieved and is provided to the next phases as input in the form of tags.

1. **Hashing** - It is a search technique used for searching data items using key-value pairs. Input is said to be the "key" which is given to a function known as hash function. This function processes the key value to provide an output which is an index in a restricted domain. This index is used to retrieve the value present in the database, narrowing the search area to a single row. This function uses $O(1)$ time for search, and is a useful mechanism to search large file structures such as databases and datasets Fig. 3.

3.2 Tag Extraction Using Sentiment Analysis

In this phase, we extract tags based on the emotion associated with the lyrics of a song. Here, we use language tags from phase 1 for speech recognition using NLP to convert lyrics into textual format. This textual format is optimised to keywords upon which we apply sentiment analysis to obtain the emotion of the song [7].

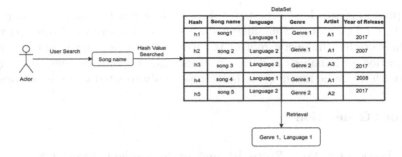

Fig. 3. Tag extraction using Hashing

Speech to Text Conversion. The audio input received from phase 1 is converted into text by using Pyaudio and Wave. Pyaudio is a Python library which is used to play and record music on various platforms like Windows, Mac, Linux etc. Wave is a Python library, it provides an interface to the WAV audio format. Wave can also read the properties of a WAV file and write audio data in raw format to a file. We have also utilized Speech-Recognization and pydub libraries which split large audio files into chunks and apply speech recognition on each of these chunks. We have also used Google recognize to get the transcription of the audio chunk and convert them into text format.

Tokenization. In this phase, we are splitting paragraphs into sentences which are further split into a set of words. These words are known as tokens. This process of tokenization is applied on lyrics extracted from the process of speech to text conversion in the previous step e.g. "Amaro porano jaha chai" becomes "Amaro", "porano", "jaha", "you", "chai".

Cleaning the Data. The set of tokens may contain many special characters like !,',/ etc. All these characters are removed from all sets of tokens as they don't have any meaning or sentiment attached to them and they don't add value in sentiment analysis. Also, uppercase letters are also converted into lowercase letters. e.g. "Tumi", "robe", "nirobe!!" becomes "tumi", "robe", "nirobe".

Removing the Stop Words. Words like "is", "a", "the", "are" and etc. are known as stopwords. They carry very little value in analysis. Hence, stop words are eliminated and size of input is reduced which results in faster computation and analysis.

Lemmatization. We are now left with meaningful words. However, to accurately count the number of words present we have to transform words into their original form (root word form). Hence, we apply lemmatization. Lemmatization is the process in which we convert words to their original lemma (word or phrase defined in a dictionary). Stemming can also be used where words are converted into their original linguistic root of the word. This is a crucial step for proper classification and analysis of data. e.g. tumi, tomar, tomader, ami, amra. Here, words with the same meaning are being repeatedly counted which is not desired.

Keyword Generation

Vectorization or Word Embeddings. In this method, words or phrases from vocabulary are mapped to a corresponding vector of real numbers which are used to find word predictions, similarities/semantics. In other words, it produces numerical features to classifiers.

Vectorization is of two types:

1. Count vectorizer: It converts a lyric into a matrix with token count. The values are assigned based on the number of occurrences of each token. tum ham pyar kushi dukhi asu Data 3 4 4 2 1 1
2. TF-IDF (Total Frequency - Inverse Document Frequency) It measures the originality of a word by comparing the number of times a word appears in a doc with the number of docs the word appears in.

$$w_{ij} = tf_{ij}log(\frac{N}{df_i}) \tag{1}$$

Sentiment Analysis. Sentiment analysis is the computational process which is used to detect sentiment, emotions and attitudes of people towards a product, topic or person from given inputs like text, audio, images and videos. Sentiment analysis is often performed on textual input. It has a wide range of applications like user satisfaction with a product for enhancement of business, detecting emotions of users for better social media experience, improved customer service etc. For this analysis, we are using naïve bayes classifiers.

Naïve Bayes'. We use Naïve Bayes' algorithm to classify keywords and identify the emotion of a song. Naïve Bayes' is a simple probabilistic classifier which works based on Bayes' theorem. Here, we utilise the keywords generated from vectorization and apply Naïve Bayes' classification on them [1]. All keywords are given equal weightage to calculate the probability of the lyrics being associated with a particular emotion. The probability of a song having a particular emotion is identified by mapping the probability to Thayer emotion model based on which the emotions present in song are identified [1].

3.3 Tagging Extraction Based on Audio Features

In this phase, we obtain tags based on the music present in a song. Sound is generated by creating difference in pressure levels. So, the related frequency and

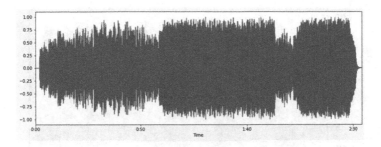

Fig. 4. Waveform of audio file

energy levels of the sounds generated in the music are used for obtaining various features of the music.

In this process, we initially obtain the audio file of the music in WAV format. This file consists of various sampling frequencies within a specified time slot Fig. 4. Then, we can present a waveform visualization of the file with respect to amplitude and time. By using python libraries - **Matplotlib** and **Librosa**, we plot the Spectrogram of the file, where we see the variation of energy levels with respect to time.

Then we need to digitize the audio file for further processing which is done by using **Numpy** array with the audio file frequency and sample rate. Then we start pre-processing of audio signals which is done in two stages that is normalization and pre-emphasis [12].

Normalization. Here we normalize the audio file into a standard format so that we can exclude the noisy environment and outliers for better pre-processing of data. Here, we use sklearn python library for the normalization of the file to a standard set Fig. 5.

Pre-emphasis. In this stage, the high frequency sounds which usually get compressed when humans sing, will be normalized. So, the lower frequency sounds stay at their original form and high frequency sounds gets boosted. After these steps, the file can used for feature extraction.

Feature Extraction. Sounds generated usually tend to have various energy levels. These variations observed here are useful in differentiating one genre or emotion from another. Here, we used six feature extractions which are given as input for our model to generate output classes. These output classes act as tags from phase-3.

Zero Crossing Rate. Here, we calculate the variation of signal's amplitude. This shows the rate of change of signal sign for a period of time that is from

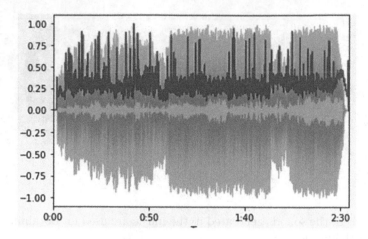

Fig. 5. Normalized audio file

positive to negative. Rapid change of signal indicates high frequency information. Music genres such as hip-hop, rock, folk comes under this high frequency. Similarly, for every genre, the rate of change of sign varies.

Spectral Rolloff. Spectral rolloff indicates the frequency level under which whole energy is present. Moreover, this process tends to differentiate the noisy data from the file so that we can concentrate only on harmony and rhythm of the music. Usually, classical music tends to have high frequency rolloff compared to folk music. This way we extract this feature to see the variation of frequency levels based on energy.

MFCC. Mel-Frequency Cepstral Coefficients (MFCC) consist of 39 features. Due to these limited features, it gets easier for the model to learn information. MFCC generates coefficients which are used in building Mel-Frequency Cepstrum (MFC). MFC is a power spectrum of sound which is built from the derivations of type of cepstral representation of audio file. This feature extraction helps in genre classification and audio similarities which help in finding the emotions Fig. 6.

Spectral Centroid. Spectral Centroid characterizes the spectrum of audio file based on center of mass. Here we indicate the location of center of mass of spectrum, that is, it usually represents the weighted mean formula 1 of the frequencies present in the signal.

$$f_c = \frac{\sum_k S(k)f(k)}{\sum_k S(k)} \tag{2}$$

```
[[-4.6509814e+02 -4.4060864e+02 -4.1775751e+02 ... -2.7338278e+02
  -3.2454871e+02 -4.5604153e+02]
 [ 2.4721164e-01  2.7963623e+01  5.4092018e+01 ...  1.7004318e+02
   1.3431506e+02  1.2559573e+01]
 [ 2.1746251e-01  1.6825876e+01  3.1683426e+01 ...  3.2062195e+01
   3.9420727e+01  1.1154607e+01]
 ...
 [ 2.2083938e-02  2.5636811e+00  1.2436292e-01 ... -2.7527070e+00
   3.0280840e-01  6.0815167e+00]
 [ 9.2635781e-02  8.2856255e+00  4.8985329e+00 ...  5.7201934e+00
   2.5712476e+00  6.1122932e+00]
 [ 1.5585655e-01  7.4691539e+00  5.0613451e+00 ...  7.5841684e+00
   5.6965923e+00  5.7118168e+00]]
```

Fig. 6. Values of MFCC

Spectral Flux. Rate of change of power spectrum is calculated in spectral flux. This is done by calculating the Euclidean distance between the two normalized spectrum. The timbre of audio file can be detected, that is, the tune color and quality of audio can be obtained. So, we can easily differentiate sound productions such as choir notes and musical instruments.

Spectral Contrast. In a spectrum, the highs and lows of the frequencies help in finding the contrast of musical sound. This difference between the peaks and valleys vary for various genres. For example, pop consists of low special contrast compared to rock music [6].

Now that all the features are extracted, these are given as input to the model and the output class generates the genre and emotion of the music from the data set present [11]. These output classes are taken as Tag-3 from last phase Fig. 7.

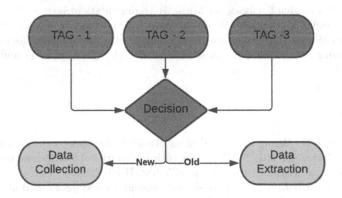

Fig. 7. Tag classification

4 Conclusion

The systems present currently help to classify and recommend music based upon various song metadata like artist, language, genre etc. Also, various feature extraction systems are based on the parameters or features of a song that the user is currently listening to, like the tempo, melody, pitch and so on. All these existing classification models are performing well in that specific classification domain but those can further be enhanced by combining the best features of above stated models, and that is what is being have proposed in this research work. Through this hybrid approach of combining various parameters of music, feature extraction as well as classification based on metadata and sentimental analysis, we are able to propose a better dataset for Indian music recommendation system.

5 Future Work

The proposed system is limited to songs containing various instruments and voice and can be further expanded to include instrumental music which can enhance the recommendation system in terms of emotion based classification. The research work can further be expanded to include more and more Indian language songs as well as local and folk music. There is a limitation on availability of audio libraries for various Indian languages processing which can be made in future to cover different Indian regional language processing for sentimental as well as emotional analysis.

Acknowledgement. This research work is an outcome of course - Problem-Solving Methodologies using AI, at the University of Hyderabad. The authors would like to thank Prof. Chakravarthy Bhagvathy, Dean, SCIS, for his support and feedback towards the research. The authors also thank the University of Hyderabad for facilitating the lab environments, and seniors Anjali Hembrome and Ritika Sinha who have provided their valuable feedback on Music Recommendation System. Their feedback helped us to build a strong basis for carrying out the research. Lastly, the authors would like to extend their gratitude to Chhanda Saha, the teaching assistant of the Problem-Solving Methodologies course, who has guided us to prepare and shape the paper.

References

1. An, Y., Sun, S., Wang, S.: Naive Bayes classifiers for music emotion classification based on lyrics. In: 2017 IEEE/ACIS 16th International Conference on Computer and Information Science (ICIS), pp. 635–638. IEEE (2017)
2. Chen, H.-C., Chen, A.L.P.: A music recommendation system based on music data grouping and user interests. In: Proceedings of the Tenth International Conference on Information and Knowledge Management, pp. 231–238 (2001)
3. Chen, H.-C., Chen, A.L.P.: A music recommendation system based on music and user grouping. J. Intell. Inf. Syst. **24**(2), 113–132 (2005)
4. El Saddik, A.: Digital twins: the convergence of multimedia technologies. IEEE Multimed. **25**(2), 87–92 (2018)
5. Hu, Y., Ogihara, M.: Nextone player: a music recommendation system based on user behavior. In: ISMIR, vol. 11, pp. 103–108 (2011)

6. Jiang, D.-N., Lu, L., Zhang, H.-J., Tao, J.-H., Cai, L.-H.: Music type classification by spectral contrast feature. In: Proceedings of the IEEE International Conference on Multimedia and Expo, vol. 1, pp. 113–116. IEEE (2002)
7. Kao, A., Poteet, S.R.: Natural Language Processing and Text Mining. Springer, Heidelberg (2007)
8. Lee, J.S., Lee, J.C.: Context awareness by case-based reasoning in a music recommendation system. In: Ichikawa, H., Cho, W.-D., Satoh, I., Youn, H.Y. (eds.) UCS 2007. LNCS, vol. 4836, pp. 45–58. Springer, Heidelberg (2007). https://doi.org/10.1007/978-3-540-76772-5_4
9. Pandeya, Y.R., Lee, J.: Deep learning-based late fusion of multimodal information for emotion classification of music video. Multimed. Tools Appl. **80**(2), 2887–2905 (2020). https://doi.org/10.1007/s11042-020-08836-3
10. Park, H.-S., Yoo, J.-O., Cho, S.-B.: A context-aware music recommendation system using fuzzy Bayesian networks with utility theory. In: Wang, L., Jiao, L., Shi, G., Li, X., Liu, J. (eds.) FSKD 2006. LNCS (LNAI), vol. 4223, pp. 970–979. Springer, Heidelberg (2006). https://doi.org/10.1007/11881599_121
11. Rosa, R.L., Rodriguez, D.Z., Bressan, G.: Music recommendation system based on user's sentiments extracted from social networks. IEEE Trans. Consum. Electron. **61**(3), 359–367 (2015)
12. Rosner, A., Kostek, B.: Automatic music genre classification based on musical instrument track separation. J. Intell. Inf. Syst. **50**(2), 363–384 (2017). https://doi.org/10.1007/s10844-017-0464-5

Interactive Visualization and Capture of Geo-Coded Multimedia Data on Mobile Devices

Deepshikha Bhati[1]([✉]), Md Amiruzzaman[2], Suphanut Jamonnak[1], and Ye Zhao[1]

[1] Kent State University, Kent, OH 44242, USA
dbhati@kent.edu
[2] West Chester University, West Chester, PA 19383, USA

Abstract. In digital community applications, geo-coded multimedia data including spatial videos, speech, and geo-narratives are collected and utilized by community users and researchers from multiple fields. It is often preferred that these data can be captured, visualized, and explored directly on mobile phones and tablets interactively. In this paper, we present a Geo-Video Mobile Application (GVM App) that collects geo-coded multimedia data for experts to process and analyze over an interactive visual exploration. This mobile App integrates user interactivity, AI-based semantic image segmentation, and audio transcription for effective data extraction and utilization. Then visualization functions are designed to quickly present geographical, semantic, and street view visual information for knowledge discovery. The users of this tool can include community workers, teachers, and tourists, and also span across multiple social disciplines in digital humanity studies.

Keywords: Deep learning · Human-Computer Interaction · Interactive · Interface · Mobile · Social · Spatial

1 Introduction

Digital humanities applications of a community or city often need to collect multimedia data associated with geographical dimensions. Important knowledge can be acquired from street view images, spatial videos (SV), and geographical narratives (GN). GN is spatial video-based multimedia data that accompanies audio narratives and geo-location information. While the imagery data associate visual information of geographical objects, GN can further accompany them with knowledge and opinions from residents, tourists, and domain experts. Effective analysis of such data could provide context to help people understand a community such as its development, problems, environment, and many social factors. In existing approaches, users often capture SV and GN data with mobile devices or specific video camera kits. The large-scale multimedia data are then uploaded and transformed to desktop platforms for storage, processing, and exploration. In some applications where users prefer to investigate the captured data on-site and in a timely manner (e.g., field studies), the current tools cannot satisfy the demand. There is a lack of visualization tools that can meet the requirement

J.-H. Kim et al. (Eds.): IHCI 2021, LNCS 13184, pp. 260–271, 2022.
https://doi.org/10.1007/978-3-030-98404-5_25

to support mobile-based data collection, processing, and visualization of geo-coded SV and GN datasets.

We have consulted with a group of community practitioners and social scientists in the fields of urban study, public health, criminology, landscaping, and geography. They have expressed a need for integrating data collection and visualization on mobile devices with the following features:

- The visualization tool is seamlessly linked to multimedia data capture in field.
- Multimedia data processing is incorporated to extract visual and semantic information from raw video and audio data files.
- The geographical context is well integrated for geo-based visual study.
- The visualization and interaction functions are easy to operate and understand for general public users.

In this paper, we present a new mobile-based visualization tool as a mobile App, named as GVM (Geo-Video Mobile) App, to satisfy the specified requirements. While the comprehensive desktop-based tools can process large volume data, this new tool can help users achieve fast velocity and performance with prompt data utilization. It thus can compensate the desktop-based tools by mitigating some social study tasks to the situations in an appropriate context.

Introducing visualization techniques to mobile devices, such as cell phones and tablets, can leverage the visualization power in many mobile applications in addition to traditional visualization estates. However, the limitation of mobile devices attributed to restrained computing power, small screen size, and moderate storage capacity, often hinders the development of mobile-based visualization. For the geo-coded SV and GN data, it is even more challenging since an effective visualization interface must integrate the multimedia data with spatial context, and present effortless interactive operations. GVM App addresses the challenges with the following contributions:

- The geo-coded multimedia data can be conveniently captured and then immediately shared and analyzed with the mobile App.
- AI-based data processing tools are applied to process the video and audio data to extract frame pictures, segmented visual categories, texts and keywords, with respect to the geographical locations.
- Mobile-based visualizations are designed and developed for presenting these heterogeneous information on the mobile interface, enabling users to perform interactive exploration.

2   Related Work

Spatial videos (SV) are geo-coded videos that create geographic layers for GIS analysis [8, 18]. Geo-narratives (GN) further add contextual information to spatial videos with human interviews and comments [9, 15]. These multimedia data associated with geographical environments provide digital data resources for social science studies and applications of the built infrastructures and environments with social factors of public health, crime [3], and homelessness [9, 25]. The visual and spatial richness of these

Fig. 1. Data capture on GVM App: (A) Map view showing current location and data capture trajectory; (B) List view of captured videos; (C) Video player with corresponding trajectory view on map.

geographical multimedia data are important for field and community study [3, 15], but the existing work often needs to upload captured data from video cameras and perform heavy post-processing before visualizing. This paper instead presents a mobile-based visualization tool that takes advantage of the camera-equipped with GPS location services on a mobile device to conduct an onsite and instantaneous study of geographical multimedia data.

Mobile devices are becoming increasingly popular because of their versatility [17]. Designing good information visualization techniques remain challenging [5]. Geo-data visualization on mobile devices has become an important topic due to the ubiquitous nature of mobile phones. Tourist-oriented systems (e.g., [24, 29]) visualize user place, time, and location, the task at hand, to provide tourist services. More examples are Cyberguide [1], GUIDE [7], CRUMPET [20] and Lol [11], which are widely known as virtual tourist guides. Minimap [23] presents a special web-based visualization. Baus et al. [4] offer an overview of the principal features of mobile guides. GiMoDig presents alternative map designs in the geospatial info-mobility service [19]. Chalmers et al. [6] tailor the map content to various bandwidths. Reichenbacher [22] presents mobile App-based SVG maps. Zipf and Richter [28] offer adaptive maps with culture-specific map coloring, map generalization, user-oriented maps, and focus maps. In the MoVi project [21], fisheye views of town maps were examined. The city map has a normal scale in the focus area (usually in the center of the map) and is skewed by smaller scales in the other sections of the map. Harrie et al. [14] generate variable-scale maps while Dillemuth presented a debate on the creation and usage of map representations on mobile devices [10]. Agrawala and Stolte [2] improve the usability of road navigation maps on mobile devices. Sester and Brenner [26] and Hampe et al. [13] present techniques for real-time generalization in mobile App. The existing systems do not process and visualize the geographical multimedia data integrated with the geo-context, which is the focus of this paper.

3   Data Capture and AI-Based Processing

3.1   Data Capture

GVM App is designed to collect spatial videos together with audio narratives. The videos and audios are associated with GPS trajectory locations, dates, and timestamps. GVM App stores the data in mobile device's internal memory for further analysis and exploration which can also be easily shared among devices.

GVM App allows users to capture spatial videos and narratives with a few simple steps. Once the GVM App is started (Fig. 1(A)), users can see their current location, which indicates that the App is ready to use. Users can click the capture button to start recording the video in the community. Their moving trajectories are recorded and matched with the captured video. GVM App also allows users to check the list of previously recorded videos (Fig. 1(B)). When they click to play a video, the associated trajectory is also shown on the map view (Fig. 1(C)), while an icon moves along the trajectory to show the current location of video content.

3.2   Video Processing and Image Segmentation

The captured video includes landscape views, and the audio often includes narrative speech. They should be processed to extract visual information and textual information to facilitate visual analysis. GVM App integrates AI-based data processing steps to extract the information for effective data exploration.

A video is first processed to extract main frames in every five seconds (this can be adjusted). Then, semantic image segmentation [27] is applied to these image frames. For each image, its visual contents are detected as multiple categories including road, sidewalk, sky, building, etc. Each visual category has an occupation percentage value which is computed as the number of pixels of this category over the total number of pixels in the image. Consequently, a visual information vector (of 19 categories) is achieved which represents street-view appearance at the associated location. Such positional visual information summarizes SV data and can be used in visual exploration. In the implementation, the segmentation is applied by using a popular AI model, PSPNet, which is built upon a Pyramid scene parsing network [27] on a remote server. It takes approximately couple of seconds to process one image and the server sends back the results in JSON format to the mobile device.

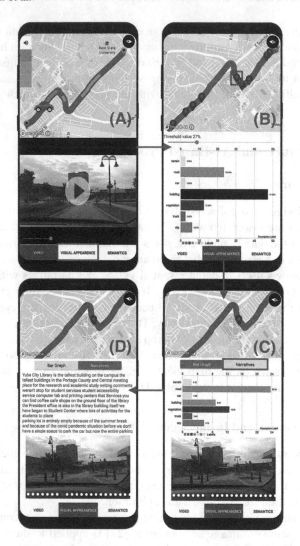

Fig. 2. Exploring community videos with visual information view: (A) Visualize trajectory with cues of geo-narratives on the map while playing the corresponding video. (B) Show the distribution of visual categories on the whole trajectory. Locations with a selected category highlighted on the map. (C) Select one location of interest, and view street view image at this location. (D) Study the narratives at this location.

3.3   Geo-narratives and Speech Transcription

Audio tracks are extracted using an open-source library, FFmpeg [16]. Then, we utilize the DeepSpeech model [12] for automatic speech transcription. Instead of pushing a whole audio file of recorded video into DeepSpeech, each audio file is broken down into smaller chunks which can be processed in parallel for faster processing.

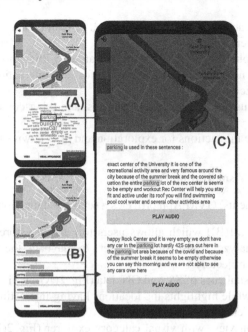

Fig. 3. Exploring geo-narratives with interactive word explorer: (A) Find interesting keywords with word cloud; (B) Find interesting keywords with word list; (C) Visualize the locations of the selected keywords and study their audio transcripts.

After geo-narrative is achieved in text from DeepSpeech, we use the Natural Language processing ToolKit (NLTK) to extract important keywords. In particular, "stop words" are removed, and then the keywords are ranked based on the Term Frequency-Inverse Document Frequency (TF-IDF). The auto-transcription is also performed on the remote server. The processing time to extract the audio chunks and extract the narrative takes approximately a few seconds for a couple of minutes of audio. Then, the narrative and keywords are stored and linked with geo-locations.

In the two AI-based processing steps, we use PSPNet and DeepSpeech models because both models are open-source and free to use.

4 Mobile Based Visualization

The GVM App visualization interface is designed for general users to quickly and easily form insights with effortless interaction on various mobile devices.

4.1 Multi-type Data and Visualization Tasks

GVM App allows users to visually explore the geo-coded images and their visual categories, the video clips, the transcribed text, and also listen to the vocal clips. These heterogeneous data should be visualized on the mobile screen. The following requirements of visual design need to be fulfilled:

- Enabling users to access both spatial-temporal, semantic, and multimedia information on mobile interfaces.
- Visualizing multiple types of data and their relations with an integrative interface.
- Providing visual cues on geographical context for easy interaction, since all the data cannot be visualized together.
- Promoting quick understanding of text, images, and other contents, on the limited display estate.
- Allowing intuitive interactions for exploration and drill-down study.

4.2 Mobile-Based Visualization Design

To meet the requirements, GVM App provides a set of visualization functions as:

- Trip manager (Fig. 1(B)) which allows users to load and store multiple trips and select a trip to analyze. It also supports users to playback the whole SV with the icon moving on a trajectory.
- Map view with visual cues of SV and GN data (Fig. 2(A)). It visualizes trip trajectories on the map, while highlights the locations having interesting information from SV and GN for interactive study.
- Visual information view with visual category explorer (Fig. 2(B)-(D)). It displays segmentation results, i.e. the visual categories content, of video frames. It allows users to interactively study the related narratives, video clips, and locations based on the visual categories.
- Geo-narrative view with interactive word explorer. It visualizes important keywords extracted from the narratives (Fig. 3(A)-(C)). Users can select or input terms of interest to study GN contents and the associated visual information and locations.

These functions are integrated into one mobile screen interface with smooth interactions.

4.3 Trip Manager

The trip manager shows a list of videos along with other related information (Fig. 1(B)). Users can select a video and explore its contents. Moreover, users can perform AI-Based video segmentation and speech transcription of the videos. Then, users can start an interactive visual analysis with the extracted visual information of segmented categories and the semantics of geo-narratives.

4.4 Map View with Data Cues

The goal of this view is to visualize the spatial information on a map while visual cues of SN semantics are presented. It is important to couple such cues over the geo-context within the limited map space on the screen. However, unlike large-screen visualization, the mobile interface may not effectively display labels, texts, or glyphs on the map together, because they will easily trigger visual cluttering. Therefore, after first plotting video trajectories as polylines, we overlay a layer of colored segments to indicate where

GN data are recorded as shown in Fig. 2(A). Here, three colored segments show three parts of the recorded geo-narratives. The moving icon indicates the current location under study. The video clip is played below the map, while the icon moves along the trajectory to link the video content with geo-spatial location. In addition, users can drag the icon on the map, or drag the video player, to quickly move to their preferred location for drill-down study.

4.5 Visual Information View

The visual information view displays the segmented categories from the video contents as bar charts. Each category, such as building, sidewalk, road, vegetation, car, and so on, is displayed as a bar with a specific color, as illustrated in Fig. 2(B). The bar size represents the percentage value of the corresponding category. In this figure, the bar chart shows the accumulated distribution of different visual categories for one whole video, which is computed by summing the segmentation results along with sampling locations (i.e., each video frame) on the trajectory.

Users can select a category and utilize the percentage slider to set a threshold. This helps users to find locations where the visual category percentage is higher than the threshold. As shown in Fig. 2(B) a user defines a threshold of 27% for the "building" category, so that only the locations with more than 27% buildings are highlighted on the trajectory over the map with blue markers. A user can further drill down to any location to inspect the location with the narrative text and the visual content as shown in Fig. 2(C) and 2(D). Here, the bar chart view of Fig. 2(C) shows the visual category distribution for the selected location (based on its street view image frame).

4.6 Geo-narrative View

The extracted keywords from GN is summarized and visualized by an interactive word explorer. The word explorer allows users to select any keyword of interest. The explorer is designed to provide two alternative visualizations: a word cloud (Fig. 3(A)) and a keyword list (Fig. 3(B)). Top keywords are ranked based on TF-IDF weights in the narratives, and are shown by different word sizes. A selected keyword (e.g., "Parking") is linked to spatial locations where the GN includes the keyword. These locations are visualized on the map and users can study the corresponding narratives and play recorded audio files.

5 Use Scenarios

We present two cases where GVM App helps users capture real-world SV and GN data and to perform interactive data exploration. The data and examples throughout this paper are generated by the authors for presentation only, and all names below are fictitious.

5.1   Case 1: Virtual Campus Tour

GVM App is used by a university student (Alice) to capture campus videos and record some introductory descriptions about the campus. Her parents can interactively explore the campus for an interactive virtual tour on their phones.

As shown in Fig. 2(A), Alice's trajectory along a main street of the campus is shown on the map. She talks during video capture, which are highlighted as three segments along the trajectory. By selecting "visual appearance", her parents can study her data by visual category information. In Fig. 2(B), it shows the major visual contents along this trajectory are "buildings" and "roads".

Alice's parents want to explore the campus buildings. By selecting this category and dragging the slider to set a threshold. This figure shows the locations with more than 27% building identified by AI segmentation. By clicking one location on the map, Fig. 2(C) shows its street view image. This view shows one of the tallest buildings on the campus. Meanwhile, visual categories of this image is displayed. The parents further click the "naratives" button to view the transcript of Alice's description about this building (Fig. 2(D)). By reading the text and listening to the audio, they obtain the information that this is the university library and it is the center of the campus life in this university.

5.2   Case 2: COVID Impact on Neighborhood

During the pandemic of COVID-19, a staff of the college town uses GVM App to record daily videos around neighborhoods while describing his view along the route. Then, the staff shares the recorded videos with town managers, so the managers can easily analyze the impact on their phones or tablets.

Figure 3 shows an example of study based on the geo-narrative view. With the world cloud of Fig. 3(A), a manager (John) can investigate top keywords about neighborhood situation. This can also be done by using the word list (Fig. 3(B)) if he prefers. Here, John wants to learn issues about parking which is a key topic of city management. Once he selects the keyword "Parking", the corresponding locations are visualized with the blue marker on the map and John can browse the related narratives of these locations, as shown in Fig. 3(C)).

Then, John selects one location which he knows is a very busy parking lot in normal times. As shown in Fig. 4(A), this location is generally empty while the visual distribution chart shows the "car" category has 2.58% out of the whole image. So John observes the parking lot and finds a few cars on a corner. He recalls that the building parking lot is not completely empty like this even during the pandemic. So John further clicks to see the narrative details (Fig. 4(B)), where he learns that the close department buildings may be closed due to summer.

6   GVM App Implementation and Accessibility

GVM App is currently implemented on the Android platform using the Android Studio which is a cross-platform integrated development environment (IDE). For video capture, we used the android.hardware.camera2 library. The geo-coded multimedia datasets

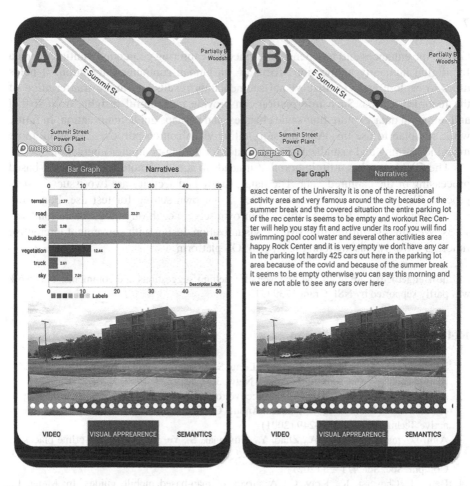

Fig. 4. Drill-down study of one location based on keyword selection. (A) Study the location with the street view image and its visual categories; (B) Read the associated narrative content.

are stored on mobile devices using the SQLite database. The visualization of trajectories and visual cues on the map is implemented with the MapBox Android library. Furthermore, the views of bar charts, word clouds, and lists, are implemented by the WMPAndroidChart and AnyChart supported libraries. The App has been tested with different models of Android mobile devices, such as Galaxy J7 Max, Samsung Galaxy S9+, OnePlus 7.

GVM App has been used by a group of domain users for test and feedback. These experts work in the fields of urban study, planning, landscaping, and geography. They are using the tool in a set of applications, such as studying walkability of community sidewalks; analyzing community infrastructure status, and so on. Based on the preliminary feedback, the experts praise GVM App for its capacity and benefits in convenient data capture and analysis. We are conducting further user evaluation to improve the system. Then the App will be released for public access.

7 Conclusion and Limitation

GVM App enhances and broadens the services of capturing geo-coded multimedia data for digital humanity applications focusing on human-computer interaction. It helps users to explore and visualize visual segmentation results and audio transcription of the recorded videos. Such information can provide meaningful insights from spatial and temporal data, capture fine-scale changes, and perhaps guide intervention. In future work, we plan to use this App for storytelling visualization purposes, integrate more machine learning and visualization techniques for human-computer interaction.

The GVM App has a limitation that it needs to access remote servers for AI-based processing of the captured data. The data privacy and security are two issues in such process. We currently establish the server in our own setting for test use. For wider use, users may be guided to establish their own servers or through their own cloud services. We will also further improve the visualization design with convenient interactive functions. We will also extend the App to iOS platform.

Acknowledgement. We thank the reviewers for helpful suggestions and comments. This work was partly supported by NSF Grant 1739491.

References

1. Abowd, G.D., Atkeson, C.G., Hong, J., Long, S., Kooper, R., Pinkerton, M.: CyberGuide: a mobile context-aware tour guide. Wirel. Netw. **3**(5), 421–433 (1997)
2. Agrawala, M., Stolte, C.: Rendering effective route maps: improving usability through generalization. In: Proceedings of the 28th Annual Conference on Computer Graphics and Interactive Techniques, pp. 241–249 (2001)
3. Amiruzzaman, M., Curtis, A., Zhao, Y., Jamonnak, S., Ye, X.: Classifying crime places by neighborhood visual appearance and police geonarratives: a machine learning approach. J. Comput. Soc. Sci. **4**, 1–25 (2021)
4. Baus, J., Cheverst, K., Kray, C.: A survey of map-based mobile guides. In: Meng, L., Reichenbacher, T., Zipf, A. (eds.) Map-Based Mobile Services, pp. 193–209. Springer, Heidelberg (2005). https://doi.org/10.1007/3-540-26982-7_13
5. Blumenstein, K., Niederer, C., Wagner, M., Schmiedl, G., Rind, A., Aigner, W.: Evaluating information visualization on mobile devices: gaps and challenges in the empirical evaluation design space. In: Proceedings of the Sixth Workshop on Beyond Time and Errors on Novel Evaluation Methods for Visualization, pp. 125–132 (2016)
6. Chalmers, D., Sloman, M., Dulay, N.: Map adaptation for users of mobile systems. In: Proceedings of the 10th International Conference on World Wide Web, pp. 735–744 (2001)
7. Cheverst, K., Davies, N., Mitchell, K., Friday, A.: Experiences of developing and deploying a context-aware tourist guide: the guide project. In: Proceedings of the 6th Annual International Conference on Mobile Computing and Networking, pp. 20–31 (2000)
8. Curtis, A., Fagan, W.F.: Capturing damage assessment with a spatial video: an example of a building and street-scale analysis of tornado-related mortality in Joplin, Missouri, 2011. Ann. Assoc. Am. Geogr. **103**(6), 1522–1538 (2013)
9. Curtis, A., Felix, C., Mitchell, S., Ajayakumar, J., Kerndt, P.R.: Contextualizing overdoses in Los Angeles's skid row between 2014 and 2016 by leveraging the spatial knowledge of the marginalized as a resource. Ann. Am. Assoc. Geogr. **108**(6), 1521–1536 (2018)

10. Dillemuth, J.: Map design evaluation for mobile display. Cartogr. Geogr. Inf. Sci. **32**(4), 285–301 (2005)
11. Gartner, G., Uhlirz, S.: Cartographic concepts for realizing a location based UMTS service: Vienna city guide lol@. In: Proceedings of the Cartographic Conference, pp. 3229–3239 (2001)
12. Hafidh Firmansyah, M., Paul, A., Bhattacharya, D., Malik Urfa, G.: AI based embedded speech to text using deepspeech. arXiv e-prints, arXiv-2002 (2020)
13. Hampe, M., Anders, K.H., Sester, M.: MRDB applications for data revision and real-time generalisation. In: Proceedings of the 21st International Cartographic Conference, pp. 10–16 (2003)
14. Harrie, L., Sarjakoski, L.T., Lehto, L.: A variable-scale map for small-display cartography. Int. Arch. Photogrammetry Remote Sens. Spat. Inf. Sci. **34**(4), 237–242 (2002)
15. Jamonnak, S., et al.: GeoVisuals: a visual analytics approach to leverage the potential of spatial videos and associated geonarratives. Int. J. Geogr. Inf. Sci. **34**(11), 2115–2135 (2020)
16. Lei, X., Jiang, X., Wang, C.: Design and implementation of a real-time video stream analysis system based on FFMPEG. In: 2013 Fourth World Congress on Software Engineering, pp. 212–216. IEEE (2013)
17. Magnisalis, I.D., Demetriadis, S.N.: Mobile widgets to support peer interaction visualization. In: 2014 IEEE 14th International Conference on Advanced Learning Technologies, pp. 191–193. IEEE (2014)
18. Mills, J.W., Curtis, A., Kennedy, B., Kennedy, S.W., Edwards, J.D.: Geospatial video for field data collection. Appl. Geogr **30**(4), 533–547 (2010). https://doi.org/10.1016/j.apgeog.2010.03.008. Climate Change and Applied Geography - Place, Policy, and Practice
19. Nissen, F., Hvas, A., Münster-Swendsen, J., Brodersen, L.: Small-display cartography. GiMoDig Scientific Report (2003)
20. Poslad, S., Laamanen, H., Malaka, R., Nick, A., Buckle, P., Zipl, A.: CRUMPET: creation of user-friendly mobile services personalised for tourism. In: IET Conference Proceedings, pp. 28–32(4) (2001)
21. Rauschenbach, U., Jeschke, S., Schumann, H.: General rectangular fisheye views for 2D graphics. Comput. Graph. **25**(4), 609–617 (2001)
22. Reichenbacher, T.: SVG for adaptive visualisations in mobile situations. In: SVG Open Conference, Zürich (2002)
23. Roto, V., Popescu, A., Koivisto, A., Vartiainen, E.: Minimap: a web page visualization method for mobile phones. In: Proceedings of the SIGCHI Conference on Human Factors in Computing Systems, pp. 35–44 (2006)
24. Schmidt-Belz, B., Laamanen, H., Poslad, S., Zipf, A.: Location-based mobile tourist services: first user experiences. In: Proceedings of the International Conference on Information and Communication Technologies In Tourism, ENTER 2003: 10th International Conference on Information Technology in Tourism (2003)
25. Schuch, L., Curtis, A., Davidson, J.: Reducing lead exposure risk to vulnerable populations: a proactive geographic solution. Ann. Am. Assoc. Geogr. **107**(3), 606–624 (2017)
26. Sester, M., Brenner, C.: Continuous generalization for visualization on small mobile devices. In: Sester, M., Brenner, C. (eds.) Developments in Spatial Data Handling, pp. 355–368. Springer, Heidelberg (2005). https://doi.org/10.1007/3-540-26772-7_27
27. Wang, W., Yang, J., You, X.: Combining ElasticFusion with PSPNet for RGB-D based indoor semantic mapping. In: 2018 Chinese Automation Congress (CAC), pp. 2996–3001. IEEE (2018)
28. Zelenka, J.: Information and communication technologies in tourism-influence, dynamics, trends. Ph.D. thesis, Technická univerzita v Liberci (2009)
29. Zipf, A., Malaka, R., et al.: Developing location based services for tourism: the service providers' view. In: ENTER, vol. 2001, pp. 83–92. Citeseer (2001)

Application of VR to Educational System of Korea

Yeun Soo Choi, Mingeon Kim, Ahhyun Ryu, Seowon Park[✉], and Sunwoo Kim

Cogito Research, Seoul, Republic of Korea (South Korea)
seowon.park22@gmail.com

Abstract. Since the breakout of Covid-19, the number of online classes skyrocketed as conducting in-person classes in school has been discouraged. This led to the sudden shift into the adaption of online classes, blurring the line between traditional in-person classes and modern technology. In the Republic of Korea, the nation where it is known for its speed of Internet and high rate of digital natives amongst its citizen, there have been numerous attempts to incorporate virtual reality (VR) into the existing curriculum but has not been getting satisfactory results back. Through interviews and research, this paper tries to assess the current position of VR in the marketplace and suggest possible solutions that can support the expansion of the system into the school. The main purpose of this essay is to analyze whether Google Arts and Culture, one of the most accessible VR assimilated educational platforms, can be blended into the Korean education programs.

Keywords: Virtual reality · 3D modeling · Mouse movement detective program

1 Introduction

Following the breakout of Covid-19, holding classes in an in-person format has been challenging, affecting nearly 1.6 billion learners globally, closing schools, institutions, and other learning spaces that hindered more than 94% of the world's student population [12]. However, education has to be continued; therefore, the situation led educational institutions to implement advanced technology faster than previously anticipated, rendering them to conduct online classes [12]. As the usage of telecommunication in the school system has been generalized, VR is a ground that numerous futuristic entrepreneurs are targeting [7]. One of the illustrations is that Stanford Medicine is "using a new software system that combines imaging from MRIs, CT scans, and angiograms to create a three-dimensional model that physicians and patients can see and manipulate" [5]. Steinberg, the Bernard and Ronni Lacroute-William Randolph Hearst Professor in Neurosurgery and Neurosciences, commented how the virtual reality system is assisting to train residents, bolstering surgeons in their steps of planning forthcoming operations, and educating patients on how the operations would be conducted. To assimilate the VR system in compulsory educational courses, the following three environmental factors are necessary: digital native, fast internet speed, and the abundance of content. In the case of Korea, it already meets two of those criteria since 92.7% of its youth are digital natives

© Springer Nature Switzerland AG 2022
J.-H. Kim et al. (Eds.): IHCI 2021, LNCS 13184, pp. 272–281, 2022.
https://doi.org/10.1007/978-3-030-98404-5_26

according to the Youth Mobility Index of 2018 and is ranked top in the 2017 Global ICT Development Index [9, 16]. However, the remaining factor, amounts of content, lacks to consider VR as an eligible option to be integrated into the education system [8]. This paper would mainly focus on how students would respond when one of the accessible VR platforms, Google Arts and Culture, gets introduced in a Korean educational setting. We hope to scrutinize the current position of VR and think of a way to apply the program to the current educational system of Korea.

2 Literature Review

2.1 High Anticipation on the Application of VR in Curriculum

Research was conducted by YouGov and Terrapin across 12 markets in the Asia Pacific during May 2021, the study examined 783 educators in the Asia Pacific, along with 669 parents and 1,935 students aged 16 to 25 above to figure out their assessment on e-learning [13]. More than 80% of students and 95% of educators reported their technology usage rate has increased during the pandemic, in 2020 [13]. This trend would continue in the coming years since 66% of students and 86% of educators responded that they are expecting a further increase in their spending on learning technology in the future [13]. It has also been figured that approximately 78% of parents are wanting to see some form of digital devices being incorporated into classroom learning; 47% are looking forwards to schools blending the smart devices into learning even after the pandemic is over [13]. On the topic of digital integrated learning, educators revealed their strong enthusiasm for it with 54% being supportive of a permanent shift to employing online services in the traditional classroom setting [1]. Especially in regard to VR, 54% of teachers and 41% of parents said they have high hopes for an increased presence of virtual reality (VR) and augmented reality (AR) solutions in the classroom [1].

Furthermore, an infographic released by Samsung regarding the effects of VR in education has shown that 85% of US K-12 teachers who are surveyed agreed upon the beneficial outcomes of educating their pupils by conjugating VR devices, where 2% of them are already using the technology. Teachers were most interested in simulating co-relative contents, exploring inaccessible terrains, traveling to different landmarks, and supplementing the existing syllabus for better comprehension of concepts. The infographic further shows how teachers are interested in better understanding, greater collaboration, and increased motivation through the implementation of virtual reality [15].

2.2 Factors to Be Resolved Before the Application of VR into the Educational System

One of the immediate issues is the teachers' burden to acquire knowledge on operating VR systems for smooth execution. For teachers, when a new technology needs to be practiced, it denotes a significant reform in previous teaching curriculum and strategies. According to research carried out by Dankook University, which surveyed 100 English teachers, half of the teachers felt the psychological burden. Furthermore, 80%

of teachers who provided moderate answers stated that the majority of educators are stressed about teaching using virtual reality [11]. When they were asked a reason for such a psychological pressure, about 31% stated the time constraints and stress on new class design, and 23% selected the absence of an official curriculum or scoring method for English classes in a virtual environment [11]. For effective English education using virtual reality, the substantialization of virtual reality-based educational content and the establishment of an accessible virtual learning environment were found to be compelling factors. Based on these data, it can be deduced that for efficient implementation of virtual reality education, developing a framework that eases educators' learning on the system and the assistance program needs to be set before the expansion of the virtual reality service.

Lack of VR-based educational content is another issue preventing the generalization of the system. In particular, in regard to other entertainment fields including gaming, the education market is lagging behind in the number of content that can be synergistic with the existing system. As stated in the paper, "A Study on the Revitalization of Virtual Reality-Based Education," which scrutinized the application of VR especially in the Korean setting, the domestic demand for VR education is comparatively low while taking into consideration that for the past decade, virtual and augmented reality-related movements have faced drastic expansion in various industries in Korea [8]. A possible explanation is that VR applications or platforms are costly to produce, inducing that they are oftentimes created from superpower nations, namely the United States. Meaning that the service is mainly available in English, a lingua franca, limiting their usage for foreign students who speak in different mother tongues [2]. The aforementioned data suggest a lack of development in educational content as the primary root drawing back the popularization of VR.

Moreover, there prevail adversities while collecting data from VR: hardware challenges, monitoring and evaluating challenges, and data storage challenges. The supply and distribution of bespoke hardware for students to conduct remote studies is a predominant issue regarding the arduous duty of ensuring devices' formal operation in users' environments. In the context of XR technologies, professionals voice their apprehensions about the possibility that temperamental system issues might arise, principally towards the already laborious demands of PC-based VR on consumer-level XR hardware. Along with the hardware, the installment of data-collection measures including video recording and motion tracking in the households would be deemed as an unreasonable prerequisite for the general users. Also, the storage and treatment of the collected informal data including facial expressions, body language, casual conversations. Additionally, there is an active dispute over the effective measures to encapsulate data from the VR experience as a recent study proclaimed the variability of collected data depending on whether it is recorded from inside the VR experience or in the real-world setting. Since there is yet to exist a definite way of collecting, transferring, and analyzing the compelling amounts of data from the collective groups, users are continuously suggesting queries portraying the lack of reliability over the VR device [14].

2.3 Increased Usage of VR in Korean Educational Institutions

In Korea, despite the conventional belief that VR is utilized for gaming purposes, the usage for educational purposes has been ranked at the top by 52.4%, gaming following as 46.6%. Such effects are expected to trickle down to secondary education as well. As of 2019, VR was already being experimented with throughout the Korean public educational system. For instance, elementary school students utilized VR to expand possibilities for students who are physically challenged. Elementary education also utilized VR to explain specific concepts such as exploring natural conditions and space exploration. Secondary school students utilized VR to experience conditions that are difficult to experience in reality. Some industry high schools also teach students how to create VR content, allowing for more people to be interested in creating content for the VR environment [3].

With support for cloud storage from private enterprises, the Seoul Education Office created a VR platform called New SSEM, that can accommodate up to 1000 participants. Through this platform, students were able to engage in activities by answering questions through interactions, staying focused as if they were in a physical classroom setting regardless of their spatial limitation due to COVID-19, and communicating with instructors through various means. Instructors were able to adjust volumes, cameras, and microphones to increase student concentration, and it is expected to be implemented in140 public schools towards the end of 2021 [6].

Furthermore, the local government of Songpa-gu allowed students to experience different kinds of jobs by utilizing VR. Through VR, students of the first year in middle school were able to experience jobs as if they were on the field. The local government said that this differentiation would be able to support students in their journey of discovering their interests and exploring careers of interest so that it would be possible for them to set their path in advance [10].

3 Research Question

What are the elements that can be improved in Google Arts and Culture to be implemented into the Korean school system? What are the benefits of using VR in the educational process?

4 Methodology

Our research will consist of two main components. First, content analysis will be utilized to identify and cross-examine the merits, demerits, and limitations in the process of being assimilated into the Korean educational system. Based on survey data released by government agencies, corporations, and research institutes, we will gather quantitative data on the subject. Following quantitative data research, we will gather qualitative data via examining the interviews or cases published by credible research organizations or news sources.

In total, 12 interviews were conducted from September 18 to November 12th, to collect data on user perceptions on one of the most accessible VR educational platforms, the Google Arts & Culture, and to figure out their assessment of the platform and perspectives on the application of VR services in Korean instructional programs. The majority of interviewees are undergraduate students considering the research conducted in 2016 which revealed positive responses from Generation Z and Millennials on the matter of adaptation of VR vehicles in their daily lives [4]. Following are the questions that were asked to the interviewees:

1. Do you use VR platforms or devices in your daily lives?
2. (Show the interviewees the google arts and culture. Let them explore for about 10 min)

   a. What do you think of this website? Is it easy to use or not? Please explain why.

3. Do you think this may serve well as an educational service or program to be used in school?
4. What would be the benefits?
5. What would be the difficulties? How can those issues be solved?
6. What functions would enable a more intuitive and effective usage of the website?
7. Do you think the usage of VR will expand in Korean educational programs?

5 Results

5.1 Increased Interest in the Application of VR in the School System

Before letting the interviewees explore the Google Arts & Culture app, when they were asked about their general perception of VR, one of the participants commented that the demerit of VR is appealing to the relatively younger generations of the contemporary era such as Generation Z and Millennials since the curriculum could be modified into a more relevant form that is more interactive with the course material students are learning. After using the Google Arts & Culture app, the participant especially praised the availability of users to become the subject of the artwork itself, which would spike interest among students.

5.2 Looking at Artworks from Multiple Angles

The platform, Google Arts and Culture provides numerous services including gallery functions that enable users to be immersed in virtual reality to explore the digital replica with the high pixeled image of the artworks. The majority of the interviewees, eight out of twelve mentioned being able to see multiple facets of the sculptures is a beneficiary factor as to when studying with two-dimensional textbooks, the visual data on paper only shows one side, usually, the front, hindering students from having a throughout look and understanding of the work. Numerous individuals showed interest in seeing the statues from the back saying that they were not given a chance to examine the works from the back unless visiting the gallery or museums physically which is a limited option, especially during the pandemic era. One of them explicitly commented, "for some reason, I have never thought of seeing the works from the side, and it is a new experience to observe the statues in 360°." Others also mentioned that three-dimensional artworks look more realistic, or their actions seem to be more dynamic after looking at the work thoroughly. However, some of the interview participants figured that for those that are placed next to the wall, the website did not allow users to rotate the perspective around the statue which is disappointing. Furthermore, based on the researcher's and interviewee's exploration of the website, it is highly likely that all of its views function horizontally, not letting users look up or down. One of the interviewees tried to look at how the top of the pyramid looks using the website; however, the platform only offers a horizontal view of the location, minimizing the sense of reality.

5.3 Observing Artworks at a Close Distance

One of the interviewees shared one's experience of visiting the Louvre museum yet not being able to see the Mona Lisa with bare eyes since the size of a crowd lining up to see the work was absurd. However, through Google Arts and Culture, one does not need to worry about waiting in line, or not being able to look at the art piece. More than half of the interviewees were surprised to see how the visual data of the works are high pixelated that the image does not crack or blur when zooming into the detail. Such competence is impressive as even if individual visits the gallery and tries to look into the work, it is either mandatory or encouraged to keep a certain distance away from the works since the body temperature of human or an accident of colliding against the celebrated can cause catastrophes. Without worrying about damaging the work or letting others take turns investigating the piece, this website promises its user as much time needed for one to embrace the work. Four of the interviewees highlighted that being able to take a close

Fig. 1. *Bourke Street East Painting* from Google Arts and Culture Website

look at the art piece is useful especially when the piece is drawn on a ceiling. As the public is not easily given the opportunity to climb up to a ceiling and closely observe the art, Google Arts and Culture's feature is compelling (Fig. 1).

5.4 Immersive Experience

An interviewee participant mentioned how the potential of the Google Arts & Culture platform has been maximized through VR as it is not only displaying artworks but also allows users to feel as if they are physically touring the art museums, like first-hand experience. The participant noted that the Google Arts & Culture website would serve as an embodiment that sheds light on the possibility of educational trips or physical interactive experiences even during the times of COVID-19. Another participant said that VR is more impactful and grants a more immersive experience than beholding a still image. Google Arts & Culture allows students to move around 360° offering a chance for the students to have a sensation of being in the simulated area of the application. This allows for a more immersive experience than staring at a low-fidelity image of the artworks from the textbook.

5.5 Abrupt Transition by Clicking Arrows

When pressing the arrows that are placed at the bottom of the page, it abruptly shifts the user's surroundings. During the interview, five of the interviewees pointed out that the transition from one location to another is not smooth to the point that the website does not look professional. One of the interviewees said, "I think it is great how the website provides its user a sense of vacation or a trip of traveling to foreign nations, but those precipitous change of scenery breaks the mood." Furthermore, oftentimes the

Fig. 2. The position of arrows

arrows cannot be even pressed properly because they are positioned so closely with a button that makes the slide go to the next page. Such an issue occurred with six of the interviewees (Fig. 2).

5.6 Technological Limitations and Need for Assisting Service for Teachers

An interviewee expressed one's concern about technical obstacles to occur in the practice of supplying and delivering devices where the VR experience can operate amicably. The participant shared an experience of one's personal smart devices stuttering when operating the VR program and noted the fact that Korean public schools tend to limit accessibility to high-performance devices. The interviewee also commented on the fact that VR hardware and its contents are primarily designed for entertainment purposes and require technical skills that many instructors would have limited knowledge to fully incorporate VR into their curriculums. Teachers would have to stay in management for hardware, software, procurement of class-related contents, profile logins, saves; furthermore, they would have to manage some head-mounted virtual equipment as the setting would be a collective classroom environment. These are the burdens that educators need to carry on their own based on the current educational system.

6 Implication

6.1 3D Modeling the Artworks

As a measure to provide a more intuitive learning experience to the students, one of the solutions that would enable the complete view of the artwork is scanning the work, saving the data, and applying it to the website. In this case, the users would be able to observe the work from multiple angles regardless of where it is positioned in the gallery or how it is presented. Within this essay, the main purpose of the Google Arts and Culture website is to be assimilated into the existing curriculum meaning that the mood or details of the gallery or museum are secondhand issues, but a factor to be prioritized is the extent of details the VR platform can provide.

6.2 Implementing Mouse Movement Detective Program

Instead of pressing arrows, the movement of the user would be more natural when the website uses a mouse movement detection system to move around. This system is mainly used in gaming services and the change of scenery would be smooth. One of the main characteristics of Google Arts and Culture is that it provides its users a travel-like experience by enabling them to virtually walk down the streets of other nations. Currently what it presents is simply a continuation of street images, rather than an experience. Therefore, instead of arrow keys, mouse movement detection programming needs to be implemented.

6.3 Establishing New Department for Teacher's Assistant

As a high number of educators noted that they receive a significant amount of stress in order to prepare classes that use virtual reality platforms, it would be useful for Google to formulate a specialized department that supports teachers. Programming a chatbot that provides answers to simple and frequently asked questions on the right corner of the screen would alleviate the burden of many teachers. When an education specialized sector is established, it would be possible for teachers to learn programs on their own and use the service whenever they have difficulties leading the class.

7 Conclusion

This research aimed to provide insights into the possibilities and limitations of VR, especially Google Arts and Culture, as a non-conventional way for students to understand concepts in a first-hand manner and explore subjects creatively. In Korea, the hardware and software for VR are continuously improving, making it more accessible to the masses; what used to require high-end computers with graphics cards is now becoming an all-in-one system. Nonetheless, the area of virtual reality as a mass educational platform is still in its infancy, and there are not enough case studies compared to conventional ways of learning. This is especially true in the context of Korea where there is not an abundance of content that users can consume due to language barriers.

The selected website for this paper, Google Arts and Culture encompasses numerous strengths such as the high resolution of visual data, being able to observe the statue in 360°, and being immersed into the moment. However, it lacks in services such as not all statutes can be viewed in numerous facets, the stuttering transition of scenery, and the lack of support system that teachers who do not feel comfortable using VR can use. For the further expansion and application of the website into the global educational field, including Korea, such aforementioned factors need to be visited beforehand.

For further research, more VR-based educational platforms need to be investigated since this paper primarily focuses on Google Arts and Culture. Instead of focusing on subjects that are artistic or culturally valued, analyzing how the system can be incorporated when teaching science and math classes would be beneficial as those subjects' curriculums differ greatly from art-related courses. In order to implement VR service to the whole educational system, such a study would be necessary.

References

1. An, M.: Problems and directions of development through analysis of virtual reality-based education in Korea. Int. J. Inf. Educ. Technol. **10**(8), 552–556 (2020)
2. Blyth, C.: Immersive technologies and language learning. Foreign Lang. Ann. **51**(1), 225–232 (2018)
3. Buhm, W.: Assessing policies regarding tangible educational contents through the utilization of VR·AR and an analysis of examples. NIPA Issue Rep. **2019**(15), 1–19 (2019)
4. Touchstone Research. https://touchstoneresearch.com/vr-and-consumer-sentiment/. Accessed 09 Nov 2021

5. Stanford Medicine News Center. https://med.stanford.edu/news/all-news/2017/07/virtual-rea lity-system-helps-surgeons-reassures-patients.html. Accessed 02 Nov 2021
6. Asia Economy. https://view.asiae.co.kr/article/2020120812063489325. Accessed 09 Nov 2021
7. CNBC. https://www.cnbc.com/2020/07/04/virtual-reality-usage-booms-in-the-workplace-amid-the-pandemic.html. Accessed 09 Nov 2021
8. Lee, J.: A study on the revitalization of virtual reality-based. J. Korean Soc. Des. Cult. **25**(1), 357–366 (2019)
9. The International Telecommunication Union ICT Development Index 2017 IDI 2017 Rank. https://www.itu.int/net4/ITU-D/idi/2017/index.html. Accessed 10 Nov 2021
10. Seoul Public News. https://go.seoul.co.kr/news/newsView.php?id=20210830011012& wlog_tag3=naver. Accessed 02 Nov 2021
11. Kim, J.: Investigating the perception of instructors on the use of virtual reality education. J. Digit. Convergence **19**(7), 11–19 (2021)
12. Pokhrel, S.: A literature review on the impact of COVID-19 pandemic on teaching and learning. High. Educ. Future **8**(1), 133–141 (2021)
13. The Lenovo Foundation. https://news.lenovo.com/pressroom/press-releases/study-one-year-later-students-educators-in-asia-pacific-crack-code-online-learning/. Accessed 09 Nov 2021
14. Ratcliffe, J.: Extended Reality (XR) remote research: a survey of drawbacks and opportunities. In: CHI 2021, no. 527, pp. 1–13 (2021)
15. Samsung Electronics America Insights. https://insights.samsung.com/2016/06/27/teachers-ready-for-virtual-reality-in-education/. Accessed 10 Nov 2021
16. Youth Mobility Index Ymi 2018 report. https://www.youthmobility.asia/ymi-2018-report/. Accessed 09 Nov 2021

Architectural View of Non-face-to-face Experiential Learning Through the Immersive Technologies

Vinayak V. Mukkawar[1] , Laxman D. Netak[1(✉)] ,
and Valmik B. Nikam[2(✉)]

[1] Department of Computer Engineering,
Dr. Babasaheb Ambedkar Technological University, Raigad, Lonere 402103, India
{mukkawar.vv,ldnetak}@dbatu.ac.in
[2] Department of Information Technology, Veermata Jijabai Technological Institute,
Mumbai 400019, India
vbnikam@it.vjti.ac.in

Abstract. The significant disruption caused by the COVID-19 pandemic prohibits the face-to-face teaching-learning process. This pandemic forced the students to utilize online i.e. non-face-to-face mode of education via different platforms available on the internet. The use of the internet allows students to use e-learning resources to learn things from anywhere and at any time. The ease of use makes these systems more favorable amongst the learner. The traditional way of face-to-face teaching-learning with the utmost learning rate is no longer beneficial in the pandemic situation. Many of the teaching institutes use online aids for content delivery. No doubt, all these platforms are far better to provide knowledge and educate the students, but these platforms do not focus on the active participation of students in an online class like teacher observe the students concentration in a physical classroom. Monitoring the engagement of students in the online mode of education seems to be difficult, but can be achieved through the use of immersive technology. This paper provides an architectural view of the online teaching-learning system with the use of Virtual Reality to achieve better engagement of students in the virtual classroom through immersion.

Keywords: Immersive technology · Virtual reality · Experiential learning · Virtual classroom

1 Introduction

The Covid-19 pandemic changes the way of teaching-learning. The institutes nowadays are taking advantage of the online teaching-learning process. Covid-19 forces the user to move from traditional classroom teaching-learning to the online mode of teaching-learning. Different tools are available for such kind of learning process. These tools are much better and easy to use but do not provide active engagement of participants.

© Springer Nature Switzerland AG 2022
J.-H. Kim et al. (Eds.): IHCI 2021, LNCS 13184, pp. 282–291, 2022.
https://doi.org/10.1007/978-3-030-98404-5_27

It's challenging to monitor the engagement of students through online mode. Active participation of students leads to a greater understanding as observed in the traditional way of teaching. Online platforms used to conduct classes do not guarantee the complete immersion of students in class. The immersion of students in online classes can be achieved through the use of Virtual Reality. Initially, Virtual Reality and Augmented Reality were used for game development. Later on, Virtual Reality places its roots in various application domains such as data and architectural visualization [11], scientific visualization [12], Medicine and Surgery [14], Training [20], Telepresence [10], and Entertainment [17]. Low-cost implementation of Virtual Reality in the classroom through Google Cardboard can be seen in [18]. Virtual Reality applications help the person with Autism Spectrum Disorder to learn the things [13,22,23].

It is observed that video-based and game-based learnings are far better than the traditional way of learning. [9,19] shows the use of immersive 360 degree videos. The AulaVR [21] and Revolutionary Interactive Smart Classroom (RISC) [15] provides novel way to interact between students. Both the techniques are applicable for distance learning and provide a way to interact among the students and teachers. VREdu [16] is a framework that allows developers to include standard components needed for developing VR-based lectures.

The implementation given in [18] limited to the display of the 3-D contents to the students. With the help of Google Cardboard, it is tedious to track the head motion of students, eye positioning of students, and interactive communication. Similarly, [9,19] also utilizes the video and does not provide a way to interact between them. The AulaVR [21], RISC [15], and VREdu [16] provide the way of interaction and fail to monitor the student head position. To monitor the head position of students, the Head Mounted Display must be configured with Accelerometer, magnetometer, and gyroscope. The proposed architecture in this paper is developed using the HMD having Accelerometer, magnetometer, and gyroscope.

2   Components of Virtual Reality Application

Before exploring the proposed architecture, firstly understand the components of any general Virtual Reality Application. The components required to build a Virtual Reality system is divided into two parts, as shown in Fig. 1.

2.1   Hardware Components

Hardware components of a VR system are divided into four types. In addition to these four types of hardware, a high-end system with higher RAM and graphics compared to any personnel system is required. The high-end system works as a workstation for the Virtual Reality application. These computers are responsible for handling all I/O devices and results in immersive experiences for users in the virtual world.

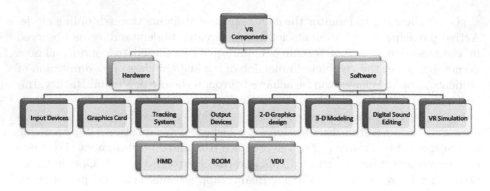

Fig. 1. VR system component

1. *Input Devices*: Input devices are used to interact with a synthetic environment. It is not possible with touch-typing devices like a mouse to interact with the virtual world. Hence, devices having tracking facilities are used. The devices act like a wand having a tracking capability that can be used for interaction. The wand allows a user to navigate in a virtual system, it also helps to insert the virtual object and to rotate the virtual objects in an imaginary world. The wand must have 6-degree of freedom since it has to operate in a 3-D environment. Data glove is another input device having tracking sense, it senses the position and orientation of the user's hand. It can also have a flex sensor to measure the bend of a finger. Voice command can also be used as input in some VR applications.
2. *Graphics cards*: These are the process acceleration cards used to update the display with sensory information. A workstation with the GPU performs better as compared with a workstation without GPU. A 3-D sound card may also increase the sense of position based on the intensity of sound.
3. *Tracking System*: A tracking system is used to measure the position and orientation of the user. This measurement helps the computer to determine the contents to be shown to the user in the virtual world. If we consider the HMD as a tracking device, and the user moves his head, the system has to show a viewpoint as per the movement. The refresh rate for a standard tracking device to take the measurement is 20 times per second. The tracking system may be mechanical, electro-magnetic, ultrasonic, or infrared.
4. *Output device*: Displays are output devices. These are used to display the simulated world to the user. Commonly HMD (Head Mounted Display) having an inbuilt headphone is used for sight and sound in the virtual environment. These devices look like eyeglasses or more like a helmet. As a human having two eyes, HMD also has two screens that display stereoscopic images that lead to building a 3-D environment. HMD always shows the screen in front of the user's eyes. Immersive rooms are another example of output devices. An immersive room displays various images on the wall based on the situation inside the virtual world. Such a room can be used in simulations. Binocular

Omni-Orientation Monitor (BOOM) is assembled on a mechanical arm having a tracking sensor. The user can hold their face in front of this stereoscopic device to observe the virtual environment. The Video Display Unit (VDU) is yet another output device. CRT, LCD, TFT, and LED monitors are examples of VDU.

2.2 Software Used in Virtual Reality

Virtual Environments are completely imaginary. Hence, each part of the virtual world needs to be manually designed. The virtual world contains 2-D, 3-D images, and sound. So the software is required to build these objects. Based on object design supported by software, the software can be categorized into four categories (i) 2-D Graphics design, (ii) 3-D modeling, (iii)Digital sound editors, and (iv)VR simulation software. In recent times all these kinds of software are integrated into one. The following section describes the various frameworks used in virtual reality for content development as well as simulation. Some of them are open source or free and some of them are proprietary.

1. *Blender*: It is an Open-source software for 2-D and 3-D design [2]. This software seamlessly runs on all operating systems. Blender software is written in Python. In addition to 2-D design and 3-D modeling, Blender supports lighting, simulation, rendering, and animation. It provides better tool connectivity by supporting plugins and various formats of the virtual object. Blender also supports video editing tools and other necessary tools required to design VR video games.
2. *Google VR*: Google VR is commonly used to develop mobile VR applications. Google offers Daydream and Cardboard platforms for mobile VR development [3]. Both the platform provides Asynchronous reprojection, WolrdSesne tracking, and 6DOF. Asynchronous reprojection ensures high-performance VR rendering. It assures consistent motion when the user performs their moves. Positional tracking can be done with WorldScene.
3. *3DS Max*: Autodesk provides this great paid software for 3-D modeling and rendering [1]. It provides tools to create 3-D models and 3-D animation. It can also be used to develop VR games with the support of powerful scene modeling, dynamic visual content, and customizable pipeline integration features.
4. *Unity*: This is the most widely used gaming engine and it supports both AR and VR [7]. Unity engine is also used to provide VR solutions for automotive, transportation, manufacturing, and engineering fields. To develop the VR objects Unity provides a powerful editor, designer tool, CAD tool, and collaboration tool. Unity also provides direct VR mode to see object rendering in HMD at the time of development like any simple console application development and execution.
5. *Maya*: Software by Autodesk is useful to draw and render the jagger-free 3-D scene [5]. This software supports 3-D modeling, lighting, animation, and VFX. Maya also provides a bunch of tools used for dynamics, 3-D shading, pipeline integration, and many more.

Table 1. Comparison of VR software

Development tools	OS platforms	Open-Source	Programming languages	Main features
Blender	Windows, Linux, Android, iOS	Yes	Python	Object rendering and animation
Google VR	Android, and Browser support	Daydream Free, and Cardboard open source	Java	Asynchronous reprojection, WolrdSesne tracking, and 6DOF
3DS Max	Windows, Linux, Mac OS	Paid software	MAXScript and Python	scene modeling, dynamic visual content, and pipeline integration
Unity	Windows, Linux, and Web based	Free	C#, Java Script	Powerful toolbox, VR mode to see object rendering
Maya	Windows, Linux, and Mac OS	Paid Software	Maya Embedded Language (MEL)	Animation, VFX, Dynamics, and pipeline integration
Unreal Engine	Windows or Mac OS	Free	C++	Blueprint Visual Scripting, pipeline integration, and Unreal motion graphics
OpenSpace3D	Android, Raspberry, iOS, Windows, Linux, Mac OS	Yes	Scol, Java	Object detection and tracking, low-end devices application development
GuriVR	Web-based	Yes	WebGL and OpenGL	Conversion of text description to 3-D Scene

6. *Unreal Engine*: With help of Unreal Engine, a developer can work on various VR platforms [8]. Popularly used to develop VR games for VR platforms like Oculus, Sony, Samsung, Android, and iOS. With the help of Blueprint, the Visual Scripting tool provided by Unreal developers can easily create a prototype.

7. *OpenSpace3D*: It is a free and open-source virtual reality development platform [6]. It can also be used to develop VR games. AR application can also be developed using OpenSpace3D. Google Cardboard, HTC Vive, Oculus-like simulation devices are provided by OpenSpace3D. It provides a scene editor, programming editor, 3-D model exporter. The 3-D model exporter is used

to export the 3-D model developed in 3DS Max, Maya, and Blender. This software is basically used to develop VR applications on low-end devices.

8. *GuriVR*: GuriVR is a powerful open-source tool to develop a VR experience. It has the feature of converting text descriptions of a 3-D scene into a 3-D VR-ready scene [4]. Web-based tool to develop VR applications that use Mozilla A-Frame (Browser-ready Virtual Reality and Mix Reality development framework) and WebGL to generate a rich virtual experience for web apps and websites. To generate a desktop VR application it uses OpenGL.

A comparative evaluation of all these development tools used to design VR-based applications is provided in Table 1.

3   Proposed Architecture for Virtual Reality Classroom

The proposed architecture is shown in Fig. 2.The use of such architecture is the same as that of regular online classes through Google Meet and Zoom meetings, except the user, has to wear a head-mounted display.

3.1   Structure

As shown in Fig. 2 the architecture of virtual class having only two users, one is a teacher and the other is a student. Both the user requires Input and Output devices. In the case of the teacher, the input device is a microphone, any haptic device, and an additional controller will act as an input. While in the case of students the input devices are microphones as well as displays. Displays are nothing but cell phone screens that are placed inside of Head Mounted Display. The complete virtual classroom and its mobile version can be created using any software mentioned in Table 1 but to render the whole scenario the developer has to use either Unity engine or Unreal engine.

Both users have to wear Head Mounted Display. In addition to students, the teacher requires a controller for body motion tracking. The action performed by the teacher is processed by the server and forwarded to all students.

3.2   Working

Initially, assets for virtual classrooms must be created, these assets include blackboard, chalk, chair, table, wall, and windows. Based on these assets virtual classroom is rendered. To create such assets one can use the software listed in Table 1. As Virtual Reality allows physical existence in the logical world, students wearing the head-mounted display feel that they are present in the virtual classroom.

To make it more realistic students can join the classroom by using their avatars. To use and create avatars assets should be developed first. The teacher will use their avatar available in assets. In addition to the head-mounted display, a teacher has to use the controller. This controller is used to track the motion of the teacher, through which students can understand the action performed by the teacher.

The traditional teaching-learning process gives you the way to monitor the active participation of students in the classroom through overall observation by faculty. In regular online teaching-learning, this could be a tedious job. Students are present in the class, but the faculty is unable to monitor him, his reaction, and his responses through facial expressions. Even the faculty don't know whether students are listening to them or not as students videos are off to save the Bandwidth. Monitoring the students in the virtual environment can be addressed through the use of Virtual classrooms and Head-Mounted Displays. The cellphone of students is placed inside HMD and students have to wear this HMD. This itself results in the better concentration of the student in the virtual classroom.

Different position tracking algorithms are available to accurately track the position of Head-Mounted Displays like Wireless Tracking, Optical Tracking, and Inertial Tracking. Wireless tracking involves anchor installation around the perimeter of the tracking environment. Wireless tracking is not suitable for our application. Optical tracking requires the cameras to be installed on HMD to track position and orientation using Computer Vision algorithms. Optical tracking is expensive in terms of money and time. Inertial tracking uses data of accelerometer and gyroscope. It can track the position by calculating roll, pitch, and yaw. Inertial tracking is cost-effective and used in this application.

The HMD in combination with an accelerometer, magnetometer, and gyroscope, must wear by students in our scenario. Also, the students and faculty have to enter the classroom through their avatars. The accelerometer, magnetometer, and gyroscope are used to trace the head position and head movement of avatars and ultimately the head position of students. So, if faculty, as stated earlier, having a controller device may change their position in a virtual environment using their avatar, now it's time to look towards students HMD position and faculty have to trace the movement in students avatar. This is as easy as monitoring students' heads inside a physical classroom.

The same application may be used for gesture recognition through the movement of the avatar. Tracing the HMD position using an accelerometer, magnetometer and, gyroscope gives proper understanding to faculty that students are actively present in the classroom or not.

The flow of utilization of this architecture is shown in Fig. 3. The teacher will create room for communication like any other online platform and enters the virtual world employing his/her avatar. The teacher will allow the students to enter the classroom by their avatar. Input and output devices work accordingly to convey the knowledge from teachers to students through online virtual mode. The Head positioning system allows the teacher to monitor virtual students. At the end of the class teacher and student can leave the virtual classroom.

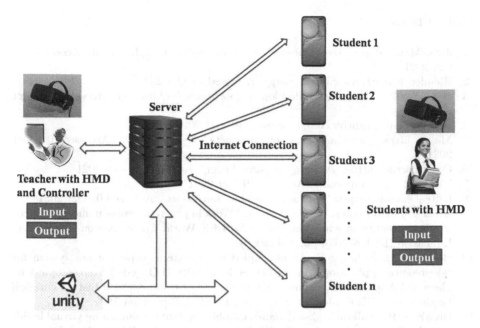

Fig. 2. Proposed architecture for virtual reality classroom

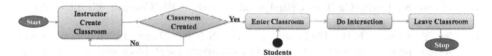

Fig. 3. Activity flow of virtual reality classroom

4   Conclusion

The paper describes the utilization of immersive technology in the field of education to enhance the teaching-learning process. Virtual Reality allows the immersion of the user in the new synthetic world. The full immersion of the user increases the concentration and understanding ability of the user.

The use of avatars for teachers advances us to provide the action of a teacher to students rather than providing only voice like any other online platform used for content delivery. The use of avatar and head moment tracker of students provides better control to the teacher to monitor the class as like physical class. The students are available with full concentration as their cellphones are kept in the head-mounted display.

References

1. 3DS Max. https://www.autodesk.in/products/3ds-max/free-trial. Accessed 01 Oct 2021
2. Blender. https://www.blender.org/. Accessed 01 Oct 2021
3. Google VR SDK. https://developers.google.com/vr/discover. Accessed 01 Oct 2021
4. Gurivr. https://gurivr.com/. Accessed 01 Oct 2021
5. Maya. https://www.autodesk.com/products/maya/overview. Accessed 01 Oct 2021
6. Openspace3d. https://www.openspace3d.com/. Accessed 01 Oct 2021
7. Unity. https://unity.com/. Accessed 01 Oct 2021
8. Unreal engine. https://www.unrealengine.com/en-us/. Accessed 01 Oct 2021
9. Alvarez, J., Rodríguez, R., Martínez, M.: Work in progress - use of immersive videos of virtual reality in education. In: 2020 IEEE World Conference on Engineering Education (EDUNINE), pp. 1–4 (2020)
10. Bolas, M.T., Fisher, S.S.: Head-coupled remote stereoscopic camera system for telepresence applications. In: Fisher, S.S., Merritt, J.O. (eds.) Stereoscopic Displays and Applications, volume 1256 of Society of Photo-Optical Instrumentation Engineers (SPIE) Conference Series, pp. 113–123, September 1990
11. Brooks, F.P.: Walkthrough-a dynamic graphics system for simulating virtual buildings. In: Proceedings of the 1986 Workshop on Interactive 3D Graphics, I3D 1986, pp. 9–21. Association for Computing Machinery, New York (1987)
12. Bryson, S., Levit, C.: The virtual wind tunnel. IEEE Comput. Graphics Appl. **12**(4), 25–34 (1992)
13. Cai, Y., Chia, N.K.H., Thalmann, D., Kee, N.K.N., Zheng, J., Thalmann, N.M.: Design and development of a virtual Dolphinarium for children with autism. IEEE Trans. Neural Syst. Rehabil. Eng. 21(2), 208–217 (2013)
14. Hunter, I.W., et al.: A teleoperated microsurgical robot and associated virtual environment for eye surgery. Presence Teleoperators Virtual Environ. **2**(4), 265–280 (1993)
15. Memos, V.A., Minopoulos, G., Stergiou, C., Psannis, K.E., Ishibashi, Y.: A revolutionary interactive smart classroom (RISC) with the use of emerging technologies. In: 2020 2nd International Conference on Computer Communication and the Internet (ICCCI), pp. 174–178 (2020)
16. Misbhauddin, M.: VREdu: a framework for interactive immersive lectures using virtual reality. In: 2018 21st Saudi Computer Society National Computer Conference (NCC), pp 1–6 (2018)
17. Onyesolu, M.O., et al.: Virtual reality: an emerging computer technology of the 21st century. Electroscope J. **1**(1), 36–40 (2016)
18. Ray, A.B., Deb, S.: Smartphone based virtual reality systems in classroom teaching - a study on the effects of learning outcome. In: 2016 IEEE Eighth International Conference on Technology for Education (T4E), pp. 68–71 (2016)
19. Seo, J.H., Kicklighter, C., Garcia, B., Chun, S.W., Wells-Beede, E.: Work-in-progress-design and evaluation of 360 VR immersive interactions in nursing education. In: 2021 7th International Conference of the Immersive Learning Research Network (iLRN), pp. 1–3 (2021)
20. Vince, J.: Virtual reality techniques in flight simulation. In: Virtual Reality Systems (1993)

21. Jonathan, Y., Guevara, L., Guerrero, G.: Aulavr: virtual reality, a telepresence technique applied to distance education. In: 2020 15th Iberian Conference on Information Systems and Technologies (CISTI), pp. 1–5 (2020)
22. Zhang, L., et al.: Cognitive load measurement in a virtual reality-based driving system for autism intervention. IEEE Trans. Affect. Comput. 8(2), 176–189 (2017)
23. Zhao, H., Swanson, A.R., Weitlauf, A.S., Warren, Z.E., Sarkar, N.: Hand-in-hand: a communication-enhancement collaborative virtual reality system for promoting social interaction in children with autism spectrum disorders. IEEE Trans. Hum.-Mach. Syst. 48(2), 136–148 (2018)

The Role of Artificial Intelligence (AI) in Assisting Applied Natya Therapy for Relapse Prevention in De-addiction

Dimple Kaur Malhotra[✉]

Imatter Institute of Counselling and Behavior Sciences,
Sumangali Arts LLC, Irvine, CA, USA
dimple@dimplekaur.com

Abstract. This paper is about exploring the role of Artificial Intelligence in therapy for drug addiction and relapse. This paper also investigates the results of timely interventions through sensing the changes in the body as a result of thoughts, learnt behaviour, and emotional responses during trauma, and stress-inducing situations. One of the possible solutions we propose is exploring the principles of Applied Natya Therapy (ANT) and integrating it with Artificial Intelligence (AI) to assist with the Therapy and Rehabilitation for the patients with drug and substance abuse, as well as drug relapse. For a long time, scientists have been observing and replicating every physical aspect of the body's movements, and have successfully replicated and applied it in robots. However, translating human emotion into machine learning is what is the next frontier of scientific research as it will open up significant opportunities in overall health and emotional well-being. The key element in any treatment is the prevention of relapse especially with the patients of drug and substance abuse. Relapse is the most dreaded condition for the patient as well as for family and the caretakers of the patients of drug addiction. Addictions are difficult to treat because we need to focus on the time window before the relapse and not after. Recent findings corroborate the characterizations of delay discounting as a candidate behavioral marker of addiction and may help identify subgroups that require special treatment or unique interventions to overcome their addiction. In a study published in the January 5 Molecular Psychiatry, researchers found that machine learning could not only help predict the characteristics of a person's depression, but also do this more effectively, and with less information, than traditional approaches [1]. The authors concluded that machine learning could be a clinically useful way to stratify depression [4] This exploration will assist in capturing data for emotions and expressions generated during Applied Natya Therapy Techniques that can be captured in real time to be utilized in devising aids for relapse prevention.

D. K. Malhotra—Director.
The paper was partly funded by IGNCA - Indira Gandhi National Centre for the Arts, New Delhi.

J.-H. Kim et al. (Eds.): IHCI 2021, LNCS 13184, pp. 292–298, 2022.
https://doi.org/10.1007/978-3-030-98404-5_28

Keywords: De-addiction therapy · Rehabilitation · Relapse
prevention · Emotions · Depression · Anxiety · Applied Natya Therapy

1 Introduction

Let's begin with understanding the key issues in the areas of therapy and rehabilitation. The DSM-5 discusses three separate categories of mental health disorders. First, trauma and stress related disorders ranging from attachment disorders to social engagement disorders. Second, neurodevelopmental disorders such as autism spectrum disorder and attention deficit hyperactivity disorder (ADHD) which have the challenges of learning intelligence and communication. Third, disruptive impulse control or conduct disorders, oppositional defiant disorder, and body and impulse control.

Psychological stress is experienced when patients feel that life situations are not what they expected or that they have no control over what is happening to them. It can be compared to standing in a building on fire, or it can be the feeling of being robbed at gunpoint, or any other horrors of life and death such as war tragedy, heart attacks, losing a limb, rape, etc. We have heard rape survivors reporting their feelings of numbness and feeling frozen in the moment of losing control and ownership of their bodies. An example of such a report is written by Franca Rame [7] who in her monologue Stupor writes about her feelings of how she survived that physical and mental trauma of rape and describes the feelings of being frozen and numb and being dissociated from her body. She felt as if she lost her voice. In retrospect and as therapists we now know that these were the body's mechanisms to help her stay alive in that moment and protect her to overcome the fear during the trauma. All these situations mentioned above are stress and trauma inducing, and lead to a very strong emotional reaction or even psychological disorders such as Post Traumatic Stress Disorder (PTSD). In all these scenarios, the event happens once and happens very quickly in cases like a gunshot. It is not a long process, it is just a few seconds. An accident is not a long drawn process but happens in a split second and you break a bone, someone dies, you lose a limb; all these tragedies happen very quickly, and research has shown the link between stress induced trauma and PTSD [3]. Depression and Anxiety are the most common comorbid disorders. Therefore, this study will explore these two conditions and the presenting emotions as well as the reduction in the intensity after providing intervention through Applied Natya Therapy.

2 Brain Pathology and Background

The fear and pain of the moment seem to have embedded itself in this one physical response of the body. The major areas of the brain related to psychological stress and trauma are: 1) Sensory motor cortex, 2) Thalamus, 3) Para hippocampal gyrus, 4) Hippocampus, 5) Amygdala, 6) Orbitofrontal cortex, 7) Prefrontal cortex, 8) Anterior cingulate cortex, and 9) Fear response.

Other areas also include networks involved in anxiety and anxiety induced disorders, error detection, executive control, detecting new stimuli and internal processing, yps inferior temporal cortex, natural parietal cortex, anterior insula, and posterior singlet cortex. All these areas of the brain are affected by trauma for a much longer term even though the physical injury heals. More often than not these psychological wounds go undiagnosed, unchecked, and untreated. These psychological wounds manifest themselves later on as stress and anxiety induced disorders. It could be as simple as being unable to speak in public, stage phobia, or as serious as social anxiety, PTSD, and substance and drug abuse. Over the years that I have worked with drugs and substance disorders, the underlying problem was always fear, low self-esteem, and low self-confidence manifesting and masking as Depression and Anxiety.

3   General Therapy Methodologies

Participation in both studies was voluntary. In order to measure the impact of ANT, Depression and Anxiety test was administered to a control group where the pre and post intervention state was measured. The results show a significant drop in Depression and Anxiety, establishing the therapeutic value of the process which ANT Uses. A total of 50 participants completed the assessment. Inclusion criteria required that participants be 18 years or older and self-report recovery from one or more SUDs, depression, anxiety. For the purpose of measurement, we used Beck's Depression inventory method; for Anxiety we used the Self-Rating Anxiety Scale (SAS) method. By using commonly used and established scale, we wanted to ensure that the data collected is as accurate and applicable as possible.

4   Study Measures

Various demographic data including age, ethnicity, annual income, gender, marital status, and education level were collected using a standardized questionnaire.

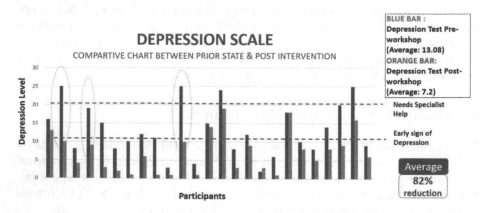

Fig. 1. Depression test comparison between pre & post ANT intervention

All participants self-reported being in recovery from at least one substance addiction. The primary areas requiring treatment were determined using the questions and the insights generated through application of Applied Natya Therapy techniques.

Evidence Based Findings: The group was instructed regarding the test and were guided through the process of self rating. Pre Intervention Test forms were filled up before the intervention through ANT to gather data based on the self assessed tests. The next step involved the learning and practice of various specific designed movements and activities derived from Natya Shastra. The participants were asked to practice them during the course of the workshop. Qualitative data regarding their experiences based on responses generated through the activities was collected. during the course of practice and reflections. At the end of the workshop, participants were given the same test to be filled post intervention and data was collected as Post Intervention Test.

Figure 1 shows the mental state of the group prior to intervention. As demonstrated, the significant number of subjects were in need of help given there stage of moderate to severe depression (n = 50). X is representing the participants; y is representing the test scores of Depression test and Anxiety tests as individually evaluated through self rating scale across the control group. In majority cases there was a significant drop in the depression level post Intervention. In some cases the drop is from Extreme depression to absolutely normal levels. This evidence proves that ANT helps reduced depression significantly.

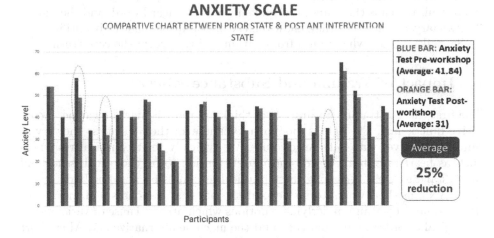

Fig. 2. Anxiety test comparison between pre & post ANT intervention

Figure 2 depicts the mental state of the group prior to intervention. As indicated, the significant number of subjects were in need of help given there stage of high level of Anxiety (n = 50). The same group post ANT shows significant drop in Anxiety and the comparative anxiety levels pre- and post-interventions are provided in graph at Fig. 2.

5   Integrating Therapy with Natya Shastra

The moment prior to loss of executive control and the way their brains react to triggers is where integration of AI can help them foresee and recall and take action before relapsing into substance abuse. Data already shows that body movement and exercise helps with the release of positive neurotransmitters, however, these specific dance movement therapies takes it one step further in bringing about a personality change in the long term resulting in increased productivity, happiness, satisfaction, and an overall improved quality of life. These are the areas that are lacking when the patients enter rehabilitation. The text used here to generate these results relies on the principles of Natya Shastra [2]. Natya as a term means the integration of multiple expressive arts into an integrated whole system to present art to others or practice for self. Over time, the whole system of Natya Shastra was reduced to just dance performance and specifically: stage performance. However, it has proven to have a much deeper application of the codified body movements and facial expressions in changing human personality and cognition. The application has also been applied for enhancing performance in all spheres of life ranging from executive functioning, resilience, happiness, or self-fulfilment. A self-fulfilled person, a self-driven person, a self-motivated person is more productive than a person with a neuropsychological disorder. Natya is based on four principles or four different pillars [5].

1. Angika: which means the body, how the body moves, the rules of the body, and how we can play with it.
2. Vaachika: means the sound, the spoken word, the heard word, and the music.
3. Aahaarya: means the ornamentation, the presentation, and the beautification.
4. Saatvika: means what comes from within and the truth: the core truth.

6   Impact of Trauma and Substance Abuse

The first effect of trauma is paralysis of thinking- there is marked decline in cognitive functioning. The pain is too much to handle for the patients so they try to numb themselves with substance abuse. We typically relate physical responses such as heart rate, brain waves and muscle tension to psychological issues and understanding what is causing these physical responses because the body senses first. ANT method works to go beyond the physical responses and metrics to understand deeper and underlying emotions which are the cause of various psychological disorders. Our goal is to find the machine alternative and AI support to the widespread issue of drug addiction and relapse prevention. When dealing with drug addiction, specifically in the LGBTQ community, the clinical diagnoses in majority of cases are anxiety, social anxiety, PTSD, and sexual abuse, along with dysfunctional coping mechanisms. Enabling the individual to reach one's core truth is the whole power and process of Applied Natya Therapy. The biggest challenge is that people are not allowed to express the multidimensional way in which they think. There is a complete disintegration and dissociation of all these aspects of human functioning. A person's Saatvika, their true self, gets suppressed under fear and anxiety when such a dissociation is displayed in a patient. Thus, Natya Therapy integrates all these elements and pillars of Natya with therapy, and applies these codified movements and gestures from the text to reach a patient's core truth and self to gain control over emotions and situations. Taking the sample of 50 patients in a recovery outpatient centre, the biggest issue in tackling drug addiction is about relapse. The window of saving the patients from relapse is small but has a prominent pattern, which if monitored and calculated fast, can help both - patient as well as the therapist to take a quick and timely action towards prevention of relapse. Difficulty in maintaining their control in high stress and social situations triggers individuals in recovery to fall back into their addictive state.

7   General Discussion

The present study examined the association between depression, anxiety, substance abuse and the role of ANT in expressing the underlying emotions in a sample of individuals in recovery. The results indicate significant associations between depression, anxiety and relapse. Higher relapse was observed among those with higher levels of depression and anxiety. In addition, the current findings also indicated the lowering of the intensity in depression and anxiety through ANT leading to being more aware with a possibility of recovery and relapse prevention. These results extend the findings by reporting a significant association between depression, anxiety and relapse due to triggers that could not be predicted among individuals in recovery from substance dependence. Once the person relapses, it is difficult to gather further data as many times guilt, shame, exhaustion, homelessnes prevents the individual to seek therapy further. Death due to overdose during such relapse episodes is also reported. The reason why the therapists need AI is because successful therapy depends on lot of factors: Therapist's individual expertise is needed, requires 10 years to make one therapist, data of depression and other disorders is hard to quantify, cost of treatment is high, therapy is a long-term treatment, and therapy wains off without consistency. Even though no previous study has examined the relationship between ANT and individuals in recovery from substance use disorders, the association between physical health-related indicators and treatment effectiveness has been established. Physical activity, for example, is often used as an adjunctive approach to substance use treatment to improve physical health amid other outcomes [8]. Interestingly, one study showed that differences in global functioning between adults submitted to a treatment program and population norms were initially verified but vanished three months after treatment commenced. Therefore, detection of early symptoms of triggers during recovery can help participants in recovery to observe the changes when they are without supervision which can help in their taking the action to curb the cravings and the triggers by taking timely actions and notify the therapist or seek other support. The window to prevent the relapse is very small and it requires urgent and immediate recognition of changes that occur within the mind and body, the sensory changes need to be recorded and a warning signal be sent to the patient to help the recall. Machine learning tools have the ability to speedily process huge amounts of data, without human fatigue. The future lies in capturing the data sets of deeper layers emotions and triggers that are elucidated during the course of therapy and creating a rapid machine computational solution for timely intervention for relapse prevention.

8 Conclusion

The path to obtaining successful results and a long-term recovery for patients with drug addiction and history of relapse is a sustained model of therapy with the inclusion of body movements and using data from triggers and neural networks to predict loss of executive control and relapse. Reminders need to be used in all of these aspects to train the patients to remember the path they are on and acknowledge the triggers rather than give in to them. Immediacy of the reminders is crucial and the therapist and AI can be used to tabulate the timings and individualize those reminders per patient. Applied Natya Therapy [6] can be used for integrating and reconnecting their physical and detached emotional states and bridge the gap in that dissociation. Artificial Intelligence will help with the need for capturing the data in real time to assess the brain data and predict relapse causes and the time window in which the therapeutic interventions could be the most beneficial for the patients. The applications can be applied to future research as a longer-term trajectory of the recovery process by understanding the relationships between the triggers, response window and relapse prevention.

References

1. Athamneh, L.N., Freitas Lemos, R., Basso, J.C.T.D.C., Craft, W.H., Stein, M.D., Bickel, W.K.: The phenotype of recovery II: the association between delay discounting, self-reported quality of life, and remission status among individuals in recovery from substance use disorders. Exp. Clin. Psychopharmacol. (2020). https://doi.org/10.1037/pha0000389
2. Bharata, M., Iyengar, G.R.S.: Natyasastra: translation of Bharatha Natyasastra. Suvani Prakasana, Bangalore (1977)
3. Carlson, N.R.: Physiology of Behavior, 6th edn. Allyn & Bacon, Boston (2010)
4. Edgcomb, J.B., Zima, B.: Machine learning, natural language processing, and the electronic health record: innovations in mental health services research. Psychiatric Serv. (Washington D.C.) 346–349 (2019). https://doi.org/10.1176/appi.ps.201800401
5. Ghosh, M.: The Nāṭya Śāstra. https://jambudveep.files.wordpress.com/2012/03/natyashastra.pdf. Accessed 14 Nov 2021
6. Malhotra, D.K.: Applied Natya Therapy. http://www.appliednatyatherapy.com/. Accessed 14 Nov 2021
7. Rame, F.: The Rape. http://www.geocities.ws/dariofoarchive/rape.html. Accessed 14 Nov 2021
8. Wang, F., Pandika, D., Chassin, L., Lee, M., King, K.: Testing the relations among family disorganization, delay discounting, and adolescent alcohol use: a genetically informed study. Alcohol. Clin. Exp. Res. **40**, 846–856 (2016). https://doi.org/10.1111/acer.12999

Immersive and Tangible Interface

Design of a Smart Puppet Theatre System for Computational Thinking Education

Raghav Kasibhatla, Saifuddin Mahmud, Redwanul Haque Sourave, Marcus Arnett, and Jong-Hoon Kim(✉)

Advanced Telerobotics Research Lab, Computer Science, Kent State University, Kent, OH, USA
jkim72@kent.edu

Abstract. Many efforts have failed to achieve tangible models of a robotic theatre, as opposed to virtual or simulated theatres, despite many attempts to merge the progress of robotics with the growth of theatre and the performing arts. Many of the initiatives that have achieved significant progress in these domains are on a considerably larger scale, with the primary goal of entertaining rather than demonstrating the interdisciplinary nature of Robotics and Engineering. The purpose of this paper is to correctly unite the principles of Science, Technology, Engineering, Arts, and Mathematics in a small size robotic theatre that will allow for a more portable and changeable exhibition. The Tortoise and Hare play will be performed in the theatre, which is made up of both stage and puppet elements. A pan and tilt lighting system, audio integration via an external device, automated curtains with stepper motors, props, and a grid stage are among the stage's components. A camera tracking module in the light system detects the location of a robot and communicates with the light fixtures to angle the spotlight. A transportable module that interacts wirelessly with its environment, as well as simple-moving, decorative puppet cutouts protruding from the module, make up the smart puppets. The mBlock IDE is used to edit the story in the theatre software, providing for a simple technique of programming the scene. The Smart Mini Theatre's production of the Tortoise and Hare play intends to encourage performing arts students to experiment with robots and programming to create their own shows, in the hopes of inspiring them to pursue Robotics and Engineering as a potential career choice.

Keywords: Virtual coding · Human-robot interaction · Smart theatre · Object detection

1 Introduction

1.1 Background

Computational thinking (CT) is a critical talent for students in the digital age, as more than 65% of students will work in jobs that do not exist today [1]. This

J.-H. Kim et al. (Eds.): IHCI 2021, LNCS 13184, pp. 301–312, 2022.
https://doi.org/10.1007/978-3-030-98404-5_29

methodical approach to problem resolution lies at the heart of not only computer science, but also a wide range of other disciplines, including the arts. To teach kids interested in the performing arts, the mini-theatre initiative uses computer technology and computational thinking. It aims to engage people who aren't interested in coding or robotics by focusing on their artistic interests and incorporating STEAM (Science, Technology, Engineering, Arts, and Mathematics) into their curriculum.

With this in mind, the proposed system incorporates ideas and research from the interdisciplinary disciplines of performing arts and robotics, particularly research on collaborative action and aesthetic design. The design and development of the "Smart Mini Theatre," as well as its similarities and differences to related projects, will be described in the following sections. This includes the creation of intelligent puppets, stage design, precise lighting, and scene rotation.

1.2   Motivation

The goal of "Smart Mini Theatre" is to inspire kids who are interested in performing arts to think about engineering and computer science as career options. Students in grades K-12 participate in a variety of creative art genres, according to study. This encompasses music, dancing, photography, and theater [2], as demonstrated by a five-day Robotic Music Camp that uses inexpensive NXT robots to teach text-based languages, Java, and MIDI [3]. Some of these applications, such as the Arts & Bots toolkit, have matured into classroom aids that include hardware, software, and integrated components at levels that even AP Computer Science students in high schools utilize in the classroom [4]. Others have taken place in rural classrooms, with day-long classes teaching elementary pupils about acting, dancing, sound, and painting using programmable humanoid robots [5]. The Animatronics High School Workshop is an excellent workshop experience that reflects the Smart Theatre Project's goals.

This project at Trinity Valley High School mixes components of three separate fields into a single goal, allowing students with varied expertise to collaborate on that assignment while also learning about other fields. 14 high school students were given puppets, aluminum strips, servo motors, software tools, and some access to their own materials to put together an original animatronics show for an audience during this three-day workshop. It was overseen by an electrical and mechanical engineer from Disney, as well as English, theatre, and computer science faculty members.

This task, which was completed in a short amount of time, required students to adhere to a strict schedule each day, which included times for plot development, puppet mechanism development, set building, programming, and voice recording in order to expose all students to the requirements of these interdisciplinary skills. It included creative writing from English majors, robot design and construction from engineering majors, and sound and motion programming from both theatre and computer science majors [6].

The Robot Opera Program in elementary schools is the result of similar initiatives. The program teaches kids about acting, robot characteristics, and how to manipulate robotic motions and speech. The application uses little robots that are about a foot tall and includes dancing, sound, and sketching modules. The program attempts to achieve STEAM goals by giving kids access to pre-designed block coding for dance, sonification mapping for sound generation, and vehicle bots that allow students to sketch on a huge canvas using a customized GUI [7].

The Robot Opera Program in elementary schools is the result of similar initiatives. The program teaches kids about acting, robot characteristics, and how to manipulate robotic motions and speech. The application uses robots that are about a foot tall and includes dancing, sound, and sketching modules. The program attempts to achieve STEAM goals by giving kids access to pre-designed block coding for dance, sonification mapping for sound generation, and vehicle bots that allow students to sketch on a huge canvas using a customized GUI. It can be a medium for students to explore creative freedom while also having the opportunity to program and change their projects in the classroom.

2   State of the Art Theatre

Many robotics initiatives have the goal of educating people. Because advanced robotic projects are designed to wow audiences seeking advanced functionality, they divert attention away from affordability and accessibility.

For example, the Roboscopie project includes a single, big robotic performer as well as a stage. It exemplifies the concept of a robotic play in which a big audience is used to observe human interactions. Using the LAAS/CNRS PR2 robot, the project shifts the robotic theatre's attention to human interaction. The robot becomes highly aware of its surroundings and responds when a human actor interacts with it using cameras and specialized modeling tools [8]. Roboscopie represents a considerably larger size than the "Smart Mini Theatre". However, in addition to utilizing cutting-edge technology that is out of reach for most schools, these initiatives operate on a far wider scale that cannot be replicated in classrooms.

The software's simplicity is just as crucial as the hardware's cost efficiency. Webots, a software that processes C++, Java, MATLAB, Python, and other more advanced programming languages, is used to program the turtle robot built by Shenzhen Engineering Laboratory [9]. This project combines a complicated robotic structure with an equally complex programming language as an educational aid for advanced computer science and robotics students. It may, however, not be a useful pedagogical tool for first-year students with little expertise. Rather, to control stepper and servo motors, the "Smart Mini Theatre" uses a simple block coding interface.

Part of the goal for the "Smart Mini Theatre" is to design mechanics that are advanced enough to meet the demands of a great theatrical performance while still using cost-effective parts to enable for inexpensive and effective recreations. Other attempts to create robotic theaters, despite being more advanced and larger in size and purpose, have failed to achieve this. They either strive to be primarily entertaining or do not include certain elements that might pique the interest of targeted pupils in learning.

2.1   Human-Robot Interactions

The Multi Robot Theatre, another study focused on interaction, studies robots' natural, humanoid behavior as well as their emotional and dramatic responses to children. Their mental and physical reactions were documented, and t The form and hue of the robots' eyes were used to represent their emotions [10].

Multiple sophisticated, autonomous robotic actors were featured in the multi-robot theatre project. While the study's main focus is Human-Robot Interaction (HRI), it is largely a behavioral response experiment in youngsters. It is also limited to simulation rather than a physically performing theater because it lacks any stage or theatre-like qualities.

Nonetheless, there are a few key factors to the multi-robot theatre endeavor. The robots' designs vary in speed, direction, and traveling path to accommodate for the plot of a scene, a character's role, and the emotion that the character is portraying. The tortoise and hare plot for the "Smart Mini Theatre" project includes emotional and character role dynamics that necessitate minute motion distinctions.

Similarly, NAO robotic characters' robotic performance, "I Sing the Body Electric," depicts the interactions between two robots and their lifelike traits. For example, the robots featured distinct colored eyes, various voice shape, and different and recognizable gestures to differentiate between genders [11].

This performance highlights the robot's features, such as LEDs that flash specific lights to explain specific components of the performance. The lighting system for the "Smart Mini Theatre" alters the intensity of a light to represent the time of day. The smart puppets will also include LEDs that indicate simple gestures like eye movement.

2.2   Robot-Stage Interactions

One of the difficulties in designing the Smart Mini Theater project's stage is that mobile interaction with the stage must be anticipated, path planning procedures must account for obstacles, robot-robot interactions must be in sync, and slight inclines in the stage plane may cause motion planning and spotlight positioning issues later on. A report on autonomous robots as performers in robotics theatre, analyzing the special communication between the Pepper and NAO humanoid robots in theatre, was motivated by Karel Capek's play, "Rossum's Universal Robots" [12].

The IbnSina Center has been working on developing an Augmented Reality (AR) theatre that incorporates robotic and human presentations, similar to the project's pivot from a large-scale theatre. A holographic screen that can display static and moving images, sensors that identify objects that occupy areas on stage, and a seating area for the audience are all included in the 10 meter stage. With these components in place, a wide range of performances and presentations including human-robot interaction can be created [13].

Human interaction with the robot and stage is the focus of the IbnSina Center theatre. The theatre's screen is extremely advanced, capable of hosting programs and virtual worlds. This is similar to the project's background function, which revolves around static graphics. Although the backdrop images do not move, they can be replaced independently because of the rotation of stepper motors.

Navigation system, obstacle avoidance, robot detection and interaction, and robot communication with other units are among the controls for robots onstage. The "Smart Mini theatre" takes into account several of these elements. The autonomous robots interact with one another, use light sensors to follow lines on the stage, and communicate with other mobile robotic devices on stage, such as obstacles or other characters. Their ability to fully mimic the complexities of human behavior, emotion, and response, on the other hand, can be questioned.

A HRI theatre study delves deeper into robots' ability to mimic the emotions of actual actors. Motion tracking with cameras is utilized to transmit data to the robot that allows it to duplicate certain behaviors in order to pinpoint the responses to those behaviors [14]. Similarly, in the smart theatre, a camera drives the lighting system to follow the robots' various moves. Some movements will be swift to convey energy and force, while others will be sluggish to convey a solemn and tense tone. Specific path planning techniques for more dynamic situations will be built into the smart puppet modules for continued advancement in the project, as well as for performing arts students to create higher level performances.

The autonomous robots' primary strength is creating interest in robotics research and, in the future, applying it to robotic theatre, which is comparable to the project's goal of raising interest in robotic areas. Although the Pepper and NAO robots are significantly larger in scale, the vocal exchanges and communications between the robots, stage, and props are equally important. The most effective and sociably appealing robots, as the development of The Public Anemone Robot has focused on, must maintain fast physical interactions with their environment as well as with other robots. The project places a strong emphasis on expression rather than robot quality.

The produced robotic figure is a snake-like construction with tentacles projecting from one end of the robot. It has a lifelike quality due to the serpentine quality, and the movement of the tentacles demonstrates expression. It has numerous servo motors and highly articulated movement, allowing it to move in a wide range of directions [15]. Regardless of their simplicity, the robotic characters utilized should have a communication and mobility acuity that is similar to that of living performers.

3   System Overview

In this work, a small scale robotic theatre with programmable micro stage components, a re-configurable stage, a scene play control system, rotating curtains, moving backgrounds, and an AI based spotlighting system is further developed to bridge the gap between STEM and STEAM.

The smart puppet theatre contains a light system that uses pan and tilt motions with servos, an audio system functioning through an external source, stage backgrounds and curtains, props, joysticks, an OLED display, webcams,

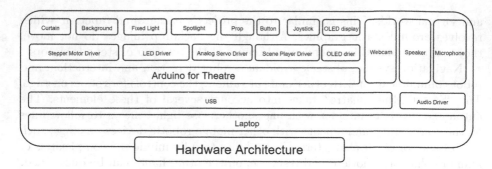

Fig. 1. Hardware architecture of theatre

speakers, and microphones, shown in Fig. 1. These parts are connected to an Arduino, which is immediately connected to a laptop through USB. The smart puppet will be a robotic module that can be programmed and interacted with. A wireless connection module, wheels, visual (line) sensors, a puppet, LEDs, and a servo will all be included in each smart puppet.

While the first three pieces have a role in the robots' mobility, the last three, such as eyes, rotation, and shape, are decorative and theatrical embellishments. Stepper motors control the curtains and the backdrop scenery. The lighting system is divided into discrete fixtures that fit into the frame. Servo motors move these fixtures, which rotate in vertical and horizontal panning motions. The light system's objective is to draw attention to the robots as they move around the stage, as well as to illuminate portions of the stage for dramatic effect. For proper illumination, webcams are employed to establish the positions of the robots.

The smart theatre's hardware components are controlled by visual block coding, which communicates with the software components and drivers, and in turn controls the hardware. Visual coding is done with mBlock.

Modules for various sections of the smart theatre are included in the software component. It includes modules that control the lighting, curtains, and backdrop systems, for example. The spotlight event handler receives the positions of the robots and directs the spotlights to them. The curtain event handler is used to handle events that require the stage curtain to be controlled. The background event handler is responsible for occurrences that require the stage background to be changed. Other communication modules are included in the software architecture, which specify the communication protocol and perform message passing and coordination between different software modules.

3.1 Light, Sound, and Scenes

While the spotlight's capacity to illuminate the stage is aesthetic, its purpose is to call attention to the finer aspects of a performance. In the "Smart Mini Theatre," the spotlight works in tandem with the smart robots, following their movements. To do this, the prototype includes a coordinating system for the

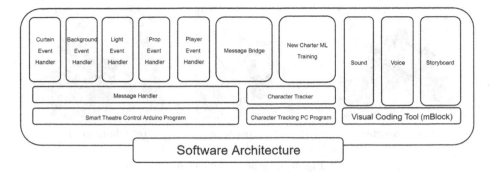

Fig. 2. Software architecture of theatre

smart puppets to maneuver on the stage. Two DXW90 Servo Motors connect together in a pan and tilt fixture to make up the light system.

The positions on the coordinate system can be used to compute the minor changes that the servo motors need to make. Two angles are required in this three-dimensional stage: the vertical tilting angle and the horizontal panning angle. Trigonometric functions and distance measurements can be used to calculate these figures.

A grid on the stage ground allows the lights to be positioned accurately. As a result, the required angles from the servo motors are moved straight to the grid points. A camera near the light fixture will be connected to a computer in a prototype for the light system. This camera will record movement and gather information on where the spotlights should be directed.

3.2   Localization for Spotlighting Targets

The theater employs a tracking device that can monitor the characters in order to highlight the objective. This system consists of a webcam that is directly connected to a PC and a YoloV3-based machine learning module. To detect an item, that module employs a deep Convolutional Neural Network (CNN).

A data set of roughly 500 photos was obtained for this study in order for the YoloV3 network to recognize the characters illustrated in Fig. 3. Google Colab, a Machine Learning/Artificial Intelligence research tool designed to provide researchers with an infrastructure as a service (IAAS) platform to train their network models on, and various other data science services the platform offers that are not relevant to the current project, were used to assist with data set training. After the model has been trained, it will be able to detect specific characters and their location on the floor plane in a 2D environment in real-time. The spotlight can then be focused on that exact position when the position and character have been identified and calculated.

(a) Character1   (b) Character2   (c) Character3

Fig. 3. Character detection

3.3   Motion Planing and Control of Spotlights

The incorporation of a spotlight system has been a key priority in the project's completion. In the "Smart Mini theatre," the spotlight works in unison with the smart robots. To do this, the prototype includes a coordinating system for the smart puppets to maneuver on the stage.

The positions on the coordinate system can be used to determine the minor modifications performed by the servo motors. Two angles are required in this three-dimensional stage: the vertical tilting angle and the horizontal panning angle. Trigonometric functions and distance measurements can be used to calculate these figures. A grid is placed on the stage ground to ensure that the lights are aimed appropriately and accurately. The angles required from the servo motors can now be moved straight to the grid points as shown in Fig. 4.

In the first model, although "z" represents the height, the puppets stay on the ground, so "z" is zero for all the coordinates that matter. In the second model, at a certain point (6, 0), the panning angle can be found by taking the inverse tangent of (b/a), with "b" being the vertical coordinate and "a" being the horizontal coordinate. In the last model, at a point (6, 6), the tilting angle can be found by taking the inverse tangent of (f/g), with "f" being the horizontal coordinate on the grid, and "g" being the vertical distance between the grid and the light fixture.

A camera near the light fixture that is connected to a computer will be used for motion planning. This camera can track movement and collect information about the robot's location on the grid.

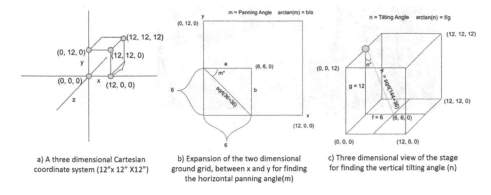

a) A three dimensional Cartesian coordinate system (12"x 12" X12")

b) Expansion of the two dimensional ground grid, between x and y for finding the horizontal panning angle(m)

c) Three dimensional view of the stage for finding the vertical tilting angle (n)

Fig. 4. Spotlighting system calculation

3.4   Scene Play Control System

Students will be able to design their own shows using a prototype of the scene control system that is currently being developed. Users will be able to control different portions of the theatre via a GUI using this scene play control system. For each of the smart mini theatre's components, the GUI has a timeline function. The learner will be able to instruct the various components of the theatre at a specific point in the show by using the timeline tool. It now allows users to add components to the smart theatre, and after doing so, the user will be presented the component's timeline, where they

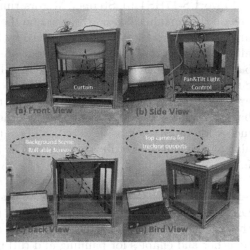

Fig. 5. Smart puppet theatre prototype

can add commands/events. The PyQt5 framework was used to create this user-friendly prototype GUI, as illustrated in Fig. 6.

4   Implementation of Smart Theatre

As shown in Fig. 5, the "Smart Mini Theatre" prototype comprises of numerous components that work together to generate a functional performance. The frame is made out of aluminum bars with slots that allow things to be moved along the bars. The actual stage takes up 17.5 in. of the cube's length, with 2.5 in. of space beneath it for electrical components. The prototype's walls are made of 16 in.^{2} cardboard that has been sliced to accommodate different components that intersect.

Fig. 6. Scene play control system

Two US-17HS4401 Stepper Motors run down the bottom of the right wall, one on the curtain side and the other on the backdrop side. These stepper motors are 1.5-in. cubes that are kept in place by 3D printed fittings that fit along the aluminum frame. The Stepper motors are connected to the rods by 14 in. × 5 mm rods with bearings on both ends. These rods can be seen on both the curtain and backdrop sides. There are also rods at the top of the theatre that are the same length as the lower rods and run parallel to them. These rods also have their own bearings, connected to the lower rod bearings with a quarter inch-wide timing belt as depicted at Fig. 5 (c). The stage of the Smart theatre is also a 16 in. length cardboard square. The stage has a 12 in. × 12 in. grid, with increments every inch.

The lighting system is installed on the right and left sides of the theatre's roof. Each side has a pair of DXW90 servo motors that sit just below the top of the frame. A 3D printed attachment holds each pair together and enables for panning and tilting actions (see Fig. 7). The curtain at the front of the theatre is a fabric that runs up and along the top of the smart tiny theatre and is attached to the front timing belt. The stage is revealed or hidden by moving the curtain vertically. Similarly, the background rotation system has a plastic sheet that adheres to the multiple-sectioned time. Magnets can be placed around the plastic's edges to attach papers that can be rotated onto the stage's background.

Fig. 7. Theater light pan & tilt fixture

5   Evaluation

The smart tiny theatre's components have been put through preliminary functional testing, which has revealed their capabilities and areas for improvement.

The curtain, backdrop system, and light system are among the various functions that testing is concerned with.

Both the curtain and background systems use US-17HS4401 Stepper motors with several thin timing belts and two rods to move them. The belts' motion and the stepper motor's speed can only be sustained if a specific amount of weight is carried. At the moment, the prototype has a 327-g curtain that moves at 3200 steps /s. A single motor can move a maximum of 535 g at this speed to sustain it.

Apart from the narrowing component that concentrates the beam on specified locations, the light system is almost weightless. The panning and tilting motions are controlled by DXW90 servo motors, which can operate at different rates depending on how they are programmed. Each servo has a range of motion of just over 180 °. The spotlight moves in roughly 0.1 s from the top right corner, (12, 12), to the bottom left corner, (0, 0), within the set coordinate grid. To follow the puppets, this movement can be slowed down.

6 Discussion and Future Developments

The design and robotic execution are to be improved with a greater understanding of projects running concurrently with the "Smart Mini Theatre." The cardboard walls might be replaced with a firmer and more appealing material for a more mood-setting theatre. The smart robotic puppets are still being developed at this time. HRI and puppet design studies show that a smaller, more realistic robotic puppet is more effective. This design may contain a three-dimensional shape that corresponds to the puppet's theme and a modulating pace to emulate the theme's suitable movements.

For performances, the stage will include an integrated speaker. The lighting system will include a camera and sensor system that will allow the fixture to move along with the robot as it detects it on the grid. This camera will enable direct targeting as well as lighting that can be regulated more precisely (e.g., smooth panning, narrow lighting).

A module will be designed to allow the smart theatre to interface with the mBlock IDE. This will also allow users to operate the smart theatre in real time via a web browser. The smart theater will be more user-friendly thanks to visual coding.

7 Conclusion

The purpose of this project is to encourage students interested in or presently enrolled in performing arts programs to use computational thinking, making, and acting. It is intended to demonstrate how to decompose a problem, identify the variables involved using data representation, and write and compute algorithms by dissecting a problem. Its purpose is to introduce the implementation of a CT-derived solution. It can also be utilized to implement computational making solutions in order to generate secondary creative solutions. For teens, high school students, and performing arts students, the "Smart Mini Theatre" initiative serves as an interdisciplinary representation of STEAM. Students can use block coding to explore their own theatrical imagination with this project, which mixes robotic stage components and smart puppets.

References

1. Schwab, K., Samans, R.: Chapter 1: the future of jobs and skills, January 2016. https://reports.weforum.org/future-of-jobs-2016/chapter-1-the-future-of-jobs-and-skills/
2. Kuhn, M., Greenhalgh, S.D., McDermott, M.A.: Using creativity from art and engineering to engage students in science (2016)
3. Chung, C.J.C.J., Cartwright, C., Chung, C.: Robot music camp 2013: an experiment to promote stem and computer science. In: 2014 IEEE Integrated STEM Education Conference, pp. 1–7 (2014). https://doi.org/10.1109/ISECon.2014.6891012
4. Hamner, E., Cross, J.: Arts & Bots: techniques for distributing a steam robotics program through K-12 classrooms. In: 2013 IEEE Integrated STEM Education Conference (ISEC), pp. 1–5 (2013). https://doi.org/10.1109/ISECon.2013.6525207
5. Barnes, J., FakhrHosseini, S.M., Vasey, E., Park, C.H., Jeon, M.: Child-robot theater: engaging elementary students in informal steam education using robots. IEEE Pervasive Comput. **19**(1), 22–31 (2020)
6. Alford, J.G., Jacob, L., Dietz, P.: Animatronics workshop: A theater + engineering collaboration at a high school. IEEE Comput. Graphics Appl. **33**(6), 9–13 (2013). https://doi.org/10.1109/MCG.2013.86
7. Jeon, M., Barnes, J., FakhrHosseini, M., Vasey, E., Duford, Z., Zheng, Z., Dare, E.: Robot Opera: a modularized afterschool program for steam education at local elementary school. In: 2017 14th International Conference on Ubiquitous Robots and Ambient Intelligence (URAI), pp. 935–936 (2017)
8. Lemaignan, S., Gharbi, M., Mainprice, J., Herrb, M., Alami, R.: Roboscopie: a theatre performance for a human and a robot [video abstract]. In: 2012 7th ACM/IEEE International Conference on Human-Robot Interaction (HRI), pp. 427–427 (2012). https://doi.org/10.1145/2157689.2157831
9. Wenfu, X., Yanning, Z., Erzhen, P.: Design and simulation of a turtle performing robot for robotic theater. In: 2015 34th Chinese Control Conference (CCC), pp. 6049–6054 (2015). https://doi.org/10.1109/ChiCC.2015.7260586
10. Peng, Y., Feng, Y.L., Wang, N., Mi, H.: How children interpret robots' contextual behaviors in live theatre: gaining insights for multi-robot theatre design. In: 2020 29th IEEE International Conference on Robot and Human Interactive Communication (RO-MAN), pp. 327–334 (2020). https://doi.org/10.1109/RO-MAN47096.2020.9223560
11. Zlotowski, J., Bleeker, T., Bartneck, C., Reynolds, R.: I sing the body electric an experimental theatre play with robots [video abstract]. In: 2013 8th ACM/IEEE International Conference on Human-Robot Interaction (HRI), pp. 427–427 (2013)
12. Petrović, D., Kićinbaći, L., Petric, F., Kovačić, Z.: Autonomous robots as actors in robotics theatre - tribute to the centenary of ruR. In: 2019 European Conference on Mobile Robots (ECMR), pp. 1–7 (2019). https://doi.org/10.1109/ECMR.2019.8870908
13. Mavridis, N., Hanson, D.: The IbnSina center: An augmented reality theater with intelligent robotic and virtual characters. In: RO-MAN 2009 - The 18th IEEE International Symposium on Robot and Human Interactive Communication (2009)
14. Lu, D.V., Smart, W.D.: Human-robot interactions as theatre. In: 2011 RO-MAN, pp. 473–478 (2011). https://doi.org/10.1109/ROMAN.2011.6005241
15. Breazeal, C., et al.: Interactive robot theatre. Commun. ACM **46**, 76–85 (2003)

Smart Trashcan Brothers: Early Childhood Environmental Education Through Green Robotics

Marcus Arnett, Saifuddin Mahmud, Redwanul Haque Sourave,
and Jong-Hoon Kim[✉]

Advanced Telerobotics Research Lab, Computer Science, Kent State University,
Kent, OH, USA
jkim72@kent.edu

Abstract. One of the main concerns of modern life would be the potential risk of irreversible ecological damage. However, due to the lack of focus on the subject within education, this type of risk will only get worse when being left unattended. This is where the robotics system, known as the "Smart Trashcan Brothers", can provide better environmental consciousness with the current, younger generation attending primary school. This paper goes over the concepts that make up the Smart Trashcan Brothers system, as well with a functional evaluation to verify that the described parts of the robotics system function as intended. From there, a discussion of future works will be brought up with regards to further Child Human Interaction works.

Keywords: Recycling robot · Smart trash can · Trash can robot · Human-robot interaction · Machine learning · Image processing

1 Introduction

Within the last couple centuries, pollution has risen to the status of a major issue that has harmed the environment. Waste production has risen rapidly in tandem with the global population growth. The growing number of people, all over the world, puts a strain on Waste Management efforts; and that humanity, wildlife, and the environment have all suffered as a result. Trash is either the product of human activity, or the outcome of natural ecological processes. As many individuals neglect the garbage management issue, it results in horrible waste conditions and environmental calamities including: floods, pollution, rising global temperatures, increase in other natural disasters, and a host of illnesses.

Trash is divided into various categories, of which are recyclable, non-recyclable, and hazardous garbage. The term "recyclable waste" refers to waste that may be treated for repurposing. Certain plastics, bottles, glass, iron, and a variety of other materials are among the numerous types of trash generated, are examples of recyclable trash. Non-recyclable trash, on the other hand, can

J.-H. Kim et al. (Eds.): IHCI 2021, LNCS 13184, pp. 313–324, 2022.
https://doi.org/10.1007/978-3-030-98404-5_30

almost never be recycled again. Items that can't be recycled are things like leaves, fruits, animal corpses, and even pet waste. As well, there is a third category known as the hazardous materials, which makes up items such as batteries, chemical bottles, used menstrual products, and radioactive waste.

In order to maintain a green environment that is sustainable, we must manage trash and distinguish between them. It can be made much easier by utilizing cutting-edge technology, such as with using robotic systems; or robots for short. These robots can be used to further engagement between the human user and itself using artificial intelligence (AI). And, in the current generation, these robots play a main, head role with various occupation sectors; which includes the environmental sector, especially for trash collection. So to meet these demands, the robotics industry is in desperate need of experts and other skilled professionals.

As of late too, due to the advancement of technologies and research, Child-Robot Interaction (CRI) has risen to the top of the evolution of Human-Robot Interaction (HRI). However, more work must be done to make use of CHI to help young people learn about environmental literacy. In addition, social and economical development has put forth urgent requirements for robotics education. We need to provide education on robotics to our children to fulfill the future social and economic need to make the environment sustainable.

In order to educate children about robotics, the robot must be visually appealing and be able to interact with people. In addition, actual application is the most effective way to meet the requirements of young students. There are several uses for a garbage can robot in this aspect, including being very productive. This is where a robotic trashcan can be used to further interest young individuals into learning more about being environmentally conscious.

"The Smart Trashcan", the series of devices used for teaching environmental consciousness, will feature programming components that will let students take control on how it will behave. And with that factor, it will need to live up to the creative criteria set out in the aforementioned study; in which it drew various young students in, and increased their learning capabilities when it came to environmental consciousness. Accordingly, the Smart Trashcan's major goal is to teach recycling values to children in an engaging and memorable way.

In this paper, a group of inexpensive and interactive mobile robot, the "Smart Trashcan Brothers", are designed to teach the ideals of recycling to young school children. Open-source hardware was used to build the robot, which was relatively low-cost, but yet functional. The Smart Trashcan's motions and gestures can also be controlled via a visual programming interface. While engaging with the Smart Trashcan, students and teachers can use the Visual Programming interface to try out different methods to programming.

The Smart Trashcan's software and hardware are also reasonably priced, making it a financially feasible teaching tool for schools. The Smart Trashcan aims to educate kids and educators about STEM and Computer Science while also creating a more environmentally conscious future generation. Educating young children about recycling can help establish these values in them from an early age.

This paper will be discussing the related works used in reference for our current implementation in Sect. 2, then details of the Smart Trashcan Brothers system will be described in detail in Sect. 3; next, the discussion of the stakeholder evaluation and functional evaluations will be on Sect. 4, finally ending with conclusions and future work for this project.

2 Related Work

The overall research done using networked robotic systems or HRI mental models is fairly well documented, as the core concepts of mental models are intertwined with HRI research. Mainly this research is dedicated to the discussion of, and study of, the three state agent model; which comprises of the robot, human, and environment agents. There are several papers support this theoretical model, including one published by Talamadupula et al. [11]. There, they test and study this three agent model in an automated planning system with real robot agents. Their conclusion for the paper was that having and implementing the model system proposed shown improvements in the studies they had conducted.

Another paper published in 2019 by Ferranti et al. [3] goes more in depth with an infrastructure-less architecture for their proposed robotic network, HIRONET. The paper brings up that, thanks to the emerging mobile phone technology of the past decade, robotics can now become a much more low powered, efficient, and infrastructure-less system; and with such a system they propose that using it in the case of disaster-relief is one of the more probable, and best, purposes for such a network. Their conclusion came down to the various studies and simulations performed with such a system, which showed potential improvements with response times; and had gone further to propose future works using HIRONET.

Getting deeper with general education robotics, a paper published in 2010 by Machorro-Fernandez et al. [6] describes a robot system that is able to train human subjects to do certain tasks that require empirical knowledge. The paper goes in depth with how the robot itself can start to monitor users that are considered "students"; where the role is determined by how good the performance was. The results of their research shown some promise when a human trainee gets feedback from this robotic system. This paper shows that a robotic system developed for training motor skills for humans is fairly non-complex to develop.

Further readings with the paper written by Hwang et al. in 2005 [4] explains the three model system, as well with the discussion of, and experimenting of, mental models within such a system. They have a discussion in regards to how mental models function within an HRI study, being that they can affect the overall outcome of such an interaction; along with that, they also propose a very similar three model system as also proposed by Talamadupula et al. [11]. However, one thing that separated their model from the previously mentioned model is the use of symbols and "shared ground", as described in the paper; as visual images for the human subject would reduce the barrier of translation between them and the robot subject. Finally, their paper ends with a pilot experiment in which subjects were to describe the functionality of a robot before and after they used it; and the results of that experiment shown that their model did help in broadening the subjects' view of the abilities of the robot.

Lastly a paper from Hyun et al. from 2010 [5] goes on to summarize their research towards educational HRI devices with children who attend early education facilities. Their results shown that vocal feedback is the best with communicating ideas. Thus, it would be one of the mandatory factors to discuss and develop a synthesized vocal feedback system for the proposed robotics system. One other paper from Nasi et al. [7] proposes a robotic solution for education; specifically for algorithmic and social skills. Lastly to mention a paper from Barnes et al. [2] brings up using robotic systems for the purposes of musical theatre education.

The collective reading of the papers discussed above proved to further push the concept of using a three model system to both improve the design and functionality of the Smart Trashcan Brothers; along with having a more grounded perspective on how to conduct further studies if need be.

3   The Smart Trashcan Brothers

This robotic system was based on the previous paper from Arnett et al. [1], in that these robots incorporate a more feature-rich system. Each of the individual trash cans, or brothers for the naming standard, in the network have a singular servo motor attached to their corresponding Arduino Micro 33 IoT board; as well with having a crank system to lift the lid open. All three of the trash cans are connected to a singular Raspberry Pi 4 board, and in turn also having an Intel RealSense D435 Camera wired up for use with the machine learning model to detect if items are recyclable, non-recyclable, or hazardous. The overall connection between each of the trash cans are centralized to the singular Raspberry Pi 4 board via Wi-Fi, and use a star mesh architecture to prevent any single point of failure issues.

Lastly, each of the three trash cans will also be equipped with an ultrasonic sensor, for detecting the user's hand presence, and an OLED screen, to indicate if the user is at the correct or incorrect trash can. These both are used for the purposes of building the fundamental robotic system for the Smart Trashcan Brothers, along with visualizing the resulting output from the user's input.

The next following sections will talk about the state case system for the Smart Trashcan Brothers, along with the physical design, trash classification model, motion and gesture planning, communication protocol, voice feedback system, and the visual programming interface.

3.1   State Cases

The 3-fold system would be the median response model for this network. The user would be the initiator of the system, starting by bringing the item up close to the camera's view to determine the object's state. The second interaction would be the corresponding trash can opening, coming in as a command wirelessly via the Raspberry Pi 4. The whole sequence fits into the trash type detection case.

The user's next interaction would be to drop their item into the corresponding trash can that opened; with the resulting mental model fitting into object recognition, with the item in question matched to its recyclable state; in which this would be audibly and visually supported towards the user by directing them towards that associated trash can. Finally the fourth state would be the trash can closing after the user moves their hand away from the trash can. This is the sequence for the correct trash case.

However, if the user picks the wrong trash can, provided that they're within the mental model to do such; then an incorrect soundbite, along with a visual indication on the OLED screen, will show the user they're incorrect to choose that trash can. They will be then mentally drawn to the correct trash can to put the associated trash object into. This sequence is the incorrect trash case.

The sequence above is shown within the diagram in Fig. 1.

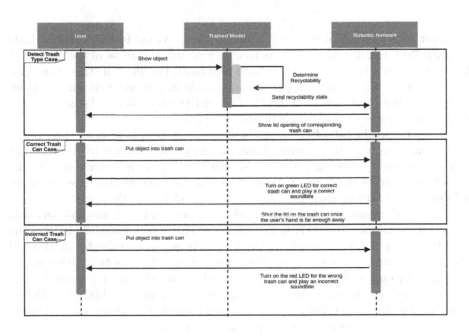

Fig. 1. Sequence diagram for the smart trashcan brothers

3.2   Physical Design

The trashcans themselves take on a more alien and robotic theme for their appearance, being that the trashcans themselves are alive and aware to the user who uses them; supporting this with the other visual and audio stimulus to

Fig. 2. Proof of concept of the smart trashcan brothers system

help out with the appearance (e.g., voice feedback, visual feedback from OLED screen). With the ultrasonic sensors too, they're designed to be in the place that the trash can has the user put their hand near most, the lid of the trash can. This is done for having an optimal performance while in use; as same reasoning can be said for the Intel RealSense D435. The OLED screen is also facing upwards to the user for the optimal angle of visual feedback.

There is also the Intel RealSense D435 Camera put in front of all three of the trash cans, signifying to the user to put the object near it for it to classify what object it is; and to determine what trash can lid to open, in accordance with the recyclability factor the object persists with. For the voice feedback, we are using a basic PC speaker system that meets the needs of the synthesized vocals.

As well, there are three of them lined up, as seen in Fig. 2; and this serves as the main mechanism for teaching the concepts. This sets the mental model of the user to figure out what type of recyclability their object pertains to. However, if the main instructor is wanting to, they can separate the robots at other points within the room to have a form of gamification for the main interactee. The trashcans are also decorated to be more appealing to a general children audience, however the trash can robots can be designed however the owner wants them to look; or to fit the appeal of a certain holiday or event.

3.3 Trash Classification

The trash classification module consists of Raspberry Pi 4, a Intel RealSense camera, and an OLED screen for additional user feedback. The trash classification module begins blinking when the RealSense camera in front of the trash can brothers detect the presence of a human being in the vicinity. The Google Voice Assistant also starts to engage with individuals and asks them to hold the trash in front of the camera near the camera. Once it identifies the waste, the waste classification procedure commences. The waste classification module divides the waste into one of three categories: recyclable, non-recyclable and hazardous. Based on the waste category, one of the trash can among the Trash Can Brothers start conversing by producing various sorts of movements, gestures and voices. We utilized YoloV3 [10], a Convolutional Neural Network (CNN), for garbage identification and categorization.

We have trained YoloV3 using our own dataset. To prepare the dataset for the trash we have collected 1500 images of each category, recyclable, non-recyclable and hazardous materials. In this dataset there are 30 different types of objects, 10 in each category. For training the YoloV3 network, we have used Google Colab, a machine learning research tool, which is a free cloud service and supports GPU processing for free. After the training process is done, we have deployed it to the trash can robot to make it smart. During operation the robot detects the objects, classifies them in real-time and shows the accuracy of the classification which will be tested later with the functional evaluation.

3.4   Motion and Gesture Planning

A lot of the motion and gesture planning will come from what the user decides to do once the item is scanned in and recognized. The camera module attached will be sending a live video feed to the Raspberry Pi 4, with the corresponding recorded input being processed into the trained model to classify the object's recyclability, as described before.

Another gesture planning event, that happens asynchronously with the event described beforehand, is with playing vocal feedback lines to the user using a voice synthesizer; which the output from the synthesizer depends on the user's input (e.g., what type of trash they have).

Then, once the recyclability is determined, the resulting output will be sent to the Arduino Micro 33 IoT modules that each of the trashcan robots have; with the output for the user being vocal feedback of what recyclability state the item is in, visually showing them where to throw the object into. From there, the user's input (e.g., selecting the correct or incorrect trashcan) will determine what type of case will be triggered for the according trashcans.

3.5   Robot to Robot Communication

The communication protocol each of the robots use within the system is the Bluetooth 4.2, since the network will be using a centralized star mesh topology. Our purpose for using this topography comes from a study conducted with Poncharernpong et al. [9]. The central point for the system will be the Raspberry Pi 4, and will serve the role of getting input from the camera module, processing the input through the trained model, and outputting the results wirelessly to the trashcan robots.

3.6   Voice Feedback

After trash detection and classification, the trashcan will generate a voice feedback. Depending on the trash, the robot will say, "Recyclable trash detected", "Non-recyclable trash detected" or "Hazardous trash detected". After that the appropriate trashcan will give the voice feedback "Please use me for this trash". When the trash has been put in correct bin, the robot will give a positive voice feedback like "Good job", "Great job", and "You have helped to keep the environment safe". It will select a positive feedback randomly among a set of positive feedback.

For voice feedback generation, we use the Text to Speech API for Google Cloud. There are more than 220 voices in 40+ languages. It employs "WaveNet voices" [8] that produce more lifelike sounding talks. It sounds more natural and humane than synthetic speech.

3.7   Visual Programming Interface

A major motivation of our work is to make our robot programming easy. Our trash can robot provides a mechanism to be connected to the Block-Based Programming Interface. Here we have used Makeblock (mBlock) programming interface so that students or teachers can watch and interact with the robot when used to promote engagement with programming. This programming interface contains blocks that can perform certain actions on the robot. Block instructions may be put directly into the Arduino boards placed on the robots from the local PC. With the visual programming interface based on blocks, the programming of individuals with little or nothing programming expertise seems less scary. The visual interface allows educators and elderly pupils to drag blocks and construct commands that the Smart Trashcan performs with the visual programming interface.

Examples of commands include "moveArm", "openHead" and "rotateWheel" among many other current and future commands. In addition, a API has been developed so that student can easily integrate machine learning based complex trash classification using block programming. Not only will the Smart Trashcan function as an environmental education tool, but it will also function as a tool that will teach students and educators the basics of programming in an appealing and interactive manner.

4   Stakeholder Evaluation

The Smart Trashcan Brothers is targeting the demographic of primary school students who would be needing this type of environmental consciousness education. The schools would benefit from having a more open sourced device for the students to learn STEM concepts from, along with any researchers who are interested in deploying pilot studies using this system. And while this type of robotic system is aimed at a younger demographic, the aesthetic changes that the robot can inherit can become a tool for anyone to learn environmental consciousness from.

4.1   Functional Evaluation

The main functional evaluation to be performed is to determine that:

1. If the mechanisms per each robot (e.g., ultrasonic sensor, OLED screen, motor) work synchronously,
2. if the three robots making up this robotic system are able to pass information between each other, and
3. if the machine learning model detects the correct type of trash within a tolerable error range.

After evaluating both of these cases several times, it can be confirmed that the first two items are true for the robots in the system. As for the third item, we have used various items for the test shown in figure set 3. The trial run results are shown in Table 1; and from the results, it can also be concluded that the third item is met and satisfied for the evaluation.

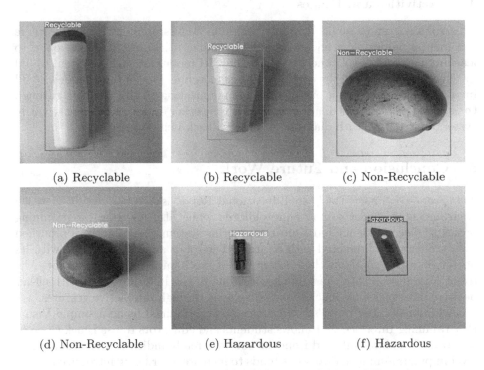

(a) Recyclable   (b) Recyclable   (c) Non-Recyclable

(d) Non-Recyclable   (e) Hazardous   (f) Hazardous

Fig. 3. Trash classification: recyclable, non-recyclable and Hazardous

Table 1. Overall performance of the proposed system

Target object	No. of trials	Reference object	Success rate of target object detection	Success rate of reference object detection	Reference object	Success rate of target object detection	Success rate of reference object detection	Average accuracy (%) for relative location information extraction
Sunglasses	20	Bedside table	19	18	Sofa	20	19	90
Water bottle	20	Chair	20	19	Chair	20	19	95
Mask	20	Bedside table	19	18	Sofa	20	19	90
Phone	20	Chair	19	19	Chair	20	19	95
Key ring	20	None	19	N/A	None	20	N/A	95

4.2   Activities and Usages

This robotic system would be easily usable in a classroom environment, where the mental models of students would be similar in regards to being open to learning new and novel concepts; thus, the CRI model for such a system would be effective for teaching the core concepts of recycling. One of these models could involve the teacher being out of sight communicating to the students through the synthesized voice feedback system; with the other option of having the entire system automated, with dialogue for the feedback being prescripted.

5   Conclusion and Future Work

The proposed Smart Trashcan Educational Robot is a robot meant to teach environmental education to young children while also teaching programming basics to older students and educators. In this system, the robot is approached by a student and presented with an item. The robot analyzes the item with its object detection methods then determines if the item is recyclable or not. The robot then responds to the student according to the item presented with either positive or negative feedback that is displayed through interactive gestures.

Additionally, the robot's actions can be programmed using a simple Visual Programming Interface that allows students and educators to use Block Code to program. The data collected from the survey already indicates that the interest level in programming and robotics tends to increase after being introduced to the idea of the Smart Trashcan Educational Robot. The proposed system is intended to be used as a teaching tool in educational institutes for both environmental and computer science education. Not to mention, the Smart Trashcan is made of inexpensive components which makes it more appealing as a learning tool for schools.

The Smart Trashcan Educational Robot's current prototype has the basic mechanical features implemented, a visually appealing dinosaur design, a block based visual programming interface used to control it, and object detection methods to determine the difference between recyclables and non-recyclables. Additionally, there are still future implementations to be made as well especially in the areas of gestures and in refining the visual programming interface. Google voice assistant will be integrated to make the robot more interactive. In conclusion, there is much potential to be had for the Smart Trashcan Educational Robot in the areas of environmental and STEM education.

This robotic system would make for an excellent solution towards benefiting both the daily curricular activities within an elementary school, along with furthering CRI research through allocating less time towards finding the right technology and more time gathering, evaluating, and discussing the data gathered. The device can have a huge benefit for children by teaching them ecological and environmental literacy skills to further reduce pollution within our current world.

The future work for the Smart Trash research will be further integration with more automation technology, such as a manipulator for picking up trash; and as well with a possible mobile autonomy to allow the robots to move around their environment for further engagement. We will also further develop on using different computer vision and machine learning algorithms to increase performance and decrease recognition latency.

References

1. Arnett, M., Luo, Z., Paladugula, P.K., Cardenas, I.S., Kim, J.-H.: Robots teaching recycling: towards improving environmental literacy of children. In: Companion of the 2020 ACM/IEEE International Conference on Human-Robot Interaction, HRI 2020, pp. 615–616. Association for Computing Machinery, New York (2020)
2. Barnes, J., FakhrHosseini, S.M., Vasey, E., Ryan, J., Park, C.H., Jeon, M.: Promoting steam education with child-robot musical theater. In: 2019 14th ACM/IEEE International Conference on Human-Robot Interaction (HRI), pp. 366–366 (2019)
3. Ferranti, L., D'Oro, S., Bonati, L., Demirors, E., Cuomo, F., Melodia, T.: Hiro-net: self-organized robotic mesh networking for internet sharing in disaster scenarios. In: 2019 IEEE 20th International Symposium on "A World of Wireless, Mobile and Multimedia Networks" (WoWMoM), pp. 1–9 (2019)
4. Hwang, J.-H., Lee, K.W., Kwon, D.-S.: The role of mental model and shared grounds in human-robot interaction. In: ROMAN 2005. IEEE International Workshop on Robot and Human Interactive Communication, pp. 623–628 (2005)
5. Hyun, E., Yoon, H., Son, S.: Relationships between user experiences and children's perceptions of the education robot. In: 2010 5th ACM/IEEE International Conference on Human-Robot Interaction (HRI), pp. 199–200 (2010)
6. Machorro-Fernandez, F., Parra-Vega, V., Lopez-Juarez, I.: Human training using HRI approach based on fuzzy ARTMAP networks. In: 2010 5th ACM/IEEE International Conference on Human-Robot Interaction (HRI), pp. 113–114 (2010)
7. Nasi, L., Nasi, Y., Aydin, C., Taki, R., Byaraktar, B., Tabag, E., Yalcin, S.: Pomelo, a collaborative education technology interaction robot. In: 2019 14th ACM/IEEE International Conference on Human-Robot Interaction (HRI), pp. 757–758 (2019)
8. van den Oord, A., et al.: Wavenet: a generative model for raw audio (2016). arxiv:1609.03499

9. Poncharernpong, N., Charanyananda, S., Silakam, Y., Klomkarn, K., Sooraksa, P.: Communication network structure for robotic manipulators. In: TENCON 2014–2014 IEEE Region 10 Conference, pp. 1–4 (2014)
10. Redmon, J., Farhadi, A.: Yolov3: an incremental improvement (2018)
11. Talamadupula, K., Briggs, G., Chakraborti, T., Matthias, S., Kambhampati, S.: Coordination in human-robot teams using mental modeling and plan recognition. In: 2014 IEEE/RSJ International Conference on Intelligent Robots and Systems, pp. 2957–2962 (2014)

Effects of Computer-Based (Scratch) and Robotic (Cozmo) Coding Instruction on Seventh Grade Students' Computational Thinking, Competency Beliefs, and Engagement

Shannon Smith(✉) ⓘ, Elena Novak, Jason Schenker, and Chia-Ling Kuo

Kent State University, Kent, OH 44242, USA
ssmith18@kent.edu

Abstract. The purpose of this pre-/posttest quasi-experimental study was to examine the effects of coding activities supported by the emotional educational robot Cozmo on seventh grade students' computational thinking, competency beliefs, and engagement compared to the computer-based program of Scratch. Two versions of the coding curriculum were developed that shared the same content and instructional features but differed in the code blocks used in each program. Two intact classes at a public middle school in the Midwestern United States participated in the study during the regularly scheduled Technology course. One class received the Scratch coding curriculum ($n = 21$), and the other class received the robotics coding curriculum ($n = 22$).

Results revealed non-significant posttest differences in computational thinking and competency beliefs among the Scratch and Cozmo interventions. However, students found Cozmo to be significantly more engaging than Scratch. Both interventions significantly improved students' computational thinking and competency beliefs from pre- to posttest.

This study contributes to the emerging literature on coding education in a public school setting. The positive gains in the cognitive and affective domains of learning can serve as a point of reference for researchers, designers, and educators with the desire to introduce students to coding.

Keywords: Educational robotics · Scratch · Cozmo · Computational thinking · Competency beliefs · Engagement

1 Introduction

The U.S. Bureau of Labor Statistics (2020) projected a much faster than average increase for computer occupations (11%) than all others from 2019 to 2029. Yet it has been found that high school students have negative attitudes toward computer science [1] and middle school students perceive programming as less meaningful and themselves less competent than younger students [2]. Researchers suggest early STEM exposure to attract students to these fields later on [3]. This study developed and implemented a coding curriculum

© Springer Nature Switzerland AG 2022
J.-H. Kim et al. (Eds.): IHCI 2021, LNCS 13184, pp. 325–336, 2022.
https://doi.org/10.1007/978-3-030-98404-5_31

for seventh grade students to increase interest and participation in computer science. Specifically, we examined the educational benefits of two block-based coding activities using Cozmo, an emotional educational robot, and a more traditional approach of Scratch.

The visual programming language Scratch is a common approach to introduce younger students to coding [4] because Scratch blocks fit together only in syntactically correct ways, eliminating the need to learn complex syntax required by traditional programming languages. But, student interviews showed conceptual gaps, the inability to explain how code worked [5] and lack of computational concepts in projects [6]. Robots are also used to introduce coding to novices because they reify code rather than just using virtual characters like Scratch [7] and robots provide direct evidence of solution accuracy making it faster and easier to find and fix errors [8]. However, research on emotional educational robotics is relatively limited [9] and classroom implementation focuses mainly on robotics research goals rather than introducing the robot into regular teaching practice [10].

1.1 Theoretical Foundation

Constructionism paradigm of Papert has been adopted in numerous robotic curricula because it engages students in a process-oriented task and makes the process of thinking and learning visible [11]. Constructionism suggests that people learn by doing [12] and Papert proposed using new technologies (e.g., computers and robots) to change the nature of learning at school [13]. Technological advances in affective computing are demonstrating the potential of emotional (social) educational robots.

People typically have positive feelings and are willing to interact with social robots [14]; however, examination of teen-robot interaction has been limited compared to other age groups [15]. Many studies of social robots in education compare versions of the same robot with different behaviors rather than against an alternative (e.g., computer-based) [16]. The limited studies comparing robots found a positive contribution with a medium effect size for affective and cognitive outcomes largely because of the physical presence of the robot [16].

This study examined the effects of using the emotional educational robot Cozmo to teach coding skills to seventh grade students. Code Lab is part of the Cozmo app that can run on a smartphone or tablet. It uses Scratch Blocks, making it similar to coding in Scratch. Dragging and dropping colorful blocks allows the user to get Cozmo to do many custom behaviors (e.g., controlling body, navigation, speech, and accessing facial recognition and emotion engine that replicates personality traits and behaviors).

Cozmo is proving to be beneficial for a variety of applications [17–20]; however, none of these studies took place in public schools or with students who had not self-selected into special camps or programs. Researchers found a positive influence of using Cozmo to teach math to middle school students [21], but there were only eight students who self-rated their knowledge gains. Moreover, a review of social robots in classrooms revealed lack of an appropriate curriculum and methodology for involving robots in learning activities, and most research is still focused mainly on further developing robotic technology rather than implementing it for educational purposes [10].

1.2 Research Goals

This study examined the effect of coding activities supported by the emotional educational robot Cozmo on seventh grade students' computational thinking, competency beliefs, and engagement compared to the more traditional computer-based program of Scratch with the following three working hypotheses:

Hypothesis 1: Cozmo will produce greater gains in computational thinking than Scratch.
Computational thinking is operationally defined as "the ability to formulate and solve programs by relying on the fundamental concepts of computing, using logic-syntax of programming languages: basic sequences, loops, iteration, conditionals, functions and variables" [22]. Empirical findings show improved computational thinking using robots compared to virtual environments [23]. Direct comparison of user interface on computational thinking found that students in the robotics group performed better on every task and mastered sequencing and debugging significantly better than the ScratchJr group [24]. The current study parallels the situation of comparing Scratch to a robotics platform except both use Scratch blocks, thus it is reasoned that robotics activities will make coding results more concrete and improve computational thinking compared to computer-based simulations in Scratch.

Hypothesis 2: Both Cozmo and Scratch training groups will increase their competency beliefs. Competency beliefs were defined as "people's judgments of their capabilities to organize and execute courses of action required to attain designated types of performances" [25]. Empirical findings show that robotics and Scratch can increase student self-efficacy [26, 27]. In this study, it is expected that competency beliefs will increase similarly among Cozmo and Scratch learners because it is their first formal introduction to coding, and using visual programming blocks to introduce coding instead of more complex text-based programming languages can decrease cognitive load.

Hypothesis 3: Cozmo will produce greater student engagement than Scratch. Observations and reports of students and teachers participating in empirical studies show increased engagement using robotics [24, 28–30]. Teachers attributed increased learning gains after using a virtual robotics curriculum to the use of physical robots [29] compared to decreased interest using the same curriculum with simulated online robots [30]. Robot use improved student interest and enjoyment of programming [28], and robotics sessions were more popular than ScratchJr sessions [24]. Ozobots that make sounds meant to mimic human emotions elicited high student motivation [31]. Cozmo is highly interactive with more advanced features lending support to the hypothesis that it will be more engaging than working with two-dimensional Scratch characters on a computer screen.

2 Method

2.1 Participants

Two intact classes of seventh grade students enrolled in a course called "Technology" at a public middle school in the Midwestern United States participated in the study. The technology course is typically filled with students who did not select any electives or did not get their top choice(s), thus it reflects a group of students who are reluctant to be there. The technology classes that participated in the study were filled with a mix of student ability levels. The researcher did not have access to students' Individualized Education Plans (IEP) or English Language Proficiency Assessment data, so no accommodations were provided to individual students during the study. One class received a Scratch curriculum ($n = 21$), and another class received a Cozmo curriculum ($n = 22$). While all students in both classes received all of the training interventions, data are only reported for those students who returned signed Parent Consent and Student Assent forms. Table 1 presents demographic information for all study participants.

Table 1. Student demographics

Characteristic	Scratch ($n = 21$)		Cozmo ($n = 22$)	
Gender	Female = 17	Male = 4	Female = 14	Male = 8
Age	M = 12.62	SD = .109	M = 12.36	SD = .155
ELL	5		2	
Gifted	2		1	
Special Needs (IEP)	2		3	

Note. ELL = English Language Learner. IEP = Individualized Education Plan

2.2 Curriculum

The current study adapted a Creative Computing curriculum unit developed by the ScratchEd research team at the Harvard Graduate School of Education [32] to create two versions of the coding curriculum for seventh grade students. Both curricula included a series of eight lessons that used a scaffolded approach (from step-by-step tutorial to open-ended exploration) to help students become acquainted with the key computational concept of sequencing.

The Scratch group used the Creative Computing curriculum lessons without modification, and the materials for the Cozmo group were modified to fit the blocks available in the Code Lab app using the same or closest equivalent block when possible. The curriculum used a project-based learning approach and ended with an open-ended coding project. A planning sheet and rubric that outlined cohesiveness elements and types of blocks was implemented to ensure similarity between the two training conditions.

2.3 Instruments

All instruments were pilot tested before the study to ensure student understanding and attain a time estimate. Table 2 presents an overview of the study instruments.

Table 2. Study instruments

Dependent variable	Instrument	Total item number	Score range	Cronbach's alpha
Computational thinking	Computational Thinking Test (CTt) [22]	28	0–28	.78 (pre)
				.83 (post)
Competency beliefs	Technology Competency Beliefs Scale [33]*	12	12–48	.88 (pre)
				.91 (post)
Engagement	Engagement Scale [34]	8	8–32	.76 (pre)
				.89 (post)

*Some wording was changed to focus on technology and coding to fit the current study.

2.4 Procedures

Both groups completed the Demographics Survey, Competency Beliefs Survey and Computational Thinking Pretest before winter break (December) and began learning coding lessons after returning from break (January). The first, second, and last (post-testing) class periods took place in the computer lab. During class periods 3–9, the Scratch group remained in the computer lab while the Cozmo group worked in the high school library due to Wi-Fi configuration. The computer-based training method (Scratch) presented students with lessons after which they created and ran code using personal Scratch accounts on the desktop computers in the computer lab. Students were seated between friends and could collaborate as desired, but each student completed all work individually at the computer of the self-selected seat because of seating and wiring configuration constraints. The robotics-based training method (Cozmo) presented students with lessons after which they collaborated and wrote code in the Cozmo Code Lab app on an iPad with at least one other student and then tested the code on the Cozmo robot. Limited availability of bandwidth and iPads required students in the Cozmo class to work in groups (with a cap of three).

An Engagement Survey was given five minutes before the end of each day's lesson (class periods 2–9). A catch-up class period was added after period 6 (debugging lesson) for the Cozmo group because more students were absent (Cozmo $n = 9$, Scratch $n = 4$) and the Cozmo app crashed repeatedly on the older iPads used all four instructional days (Lessons 4–6) due to bandwidth reduction caused by high school classes coming to the library to use both computer labs at the same time that the intervention was taking place. The Competency Beliefs posttest was given at the conclusion of the final lesson (class period 9) and the Computational Thinking posttest was given during class period 10. Due to school scheduling, students in the Cozmo group had less time to complete the computational thinking posttest because they had to take two more non-related assessments during the class period on the day it was given.

2.5 Data Analysis

This quasi-experimental quantitative study used repeated measures analysis of variance (ANOVA) with a between-subjects factor of intervention (Scratch/Cozmo) and within-subjects factor of time (pre/posttest) to analyze the effects of the two training methods on computational thinking and competency beliefs. Two analyses were run for each variable: one for all students and one excluding scores for students with special education needs (IEP) and English Language Learners (ELL), because of comprehension issues. A linear mixed model was used to analyze the effects of the two different instructional interventions on student engagement.

3 Results

Additional demographic information was collected using a survey modeled after [27] as part of the Demographics questionnaire. ANOVA revealed no significant differences in availability of resources and types of learning assistance available at home between the Scratch and Cozmo groups. Analysis of student background questionnaires revealed that none of the participants had previous formal training in coding.

Table 3 provides a summary of means and standard deviations for pre- and posttest data for computational thinking and competency beliefs for all students and excluding ELL and IEP student data. Table 4 provides a summary of means and standard deviations for student engagement during each day of the study.

Table 3. Means and standard deviations for CTt and Competency Beliefs by intervention group

Dependent variable	Scratch				Cozmo			
	All students (n = 20)		Minus ELL/IEP (n = 13)		All students (n = 22)		Minus ELL/IEP (n = 17)	
	Pre M (SD)	Post M (SD)	Pre M (SD)	Post M (SD)	Pre M (SD)	Post M (SD)	Pre M (SD)	Post M (SD)
CTt Total score[a]	16.65 (4.31)	17.30 (5.25)	18.46 (3.53)	19.85 (4.47)	16.27 (5.07)	16.82 (5.32)	17.00 (5.45)	18.53 (4.11)
Competency Beliefs[b]	30.70 (6.66)	33.85 (7.61)	32.00 (6.61)	36.23 (7.40)	30.86 (6.62)	34.09 (6.57)	30.71 (6.90)	35.53 (6.66)

[a]Possible score range: 0–28.
[b]Possible score range: 12–48.

3.1 Assumptions

Shapiro-Wilk test showed that scores for all dependent variables did not deviate significantly from normal and Levene's test showed equal variances for all dependent variables. ANOVA revealed non-significant ($p > .05$) differences between the Scratch and Cozmo interventions for all variables measured at the outset of the study.

Table 4. Means and standard deviations for daily engagement by intervention group*

Time	Scratch		Cozmo	
	All students	Minus ELL/IEP	All students	Minus ELL/IEP
	M	M	M	M
	(SD)	(SD)	(SD)	(SD)
Period 2	(n = 19)	(n = 13)	(n = 22)	(n = 17)
	2.93	2.89	3.19	3.18
	(.51)	(.38)	(.54)	(.59)
Period 3	(n = 21)	(n = 14)	(n = 20)	(n = 15)
	3.11	3.04	3.56	3.61
	(.49)	(.49)	(.41)	(.41)
Period 4	(n = 19)	(n = 12)	(n = 21)	(n = 16)
	3.03	3.00	3.43	3.47
	(.44)	(.41)	(.43)	(.43)
Period 5	(n = 20)	(n = 13)	(n = 22)	(n = 17)
	3.05	3.07	3.35	3.39
	(.40)	(.40)	(.45)	(.44)
Period 6	(n = 21)	(n = 14)	(n = 19)	(n = 15)
	3.01	2.93	3.11	3.15
	(.46)	(.46)	(.67)	(.68)
Make-up			(n = 19)	(n = 17)
			3.13	3.06
			(.54)	(.58)
Period 7	(n = 21)	(n = 14)	(n = 21)	(n = 14)
	2.98	2.96	2.98	3.19
	(.51)	(.47)	(.69)	(.58)
Period 8	(n − 20)	(n − 14)	(n = 22)	(n = 17)
	3.06	3.02	3.26	3.30
	(.47)	(.46)	(.64)	(.67)
Period 9	(n = 19)	(n = 12)	(n = 22)	(n = 17)
	2.97	2.96	3.26	3.34
	(.50)	(.47)	(.45)	(.44)

*Scores were calculated by averaging the total number of items; possible score range: 1–4.

3.2 Computational Thinking

Using a repeated measures ANOVA with a between-subjects factor (Cozmo versus Scratch) and within-subjects factor (CTt pre-/posttest), there was a non-significant main effect of intervention when including all students in the analysis, $F (1, 40) = 0.090$, $p = .766$, $d = -.09$, and when excluding IEP and ELL student data, $F (1, 28) = 0.839$, $p = .367$, $d = -.31$, indicating insufficient evidence that posttest computational thinking scores were different between the Scratch and Cozmo groups.

There was a non-significant main effect of time when including all students in the analysis, $F(1, 40) = 1.012$, $p = .321$, $d_{Scratch} = .14$, $d_{Cozmo} = .11$; however, there was a significant main effect of time when excluding IEP and ELL student data, $F(1,28) = 4.692$, $p = .039$, $d_{Scratch} = .35$, $d_{Cozmo} = .32$, indicating that computational thinking skills improved significantly from pre- to posttest for both the Scratch and Cozmo groups.

There was a non-significant interaction between time and intervention for all students, $F(1, 40) = 0.008$, $p = .930$ and when excluding IEP and ELL student data, $F(1, 28) = 0.012$, $p = .915$, indicating that, on average, students in both interventions improved their computational thinking skills similarly over time.

3.3 Competency Beliefs

Using a repeated measures ANOVA with a between-subjects factor (Cozmo versus Scratch) and within-subjects factor (Competency Beliefs pre/posttest), there was a non-significant main effect of intervention when including all students in the analysis, $F(1, 40) = 0.012$, $p = .914$, $d = .03$, and when excluding IEP and ELL student data, $F(1, 28) = 0.202$, $p = .656$, $d = -.10$, indicating insufficient evidence that posttest competency beliefs were different between the Scratch and Cozmo groups.

There was a significant main effect of time for all students, $F(1, 40) = 10.058$, $p = .003$, $d_{Scratch} = .44$, $d_{Cozmo} = .49$, and when excluding IEP and ELL student data, $F(1, 28) = 13.563$, $p = .001$, $d_{Scratch} = .60$, $d_{Cozmo} = .71$, indicating that competency beliefs improved significantly from pre- to posttest for both the Scratch and Cozmo groups.

There was a non-significant interaction between time and intervention for all students, $F(1, 40) = 0.001$, $p = .970$, and when excluding IEP and ELL student data, $F(1, 28) = 0.058$, $p = .811$, indicating that, on average, students in both interventions improved their competency beliefs similarly over time.

3.4 Engagement

Engagement was measured each day of the intervention. A linear mixed model was performed to test the intervention's effects on engagement to avoid loss of data and provide a clearer picture of daily engagement. Intervention (Scratch versus Cozmo), class period, and the interaction of intervention by class period were set as fixed factors, and class period was set as the repeated factor with compound symmetry covariance structure. This analysis provided information about whether students found Scratch or Cozmo more engaging, which class periods students found more engaging, and whether engagement varied between the Scratch and Cozmo groups during any of the class periods.

Intervention significantly predicted engagement when including all students in the analysis, $F(1, 41.492) = 4.654$, $p = .037$, and intervention significantly predicted engagement when excluding IEP and ELL student data, $F(1, 29.544) = 6.963$, $p = .013$. Class period significantly predicted engagement for all students, $F(8, 290.547) = 4.965$, $p = .000$, and when excluding IEP and ELL student data, $F(8, 205.462) = 3.550$, $p = .001$.

The interaction of intervention and class period significantly predicted engagement for all students, F (7, 290.481) = 2.380, p = .022, but not when excluding IEP and ELL student data, F (7, 205.516) = 1.152, p = .332.

After controlling for the class period interaction, these analyses showed that intervention significantly predicted engagement for all students, b = −320, t (114.228) = −2.017, p = .046, and when excluding IEP and ELL student data, b = −.433, t (97.243) = −2.318, p = .023. Pairwise comparisons showed that the Cozmo group was significantly more engaged than the Scratch group with a medium effect d = (.45) for all students and when excluding IEP and ELL student data with a medium effect d = (.63).

4 Discussion

There was a significant pre-/posttest gain in computational thinking skills for both the Scratch and Cozmo groups when ELL and students with special education needs were excluded. However, the hypothesis that Cozmo would produce greater gains in computational thinking was not supported. These results are similar to other studies comparing computer-based and physical robots that found no significant difference in computational thinking [35]. However, the results of the present study should be interpreted with caution. The Cozmo group faced additional limitations including more absences, less accountability when students switched groups, and less time to complete the CTt posttest. Limited number of devices and school Wi-Fi configuration required students to work in small groups in the high school library, where the app crashed repeatedly during all four instructional days due to bandwidth limitations. Even with the make-up day, many students were unable to complete all of the lesson objectives. Additionally, students were administered a paper version of the CTt, which can be demotivating for students accustomed to using computers in a course [35]. It is also possible that Scratch is better aligned with the CTt because both use two-dimensional images. Additional data collection methods (e.g., interviews) could provide more information about student thought processes. In the current study, pre-/posttest gains in computational thinking combined with successful completion of student coding projects provide encouraging evidence for using Cozmo and Scratch as a learning tool for introducing middle school students to coding and enhancing their computational thinking.

The hypothesis that both the Cozmo and Scratch groups would experience an increase in competency beliefs was confirmed with practically meaningful effect sizes and a larger effect for the Cozmo group. The current study took place in a public seventh grade classroom rather than a self-selected STEM activity thus the improved competency beliefs found in both groups are reassuring. This is contrary to studies of middle school students that found decreased student self-efficacy after programming robots [27] and after using a virtual robotics curriculum [30].

While the current study was the initial exposure of both groups to coding, using the same visual programming language may have contributed to the finding of increased competency beliefs by reducing the cognitive load compared to that required for complex text-based programming languages Additionally, the curriculum used a scaffolded learning approach which may have helped build student confidence. These results are encouraging because providing students with learning opportunities that develop their beliefs about their coding abilities is important for encouraging continued participation in computer science [30].

The hypothesis that Cozmo would produce greater student engagement was confirmed. Pairwise comparisons showed that the Cozmo group was significantly more engaged than the Scratch group with a medium effect size. The high level of interactivity and emotions offered by Cozmo resulted in a higher level of engagement compared to two-dimensional Scratch characters on a computer screen. This is supported by findings that students were more engaged working with physical rather than simulated robots [36] and that emotional stimuli embedded into interfaces increase learners' engagement [37]. The Scratch group experienced no technical issues and their engagement scores were similar throughout the intervention, but engagement in the Cozmo group steadily declined on each consecutive day when the app was crashing; however, engagement scores increased after the technology began working again.

Written reflections collected at the end of the intervention provided additional support that Cozmo was more engaging. When asked what students might want to do next, responses in the Scratch group included: Nothing involving coding; Take a break from coding; Scratch is not my favorite; Scratch is boring; Try something less boring than Scratch. All feedback from the Cozmo group was positive and expressed a desire to make more complex projects with Cozmo. Several students wrote that they wanted to buy their own Cozmo, one wanted to keep Cozmo, and one wrote "Cozmo is cute and I love him."

4.1 Implications and Conclusion

There is a lack of research on integrating robotics in the classroom [38] and the outcomes reported in the literature tend to use small samples, are mostly descriptive, and are not integrated into classroom activities [9]. This study empirically investigated the use of Cozmo compared to Scratch where students did not self-select into the course. This elucidated some real-world implications of integrating robotics interventions including technical (older mobile devices, lack of adequate bandwidth), physical (limited space and classroom configurations), and scheduling (calamity days) challenges. English Language Learners and students with special needs faced challenges reading and comprehending assessments; however, they were able to successfully complete the open-ended challenge projects. Thus, using multiple means of assessment can provide a clearer picture of coding competence.

Regardless of these challenges, the Creative Computing curriculum unit used to introduce students to coding resulted in statistically significant increases in computational thinking and competency beliefs for both the Scratch and Cozmo groups. This shows that the scaffolded approach to coding instruction was effective and can be adapted to other programming languages and technologies. Clarifying an effective pedagogical approach for coding instruction is important, but so is considering the tools that can assist educators in meeting instructional goals. Cozmo proved to be an effective tool to cognitively and affectively engage students in learning and students were more engaged with Cozmo than Scratch. As such, future research is needed to investigate whether similar results can be achieved with other types of physical robots as well as realistic 3D simulated robots.

References

1. Carter, L.: Why students with an apparent aptitude for computer science don't choose to major in computer science. In: 37th SIGCSE Technical Symposium on Computer Science Education, pp. 27–31. ACM, New York (2006)
2. Kong, S., Chiu, M.M., Lai, M.: A study of primary school students' interest, collaboration attitude, and programming empowerment in computational thinking education. Comput. Educ. **127**, 178–189 (2018)
3. Tai, R., Liu, C.Q., Maltese, A.V., Fan, X.: Career choice: enhanced: planning early for careers in science. Science **312**, 1143–1144 (2006)
4. Monroy-Hernández, A., Resnick, M.: Empowering kids to create and share programmable media. Interactions **15**(2), 50–53 (2015)
5. Maloney, J., Peppler, K., Kafai, Y.B., Resnick, M., Rusk, N.: Programming by choice: urban youth learn programming with scratch. In: 39th SIGCSE Technical Symposium on Computer Science Education, pp. 367–371. ACM, New York (2008)
6. Fields, D.A., Kafai, Y.B., Giang, M.T.: Youth computational participation in the wild. ACM Trans. Comput. Educ. **17**(3), 1–22 (2017)
7. Armoni, M., Meerbaum-Salant, O., Ben-Ari, M.: From Scratch to "real" programming. ACM Trans. Comput. Educ. **14**(4), 1–15 (2015)
8. Fronza, I., El Ioini, N., Corral, L.: Leveraging robot programming to foster computational thinking. In: 9th International Conference on Computer Supported Education, vol. 2, CSEDU, pp. 109–116. Springer, Heidelberg (2017). https://doi.org/10.5220/0006310101090116
9. Pachidis, T.P., Macedonia, E., Vrochidou, E., Kaburlasos, V., Macedonia, E.: Social robotics in education: state-of-the-art and directions. In: International Conference on Robotics, July 2018
10. Rosanda, V., Starčič, A.I.: A review of social robots in classrooms: emerging educational technoogy and teacher education. Educ. Self Dev. **14**(3), 93–106 (2019)
11. Anwar, S., Bascou, N.A., Menekse, M., Kardgar, A.: A systematic review of studies on educational robotics. J. Pre-College Eng. Educ. Res. **9**(2), 19–42 (2019)
12. Papert, S., Harel, I.: Situating Constructionism. Ablex Publishing Corporation, Norwood (1991)
13. Julià, C., Antolí, J.Ò.: Spatial ability learning through educational robotics. Int. J. Technol. Des. Educ. **26**(2), 185–203 (2015). https://doi.org/10.1007/s10798-015-9307-2
14. Naneva, S., Sarda Gou, M., Webb, T.L., Prescott, T.J.: A systematic review of attitudes, anxiety, acceptance and trust towards social robots. Int. J. Soc. Robot. **12**, 1179–1201 (2020)
15. Björling, E., Rose, E., Davidson, A., Ren, R., Wong, D.: Can we keep him forever? Teens' engagement and desire for emotional connection with a social robot. Int. J. Soc. Robot. **12**(1), 65–77 (2020)
16. Belpaeme, T., Kennedy, J., Ramachandran, A., Scassellati, B., Tanaka, F.: Social robots for education: a review. Sci. Robot. **3**(21), 1–10 (2018)
17. Davide, G., Pauline, C., Federica, F., Tiziana, P., Agnieszka, W.: Follow the white robot: efficacy of robot-assistive training for children with autism-spectrum condition. Soc. Cogn. Hum.-Robot Interact. **86**, 101822 (2020)
18. Keller, L., John, I.: Motivating female students for computer science by means of robot workshops. Int. J. Eng. Pedagogy **10**(1), 94–108 (2020)
19. Jovanovic, V.M., et al.: Exposing students to STEM careers through hands on activities with drones and robots. In: ASEE Annual Conference and Exposition, Conference Proceedings (2019)
20. Szecsei, D.: Using storytelling and robot theater to develop computational thinking. In: Purdue University Symposium on Education in Entertainment and Engineering (2019)

21. Ahmad, M.I., Khordi-Moodi, M., Lohan, K.S.: Social robot for STEM education. In: ACM/IEEE International Conference on Human-Robot Interaction, pp. 90–92 (2020)
22. Román-González, M., Pérez-González, J.C., Jiménez-Fernández, C.: Which cognitive abilities underlie computational thinking? Criterion validity of the Computational Thinking Test. Comput. Hum. Behav. **72**, 678–691 (2017)
23. Özüorçun, N.Ç., Bicen, H.: Does the inclusion of robots affect engineering students' achievement in computer programming courses? Eurasia J. Math. Sci Technol. Educ. **13**(8), 4779–4787 (2017)
24. Pugnali, A., Sullivan, A.: The impact of user interface on young children's computational thinking. J. Inf. Techol. Educ. Innov. Pract. **16**(16), 171–193 (2017)
25. Bandura, A.: Social Foundations of Thought and Action: A Social Cognitive Theory. Prentice-Hall (1986)
26. Hinton, T.B.: An exploratory study of a robotics educational platform on STEM career interests in middle school students. Diss. Abstr. Int. **78**, 146 (2018)
27. Weese, J.L., Feldhausen, R., Bean, N.H.: The impact of STEM experiences on student self-efficacy in computational thinking. In: ASEE Annual Conference and Exposition, Conference Proceedings, June 2016
28. Phetsrikran, T., Massagram, W., Harfield, A.: First steps in teaching computational thinking through mobile technology and robotics. Asian Int. J. Soc. Sci. **17**(3), 37–52 (2017)
29. Witherspoon, E.B., Higashi, R.M., Schunn, C.D., Baehr, E.C., Shoop, R.: Developing computational thinking through a virtual robotics programming curriculum. ACM Trans. Comput. Educ. **18**(1), 1–20 (2017)
30. Witherspoon, E.B., Schunn, C.D., Higashi, R.M., Shoop, R.: Attending to structural programming features predicts differences in learning and motivation. J. Comput. Assistaed Learn. **34**(2), 115–128 (2018)
31. Merino-Armero, J.M., González-Calero, J.A., Cózar-Gutiérrez, R., Villena-Taranilla, R.: Computational thinking initiation. An experience with robots in primary education. J. Res. Sci. Math. Technol. Educ. **1**(2), 181–206 (2018)
32. Brennan, K., Balch, C., Chung, M.: An introductory computing curriculum using Scratch. Harvard Graduate Sch. Educ. **154**, 23–38 (2011)
33. Chen, Y.-F., Cannady, M.A., Schunn, C., Dorph, R.: Measures technical brief: competency beliefs in STEM. Activiation Lab (2017)
34. Chung, J., Cannady, M.A., Schunn, C., Dorph, R., Bathgate, M.: Measures technical brief: engagement in science learning activities. Activation Lab (2016)
35. Djambong, T., Freiman, V.: Task-based assessment of students' computational thinking skills developed through visual programming or tangible coding environments. In: 13th International Conference on Cognition and Exploratory Learning in Digital Age, Celda, pp. 41–51 (2016)
36. Merkouris, A., Chorianopoulos, K.: Introducing computer programming to children through robotic and wearable devices. In: ACM International Conference Proceeding Series, pp. 69–72 (2015)
37. Plass, J.L., Heidig, S., Hayward, E.O., Homer, B.D., Um, E.: Emotional design in multimedia learning: effects of shape and color on affect and learning. Learn. Instr. **29**, 128–140 (2013)
38. Poh, L., Toh, E., Causo, A., Tzuo, P.-W., Chen, I.-M., Yeo, S.H.: A review on the use of robots in education and young children. Educ. Technol. Soc. **19**(2), 148–163 (2016)

Design of a VR-Based Campus Tour Platform with a User-Friendly Scene Asset Management System

Stefan Hendricks, Alfred Shaker, and Jong-Hoon Kim(✉)

The Advanced Telerobotics Research Lab,
Kent State University, Kent, OH 44240, USA
jkim72@kent.edu

Abstract. Virtual reality tours have become a desire for many educational institutions due to the potential difficulties for students to attend in person, especially during the COVID-19 pandemic. Having the ability for a student to explore the buildings and locations on a university campus is a crucial part of convincing them to enroll in classes. Many institutions have already installed tour applications that they have either designed themselves or contracted to a third party. However, they lack a convenient way for non-maintainers, such as faculty, to manage and personalize their classrooms and offices in a simple way. In this paper, we propose a platform to not only provide a full virtual experience of the campus but also feature a user-friendly content management system designed for staff and faculty to customize their assigned scenes. The tour uses the Unity3D engine, which communicates to a university server hosting a custom .NET API and SQL database to obtain information about the virtual rooms through a role-based access system to the faculty and staff. We believe this system for managing tour scenes will solve both time and expense for the tour development team and allow them to focus on implementing other features, rather than having to fulfill requests for editing locations in the tour. We expect this framework to function as a tour platform for other universities, as well as small businesses and communities. We seek to demonstrate the feasibility of this platform through our developed prototype application. Based on small sample testing, we have received overall positive responses and constructive critique that has played a role in improving the application moving forward.

Keywords: Virtual reality · Tours · Spacio-temporal · User experience · Cyber-sickness · Mental models · Content management · Real-time

1 Introduction

Media and the entertainment business have always pushed technology forward. With trends leaning more towards virtual spaces, industries like tourism now

© Springer Nature Switzerland AG 2022
J.-H. Kim et al. (Eds.): IHCI 2021, LNCS 13184, pp. 337–348, 2022.
https://doi.org/10.1007/978-3-030-98404-5_32

have a greater dependency on technology. There are many opportunities for innovation with tourism, such as through virtual reality as indicated by various studies. One of the main parts of presenting media is creating content and arranging it in an appealing format. A great content management system can enhance the user experience because it can make the content well organized, have higher quality, and appear seamless when creating and modifying it. Users should not have affected the presentation of their media due to lousy content management. With this idea, we wanted to create a content management system for virtual tourism that would allow the live creation and deployment of new scenes within the virtual tour without relying on the system developers. It would also allow the modification of the tour platform in real-time without impacting the user experience by restarting to make new changes.

With virtual tourism becoming more popular and even needed to some degree [3,5], we wanted to accommodate both the users and content creators in the tour. From what is discussed later in the literature review, we realized that other virtual tour systems do not allow content creators to modify or add content while the experience is live. These applications would require paying experienced developers, taking the tour down for maintenance, and ultimately spending time and money for minor scene changes. We address these issues with our live content management system for our fully dynamic virtual tour user experience. Not only would we provide system administrators the ability to control the management of the tour content, but individual users could be assigned permissions that allow them to edit and add content to certain scenes. Ultimately, this will allow for multiple levels of authority and content management that are intuitive enough for new users to manage their respective locations within the application. Additionally, we discuss the architecture used, our design philosophies, and our current implementation.

The latest development build of the tour is used to experiment and gather data on the usability, user-friendliness, efficiency, and performance of the program. We have conducted internal testing and have received positive results and reactions for our content management system and the virtual tour from several selected faculty members and students. We are also planning to conduct large-scale studies through surveys based on our mental models for data collection, along with implementing integrated metrics within the tour that give us supplementary data about users while they travel through the tour. These will allow us to understand how users interact with the tour, and how to further improve the current implementation, which we discuss in the data analysis section. In the future works section, we discuss how we will improve from the results, and what other features we have planned to make this a better overall experience for both users and content creators.

2   Literature Reviews

Virtual Reality: Virtual reality (VR) is becoming increasingly prominent in today's society. Applications can simulate an environment as if the user were viewing it in real life by creating 360-degree panoramic photos. Some applications generate these photos either through stitching different ones together from multiple angles or by using a 360-degree camera from room to room. Examples of this technology are becoming common in several industries, from video games to advanced testing through simulations, and even through tour applications [2].

A study by Lin et al. shows the therapeutic effects of listening and playing music in a virtual world. They created an application where the user could use the VR controllers that play music to interact with instruments and listen to them in a VR environment. Those who participated in the experiment showed positive effects on their mental state [7].

Additionally, Shaker et al. conducted a study to show the therapeutic potential of virtual reality applications in treating intellectually and developmentally disabled (IDD) individuals. The VR experience was a tour of a specific setting, where they could visit different indoor locations and have the freedom to go anywhere, giving them a good idea of the layout and where the interactable objects are. The IDD individuals in the study indicated that this would be an ideal way to become familiar with a place before going there in person to reduce social stress in these situations. They also would like these VR applications to have more use-cases, such as university events and tours. The results showed that there is potential for VR in therapeutic applications for various individuals [13]. For universities, using virtual reality as a form of tourism is an increasingly common approach, but some universities want to extend the virtual reality experience to other areas of campus. Specifically, Velev and Zlateva described how virtual reality on campuses could extend to sports events and even networking opportunities [16].

Virtual Tourism: Suwarno et al. talk about virtual tours as an appealing way for universities and other institutions to allow students to explore the campus without the inconvenience of having to travel there in person [14]. These universities typically use in-person events for student engagement on their campus. Due to the COVID-19 pandemic, however, they needed a new solution for remote events. One of the significant issues for new students arriving at a university is how complex the layouts of certain buildings are, along with some students being physically unable to be on campus in person. They also need to be able to solve orientation problems across large areas on campus. Some applications attempt to solve this issue by making use of external Google Maps APIs to show the outsides of the various buildings across campus, such as a tour application developed by Bengkulu University [12]. Others like Figueroa et al. compare several virtual reality tour applications developed by other universities but cite either their expense or lack of good user experience on other platforms as deterrents for using them [10]. Additionally, Rohizan et al. highlights how it becomes essential to have a high-quality tour application for students unable to attend these tours in person so they can make an accurate decision on whether to enroll in courses [11]. Thus, some universities create virtual tours not only to enhance the user experience of the campus but to also gather research and compare it to in-person tours. These universities may have also used different methods of generating 360-degree panoramic images. The most common approach is to use 360-degree cameras in a room to create them. Another technique used by institutions, such as the Tsinghua University in Beijing, stitch images together that are taken at multiple angles to generate the effect. Wu, Shaomei et al. use mathematical equations to create the photos in a cylindrical shape, which can create a panorama as if it were a 360-degree camera [18].

Mental Models: When trying to quantify how someone feels towards something, we need to understand the various states that could be affected in the current context and how to manipulate them. We also need to understand the significance of each state. For that, we build mental models that allow us to examine and quantify the ways different agents in a cycle communicate and interact with each other, and how these affect themselves and others [15,20]. These mental models determine their state before, during, and after the trial to track the significance of these states. They could be a variety of things like anger, stress, or fatigue, which all depend on what is relevant to the context of the application they are using. In the context of virtual reality, we consider many factors that align with simulation sickness questionnaires and the things they quantify and map there, such as fatigue, headache, and eye strain. There is a study by Kim et al. which worked on creating a virtual reality sickness questionnaire that took elements of the SSQ and altered it to fit with the context of virtual reality applications [6]. These factors align more with the context of VR and will help us construct the mental model [17] that will help us understand the human state in the context of the VR application.

User Experience: To create an application that the users will enjoy, the user experience and interface design become critical. The developers must take the user's needs in the context of the application into account and design the experience to suit the user's capabilities. Some researchers such as Figueroa et al. use audio to accompany each scene to enhance the virtual reality feeling of being present [10]. Others like Giraldo et al. feature help and service modules that allow users to obtain support for the tour or other components if needed [4]. These work very well for the user, however, they rely heavily on the developers and maintainers of the tour framework to make the necessary updates. For testing, some applications not only test the usability on many platforms but also the performance load from many users viewing it at a time. A particular application created by Perdana et al. emphasized the necessity of testing the application thoroughly by including local, QA, and production builds along with using Apache JMeter for testing the application endpoints at scale from the university [9]. Additionally, some universities choose to make their scene viewing experience feel much more like a video game rather than using static 360-degree panoramic images. Maines et al. take the typical virtual reality experience further by incorporating a video game-like environment and assets into each scene through custom 3D modeling [8]. These models make the scenes much more interactive, but it also must be much more time-consuming to create each scene rather than just using a panoramic image. Other applications attempt to make the experience more immersive for the users wearing special virtual reality headsets. The tour created by Azizo et al. allows users to control it through voice commands so that they can feel much more immersed in the tour [1]. On top of this, some applications attempt to teach students about the fastest possible route to take on campus. One example, created by Yeung et al. aims to use a "Shortest Path Algorithm" to not only inform the students about the quickest routes across campus but also to caution the user about real-time emergency closures on campus that are in their path [19].

3 Design Concepts

For other university tour systems, we noticed that it is only possible for the tour system administrators and the developers themselves to manually make adjustments to particular scenes, which would require downtime and maintenance of the application. The main idea for our VR tour system is to allow the users to experience a seamless interactive tour that can be modified without impeding the user experience and assigning more work to the developers. With the way we built the system, we can have administrators change and add content, such as new hotspots to connect to scenes, changing the 360 photo of the scene, adding anchors and link buttons, all in real-time while the application continues to run for other users. This design allows for an uninterrupted touring experience, and better yet, the ability for admins to make content updates and fixes efficiently using a user-friendly UI. The goal of the UI is to make it intuitive and streamlined so that we would not need technology experts to handle content updates, but rather allow any trusted individual the ability to make changes. We want the content management system to be easy to use and make sense to anyone using it. With this in mind, we have set up the UI to allow for adding and editing various parts of the tour independently. The Content Management System (CMS) allows the user a degree of freedom with customization but also can assist in areas such as determining the exact location data of an object, associating foreign keys from the database and local scene names correctly, and handling the back-end without end-user intervention. They would not need to do any additional work in the database to get anything going, as just using the provided workflow allows the addition and editing of the content when required. Managing content this way is the core of our design and what we built the system around, as it provides a better experience for the end-users.

4 System Overview

4.1 System Architecture

The proposed VR Tour system requires various components to work together to bring the user an interactive and intuitive viewing experience while allowing administrators to add and edit content in real-time. It consists of the symbolic architecture and the system overview, shown in Fig. 1.

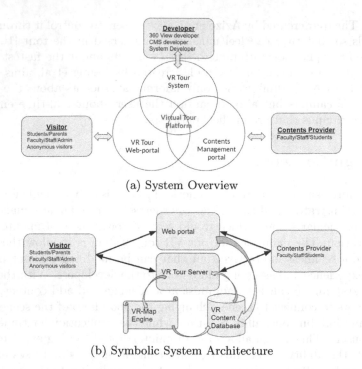

(a) System Overview

(b) Symbolic System Architecture

Fig. 1. The VR tour system's symbolic architecture and overview

The system overview shows the various systems and how they interact with each agent in the system. The developers created the dynamic 360-degree view scenes that have their content loaded from the database and CMS, along with the communication systems for the server and client VR tour system. This system allows the client to retrieve information needed for each scene from the back-end database. The back-end interaction for users with administrator access happens through the CMS on the client-side as well. The contents provider interacts with this contents management system to provide the visitors with dynamic content through the VR tour web portal (Fig. 2). These components all come together to create the VR tour platform.

The architecture shows the relationships with the various components and how they interact with each other. The visitor interacts directly with the web portal that dynamically obtains information from the VR tour server. In the case of administrators and content providers, the VR tour server provides content to the engine that runs the map generation using the VR content database, which contains information and references to all the data in the context of their scenes and locations on the map. These systems ultimately control the content that the VR tour server dynamically serves to the web portal client without interrupting the clients.

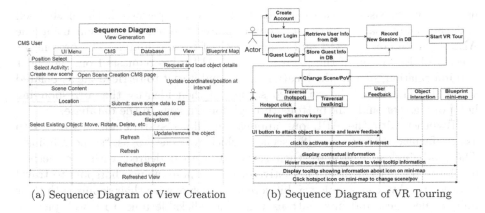

(a) Sequence Diagram of View Creation   (b) Sequence Diagram of VR Touring

Fig. 2. Illustrates the CMS content creation process and VR tour process

(a)Add contents to a scene   (b)Create hotspots in a scene   (c) Edit a hotspot

Fig. 3. The scene manager UI

5   Implementation

Compared to other university tours, our goal was to build a tour application to provide a pleasant experience to the user viewing it and for the faculty managing it. The main client runs on Unity3D, which uses WebGL to build a playable application through a browser. The client allows the users to log in as a guest, or create an account and use it to log in to the tour. Accounts have various groups that they can belong to with varying levels of authority. A regular user and a guest account cannot edit or add content, unlike an admin account.

The Unity client communicates through an ASP.NET 5 API to a MariaDB database that contains information used to display content in the scene. The 360-degree photos are stored on the server that holds the API and the web application and retrieves them when the corresponding scene loads. The API is also used for the login flow, communicating with the database stores user information, and verifying users upon login. The API functions as the middle-man and request handler of the client application. When the API receives a request, it keeps track of IP addresses to ensure that only authorized clients can access data-sensitive areas. It is also responsible for encrypting and uploading user passwords to the database, handling rate limits for endpoints, and facilitating the secure creation of new accounts through email verification. The database contains tables for users, locations, scenes, assets, feedback, and link buttons. For security, the users' table consists of two columns that store the password: the hash itself and the unique salt. These are securely stored through encryption using the AES algorithm on the API and require both of these columns to be present for successful decryption of the passwords. The API takes requests from the client and information, such as the location name, and uses it to retrieve the associated scene ID. The ID of the retrieved scene can then identify the corresponding hotspots, assets, and link buttons through foreign keys in the database.

Together with the API, our application allows system administrators to assign faculty users to specific scenes, which we refer to as "scene admins". These admins can customize their scenes to a great degree, with one method involving the placement of interactive objects. These include hotspots to travel to other nearby scenes, holographic screens to personalize their rooms with their unique messages, and link buttons which are clickable links to a web page of the administrator's choosing. They can use a role-based admin UI, which only appears in a scene they have permission in, to create and edit these props through a coordinate-based button system along with object dragging (see Fig. 3). Ultimately this saves future time and expenses by allowing designated faculty to manage scene content so that the application maintainers can focus on implementing or improving features.

These scene admins and CMS users have access to several exclusive functions. These involve being able to create, modify, and delete scene content. A typical example from the tour would be if the user wanted to create a new hotspot. From the "Select Existing Object..." sequence, the user would replicate this in the application by opening the "Add Content" section in the menu (see Fig. 3, which allows them to either create a new hotspot, anchor, or link button. When clicking the "Create Hotspot" button, a UI view appears for the user to control the placement of the hotspot and which scene to connect. Once they submit, the new hotspot is added to the database and the CMS scene will automatically refresh to reflect the new hotspot. Modifying a hotspot would follow a similar sequence to creating one. The user can click on the "Edit Hotspot" button to take them to a near-identical UI to the "Create Hotspot" UI. Through this, they would select the hotspot they wish to edit through a drop-down list and ensure that the respective hotspot would highlight green. Similarly, when they submit their changes, it would follow the sequence of updating the database and having the CMS automatically refresh the page. Additionally, scene admins can also create new scenes that they have permission for through the map, which would follow the appropriate sequence to update the database and refresh the map accordingly.

Figure 4 plans out several key functions for this user. For a typical user interacting with the tour, they would first find themselves on the login page, where they could sign in to an existing account, create a new account, or use a guest account. Creating a new account would properly store it in the database while logging in as a user or a guest would have the server store their information as a session to keep track of permissions and statistical information. Once logged in, they would find themselves at the start page, where they would have the option

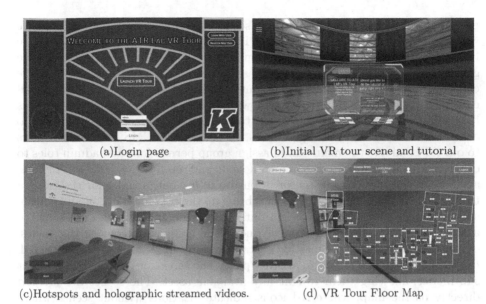

(a)Login page   (b)Initial VR tour scene and tutorial

(c)Hotspots and holographic streamed videos.   (d) VR Tour Floor Map

Fig. 4. Walk-through demonstration of the KSU VR tour system

to learn how to traverse the tour through the various hotspots or to start the tour. The tutorial provides three clickable hotspots to simulate different scenes along with holographic messages that both inform the user of the controls as well as praise them for clicking the hotspot. When the user starts the tour, they begin their journey at the start of the second floor of the Math and Sciences Building (MSB), which is near the staircase and elevators. The user can navigate through the tour either by clicking each hotspot icon (which is represented as a light-bulb with particle effects that light up when hovered on) or by accessing their map through the UI. On the map itself, there are several different actions that the user can perform depending on their role: regular user, scene admin, and system admin. Regular users can click on the blue circles on the map to transition them to any scene on a particular floor, and they can toggle buttons on the bottom of the map to change floors. Scene admins can also upload their 360-degree panoramic images to any scene with a red circle above it for the background, while system admins have this functionality for every scene.

6 Functional Verification

To verify the functionality and concepts we were going for, we conducted some in-house testing to get initial results. We had people from our lab and faculty at the university use the VR tour to navigate around and create example content in the test scenes in the application using the CMS. We instructed them how to navigate the tour and use the CMS through a live demonstration. In the demo, we navigated and added an example of each type of content: locations and the 360 photos in them, hotspots that connect scenes, holograms, and link buttons. We were confident that they at least had an idea of how to use the system, so then we let them try it themselves by giving them a link to a live demo version. They were given credentials to log in that would assign the proper permissions to manage content. Going through, they experimented with the creation of content, as well editing it, which have different workflows. We also had user group permissions that allowed certain non-admin users to act as admins for certain scenes. To control the accounts and assign admins, we created the CMS website that links to our API and lets the main admin assign group permissions and admin roles to other users. There are menus to show the map and scroll through different floors, an indication of the logged-in user, a button to log out, a slider for the camera turn speed, and two other buttons that bring up the content addition and editing sub-menus. Pressing the add content button will bring up four sub-menus, one to add locations (which contain scenes), one to add hotspots to connect the scenes, one to add holograph anchors for custom information, and one to add a link button on the screen to link to another page. The same goes for the edit content sub-menus, allowing them to edit any available asset. The scenes are created directly on the map, where red icons indicate locations without scenes where they can add a 360-degree image, and blue icons indicate locations with scenes where they can still edit the image. We explained this to the users before letting them explore on their own. For them to create content, a placeholder preview item assists the user in placing it correctly at the desired location. For editing, there is an indicator to let the user know what piece of content they selected. These are some of the ways we wanted to help make the system more intuitive and not require extensive training to use. Our demos work off of live databases to monitor if they were adding data correctly to the application. Additionally, because it used live material, it was simple to view their changes. After the demo, we asked if they could write to us about what they thought about the experience and how we could improve it. Ultimately, this allowed us to move forward with the prototype to reach a stage to publish the application.

7   Discussion

The general theme of the feedback was very positive. People enjoyed going through the virtual tour as a tourist, and they found the CMS simple and convenient. They were able to use it to create sample content in the application as well as edit it. They praised how intuitive the system workflows were for content management. We found that they had informative suggestions for improving the application in terms of its UI and functionality. Using this feedback, we iterated on these features and conducted more in-house testing to get further feedback. Generally, people agreed that this type of application helps bring interest to the university. It allows them to tour these rooms remotely in a way for each professor to customize their own space and give it a more personal touch. Being able to control the data in this way is helpful as it will not disturb their viewing experience, so people can edit this information conveniently rather than having to wait until scheduled maintenance or some other inconvenient time. The users liked the split menus and sub-menus, allowing for specific workflows that did not interfere with each other. Having the locations shown on the map made it easy to visualize where the scenes would go and made constructing the locations simpler, as they had little difficulty working with this interface. Overall, the system creates a better experience for the end-users and the content managers. Our internal testing also indicates that we are going in the right direction with our methods.

8 Conclusion

We believe that the VR Tour platform is a unique and useful application compared to existing tour applications. With its primary focus being to provide an interactive and simple user interface for scene managers, it provides the ability to customize their designated scenes without having to create inconvenience for the tour developers and administrators. Although the only customization options available currently are holographic images that can display custom text messages and custom link buttons that take you to external web pages, the team is planning on the ability to add custom assets to each scene, such as uploading an image or using a camera to scan the objects they wish to import. Additionally, the team hopes to add multiplayer support for seeing and interacting with other users in the same scene during the same session, having a survey presented when they finish the tour to gather data, and to have automatic data collection from users during their session, such as what scenes they visited and how long they visited. Ultimately, they hope that this framework will eventually become used by other buildings on campus and potentially expand to other institutions as a whole.

References

1. Azizo, A.S.B., Mohamed, F.B., Siang, C.V., Isham, M.I.M.: Virtual reality 360 UTM campus tour with voice commands. In: 2020 6th International Conference on Interactive Digital Media (ICIDM), pp. 1–6 (2020). https://doi.org/10.1109/ICIDM51048.2020.9339665
2. Burdea, G., Coiffet, P.: Virtual Reality Technology. MIT Press, Cambridge (2003)
3. El-Said, O., Aziz, H.: Virtual tours a means to an end: an analysis of virtual tours' role in tourism recovery post COVID-19. J. Travel Res. https://doi.org/10.1177/0047287521997567
4. Giraldo, F.D., Arango, E., Cruz, C.D., Bernal, C.C.: Application of augmented reality and usability approaches for the implementation of an interactive tour applied at the University of Quindio. In: 2016 IEEE 11th Colombian Computing Conference (CCC), pp. 1–8 (2016). https://doi.org/10.1109/ColumbianCC.2016.7750798
5. Huang, Y.C., Backman, S.J., Backman, K.F.: The impacts of virtual experiences on people's travel intentions. In: Gretzel, U., Law, R., Fuchs, M. (eds.) Information and Communication Technologies in Tourism 2010, pp. 555–566. Springer, Vienna (2010). https://doi.org/10.1007/978-3-211-99407-8_46

6. Kim, H.K., Park, J., Choi, Y., Choe, M.: Virtual reality sickness questionnaire (VRSQ): motion sickness measurement index in a virtual reality environment. Appl. Ergon. **69**, 66–73 (2018). https://doi.org/10.1016/j.apergo.2017.12.016
7. Lin, X., et al.: Virtual reality-based musical therapy for mental health management. In: 2020 10th Annual Computing and Communication Workshop and Conference (CCWC), pp. 0948–0952 (2020). https://doi.org/10.1109/CCWC47524.2020.9031157
8. Maines, C., Tang, S.: An application of game technology to virtual university campus tour and interior navigation. In: 2015 International Conference on Developments of E-Systems Engineering (DeSE), pp. 341–346 (2015). https://doi.org/10.1109/DeSE.2015.15
9. Perdana, D., Irawan, A.I., Munadi, R.: Implementation of a web based campus virtual tour for introducing Telkom university building. Int. J. Simul.-Syst. Sci. Technol. **20**, 1–6 (2019). https://doi.org/10.5013/IJSSST.a.20.01.06
10. Roberto, F., Mendoza, G.A., Fajardo, J.C.C., Tan, S.E., Yassin, E., Thian, T.H.: Virtualizing a university campus tour: a pilot study on its usability and user experience, and perception. Int. J. Inf. Technol. Gov. Educ. Bus. **2**, 1–8 (2020)
11. Rohizan, R.B., Vistro, D.M., Puasa, M.R.B.: Enhanced visitor experience through campus virtual tour. J. Phys.: Conf. Ser. 1228 (2019). https://doi.org/10.1088/1742-6596/1228/1/012067
12. Setiawan, Y., Erlanshari, A., Fakhrurezi, Y.M., Purwandari, E.P.: Usability testing to measure real perception generation level in introduction of Bengkulu university building based on virtual tour with 360° object modelling. In: Proceedings of the Sriwijaya International Conference on Information Technology and its Applications (SICONIAN 2019), pp. 645–648. Atlantis Press (2020). https://doi.org/10.2991/aisr.k.200424.097
13. Shaker, A., Lin, X., Kim, D.Y., Kim, J.H., Sharma, G., Devine, M.A.: Design of a virtual reality tour system for people with intellectual and developmental disabilities: a case study. Comput. Sci. Eng. **22**(3), 7–17 (2020). https://doi.org/10.1109/MCSE.2019.2961352
14. Suwarno, N.P.M.: Virtual campus tour (student perception of university virtual environment). J. Crit. Rev. (2020). https://doi.org/10.31838/jcr.07.19.584
15. Tabrez, A., Luebbers, M.B., Hayes, B.: A survey of mental modeling techniques in human–robot teaming. Curr. Robot. Rep. **1**(4), 259–267 (2020). https://doi.org/10.1007/s43154-020-00019-0
16. Velev, D., Zlateva, P.: Virtual reality challenges in education and training. Int. J. Learn. Teach. **3**, 33–37 (2017). https://doi.org/10.18178/ijlt.3.1.33-37
17. Vogt, A., Babel, F., Hock, P., Baumann, M., Seufert, T.: Prompting in-depth learning in immersive virtual reality: impact of an elaboration prompt on developing a mental model. Comput. Educ. **171** (2021). https://doi.org/10.1016/j.compedu.2021.104235
18. Wu, S., Wang, R., Wang, J.: Campus virtual tour system based on cylindric panorama (2005)
19. Yeung, C., Kan, C., Bradford, J., Wong, R.: Campus guided tour vr system for the university of hong kong pp. 77–81 (1998)
20. Zhang, T., Kaber, D., Hsiang, S.: Characterisation of mental models in a virtual reality-based multitasking scenario using measures of situation awareness. Theoretical Issues in Ergonomics Science **11**(1–2), 99–118 (2010). https://doi.org/10.1080/14639220903010027

Usability Analysis for Blockchain-Based Applications

Sanil S. Gandhi$^{(\boxtimes)}$, Yogesh N. Patil, Laxman D. Netak,
and Harsha R. Gaikwad

Department of Computer Engineering,
Dr. Babasaheb Ambedkar Technological University, Lonere-Raigad 402103, India
{ssgandhi,ynpatil,ldnetak,harsha.gaikwad}@dbatu.ac.in

Abstract. In this digitization phase, several new applications are developed by developers and used by end-users to complete their needs. But very few applications remain popular among users depending on the functional working of an application, such as the mobility of the application, its user-friendliness, pop-up advertisements. The Non-functional requirements such as space required in the memory, security aspects fulfill by application, etc. Blockchain Technology is an emerging trend in the market, and many developers are developing enormous applications in various domains. Human-Computer Interaction (HCI) will play a significant role in designing a graphical user interface. In this paper, we will discuss the opportunities and challenges faced by the developers while working on the different projects.

Keywords: Blockchain technology · Human computer interaction ·
Graphical user interface · Usability · Security · Distributed ledger
technologies

1 Introduction

The focus of all developers is to provide a sophisticated graphical user interface of an application to end-users. It plays a crucial role as the end-users using such applications who are either be literate or illiterate. The application must be easy to use for novice users, and all functionalities of the application must be available within a single click. The main focus of human-computer interaction is to design a suitable and easy-to-use graphical user interface (GUI) between the end-user and system. Adaptive systems will help to improve the usability of the system by determining essential characteristics of an end-user that affect harmony between the end-user and the system [4].

The term usability means the how easily and effectively stakeholders learn the new developed system and complete their goals efficiently. Effective, efficient, engaging, error tolerant, and easy to learn are the main characteristics that system must to satisfy and user-centered design leads to increase the stakeholders

© Springer Nature Switzerland AG 2022
J.-H. Kim et al. (Eds.): IIICI 2021, LNCS 13184, pp. 349–360, 2022.
https://doi.org/10.1007/978-3-030-98404-5_33

engagement with the system. Usability analysis helps to improve the various aspects of the system which are remains not utilize by the stakeholders.

The name HCI is composed of three different components, the first is human who is the end-user, the second is a computer that takes command from the end-user and works on it as programmed, and last is how the end-user interacts with the particular software installed on the computer. HCI assists in creating innovative interfaces and designs that boost productivity, enhance user experience and minimize the risks in systems. Eskandari et al. [13] studied key management of bitcoin wallet and concluded that due to lack of key management issues, bitcoin users lose their bitcoins due to poor usability of the bitcoin wallet, lack of knowledge, and malicious exchange of the bitcoins.

HCI researchers and designers aim to improve the usability of the computers or the various applications as per the needs of end-users. As HCI is related to the multidisciplinary science [6] such as Computer Science, Cognitive Science, Social Psychology, Ergonomics/Human Factors, Linguistics, Engineering & Design, etc. disciplines has significant contributions to HCI. HCI is a continuously evolving field as new user experience (UX) technologies come into the market from time to time [36].

HCI community is trying to provide a just and decent life to society by finding rigid solutions to the different problems and transparency in the system [15] using emerging technologies. Blockchain Technology plays a prominent role in the public domains such as education, healthcare, governance, and financial services that increases trust where people have less faith and involvement in the system [7].

The blockchain is an emerging technology, and its eminence characteristics overcome the pitfalls found in working projects or applications. And, it leads to the development of the applications for the various domains known as *DApps*. Many researchers from industries and academia are working on how to transform, collaborate, trust and perform transactions between the peers in a distributed network using blockchain as a 'General Purpose Technology' [24]. All the blockchain-based applications are in their infancy stage. Smart contracts (evolution of Blockchain 2.0) will provide an opportunity to designers as smart contracts trigger a particular action when meeting a specified condition.

It is a challenging task for the HCI researchers and designers to design a system with proper GUI so, stakeholders easily and efficiently interact with system in their day-to-day life to accomplish the various goals. Following questions must be concerned by developers when designing the system using several emerging technologies: Who is the end-user? Is there a need for emerging technologies to implement an application?

According to the most recent news published on July 15, 2021, in The Economics Times, 15 banks in India are implementing blockchain technology to eliminate paperwork and reduce transaction time for various bank activities. So, in such delegated applications, security must take into consideration. *HCISec* concerned with improving the usability of security features in the stakeholders' application. Security problems can tackle by solving the usability issues that arise due to human factors [10].

In the paper, author [11] discussed the information security aspects which is to be examined during designing and developing the user interface for the end-users. The BitBarista [35], coffee wending application was designed using the Internet of Things (IoT) and Blockchain Technology. The drawback is the interaction between an end-user and the system is not user-friendly for the particular functionality of the system.

The paper is organized as follows: In next Sect. 2, we discuss the fundamentals of the blockchain technology and findings of researchers about how and in what manner HCI might play the major role in designing the various blockchain-based applications describe in the Sect. 3. Section 4 describes the fundamental principles of HCI to design blockchain-based applications from an end-user perspective. The Sect. 5 gives the details about the usability methods for a blockchain-based application. And, in the last Sect. 6, we conclude that how to cope up with the issues and challenges that arose in the blockchain-based applications from a usability and security point of view.

2 Background

In this section, we will discuss the basic fundamentals about the blockchain technology and various conceptual things that makes blockchain more prominent technology.

2.1 Blockchain Technology

Blockchain is a share and immutable database in which data or transactions stored on the blocks and encrypted blocks are chained together sequentially. Bitcoin [29] is used as a Cryptocurrency which is the first application designed using the blockchain platform. Nodes or blocks as shown in Fig. 1 save the transactions performed by end-users in append-only mode. An adversary can not alter or delete the previous transactions or data as a whole application running on the consensus mechanism. Also, several transactions are stored in a block as per the maximum size of the block, and block size can be varied as required in the application.

The First block of the blockchain does not consist of any transaction data. All fields are initialized to either null or the default values. Except previous hash value is set to default value and block called as a *genesis block*. Decentralized, immutable, anonymity, and transparency are the characteristics of blockchain technology. The above characteristics make the system fully proof, efficient and eliminate most of the pitfalls that arose in the traditional and Internet-based centralized systems. These are described as a given below:

1. **Decentralized:** Due to single-point failure in the centralized system, many developers prefer a decentralized model to save the data. Every node in the

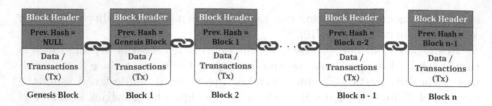

Fig. 1. Basic blockchain diagram

system saves all available data. Each transaction is validated by nodes before appending the block to the blockchain, which eliminates the need for a third party or inter-mediator.

2. **Immutable:** This characteristic guarantees that all the data in the system remains unchanged. If an adversary has more than 51% control of the system is then only the adversary can alter or delete the data or transaction. The key element behind this is cryptographic hash functions.

3. **Anonymity:** With the help of a public/private key-pair address, the original identity of the user conceals from the rest of the world. These characteristics are convenient in the applications such as fund transfer or e-voting.

4. **Transparency:** Anyone can participate in the network and view all the transactions present on the system. It helps to verify and validate the transaction in the blockchain.

Depending on how the data or transactions of the application are accessed by the end-user or types of network required, the developer prefers public blockchain, private blockchain, and consortium blockchain. Any node that can join or leave the network is the public (permissionless) blockchain, while it needs prior permission to join and leave the network is the private (permissioned) blockchain. Bitcoin [29] is an example of public blockchain, whereas Hyperledger [2], MultiChain [17] are examples of private blockchain.

As technology changes rapidly, Swan [41] described the evolution of the blockchain versions move from 1.0 to 3.0. *Blockchain 1.0* implemented the digital currency using the distributed ledger known as a cryptocurrency, i.e., Bitcoin. A smart contract defines code which executed automatically as the particular condition is satisfied. It is mostly used in the Ethereum [5] blockchain and part of the evolution of *Blockchain 2.0*. *Blockchain 3.0* describes decentralized applications known as *DApps*. In *DApps*, there is a user interface as frontend, and that calls to any function running in the backend on a decentralized network. And, currently, *Blockchain 4.0* proposed the various solutions to the business problems that arose in the *Industry 4.0*.

Distributed Ledger, Cryptography, Consensus Protocol, and Smart Contract are pillar elements to implement the blockchain technology. *Distributed Ledger (DL)* used to store the data or transactions on all the nodes which are part of the network. If anyone misleads to the previous transaction on the particular block leads to a change in all the consecutive transactions present in the blocks. *Cryptographic* algorithms such as the Paillier encryption [43], Homomorphic encryption [20], Ring signature, Blind Signature, as well as Zero-Knowledge Proof (ZKP) [31] etc. are preferred to secure systems.

Consensus algorithms used to reach a mutual agreement about the current state of the database or ledger. It helps to eliminate the double-spending attack. Bitcoin [29] uses Proof-of-Work (PoW), Ethereum [5] shifted from PoW to Proof-of-Stake (PoS), and Hyperledger prefers Practical Byzantine Fault Tolerance (PBFT) as a consensus algorithm.

As per business specifications, various consensus algorithms such as Proof of Activity (PoA), Proof of Weight (PoW), Proof of Importance (PoI), Delegated Proof of Stake (DPoS), Proof of Elapsed Time (PoET), Proof of Capacity (PoC), etc. use as per the system requirement. *Smart Contracts* executes a particular event when the system meets the predefined condition specified in the contract. Solidity, Vyper, Golang, etc., are some of the programming languages to write smart contracts.

3   Related Work

Most of the articles, research papers, or Journals [8,12,14], written by the industries or academia described the challenges and opportunities to HCI researchers in this emerging technology. In the paper [26], authors described various projects from the different domains such as education, energy, finance sector, etc. The authors also mentioned how blockchain technology would be beneficial to tackle loopholes in several areas. These all projects are in the initial phase of development. The short paper written by Foth [14] discussed how blockchain can provide opportunities and designing challenges to interaction designers. Harrison et al. [19] proposed the three paradigms of HCI that help to identify different problems and simple methods to overcome them.

The various applications of Blockchain Technology are systematically summarised into the topology [12]. For this, authors [12] analyzed about 203 different blockchain applications from the public as well as private domains and finally conclude with where to researchers have to focus on HCI methodologies by suggesting four conceptual and methodological challenges.

PowerShare [40], a peer-to-peer (P2P), decentralized energy trading system inspired the HCI community by addressing issues raised by the people in embedded complexity of distributed ledger technologies (DLT) and also, lack of understanding between DLT and peer-to-peer energy trading. In the paper [34], authors discussed and mapped blockchain elements to the functional requirements of the educational system of the University, but not describe about the how end user will access and utilize the system.

Blockchain technology has aggravated the new research areas which can bring revolution in the digital economy. Due to the complex structure of mental models of blockchain technology, it is difficult to understand. To uphold the architecture and key factors of blockchain technology, authors [25] proposed BlocKit, which is a three-dimensional physical model developed after evaluating 15 experienced bitcoin [29] users. In recent years, HCI researchers have increasingly contributed to designing physical objects, devices, sensors, etc., securely keep user's bitcoin addresses. The BlocKit is an innovative artifact that will inspire HCI researchers to engage in designing infrastructures for blockchain.

The key elements of blockchain such as anonymity, decentralized, and immutable ledger lead to new development and designing of HCI model as the previous model will work on it is questionable [39]. The third party or governing body is responsible to establish trust among the end-users in the centralized system but, in the decentralized system how to build trust among the end-users.

In most of the applications, developers are concerned only with user satisfaction by providing an easy-to-use graphical user interface but, not concerned about possible threats that remain unhindered during the development of the system. The common usability issues present in the bitcoin wallet are identified by applying the analytical cognitive walk-through usability inspection method [28].

In [42], online, open-source, and end-to-end verifiable voting platform based on blockchain technology. A benefit to using blockchain for voting purposes is the voter can audit his casted vote after the voting and at the time of the counting process. The voter has first registered himself on the system and, GUI for registration to casting the voting process is cumbersome and time-consuming. Also, the users from the non-technical ground will need the middleman to perform the initial configuration of the system. *BurstIQ* is a data management application developed for the healthcare and medical domain using a blockchain platform to save patient's health data, which is helpful for research purposes. This system will generate plenty of data, and blockchain characteristics secure patient health data.

Kainda et al. [23] proposed the security-usability threat model highlights critical factors related to non-functional requirements such as usability and security of a developed system. The author described various threat scenarios and usage scenarios that analyze, understand, and identify possible threats to the system's usability and security. In the paper [27], authors studied the two largest Bio-metric systems, i.e., India's *AADHAR* and China's Social Credit System, and found what are pitfalls in both systems. From the study, the author suggested blockchain to overcome pitfalls and opportunities for HCI designers and researchers.

Authors of [21] proposed a simple graphical user interface designed to perform pivotal functions of the *MultiChain* [17] platform to increase the usability of the system as it is easy to operate to people who are not technically sound. In [38], authors described the HCI research framework based on theoretical viewpoints to analyze trust in the Bitcoin [29].

Cila N. et al. [9] copes with design dilemmas as a solution to the distributed ledger technology (DTL) applied in the governance of artificial material commons. In this, author [9] suggested a framework comprising three processes and six design challenges that can help in the creation of local platforms for commons-based resource management by balancing opposing values and identified the lack of design principles for DLT-based platforms.

4   HCI Principles from Blockchain Point of View

As humans are developing or designing the system and services utilized by an end-user is also human. If only machines are communicating with each other, then the system definitely will foolproof the system. But, the end-user is a human who can find out loopholes present in the system by trial and error method. So, it is nearly impossible to design a foolproof system.

Industry 4.0 operating on complete automation processes in development phases, authors [37] proposed a Human Work Interaction Design (HWID) framework for such systems. In automation, robots or machines support human workers to complete tough and heavy tasks. So, there must be required smooth interaction between robots or machines and human workers.

In the development process, researchers or academia focused on issues such as data integrity, scalability, privacy, etc. but ignore the usability of the system [18]. Usability and HCI maintain the harmony of the system under development by enhancing system functionalities and assure that system fulfills the users' needs. Usability specification measures the success of the system and keeps the development of the system on the right track. HCI researchers should merge the HCI and usability in their sustainable design to improve the performance of portable devices and emerging technologies and meet users' needs [22].

4.1   Trade-off between Usability and Security

To design or develop an application or a system, usability and security principles play a vital role. Both these principles work exactly converse with each other. This means, if the designer wants higher usability of the system, it leads to compromise in the security features and vice versa. To tackle such, authors [30] proposed the use of usable security patterns to manage the trade-off between security and usability. The systematic comparison between credit/debit cards and bitcoin users was studied by [1] and showed what kind of the relationship holds by them between usability and security.

Usability principles help to developers to design a effective and easy to handle system so, novice user to complete the desired task. Flexibility and robustness qualities highlight the usability of a system, be considering user capabilities and limitations. Efficiency, Effectiveness, and satisfaction are non-functional parameters that evaluate the usability of the system.

Learnability [32] is the most crucial characteristic of usability. It means the system must be easy to learn and operate for novice people. Donald Norman [33] entitled six usability principles for the decent user interface are visibility, feedback, constraint, mapping, consistency, and affordance.

Security means to what extend the system is safe from external attackers. Numerous security features provided via GUI or via interfaces of external devices such as bio-metric detection, or the verification through message or mail, CAPTCHA (Completely Automated Public Turing Test to Tell Computers and Humans Apart), etc. reduce security attacks, such as Sybil attack, Denial-of-Service (DoS) attack, Man-in-the-middle attack, etc.

A large amount of patient health data is generated in the healthcare domain. Blockchain may address the data usability and security issues as the data collected from the different wearable, health trackers, and medical devices present at home [3]. Glomann et al. [16] identified solutions to specified four adoption problems, among which one is usability from a human-centered perspective.

Blockchain is an emerging technology and to develop an application uses different new tools (blockchain wallet or metamask, truffle, etc.), applications, or devices. Cryptokitty is a blockchain-based game in which a player must complete a series of activities such as installing metamask (a cryptocurrency wallet), purchasing bitcoin, and transferring it to a game creator. The process of performing such tasks are lengthy and time-consuming.

At the early stage of blockchain, it was challenging to design a smooth and complete working system with a sophisticated graphical user interface. The GUI helps to speed up functionalities of the system with great accuracy and increases efficiency as accomplish tasks within a stipulated period. In this article, we attempt to solve the numerous difficulties encountered by the end-user of the blockchain-based system.

5 Case Study of a Blockchain-Based Application

In this section, we analyze the usability of one of the blockchain-based applications from the different domains. We will consider several parameters such as mobility support, support to local languages (localization), context-sensitive (help), dynamic organization of user interface (UI) elements, voice-operated UI, trading to trace out the usability of an application. People from different parts of the world who use the application which must support all the local languages. Also, most people are using a mobile phone to perform various tasks, so every application should have a mobile-based application.

We consider Voatz from E-Governance, WholeCare from Healthcare, Gemini from Finance, and Civic from Social domains. For these applications, we map the parameters of usability with each of the application as describe in the Table 1.

Table 1. Non-functional requirements of existing blockchain-based e-voting systems

Name of blockchain-based application	Usability parameters					
	Mobility support	Localization support	Dynamic organization of UI element	Voice operated UI	Context sensitive	Trading
WholeCare	x				x	
Voatz	x	x			x	
Civic	x			x		x
Gemini	x			x	x	x

6 Conclusion

The first blockchain application Bitcoin make revolutionary changes in the digital economy. The process of registration on a bitcoin wallet is tedious and as cryptographic credentials are onerous to remember, need to keep it securely either in the paper or file format or in plug and play device. Therefore, the system's workflow must be user-friendly, and the system is easily accessed or operate by the stakeholders. Designers or developers have balanced weights to both the usability and security of the system.

Numerous applications in the domain of government and education sectors are in the development phase and the designer or developer has to design the system by keeping in mind non-technical end-users. Even, blockchain technology has grown dramatically, still end user-facing usability problems and there is not an actual working system based on blockchain part of a day to day life.

In this paper, we tried to find out the various challenges and opportunities for HCI researchers or designers from a blockchain point of view. This paper presents the state of the research of human-computer interaction for blockchain technology, and how to implement or design such a system from the end-user perspective.

References

1. Alshamsi, A., Andras, P.P.: User perception of bitcoin usability and security across novice users. Int. J. Hum. Comput. Stud. **126**, 94–110 (2019). https://doi.org/10.1016/j.ijhcs.2019.02.004
2. Androulaki, E., et al: Hyperledger fabric: a distributed operating system for permissioned blockchains. In: Proceedings of the Thirteenth EuroSys Conference. EuroSys '18. Association for Computing Machinery, New York (2018). https://doi.org/10.1145/3190508.3190538
3. Baumann, S., et al.: Implementing blockchain to enhance usability of patient-generated data. In: Proceedings of the Human Factors and Ergonomics Society Annual Meeting, vol. 63, no. 1, pp. 1344–1348 (2019). https://doi.org/10.1177/1071181319631275
4. Benyon, D.: Adaptive systems: a solution to usability problems. User Model. User-Adap. Inter. **3**, 65–87 (1993). https://doi.org/10.1007/BF01099425
5. Buterin, V., et al.: A next-generation smart contract and decentralized application platform
6. Carroll, J.M.: HCI Models, Theories, and Frameworks: Toward a Multidisciplinary Science. Morgan Kaufmann Publishers Inc., San Francisco (2003)
7. Chiang, C.W., et al.: Understanding interface design and mobile money perceptions in Latin America. In: Proceedings of the 8th Latin American Conference on Human-Computer Interaction, CLIHC '17. Association for Computing Machinery, New York (2017). https://doi.org/10.1145/3151470.3151473
8. Chiang, C.W., Betanzos, E., Savage, S.: The challenges and trends of deploying blockchain in the real world for the users' need. J. Cyberspace Stud. **3**(2), 119–128 (2019). https://doi.org/10.22059/jcss.2019.72454

9. Cila, N., Ferri, G., de Waal, M., Gloerich, I., Karpinski, T.: The blockchain and the commons: Dilemmas in the design of local platforms. In: Proceedings of the 2020 CHI Conference on Human Factors in Computing Systems, CHI '20, pp. 1–14. Association for Computing Machinery, New York (2020). https://doi.org/10.1145/3313831.3376660

10. Cranor, L., Garfinkel, S.: Security and Usability. O'Reilly Media Inc., Sebastopol (2005)

11. Eloff, M.M., Eloff, J.H.P.: Human computer interaction: an information security perspectives. In: Ghonaimy, M.A., El-Hadidi, M.T., Aslan, H.K. (eds.) Security in the Information Society. IAICT, vol. 86, pp. 535–545. Springer, Boston, MA (2002). https://doi.org/10.1007/978-0-387-35586-3_42

12. Elsden, C., Manohar, A., Briggs, J., Harding, M., Speed, C., Vines, J.: Making sense of blockchain applications: a typology for HCI, pp. 1–14. Association for Computing Machinery, New York (2018). https://doi.org/10.1145/3173574.3174032

13. Eskandari, S., Barrera, D., Stobert, E., Clark, J.: A first look at the usability of bitcoin key management. In: Proceedings 2015 Workshop on Usable Security (2015). https://doi.org/10.14722/usec.2015.23015

14. Foth, M.: The promise of blockchain technology for interaction design. In: Proceedings of the 29th Australian Conference on Computer-Human Interaction. OZCHI '17, pp. 513–517. Association for Computing Machinery (2017). https://doi.org/10.1145/3152771.3156168

15. Foth, M., Tomitsch, M., Satchell, C., Haeusler, M.H.: From users to citizens: some thoughts on designing for polity and civics. In: Proceedings of the Annual Meeting of the Australian Special Interest Group for Computer Human Interaction, OzCHI '15, pp. 623–633. Association for Computing Machinery, New York (2015). https://doi.org/10.1145/2838739.2838769

16. Glomann, L., Schmid, M., Kitajewa, N.: Improving the blockchain user experience - an approach to address blockchain mass adoption issues from a human-centred perspective. In: Ahram, T. (ed.) AHFE 2019. AISC, vol. 965, pp. 608–616. Springer, Cham (2020). https://doi.org/10.1007/978-3-030-20454-9_60

17. Greenspan, G.: Multichain private blockchain-white paper, pp. 57–60 (2015). http://www.multichain.com/download/MultiChain-White-Paper.pdf

18. Habibzadeh, H., Nussbaum, B.H., Anjomshoa, F., Kantarci, B., Soyata, T.: A survey on cybersecurity, data privacy, and policy issues in cyber-physical system deployments in smart cities. Sustain. Urban Areas 50, 101660 (2019). https://doi.org/10.1016/j.scs.2019.101660

19. Harrison, S., Tatar, D., Sengers, P.: The three paradigms of HCI. In: Alt. Chi. Session at the SIGCHI Conference on Human Factors in Computing Systems, San Jose, California, USA, pp. 1–18 (2007)

20. Hirt, M., Sako, K.: Efficient receipt-free voting based on homomorphic encryption. In: Preneel, B. (ed.) EUROCRYPT 2000. LNCS, vol. 1807, pp. 539–556. Springer, Heidelberg (2000). https://doi.org/10.1007/3-540-45539-6_38

21. Hossain, T., Mohiuddin, T., Hasan, A.M.S., Islam, M.N., Hossain, S.A.: Designing and developing graphical user interface for the MultiChain blockchain: towards incorporating HCI in blockchain. In: Abraham, A., Piuri, V., Gandhi, N., Siarry, P., Kaklauskas, A., Madureira, A. (eds.) ISDA 2020. AISC, vol. 1351, pp. 446–456. Springer, Cham (2021). https://doi.org/10.1007/978-3-030-71187-0_41

22. Issa, T., Isaias, P.: Usability and Human Computer Interaction (HCI). In: Issa, T., Isaias, P. (eds.) Sustainable Design, pp. 19–36. Springer, London (2015). https://doi.org/10.1007/978-1-4471-6753-2_2

23. Kainda, R., Fléchais, I., Roscoe, A.: Security and usability: analysis and evaluation. In: 2010 International Conference on Availability, Reliability and Security, pp. 275–282 (2010). https://doi.org/10.1109/ARES.2010.77

24. Kane, E.: Is blockchain a general purpose technology? Available at SSRN 2932585 (2017). https://dx.doi.org/10.2139/ssrn.2932585

25. Khairuddin, I.E., Sas, C., Speed, C.: BlocKit: a physical kit for materializing and designing for blockchain infrastructure. In: Proceedings of the 2019 on Designing Interactive Systems Conference, DIS '19, pp. 1449–1462. Association for Computing Machinery, New York (2019). https://doi.org/10.1145/3322276.3322370

26. Kiwelekar, A.W., Gandhi, S.S., Netak, L.D., Deosarkar, S.B.: Use cases of blockchain technology for humanitarian engineering, pp. 143–163. Telecommunications, Institution of Engineering and Technology (2020)

27. Manohar, A., Briggs, J.: Identity management in the age of blockchain 3.0 (2018). https://chi2018.acm.org/. 2018 ACM Conference on Human Factors in Computing Systems, CHI 2018; Conference date: 21–04-2018 Through 26–04-2018

28. Moniruzzaman, Md., Chowdhury, F., Ferdous, M.S.: Examining usability issues in blockchain-based cryptocurrency wallets. In: Bhuiyan, T., Rahman, M.M., Ali, M.A. (eds.) ICONCS 2020. LNICST, vol. 325, pp. 631–643. Springer, Cham (2020). https://doi.org/10.1007/978-3-030-52856-0_50

29. Nakamoto, S.: Bitcoin: a peer-to-peer electronic cash system. Decentral. Bus. Rev. 21260 (2008)

30. Naqvi, B., Porras, J., Oyedeji, S., Ullah, M.: Aligning security, usability, user experience: a pattern approach. In: Human Computer Interaction and Emerging Technologies: Adjunct Proceedings from, p. 267 (2020)

31. Neff, C.A.: A verifiable secret shuffle and its application to e-voting. In: Proceedings of the 8th ACM Conference on Computer and Communications Security, CCS '01, pp. 116–125. Association for Computing Machinery, New York (2001). https://doi.org/10.1145/501983.502000

32. Nielsen, J.: Usability inspection methods. In: Conference Companion on Human Factors in Computing Systems, CHI '94, pp. 413–414. Association for Computing Machinery, New York (1994). https://doi.org/10.1145/259963.260531

33. Norman, D.A.: The Design of Everyday Things. Basic Books Inc., New York (2002)

34. Patil, Y.N., Kiwelekar, A.W., Netak, L.D., Deosarkar, S.B.: A decentralized and autonomous model to administer university examinations. In: Lee, S.-W., Singh, I., Mohammadian, M. (eds.) Blockchain Technology for IoT Applications. BT, pp. 119–134. Springer, Singapore (2021). https://doi.org/10.1007/978-981-33-4122-7_6

35. Pschetz, L., Tallyn, E., Gianni, R., Speed, C.: Bitbarista: exploring perceptions of data transactions in the internet of things. In: Proceedings of the 2017 CHI Conference on Human Factors in Computing Systems, CHI '17, pp. 2964–2975. Association for Computing Machinery, New York (2017). https://doi.org/10.1145/3025453.3025878

36. Rogers, Y.: The changing face of human-computer interaction in the age of ubiquitous computing. In: Holzinger, A., Miesenberger, K. (eds.) USAB 2009. LNCS, vol. 5889, pp. 1–19. Springer, Heidelberg (2009). https://doi.org/10.1007/978-3-642-10308-7_1

37. Saadati, P., Abdelnour-Nocera, J., Clemmensen, T.: Proposed system for a socio-technical design framework for improved user collaborations with automation technologies. In: Abdelnour Nocera, J., et al. (eds.) INTERACT 2019. LNCS, vol. 11930, pp. 59–67. Springer, Cham (2020). https://doi.org/10.1007/978-3-030-46540-7_7

38. Sas, C., Khairuddin, I.E.: Exploring trust in bitcoin technology: a framework for HCI research. In: Proceedings of the Annual Meeting of the Australian Special Interest Group for Computer Human Interaction, OzCHI '15, pp. 338–342. Association for Computing Machinery, New York (2015). https://doi.org/10.1145/2838739.2838821

39. Sas, C., Khairuddin, I.E.: Design for trust: an exploration of the challenges and opportunities of bitcoin users. In: Proceedings of the 2017 CHI Conference on Human Factors in Computing Systems. CHI '17, pp. 6499–6510. Association for Computing Machinery, New York (2017). https://doi.org/10.1145/3025453.3025886

40. Scuri, S., Tasheva, G., Barros, L., Nunes, N.J.: An HCI perspective on distributed ledger technologies for peer-to-peer energy trading. In: Lamas, D., Loizides, F., Nacke, L., Petrie, H., Winckler, M., Zaphiris, P. (eds.) INTERACT 2019. LNCS, vol. 11748, pp. 91–111. Springer, Cham (2019). https://doi.org/10.1007/978-3-030-29387-1_6

41. Swan, M.: Blockchain: Blueprint for a New Economy, 1st edn. O'Reilly Media Inc., Sebastopol (2015)

42. Follow My Vote: Follow my vote (2017). https://followmyvote.com/blockchain-voting-the-end-to-end-process/. Accessed 01 Feb 2017

43. Xia, Z., Schneider, S.A., Heather, J., Traoré, J.: Analysis, improvement and simplification of prêt à voter with Paillier encryption. In: Proceedings of the Conference on Electronic Voting Technology, EVT'08. USENIX Association, USA (2008)

Permission-Educator: App for Educating Users About Android Permissions

Akshay Mathur[1], Ethan Ewoldt[2], Quamar Niyaz[2], Ahmad Javaid[1(✉)], and Xiaoli Yang[2]

[1] The University of Toledo, Toledo, OH 43606, USA
{akshay.mathur,ahmad.javaid}@utoledo.edu
[2] Purdue University Northwest, Hammond, IN 46323, USA
{eewoldt,qniyaz,yangx}@pnw.edu

Abstract. Cyberattacks and malware infestation are issues that surround most operating systems (OS) these days. In smartphones, Android OS is more susceptible to malware infection. Although Android has introduced several mechanisms to avoid cyberattacks, including Google Play Protect, dynamic permissions, and sign-in control notifications, cyberattacks on Android-based phones are prevalent and continuously increasing. Most malware apps use critical permissions to access resources and data to compromise smartphone security. One of the key reasons behind this is the lack of knowledge for the usage of permissions in users. In this paper, we introduce *Permission-Educator*, a cloud-based service to educate users about the permissions associated with the installed apps in an Android-based smartphone. We developed an Android app as a client that allows users to categorize the installed apps on their smartphones as system or store apps. The user can learn about permissions for a specific app and identify the app as benign or malware through the interaction of the client app with the cloud service. We integrated the service with a web server that facilitates users to upload any Android application package file, i.e. *apk*, to extract information regarding the Android app and display it to the user.

Keywords: Smartphone security · Android · Malware detection · App permissions · Education

1 Introduction

To combat against the rise in malware in operating systems (OS), system developers fix vulnerabilities in their systems through regular updates. With each new version of Android (OS), Google also fixes the vulnerabilities discovered in the previous versions to make it more resilient against cyberattacks and ensure the security and privacy of its users. The first line of defense in Android is Google Play Protect that identifies any malware apps on Google Play Store. However, there are several third-party app stores where malware apps can still be found. Another major contributor to its security is the permission-based resources access system, which prevents apps from gaining unauthorized access

© Springer Nature Switzerland AG 2022
J.-H. Kim et al. (Eds.): IHCI 2021, LNCS 13184, pp. 361–371, 2022.
https://doi.org/10.1007/978-3-030-98404-5_34

to resources such as camera, microphone, and internal file storage. Even with this dual-layer defense mechanism, malware attacks are still prevalent in Android.

In the permission-based system, each permission holds rights to access a specific resource. Therefore, an application needs the user's consent to use certain resources. These permissions are categorized into four levels of protection: *i) Normal, ii) Dangerous, iii) Signature*, and *iv) Signature|Privileged* [1]. Permissions categorized as *Dangerous* are the most sensitive among all of them as they manage users' personal information and they might compromise the security and privacy of users when used with malicious intent. Hence, user approval is requested for these permissions,e.g. CALL_PHONE permission that enables an app to make phone calls, or CAMERA permission to give an app access to the device camera.

A naive user might be oblivious to whether a permission is requested by a benign or malware app during installation. Malware developers employ several techniques to hide the actual intent of a malware app and deceive users by making it appeared as benign. Malware apps gain access to smartphone's resources through over-claimed permissions – requesting more permissions than required [2], drive-by-download – a malicious download link [3], or permission escalation – using other permissions used by other apps through intents [4]. Malware such as Trojan, ransomware, spyware, and worms take advantage of an uninformed user about Android's permission system and compromise user's data. Therefore, a need arises to educate users about Android permissions.

In this paper, we present a cloud-based service called *Permission-Educator* to help users understand Android permissions and their usage in apps. Permission-Educator provides an Android app as a client using which a user can select an app and see the permissions associated with the installed app on the smartphone. A web interface is developed to allow users to upload Android apps for the same purpose from a desktop system. We have also integrated Permission-Educator with an in-house developed malware detection system, NATICUSdroid [5], which can analyze an installed app's permissions and identify the app as benign or malware. The contributions of this work are as follows:

1. A cloud-based service, Permission-Educator, is developed to educate users about various permissions associated with the installed apps, with the motive to educate naive users about the importance of permissions with respect to data privacy.
2. An Android app and a website are developed as clients of the cloud-based service. The app displays all the installed apps on a user's smartphone, and the web client allows users to upload an Android *apk* file from a browser to view permissions and their purpose and identify whether the app is malware or not.
3. We bring a recently *in-house developed* malware detection system (NATICUSdroid) in production by integrating it with Permission-Educator to identify an app as benign or malware. NATICUSdroid uses the permissions of an app as features and determines whether the app is benign or malicious.

Towards this direction, the paper is structured as follows. Section 2 provides a review of related works. Section 3 and 4 discuss the architecture of Permission-

Educator and give an insight on its functionality, respectively. Section 5 concludes the paper along with the possible future works.

2 Related Work

Until Android Kitkat (Android release 4.4), apps were installed using a "take-it or leave-it" approach, where a user could either install an app with its all requested permissions or deny the installation. The app would display information on all necessary dangerous category permissions to the user before the choice is made. From Android Marshmallow (release 6.0) onward, users can either grant permission or deny it while running the app based on their judgment. One could think this choice could prevent malicious intents of apps. However, it has not made a significant change for users [6].

Another change made to facilitate this new method of granting permissions is to create permission groups. For example, GET_ACCOUNTS, READ_CONTACTS, and WRITE_CONTACTS, all are being covered by the app's request to access *Contacts*, i.e., granting all through one. While this provides a choice for granting permissions during run-time over the "take-it or leave-it" approach, the grouping may grant permissions to the app that users may not want, but just because they are in the requested permissions group. As a result of this grouping, earlier, an app needed to request solely READ_PHONE_STATE permission to find if a call is in progress or not, could now also gain access to CALL_PHONE permission that allows making phone calls without the user's knowledge. Such functionality makes this security module translucent for users as opposed to the prior take-it or leave-it model, which was more transparent regarding individual permissions [7].

While a simple solution to this could be to provide a list of permissions granted in the permission group, it would still not solve the existing problem, i.e., the user's lack of understanding of permissions and their purposes. While the permission models have changed vulnerabilities are still there and user's understanding of what all a permission does, attitude towards different permissions, and apps that request access have not varied considerably. Surveys conducted after Android Marshmallow demonstrate that even if a naive user is constantly 'nagged' by the app to grant a permission the user would give in one day without having a full understanding of them. Such a behavior of the user makes one even more vulnerable to malware infection [7].

Felt et al. surveyed 333 participants and reported that only 17% of individuals paid attention to permissions while installing an application, and only 6.6% (22 of 333) participants completely understood the utility of permissions in general [8]. Ramachandran et al. found in their survey conducted with 478 people that around 63% participants do not review an app's requested permissions diligently. They also found that if a user has downloaded apps from a category before, they hint at what permissions that app can ask. This is why they felt "very comfortable" in downloading and installing a new app from a similar category [9]. This could be an issue as such users are at risk of downloading potential malware.

Several studies have been published to better help non-tech savvy users handle apps more safely. Oglaza et al. and Scoccia et al. attempt to automate the process of permission granting by learning what permissions the user accepts or denies and automatically grant or deny runtime permission pop-ups while installing new apps [10,11]. However, this could become counter-productive if the user is not familiar with permissions in apps and encourages the model to grant all permissions to any app, including malware, automatically. A few researchers attempt to use more mathematical-based models to predict an app's credibility and, in doing so, assist the user in knowing whether an app is potentially harmful or not before installation. While Hamed et al. in [12] focuses solely on permissions requested compared to the permissions already granted to other apps on a user's phone, Moussa et al. in [13] proposed the ACCUSE model that includes an app's rating and the number of downloads as a "popularity factor." ACCUSE was even found to outperform other malware detection models when tested against 868 malware apps. However, these models and apps do not assist users in understanding why an app is requesting specific permissions and what they are used for.

Although the studies mentioned above attempted to reduce malware app installation or help in handling run-time permission pop-ups, many users still

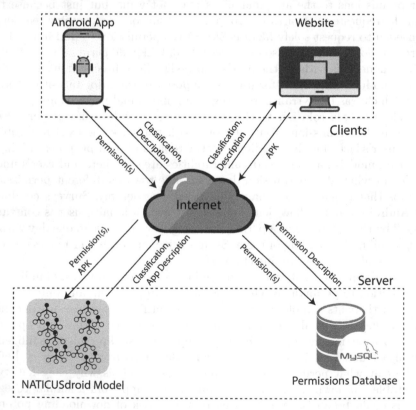

Fig. 1. Permission-Educator architecture

do not comprehend the purpose of permissions. This lack of knowledge can inhibit the previous efforts from providing sufficient protection. Consequently, *Permission-Educator* focuses on educating users about permissions and potential malware for installed apps on user's smartphones to make better decisions in granting permissions to apps.

3   Permission-Educator

We believe by educating naive users about Android and its permission-based security model we can contribute more towards preventing malware attacks. The purpose of permission educator is to inform and make users understand the role permissions play in safeguarding our data and privacy. This app not only gives a detailed description of what a permission intends to do, but also uses these permissions to detect any potential malware applications on the device. This is intended to give the user an idea as which permissions can play a crucial role in data privacy. The proposed web application also allows the user to check whether the apk at hand is malicious or not, and give a detailed description of the permissions used in apk. The source code of *Permission-Educator* is released on Github for adoption by the research community [14]. The overall architecture of Permission-Educator is shown in Fig. 1.

Algorithm 1: Pseudo code for separation of System and Store Apps

Input:

installedApps[]: **Apps installed on phone**

1 storeApps, storeAppNames, systemApps, systemAppNames = [];
2 **for** *appInfo in installedApps* **do**
3   label = pm.getApplicationLabel(appInfo);
4   **if** *appInfo.FLAGS == TRUE & FLAG_SYSTEM ==* 1 & *FLAG_UPDATED_SYSTEM_APP == 1* **then**
5   systemApps.add(appInfo);
6   systemAppNames.add(label);
7   **else if** *appInfo.FLAGS == TRUE & FLAG_SYSTEM ==* 0 & *FLAG_UPDATED_SYSTEM_APP == 0* **then**
8   storeApps.add(appInfo);
9   storeAppNames.add(label);

3.1   Clients

There are two clients of Permission-Educator – an Android app and a website – that communicate with the cloud service.

Android App: The app is developed on Android Studio and evaluated on Google Pixel 2 Android Emulator running Android 7.1.1. This app will be compatible with the latest Android versions as well. It categorizes all the apps in a user's smartphone into System and Store apps and allows them to select an app from one of these categories. *System apps* are pre-installed and signed with the manufacturer's certificate, while *Store apps* are usually installed from different app stores. This grouping was done for two reasons: i) It provides a simple method of sorting the apps into more organized groups by offering a simple user interface, and ii) it allows the user to see differences in the type, category, and frequency of permissions System and Store Apps. We separated the apps using `ApplicationInfo` class and its two flags – `FLAG_SYSTEM` and `FLAG_UPDATED_SYSTEM_APP`. The former is used to discern whether an app is installed in the device's system image, which, if set to true, the app was present when the user first booted up the device. The latter is then used to discern whether the application has been installed as an update to a built-in system application, which means system applications that the user can use. Algorithm 1 shows the pseudo-code for separating system and store apps.

The Website: The website was developed using HTML 5 and integrated with JavaScript for dynamic components. The purpose of the website is to provide a summary of any uploaded Android app (apk) from a Desktop system similar to VirusTotal [15]. It provides information for the permissions used in the app, the purpose and category of each permission, and the overall behavior of the app (malware or benign). We also used Jinja2 library [16] for integrating the website's front-end with the Python back-end.

3.2   Cloud Service

We have used a Flask server at the backend of cloud service. NATICUSdroid was hosted on the Flask server. The server receives all the queries using POST requests. The database to store permissions information was implemented using MySQL Server.

Flask Server: Flask server is a Python-based micro web framework. It is classified as a micro framework as it does not require particular tools or libraries [17]. We deployed a malware detection system, NATICUSdroid, on this server. The server receives permissions or apks from the clients and send the requested information in String format.

NATICUSdroid is an Android malware detection system that our research team has recently developed [5]. It is an adaptive, lightweight, fast, and robust ML-based framework developed to detect Android malware spreading from third-party Android app stores and phishing attacks. We analyzed an extensive and recent collection of benign and malicious Android apps and found that several 'dangerous' native and custom Android permissions were used frequently in both benign and malware apps. A rigorous feature selection process yielded a combination of 56 native and custom permissions, which were critical in the classification process. We used these as features for training a Random Forest Classifier that classifies apps with an accuracy of 96.9%. Since the classifier was trained using only permissions from both malware and benign apps, it provides the most appropriate insight on which apps could potentially be malicious.

MySQL Server: The MySQL server hosts a database that holds two tables – *permissions* and *missed_permissions*. The *permissions* table consists of three fields – perm_name, perm_about, and perm_category. perm_name stores permission name as mentioned in AndroidManifest.xml file, perm_about stores permission information retrieved from Android Developers website [1] and several other sources to have as much detail about the permission as possible, and perm_category stores permission category, i.e. *Normal, Dangerous, Signature,* and *Privileged.* The field perm_name is the primary key for this table. All three fields store string values. Once a permission is clicked on the client, the permission name is sent to the MySQL server, where a query retrieves the information and category of the permission and returns it to the client. *missed_permissions* table consists of two fields – perm_name and perm_category. Both the fields store string values and similar information as in the *permissions* table. This table is used for keeping a record of permissions which are used in apps, but do not exist in the *permissions* table, as there are several custom permissions whose information are not available easily.

4 Results

As Permission-Educator focuses on individuals who are not as fluent in Android technology and permissions, the goal is to provide a simple and informative User Interface (UI).

4.1 The App

A user interface (UI) overview of the Android client app is shown in Fig. 2. Figure 2a is the home screen of the app that provides the user a choice of selecting an app from two groups: one that comes pre-loaded on the phone during startup and whose files are not accessible by the user (System apps), and the other downloaded by the user from app stores or pre-downloaded apks that can be installed and uninstalled by the user (Store apps).

Figures 2b and 2d show the UI of "System Apps" and "Store Apps" activities. Once the user chooses system or store apps, a drop-down menu is provided listing all the apps in that category shown in Fig. 2d. Once an app is selected, we provide a clickable list of all the permissions used by the chosen app, as shown in Fig. 2b. This allows the user to see the details for each permission (either has access to or will request if it has not done so already) for the selected app. This is the first step in educating the user on app permissions, learning what an app has access to on their phone. However, that information alone is not sufficient. The users may not know the full context of every permission. For this reason, we provide the user with more information on what each permission means and what it lets the app access on the user's phone. To access this feature, the user needs to click

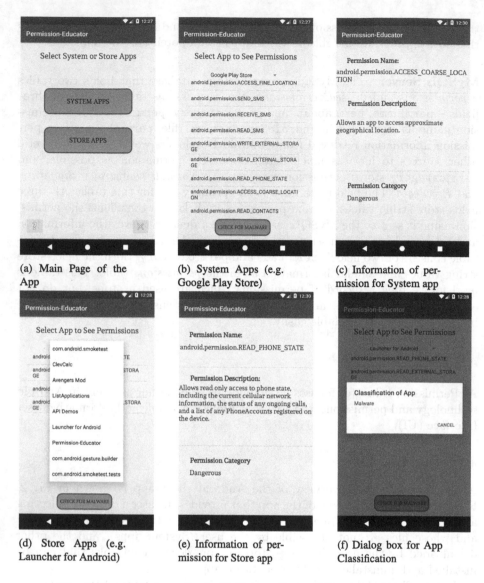

(a) Main Page of the App

(b) System Apps (e.g. Google Play Store)

(c) Information of permission for System app

(d) Store Apps (e.g. Launcher for Android)

(e) Information of permission for Store app

(f) Dialog box for App Classification

Fig. 2. User interfaces for Android app client of Permission-Educator

on the permission of their choice, and they are redirected to a new screen where the chosen permission's information is retrieved from the server database and displayed as shown in Figs. 2c and 2e.

Once the permissions of a chosen app are shown, a button at the bottom *Check for Malware* is provided that sends (when pressed) all the permissions mentioned in the app's `AndroidManifest.xml` file to the server. A permission vector is created by matching the final permissions set defined for NATICUSdroid to the permissions received at the server. This vector is then passed to the model, which classifies the permission vector as malicious or benign. The predicted class is sent back to the client, which is displayed to the user in a dialog box as shown in Fig. 2f.

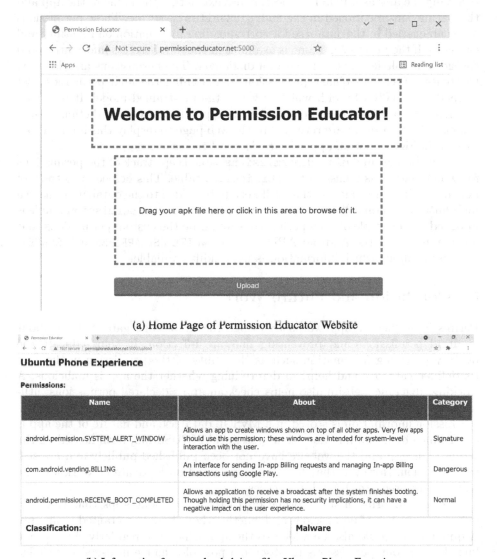

(a) Home Page of Permission Educator Website

(b) Information for an uploaded App file, *Ubuntu Phone Experience*

Fig. 3. The UI of the website

4.2 The Website

The website provides similar information as the app. Figure 3a shows the Home page of the website. The user can select or drag and drop an apk file from the system and click on "Upload" to send it to the server. The server, upon receiving the apk as a POST request, starts extracting the name of the app and the permissions mentioned in the `AndroidManifest.xml` file. These permissions are then queried in the database for corresponding information on its utility and category. If the permission name is available in the database, its information and category are retrieved and stored in a dictionary. The permissions are also used to create a vector of binary permission by matching the final permissions set defined for NATICUSdroid, which is fed to the pre-trained model. It returns a 'benign' or 'malicious' classification for the app. The permission dictionary and the classification result are returned to the web page to display this information, as seen in Fig. 3b, for an app *Ubuntu Phone Experience*.

In the background `missed_permissions` table keeps track of the permissions for which there was a miss in the `permissions` table. This helped keep track of permissions and information that still need to be added to the database to have a high hit ratio. Upon collecting several such permissions, the `permissions` table is updated. An example of such permissions would be the custom permissions that are not native to the Android APIs, such as, `WRITE_USE_APP_FEATURE_SURVEY`, and so on, about which information is not readily available.

5 Conclusion and Future Work

Permission-Educator app works to bridge the knowledge gap of users about Android permissions and preventing malware infection. It helps educate the user by providing information such as the utility of the permission in the app, its defined category and helps in determining whether the app is malicious. A working, dynamic website also helps check an app's declared permissions, utility, and nature. This is done with the help of a cloud-based service, where the permission information is stored in a MySQL database and nature of the app is determined by a malware detection system NATICUSdroid, both hosted on the server. The app and the website have not been published publicly and are still in production. However, they have been evaluated on a private network and the results presented are through test cases.

We aim to bring more information to the user about apps that can help determine the use of permissions and whether they should be granted to an app. A quiz module could also be added to the app, which can regularly check users' knowledge about permissions to observe a possible change in users' knowledge or attitude towards permissions. The app can then be released on Google Play Store. This will enable us to get more feedback from the users and improve the app over time.

Acknowledgement. This project was partially supported by National Science Foundation Grant Awards #1903419 and #1903423.

References

1. Android for Developers (2019). https://developer.android.com/. Accessed 24 Apr 2020
2. Felt, A.P., Chin, E., Hanna, S., Song, D., Wagner, D.: Android permissions demystified. In: Proceedings of the 18th ACM Conference on Computer and Communications Security, pp. 627–638. ACM (2011)
3. Schwarz, M., Weiser, S., Gruss, D., Maurice, C., Mangard, S.: Malware guard extension: using SGX to conceal cache attacks. In: Polychronakis, M., Meier, M. (eds.) DIMVA 2017. LNCS, vol. 10327, pp. 3–24. Springer, Cham (2017). https://doi.org/10.1007/978-3-319-60876-1_1
4. Mathew, R.: Study of privilege escalation attack on android and its countermeasures (2012)
5. Mathur, A., Podila, L.M., Kulkarni, K., Niyaz, Q., Javaid, A.Y.: NATICUSdroid: a malware detection framework for android using native and custom permissions. J. Inf. Secur. Appl. **58**, 102696 (2021)
6. Kelley, P.G., Consolvo, S., Cranor, L.F., Jung, J., Sadeh, N., Wetherall, D.: A conundrum of permissions: installing applications on an android smartphone. In: Blyth, J., Dietrich, S., Camp, L.J. (eds.) FC 2012. LNCS, vol. 7398, pp. 68–79. Springer, Heidelberg (2012). https://doi.org/10.1007/978-3-642-34638-5_6
7. Alepis, E., Patsakis, C.: Unravelling security issues of runtime permissions in android. J. Hardw. Syst. Secur. **3**(1), 45–63 (2018). https://doi.org/10.1007/s41635-018-0053-2
8. Felt, A.P., Ha, E., Egelman, S., Haney, A., Chin, E., Wagner, D.: Android permissions: user attention, comprehension, and behavior. In: SOUPS 2012 - Proceedings of the 8th Symposium on Usable Privacy and Security (2012)
9. Ramachandran, S., et al.: Understanding and granting android permissions: a user survey. In: Proceedings - International Carnahan Conference on Security Technology, pp. 1–6 (2017)
10. Scoccia, G.L., Malavolta, I., Autili, M., Di Salle, A., Inverardi, P.: User-centric android flexible permissions. In: Proceedings - 2017 IEEE/ACM 39th International Conference on Software Engineering Companion, ICSE-C 2017, (i), pp. 365–367 (2017)
11. Oglaza, A., Laborde, R., Benzekri, A., Barrère, F.: A recommender-based system for assisting non technical users in managing android permissions. In: Proceedings - 2016 11th International Conference on Availability, Reliability and Security, ARES 2016, pp. 1–9 (2016)
12. Hamed, A., Ayed, H.K.B.: Privacy risk assessment and users' awareness for mobile apps permissions. In: Proceedings of IEEE/ACS International Conference on Computer Systems and Applications, AICCSA (2016)
13. Moussa, M., Di Penta, M., Antoniol, G., Beltrame, G.: ACCUSE: helping users to minimize android app privacy concerns. In: Proceedings - 2017 IEEE/ACM 4th International Conference on Mobile Software Engineering and Systems, MOBILE-Soft 2017, pp. 144–148 (2017)
14. Mathur, A., Ewoldt, E.: Permission Educator App. https://github.com/akshaymathur05/Permission_Educator
15. VirusTotal. www.virustotal.com/. Accessed 05 July 2021
16. Jinja2. https://jinja.palletsprojects.com/en/3.0.x/. Accessed 05 July 2021
17. Flask (web framework) (2012). https://en.wikipedia.org/wiki/Flask_(web_framework). Accessed 05 July 2021

An Intelligent System to Support Social Storytelling for People with ASD

Rita Francese[1]([⊠]), Angela Guercio[2], and Veronica Rossano[3]

[1] University of Salerno, Fisciano, Italy
francese@unisa.it
[2] Kent State University at Stark, North Canton, USA
aguercio@kent.edu
[3] University of Bari, Bari, Italy
veronica.rossano@uniba.it

Abstract. The number of diagnoses of ASD (Autism Spectrum Disorder) is growing every day. Children suffering from ASD lack of social behaviors, which strongly impacts on the inclusion of the child and his/her own family in the community. Much scientific evidence shows that social storytelling is a valuable tool for developing pro-social behaviors in children with ASD and for articulating their emotional language, empathy, and expressive and verbal communication. To be effective, social stories should be customized for the target user since there exist different levels of ASD. To tackle this issue, this paper proposes an application that supports the semiautomatic creation of social stories. The intelligent system learns the needs of the target user over time and adapts by creating social stories tailored to the ASD level of the disorder. The editor lets non-expert caregivers select the appropriate elements and content representations to be included in the social stories.

Keywords: Autism Spectrum Disorder · Social Stories · Digital storytelling

1 Introduction

In 2020, approximately 1 in 54 children in the U.S. was diagnosed with an Autism Spectrum Disorder (ASD), referring to 2016 data[1]. According to the Diagnostic and Statistical Manual of Mental Disorders (DSM-5)[2], ASD is a class of life-long neurodevelopmental disorders characterized by difficulties in social communications, such as deficits in social-emotional reciprocity or deficits in nonverbal communicative behaviors, or in developing, maintaining, and understanding relationships; restricted, repetitive, and sensory behavior or interests, such as stereotyped or repetitive motor movements, use of objects, or speech. The term "spectrum" indicates that there exist different levels of severity. Often

---

[1] https://www.autismspeaks.org/autism-statistics-asd.
[2] https://www.psychiatry.org/psychiatrists/practice/dsm.

© Springer Nature Switzerland AG 2022
J.-H. Kim et al. (Eds.): IHCI 2021, LNCS 13184, pp. 372–378, 2022.
https://doi.org/10.1007/978-3-030-98404-5_35

these core features are accompanied by other problems, including anxiety, eating and sleep disorders, depression, attention deficit, aggressive or self-injury behavior (challenging behaviors). Challenging behaviors strongly impact social skill development, contributing to the difficulty of inclusion for the person and the entire family [15].

Social stories provide a medium and effective intervention for learning social information and reducing anxiety for people with ASD [4]. Gray provides guidelines for the construction of effective social stories [3]. Digital storytelling is a combination of traditional oral storytelling with personalized digital images, graphics and sound, widely adopted for supporting learning. Gray's social stories and digital storytelling may be combined.

In this paper, we propose an intelligent editor for social stories that follows Gray's guidelines and enables the user to customize them to the severity level of ASD of the person. The tool is currently a work-in-progress.

2 Background

2.1 Digital Storytelling

The term Storytelling indicates the most ancient practice used to transfer knowledge and culture.

Experimental evidence has shown the power of storytelling in education, as well as in complex and abstract subjects like in STEM education [10]. Bruner [1] states that stories involve the listener's mind and body by allowing one to jump in the story world, react using deep thinking, invoke the deepest emotions, and promote a deeper level of imagination. Also, AI researchers have been studying storytelling and explored how stories relate to our memory and comprehension, and how storytelling activities shape our memories. Schank states that the human interest in stories is strongly related to the nature of intelligence since they engage a listener more effectively [11]. Digital storytelling is an evolution of the old fashion storytelling. In digital storytelling interactive and personalized digital media are used to enhance the listener's experience. In addition, the story is easier to share, store, and search. Digital storytelling, as a new form of communication, has been successfully employed in several contexts including well-being [9]. Experimental experiences in health professional education have shown that the use of health professional digital stories positively enhances learning and the behavior of the caregiver towards patients [8].

2.2 Digital Social Stories

Social Stories were proposed by Carol Gray at the beginning of the 1990s [3] to positively affect the social understanding and behavior of children with ASD. A social story concerns the description of concepts of behaviors related to a specific social situation (i.e., staying inline). It aims at reassuring the person with ASD while providing social information in a simple and redundant way. As an example, changes in habits may be very difficult to deal with, even small ones like changing the path to go home, and can cause stress [2]. Some efforts have been devoted in the literature to propose social stories with digital support [6,7,12]. Zhu et al. [15] proposed an app named FriendStar adopting interactive narrative techniques with branching structures for 9–13 years old children. The Sofa app enables caregivers to create social stories for autistic children, by customizing existing stories and supporting their modification or the creation of new ones. It has been assessed in [5] when adopted by ten children on the autism spectrum attending a school summer camp with significant improvements in child understanding, anxiety, and closeness to goal. Varnava et al. [13] performed a preliminary study to design an app for supporting children with autism in coping with changes by using social stories and timetables. All these tools do not learn or adapt over time.

3   An Intelligent Editor for the Generation of Social Stories

There are AI-enabled SaaS commercial tools for the automatic creation of digital content. Some of them focus on article rewriting like the AI Article Spinner and WordAI; or ChimpWriter which uses NPL (Natural Processing Language) to search, analyze and rewrite content. The Sassbook AI Summarizer generates automatic text summaries and Articoolo and Kafkai (by Niteo) writes articles from scratch. Other tools provide proofreading and grammar checking, like Quillbot and Grammarly. These tools provide support to businesses and organizations. However, when it comes to the production of social stories for people with ASD there are no tools that reproduce ASD-tailored social stories. Due to the broad difference of abilities in the ASD spectrum, the tool should adapt to the specific autistic features of the end-user and create social stories effective for that target person. The editor presented in this paper has its primary utility at home where family caregivers have the opportunity, via this tool, to teach and communicate with the person with ASD. Consequently, it must be user-friendly and easy to learn. To this aim we followed both a user-centered design approach as well as the accessibility guidelines.

When creating social stories for people with ASD, many factors must be considered: first, the level of autism. Our editor uses the modern classification of the 3 levels of autism as developed after 2013, listed in the DSM-5, and supported by the American Psychiatric Association. Level 1 ASD refers to mild autism that requires the least amount of support. Level 2 ASD requires substantial support in some areas. Level 3 ASD requires very substantial support to perform activities of daily life. At level 1 our application creates social stories that are more descriptive and the text and phrase complexity ranges according to the level of education and age of the target user. At level 2 the social stories are simplified and integrate more flexible communications elements, for example, extensive use of audio integration for those who cannot read. At level 3, the social stories are kept very basic and short with simplified phrase structure. A database of images indexed for the appropriate level of autism is available to the editor and the content generator. Age, ability, and interests of the end-user, length of the story, sentence structure, vocabulary, font and font size, organization of the text, and illustration are all aspects considered by the editor and differ for each ASD level and/or target user.

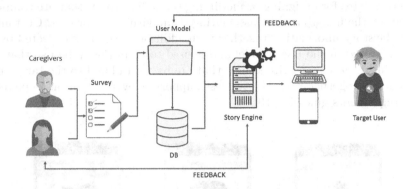

Fig. 1. The social story process from creation (caregiver-side) to its use.

The editor of digital social stories we propose uses the guidelines of Carol Gray[3] for the social story construction. The guidelines are briefly listed here: 1) Identify the Social Story Goal; 2) Two-Step Discovery (i.e., gather audience information); 3) Three Parts and a Title (i.e., determine a title, the introduction, the body, and the conclusion); 4) FOURmat (i.e., choose the format according to the abilities and interests of the audience); 5) Define Voice and Vocabulary (i.e., choose the "voice": never in 2nd person; the tense: Past, Present, Future; use a positive and patient tone; be accurate; 6) Questions Guide Story Development (i.e., the WHERE, WHEN, WHO, WHAT, HOW, and WHY of the story; 7) About Sentences; 8) A GR-EIGHT Formula; 9) Refine; 10) Guides to implementation (i.e., plan, organize, monitor, build, recycle, review, stay current).

These guidelines are implemented by the editor in the following way. Guidelines 1, 2, and 4 are fulfilled by asking the caregiver to fill in a brief questionnaire aiming at assessing the severity level of the person with ASD, collecting the end-user information, and identifying the topic and the focus of the story. The talents and/or interests of the end-user are also identified to produce a social story that grabs the end-user's attention. This information is stored in the User Model part of the system as depicted in Fig. 1. Guidelines 3, 5, 6, and 7 are integrated in the semi-automatic story generator. Plan-and-Write [14] is used as part of the story engine. To reassure, the story engine selects rhythmic and repetitive phrases, as well as coaching sentences; descriptive instead of directive terms. A positive and supporting story ending is always used. The story generator adds pictures to the story but the editor enables the caregiver's selection of pictures of the

---

[3] https://carolgraysocialstories.com/wp-content/uploads/2015/09/Social-Stories-10.0-10.2-Comparison-Chart.pdf.

end-user. Indeed, because people with autism often have difficulty in identifying the emotions of other people or understanding abstract concepts, it may be better to use their pictures to interest them more. Guideline 9 is implemented by allowing the caregiver to review the generated story and to modify it as pleased. In the design phase as well as in the customization of the story, the tool provides simple templates for designing or modifying the social stories that are composed by selecting the images and by associating them with audio or text. Customization of the story information together with additional feedback collected by the system is stored in the User Model and is used to train the system so that over time it will suggest and write stories that are better tailored to the target user. This feature, together with the process supported by the tool, as depicted in Fig. 1, implements guideline 10.

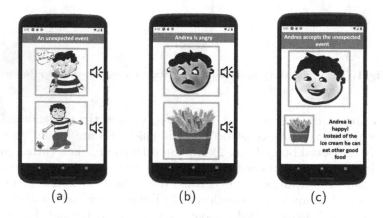

Fig. 2. Some screenshots of the social story generated by the tool.

As an example, the story in Fig. 2 has been created for Andrea, a young boy with autism who does not accept unexpected events that cause him serious challenging behaviors. This figure shows three screenshots related to the social story "An unexpected event may happen". In this story in Fig. 2, Andrea's ice cream falls, and this generates a strong sense of anger in him. The mother of the boy buys french fries for Andrea and this makes him happy. Even if Andrea did not eat the ice cream, there is always something else to eat. Andrea now is happy; he accepted the unexpected event. We decide to use a presentation modality based on slides, that the person with ASD (or his caregiver) may advance according to the specific person's learning time. The narration of the story may be provided in different modalities:

- audio, for end-users with limited reading capabilities. The audio describing an image may be listened to by pressing on the image or on the audio button.
- textual, for end-users able to read and focus their attention on the text.
- both audio and textual.

Figures 2 (a) and (b) are proposed to a person of Level 2 ASD with reduced reading ability. On the contrary, Fig. 2 (c) is created for an able reader.

The tool also enables one to reuse the elements of this story (i.e., the main character) in other unexpected events (i.e., the car breaks down or uncle William comes home) thus providing examples of similar social situations. The generated story may also be proposed in test format later, to test the end-user's comprehension by asking him/her to select the correct conclusion of the story.

4 Conclusion

In this paper, we propose an intelligent editor for generating social stories that abide by Gray's guidelines for people with ASD, considers different severity levels of ASD, and proposes different stories on the same social topic. The tool learns from the interaction with the story creator and proposes in time stories more tailored to the target user. The tool is currently a work-in-progress and in the future, we plan to evaluate it with end-users of different levels of severity and to enrich the interaction modality with a vocal chatbot.

References

1. Bruner, J.: Actual Minds Possible Worlds. Harvard University Press, Cambridge (2020)
2. Francese, R., Yang, X.: Supporting autism spectrum disorder screening and intervention with machine learning and wearables: a systematic literature review. Complex Intell. Syst. 1–16 (2021). https://doi.org/10.1007/s40747-021-00447-1
3. Gray, C.: Social Stories. Future Horizons, Arlington (1994)
4. Gray, C.: The New Social Story Book. Future Horizons (2000)
5. Hanrahan, R., Smith, E., Johnson, H., Constantin, A., Brosnan, M.: A pilot randomised control trial of digitally-mediated social stories for children on the autism spectrum. J. Autism Dev. Disord. 50(12), 4243–4257 (2020). https://doi.org/10.1007/s10803-020-04490-8
6. Karkhaneh, M., Clark, B., Ospina, M.B., Seida, J.C., Smith, V., Hartling, L.: Social stories[TM] to improve social skills in children with autism spectrum disorder: a systematic review. Autism 14(6), 641–662 (2010)
7. Li, X., Kang, X.: Combining computational thinking and Chibitronics and Makey Makey to develop a social story teaching aid system to improve social reciprocity and emotional expression skills for autistic children. In: 2021 12th International Conference on E-Education, E-Business, E-Management, and E-Learning, pp. 1–5 (2021)
8. Moreau, K.A., Eady, K., Sikora, L., Horsley, T.: Digital storytelling in health professions education: a systematic review. BMC Med. Educ. 18(1), 1–9 (2018)
9. Petrovic, M., Gaggioli, A.: The potential of transformative interactive video storytelling for improving caregivers' mental wellbeing: a research protocol. Annu. Rev. Cyberther. Telemed. 2020, 275 (2020)
10. Robin, B.R.: Digital storytelling: a powerful technology tool for the 21st century classroom. Theor. Pract. 47(3), 220–228 (2008)

11. Schank, R.C.: Tell me a Story: A New Look at Real And Artificial Memory. Charles Scribner's Sons (1990)
12. Smith, E., Constantin, A., Johnson, H., Brosnan, M.: Digitally-mediated social stories support children on the autism spectrum adapting to a change in a 'Real-World'context. J. Autism Dev. Disord. **51**, 514–526 (2021). https://doi.org/10. 1007/s10803-020-04558-5
13. Varnava, V., Constantin, A., Alexandru, C.A.: ChangeIT: toward an app to help children with autism cope with changes. In: Interactivity and the Future of the Human-Computer Interface, pp. 72–94. IGI Global (2020)
14. Yao, L., Peng, N., Ralph, W., Knight, K., Zhao, D., Yan, R.: Plan-and-write: towards better automatic storytelling. In: The Thirty-Third AAAI Conference on Artificial Intelligence (AAAI-19) (2019)
15. Zhu, J., Connell, J., Kerns, C., Lyon, N., Vecere, N., Lim, D., Myers, C.: Toward interactive social stories for children with autism. IN: CHI PLAY 2014, pp. 453–454 (2014)

Evaluating Accuracy of the Tobii Eye Tracker 5

Andrew Housholder, Jonathan Reaban, Aira Peregrino, Georgia Votta,
and Tauheed Khan Mohd[✉]

Augustana College, Rock Island, IL 61201, USA
tauheedkhanmohd@augustana.edu

Abstract. Eye-tracking sensors are a relatively new technology and currently has use as an accessibility method to allow those with disabilities to use technology with greater independence. This study evaluates the general accuracy and precision of Tobii eye-tracking software and hardware, along with the efficacy of training a neural network to improve both aspects of the eye-tracker itself. With three human testers observing a grid of data points, the measured and known point locations are recorded and analyzed using over 250 data points. The study was conducted over two days, with each participant performing four trials each. In this study, we use basic statistics and a k-means clustering algorithm to examine the data in depth and give insights into the performance of the Tobii-5 eye-tracker. In addition to evaluating performance, this study also attempts to improve the accuracy of the Tobii-5 eye-tracker by using a Multi-Layer Perceptron Regressor to reassign gaze locations to better line up with the expected gaze location. Potential future developments are also discussed.

Keywords: Tobii · Eye-tracking · Tobii eye tracker 5 · Calibration · Python · Point-of-gaze

1 Introduction

Eye-tracking as a field of study has been around since the late 1800s when Louis Emile Javal noticed strange behavior in people's eyes while reading across a page; people would spend differing amounts of time on different words instead of a smooth motion across the page. This was the first real use of eye tracking, even if it was relatively simple. Later on, Edmond Huey was able to build a device that identified what words people were pausing on for long periods of time. Huey's research cemented him as an important figure in the early days of the study of reading. Over the years, eye tracking gradually progressed from educational fields like reading into the more lucrative fields of marketing, business, and web design. By the late 1900s, eye-tracking technology became instrumental in modernizing web pages from looking like the print sources such as newspapers that were their predecessors. A study in 1991 specifically examined the use of eye-trackers as a normalized human-computer interaction technique [1]. They

© Springer Nature Switzerland AG 2022
J.-H. Kim et al. (Eds.): IHCI 2021, LNCS 13184, pp. 379–390, 2022.
https://doi.org/10.1007/978-3-030-98404-5_36

suggested that, while eye-tracking at time of writing is not accurate enough to replace or substitute standard mouse/keyboard control, eye-tracking could reasonably be used as a complement with mouse/keyboard in the future. Today, eye-tracking is finding a niche in "in-game" advertising such as product placement in movies and video games [2]. This is bringing the prediction made in 1991 come true.

Today, most companies that produce eye-tracking hardware offer eye-tracking based off of image-based techniques [3]. Less intrusive models (e.g. a device that sits on the computer) have become most popular among consumers. These devices commonly use a combination of near-infrared light and a camera to capture data. The IR light reflects off of the inside of the user's eye, where the reflected light is captured in images of the eyes. These images are then analyzed in order to produce a gaze direction. This gaze direction data is then used to provide raw input on the computer, based on the devices location on the computer.

Eye-tracking as a new technology provides human-computer interactions a new source of input in the form of the human visual experience. Because of it's potential applications in neuroscience [4], psychology [5], and computer science [6], eye-tracking has been both more prevalent and more developed in recent years. Tobii Tech, a branch of the larger tech company Tobii, has been primarily focused on evolving this technology and is currently the world leader in eye-tracking technology. It's success has only been limited by its costs; recently, however, consumer demand has brought this barrier down to the point where eye-tracking software is almost commercially available from any location. Some of the biggest companies offering eye-tracking hardware at the time this paper was written are Gazepoint (based in Vancouver, B.C., Canada), Natural Point (based in Corvallis, OR, USA), and Tobii (based in Stockholm, Sweden).

With eye-tracking hardware and software becoming more widely available, it is important that the technology is very accurate to the user's actual eye position. This paper is focused on evaluating the accuracy of the Tobii 5 eye-tracker (See Fig. 1), the most recent publicly available device at time of writing capable of tracking both head and eye movement. The device is plugged into the computer, mounted on either the top or the bottom of the monitor, and then pointed towards the user. The device then gives a visual que to where the user is looking on screen. With an operable distance of 45–95 cm, a sampling rate of 133 Hz and infrared illuminators, Tobii claims that the device is accurate and performs exceptionally well under any lighting conditions at determining an individual's point of gaze (POG). This paper will specifically provide data on the accuracy of the Tobii 5 in the different quadrants of the screen (upper left, upper right, lower left, lower right) and test whether the eye-tracker is more or less accurate towards the edges of the screen versus the center of the screen.

The testing was performed using both the Tobii 5 eye-tracker hardware and the Unity game engine. There is a free game included in Unity that tracks your POG via the Tobii 5 eye-tracker and returns the exact coordinates (in pixels) as text fields in the game. Using a combination of this game and an image

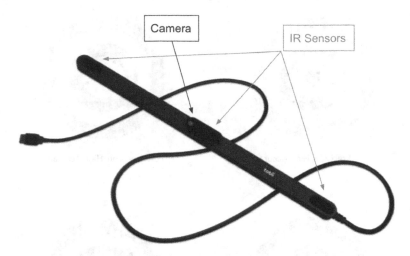

Fig. 1. A labeled diagram of the Tobii 5 eye-tracker hardware used in the experiment.

containing 21 fixed points of known location, we were able to manually collect data for testing.

Accuracy is defined in this study as the average difference between the known location and the eye-tracker's measured location. Precision is defined as the standard deviation of the data in each trial; the eye-tracker's capability in consistently producing the same output from the same location (See Fig. 2).

When examining the data from this study, we employed both basic statistics and a k-means clustering algorithm to gain insights into the performance of the Tobii 5 eye-tracker. Overall, we found that the Tobii 5 eye-tracker strays on average 35 pixels (visual angle of .74°) from the target and has a standard deviation of 18 pixels (.39°) according to the data.

The data was acquired by having 3 people each perform 4 trials in which they looked at 21 fixed points on the screen for a total of 252 points, distributed at even intervals across the screen. Next, we compared the actual location of the point in pixels to the location returned by the Tobii 5 eye-tracker and were able to do our data analysis, using both excel and python (pandas, scikit-learn, matplotlib libraries were used).

In addition to simply examining the accuracy of the Tobii-5 eye-tracker, solutions are also explored for improving the overall accuracy of the device through software and neural networks. A Multi-Layer Perceptron Regressor was implemented to determine the error for the POG anywhere on the screen. This neural network helps to provide more accuracy to the Tobii-5 eye-tracker hardware through the implementation of software.

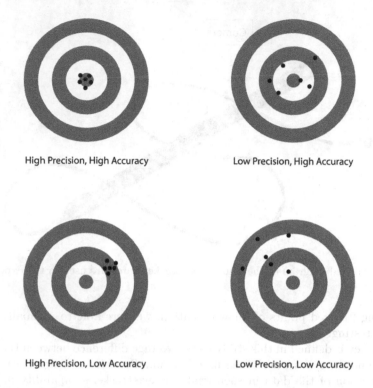

High Precision, High Accuracy   Low Precision, High Accuracy

High Precision, Low Accuracy   Low Precision, Low Accuracy

Fig. 2. Distinction between high accuracy and high precision from [7].

2   Related Work

Eye tracking technology has become a popular area of research within the field of Human Computer Interaction and new applications are emerging everyday. From research [3], to psychology [5], to making the lives of disabled people less difficult [8], a large number of people are gradually adopting eye tracking technology and making it a more prevalent tool in everyday life.

In terms of research, one subset of study focuses heavily on examining the accuracy, precision, and overall performance of the eye tracking technology [9]. These types of studies collect large amounts of data and attempt to quantify the performance of the eye tracking devices. They include studies regarding efficacy when user is wearing glasses [9], efficiency of eye tracking in comparison to other multi-modal human-computer interfaces [10], and even the accuracy between specific brands of eye-tracker [11].

Another subset examines the actual metrics used to determine what "accuracy" [12], "precision" [13], and "performance" [14] actually means in regards to eye-tracking sensors in general. The Tobii website has published their specific methodology in regards to testing their own device, with accuracy measured through Euclidean distance between points, and precision measured through the root mean square (RMS) between successive sample points [15]. Another study conducted by Microsoft uses the standard deviation to illustrate the spread of points around the "average" [16].

Beyond the examination of accuracy and precision of eye-tracking technology, work has been done to seek improvement of certain flaws that exist within eye-trackers [17]. This study made advancements in three areas of improvement: smoothing gaze data in real time, accounting for sensor lag in real time, and providing focus points for the user's eyes. Two of the three improvement attempts showed moderate success (data smoothing and sensor lag adjustments). Another study suggests a new mechanism to convert eye-gaze-tracking data to mouse-pointer data [18]. This study in particular finds that although using eye-gazing data as a primary input is fast, it is still much less accurate and stable than most other input devices [19] due to saccades, the rapid movement of eyes between two different fixation points. Saccades are the concurrent movement of both eyes and result in very unpredictable pathing from one point to another. However, the work done in the study confirms that the use of eye-gaze data as a computer input is feasible with the implementation of algorithms that reduce the effects of the jittery saccade behavior of the eye.

With the right implementation, there are some potentially useful applications of eye-tracking technology that have been discussed. Using eye gaze data as a means for target selection on a computer screen is an application that has been explored in a recent study [20].

As eye-tracking performance improves, its application to other technologies could help make new devices more accessible. One study has shown specifically that human testers using an eye-tracking device can perform just as well as human testers using mouse and keyboard [8]. The biggest impact on eye-tracking user performance is primarily precision and accuracy, rather than speed or ease of use. Users were able to quickly adjust to the eye-tracking technology.

With major advancements being made in eye-tracking technology and its applications, there are still some limitations to the type of data collected. Most eye trackers are not necessarily portable and only are for use on computer or laptop screens. One study examines how gaze data could be collected without any external hardware [21]. With a significant data set of over 2.5 million frames, this study uses the data to attempt to predict the location of the users' gaze. The overall goal of the study is to make eye-tracking technology available to all mobile devices without any sort of external hardware. This, however, is some ways away.

3   Experiment

3.1   Technology Specifications

Tobii Experience was downloaded onto a Dell PC running Windows 10 with a 3.0 GHz Intel core 2 Quad processor with 32 GB of RAM on a 24-in. thin film transistor liquid crystal display, 1920 × 1080 pixels. The Tobii 5 hardware was connected through a USB port and mounted to the bottom of the monitor facing the user. With no other operations running in the background, the test was performed using an application that plots exact x and y coordinates of the eye-tracker's calculated viewpoint. This application can be found on a project in the Tobii Unity SDK for Windows.

3.2 Procedure

For this study three participants were screened. The participants were aged in their twenties and none require glasses or wore any type of accessory that would potentially interfere with the Tobii Eye Tracker. All three consenting partici-pants were informed ahead of time about the study's methods and nature. To test the accuracy and precision of the eye-tracking technology, known locations were marked on the screen for testers to look at down to the exact pixel. Upon installation of the device drivers, the user is provided with various demo projects in Unity. One of these applications is to plot the exact x and y location, in pixels, of where the eye tracking device is reading the users point of gaze to be. Given the environment was in 1920p by 1080p, a transparent .png image was created with the matching dimensions of 1920p by 1080p with 21 predetermined points plotted out (See Fig. 3) sporadically across the screen. This image was produced fully in Adobe Photoshop. Each of the points consisted of a light blue circle with a black dot on the exact pixel of each point used for testing.

With the user seated the recommended 45–95 cm away, the participants began by calibrating the device using the native Tobii Experience calibration tool. From there, they went through each point row by row and another individ-ual recorded the determined POG by the eye tracker. This given point was then compared with the known location, and both locations were entered manually into a Microsoft Excel document.

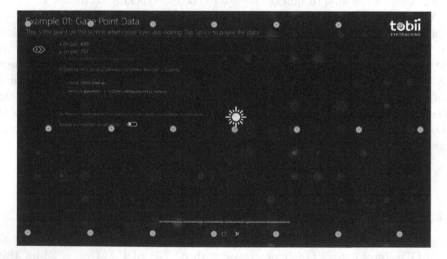

Fig. 3. The Unity environment used for obtaining data points. The user, with the eye-tracking device enabled, observes each point on the screen in reading order; left to right, top to bottom.

3.3 Data Processing

By calculating the Euclidean distance between the determined POG and the given location, the approximate accuracy of the sensor can be calculated in terms of the visual angle. The test was repeated multiple times with multiple people to compare accuracy between the middle of the screen, the four corners, the top/bottom edges, and the left/right edges.

The test used was a grid of points made in Adobe Photoshop and the accuracy was calculated using the Euclidean distance to find the visual angle between the sensor's determined point and the actual point.

The Euclidean distance can be calculated using the x and y coordinates between the determined point and the actual point using the following equation:

$$Euclidean\ Distance = \sqrt{(x_1 - x_2)^2 + (y_1 - y_2)^2} \tag{1}$$

The visual angle can be calculated using the Euclidean difference between the two points and the distance of the observer to the screen. The relationship is as follows:

$$Visual\ Angle = 2 * \arctan(\frac{\frac{Difference}{2}}{Distance}) \tag{2}$$

To evaluate accuracy, the average Euclidean distance across all test points was found using Microsoft Excel, along with the average across all corner points, the average across all points on the top/bottom edges, and the average across all points on the left/right edges.

To evaluate precision, the standard deviation of the Euclidean distance was taken across all points for each trial in the same categories as mentioned above.

The data was also processed using a neural network in python in an attempt to correct the Tobii data to display the actual coordinates where the user was looking. This neural network takes in Tobii gaze data as its input and outputs the predicted actual gaze location. The neural network is implemented in the scikit-learn package in python as an MLPRegressor.

The data was first scaled using scikit-learn's minmax scale method and then ten percent of the data was put into a test set at random while the remaining ninety percent was put into the training set. The labels for the training in test set were the known locations on the screen that the users looked at during testing and that input data was the output from the Tobii 5 eye-tracker.

One limitation to using a neural network to process this data is the amount of data collected. The amount of data collected only amounted to 252 points due to time constraints on the project. Ideally, we would want to have much more data (preferably in the thousands) with many more known points in order to get a more accurate neural network to better improve our results.

4   Results

The first set of results to look at are the statistics from the raw data from the experiment. A histogram of the calculated euclidean distances can be seen in Fig. 4. From this histogram, we can see that the distribution of euclidean distances is skewed to the right so the measure of center and spread to use are median and interquartile range. The median of this data set is 30.70 pixels (.65°) and the interquartile range is 33.37 pixels (.71°).

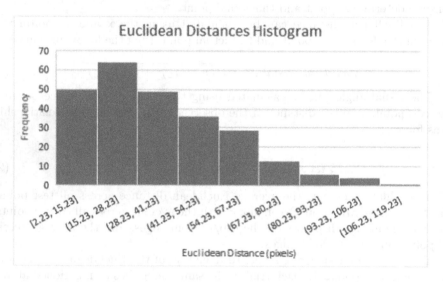

Fig. 4. Histogram of the euclidean distances between the data from the Tobii 5 eye-tracker and the actual location of the user's POG.

Using the scikit-learn KMeans clustering algorithm with 4 clusters, the clusters that appeared were the 4 different quadrants of the screen as shown in Fig. 5. The choice of 4 clusters was made after using the elbow method for KMeans clustering which showed no obvious number of clusters to use; four clusters seemed to work the most consistently though. After looking at the euclidean distances from each of the actual fixed points to each test point in each of the clusters, however, there was no significant difference in the distribution between any of the quadrants. There was a slightly higher variance in the top left and bottom right quadrants than in the top right and bottom left quadrants, but this may only be due to the amount of data points in each of the clusters.

A Multi-Layer Perceptron Regressor was also used to analyze the data. We decided not to use a CNN or RNN because our data was numeric and did not include a time component so a simple ANN would be good enough for our data set. This neural network attempts to take the Tobii-5 eye-tracker data and make it more accurate to where the user is actually looking. The neural network has a hidden layer size of 20 and a logistic activation function. The network also used

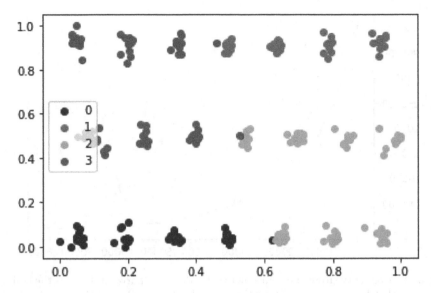

Fig. 5. A graph of the clusters that came from using the KMeans clustering algorithm.

a set random state for splitting the training and test data so it is trained on the same data every time. The loss curve from training the network can be seen in Fig. 6. After training the network, it appears to be working as intended. For example, looking at the point (1808, 48), which was given from the Tobii-5 eye-tracker when the user was looking at the point (1776, 60), the network updated this point to be (1771, 57). The euclidean distance in this case decreased from 34.18 to 5.77 (1.15° to 0.19). This decrease is similar across all data points in the test data. It is clear that the network's output is much more accurate to the actual point of gaze of the user than what the Tobii-5 eye-tracker had originally predicted.

There are some limitations to this method of improving the accuracy of the Tobii-5 eye-tracker however. One such limitation is the amount of data collected prior to training and testing. Due to time constraints on the project, only 252 data points were used for training and testing. With so few data points, it will be hard for the neural network to get highly accurate results. The data collection also only involved 21 known points. Better results could be obtained by collecting data from more known points. This would allow for us to see more clearly the accuracy of the Tobii-5 eye-tracker in different regions of the screen. Another potential limitation of the neural network is that it only seemed to work very well on points that were already inaccurate. On points that were already fairly accurate, the neural network did not improve much or got slightly worse in terms of accuracy.

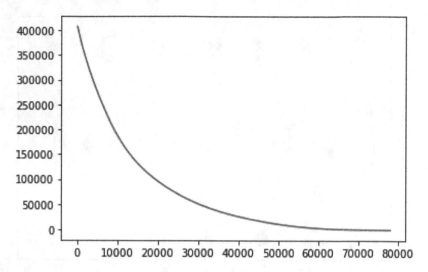

Fig. 6. The loss curve from the neural network. Along the horizontal axis is the training iterations that have occurred. Along the vertical axis is the loss of the neural network.

5   Conclusion and Future Work

From these results, we can conclude that the Tobii-5 eye-tracker is typically accurate to around 30 pixels (1.01°) of the actual point of gaze of the user. This accuracy tends to be consistent throughout the entire screen. In other words, eye-tracker does not get more or less accurate when the user looks at different regions of the screen.

As previously stated, one of the biggest limitations with the Tobii-5 to this project thus far is the number of data points collected. Only 252 data points were used for training and testing the neural network as well as collecting the accuracy data. Ideally the results would be made based off of a few thousand points; however, time constraints restricted how many data points could be collected. Many more known points on the screen would also be used to better test the accuracy in different regions in the screen.

We also plan to have more individuals participate in future studies. For this study, we only had three participants. Having closer to 20 or 30 participants would allow for even more data points and would give a better overall picture of the accuracy and precision of the Tobii-5 eye-tracker. The best case scenario would allow us to randomly select 30 participants from a large pool of individuals.

Our method of data collection was to manually record each coordinate as indicated by the Tobii-5 eye-tracker. An automatic data collection program would have been noticeably more efficient and would have allowed us to collect many more data points in a shorter time-frame.

With a larger pool of data, our results would have been considerably better and our software using the Multi-Layer Perceptron Regressor would be able to reliably correct the location of someone's gaze for any point on the screen. Currently the neural network only reliably corrects points that are very inaccurate and does not tend to improve points that are already relatively close to the actual point of gaze of the user.

It would be beneficial to study if this was consistent across a variety of screen sizes, how much the screen size affects the accuracy of the Tobii Eye Tracker 5, and then apply a dynamic progressive model to correct the areas that are typically further off from the ones that tend to be more accurate. This can be especially useful when the user is using their eyes as a mouse for example, as the buttons the user could click would be used as correction points, rather than just random points on the screen.

After finding a method to collect larger pools of data and to efficiently correct that data, we would have the opportunity to go further with our hypotheses regarding the accuracy and precision of the Tobii-5 eye-tracker. With more participants and data, we would be able to look into how optical aids such as eyeglasses and soft contact lenses effect the accuracy of eye-tracking. Though this has been done before [9], we would first be able to confirm or deny the findings of this paper by having more participants in our study. We then could also take this further by checking whether our correction algorithm would be able to also correct for inaccuracies produced by prescription eyeglasses or contacts.

References

1. Jacob, R.J.: The use of eye movements in human-computer interaction techniques: what you look at is what you get. ACM Trans. Inf. Syst. (TOIS) **9**(2), 152–169 (1991)
2. Leggett, D.: A brief history of eye-tracking: UX booth, January 2010
3. Weigle, C., Banks, D.: Analysis of eye-tracking experiments performed on a Tobii T60, January 2008
4. Hopstaken, J.F., Van Der Linden, D., Bakker, A.B., Kompier, M.A.: A multifaceted investigation of the link between mental fatigue and task disengagement. Psychophysiology **52**(3), 305 315 (2015)
5. Morgante, J.D., et al.: A critical test of temporal spatial accuracy of the Tobii T60XL eye tracker. Infancy **17**(1), 9–32 (2012)
6. Elhelw, M., Nicolaou, M., Chung, A., Yang, G.-Z., Atkins, M.S.: A gaze-based study for investigating the perception of visual realism in simulated scenes. ACM Trans. Appl. Percept. (TAP) **5**(1), 1–20 (2008)
7. GeoCue: Accuracy, precision, resolution (2015). Accessed 28 Jan 2021
8. Tall, M., et al.: Gaze-controlled driving. In: CHI 2009 Extended Abstracts on Human Factors in Computing Systems, CHI EA 2009, New York, NY, USA, pp. 4387–4392. Association for Computing Machinery (2009)
9. Dahlberg, J.: Eye tracking with eye glasses, pp. 1–66, June 2010
10. Trouvain, B., Schlick, C.M.: A comparative study of multimodal displays for multirobot supervisory control. In: Harris, D. (ed.) EPCE 2007. LNCS (LNAI), vol. 4562, pp. 184–193. Springer, Heidelberg (2007). https://doi.org/10.1007/978-3-540-73331-7_20
11. Funke, G., Greenlee, E., Carter, M., Dukes, A., Brown, R., Menke, L.: Which eye tracker is right for your research? Performance evaluation of several cost variant eye

trackers. In: Proceedings of the Human Factors and Ergonomics Society Annual Meeting, vol. 60, pp. 1240–1244. SAGE Publications, Los Angeles (2016)

12. Holmqvist, K., Nystrm, M., Anderson, H., Weijer, J.: Eye-tracking data and dependent variables. Niepublikowana praca, Lund University (2011)

13. Demšar, U., Çöltekin, A.: Quantifying gaze and mouse interactions on spatial visual interfaces with a new movement analytics methodology. PLoS One **12**(8), e0181818 (2017)

14. Goodrich, M.A., Olsen Jr., D.R.: Metrics for evaluating human-robot interactions (2003)

15. Johnsson, J., Matos, R.: Accuracy and precision test method for remote eye trackers. Sweden, Tobii Technology (2011)

16. Feit, A.M.: Toward everyday gaze input: accuracy and precision of eye tracking and implications for design. In: Proceedings of the 2017 Chi Conference on Human Factors in Computing Systems, pp. 1118–1130 (2017)

17. Kumar, M., Klingner, J., Puranik, R., Winograd, T., Paepcke, A.: Improving the accuracy of gaze input for interaction. In: Proceedings of the 2008 Symposium on Eye Tracking Research & Applications, pp. 65–68 (2008)

18. Sesin, A., Adjouadi, M., Ayala, M., Barreto, A., Rishe, N.: Effective data conversion algorithm for real-time vision based human computer interface. In: Proceedings of the 6th WSEAS International Conference on Software Engineering, Parallel and Distributed Systems, pp. 16–19 (2007)

19. Xue, J., et al.: A crucial temporal accuracy test of combining EEG and Tobii eye tracker. Medicine **96** (2017)

20. Vertegaal, R.: A Fitts law comparison of eye tracking and manual input in the selection of visual targets. In: Proceedings of the 10th International Conference on Multimodal Interfaces, pp. 241–248 (2008)

21. Krafka, K., et al.: Eye tracking for everyone. In: Proceedings of the IEEE Conference on Computer Vision and Pattern Recognition, pp. 2176–2184 (2016)

Evaluation of Accuracy of Leap Motion Controller Device

Anas Akkar, Sam Cregan, Yafet Zeleke, Chase Fahy, Parajwal Sarkar,
and Tauheed Khan Mohd[✉]

Augustana College, Rock Island, IL 61201, USA
tauheedkhanmohd@augustana.edu

Abstract. As Human-Computer Interaction has continued to advance
with technology, Augmented Virtuality (AV) systems have become
increasingly useful and improve our interaction with technology. This
article addresses the effectiveness of the Leap Motion Controller at capturing this interaction, as well as present new ways to improve the experience. First, we will present and discuss data from test trials with human
input to show how accurately the Leap Motion Controller represents
the user's hand motion. This will provide the background information
needed to understand our proposal for the potential changes and modifications to the device that would improve the Human-Computer Interaction. This will also provide insight into how implementing deep learning
could improve the accuracy of this device. Improving the accuracy of the
Leap Motion Controller could lead to an increased usage of the device
in games and it could also potentially be used for educational purposes.
While it has a long way to go, the Leap Motion Controller could potentially become an incredible source for virtual environments in academia,
the world of rehabilitation, and for recreational use.

Keywords: Augmented virtuality · Leap motion controller · Human
computer interaction · Deep learning

1 Introduction

The goal of both Augmented Reality (AR) and Augmented Virtuality (AV) is to
seamlessly combine the real world with the virtual world to create an immersive
experience for the user. However, while often confused, there is an important
distinction between augmented reality and augmented virtuality that will be
important.

Augmented reality takes place in the real world, and typically has virtual
components added into it via a projector or screen. In some cases, the real world
is mimicked by the AR application and used on the screen. Augmented virtuality exists entirely in its virtual world, with bits and pieces of the real world
added into it. M. Farshid, J. Paschen, T. Eriksson, and J. Kietzmann state the
main driver of human-computer interaction with AV is defined as "the introduction of actual elements into a possible world" [1]. The real-world component,

© Springer Nature Switzerland AG 2022
J.-H. Kim et al. (Eds.): IHCI 2021, LNCS 13184, pp. 391–402, 2022.
https://doi.org/10.1007/978-3-030-98404-5_37

or "actual elements" of AV comes from the human interaction with the device or application. R. Rouse, M. Engberg, N. JafariNaimi, and J. Bolter mention both AR and AV lie on a spectrum and can have varying levels of reality and virtuality that define them [2]. Every AR and AV application has a different mix of both, which means that no two applications have the same human-computer interaction. Figure 1 shows this spectrum [3].

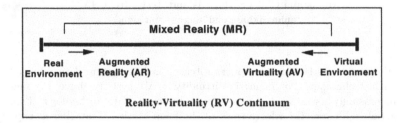

Fig. 1. The mixed reality spectrum as described by Milgram and Kashino

The device that we studied, the Leap Motion Controller, lies further towards the augmented virtuality side of the spectrum. This device operates with a completely virtual environment and adds the user's hands into the environment to allow interaction with the virtual components of the environment. The device lies face up on a table or on a flat surface. When the user's hands hover over the device, they are projected onto the screen and into the virtual environment. The projected hands are shown in Fig. 2.

Fig. 2. Hands projected from reality into a virtual environment via the Leap Motion Controller; virtual environment created in Unity.

The device allows the developer to create a virtual world with objects that can be interacted with by the projected hands. With this kind of freedom, there are endless possibilities that a creative mind could create with this technology. S. Adilkhan and M. Alimanova note it could be used for educational advancement, creating games, and for medical and rehabilitation purposes [4].

2   Related Work

2.1   Testing the Accuracy of the LMC

With the possibilities for a device such as the Leap Motion Controller appearing seemingly an endless, we aimed to find other research with a similar goal to ours in mind. What is the functionality of the Leap Motion Controller, what are its limitations, and how can we improve on this device based on our experiments? After their first release in 2013, Leap Motion Controllers have been put to test through so many experiments in order to test their accuracy and efficiency.

Generally speaking, the Leap Motion Controllers are known for being pretty accurate. However, how accurate is pretty accurate? A previous study by D. Bachmann, F. Weichert, and G. Rinkenauer has shown that the "error rate for an LMC is 7.8% while the error rate is 2.8% for the mouse device" [5]. What this is communicating to us at this point of the project is that LMC's performance won't be as accurate and precise as the mouse. However, the aim is to make this device worth it despite the drop in accuracy because of the freedom that hand tracking provides. This also communicates to us the fact that when using an LMC, fluctuations are to be expected.

The accuracy can be improved with the use of multiple devices. Research conducted by V. Kiselev, M. Khlamov, and K. Chuvilin aimed to find the optimal way to improve accuracy for this device [6]. This paper investigates the results obtained by using multiple Leap Motion controllers (up to 3 devices). Each dataset was produced by the authors by adjusting the optimal distance between the cameras and using different algorithms for recognition. Three algorithms (Logistic regression, SVC, and XGBClassifier) were used and compared to get results that showed using multiple LMC devices does increase accuracy. The recognition results gave an accuracy level below 50% when only a single device was used, however, with each additional device there was an increased accuracy level of 20%, and by using the XGBClassifier algorithm and three LMC devices they were able to achieve an accuracy of 89.32% [6].

This device is not designed to replace the mouse. Of course, it provides a very unique experience when it comes to hands-free gaming and immersion in VR. D. Bachmann, F. Weichert, and G. Rinkenauer evaluate the Leap Motion Controllers, which are normally used for hand gestures and finger point detection; however, it does have a limiting factor in tracking precise movements in the human motor system along with complications in regards to gestures which perform click movements [5]. According to Fitts law, human performance can be calculated mathematically with information and can be estimated in an index of performance of the human motor system [7]. LMCs have similar information processing to mouse devices but degrees of freedom need to be controlled with a reduction to complex movement in the coordination of the arm, hand, and fingertips. These complex movements decrease accuracy in the data collected by LMCs when compared to a mouse device. Hence the future of LMC research is focused on pointing gestures and performances. These features have massive potential and could be improved immensely with proper data collection and the help of machine learning.

2.2 Uses Beyond the Gaming Industry

Many researchers and developers are coming to the realization that this device could have a much more beneficial use to society than a cool gaming party trick. They have begun to use this device in medicinal and educational environments. Take sign language, for example, this device would help increase the accessibility of the virtual world. The LMC could aid in the teaching of sign language by recognizing signs to test students or it could assist those whose primary communication is signing. At a computer science conference in 2012, developers showed their work of attempting to recognize sign language using Microsoft's system, the Kinect [8]. While the possibility might be there for this tech to complete the job, cameras are limited in the sense that they are taking in a lot more data than the LMC which is focused on the user's hands. The conditions need to be very favorable for the cameras for them to recognize sign language with accuracy. However, when it comes to signing recognition, the LMC has advantages over the weaknesses of a typical camera and is able to translate sign language better than other devices used for the same purposes [9]. By focusing on the user's hands and creating a virtual model of them, computer algorithms can learn to accurately recognize signs.

The claim that the LMC is better equipped to recognize signs than a camera has been researched by others before. To test the limits of the recognition capabilities of the LMC, a group in the Journal of Physics: Conference Series ran an experiment testing different devices. They used a variety of devices including, sensor gloves, single cameras such as phones, and infrared-based (IR) cameras like the LMC [9]. The Leap Motion Controller can be utilized with Sign Language recognition (SLR) systems as an interaction tool for deaf people. The data (hand position of the user) is obtained by a set of left and right IR cameras of the LMC in a gray-scale format. Both D. Enikeev and S. Mustafina claim that the device has a high output rate and accuracy as bench-marking tests have shown that the camera averages 89 frames per second which allows it to make smooth images and detect complex movements [9]. LMC's also have a low tendency of being dependent on the environment it observes due to invisible IR range. The software can easily eliminate background distortions and un-trackable objects. The environment lighting rarely causes issues because of the LED brightness adjustments. However, unsuitable conditions such as complete darkness and the presence of heat-producing objects around the observable area can degrade accuracy significantly. The LMC Application Programming Interface (API) provides a large data-set that consists of skeletal data, coordinate positions, velocity, and rotation of the movements performed by the user. This allows the software to compute bulk data for statistical analysis and highlight particular qualities in the 3D structure to achieve utmost accuracy.

Another promising study showed the effectiveness of creating a database from the recognized signs. Mohamed Mohandes of King Fahd University of Petroleum and Minerals in Saudi Arabia conducted research on recording signs recognized by the LMC in the Arabic Sign Language alphabet. This work aims to recognize Arabic alphabet signs with the help of two Leap Motion Controllers placed perpendicular to each other. They took 10 samples of each of the 28 Arabic alphabet signs with 10 frames which made up 2800 frames of data. This data was further processed and analyzed in two stages, a feature extraction stage, and a classification stage. Once the feature of the hand position was extracted from the data obtained from the LMCs, it was then classified into the Arabic alphabet signs using two different methods, Linear Discriminant Analysis (LDA) and Dempster-Shafer (DS) Theory of Evidence. The results obtained from the LDA method were more promising as it yielded an accuracy level of 97.7% [10]. The LDA method is commonly used in pattern recognition and classification of patterns based on the linear combination of features to increase accuracy.

Some researchers in the medical field aim to combine the entertainment and gaming aspect of the LMC with its practical uses. Rehabilitation after a severe injury can be a draining and often very frustrating process. As someone recovers and attempts to regain dexterity in their hands and stay in the right mindset for recovery, assistance is often needed. Adilkhan and Alimanova say developers in Kazakhstan have used the LMC to create games and other virtual environments to help this process [4]. Treatment is usually a painful journey to recovery but with a little help from modern-day technology, major treatment developments have been possible. LMC can be used to improve upper body movements to track and improve body postures while VR provides an alternate universe where patients can separate themselves from the misery of treatment. Combining those aspects in a game not only facilitates physical recovery but also helps in psychological aspects in terms of positive reinforcements which enhances the patients' rewarding recovery even if it is gradual.

3 Experimental Setup

3.1 Leap Motion Controller and Unity Game Engine

The Leap Motion Controller is a hand-tracking sensor developed by Leap Motion, Inc. [11] consisting of three infrared emitters and two CCD cameras. Its primary function is gesture and finger position detection in interactive software applications. The controller is capable of tracking hands within a 3D interactive zone depth of preferred range 60 cm (23″) up to a maximum of 80 cm (31″), extending from the device in a 140° × 120° field of view, with accuracy in finger position detection of approximately 0.01 mm [11]. The LMC software is able to discern various hand elements, including bones and joints, and track them even when they are obscured by other parts of the hand.

In order to understand the Leap Motion Controller, we first needed to find a method that would best represent the abilities of this device. The device's main attraction is the hand tracking abilities and its implementation in gaming or other virtual environments. The way we went about utilizing this feature is through the program Unity. John Hass states that Unity is a platform that allows for game development in 2D, 3D, and Virtual Reality environments [12]. They have implemented features that allow for the use of the Leap Motion Controller in virtual reality and for a desktop. These implementations allow for the recreation of real-life motion in a 3D scene. The Unity game engine provides a platform to test the capabilities of the LMC. We wanted to record data on the accuracy of the tracking device. Prior to our testing, we wanted to establish a familiarity with the device and its capabilities. We developed a set of scenes designed to show different aspects of the LMC and its interaction with 3D objects. After seeing the hands and how they are tracked in the diagnostic runner, we created a virtual scene in Unity for pushing objects with the hands as rigid objects, another with a set of blocks we were able to drag and drop into a pyramid, and finally to show the full functionality; a bowling game as shown below in Fig. 3.

Fig. 3. Bowling game environment created in unity

To better understand the software behind the device as well as its abilities we used these games as a testing environment. We downloaded the necessary Software Development Kits (SDK) that Unity requires to implement Leap Motion Controller functionality and we designed bowling pins using Autodesk Inventor before we imported them on the Unity UI. Following this, we downloaded a set of modules, plugins, and assets within Unity to improve the virtual environment we were creating to better analyze the device. These modules were the Core Unity package, Hands Unity package, and Interaction Engine Unity package. The Core package provided a foundation for developing in Unity by allowing simpler and smoother interaction between Unity and the LMC. The Hands module allowed us to better visualize our hands and their live tracking within the program. As seen in Fig. 2 above, the hand models are marked with purple and yellow dots on the tracking points on the left and right hand respectively. The Interaction Engine module allows for more direct interaction between the hand tracking models and the 3D objects we placed in our game. Prior to these modules being implemented, we were only able to interact with the objects with static hands. The replicated hands in the game could push the objects as though our hands were solid blocks but, without this engine, could not replicate any other function.

Weichert *et al.* [13] discuss an important factor that should be taken into consideration when dealing with hand gesture-based interfaces (which the applications designed for the Leap Motion Controller primarily are) - the accuracy of measurement of the hand's motion. This is affected by tremors, the involuntary and somewhat rhythmic movements of muscles. Tremor varies with age and even among individuals. However, since the majority of the subjects involved in our testing fall within a narrow age range, we will assume an accuracy of ± 0.2 mm [14].

For this experiment, the setup consisted of the Leap Motion Controller and Java software used for calibration, measurement, and data collection. The Leap Development Kit version 4.1.0 was used, mainly for the purposes of troubleshooting and calibration. While the Kit version 3.2.1 was used to track raw data. Additionally, we used Eclipse Java and Java 7 in order to collect data, and Unity 2020.2.1 Personal for designing an environment in which we could test the accuracy and capabilities of the Leap Motion Controller.

3.2 Testing and Data Collection Setup

A scene consisting of interactive objects with realistic physics applied was created in Unity - this served as the testing setup. Various objects, such as spheres and cubes were added to the scene to be interacted with using hand gestures, and other structures were placed in the scene in order to observe how the interactive objects would affect or interact with them. In Eclipse, a method was coded which enabled us to collect data of the hand movements and individual finger positions, as well as specifying whether it was the left or right hand.

We were able to track the motion of the user's hand over a set of objects placed on a desk with the LMC. A small rectangular box of length 12.4 cm was placed 20 cm in front of the LMC. The test involved the user placing their hand on the front left corner of this box while the device was calibrated and executing the Java code. This setup can be seen in Fig. 4.

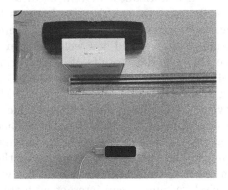

Fig. 4. Desk setup for recording location data.

On execution, the code would begin to print out X, Y, and Z coordinates of the tip of the finger that the LMC is tracking. The LMC device is the point of origin of our coordinate system. These (X, Y, Z) coordinates translate to the distance in millimeters of the tip of our index finger being moved in real life. As the user moved their finger left and right, the X coordinate would reflect the distance in millimeters. The same can be said about moving the finger forward and backward for the Y coordinate and up and down for the Z coordinate. Once the program showed that the pointer finger was recognized and it was at the starting X coordinate of 0, the user would slowly track their finger along the edge of the box. They were instructed to run their pointer finger along the edge of the box until they reached the leftmost edge. When they stopped their finger, the X coordinate was recorded and the distance between the coordinates was converted to millimeters. For example, the data may show the pointer finger was being recorded at (0, 187, 75) and would end at (−121, 209, 70). This would be recorded as the finger traveling 12.1 cm to the left, with minor adjustments in tracking up and down, as well as forward and back that are associated with the user's tremor. We ran 5 trials for each of the 3 testing users.

3.3   Accounting for Errors

While we attempt to create and conduct the perfect experiment to measure the accuracy of the LMC, we must acknowledge the faults and issues that arise. Human error plays a large part in this experiment. While each user was instructed to begin and end at the same place, there is going to be some margin of error there that will ultimately affect the results.

4   Experimental Results

The purpose of our first experimental setup was to measure the precision of the Human-Computer Interaction with the Leap Motion Controller. Ideally, the experiment would result in a horizontal movement distance of 12.5 cm every time, since that is the distance, we asked our volunteers to move their finger along the box. However, our experiment showed that there is some variability in how the LMC measures distance, and how well a human using the device can represent this distance virtually. The results of our experiment with three test subjects with five trial runs each are shown below in Fig. 5.

This data does not give us the pure accuracy of the LMC. As stated by the LMC website, the device is accurate within 0.01 m, which we have no reason to doubt based on this experiment. We cannot judge the accuracy of the actual device purely based on these results as we have to account for the element of human error. For example, the volunteer may have put their finger farther to the side of a corner in one trial than another user. What we can gain from this experiment is how precisely a human can interact with this device when asked to move a fixed distance in any direction, and how well moving a fixed distance is translated by the LMC.

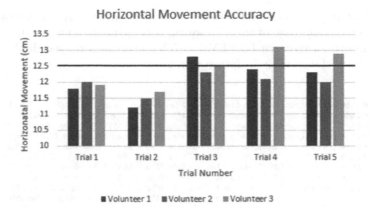

Fig. 5. Data from the accuracy experiment. The horizontal red line is the actual distance. (Color figure online)

This experiment shows us that the Human-Computer Interaction with the LMC is within one centimeter of accuracy. This means that when a user is asked to move to a specific point in the real world, the virtual accuracy of this with the LMC is within one centimeter of where it should be in the virtual world.

4.1 Introducing the Use of Convolutional Neural Networks

Machine learning promises to reduce the efforts of learning by making the machines learn through experience [15]. Conventional machine learning techniques need feature extraction as the prerequisite. This involves learning the coding of an initial set of collected data to derive new data (features).

Convolutional neural networks (CNNs), often called ConvNet, is a deep learning approach that is widely used for solving complex problems [16]. For CNNs, the number of features needed to be extracted is substantially reduced. Subsequently, due to lesser parameters, CNNs can be trained quite smoothly [17].

CNNs transform an input by putting it through a series of hidden layers organized in 3 dimensions: width, height, and depth. Every layer is made up of a set of neurons, but unlike regular neural networks (RNNs), the neurons in one layer do not connect to all the neurons in the next layer but only to a small region of it. The final output will then be reduced to a single vector of probability scores, organized along the depth dimension. Afterward, the network will perform a series of convolutions and pooling operations during which the features are detected. If shown a picture of a zebra, this is where the network would recognize its stripes, two ears, and four legs [18].

In our measuring experiment, there was some sort of inaccuracy or error. Consequently, to train our CNN, one process that comes to mind is to feed its outputs and add the calculated error component. By performing the same steps until the efficacy is observed, we should be able to train our machine to produce outputs closer to the target outputs.

Unfortunately, we were not able to set up and analyze the result of such a process due to a shortage of time. However, this opens up on this new combination of subjects of research (the LMC, CNNs, and machine learning) that will be the subject of dissection in future work.

Hand type: Left Hand, hand ID: 12, palm position: (-61.0768, 185.384, 87.8216), Timestamp: 336754357051
Hand type: Left Hand, hand ID: 12, palm position: (-60.479, 186.017, 87.5297), Timestamp: 336754365797
Hand type: Left Hand, hand ID: 12, palm position: (-59.8042, 186.708, 87.1515), Timestamp: 336754374453
Hand type: Left Hand, hand ID: 12, palm position: (-59.1742, 187.729, 86.637), Timestamp: 336754383175
Hand type: Left Hand, hand ID: 12, palm position: (-58.5317, 188.924, 86.038), Timestamp: 336754391822
Hand type: Left Hand, hand ID: 12, palm position: (-57.8951, 190.352, 85.4757), Timestamp: 336754400524
Hand type: Left Hand, hand ID: 12, palm position: (-57.3764, 191.833, 84.8842), Timestamp: 336754409172
Hand type: Left Hand, hand ID: 12, palm position: (-56.842, 193.589, 84.2876), Timestamp: 336754417844
Hand type: Left Hand, hand ID: 12, palm position: (-56.5367, 195.864, 83.9251), Timestamp: 336754426423
Hand type: Left Hand, hand ID: 12, palm position: (-56.2699, 198.708, 83.5187), Timestamp: 336754435109
Hand type: Left Hand, hand ID: 12, palm position: (-55.8892, 200.95, 82.9668), Timestamp: 336754443755
Hand type: Left Hand, hand ID: 12, palm position: (-55.6608, 203.452, 82.0831), Timestamp: 336754452469
Hand type: Left Hand, hand ID: 12, palm position: (-55.3083, 205.967, 81.3612), Timestamp: 336754461105
Hand type: Left Hand, hand ID: 12, palm position: (-54.9479, 208.661, 80.5926), Timestamp: 336754469803
Hand type: Left Hand, hand ID: 12, palm position: (-54.43, 211.464, 79.996), Timestamp: 336754478441
Hand type: Right Hand, hand ID: 14, palm position: (-53.7878, 239.06, 73.4238), Timestamp: 336754487142
Hand type: Right Hand, hand ID: 14, palm position: (-51.859, 225.206, 66.5563), Timestamp: 336754496048
Hand type: Right Hand, hand ID: 14, palm position: (-50.735, 219.605, 64.2336), Timestamp: 336754504932
Hand type: Right Hand, hand ID: 14, palm position: (-50.3963, 219.672, 62.9839), Timestamp: 336754513189
Hand type: Right Hand, hand ID: 14, palm position: (-50.2822, 222.763, 62.0327), Timestamp: 336754522321
Hand type: Right Hand, hand ID: 14, palm position: (-49.7995, 226.704, 60.9464), Timestamp: 336754530718
Hand type: Right Hand, hand ID: 14, palm position: (-49.5471, 231.92, 60.0206), Timestamp: 336754539336
Hand type: Right Hand, hand ID: 14, palm position: (-49.257, 237.091, 59.1453), Timestamp: 336754548029
Hand type: Right Hand, hand ID: 14, palm position: (-49.1767, 242.589, 58.4421), Timestamp: 336754556664
Hand type: Right Hand, hand ID: 14, palm position: (-49.0354, 248.161, 57.8158), Timestamp: 336754565348
Hand type: Right Hand, hand ID: 14, palm position: (-48.8029, 253.546, 57.0311), Timestamp: 336754573818
Hand type: Right Hand, hand ID: 14, palm position: (-48.573, 258.942, 56.246), Timestamp: 336754582533
Hand type: Right Hand, hand ID: 14, palm position: (-48.3165, 264.548, 55.4744), Timestamp: 336754591201

Fig. 6. This set of data shows the LMC calibrating itself and switching from right hand to left as it begins to recognize the user's input.

5   Conclusion and Future Work

From our research and our experiment, we can conclude that the Leap Motion Controller is very competent when it comes to Human-Computer Interaction. Based on our results, with acknowledgment of human error, the device is accurate within one centimeter. The LMC controller is a step towards greater and more immersive interaction with computers not only for games, but for practical use as well. For example, A. Borrero proposes the use of Augmented Reality and Augmented Virtuality to allow electrical engineering students to do labs from home, improving their remote learning experience [19]. This would be especially useful now that remote learning has become more common due to the Covid-19 pandemic. It will probably continue to be utilized in public schools for economic and social reasons, flexibility, and a variety of other student needs [20].

One of the impressive things about the Leap Motion Controller that we studied is that it is self-correcting. It is constantly re-calibrating itself to provide accurate feedback to the user. This can be seen in the raw data taken from the user's hand position in a test trial, shown in Fig. 6.

Figure 6 shows that when the controller first recognized user input, it believed that it was seeing the user's left hand, and projected a left hand onto the screen. Then, as it read the hand motion more, it self-corrected to realize that the hand was a right hand, which the data reflects. While this is a current attribute of the device, it is this sort of re-calibration that implementing deep learning, more specifically Convolutional Neural Network (CNN), could potentially improve upon. Convolutional Neural Networks, typically used for analyzing visual data, could take the LMC to the next level of technology.

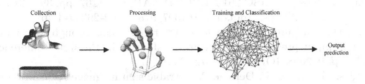

Fig. 7. This image shows a visualization of the machine learning process of the LMC.

We collected a small amount of data for our experiment. If that data is amplified and refined, we could make immense improvements to the image recognition of the LMC. Figure 7 above shows a simplified version of the process used to improve real-time recognition using machine learning [21]. As seen in some of the related work on sign language recognition using the LMC; by collecting large amounts of data, the device could become more accurate in recognizing smaller differences in gestures. This would in turn extend the range of possibilities into something beyond a gaming gadget. This device could become everyday use in the education and medical fields. We could use CNN to improve the image recognition of the LMC. Using more location data as well as the other positional data provided by the device, we could improve the image recognition of the LMC. This would lead to more fluidity in the gaming aspects of the device, more recognition capabilities in the educational uses, and accurate recreations of real-life movements in gestures in medical practice using the device. The deep learning algorithms we would perform on this device using CNN would lead to more accurate predictions and an overall increase in productivity from the LMC.

References

1. Farshid, M., Paschen, J., Eriksson, T., Kietzmann, J.: Go boldly!: Explore augmented reality (AR), virtual reality (VR), and mixed reality (MR) for business. Bus. Horiz. **61**(5), 657–663 (2018)
2. Rouse, R., Engberg, M., JafariNaimi, N., Bolter, J.D.: MRX: an interdisciplinary framework for mixed reality experience design and criticism. Digit. Creat. **26**(3–4), 175–181 (2015)

3. Moore, H.F., Gheisari, M.: A review of virtual and mixed reality applications in construction safety literature. Safety **5**, 51 (2019)
4. Adilkhan, S., Alimanova: Gamification of medical processes
5. Bachmann, D., Weichert, F., Rinkenauer, G.: Evaluation of the leap motion controller as a new contact-free pointing device. Sensors **15**(1), 214–233 (2015)
6. Kiselev, V., Khlamov, M., Chuvilin, K.: Hand gesture recognition with multiple leap motion devices. In: 2019 24th Conference of Open Innovations Association (FRUCT), pp. 163–169. IEEE (2019)
7. MacKenzie, I.S.: Fitts' law as a research and design tool in human-computer interaction. Hum.-Comput. Interact. **7**(1), 91–139 (1992)
8. Lang, S., Block, M., Rojas, R.: Sign language recognition using kinect. In: Rutkowski, L., Korytkowski, M., Scherer, R., Tadeusiewicz, R., Zadeh, L.A., Zurada, J.M. (eds.) ICAISC 2012. LNCS (LNAI), vol. 7267, pp. 394–402. Springer, Heidelberg (2012). https://doi.org/10.1007/978-3-642-29347-4_46
9. Enikeev, D., Mustafina, S.: Sign language recognition through leap motion controller and input prediction algorithm. In: Journal of Physics: Conference Series, vol. 1715, p. 012008. IOP Publishing (2021)
10. Mohandes, M., Aliyu, S., Deriche, M.: Arabic sign language recognition using the leap motion controller. In: 2014 IEEE 23rd International Symposium on Industrial Electronics (ISIE), pp. 960–965. IEEE (2014)
11. Ultraleap: Digital worlds that feel human
12. Haas, J.: A history of the unity game engine. Diss, Worcester Polytechnic Institute (2014)
13. Weichert, F., Bachmann, D., Rudak, B., Fisseler, D.: Analysis of the accuracy and robustness of the leap motion controller. Sensors **13**(5), 6380–6393 (2013)
14. Bachmann, D., Weichert, F., Rinkenauer, G.: Review of three-dimensional human-computer interaction with focus on the leap motion controller. Sensors **18**(7), 2194 (2018)
15. Carbonell, J.G., Mitchell, T.M., Michalski, R.S.: Machine Learning. Springer, Heidelberg (1983). https://doi.org/10.1007/978-3-662-12405-5
16. Indolia, S., Goswami, A.K., Mishra, S., Asopa, P.: Conceptual understanding of convolutional neural network - a deep learning approach. Proc. Comput. Sci. **132**, 679–688 (2018). International Conference on Computational Intelligence and Data Science
17. Smirnov, E., Timoshenko, D., Andrianov, S.: Comparison of regularization methods for ImageNet classification with deep convolutional neural networks. AASRI Proc. **6**, 89–94 (2014)
18. Cornelisse, D.: An intuitive guide to convolutional neural networks
19. Borrero, A.M., Márquez, J.A.: A pilot study of the effectiveness of augmented reality to enhance the use of remote labs in electrical engineering education. J. Sci. Educ. Technol. **21**(5), 540–557 (2012)
20. Superville, D.R.: Remote learning will keep a strong foothold even after the pandemic, survey finds. Educ. Week (2020)
21. Yang, L., Chen, J., Zhu, W.: Dynamic hand gesture recognition based on a leap motion controller and two-layer bidirectional recurrent neural network. Sensors **20**(7), 2106 (2020)

A Comparison of Input Devices for Gaming: Are Gamepads Still Useful in PC Environment?

Yunsun A. Hong[1]([✉]) [ID], Soojin O. Peck[1] [ID], and Ilgang M. Lee[2] [ID]

[1] Cognitive Engineering Lab, Department of Psychology, Yonsei University, Seoul,
Republic of Korea
ramuneiro9@gmail.com
[2] Department of Psychology, Yonsei University, Seoul, Republic of Korea

Abstract. As the PC has emerged as a new video game platform since its rapid performance progress, the cross-platform compatibility has grown to prominence for developers and designers. Besides, the number of users who want to use their gamepads, which is the conventional input devices of video game consoles, has been gradually increasing. This study was designed to compare the performance and usability of two input devices, the gamepad and the keyboard-mouse setup, the traditional setup used by most PC users, by task type and difficulty level. The goal of this study is to explore the interface design guidelines for each device. In this study, we measured the reaction time for the performance and the perceived workload for usability. The results indicated that the keyboard-mouse setup showed higher performance than the gamepad in general, and that the difference by the difficulty level was intensified in the physical task group. However, this tendency was not found in the cognitive task group. The keyboard-mouse setup also showed lower mental demand and physical demand than the gamepad. This result suggests that designers should not require too many simultaneous inputs when designing interfaces for gamepads, and that users should understand the characteristics of each device, in order to choose the one appropriate for their intended goals.

Keywords: HCI · User experience · Hardware interface · Input device · Gamepad · Keyboard-mouse

1 Introduction

The market size of the video game industry has seen immense development over the past few decades. The market size of the video game in the United States reached 66.9 billion USD in 2020, and predicted it will exceed 65.5 billion USD in 2021 [1] and while the number of video game consoles sold worldwide drastically declined once from 89.2 million in 2008 to 37.7 million in 2016, it recovered up to 45.7 million in 2018 [2]. At the same time, due to the improvements of PC (Personal Computer) performance, it became much easier to attract new users who do not possess a video game console. As a result of this, cross-platform compatibility has emerged as a major trend to attract new users and to maximise the profit. According to this trend, many video game digital

© Springer Nature Switzerland AG 2022
J.-H. Kim et al. (Eds.): IHCI 2021, LNCS 13184, pp. 403–416, 2022.
https://doi.org/10.1007/978-3-030-98404-5_38

distribution services provide a configuration that enables users to use gamepads in their PC environment. Over 30 million users have registered at least one gamepad to the Steam platform and over 15 million of those users have registered more than one [3]. The gamepads exceed the intrinsic restriction of the limited compatibility, and they are adopted as a new input device for the most powerful general-purpose machine.

However, not enough research has yet been done about the performance and usability between the gamepad and the keyboard-mouse setup, which has been the traditional input device setup of the PC. Alternatively, there were several studies which investigated the performance and usability of the gamepad itself alone, or which compared the gamepad with the other devices. For example, users have reported greater feelings of control and enjoyment with a gamepad, which has a traditional control scheme than with a game controller, which has a more technologically advanced control scheme [4]. Cardoso [5] also found that the gamepad control technique is both faster and more comfortable than either the Leap Motion-based or the gaze-directed techniques. The gamepad had lower tracking errors and trended towards lower workloads and a slightly higher usability score as measured by the system usability scale, therefore the gamepad may be a viable control interface even for more complex human system interaction tasks [6]. In addition, several users reported preferring using a gamepad over naturally-mapped VR controllers [7] and experienced users performed significantly better when using the gamepad than when using a multi-touch device, compared to casual users [8].

Results of the previous research, however, were not sufficiently consistent and it was assumed that this inconsistency stemmed from the attribute of the task used. Previous research used various and unique task for measuring, and to our best knowledge, there was no research which considered the attribute of the task itself as a variable. Therefore, we designed two types (physical/cognitive) and two difficulties (easy/hard) for the task and compared the performance and usability between a gamepad and a keyboard-mouse setup. Firstly, we assumed that due to the inherent restrictions in the ways to hold a gamepad, there would exist a physical upper limit on the possible numbers of simultaneous inputs. Mustaquim and Nystrom [9] found that the user's perceived level of familiarity and difficulty can be influenced by game control dimensionality; the degree of complexity inherent in a control mechanism. When the task is physically hard, in other words, the low performance and usability of the gamepad may be a result overwhelmingly influenced by the control dimensionality compared to any other factors and suggesting this is a way to possibly improve the performance and usability of a gamepad. On the other hand, the gamepad has far fewer buttons compared to the keyboard-mouse, making users spend less time finding the target button, and the arrangement of the buttons is both symmetric and intuitive. For example, the labels of the directional pad (D-pad) are arrows which represent each direction literally. Face buttons refer to the buttons on the front of the gamepad, and the shoulder buttons are the buttons on top of the gamepad. This arrangement provides users with cognitive benefits by associating a button's label and its form or function. Thus, we assumed that when the task requires cognitive processing, the performance and usability of the gamepad will be higher than when using keyboard-mouse.

In this study, we compared the performance and usability between gamepad and keyboard-mouse, and investigated which device is more suitable for each task type and difficulty. The following are the hypotheses of this study:

- H1. When the task is physically easy or hard, the performance of the gamepad will be lower than the keyboard-mouse.
- H2. When the task gets physically hard, the difference of the performance between the gamepad and keyboard-mouse will increase.
- H3. When the task is cognitively easy or hard, the performance of the gamepad will be higher than the keyboard-mouse.
- H4. When the task gets cognitively hard, the difference of the performance between the gamepad and keyboard-mouse will increase.
- H5. The gamepad will show lower mental demand than the keyboard-mouse.
- H6. The gamepad will show higher physical demand than the keyboard-mouse.

2 Method

2.1 Experiment Design

The experiment was designed with a $2 \times 2 \times 2$ mixed factorial design. Task type (Physical/Cognitive) was set as a between-subject factor and the device (Gamepad/Keyboard-Mouse) and difficulty (Easy/Hard) were set as within-subject factors. We measured reaction time in seconds as a dependent variable for the performance and investigated how the device, difficulty, and task type affected reaction time.

2.2 Participants

61 undergraduate students of Yonsei University participated in the experiment, and received course credits or monetary compensation. All participants had Korean as their first language, reported normal vision and no restrictions of moving their upper body. One participant's data was detected as an unreliable response, and was excluded from the analysis as there was a numerical discrepancy between its Cook's distance value and the others. the average age of the male participants (n = 27) was 22.96 (SD = 2.65), and the one of female participants (n = 33) was 21.48 (SD = 2.06). All participants were randomly assigned into two task type (Physical/Cognitive) groups.

2.3 Materials

A PlayStation DualShock 4 gamepad and a Logitech MK120 keyboard-mouse were used for this experiment. The experiment was conducted on an Intel i5 processor level computer and operated via PsychoPy3. Tasks were presented on a 21.5-in. LED monitor with a 1920 * 1080 resolution and 60 Hz refresh rate. Participants were assigned to the one task type group (i.e. physical or cognitive), and they conducted four task blocks including all combinations of the device types and difficulty levels. Tasks were counterbalanced by the device type, whereas the difficulty level was fixed in order from easy to hard.

In order to control the relative complexity of each input method, 10 keys were used for each controller setup in the experiment. For the gamepad, four D-pad buttons (→/↓/↑/←), four face buttons (○/✕/△/□), and two shoulder buttons (L/R) were used, while eight keyboard keys (Q/W/E/R/A/S/D/F) were used together with two mouse buttons (←/→) with the keyboard-mouse setup. In the physically easy task, one of the ten keys was presented on the screen as a target and participants were required to simply press the indicated key. In physically hard task, instead, a combination of the three keys was presented on the screen and participants were required to press the indicated keys in the order presented. Each key of each combination was from one specific position set (i.e. D-pad buttons, face buttons, or shoulder buttons for the gamepad, and upper row keys, lower row keys, or mouse buttons for the keyboard-mouse), so the participants did not need to change their grip or hand positioning to press the buttons.

The cognitively easy task required the participants to press a single key presented, similar to the physically easy task, while also providing a cognitive cue in two different colours; red and blue. A target key presented in red meant that the indicated key was on the left side of the gamepad and mouse, or in the upper row of keys on the keyboard, whereas a blue target key meant that the indicated key was on the right side of the gamepad and mouse, or the lower row of keys on the keyboard. This time, the cognitively hard task presented just one target at a time and required participants to press a single key, but it imposed a condition in two different colours; green and yellow (see Fig. 1). The target key being shown in green meant that participants had to press the within-side transposed keys for the gamepad, and the horizontally transposed keys for the keyboard-mouse. In the case of using the gamepad setup, for example, four D-pad keys (→/↓/↑/←) had to be pressed in the opposite direction (←/↑/↓/→), and the left shoulder button should be input by the left shoulder key, and vice versa. In the case of using the keyboard-mouse setup, the four upper row keys (Q/W/E/R) had to instead be input by using the lower row keys (A/S/D/F) and the left mouse button had to be input using the left mouse button and vice versa. On the other hand, if the target key appeared in yellow, the participants had to press the between-side transposed keys for the gamepad setup and the vertically transposed keys for the keyboard-mouse setup instead. In the case of using the gamepad setup, for example, four D-pad keys (→/↓/↑/←) had to be input by using the face buttons in equivalent positions (○/✕/△/□), and the left shoulder button had to be input by using the right shoulder key and vice versa. In the case of using the keyboard-mouse setup, four upper row keys (Q/W/E/R) had to be input in reverse order using the upper row keys (R/E/W/Q), and the left mouse button had to be input using the right mouse button and vice versa.

Lastly, a questionnaire was conducted after the experiment via Qualtrics. It was composed of three sections, each section containing questions about demographic information, prior experience with gamepads, and subjective experience regarding the usability of the device. NASA Task Load Index (NASA-TLX) [10] was used to measure perceived workload as usability of the device. In addition, participants had an optional choice to answer a descriptive question about overall experience of using the devices.

Cognitively Hard Task

Target colour: Green	Target colour: Yellow

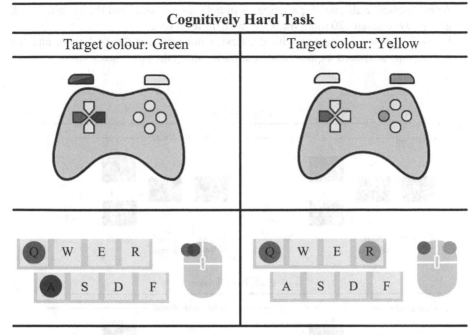

Fig. 1. Example of the Cognitively Hard Task. The green target key required participants to press the within-side transposed keys for the gamepad, and the horizontally transposed keys for the keyboard-mouse. The yellow target key, whereas, required participants to press the between-side transposed keys for the gamepad, and the vertically transposed keys for the keyboard-mouse. (Color figure online)

2.4 Experimental Procedure

The following is the procedure of entire experiment session (see Fig. 2):

1. Prior to the experiment, participants completed an informed consent form, and received an explanation of the tasks by the researchers.
2. Participants in the physical task type group were given 10 practice trials, and participants in the cognitive task type group were given 24 practice trials for the easy level task.
3. After the practice trials, the participants in both the physical and the cognitive task groups were given 120 main trials for the easy level task.
4. After a short break, participants in the physical task group were given 20 practice trials and participants in the cognitive task type group were given 40 practice trials for the hard level task.

5. After practice trials ended, participants in both the physical and the cognitive task groups were given 120 main trials for the hard level task.
6. Steps 2 to 5 were repeated with the device not used for the first time, and the participants answered a questionnaire after finishing the entire session.

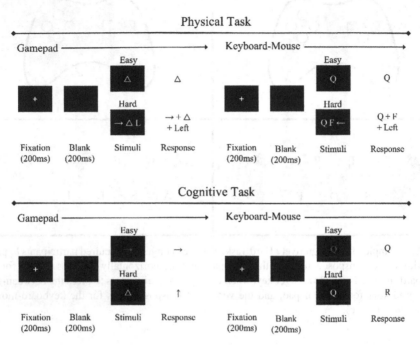

Fig. 2. Example of stimuli and procedures

2.5 Data Analysis

To prevent influence of statistical outliers in measured reaction time value, median values of each participant's reaction time were used for analysis. A repeated-measure analysis of variance (ANOVA) was conducted for both the reaction time data and perceived workload data via IBM SPSS Statistics 26 [11].

3 Results

3.1 Reaction Time

A repeated-measures ANOVA was conducted on the experiment data to investigate how the device type, difficulty level, and task type affect the reaction times (RTs) (see Fig. 3). The result indicated that the RTs were significantly higher with the gamepad ($M = 1.04$, $SD = 0.36$) condition compared to the keyboard-mouse ($M = 0.86$, $SD = 0.33$)

condition, $F(1, 58) = 117.77$, $p < .001$, $\eta_p^2 = 0.67$. The hard level ($M = 1.25$, $SD = 0.24$) condition also showed significantly higher RTs than the easy level ($M = 0.65$, $SD = 0.14$) condition, $F(1, 58) = 1400.67$, $p < .001$, $\eta_p^2 = 0.96$. However, there was no significant difference in the RTs between the physical task ($M = 0.94$, $SD = 0.34$) group and the cognitive task ($M = 0.96$, $SD = 0.37$) group, $F(1, 58) = 0.23$, $p = .63$, $\eta_p^2 = 0.004$.

In addition, there was a significant interaction between the device type and the difficulty level, $F(1, 58) = 10.42$, $p = .002$, $\eta_p^2 = 0.15$. In the hard level condition, the difference between the gamepad ($M = 1.36$, $SD = 0.22$) condition and the keyboard-mouse ($M = 1.14$, $SD = 0.21$) condition was larger than the difference between the gamepad ($M = 0.73$, $SD = 0.12$) condition and the keyboard-mouse ($M = 0.58$, $SD = 0.12$) condition in the easy level condition. There was also a significant interaction between the device type and the task type, $F(1, 58) = 6.04$, $p = .017$, $\eta_p^2 = 0.09$. The difference between the gamepad ($M = 1.05$, $SD = 0.36$) condition and the keyboard-mouse ($M = 0.83$, $SD = 0.29$) condition of the physical task group was larger than the difference between the gamepad condition ($M = 1.03$, $SD = 0.36$) and the keyboard-mouse ($M = 0.89$, $SD = 0.37$) condition of the cognitive task group. However, there was no significant interaction between the difficulty level and the task type, $F(1, 58) = 3.51$, $p = .07$, $\eta_p^2 = 0.06$. Lastly, the three-way interaction among the device type, difficulty level, and task type, $F(1, 58) = 18.86$, $p < .001$, $\eta_p^2 = 0.25$. The interaction between the device type and difficulty level in the physical task group was statistically significant, $F(1, 29) = 28.21$, $p < .001$, $\eta_p^2 = 0.49$, whereas the interaction in the cognitive task group was not, $F(1, 29) = 0.63$, $p = .43$, $\eta_p^2 = 0.02$. When the task was physically hard, the difference between the gamepad ($M = 1.37$, $SD = 0.20$) condition and the keyboard-mouse ($M = 1.08$, $SD = 0.20$) condition was larger than the difference between the gamepad ($M = 0.73$, $SD = 0.10$) condition and the keyboard-mouse ($M = 0.59$, $SD = 0.10$) condition when the task was physically easy.

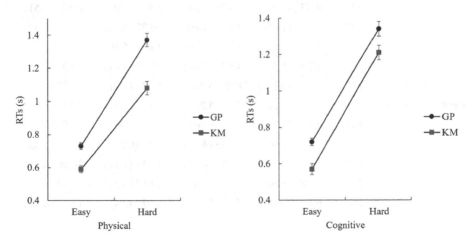

Fig. 3. RTs in each condition of the experiment. Reaction times (RTs) from the case of using each device (GP/KM) grouped by difficulty level and task type. Error bars represent standard errors of the means.

3.2 Perceived Workload

A repeated-measures ANOVA was conducted on six subscales of NASA-TLX data to investigate how device type, difficulty level, and task type affect perceived workload. Descriptive statistics for each device type, difficulty level, and task type are presented in Table 1 and the results of ANOVA are summarised in Table 2. The results (see Fig. 4) indicated that the gamepad condition showed significantly higher mental demand and physical demand than the keyboard-mouse condition, whereas there were no statistically significant differences between the gamepad and the keyboard-mouse condition in temporal demand, overall performance, effort, or frustration. The hard level condition showed significantly higher mental demand, physical demand, temporal demand, effort, and frustration, as well as lower overall performance than the easy level condition. The cognitive task group showed higher mental demand and frustration than the physical task group and there were no significant differences in physical demand, temporal demand, overall performance, or effort. Furthermore, there were no significant interactions between the device type and the difficulty level, or between the device type and the task type in any of the subscales. There was a significant interaction, however, between the difficulty level and the task type in all subscales. Lastly, the only statistically significant three-way interaction among the device type, difficulty level, and task type was in temporal demand.

Table 1. Means and standard deviations of the six subscales of NASA-TLX

Device		Physical		Cognitive	
		Easy	Hard	Easy	Hard
		M (SD)	M (SD)	M (SD)	M (SD)
Gamepad	MD	6.60 (4.48)	9.53 (5.49)	7.10 (4.87)	14.50 (4.01)
	PD	4.83 (4.84)	6.80 (5.65)	5.87 (5.40)	9.83 (6.35)
	TD	11.27 (4.88)	13.00 (4.60)	10.77 (5.04)	13.47 (4.40)
	OP	14.17 (3.51)	12.07 (3.70)	13.77 (5.10)	9.67 (4.22)
	EF	12.47 (5.36)	13.77 (4.64)	10.93 (4.81)	15.37 (3.60)
	FR	6.60 (5.11)	8.80 (5.77)	7.23 (4.09)	13.73 (4.38)
Keyboard-mouse	MD	5.87 (5.22)	7.77 (5.26)	5.93 (5.05)	12.77 (3.61)
	PD	4.10 (4.57)	6.57 (5.10)	4.10 (4.78)	8.70 (5.96)
	TD	12.07 (5.00)	12.13 (4.61)	9.73 (6.08)	12.70 (3.83)
	OP	14.03 (3.70)	12.73 (4.13)	14.37 (4.71)	10.20 (4.44)
	EF	12.77 (5.56)	13.37 (4.82)	10.17 (6.22)	14.83 (3.32)
	FR	6.47 (5.31)	7.97 (5.40)	6.07 (5.04)	12.93 (4.42)

Table 2. The result of ANOVA

Source		df	F	P	η_p^2
Between-subjects effects					
Task	MD	1	6.34	.01	0.10
	PD	1	1.62	.21	0.03
	TD	1	0.17	.68	0.003
	OP	1	1.73	.19	0.03
	EF	1	0.06	.81	0.001
	FR	1	5.15	.03	0.08
Error (Task)	MD	58			
	PD	58			
	TD	58			
	OP	58			
	EF	58			
	FR	58			
Within-subjects effects					
Device	MD	1	13.39	.001	0.19
	PD	1	4.81	.03	0.08
	TD	1	1.71	.20	0.03
	OP	1	1.67	.20	0.03
	EF	1	1.05	.31	0.02
	FR	1	3.88	.05	0.06
Device × Task	MD	1	0.07	.79	0.001
	PD	1	1.20	.28	0.02
	TD	1	1.48	.23	0.02
	OP	1	0.22	.64	0.004
	EF	1	0.77	.38	0.01
	FR	1	0.45	.50	0.01
Error (Device)	MD	58			
	PD	58			
	TD	58			
	OP	58			
	EF	58			
	FR	58			

(continued)

Table 2. (*continued*)

Source			df	F	P	η_p^2
Difficulty	MD		1	99.47	<.001	0.63
	PD		1	55.72	<.001	0.49
	TD		1	16.77	<.001	0.22
	OP		1	74.15	<.001	0.56
	EF		1	38.68	<.001	0.40
	FR		1	93.88	<.001	0.62
Difficulty × Task	MD		1	24.18	<.001	0.29
	PD		1	5.63	.02	0.09
	TD		1	4.50	.04	0.07
	OP		1	12.90	.001	0.18
	EF		1	16.57	<.001	0.22
	FR		1	30.12	<.001	0.34
Error (Difficulty)	MD		58			
	PD		58			
	TD		58			
	OP		58			
	EF		58			
	FR		58			
Device × Difficulty	MD		1	2.22	.14	0.04
	PD		1	1.63	.21	0.03
	TD		1	3.45	.07	0.06
	OP		1	0.50	.48	0.01
	EF		1	0.20	.65	0.003
	FR		1	0.10	.75	0.002
Device × Difficulty × Task	MD		1	0.19	.67	0.003
	PD		1	0.02	.88	0.000
	TD		1	6.58	.01	0.10
	OP		1	0.70	.41	0.01
	EF		1	0.81	.37	0.01
	FR		1	1.04	.31	0.02
Error (Device × Difficulty)	MD		58			
	PD		58			

(*continued*)

Table 2. (*continued*)

Source		df	F	P	η_p^2
	TD	58			
	OP	58			
	EF	58			
	FR	58			

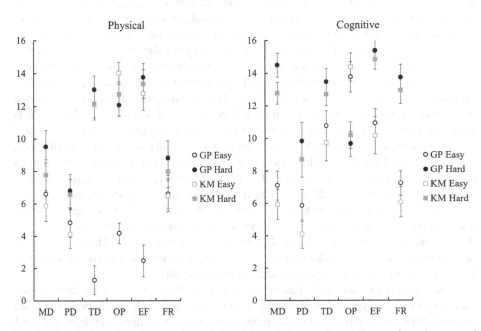

Fig. 4. Perceived workload scores in each condition of the experiment. Scores from the case of using both devices (GP/KM) in each difficulty level (Easy/Hard) grouped by task type. Error bars represent standard errors of the means.

4 Discussion

This study was designed to investigate the performance and usability of the gamepad and the keyboard-mouse setup by task type and difficulty level. Researchers found that the keyboard-mouse setup showed higher performance in general, compared to the gamepad in both task types, so hypothesis 1 was supported and hypothesis 3 was rejected. This tendency was intensified when the task was difficult or when the task was physical. With the physical task, more specifically, the difference of performance between the gamepad and the keyboard-mouse setup tended towards being higher when the task was difficult compared to when it was easy. Therefore, hypothesis 2 was supported. This tendency was not observed, however, during the cognitive task, so hypothesis 4 was rejected. The keyboard-mouse setup also showed lower mental demand and physical demand than the gamepad, thus hypothesis 5 was rejected and hypothesis 6 was supported. Hence, we carefully bring this study to a conclusion that the keyboard-mouse setup still has better performance in general than the gamepad, and that the performance of the gamepad deteriorates when the task becomes physically demanding.

Since there are some limitations to this study, we want to suggest some follow-up studies which can make up for these limitations. Firstly, most participants were not accustomed to the gamepad. 14 (23.3%) participants answered that they have never used any gamepads before, and 40 (66.7%) participants who have prior experience with gamepads answered that they used them very infrequently. In other words, 90% of the participants were not accustomed to the gamepad, thus a large amount of cognitive resources were required, and the participants had to concentrate more to perform the task while using the gamepad. On account of the possibility that the longer reaction time was caused by such processing delays, it is recommended to test proficient gamepad users for follow-up studies, or alternatively use the position of buttons as an input command indicator, instead of the label of buttons. Secondly, even though the differences in reaction times were statistically significant, it is still controversial whether this difference is sufficiently large. The difference in reaction time between the gamepad and the keyboard-mouse setup in all four conditions, consisting of two difficulty levels and two task types, ranged from 0.14 s to 0.29 s. These values can take on different meanings depending on the situation they are used in, therefore it should be interpreted carefully. Lastly, the task used in this study was quite different to real-world situations (e.g. video games). In this study, the key labels were the only indicators for the task. Real-life situations, where the gamepad and the keyboard-mouse setup are used, however, can include more well-defined indicators which are designed to strengthen the affordance. Thus, we strongly recommend conducting a follow-up study which includes various assistive indicators to find out ways to improve the performance of the gamepads.

This study is the first study that investigates how the usability of the input device varies with the task type and the difficulty level to our best knowledge. In conclusion, we suggest that inordinately complicated input requests (i.e. too many simultaneous input requests) should be refrained from for the gamepad interface. Interface designers should actively consider innate physical restrictions or workloads of the device, and optimise their software interface with the hardware interface used. The users also have to choose input devices fit for their using purpose with discretion. Although a difference of less than a second generally can be deemed a small gap, it is possible that even very slight differences can have powerful leverage in some circumstances.

5 Conclusion

This study was designed to find out which of the two input methods (i.e. gamepad, keyboard-mouse) are the more appropriate input device for various situations, by comparing performance and usability of each setup. Contrary to the increasing demand of gamepads, the number of previous studies was not sufficient, and the results of them were not consistent. In particular, researchers expected that the main factors affecting the inconsistency of the results might be the task type and task difficulty. The experimental results of our study showed that the performance of the gamepad was lower in general than the keyboard-mouse setup, and deteriorated especially drastically in the physically hard task. The questionnaire result, however, showed that only mental demand and physical demand were higher with the gamepad setup, and that there was no significant difference in perceived overall performance, effort, or frustration levels between the two. Additionally, there was no tendency of deterioration in the usability by task type and task difficulty in the questionnaire response, which existed in the actual performance of the physically hard task. When considering these results, it shows that the performance difference was affected by the task type and the task difficulty, while the difference in usability was not affected. To the best of our knowledge, our study was the first study which included the task type and the task difficulty as factors which had not been considered in previous studies, as well as using experimental tasks similar to real-world situations. Furthermore, the result of this study has not only an academic implication, but also several practical implications. Firstly, it suggests that interface designs should not require too many simultaneous (i.e. physically hard) key inputs for the gamepad. Secondly, this might be the beginning of a discussion to find a way to overcome the intrinsic weaknesses of the gamepad within the framework of product design. Lastly, it helps users choose a more suitable input device for the situation they are in.

References

1. Clement, J.: Market size of the video games industry in the United States from 2010 to 2021. Statista (2021). https://www.statista.com/statistics/246892/value-of-the-video-game-market-in-the-us/
2. Feldman, S.: What Is the Game Console's Future? Statista (2019). https://www.statista.com/chart/17465/video-game-console/
3. Valve. Controller Gaming on PC. Steamcommunity (2018). https://steamcommunity.com/games/593110/announcements/detail/1712946892833213377
4. Limperos, A.M., Schmierbach, M.G., Kegerise, A.D., Dardis, F.E.: Gaming across different consoles: exploring the influence of control scheme on game-player enjoyment. Cyberpsychol. Behav. Soc. Network. 14(6), 345–350 (2011)
5. Cardoso, J.C.: Comparison of gesture, gamepad, and gaze-based locomotion for VR worlds. In: Proceedings of the 22nd ACM Conference on Virtual Reality Software and Technology, pp. 319–320 (2016)
6. Rupp, M.A., Oppold, P., McConnell, D.S.: Comparing the performance, workload, and usability of a gamepad and joystick in a complex task. In: Proceedings of the Human Factors and Ergonomics Society Annual Meeting, vol. 57, no. 1, pp. 1775–1779. SAGE Publications, Sage CA: Los Angeles, CA (2013)
7. Ali, M., Cardona-Rivera, R.E.: Comparing gamepad and naturally-mapped controller effects on perceived virtual reality experiences. In: ACM Symposium on Applied Perception 2020, pp. 1–10 (2020)
8. Ortega, F.R., Williams, A.S., Tarre, K., Barreto, A., Rishe, N.: 3D travel comparison study between multi-touch and GamePad. Int. J. Hum.–Comput. Interact. 36(18), 1699–1713 (2020)
9. Mustaquim, M.M., Nyström, T.: Video game control dimensionality analysis. In: Proceedings of the 2014 Conference on Interactive Entertainment, pp. 1–8 (2014)

10. Hart, S.G., Staveland, L.E.: Development of NASA-TLX (Task Load Index): results of empirical and theoretical research. In: Advances in Psychology, vol. 52, pp. 139–183. North-Holland (1988)
11. IBM Corp. IBM SPSS Statisctics for Windows (Version 26.0) [Computer software]. IBM Corp, Armonk, NY (2019). https://www.ibm.com/analytics/spss-statistics-software

The Value of eCoaching in the COVID-19 Pandemic to Promote Adherence to Self-isolation and Quarantine

Jan Willem Jaap Roderick van 't Klooster[1]($\boxtimes$), Joris Elmar van Gend[1],
Maud Annemarie Schreijer[2], Elles Riek de Witte[1], and Lisette van Gemert-Pijnen[2]

[1] BMS LAB, Faculty of Behavioural, Management, and Social Sciences, University of Twente, Enschede, The Netherlands
j.vantklooster@utwente.nl

[2] Department of Psychology, Health, and Technology, Faculty of Behavioural, Management, and Social Sciences, University of Twente, Enschede, The Netherlands

Abstract. A Digital electronic Coach (eCoach) app was built and evaluated during the Covid-19 pandemic in The Netherlands. Its aim was to provide support for individuals that had to either quarantine or self-isolate after a positive corona test or an indication of a heightened risk of infection. The coach ("IsolationCoach"), its value and uses were evaluated in 29 semi-structured interviews with individuals who had quarantined or isolated themselves or were part of the general Dutch public. Three main findings emerge. First, participants found value in a digital coach that would help them comply with quarantine or isolation instructions and provided information on the practical challenges of organizing their quarantine or isolation. Second, the usage of the app, which gradually and conditionally provides relevant information as opposed to conventional paper pamphlets/email, was greatly appreciated. Third, participants experienced a need for mental support during their period of isolation or quarantine, and this could at least partially be filled by the eCoach, which provided emotional support through a Socratic method styled form of self-reflection. It was beneficial that the app was implemented rapidly within weeks using a ready-to-use platform and that its content was assessed by experts from various health-related disciplines prior to rollout. Yet, for large-scale implementation, an integrated vision and digital strategy is needed to align forms of support by the health authorities.

Keywords: Isolation · Quarantine · COVID-19 · Ecoaching

1 Introduction

The ongoing corona pandemic and associated crises caused by the Novel Coronavirus presents the world with many new challenges [1]. One challenge of key importance is to limit contact between people to prevent further spread of the virus, also known as social distancing. Tried and tested public health measures such as campaigns promoting hygiene, information campaigns and contact tracing have been used to promote healthy

© Springer Nature Switzerland AG 2022
J.-H. Kim et al. (Eds.): IHCI 2021, LNCS 13184, pp. 417–422, 2022.
https://doi.org/10.1007/978-3-030-98404-5_39

behaviour and reduction of viral spread. The pandemic has seen the development and deployment of more novel approaches as well, such as digital (and anonymized) contact tracing through apps, large scale (partial) lockdowns and mass testing [2, 3].

Infected individuals or individuals of which it is suspected that they are infected, however form an essential but specific group. The limiting or removing of their contact with other people is both essential and has proved challenging [4]. The effectiveness of measures aimed at limiting their contact with the general population in many cases hinges upon the individual's participation.

Research from the Duth Healthcare Authority's Behavioural Unit [4] showed that quarantaine obligation is oftentimes not adhered to. In particular non-adherence is: after travelling to high-risk foreign countries (70.5%); when experiencing symptoms (68,2%); when a member of the household has symptoms (53%); after local health authority notification (e.g. contact tracing) 41.4%; when a member of the household tested positive (34.5%); when tested positive oneself (17.8%). These number clearly demand multiple interventions aimed at improving adherence.

In this paper, a novel method to promote social distancing and advised behaviour for people that should quarantaine or self-isolate is introduced, using personalised app-technology to promote the advised behaviour for these people-at-risk. As such, this app provides an innovative way to promote and facilitate self-isolation rules during the pandemic and in the process provide value in both practical and emotional support to users.

The rest of this paper is structured as follows. In the following section, the methods that led to the design and implementation of the app are described. Then, the main results are described. Finally, a discussion and conclusion are presented as well as possibilities for future work.

2 Methods

Using the configurable app platform TIIM [5, 6], an ecoach was created. Two brainstorm sessions were held with health psychologists, computer scientists and ehealth experts to come to the design of the ecoach and a set of modules to provide elearning on various aspects. These modules included knowledge transfer on self-isolation, hygiene, work, shopping, seeing family, a quiz to test knowledge, and the possibility to reflect upon the situation. The latter aspect is based upon the Socratic method [7], entailing that expressing feelings about one's situation helps coping with them. The content texts in the ecoach were discussed with experts from the Dutch Municipal Health Services (GGD) and national health authority (RIVM) before implementation.

After a pilot test, implementation was done in the municipality of Dronten, The Netherlands, where the app (see Fig. 1) was tested among other health interventions. A reminder mechanism using push notifications was used to send users of the app reminders after a few days when new modules became available. To evaluate the app, interviews with users of varying age groups were held. The evaluation consisted of n = 29 interviews with both indices (persons) tested positive, as well as people that had to adhere to a quarantaine period. The interviews focused on perceived value, usability of the tool, and potential for improved adherence to the isolation rules. A questionnaire to obtain metrics about the app appreciation was given at the end of the interview to obtain standardized metrics including the Net Promotor Score. The complete procedure of the evaluation was assessed by the Ethics Committee of the University of Twente under no. 210075.

Fig. 1. Screenshots of parts of the isolation coach app. Left: Start screen with different active modules, made available over course of time, with a.o. practical tips and reflection tasks. Middle: a self-reflection module with a question to be answered by users on barriers experienced. Right: informative video on isolation and applicable measures.

3 Results

In total, 29 Dutch speaking individuals were interviewed. Participants were gathered through convenience sampling at a pilot event lasting more than a month held by the Dutch Municipal Health services in the Dutch municipality of Dronten. The event aimed to test and retest the entire population of Dronten in a time window of six weeks as a means of identifying and containing a local severe outbreak. All participants had needed to quarantine or isolate themselves in the period in which the study was conducted. Slightly more than half (n = 17) identified as female, the others as male. The youngest participant was 22 and the oldest 86 (SD = 18.5). Participants predominantly enjoyed a high level of education with 18 participants having followed university level education or equivalent. A smaller group (n = 6), were educated up until high school or trade school. Lastly, 5 participants had elementary school level education, mid school or a basic qualification (MBO level 1 or 2). The sample was not representative of the Dutch population.

Overall, the participants evaluated the Isolation Coach positively, rating it with a mean score of 7.7 (SD = 1.07) out of 10. Participants rated the coach on several sub aspects as well. Most positively rated was the user friendliness with a mean of 8.1 (SD

= 1.34). The contents were rated with a mean score of 7.5 (SD = 1.19) and the design with a mean of 7.7 (SD = 1.07). Participants evaluated four modules with each their own purpose as well. First, they rated the personalisation and length of generic quarantine and isolation instructions with a mean score of 7.6 (SD = 0.093). Second, the practical information aimed at supporting participants in reorganizing their lives and safeguarding their income was rated with a mean score of 7.4 (SD = 1.05). Third, the regular check-ups and mental support was rated with a mean score of 7.1 (SD = 1.74). Fourth, the module checking whether they had met the conditions to leave quarantine or isolation and which contained follow-up instructions was rated with a mean score of 7.4 (SD = 1.60).

Participants were asked to indicate what brought value to their experience with the IsolationCoach. The bite sized and contextually relevant instructions were most often mentioned (n = 18) as a value adding factor. The use of an interactive app as the platform (n = 8) was mentioned second most often and the additional (mental) support (n = 5) third most often.

Participants were overwhelmingly positive about the overall value of the Isolation-Coach. A large majority (n = 22) would surely (n = 10) or probably (n = 12) recommend the IsolationCoach to others. A smaller subset of 5 participants would not recommend the IsolationCoach to others.

A survey conducted during the pilot amongst the general population of the munici-pality of Dronten helped provide an image of the motivations of those who hadn't used the IsolationCoach. Amongst all participants in the larger municipality wide trial who returned the questionnaire (n = 134), most often mentioned as reason for not using the IsolationCoach was the lack of a motivation to do so. The app was deemed not necessary (n = 18) or lacked clear value (n = 8) to them. Others were unaware of its existence (n = 4) or forgot (n = 3) to use the app. There were no promotional activities under-taken for the coach and thus participants needed to actively download the app to start. Moreover, during the pilot it was established that 1% of the people who tested positive for COVID would download and use the IsolationCoach. A physical isolation coach that would regularly call and offer support to those in isolation or quarantine received similar support from the general public.

4 Discussion

In general, the Digital Isolation Coach was perceived positively by the participants. Both the app's user friendliness and value were rated highly. The eCoach was shown to be a tool with which instructions which were otherwise perceived as complex, could be chopped up in digestible chunks which were relevant for the individual participant's evolving context (e.g.when they would move from quarantine to isolation due to receiving a positive test). The possibilities concerning the use of multimedia content was a large part of what participants appreciated. Moreover, the psychological support provided through the invitation to participants to contextualize and evaluate their own situation, was greatly appreciated. Participants indicated to have a latent need in this area.

The usage of a generic ready-to-use app framework that allowed the establishment of the tailorable ecoach, without programming and within 2 weeks lead time, worked out great and was very valuable for this project.

For organizations active during a pandemic or health crisis, the IsolationCoach provides evidence of the effectiveness of eCoaching as scalable and personalizable instrument for both the increase in compliance and improving the general information position of affected individuals. Moreover, the digital nature of the coach means that it can be updated to reflect the latest information, instructions and advice to work optimally in the current situation. This provides a clear benefit in fast moving crises, like the Covid-19 pandemic. Already, quarantaine rules are changing (e.g. because of vaccination) and hence become unclear to the general public. An important note for organizations responsible for the creation or implementation of an eCoach, is that they should do so with a distinct awareness of the whole context in mind. That is to say that such a tool's effectiveness is believed to be optimal when integrated in a broader toolset which has a clear goal and narrative [8–10].

Although 'a coach in your pocket' can provide clear benefits over static text, leveraging knowlegde testing, interactive media, and reminders, solely providing it to the audience without further implementation and guidance has only limited benefits over the standard email text with instructions sent to the index.

5   Conclusions and Directions for Further Research

The app tested in this research, offers interactive information of the policies valid for self-isolation and quarantine. The app offers multimodal, practical information tailored at the personal situation (e.g. freelancer vs employed). Using the app, knowledge can be accessed in the right portion at the right time. Also, the app offered moral support and self-reflection support using the socratic method.

The app was designed from the knowledge that adherence to covid rules is poor. Although developed under time pressure, it was beneficial that the content was assessed by various experts, including medical experts, behavioural scientists, health scientists, ehealth specialists and psychologists. Also, a ready-to-use platform to be able to deploy the ecoach was crucial.

In this research, the ecoach developed was shown to be appealing and user friendly, based on 29interviews with end users, from varying educational levels.

In a next phase, the scaling up of digital support in the pandemic should be research more widely as well as a controlled test for effectivity. This will be challenging as the local health authorities face difficulties in implementing change and lack the embracement of an innovative culture. As pointed out by [8], there is a lack of an integral view on the implementation of an effective digital strategy, and a standalone rather than an integrated approach is being followed. The support by the app should be aligned with other forms of support by the health authorities, and not via additional chains and institutions. Otherwise, the low uptake (1%, comparable to physical isolation coaches) seen in this pilot study will likely not be improved, because of fear of data privacy, hesistance, and resistance to the unknown.

References

1. World Health Organization. COVID-19. https://www.who.int/emergencies/diseases/novel-coronavirus2019. Accessed 6 Jan 2022

2. van 't Klooster, J.W.J.R., Slijkhuis, P.J.H., van Gend, J., Bente, B., van Gemert-Pijnen, L.: First eyetracking results of dutch coronamelder contact tracing and notification app. In: Singh, M., Kang, D.-K., Lee, J.-H., Tiwary, U.S., Singh, D., Chung, W.-Y. (eds.) IHCI 2020. LNCS, vol. 12616, pp. 199–207. Springer, Cham (2021). https://doi.org/10.1007/978-3-030-68452-5_21

3. Bente, B.E., et al.: The dutch COVID-19 contact tracing app (the CoronaMelder): usability study. JMIR Format. Res. **5**(3), e27882 (2021). https://doi.org/10.2196/27882

4. RIVM Behavioural Unit. https://www.rivm.nl/gedragsonderzoek/over-corona-gedragsunit. Accessed 6 Jan 2022

5. Lentferink, A., et al.: On the receptivity of employees to just-in-time self-tracking and eCoaching for stress management: a mixed-methods approach. Behav. Inf. Technol. (2021). https://doi.org/10.1080/0144929X.2021.1876764

6. TIIM (Twente Intervention and Interaction instruMent). https://bmslab.utwente.nl/knowledge base/tiim/. Accessed 6 Jan 2022

7. Oyler, D.R., Romanelli, F.: The fact of ignorance: revisiting the Socratic method as a tool for teaching critical thinking. Am. J. Pharm. Educ. **78**(7), 144 (2014). https://doi.org/10.5688/ajpe787144

8. Ebbers, W.: Eindrapportage Evaluatie CoronaMelder-meldingen van kans op besmetting (2021). https://www.rijksoverheid.nl/onderwerpen/coronavirus-app/nieuws/2021/03/23/ond erzoek-toont-coronamelder-helpt-ggd-bij-voorkomen-verspreiding

9. Roadmap to Pandemic Resilience: Massive Scale Testing, Tracing, and Supported Isolation (TTSI) as the Path to Pandemic Resilience for a Free Society. Harvard. https://ethics.harvard.edu/covid-19-response. Accessed 6 Jan 2022

10. Tanwar, G., Chauhan, R., Singh, M., Singh, D.: Pre-emption of affliction severity using HRV measurements from a smart wearable; case-study on SARS-Cov-2 symptoms. Sensors. **20**(24), 7068 (2020). https://doi.org/10.3390/s20247068

Signal Processing and Complex System

Methods of Constructing Equations for Objects of Fractal Geometry and R-Function Method

Sh. A. Anarova[1]($\boxtimes$) (iD) and Z. E. Ibrohimova[2]($\boxtimes$) (iD)

[1] Tashkent University of Information Technologies, 100200 Tashkent, Republic of Uzbekistan
shahzodaanarova@gmail.com
[2] Research Institute for the Development of Digital Technologies and Artificial Intelligence,
Tashkent, Uzbekistan
zulayhoibrohimova90@gmail.com

Abstract. The paper discusses methods for constructing equations for objects of fractal geometry and method of R-functions. Basic concepts of the theory of fractals, areas of application and their types have been presented. The basic methods of constructing fractals are taken into account: L-system method, system of iterating functions, set theory method, and the R-function method. Equations of complex structures of fractal geometry have been developed based on the R-functions method. Using the of straight-line equation, the equation of a circle and constructive means of the method of R-functions R0: R-conjunctions and R-disjunctions are constructed various kinds of fractals, equations of fractals consisting of intersections of lines, tangencies of circles. Based on these equations, various prefractals were generated by specifying the number of iterations n and the angle of inclination. Equations are constructed for fractal antennas based on the "Cayley tree", fractal ring monopolies and the Sierpinski curve that are used in antenna design. These fractals are very beautiful, which can be used in the creation of computer landscapes, in various illustrations, in telecommunications, in the textile industry, in drawing patterns in ceramic and porcelain products, as well as in the development of patterns for the modern design of Uzbek national carpets, fabrics, costumes, etc.

Keywords: Fractal · Self-similarity · L-systems · Cantor set · IFS · R-function method · R-conjunctions · R-disjunctions · Pre-fractal · Sierpinski curve

1 Introduction

Fractal geometry originated in the 19th century. Cantor by using a simple repeating procedure, turned the line into a set of unconnected points, thus obtained the so-called Cantor dust [1].

The word "fractal" was introduced by Benoit R. Mandelbrot from the Latin word "fractus", which means broken, i.e. divided into parts [1]. One of the definitions of a fractal is as follows: A fractal is a geometric shape made up of parts that can be divided into parts, each of which will represent a reduced copy of the whole. Namely, a fractal is an object for which it does not matter with what magnification it is viewed

© Springer Nature Switzerland AG 2022
J.-H. Kim et al. (Eds.): IHCI 2021, LNCS 13184, pp. 425–436, 2022.
https://doi.org/10.1007/978-3-030-98404-5_40

through a magnifying glass, but with all its magnifications, the structure remains the same. Large-scale structures completely repeat smaller-scale structures.

Self-similarity is one of the main properties of fractals. The dimension of an object shows by what law its internal area grows. Similarly, the "volume" of a fractal increases with an increase in its size, but its dimension is not an integer value, but a fractional one. Therefore, the border of a fractal figure is not a line: at high magnification, it becomes clear that it is blurred and consists of spirals and curls, repeating the figure itself on a small scale.

Currently, fractals have found wide application in various fields of science and technology: computer graphics, radio engineering, telecommunications, television, physics and other natural sciences, textile and light industry, urban planning and architecture, medicine, etc. [1–5].

Research related to fractals changes a lot of the usual ideas about the world around us, about the most common objects such as clouds, rivers, trees, mountains, grasses, etc. [1–5].

1.1 Types of Fractals

Most scientists and authors identify the main large groups of fractals: geometric, algebraic (dynamic), stochastic and natural [1–5].

Geometric Fractals: Geometric fractals were studied by mathematicians in the 19th century. Fractals of this class are the most illustrative, because self-similarity is immediately visible in them. An object is called self-similar when the enlarged parts of the object resemble the object itself and each other. In the two-dimensional case, geometric fractals are obtained by specifying a certain broken line (or surface in the three-dimensional case), called a generator. In one step of the algorithm, each of the segments that make up the polyline is replaced by a polyline - a generator, in the appropriate scale. As a result of an infinite number of repetitions of this procedure, a fractal curve has been obtained, i.e. geometric fractal. With the apparent complexity of the resulting curve, its general appearance is set only by the shape of the generator. Examples of such curves are the Koch curve, the Levy curve, the Minkowski curve, the Peano curve, the Harter-Heitway curve. Geometric fractals also include the Sierpinski triangle, Cantor set, Sierpinski carpet, Menger sponge, Pythagoras tree.

Algebraic Fractals (Dynamic Fractals): Mandelbrot set, Julia set, Newtonian basins (fractals), biomorphs, Sierpinski triangles. Fractals of this type are obtained using nonlinear processes in n-dimensional spaces (nonlinear dynamical systems). Based on this, the name of the group describes the fractals themselves. Science is currently the most studied two-dimensional processes. This is the largest group of fractals. They also owe their name to the fact that they are built on the basis of algebraic formulas as one of the methods. Nonlinear dynamical systems have several stable states - attractors. The state in which a dynamical system finds itself after a certain number of iterations or a certain number of changes depends on its initial state. As a consequence, each stable state will have a certain region of initial states, from which the system will get to the final states.

Stochastic Fractals. Fractals, during the construction of which some parameters are randomly changed in the iterative process. A typical representative of this class of fractals "Plasma". To construct it, take a rectangle and define a color for each corner. Next, we find the center point of the rectangle and paint it in a color equal to the arithmetic mean of the colors at the corners of the rectangle plus some random number. Two-dimensional stochastic fractals are very often used to model the terrain and sea surface.

Stochastic algorithms give a greater variety of shapes due to elements of controlled randomness. The fractal image turns out to be unique, which is sometimes a disadvantage due to the impossibility of foreseeing the results of a long calculation in advance. The transformed elements in the process of fractal construction can move, rotate, shrink, reflect.

Natural Fractals. Natural fractals are objects in nature that have fractal properties. For example, in nature, such fractals include the human circulatory system, lungs and the structure of the eye. And also, the crowns and leaves of trees. It also includes starfish, sea urchins, corals, seashells, and some plants such as cabbage and broccoli. If we consider inanimate nature, then there are much more interesting examples there than in living nature. Lightning, snowflakes, clouds, well-known to all, patterns on windows on frosty days, crystals, mountain ranges - all these are examples of natural fractals from inanimate nature. But the most interesting fractals are natural ones.

However, today there is no unified approach to the classification of fractals. For example, A.A. Potapov, one of the leading specialists in the theory and practice of fractals, gives other forms of classification of fractals [3] This classification was approved by B. Mandelbrot himself, who is the father of the general concept of fractals.

At the IREE named after Kotelnikov RAS, research was carried out on the following tasks of fractal radio physics and fractal radar:

- texture and fractal image processing and fractal detection of ultra-weak signals in intense non-Gaussian interference and noise;
- rejection of Gaussian statistics in experiments. Fine structure of reflected impulse signals and a new class of features;
- Fractal signatures and their application in signal processing;
- fundamentals of methods for constructing fractal signals and fractal methods of information transmission;
- fractal electrodynamics and fractal "smart" materials;
- scaling of a rough layer and fractal signatures in the problems of evaluating the microrelief of machined surfaces;
- fractal impedances and fractional operator modeling. First fractal capacitor;
- basic methods for constructing fractal impedances and their promising fields of application;
- dynamic fractal models of wave propagation and scattering by randomly inhomogeneous media;
- The concept of fractal radioelements and fractal radio systems.

In Uzbekistan, the theory of fractals and its applications was studied by academician B.A.Bondarenko [6]. He investigated the classical and new arithmetic, geometric and combinatorial properties of arithmetic triangles and pyramids that generalize Pascal's triangle. The problems of divisibility and distribution of elements of generalized triangles and Pascal pyramids modulo p are studied. On the basis of this, flat and spatial classes of fractals and generalized arithmetic graphs, which are discrete mathematical models of some structures and processes of technology and natural science, have been constructed and investigated. He developed combinatorial algorithms for using arithmetic triangles for constructing non-orthogonal polynomials and using them to solve problems in mathematical physics [7, 8].

2 Methods for Constructing Fractals

Currently, there are various methods for constructing fractals [1–6, 13–18].

2.1 L-System Method

The concept of L-systems, closely related to self-similar fractals, appeared only in 1968 thanks to Aristrid Lindenmayer. Initially, L-systems were introduced in the study of formal languages, and were also used in biological models of selection. They can be used to construct many well-known self-similar fractals, including the Koch snowflake and the Sierpinski carpet [11–13]. Some other classical constructions, for example Peano curves (works of Peano, Hilbert, Sierpinski), also fit into this scheme. And, of course, L-systems open the way to an infinite variety of new fractals, which is the reason for their widespread use in computer graphics for constructing fractal trees and plants. Our presentation of L-systems follows mainly from the work of Pruzinkevich and Canaan [11] and is limited to the case of deterministic L-systems and graphics on the plane.

For the graphical implementation of L-systems, the so-called turtle (turtle) is used as an inference subsystem. In this case, the point (turtle) moves across the screen in discrete steps, as a rule, tracing its own trail, but if necessary, it can move without drawing. We have at our disposal three parameters (x, y, α), where x, y are the coordinates of the turtle, α is its direction. The turtle is trained to interpret and execute a sequence of commands given by a code word, the letters of which are read from left to right. The code word is the result of the L-system and may include the following letters:

F – move forward one step, drawing a trail;
b – move forward one step without drawing a trace;
[– open a branch (see below for details);
] – close branch (see below for details);
+ – increase the angle α by θ;
− – decrease the angle α by the value θ.

The step size and the value of the increment in angle θ are predefined and remain unchanged for all movements of the turtle. If the initial direction of motion α (the angle measured from the positive direction of the X-axis) is not indicated, then we assume α equal to zero.

Several examples illustrate the use of branch commands (denoted by], [) and auxiliary variables (denoted by X, Y, etc.). Branching commands are used to build trees and plants, and auxiliary variables make it much easier to build some L-systems.

A formally deterministic L-system consists of an alphabet, an initialization word, called an axiom or initiator, and a set of generative rules that indicate how the word should be transformed when moving from level to level (from iteration to iteration). For example, you can replace the letter F with the generative rule $newf = F\text{-}F ++ F\text{-}F$, which corresponds to the Koch snowflake L-system discussed below. Symbols $+$, $-$,], [are not updated, but simply remain in the places where they met. The renewal of a letter in a given word is assumed to be simultaneous, i.e. all letters of a word of one level are updated before any letter of the next level.

2.2   Iterated Function Systems (IFS)

Iterated Function Systems is a collection of contracting affine transformations. As you know, affine transformations include scaling, rotation, and parallel translation. An affine transform is considered to be compressive if the scaling factor is less than one [1, 4, 5].

Let us consider in more detail the construction of the Koch curve using affine transformations [16, 17].

Each new curve element contains four links derived from the generating element using scaling, rotation, and translation.

1.   To obtain the first link, it is enough to compress the original segment three times.
2.   The next link is constructed using all possible transformations, namely: parallel translation by *1/3* along the *OX* axis, rotation by *60°* (counterclockwise) and compression by three times.
3.   The third link is constructed similarly to the second one: parallel transfer by *2/3* along the *OX* axis, rotation by *60°* (counterclockwise), compression by *3* times along the *OY* axis and compression by *3* times along the *OX* axis.
4.   The last link: parallel transfer by *2/3* along the *OX* axis, compression by *3* times.

Now we can find a system of iterating functions to describe the Koch curve. It remains only to perform a superposition of affine transformations - scaling, rotation and parallel translation.

Formulas for calculating new coordinates x', y' under affine transformations are known from the course of analytical geometry [11]:

$$x' = x * a + y * b + e, \quad y' = x * c + y * d + f. \tag{1}$$

If we agree to consider only such coordinate systems for which the shortest rotation from the first basis vector to the second occurs counterclockwise (we will call such systems right-handed), then any coordinate transformation will be determined by the formulas:

$$a = \cos(\text{alpha}) * \text{scale\_}x,$$

$$b = -\sin(\text{alpha}) * \text{scale\_}x,$$

$$c = \sin(\text{alpha}) * \text{scale}\_y,$$
$$d = \cos(\text{alpha}) * \text{scale}\_y,$$
$$e = \text{move}\_x, f = \text{move}\_y \qquad (2)$$

where $scale\_x$ - scaling along the OX axis; $scale\_y$ - scaling along the OY axis; $alpha$ - rotation angle (counterclockwise); $move\_x$ - parallel move along the OX axis; $move\_y$ - parallel move along the OY axis.

The obtained coefficients a, b, c, d, e, f for each link will form the required system of iterating functions.

IFS can be implemented by various methods [4, 7–10]: deterministic algorithm, randomized algorithm. In addition, when drawing objects of fractal geometry, you can use the IFS with condensation, with which you can build a huge number of different fractal configurations [7–10].

2.3 Set Theory Method

Let us construct the Contor set equation. The classical Cantor set (or Cantor dust) is well known from the course of mathematical analysis as an example of a set of zero Lebesgue measure, whose cardinality is equal to the cardinality of the continuum [0, 1]. The fractal properties of Cantor's dust are of great importance, especially considering the fact that many of the known fractals are close relatives of this set [1, 2, 4, 5].

The construction of the classical Cantor dust begins with throwing out the middle third (excluding the ends) of a unit segment. That is, the original set is the segment [0, 1], and the first step is to delete the open interval (1/3, 2/3). At the next and all other steps, the middle third (not including the ends) of all segments of the current level is thrown out. Thus, we get a sequence of sets:

$$C_0 = [0, \ 1];$$
$$C_1 = [0, \ 1/3] \cup [2/3, \ 1];$$
$$C_2 = [0, \ 1/9] \cup [2/9, \ 1/3] \cup [2/3, \ 7/9] \cup [8/9, \ 1];$$
$$\dots$$
$$C.$$

The limit set C, which is the intersection of the sets C_n, $n = 0, 1, 2, \ldots$, is called the classical Cantor dust or simply Cantor dust.

The Cantor set of dimension $d \approx 0.9542$. Consider an example of a self-similar fractal that is the Cantor set of fractal dimension $d = \log(9)/\log(10) \approx 0,9542$ (while the dimension of Cantor dust is $d \approx 0.6309$).

Let X denote the set of all real numbers of the segment [0, 1], in decimal representation of which

$x = 0, \ x_1 x_2 x_3 \ldots$ any number is missing, say, number 7. For example, numbers

$$0 = 0,0000\ldots \quad 1 = 0,9999\ldots \quad 1/4 = 0,2500\ldots$$

belong to the set X. X also belongs to the number 0.7, since we can write it as follows: $0,7 = 0,6999\ldots$, that is, without using the number 7.

After some reflection, it becomes clear how to construct the set X. Let $X_0 = [0, 1]$. Divide X_0 into ten equal intervals. The number x_1 indicates which of the intervals x belongs to. If $x_1 = 0$, then x falls into the first interval, etc. Ambiguity arises only when x coincides with the end of a segment. Then there are two possible representations of the number x: one ends with all zeros, the other with all nines. However, this does not create any problems, since we agreed in advance that no digit x_i is equal to 7. Since $x_1 \neq 7$, then x does not fall into the eighth interval, that is, x does not belong to the interval $(0.7;\ 0.8)$. We drop this interval and denote the remaining set by X_1. Divide each of the nine remaining intervals into ten equal parts. Since $x_2 \neq 7$, we can discard every eighth of the resulting intervals. Let us denote the new set by X_2. Repeating the described procedure an infinite number of times, we obtain a sequence of nested sets.

It follows from the construction that X is a union of $N = 9$, 10 times smaller $(r = 1/10)$ copies of itself. Thus, X is a self-similar fractal, and its fractal dimension is equal to

$$d = \log(9)/\log(10) \approx 0,9542.$$

Cantor set of dimension $d = 1$. Passing from a straight line to a plane, one can construct a Cantor set of dimension $d = 1$. The next example belongs to Magdi Mohammed. Let the original set be a unit square on the plane with vertices at the points $(0, 0)$, $(1, 0)$, $(1, 1)$ and $(0, 1)$. At each step, the existing squares are replaced by four smaller ones, as shown in Fig. 1. The limiting set of this construction is a self-similar fractal with $N = 4$ and the similarity coefficient $r = 1/4$. Therefore, its dimension is equal to

$$d = \log(4)/\log(4) = 1.$$

It follows from the construction that the resulting set is a Cantor set, since it is compact, perfect, and completely discontinuous.

2.4 Method of R-Functions for Constructing Fractal Equations

In the method of R functions (RFM) problem [9, 10], the construction of equations for a number of geometric objects.

Consider the construction of the equations of the geometry of the regions:

1. Cayley Tree Fractal Antennas. A fractal antenna is a series of wire sections of different lengths. With each new iteration, segments of a certain length are added to the antenna, so that for each odd iteration, the length remains the same, and with each even iteration, the length is halved (Fig. 1). In [3], the distributions of the current in the Kayley tree antenna of the 6th order were investigated. New sections of the aperture begin to play a role in the formation of the antenna parameters (Fig. 1).

Now let's construct the Cayley tree equation based on the R-function method. Let's construct the Cayley tree equation.

Step #1.

$$i = 1;\ a_1 = l/2;\ b_1 = l/2;$$

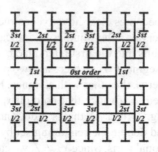

Fig. 1. Cayley tree of the 6th order

$$f_{oe}(x, y) = \frac{a_{11}^2 - (x + a_1)^2}{2a_{11}} \geq 0, \ (a_{11} - \text{small number}),$$

$$f_{op} = \frac{a_{11}^2 - (a_1 - x)^2}{2a_{11}} \geq 0, \quad \varphi_0(x, y) = \frac{b_1^2 - y^2}{2b_1} \geq 0;$$

$$f_1 = f_{oe}(x, y) \wedge \varphi_0(x, y) \geq 0, f_2(x, y) = f_{op}(x, y) \wedge_0 \phi_0(x, y) \geq 0, \tag{3}$$

$$\omega_{01}(x, y) = f_1(x, y) \vee_0 f_2(x, y) \geq 0,$$

$$f_3(x, y) = \frac{a_1^2 - x^2}{2a_1} \geq 0, \quad f_4(x, y) = \frac{b_{11}^2 - y^2}{2b_{11}} \geq 0, \tag{4}$$

(*b_{11}-sufficiently small number*),

$$\omega_{02}(x, y) = f_3(x, y) \wedge_0 f_4(x, y) \geq 0,$$

$$f_{1ay}(x, y) = \frac{b_{11}^2 - (y + b_1)^2}{2b_{11}} \geq 0, \quad f_{1by}(x, y) = \frac{b_{11}^2 - (b - y)^2}{2b_{11}} \geq 0, \quad c = b_1/2,$$

$$\varphi_{1lx}(x, y) = \frac{c^2 - (x + a_1)^2}{2c} \geq 0, \quad \varphi_{1px} = \frac{c^2 - (x - a_1)^2}{2c} \geq 0,$$

$$\omega_{03}(x, y) = \left(f_{1ay}(x, y) \wedge_0 \varphi_{1lx}(x, y)\right) \vee_0 \left(f_{1ay}(x, y) \wedge_0 \varphi_{1px}(x, y)\right) \vee_0$$

$$\vee_0 \left(f_{1by}(x, y) \wedge_0 \varphi_{1lx}(x, y)\right) \vee_0 \left(f_{1by}(x, y) \wedge_0 \varphi_{1px}(x, y)\right) \geq 0,$$

$$\omega_1(x, y) = \omega_{01}(x, y) \vee_0 \omega_{02}(x, y) \vee_0 \omega_{03}(x, y) \geq 0 \tag{5}$$

Step #2.

$$i = 2; a_1 = a_1/2; b_1 = b_1/2; \tag{6}$$

$$\omega_2(x, y) = \omega_1(x - a_1, y - b_1) \vee_0 \omega_1(x + a_1, y - b_1) \vee_0 \omega_1(x + a_1, y + b_1) \vee_0$$

$$\vee_0 \omega_1(x - a_1, y + b_1) \vee_0 \omega_1(x, y) \geq 0.$$

Now we build an iterative process, and as a result we get

$$i = k; a_1 = a_1/2; b_1 = b_1/2; \tag{7}$$

$$\omega_k(x, y) = \omega_{k-1}(x - a_1, y - b_1) \vee_0 \omega_{k-1}(x + a_1, y - b_1) \vee_0 \omega_{k-1}(x + a_1, y + b_1) \vee_0$$
$$\vee_0 \omega_{k-1}(x - a_1, y + b_1) \vee_0 \omega_{k-1}(x, y) \geq 0, \ k = 3, 4, 5,...$$

In this: i-step, k-number of iterations, l-initial line length, a_1, a_{11}, b_1, b_{11} - the length of the shrinking segments in the left and right branches, f_1, f_2, f_3, f_4 - functional equation of each branch, ω_i-generalization function.

The calculation results for different values of k are shown in Fig. 2.

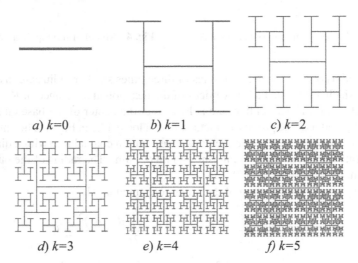

a) k=0   b) k=1   c) k=2

d) k=3   e) k=4   f) k=5

Fig. 2. Cayley tree: in different values of n. n-number of iterations

2. Fractal Ring Monopolies. The study of fractal ring structures, first proposed by the authors of [3], was carried out using CAD Antsoft HFSS, thanks to the convenient design interface of which it is easy to create ring structures, taking into account the properties of symmetry and similarity.

As the basic element of the fractal antenna structure of the first iteration $A1$, we took a ring with a radius of *11* mm, a thickness of *0.4* mm along the *OX* axis and *0.2* mm along the radius. The algorithm for constructing the structure of the fractal aperture shown in Fig. 3 is as follows.

Inside the base element of the zero iteration, there are seven rings with a radius three times smaller than the original element. The rest of the parameters (width and thickness of the base element ring) are left unchanged. The centers of the six small circles are located at a distance of $R * 2/3$ at the vertices of the hexagon. The center of the seventh circle coincides with the center of the main antenna. We will call this construction the first iteration cycle of the construction algorithm, and the antenna will be briefly designated by the abbreviation $A1$ [3, 19, 20].

To construct the ring monopoly of the second iteration $A2$, the same algorithm [9] was used as for model $A1$ (Fig. 4).

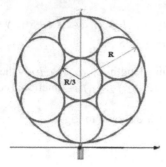

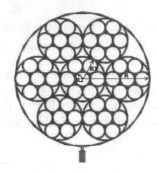

Fig. 3. Model of mono-pole antenna A1   **Fig. 4.** Model of monopole antenna A2

In the radius of each circle, six circles of three times smaller radius are inserted, the centers of which are located at the vertices of the hexagon at a distance of $R * 2/3$ from the original radius. The seventh circle is located at the center of the base circle. Thus, the resulting model of the proposed fractal antenna looks like in Fig. 4. The antenna curl is made in the same way as in the previous cases, with a coaxial line with a diameter of 0.5 mm. Antenna thickness 0.4 mm, rings width 0.2 mm. The radius of the outer circle $R = 11$ mm, $R1 = R/3$, $R2 = R/9$ (Fig. 4).

Let us construct the equation of the monopole antenna $A1$:

$$\omega_0 = \frac{R_0^2 - x^2 - y^2}{2R} \wedge_0 \frac{x^2 + y^2 - (R - dr)^2}{2R} \geq 0,$$

$$r_1 = \frac{1}{3}R_0, \quad a_1 = \frac{2}{3}R_0, \quad dx = \frac{\sqrt{3}}{3}R_0, \quad dy = \frac{1}{3}R_0,$$

$$\omega_{10} = \omega_0(r_1, x, y), \quad \omega_{11} = \omega_0(r_1, x, y - a_1), \quad \omega_{12} = \omega_0(r_1, x, y + a_1),$$

$$\omega_{13} = \omega_0(r_1, x + dx, y - dy), \quad \omega_{14} = \omega_0(r_1, x + dx, y + dy), \qquad (8)$$

$$\omega_{15} = \omega_0(r_1, x - dx, y + dy), \quad \omega_{16} = \omega_0(r_1, x - dx, y - dy),$$

$$\omega_1 = (\omega_{00} \vee_0 (\omega_{10} \vee_0 \omega_{11} \vee_0 \omega_{12} \vee_0 \omega_{13} \vee_0 \omega_{14} \vee_0 \omega_{15} \vee_0 \omega_{16})),$$

where dr is small number circle thickness.

To obtain a monopole antenna $A2$ and generalize it, we construct an iterative process.

$$r_i = \frac{1}{3}r_{i-1}, \quad a_i = \frac{2}{3}r_{i-1}, \quad dx = \frac{\sqrt{3}}{3}r_{i-1}, \quad dy = \frac{1}{3}r_{i-1},$$

$$\omega_{i0} = \omega_{i-1}(r_i, x, y), \quad \omega_{i1} = \omega_{i-1}(r_i, x, y - a_i), \quad \omega_{i2} = \omega_{i-1}(r_i, x, y + a_i),$$

$$\omega_{i3} = \omega_{i-1}(r_i, x + dx, y - dy), \quad \omega_{i4} = \omega_{i-1}(r_i, x + dx, y + dy), \qquad (9)$$

$$\omega_{i5} = \omega_{i-1}(r_i, x - dx, y + dy), \quad \omega_{i6} = \omega_{i-1}(r_i, x - dx, y - dy),$$

$$\omega = (\omega_{00} \vee_0 (\omega_{i0} \vee_0 \omega_{i1} \vee_0 \omega_{i2} \vee_0 \omega_{i3} \vee_0 \omega_{i4} \vee_0 \omega_{i5} \vee_0 \omega_{i6})) \; i = 2, 3, 4, \ldots$$

It should be noted that for $i = 2$ we obtain the antenna equation A2, the calculation results for $k = 0, 1, 2, 3$ are shown in Fig. 5.

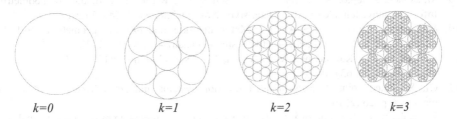

$k=0$ $k=1$ $k=2$ $k=3$

Fig. 5. Monopole antenna A2 for different values of n. n-number of iterations

3 Conclusion

The fractal equation and recursive algorithms have been developed using L-system, IFS, set theory and RFM. On the basis of the RFM, an automated technology for describing the boundaries of complex shapes has been developed. A technology has been developed for geometric modeling of complex fractal structures using the capabilities of the R-function method to create fractal designs.

In this paper, equations of only some types of fractals are constructed, which indicates that this problem is poorly investigated from the point of view of the analytical description of the equations of fractals. Currently, there are many types of fractals. In order to construct their equation, it is necessary to conduct serious scientific research on the construction of fractal equations based on the constructive method of R-functions by V. L. Rvachev.

References

1. Mandel'brot, B.: Fraktalnaya geometriya prirodi: Per. s angl. M.:Institut komp'juternyh issledovanij, p. 656 (2002)
2. Edgar, G.: Measure "Topology and Fractal Geometry," p. 293. Springer, Heidelberg (2008)
3. Potapov, A.A.: Fraktaly, Skejling i drobnye operatory v radiotehnike i elektronike: Sovremennoe sostojanie i razvitie. Žurnal radioèlektroniki, no. 1, Moskva (2010)
4. Balhanov, V.K.: Osnovy fraktal'noj geometrii i fraktal'nogo isčislenija, p. 224. Izd-vo Burjatskogo gosuniversiteta, Ulan-Udi (2013)
5. Falconer K.: "Fractal Geometry": Mathematical Foundations and Applications, p. 400 (2014)
6. Bondarenko, B.A.: Generalized Pascal Triangles and Pyramids, their Fractals, Graphs, and Applications., 3rd edn., p. 296. Fibonacci Associations, Santa Clara (2010)

7. Anarova, S., Nuraliev, F., Narzulloev, O.: Construction of the equation of fractals structure based on the rvachev r-functions theories. In: Journal of Physics: Conference Series, vol. 1260. Institute of Physics Publishing (2019). https://doi.org/10.1088/1742-6596/1260/7/072001

8. Murodillayevich, N.F., Amanbayevna, A.S., Mirzayevich, N.O.: Mathematical and software of fractal structures from combinatorial numbers. In: International Conference on Information Science and Communications Technologies: Applications, Trends and Opportunities, ICISCT 2019. Institute of Electrical and Electronics Engineers Inc. (2019). https://doi.org/10.1109/ICISCT47635.2019.9012051

9. Maksimenko Šejko, K.V., Tolok, A.V., Šejko, T.I.: R-funkcii v fraktal'noj geometrii. Informacionnye tehnologii. M.: Izdatel'stvo "Novye tehnologii 7, 24–27 (2011)

10. Maksimenko Šejko, K.V., Šejko, T.I.: Matematičeskie modelirovanie geometričeskih fraktalov s pomoš'ju R-funkcij. Kibernetika sistemnyj analiz 4, 155–162 (2012)

11. Kal'mikov, A.V., Kal'mikov, L.V., Kešelova, A.V.: Neskol'ko novyh biopodobnyh L-sistem. MKO-10, pp. 50–63 (2002)

12. Qi, X.: Fixed points fractals, iterated function systems and generalized support vector machines, p. 26 (2016)

13. Zaynidinov, H., Zaynutdinova, M., Nazirova, E.: Digital processing of two-dimensional signals in the basis of Haar wavelets. In: ACM International Conference Proceeding Series, pp. 130–133. Association for Computing Machinery (2018). https://doi.org/10.1145/3274005.3274023

14. Garg, A., Agrawal, A., Negi, A.: Review on natural phenomenon of fractal geometry. Int. J. Comput. Appl. 86(4) (2014). www.ijcaonline.org

15. Waghmare, G.B., Nadaf, A.J., Korake, P.M., Bhanarkar, M.K.: Square spiral curve fractal antenna for multiband wireless communication. Int. J. Adv. Res. 3(4), 743–748 (2015). http://www.journalijar.com

16. Wang, W., Zhang, G., Yang, L., Wang, W.: Research on garment pattern design based on fractal graphics. EURASIP J. Image Video Process. 2019(1), 1–15 (2019). https://doi.org/10.1186/s13640-019-0431-x

17. Gelashvili, D.B., Iudin, D.I., Rozenberg, G.S., Yakimov, V.N., Solnsev, L.A.: Fraktali i mulg'tifraktali v bioekologii. Monografiya, p. 370. Izd-vo Nijegorodskogo gosuniversiteta, Nijniy Novgorod (2013)

18. Novikov, O.B.: Fraktalniy splayn kak model fraktalnix funksiy dlya generirovaniya fraktalmnix signalov. Kompyuternie isslidovaniya modelirovaniya 5(4), 583–587 (2013). https://doi.org/10.20537/2076-7633-2013-5-4-583-587

19. Anarova, S.A., Ibrohimova, Z.E., Narzulloyev, O.M., Qayumova, G.A.: Mathematical modeling of pascal triangular fractal patterns and its practical application. In: Singh, M., Kang, D.K., Lee, J.H., Tiwary, U.S., Singh, D., Chung, W.Y. (eds.) IHCI 2020. LNCS, vol. 12615, pp. 390–399. Springer, Cham (2020). https://doi.org/10.1007/978-3-030-68449-5_39

20. Singh, D., Singh, M., Hakimjon, Z.: One-dimensional polynomial splines for cubic splines. In: Singh, D., Singh, M., Hakimjon, Z. (eds.) Signal Processing Applications Using Multidimensional Polynomial Splines. Springer Briefs in Applied Sciences and Technology, pp. 21–26. Springer, Singapore (2019). https://doi.org/10.1007/978-981-13-2239-6_3

Determination of Dimensions of Complex Geometric Objects with Fractal Structure

Kh. N. Zaynidinov[1](✉) ⓘ, Sh. A. Anarova[2](✉) ⓘ, and J. S. Jabbarov[3](✉) ⓘ

[1] Tashkent University of Information Technologies named after Muhammad Al-Khwarizmi, 100200 Tashkent, Republic of Uzbekistan
tet2001@rambler.ru
[2] Tashkent University of Information Technologies, 100200 Tashkent, Republic of Uzbekistan
shahzodaanarova@gmail.com
[3] Samarkand State University, Samarkand, Uzbekistan
jamoliddin.jabbarov@mail.ru

Abstract. This article is given to the assurance of the dimensions of complex geometric objects with fractal structures. A detailed depiction of the different mathematical methods for deciding the dimensions of complex geometric objects with a fractal structure and the investigation of errors in determining the fractional measure of complex geometric objects are displayed. The article presents the concept of fractal estimation, properties, topological estimation, estimations of designs and scenes in nature, differences between Hausdorf-Bezikovich measurement and Mandelbrot-Richardson measurement, fractal measurements. Dimensions of complex geometric objects with several fractal structures have too been identified. In particular, the Mandelbrot-Richardson scale was used to calculate the fractal dimensions of four-sided star fractals, eight-sided star fractals, the Cox curve, and the Given (cap) curves. Hausdorf-Bezikovich and Mandelbrot-Richardson measurements were used to determine the fractal scale. Most articles describe the study of the properties of complex objects in graphical form. In this article, the measurement properties of complex objects are studied on the premise of mathematical equations and special methods are used to compare and calculate the fractional measurements of fractal structures, as well as the results of a number of experiments at each iteration, which are presented in formulas and charts. In addition, different methods of measuring fractal structure images are presented, as well as information on their practical application.

Keywords: Fractal · Fractal dimension · Topological dimension · Hausdorf-Bezikovich dimension · Mandelbrot-Richadson dimension · Cox curve · Given (hat) curve

1 Introduction

The purpose of this article is to extend the precision of the calculation of fractal measurements in images of fractal theory. The measurement depends exceptionally much on the method of measuring it. This implies that in addition to the formulas for calculating

© Springer Nature Switzerland AG 2022
J.-H. Kim et al. (Eds.): IHCI 2021, LNCS 13184, pp. 437–448, 2022.
https://doi.org/10.1007/978-3-030-98404-5_41

the scale, it is necessary to clearly characterize certain methods of measuring and deciphering the measurements. Traditionally, measurement has been related to the number of independent parameters required to determine the position of a point in space [1]. For example, the position of a point in a plane bounded by a square can be determined by two dimensions, so that its dimension is equal to two.

A fractal measurement can be described as a measure of filling a plane with a specific shape, which shows what fractional measure the shape is equal to depending on the size. Using fractal measurements, volumes can also be calculated with high accuracy [2, 4]. Fractal pictures are comparative in nature, and this is a geometric shape, the exact part of which is repeated over and over again as the dimensions alter [1, 11, 12]. The structures of fractals at a certain scale are similar to its structure on another bigger scale, that's, in case an element of a fractal structure is amplified a few times, it again shows the same fractal structures [18–20]. If one looks closely, one can see many angles of self-similarity within a fractal, so fractal estimations are broadly utilized to decide the fractional measurements of parts of normal objects that regular or fragmented shapes cannot be analyzed by Euclidean geometry. As a result of calculating the fractal dimensions of naturally occurring self-similar structures, numerous objects (e.g., plants) consist of a set of fractals included to each other, each fractal having its own dimension that differs from the others [5, 9, 20], based on fractal measurements determination of fractional measurements of plants with complex structure in nature. However, fractals are not as it were complex shapes, but are too utilized in the utilize of images for digital handling, analysis, and classification [3–6].

2 The Main Findings and Results

B. Mendelbrot expressed: "One of the most highlights of a fractal is its length" and its dimensions must be entirely less than the topological dimension [1]. The distinction between fractional measurements and other measurements is that the obtained measurement must be smaller than the total degree of the fractal, i.e., if $l_{min} < l < l_{max}$ inequalities are winged [1, 2, 5, 7], the obtained length must be greater than the smallest of the fractions and less than the overall length. Based on the earliest concepts of Euclidean geometry, a straight line is one-dimensional, straight shapes are two-dimensional, bodies are three-dimensional, and are only utilized to determine the size of geometric objects. Topological measure is a whole number but a fractional measure is a fractional number, if we define the Fractal measure as Φ_p, length l, surface S, volume H, we get the following inequality: $0 < \Phi_p < l, l < \Phi_p < S, S < \Phi_p < H$. It is known from the above inequalities that the fractal measurement is a fraction [8, 10, 14–16]. We consider the following two methods of determining the fractal scale: the Hausdorf-Bezikovich scale and the Mandelbrot-Richardson scale.

Hausdorf-Bezikovich measurement. To form this scale, the length of a given fractal is scaled to m as follows: that is,

$$m = \frac{L}{N},$$ (1)

where N is the number of pieces of a straight line m and the number N is arbitrary, but m is the initial length. Accordingly,

$$L(m) = m * N. \tag{2}$$

In that case the face of the field is

$$S = L(m) * m, \tag{3}$$

because (1) to

$$S = m^2 * N = \left(\frac{L(m)}{N}\right)^2 * N = \frac{L(m)}{N} * \frac{L(m)}{N} * N = L(m) * m. \tag{4}$$

For size

$$V = m^3 * N = L(m) * m^2.$$

Thus, this rule reduces the given scale by χ times. Hence, $m = \frac{L(m)}{\chi}$ is substituted for m in formula (2):

$$S = L(m)^2 * \frac{N}{\chi^2},$$

$$V = L(m)^3 * \frac{N}{\chi^3},$$

So the similarity coefficient is $\eta = \frac{1}{\chi}, \eta = \frac{1}{\chi^2}, \eta = \frac{1}{\chi^3}, \ldots\ldots, \eta = \frac{1}{\chi^n}$.
Now if the given length m is considered to be 1 unit, that is, $m = 1$ is

$$N = \chi^{-d},$$

and we express both sides in the form of a natural logarithm:

$$d = \lim_{k \to \infty} \frac{\ln(N)}{\ln\left(\frac{1}{\chi}\right)}. \tag{5}$$

This scale was determined differently by Hausdorf and Bezikovich [13, 16, 18], and a fractional measurement of complex geometric fractals is found based on formula (5). Therefore, the above measurement differs from other measurements by its fractionality. χ – similarity coefficient in the formulas, N – number of copies generated.

The Mandelbrot-Richardson scale. Complex geometric objects with fractal structures can be depicted and studied by mathematical methods. The reality is that pictures of fractal geometric objects are as a rule continuously considered to be within the plane [2]. We can see how much area fractal images possess within the plane. To do this, divide the plane into grids, the estimate of which is denoted by a, and calculate how many cells intersect the fractal images.

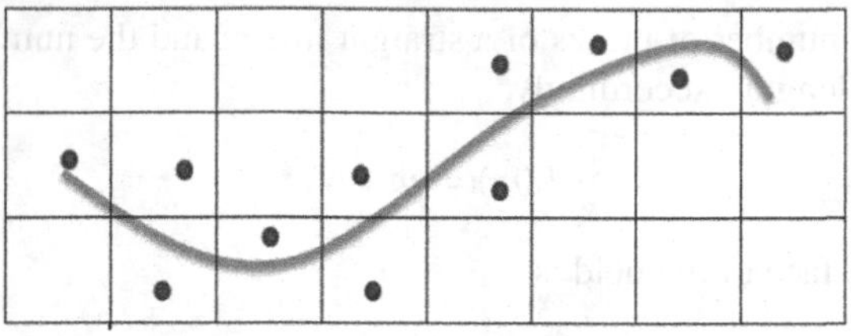

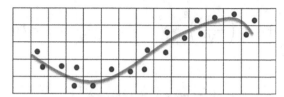

Fig. 1. a is the size of the cell, conditionally 3 cm, and the number of cells in the drawing is N = 11

Fig. 2. a is the size of a cell, conditionally 1.5 cm, and the number of cells in the drawing is N = 19

Table 1. Length measurement by counting cells containing a line

The size of the cell a	1.5	3
Number of cells H	19	11
$y = \ln N$	1,2787	1,0413
$x = \ln a$	0,1760	0,4771

The above N and a are related to the Mandelbrot-Richardson formula: That is,

$$N = C * a^{-D}, \tag{6}$$

here, D – is the fractal dimension, C – is the magnitude characteristic of fractal geometry. The fractal measurement indicates the degree to which a flat surface is filled with a fractal drawing.

The method of calculating fractal measurements is discussed in detail within the example of Figs. 1 and 2. The results of measuring the number of cells in which the lines of the drawing are located depend on the cell size are given in Table 1. Based on these, logarithmic values were also calculated [12, 15, 19]. As can be seen from the chart, a straight line is formed between the two focuses. That's,

$$y = -D \cdot x + c, \tag{7}$$

This is the D – sought fractal measure in the formula. Now we add all x and y in Table 1:

$$\sum_{i=1}^{n} y_i = n \cdot c - D \cdot \sum_{i=1}^{n} x_i, \tag{8}$$

(8) Multiply both sides of the formula by $\sum\limits_{i=1}^{n} x_i$:

$$\sum_{i=1}^{n} x_i y_i = c \cdot \sum_{i=1}^{n} x_i - D \cdot \sum_{i=1}^{n} x_i^2, \tag{9}$$

From formulas (8) and (9) we obtain the formula for finding the fractal scale using the `Mandelbrot-Richardson` scale.

$$D = \frac{\sum\limits_{i=1}^{n} x_i \sum\limits_{i=1}^{n} y_i - n \sum\limits_{i=1}^{n} x_i y_i}{n \sum\limits_{i=1}^{n} x_i^2 - \left(\sum\limits_{i=1}^{n} x_i\right)^2}. \tag{10}$$

The fractional measurement of complex fractal objects was determined using the `Hausdorf-Bezikovich` scale and the `Mandelbrot-Richardson` scale above (Table 2).

Table 2. Fractal measurement of the Cox curve using the Hausdorf-Bezikovich measurement

Step 1	x=60 y=150 l=400 u=0 t=0		$N_1 = $, $\chi_1 = $;
Step 2	x=60 y=150 l=400 u=0 t=1		$N_2 = $, $\chi_2 = \dfrac{1}{3}$;
Step 3	x-60 y=150 l=400 u=0 t=2		$N_3 = 16$, $\chi_3 = \dfrac{1}{9}$;

x – The abscissa of the first point of the Cox curve;
y – The ordinate of the first point of the Cox curve;
l – The length of the Cox curve;
u – The degree of rotation of the Cox curve;
t – Number of steps.
Step n is equal to $N_n = 4^n$ $\chi_n = \frac{1}{3^n}$. In this case, the fractal dimension of the Cox curve is (Fig. 3):

$$D = \lim_{x \to \infty} \frac{\ln(N)}{\ln\left(\frac{1}{x}\right)} = \lim_{n \to \infty} \frac{\ln(4^n)}{\ln\left(\frac{1}{1/3^n}\right)} = \frac{\ln 4}{\ln 3} = 1.26186. \tag{11}$$

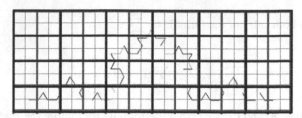

Fig. 3. Determination of the fractal scale of the Cox curve using the Mandelbrot-Richardson scale

Cells of three different sizes are drawn over the Cox curve. From this it was determined (Table 3):

Table 3. Length measurement by counting cells containing a line

The size of the cell a	12.5	25	50
Number of cells H	52	19	8
$y = \ln N$	1,7160	1,2787	0,9030
$x = \ln a$	1,09691	1,3979	1,6989

If the results are given in formula (10), the result is as follows (Table 4):

$$D = \frac{\sum\limits_{i=1}^{n} x_i \sum\limits_{i=1}^{n} y_i - n \sum\limits_{i=1}^{n} x_i y_i}{n \sum\limits_{i=1}^{n} x_i^2 - \left(\sum\limits_{i=1}^{n} x_i\right)^2} = 1.3502 \tag{12}$$

Table 4. Fractal measurement of the Given (hat) curve using the Hausdorf-Bezikovich scale

Step 1		$N_1 = \ , \ \chi_1 = \ ;$
Step 2		$N_2 = \ , \ \chi_2 = \dfrac{1}{4};$
Step 3		$N_3 = 64, \ \chi_3 = \dfrac{1}{16};$
....	.	....

If we continue the number of steps in step n – the following result is obtained $N_n = 8^n$, $\chi_n = \frac{1}{4^n}$, then the fractal dimension of the Given curve is equal to:

$$D = \lim_{\chi \to \infty} \frac{\ln(N)}{\ln\left(\frac{1}{\chi}\right)} = \lim_{n \to \infty} \frac{\ln(8^n)}{\ln\left(\frac{1}{\frac{1}{4^n}}\right)} = \lim_{n \to \infty} \frac{\ln 2^{3n}}{\ln 4^{2n}} = \frac{3}{2} = 1.5. \tag{13}$$

Fractal measurement of the Given (hat) curve using the Mandelbrot-Richardson scale (Fig. 4):

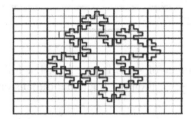

Fig. 4. Fractal measurement of the Given (hat) curve using the Hausdorf-Bezikovich scale

Three different sized squares are drawn over the Given (hat) curve. From this it was determined (Table 5):

Table 5. Length measurement by counting cells containing a line

The size of the cell a	12.5	25	50
Number of cells H	108	30	13
$y = \ln N$	2,0334	1,4771	1,1139
$x = \ln a$	1,09691	1,3979	1,6989

The results are given in formula (14) as follows (Table 6):

$$D = \frac{\sum_{i=1}^{n} x_i \sum_{i=1}^{n} y_i - n \sum_{i=1}^{n} x_i y_i}{n \sum_{i=1}^{n} x_i^2 - \left(\sum_{i=1}^{n} x_i\right)^2} = 1.5272, \tag{14}$$

n – is the number of steps;

x – is the point abscissa at the center of the quadrilateral stellate fractal;

y – is the ordinate of the point where the center of the quadrilateral star fractal is located;

a – is the distance from the center of the four-pointed star to the farthest ends.

Table 6. Measurement of a quadrilateral star-shaped fractal using the Hausdorf-Bezikovich scale

Step 1	n=1 x=230 y=230 a=50	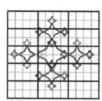	$N_1 = \ , \ \chi_1 = \ ;$
Step 2	n=2 x=230 y=230 a=50		$N_2 = \ , \ \chi_2 = \dfrac{1}{4^2};$
Step 3	n=3 x=230 y=230 a=50		$N_3 = 21, \ \chi_3 = \dfrac{1}{4^3};$

....

If we continue the number of steps in step n –, the following result is obtained: $N_n = 4^{n-2} * 5 + 1$, $\chi_n = \frac{1}{4^{n-1}}$, then the fractional dimension of the quadrilateral star fractal is equal to:

$$D = \lim_{x \to \infty} \frac{\ln(N)}{\ln\left(\frac{1}{x}\right)} = \lim_{n \to \infty} \frac{\ln(4^{n-2} * 5 + 1)}{\ln\left(\frac{1}{1/4^{n-1}}\right)} = \lim_{n \to \infty} \frac{\ln(\frac{5}{4} * 4^{n-1} + 1)}{\ln(4^{n-1})} = \lim_{n \to \infty} \frac{1}{\ln 4} \frac{\ln(4^{n-1}(\frac{5}{4} + \frac{1}{4^{n-1}}))}{n-1}$$

$$= \lim_{n \to \infty} \frac{1}{\ln 4} \left(\frac{\ln 4^{n-1}}{n-1} + \frac{\ln(\frac{5}{4} + \frac{1}{4^{n-1}})}{n-1} \right) = \lim_{n \to \infty} \frac{1}{\ln 4} \left(\frac{(n-1)\ln 4}{n-1} + \frac{4^{n-1}\ln(\frac{5}{4} + \frac{1}{4^{n-1}})}{4^{n-1}(n-1)} \right) = 1. \quad (15)$$

Measurement of a quadrilateral star-shaped fractal using the Mandelbrot-Richardson scale (Fig. 5 and Table 7):

Fig. 5. Grids of three different sizes are drawn over the four-sided star-shaped fractal. From this it was determined

If the results are given in formula (16), the result is as follows (Table 8):

$$D = \frac{\sum_{i=1}^{n} x_i \sum_{i=1}^{n} y_i - n \sum_{i=1}^{n} x_i y_i}{n \sum_{i=1}^{n} x_i^2 - \left(\sum_{i=1}^{n} x_i\right)^2} = 1.04373. \quad (16)$$

n – is the number of steps;

x – is the point abscissa at the center of the octagonal star fractal;

Table 7. Length measurement by counting cells containing a line

The size of the cell a	12.5	25	50
Number of cells H	68	15	16
$y = \ln N$	1,8325	1,1760	1,2041
$x = \ln a$	1,0969	1,3979	1,6989

Table 8. Measurement of an octagonal star fractal using the Hausdorf-Bezikovich scale

Step 1	$n=1$ $x=260$ $y=50$ $a=32$ $r=48$		$N_1 = ,\ \chi_1 = 1;$
Step 2	$n=2$ $x=260$ $y=50$ $a=32$ $r=48$		$N_2 = ,\ \chi_2 = \dfrac{1}{3};$
Step 3	$n=3$ $x=260$ $y=50$ $a=32$ $r=48$		$N_3 = 64,\ \chi_3 = \dfrac{1}{3^2};$

y – is the ordinate of the point where the center of the octagonal stellar fractal is located;

a – is the side length of an octagonal stellar fractal;

r – is the distance from the center of the eight-pointed star to the farthest ends.

If we continue the number of steps in step n –, the following result is obtained: $N_n = 4^n$ $\chi_n = \frac{1}{3^n}$, then the fractional dimension of the octagonal fractal is equal to:

$$D = \lim_{\chi \to \infty} \frac{\ln(N)}{\ln\left(\frac{1}{\chi}\right)} = \lim_{n \to \infty} \frac{\ln(4^n)}{\ln\left(\frac{1}{\frac{1}{3^n}}\right)} = \frac{\ln(4)}{\ln(3)} = 1.26186. \tag{17}$$

Measurement of an octagonal stellar fractal using the Mandelbrot-Richardson scale (Fig. 6 and Table 9):

If the results are given in formula (18), the result is as follows (Table 10):

$$D = \frac{\sum_{i=1}^{n} x_i \sum_{i=1}^{n} y_i - n \sum_{i=1}^{n} x_i y_i}{n \sum_{i=1}^{n} x_i^2 - \left(\sum_{i=1}^{n} x_i\right)^2} = 1.29248. \tag{18}$$

Fig. 6. Grids of three different sizes are drawn over the octagonal star-shaped fractal. From this it was determined

Table 9. Length measurement by counting cells containing a line

The size of the cell a	12.5	25	50
Number of cells H	48	15	8
$y = \ln N$	1,6812	1,1760	0,9030
$x = \ln a$	1,0969	1,3979	1,6989

Table 10. Comparison of the accuracy of fractal measurements

	Topological measurement	Hausdorf-Bezikovich measurement	The degree of accuracy of the fractional measurement	The Mandelbrot-Richardson scale	The degree of accuracy of the fractional measurement
Cox curve	1	1,2619	0,2619	1,3502	0,3502
Given (hat) curve	1	1,5	0,5	1,5272	0,5272
Four-sided star-shaped fractal	1	1	0	1,04373	0,0437
An octagonal star-shaped fractal	1	1,2618	0,26186	1,29248	0,2924

As can be seen from the table above, the Mandelbrot-Richardson scale is more precise than the Hausdorf-Bezikovich scale in determining the dimensions of complex geometric objects with fractal structures. However, taking into consideration the structure of fractal objects, the degree of precision of these measurements varies [11–17].

3 Conclusion

To conclude, it can be said that this study is dedicated to determining the dimensions of complex geometric objects with fractal structures. Various mathematical methods for determining the fractional dimensions of a wide range of classes of fractal geometric objects are described in detail. For example, the Mandelbrot-Richardson scale is more accurate than the Hausdorf-Bezikovich scale, and the analysis of errors in determining the fractional size of complex geometric objects is 0.3502 for the Cox curve, 0.5272 for the Given curve, 0.04 for the four-sided stellar fractal, 0.04 for a faceted stellar fractal, the equation is 0.2925. Fractional measurements of complex geometric objects with several fractal structures have also been identified. In particular, using the Mandelbrot-Richardson scale, we determined that a) a quadrilateral star-shaped fractal has a fractal structure, that it can be constructed, and that it is a fractional measure, b) we found that an octagonal star has a fractal structure, that it can be constructed, and that it has a fractional dimension. Based on these fractals, it was shown to determine the fractional dimensions of complex geometric objects and the existence of similar fractals in nature. As a result of the use of Hausdorf-Bezikovich and Mandelbrot-Richardson measurements, the rate of detection of complex geometric objects with fractal structures increased by ~25%. It should be noted that currently in the world to determine the fractal size of the organs that have a fractal structure in the human body; on this basis it is important to help to predict and treat various diseases in humans. Therefore, we have shown in the article that the fractal measurement must have a high degree of accuracy and that positive results can be obtained using fractals when measuring the dimensions of some geometric objects in nature.

References

1. Mandelbrot, B.B.: Les Objects Fractals: Forme, Hasardet Dimension. Flammarion, Paris (1995)
2. Balkhanov, V.K.: Fundamentals of Fractal Geometry and Fractal Calculus. Resp. ed. Ulan-Ude, p. 224. Publishing House of the Buryat State University (2013)
3. Bozhokin, S.V., Parshin, D.A.: Fractals and Multifractals. "Regular and Chaotic Dynamics". Izhevsk, Moscow (2001)
4. Kronover, R.M.: Fractals and Chaos in Dynamical Systems. Postmarket (2000)
5. Morozov, A.D.: Introduction to the Theory of Fractals. Nizhny Novgorod State University, Nizhny Novgorod (1999)
6. Kononyuk, A.E.: Discrete - continuous mathematics. (Surfaces). In: The 12th Book. Book 6. Part 2, p. 618. Osvita of Ukraine, Kiev (2016)
7. Potapov, A.A.: Fractal Theory: Sampling Topology, p. 868. University Book (2005)
8. Pererva, L.M., Yudin, V.V.: Fractal modelling. In: Gryanika, V.N. (ed.) Tutorial Under Total, p. 186. Publishing House of the Vladivostok State University of Economics and Service, Vladivostok (2007)
9. Cronover, R.M.: Fractals and chaos in dynamical systems. Fundamentals of the theory, p. 350. POSTMARKET, Moscow (2000)
10. Feder, E.: Fractals. Translated from English, p. 254. Mir, Moscow (1991). (Jens Feder, Plenum Press, NewYork 1988)
11. Bondarenko, B.A.: Generalized Pascal's Triangles, their Fractals, Graphs and Applications, p. 192. Fan., Tashkent (1990)
12. Bondarenko, B.A.: Generalized Pascal Triangles and Pyramids, their Fractals, Graphs, and Applications, 3rd edn., p. 296. Fibonacci Associations, Santa Clara (2010)
13. Elgar, G.: Measure, Topology, and Fractal Geometry, 2nd edn., p. 272. Springer, Heidelberg (2008)
14. Falconer, K.: Fractal Geometry. Mathematical Foundations and Applications, 3rd edn., p. 400. University of St Andrews UK. Wiley (2014)
15. Wellestead, S.: Fractals and Wavelets for Image Compression in Action. Study Guide, p. 320. Triumph Publishing House, Moscow (2003)

16. Anarova, S., Nuraliev, F., Narzulloev, O.: Construction of the equation of fractals structure based on the Rvachev R-functions theories. In: Journal of Physics: Conference Series, vol. 1260, no. 7, 072001 (2019)
17. Nuraliev, F.M., Anarova, Sh.A., Narzulloev, O.M.: Mathematical and software of fractal structures from combinatorial numbers. In: International Conference on Information Science and Communications Technologies ICISCT 2019 Applications, Trends and Opportunities 4th, 5th and 6th of November (2019). Tashkent University of Information Technologies TUIT, Tashkent, Uzbekistan (SCOPUS) (2019)
18. Zaynidinov, H.N., Juraev, J.U., Yusupov, I., Jabbarov, J.S.: Applying Two-dimensional piecewise-polynomial basis for medical image processing. Int. J. Adv. Trends Comput. Sci. Eng. (IJATCSE) – Scopus 9(4), 5259–5265 (2020). https://doi.org/10.30534/ijatcse/2020/156 942020
19. Potapov, A.A.: Fractals, scaling and fractional operators in radio engineering and electronics: current state and development. Radioelectronics J. 1, 1–100 (2010)
20. Zainidinov, Kh.N., Anarova, Sh.A., Zhabbarov, Zh.S.: Fractal measurement and prospects for its application. Probl. Comput. Appl. Math. J. Toshkent 3(33), 105–114 (2021)

Performance Analysis of the IBM Cloud Quantum Computing Lab Against MacBook Pro 2019

Alvaro Martin Grande, Rodrigo Ayala, Izan Khan, Prajwal Sarkar,
and Tauheed Khan Mohd(✉)

Department of Mathematics and Computer Science, Augustana College,
Rock Island, IL 61201, USA
tauheedkhanmohd@augustana.edu

Abstract. Quantum Computing is the conjunction of Quantum Physics, Computer Science, Mathematics and Nanotechnology. While this technology is extremely complex and unexplored, this paper addresses and explains the basic functioning of these devices. Additionally, it covers its most tangible applications nowadays, as well as the short-term implementation and development of these ones. Our research reflects the experimental performance of IBM's Quantum Computer Cloud Lab. This is an environment designed to interact with IBM's Quantum Computer by using the *Jupyter Notebook* interface, *Conda* package and environment manager, and Python. The results of different computations were mirrored on a 2019 MacBook Pro. The outcomes of these experiments were unexpected due to the low performance of this tool.

Keywords: IBM quantum lab · Quantum computing · Quantum computing performance · Introduction to quantum computing

1 Introduction

Quantum computing opens new realms to technology in ways that we had never imagined before. This new world is based on the foundations of Quantum Mechanics and Mathematics, and our understanding is crucial to develop these new types of machines. Quantum Computation terminates Moore's Law (computer power doubles every eighteen months, valid since 1965) [1] since silicon cannot longer be used to develop better classical machines [1]. However, there exists an ultimate limit, dictated by the Laws of Thermodynamics and Quantum Physics which was predicted by Moore. This fundamental barrier lies on the size of electronic microprocessors ruled by "the speed of light and the atomic nature of matter", Stephen Hawking.

A quantum computer is not an enhanced classical supercomputer which its functioning is based on bits, but a completely new different type of computer which uses the super-positioning of bits, called *qubits.* Using the double nature

J.-H. Kim et al. (Eds.): IHCI 2021, LNCS 13184, pp. 449–459, 2022.
https://doi.org/10.1007/978-3-030-98404-5_42

of the spin of an electron, it allows to perform certain types of computations more efficiently. It is crucial to understand these computers do not follow the Laws of Classical Mechanics since they are not able to describe the Quantum world. Richard Feynman, at the MIT Physics of Computation Conference in 1981, stated: "Nature isn't classical... and if you want to make a simulation of Nature, you'd better make it quantum mechanical" [2].

These machines use the principles of the Quantum Theory. They can accurately compute reality, and they will eventually let us travel beyond the classical computer limits. They can perform calculations in millions of different parallel universes of probability and make them reveal a result when it is obtained in one of them. To perform such calculations, these devices use *qubits* capable of interacting with each other at the same time, as well as super-positioning their states. Therefore, they must not be understood as classical bits. A bit is a binary digit and the most basic unit of information in computing. It allows only two possible values, 0 or 1. Although, a *qubit* or quantum bit may adopt values of 0 or 1, or both at the same, or neither of these ones. These terms are discussed on more detail on the next sections.

Due to the nature of Quantum Mechanics, this technology has a wide variety of uses and applications such as the creation of enhanced machine learning algorithms, the improvement and rapid training of neuronal networks, the calculation and simulation of cancer propagation, the calculation and replication of molecular reactions, the ability to quantize cybersecurity and blockchain algorithms, the improvement of financial modeling or the creation of solutions for unsolved mathematical models, among others [3].

2   Related Work

Research about the impact of the quantum computing technology on future developments addresses how the use of these ones can impact other types of scientific developments. Nowadays, high-technological companies such as Google, IBM, or Intel, are investing significant economic resources to develop this technology. According to certain experts, the main motivation for these companies to invest on quantum computing is to decipher public-key cryptosystems using the RSA scheme. This is a type of encryption which is commonly used to protect a wide variety of data, from text messages to digital transactions over the Internet.

Regarding the future of these systems, this paper addresses the need of improvements on their processors' architecture to operate at lower temperatures, and eventually, to become frequently used for cloud computing services. While these devices are mostly used for scientific purposes such us Computer Science, Physics, Biology, Medicine, or engineering, it is necessary to highlight their limitations and to understand large efforts must be done to discover more of their properties and applications. In addition, at this moment, it is fundamental to establish a standardized programming language and a compiler to organize and structure the different methodologies for computer scientists to successfully implement code to communicate with the quantum processor.

The current state of Quantum Computing is comparable to the beginning of classical computers development at the end of the 20th century [4]. Developing, programming, and constructing quantum devices is an arduous task. Quantum Physics is a field of study which has been recently developed. Furthermore, our current understanding about it is limited, and its math is highly complicated. The Quantum world does not behave as the world we can see and Classical Physics is able to describe. This makes quantum computers difficult to build and to understand.

Nevertheless, the process of developing a quantum machine is surprisingly similar to building a classical one. Processors, memory, disks, compilers, and machine language are needed to build these devices. The compiler and other high-level elements run on a standard computing system. The machine language instructions are translated via a digital control unit to analog control signals, like the voltage pulses and microwave bursts, which are sent to the *qubits* via conventional transmission lines. The signals for *qubit* control are generated using conventional electronics. Although, a *qubit* is defined as a microwave function [5], it can be written as a linear combination of states, using the next quantum function (*Eq.* 1):

$$|\psi> = \alpha|0> + \beta|1> \tag{1}$$

As it can be observed, a *qubit* is strictly described as a wave. While this equation not only encloses the classical states of a bit (either 0 or 1), but it also uses the complex numbers α and β to let these ones accept quantum states. This characteristic will allow a *qubit* to behave as a linear combination of both states of a classical bit. Consequently, a *qubit* can potentially behave as 0, 1, both at the same time, or maybe neither of them. The need to use classical binary bits to describe the state of *qubits* points out that a classical system approach is required to successfully design and operate a quantum computer. Therefore, this indicates *qubits* are only one part of the entire system, and therefore, the bulk of the system is still classical.

Furthermore, *qubits* require vast memory usage. We notice storing the quantum state of just 50 quantum bits, already exceeds the memory of today's most powerful classical supercomputers. Therefore, classical technologies such as RAM and ROM must be further developed and improved to successfully operate with a quantum device. Every additional *qubit* doubles the memory, and consequently the processing power required by a classical supercomputer to calculate the behavior of these ones. This makes possible the computation of certain tasks that are far beyond the scope of today's supercomputers such as simulating quantum chaotic evaluations or cancer propagation. These tasks could be achieved only by using 50-*qubit* systems. The superposition of quantum bits opens the possibility to make extremely complex probability calculations based on the Quantum Theory. Moreover, we encounter the concept of trapped nuclear particles that give one of the main reasons to build a completely practical quantum computer [6].

Currently, there exist different programmable quantum computer models which allow users to have a great degree of flexibility to compute different algorithms and operations without modifying the machine's hardware [7]. This relatively new feature is extremely compelling, and we exploited it to perform a wide variety of computations on IBM's Quantum Lab which will be described in the next sections.

Even though the number of quantum computers available now in the world is limited, there exist two different platforms: trapped atomic ions and super-conducting circuits [8]. While the first platform stores the states of *qubits* in different ions and transfers information through the interactions and motions of these ones, the second one varies the energy states of thousands of nano-LC circuits to represent *qubits* by manipulating their energy levels at extremely low temperatures. In addition to this, recently quantum reenactments have further been acquiring consideration with regards to significant uses of quantum process-ing. First noted by Feynman and Manin [9], a quantum computer is required to be especially appropriate for reenacting different quantum mechanical mar-vels, similar to how an old style computer is valuable for reenacting different traditional mechanical wonders. A large group of fascinating issues which have been not realized how to address proficiently with traditional computers might be effectively tackled with quantum reenactments performed on a quantum com-puter. A few examples include, in increasing order of difficulty and impact, the following: 1) more profound comprehension of many body physical science and emphatically corresponded matter, with potential applications in the plan of room-temperature superconductors or materials with good electrical properties; 2) highly-accurate chemistry computations for growing new impetuses and syn-thetic cycles, with significant applications, for example, finding a swap for the Haber process for nitrogen fixation (NF) utilized in the synthesis of fertilizers; 3) large scale, exceptionally precise sub-atomic elements reproductions to con-template issues in protein folding and drug design.

3   Theory and Encryption

Quantum Computing Performance Theory. The principal goal of our research is to analyze and compare the performance of a quantum computer over a classical one. The idea of quantum computers was introduced by thinking that it could be possible to reduce the time complexity of algorithms, as well as to perform certain statistical operations which could transform several sci-ence fields because of the revolutionary computational power. Researchers have been developing Quantum Processing Units (QPU) which could be allocated in high-performance computers. However, some of the features that should be incorporated in those QPU's have very specific settings and further research is needed in order to obtain proper configurations [10]. Indeed, the important question and concern is to find out how much efficient quantum devices can be, and if it is worth to spend so many resources on attempting to achieve quan-tum supremacy. To accomplish such a goal, certain simulations must be run on both types of machines. Moreover, the complexity of the circuits used by these ones should increase exponentially until classical machines cannot longer per-form computations. Consequently, we would reach the state of supremacy when the quantum computer is the only device capable of carrying and executing the given tasks.

Encryption. The question of whether quantum computers are powerful enough to break encryption algorithms is one of the main concerns for researchers, as it was mentioned previously. Cybersecurity is now required for the majority of data that individuals like to share through the Internet. Currently, many different sensitive tasks can be done in the Internet by just by clicking a button, from money transactions to access to private information. In order to keep privacy, and therefore this information safe, encryption must be used. This process consists on encoding information by transforming the data to cipher text. Only authorized parties can decipher this text, to then be able to access the desired information. The authorized parties will need to have a key or gain access to the decipher algorithm in order to obtain the information. The ability for quantum computers to decipher data could breakdown the current algorithms and the most commonly used methods of encryption to secure data such as RSA and Elliptic Curve Cryptosystems. Moreover, these two types of public-key algorithms could be easily bypassed by using Grover's and Shor's techniques in fully operative quantum computers [11]. Grover's algorithm is characterized by its efficacy to find encrypted data and files on databases. Therefore, sophisticated encryption systems such as AES (Advanced Encryption Standard) could be negatively affected due to the performance of a quantum computer debilitating the security system [12]. On the other hand, Shor's algorithm is a well-known technique in computer science to efficiently encrypt data. While this encrypted data would take years to be hacked by classical systems, quantum computers would be able to rapidly decipher it by performing large-integer factorization. Therefore, current encrypted data by this technique would be seriously threatened. Consequently, some researchers are attempting to implement variations of Shor's technique which cannot be attacked by quantum devices. In addition, certain researchers suggest to enhance the security of quantum data by designing novel logic circuits such as the linear-nearest-neighbor *qubit*-array architecture [13].

The age of practical quantum computers has been heralded by technological breakthroughs such as the Transmon cryogenic 5-*qubit* machines [14]. Nowadays, many different researchers are working to enhance the mass production of multi-*qubit* devices, to eventually assemble quantum computers with millions or billions of *qubits* [15]. In addition, it is critical to develop a quantum ecosystem which includes standardized quantum programming languages [16], compilers, and debuggers [17], as well as hardware that enables single programs to be compiled. Furthermore, since all *qubit* technologies available today are fragile and vulnerable to errors, quantum computers will need extra effort to detect and correct these ones.

4   Experimental Setup

Throughout our research, we have learnt high performance and speed are two of the most important characteristics of quantum computers. We are aware that there are many other factors which condition performance while executing certain scripts or algorithms, such as available memory and disk or processor power. Nevertheless, testing certain algorithms, techniques and tasks using quantum computers is valuable to analyze how these machines could eventually be operated by regular users. As it is impossible for this research team to directly access a quantum computer, an online tool created and developed by IBM was used to perform the next experiments. This tool makes usage of their superconducting IBM Q device, and it allows users to easily compile code with it by using *Jupyter* and Python. Clients can gain access to this service through the Internet from their own personal computers using any operating system.

Our code was implemented in Python, and three different tests using the *timeit* library were performed. This library implements software profiling in order to calculate the performance of a given piece of code. This analysis can measure the resources used by the CPU and the memory, frequency or duration of the function calls or wall clock execution time for a piece of code [18]. Our idea is to utilize this module to compare the performance of a regular personal computer versus IBM's Cloud Quantum Computer Lab. The computer used throughout the experiment was a MacBook Pro 2019 mounting a 1.4GHz Quad-Core Intel Core i5 processor, and 8 GB 2133 MHz LPDDR3 of RAM Memory. As *Jupyter* Notebooks is used to run our code in the Quantum Computer Lab, *Anaconda* and *Jupyter* were used on our local machine, as well.

It is important to highlight why we use this method. A primitive version of our experiment was tested just using the *time* library. This library is extensively known along Python users. This software allows programmers to easily measure the running time of their software. It is implemented as a stopwatch, initialized at the beginning of the scrip, and stopped at the end of this one [18]. This method is extremely convenient to test certain pieces of code or applications in given specific environments and conditions. Nevertheless, this technique is not completely accurate. It fails to discriminate the conditions which make the running time of a script change. Thus, this method does not implement any performance calculation, but only a mere time measurement. This is the reason why *timeit* is used. This software can test hypotheses regarding algorithms and Python idioms efficiency. In addition, *timeit* tests each piece of code 100,000 times by default using the *lambda* function defined by this library. By following the online documentation, users can vary this number of times.

4.1 Massive Random Numbers Generation

To start testing the IBM Cloud Quantum Computer Lab, a script was designed to generate 100 decimal random numbers from 0 to 1 by using the *random* library in Python. This piece of code was set into a loop. The user can decide the times this loop is executed. As an example, if the user were to enter 100, the loop would execute the code 10,000 times. *timeit* is used to measure the performance of this code an average of 100, 000 times by default. This increases the difficulty of the calculations significantly.

The next measurements were taken (Table 1) after performing this task different times. These results will be discussed in the next section.

Table 1. Massive random number generator testing comparison.

Rand. numbers	IBM's quantum (s)	Mac pro 2019 (s)
10	1.019	0.943
100	7.473	6.476
1000	81.259	72.277
10000	820.639	744.823

It is important to highlight the difficulty found to perform certain types of computations in the IBM computer. It was impossible to overpass the 100,000 iterations.

4.2 Classic Algorithms Performance

Secondly, a similar process is followed to calculate the efficiency of two of the most well-known algorithms in the computer science field: Linear Search and Binary Search. Linear Search is frequently used to locate a target value in certain types of data structures, usually arrays or lists, depending on the programming language used. This method examines each of the elements, from the first one to the last one. This algorithm has a complexity of $O(n+1/2)$ [19]. On the other hand, Binary Search is a frequently used algorithm which locates a target value in an array or a list by successfully eliminating half of the structure from consideration. This algorithm has a complexity of $O(logN)$ [20].

Then, by using the *timeit* library, these searching techniques were tested with random data structures. As we can see, the complexity of Binary Search is lower than Linear Search, and therefore, we expect to obtain faster runtimes for this one. Each of the techniques was tested ten different times in each machine. The average of both was calculated (Table 2):

Table 2. Classical algorithm performance.

Algorithm name	IBM's quantum (s)	Mac Pro 2019 (s)
Linear search	3.87	4.48
Binary search	2.87	3.50

4.3   *For* Loop Concatenation

Finally, a script was designed to run a certain *for* loop structures for 100 times. Afterwards, this loop was additionally run different times. For the purpose of our experiment, we went from 10 to 10,000 iterations. Again, *timeit* was used to accurately calculate the performance of this piece of code. The results obtained can be found on the next table (Table 3):

Table 3. Massive for-loop concatenation.

Times looped	IBM's quantum (s)	Mac Pro 2019 (s)
10	11.675	12.524
100	115.437	119.936
1000	1238.029	1216.072

5   Analysis

The nature of the results obtained was compelling. It was not expected to find such a wide variety of outcomes. The analysis will be divided into three different sections to discuss each of the experiments' performance.

5.1   Massive Random Number Generation

As it was previously explained, *timeit* library was used to measure the performance of our code while generating a vast number of random digits from 0 to 1. It can be clearly understood on Table 1 that our computer (in orange) performs better runtimes than the IBM Quantum Lab (in blue). This is remarkable since the cloud computer was expected to perform exactly the same operations in a shorter period of time.

On the next figure, it can be observed the time needed to perform each of the tasks in comparison to the amount of random numbers to be generated for each of them (Fig. 1).

Both systems had performed similar while generating random numbers from 10 to 1,000 times. Later, while attempting to generate 10,000 different digits, the IBM Lab environment clearly slowed down. On the next figure (Fig. 1), it is shown how the blue line slightly diverged from the orange one. This points out the MacBook Pro needed less time than the other machine to compute the results. In addition, it is important to highlight neither of the devices were able to generate more than 10,000 numbers. While the Quantum Lab was expected to perform these computations easily and efficiently, it was shown this environment was unable to reach such expectations. Furthermore, it is necessary to point out the lines obtained follow a linear tendency. Thus, by calculating the slope of these ones, the run time needed for these machines to carry out the generation of random numbers could be theoretically predicted.

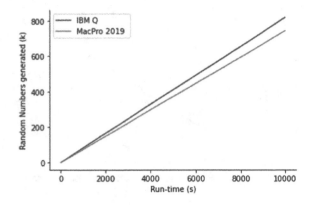

Fig. 1. Massive random number generator test (0, 1) - MB Pro 2019 VS IBM cloud quantum computer

5.2   Classic Algorithms Performance

The results obtained for this part of the experiment verified the complexity of the tested algorithms. We could observe Binary Search performed faster than Linear Search. This is caused due to the characteristics of each of these techniques. The Binary Search does not iterate through all the structure, but just half of it. This is the reason why it has a complexity of $O(logN)$. The Linear Search algorithm has a complexity of $O(n + 1/2)$, and therefore slower runtimes were expected.

Our experiment concludes, in this case, that the Quantum Computer averagely performs faster searches than our computer. It can perform Binary Searches in less than 2.87 s.

5.3   *For* Loop Concatenation

The results obtained for the *for loop concatenation* experiment were compelling. This task required more complex computations, and therefore, longer runtimes were needed than in the previous experiments. While we expected to find quadratic tendencies (Fig. 2) due to the complexity of concatenating different loops together, the results shown on Fig. 2 are linear. Therefore, we understand these ones are erroneous. We attribute these errors to the low number of trials performed by the devices used.

By the end of this experiment, we could just compare three different data points, as it can be observed on Table 3. Again, it was impossible for our device and the IBM Lab to perform more complex calculations.

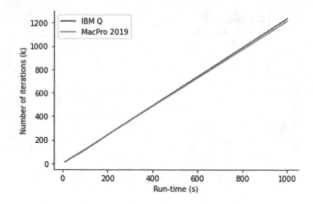

Fig. 2. For loop concatenation test - MB Pro 2019 VS IBM Q cloud quantum computer

6 Conclusions

The results obtained throughout the experimental phase did not satisfy our expectations. We expected to find extremely low runtimes using the IBM Cloud Quantum Computer Lab. Obtaining more data would dramatically improve the results, as well as the accuracy of our experiment. We propose the idea that the performance of random number generation vs. runtime, as well as times-looped vs runtime could be predicted by calculating the slope produced by the data gathered. Therefore, this would proof the linearly behavior of the Quantum Lab to perform the required tasks during our experiment. In addition, this could eventually point out the computational power available for the user by calculating how many tasks can be performed in a specific period of time. Although, we do not have the capacity to test if this thesis is valid and would apply to more complex versions of our experiments.

We understand the processing power of a Quantum Computer is superior to the power of a classical device, as it was explained throughout this paper. This is the reason why we cannot attribute the error to the Quantum Computer but to the interface used to interact with this one. We believe the IBM's Cloud Service Lab environment does not take advantage of all the computational power available to run code. Therefore, IBM limits the power available to the user. Furthermore, we ignore if the fluctuations on our internet connection or the browser used are elements which would potentially alter the performance of the Quantum Lab since this one is accessed through the Internet. Moreover, we encountered a wide variety of anomalous runtimes while performing similar tasks using the Quantum Lab. Additionally, while attempting to conduct different experiments, we found IBM's software to fail in numerous occasions, as well as we experienced extremely long runtimes to compile simple pieces of code. Consequently, we do not find the IBM Quantum Lab to be reliable as a daily coding tool neither as an online compiler.

In conclusion, we doubt the real usefulness of the IBM Quantum Lab. Faster runtimes can be obtained using a regular desktop machine by running *Jupyter*

Notebooks and *Anaconda*. On future work, we expect to address IBM Quantum Lab environment issues, as well as to understand the reason why the processing power is so limited.

References

1. Powell, J.R.: The quantum limit to Moore's law. Proc. IEEE **96**(8), 1247–1248 (2008)
2. Los Alamos Scientific Laboratory and Los Alamos National Laboratory: Los Alamos Science. No. 27–28, The Laboratory (2002)
3. Cho, A.: Google claims quantum computing milestone (2019)
4. Möller, M., Vuik, C.: On the impact of quantum computing technology on future developments in high-performance scientific computing. Ethics Inf. Technol. **19**(4), 253–269 (2017). https://doi.org/10.1007/s10676-017-9438-0
5. Steffen, M., DiVincenzo, D.P., Chow, J.M., Theis, T.N., Ketchen, M.B.: Quantum computing: an IBM perspective. IBM J. Res. Dev. **55**(5), 13-1 (2011)
6. Monroe, C., Kim, J.: Scaling the ion trap quantum processor. Science **339**(6124), 1164–1169 (2013)
7. Debnath, S., Linke, N.M., Figgatt, C., Landsman, K.A., Wright, K., Monroe, C.: Demonstration of a small programmable quantum computer with atomic qubits. Nature **536**(7614), 63–66 (2016)
8. Merrill, J.T., et al.: Demonstration of integrated microscale optics in surface-electrode ion traps. New J. Phys. **13**(10), 103005 (2011)
9. Feynman, R.P.: Simulating physics with computers. Int. J. Theor. Phys. **21**(6/7) (1982)
10. Britt, K.A., Humble, T.S.: High-performance computing with quantum processing units. ACM J. Emerg. Technol. Comput. Syst. (JETC) **13**(3), 1–13 (2017)
11. Mavroeidis, V., Vishi, K., Zych, M.D., Jøsang, A.: The impact of quantum computing on present cryptography. arXiv preprint arXiv:1804.00200 (2018)
12. Sakhi, Z., Kabil, R., Tragha, A., Bennai, M.: Quantum cryptography based on Grover's algorithm. In: Second International Conference on the Innovative Computing Technology (INTECH 2012), pp. 33–37. IEEE (2012)
13. Fowler, A.G., Devitt, S.J., Hollenberg, L.C.: Implementation of Shor's algorithm on a linear nearest neighbour qubit array. arXiv preprint quant-ph/0402196 (2004)
14. Fu, X., et al.: A heterogeneous quantum computer architecture. In: Proceedings of the ACM International Conference on Computing Frontiers, pp. 323–330 (2016)
15. Lekitsch, B., et al.: Blueprint for a microwave trapped ion quantum computer. Sci. Adv. **3**(2), e1601540 (2017)
16. Balensiefer, S., Kregor-Stickles, L., Oskin, M.: An evaluation framework and instruction set architecture for ion-trap based quantum micro-architectures. In: 32nd International Symposium on Computer Architecture (ISCA 2005), pp. 186–196. IEEE (2005)
17. JavadiAbhari, A., et al.: ScaffCC: scalable compilation and analysis of quantum programs. Parallel Comput. **45**, 2–17 (2015)
18. Christopher Barker, M.M., Sheedy, J.: Performance and profiling (2015)
19. Kamara, S., Moataz, T.: Boolean searchable symmetric encryption with worst-case sub-linear complexity. In: Coron, J.-S., Nielsen, J.B. (eds.) EUROCRYPT 2017. LNCS, vol. 10212, pp. 94–124. Springer, Cham (2017). https://doi.org/10.1007/978-3-319-56617-7_4
20. Tarjan, R.E.: Amortized computational complexity. SIAM J. Algebraic Discrete Methods **6**, 306–318 (1985)

Algorithms and Service for Digital Processing of Two-Dimensional Geophysical Fields Using Octave Method

H. N. Zaynidinov[1] (iD), Dhananjay Singh[2](✉) (iD), I. Yusupov[1] (iD),
and S. U. Makhmudjanov[1] (iD)

[1] Tashkent University of Information Technologies named after Muhammad al Khwarizmi, Tashkent, Uzbekistan
[2] Department of Electronics Engineering, Hankuk University of Foreign Studies, Seoul, South Korea
dsingh@hufs.ac.kr

Abstract. This paper covers new algorithms for digital signal processing of two-dimensional geophysical fields using octave method, which predicts the mineral value of the field in terms of signal energy value. In addition, it addresses and shows a functional scheme of the platform service based on cloud technologies. The essence of the work is that the geophysical data are two-dimensional, so their volume is very large. This requires the use of fast algorithms for digital processing of large amounts of data. Therefore, if we use the octave method effectively, the required result is obtained by calculating the value of the signal energy and comparing the finite difference of these values with its previous value.

Keywords: Morlet wavelets · Fure spectrum · Haar wavelet-coefficient · Haar fast transformation · Shannon wavelets · Two-dimensional signals

1 Introduction

The fast growth of geophysical data in the world has led to the digital processing with the application of modern technologies and increase the speed of processing, in particular, the identification of reserves of various minerals. There is a need to develop mathematical models and optimal methods of digital processing of data obtained as a result of geophysical research to solve forecasting problems. To date, the volume of geophysical data has almost tripled over the past 5 years, and this data will increase 5 times by the year 2024 [15]. Many problems can also be solved today by digital processing of two-dimensional signals. In particular, the issues of identification and forecasting of mineral resources are among them. Digital processing of two-dimensional signals is the processing of data presented in the form of arrays of two-dimensional numbers, for example, data entered from multiple sources is the result of continuously changing data in time and space. Significant differences in the processing of two-dimensional signals relative to one-dimensional signals have been based on the following key factors:

J.-H. Kim et al. (Eds.): IHCI 2021, LNCS 13184, pp. 460–470, 2022.
https://doi.org/10.1007/978-3-030-98404-5_43

- As the size of the data increases, the amount of digital data increases dramatically.
- Mathematical processing methods become more complex, resulting in an increase in errors as a rule, a decrease in the reliability of the results.

The simplest and most traditional way to organize two-dimensional samples is by right-angled sampling when the surface data carrier is square and right-angled and in large-volume space when there are parallelepipeds and hypercube. As many experts in one-dimensional signal processing have pointed out the time function spectrum limit principle is very effective. Its limitations are usually satisfactory in the processing of one-dimensional processes, and this works differently in multidimensional fields, where "space-time" must be measured in physical quantities. There are also cases that preclude taking into account time to find a reliable solution to spatial problems.

2 Calculating of Signal Spectral Energy

The significant increase in the use of wavelets in different applications is primarily due to the availability of fast algorithms for spectral discrete changes and a significant increase in the class of fast transformation based on complex performance of functions. To solve the problem of organizing the minimum signal patterns that provide the desired recovery point, it is necessary to study the specific spectral wavelet coefficients. Derivatives of the Gaussian function, Morlet wavelets, Shannon wavelets, and other similar wavelet functions are theoretically defined on all axes, but they can be considered local [1, 4, 11].

However, orthonormal wavelet basis in a compact environment play an important role in discrete wavelet fast transformation (WFT). Two basic operators will be required to apply the energy measurement accuracy of signal recovery on wavelet coefficients: multidimensional analysis and calculation of octave energy spectrum. The advantage of the octave spectrum is that, like the Fure spectrum, it has the property of invariance with respect to the shifts of time-constant signals [3]. Features of multidimensional analysis in the example of Shannon Wavelets t ϵ $(-\infty, \infty)$ has some Wavelets that can be studied on all axes [13]. We convert F (x) to a continuous signal in a discrete view, represented as a vector array of f_i, i = 0, 1, ..., n − 1 n integers (Fig. 1).

In fact, the integer iteration of a single $D\sigma(\sigma > 1)$ scale operator is used in wavelet fast conversion algorithms [7]. Typically, $\sigma = 2$ scale is used:

$$D_2 \psi(t) = \sum_{k=0}^{n-1} c_k \psi(t - k). \tag{1}$$

The wavelet coefficients for the function fϵL2(R) are interpreted as the difference between the sum of the fractions c_k, 2^{-j+1}, and 2^{-f}, and the short-scale analysis uses the sets of the approximation grid. 2^{-j}-dimensional approximation contains all the necessary data to approximate the 2^{-j-1} dimension [1, 14].

Figure 2 a histogram showing the half-value of the Haar fast transformation (HFT) coefficients of the input vector $\{f_i\}$ containing the sample N = 2^p, N = 128.

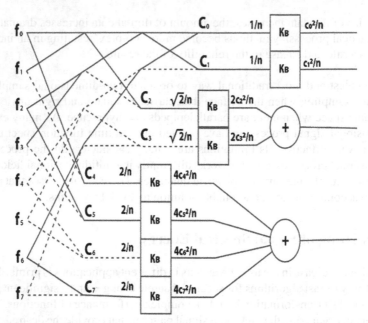

Fig. 1. Haar fast transformation graph: c_k – Haar coefficients, K_B – square, E_S – the octave values that make up the spectral energy of a discrete signal.

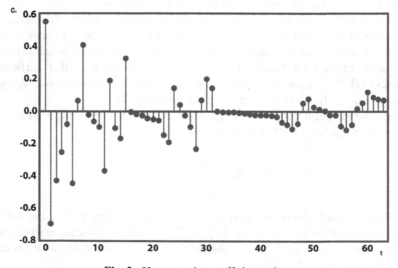

Fig. 2. Haar wavelet-coefficient values.

Here, the signal length is assumed to be 128. The p-level indicator, which represents the maximum number of iterations, is called a discrete change order. The total value of the spectral energy of the vector of $\{c_k\}$ Haar coefficients on all octaves represents the sum of the squares.

$$E_\varepsilon = ((c_0^2 + c_1^2) + 2^{-1}(c_2^2 + c_3^2) + 2^{-2}\sum_{k=4}^{2^{p-4}-1} c_k^2 + 2^{-3}\sum_{k=8}^{2^{p-3}-1} c_k^2 + ... + 2^{-p}\sum_{k=2^{p-1}}^{2^p-1} c_k^2)n.$$

(2)

Here are c - spectral coefficients, k, p - integer, n - input signal value. Its numerical value is $E_e = 136{,}887$.

For the sample grid, we repeat the Haar fast transformation, doing twice less for the even values of the previous signal vector (the signal length is 64). In this case (2) the energy value is $E_e = 136.375$.

3 Performance Analysis

Wavelets as a class of mathematical functions were discovered by geophysicists Morle and Grossman during the study of seismic waves. Seismic prospecting is one of the areas of application of mathematical methods in solving geophysical problems of mineral exploration, including gravitational prospecting, electric search and magnetic search (Fig. 3).

Magnetic reconnaissance is the most effective method in terms of high efficiency, measuring the parameters of physical fields on the earth's surface [15].

It can be done by aeromethodes and significantly covers tens, hundreds of km^2. The basis of mathematical transformations consists of methods of solving systems of equations in partial products and is expressed in the following form:

$$\frac{\partial^2 F_i(x, y, z, t)}{\partial x \partial y} = f_i(x, y, z, t), \quad i = 1, 2, ..., N,$$

(3)

Where x, y, z are the spatial coordinates of the four-dimensional constant, and t is time. Search methods include the detection of geophysical anomalies in signals. This requires the exclusion of time as a factor that interferes with the constant available space in the study, and only the spatial variables should be left in the equations. For example, it is necessary to exclude from the data of magnetic measurements the factors influencing the following magnetometer readings:

- the secular direction of the magnetic field (displacement of the pole);
- change of magnetic field over time (oscillations during the day);
- the functional dependence of the deviation resulting from the effect of the magnetic field, and so on.

At the Fig. 4, one section of the earth's surface shows a complex field image of magnetic induction values measured by the method of aeromagnetic studies. The unit of

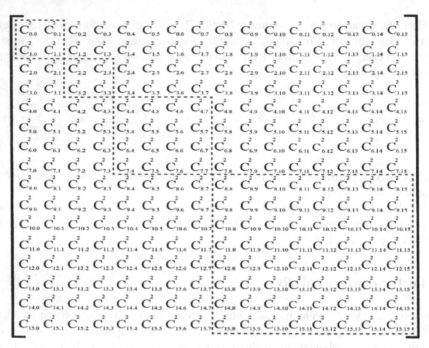

Fig. 3. Octave of two-dimensional signal spectrum.

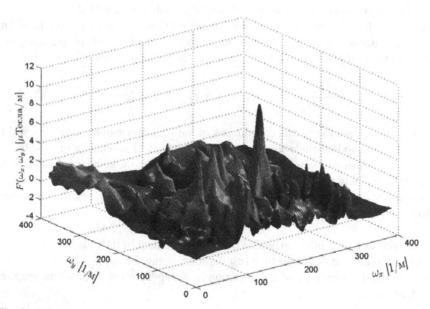

Fig. 4. Field graph of magnetic induction values measured by aeromagnetic survey method.

measurement is the microTesla. The two-dimensional array f (x, y) contains 300 × 300 samples with a distance of 1 km between adjacent samples. In the Fig. 4, we define a square area of 16 × 16 containing one local maximum volume of the function and apply the formula for estimating the accuracy of spectral energy calculations using the two-dimensional Haar wavelet method [14]. Magnetometers can accurately measure field intensity up to 6 decimal places after the point. The graph of the section in this field is shown in Fig. 5.

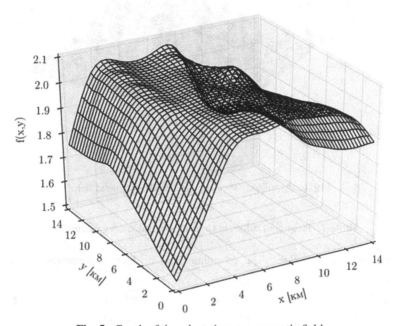

Fig. 5. Graph of the selected square magnetic field

Let us calculate the accuracy of the function samples f (x, y) given in an area of 16 × 16 km². Taking into account the weights of the octaves, the energy value of the sum of the squares of the 256 wavelet coefficients was E = 949,376. It is related to the total energy calculated at the level of E = 955.403. An error was equal to e = 0.6%. If we take 2 times less sample signal (only even values on each horizontal axis), then the measured value of the spectral energy will be E = 943.976. In this case, the error is equal to e = 1.2%. Thus, as the number of binary samples increases, the transition to full energy becomes clear (Fig. 6).

In addition, the methods of compact carrier wavelet functions can provide several advantages over theories that use limited spectral principles in solving problems of signal pattern theory [2].

$$\Delta E = |E_i - E_{i+1}| \leq E_i * 10^{-2}; \quad i - 1, 2, \ldots \text{ - relative error.}$$

This table shows the energy values of the one- and two-dimensional signals at different steps. Iteration continues until the energy difference (relative error) exceeds one

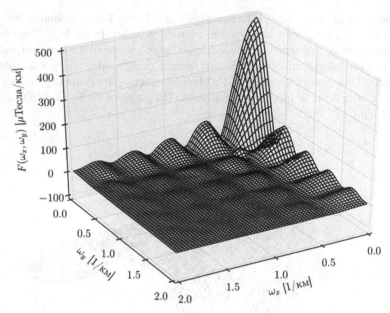

Fig. 6. Amplitude spectrum graph of a magnetic field

Table 1. Results of different steps of spectral energy calculation.

No	Number of signal values	E_i (one dimension)	E_{ij} (two dimension)	Step h
1	128	137.498	955.403	1
2	**64**	**137.158**	**949.376**	**2**
3	32	121.345	943.976	4

percent. In the Table 1, we can see that the iteration has been stopped at the expense of a relative error of more than 1 per cent in the second step. This result, which is the basis for the presence of the necessary mineral in this range.

The finite principle of carrier signals leading to the infinite spectrum can be put first. The advantage of finite base function method is that, unlike the practice of interpolation approximation considered in the application of the theory of finite spectral functions, it allows the recovery of signals by different criteria that minimize interpolation and quadratic functions.

4   Service Organization and Functional Scheme

Based on these methods, the application of modern technologies in the industry and the creation of services can save resources and achieve fast and efficient data processing. In this paper, a service was created using cloud technologies, which was presented as a software package "Cloud_tech_service" and hosted on an internal server as PS. At the same time, unlike other systems, using VMware ESXi, CentOS7 was installed and we launched this software package as a service.

Figure 7, below shows the high-level architecture of the PaaS and the functional scheme of the cloud service we offer. The architecture of the PaaS and through the digital processing of two-dimensional signals and the organization of services using cloud technologies [5, 6]. We can achieve such achievements as saving computer resources, preventing addiction, providing security.

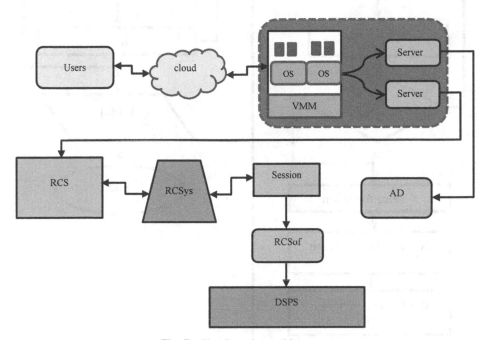

Fig. 7. Cloud service architecture.

OS-operation system, VMM – virtual machine, RCS - remote control service, RCSys - remote control system, RCSof - remote control software, DSPS - digital signal processing software, AD – active directory.

This figure shows the scheme of using the software product as a service, created based on the developed algorithm. This allows the user to use the computing system and the existing experimental database at the same time. Besides, it allows experts who are working in the field and those engaged in scientific research to compare their results with the existing database on the server and compare of them with their results.

In addition, for this service computing systems from the service model to the platform implementation model as a service, based on the public "Cloud_tech_service" software package was formed and placed on the server as a service (Fig. 8).

The proposed service is a cloud service, in which experts of the field safely use the obtained experimental data in the use of the proposed fast algorithms to obtain results quickly and accurately, using optional devices (Fig. 9).

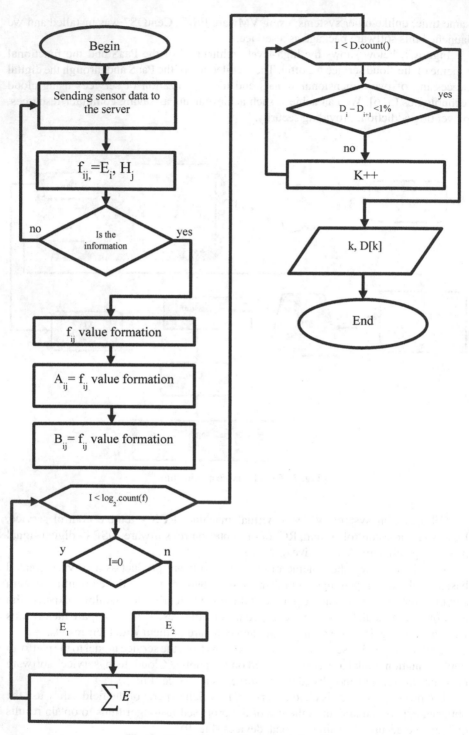

Fig. 8. Block scheme of proposed algorithm.

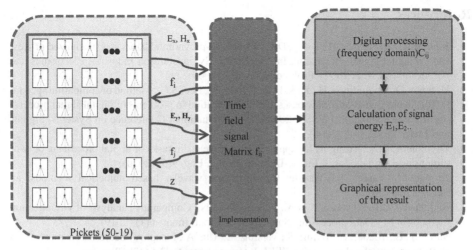

Fig. 9. Software interface performed using proposed algorithm.

The information coming from the pickets in the area marked in the system is generalized and sent to the hardware. These data count the electric and magnetic fields coming from the sensors and form the resulting matrix f_{ij}. In processing this data, a transition is made from the time field to the frequency field [9]. In this case, C_{ij} is calculated and the signal energy E_1, E_2 are determined. Based on these energy values, the optimal sampling step of the defined area is determined. The service is installed on CentOS7 operating system using VMware ESXi, the platform is hosted on an internal server as a service (PaaS), and a program for digital processing of one and two-dimensional signals based on cloud technology "Cloud_tech_service" was created.

5   Conclusion

The results obtained throughout the experiment based on the development of algorithms for digital processing of two-dimensional signals in the octave method, the error is reduced and services for digital processing of one and two-dimensional signals have been offered by using cloud technology. An algorithm for digital processing of geophysical signals using the octave method used for calculate the accuracy of f (x, y) signal samples given in $16 \times 16 \ km^2$ that is allowed to determine the optimal sampling step by determining the values. We propose new algorithm and cloud service for digital processing of one and two - dimensional geophysical signal that is methods for determining mineral reserves based on the calculation of the optimal sampling step and the calculation of spectral energies. These results were compared with the systems used in Uzbekistan and showed real performance. In particular, the results obtained in practice in the state institution "HYDROENGEO INSTITUTE". It can be seen that the accuracy and speed of the results have increased due to the new algorithm in the program.

References

1. Kew, H.P., Zaynidinov, H., Jeong, D.U.: Piecewise-polynomial bases and specialized processor for digital signal processing. In: 2009 IEEE Symposium on Industrial Electronics and Applications, ISIEA 2009 - Proceedings, vol. 2 (2009)
2. Hidayov, O., Zaynidinov, H., Park, H.C., Pravin, K., Lee, S.G.: Method of computing spectral factors in piecewise-quadratic bases and its application in problems of digital signal processing. In: Proceedings of IWSSIP 2008 - 15th International Conference on Systems, Signals and Image Processing (2008)
3. Zaynidinov, H.N., Yusupov, I.: Applying haar wavelets in tasks of digital processing of two-dimensional signals. Int. J. Innov. Technol. Explor. Eng. **9**(6) (2020)
4. Kumar, M., Pandit, S.: Wavelet transform and wavelet based numerical methods: an introduction (2012)
5. Radchenko, G.I., Alaasam, A.B.A., Tchernykh, A.N.: Comparative analysis of virtualization methods in Big Data processing. Supercomput. Front. Innov. **6**(1) (2019)
6. Van Eyk, E., Toader, L., Talluri, S., Versluis, L., Uta, A., Iosup, A.: Serverless is more: from PaaS to present cloud computing. IEEE Internet Comput. **22**(5) (2018)
7. Zaynidinov, H.N., Yusupov, I., Juraev, J.U., Jabbarov, J.S.: Applying two-dimensional piecewise-polynomial basis for medical image processing. Int. J. Adv. Trends Comput. Sci. Eng. **9**(4) (2020)
8. Odun-Ayo, I., Ananya, M., Agono, F., Goddy-Worlu, R.: Cloud computing architecture: a critical analysis. In: Proceedings of the 2018 18th International Conference on Computational Science and Its Applications, ICCSA 2018 (2018)
9. Hiregoudar, S.B.: Cloud computing: overview of PaaS with Force.com platform. Int. J. Res. Appl. Sci. Eng. Technol. **8**(9) (2020)
10. Haver, T.O.: A Pragmatic Introduction to Signal Processing. University of Maryland at College Park (2014). http://terpconnect.umd.edu/~toh/spectrum/TOC.html
11. Sundararajan, D.: Fundamentals of the Discrete Haar Wavelet Transform. Dsprelated.Com (2011)
12. da Rosa, M.M., Seidel, H.B., Paim, G., da Costa, E.A., Almeida, S., Bampi, S.: An energy-efficient haar wavelet transform architecture for respiratory signal processing. IEEE Trans. Circuits Syst. II Express Briefs (2020)
13. Kravchenko, V.F., Churikov, D.V.: Two-dimensional analytical Kravchenko-Rvachev wavelets in digital signal and image processing. In: Proceedings of the International Conference Days on Diffraction 2011, DD 2011 (2011)
14. Zaynidinov, H., Zaynutdinova, M., Nazirova, E.: Digital processing of two-dimensional signals in the basis of Haar wavelets. In: ACM International Conference Proceeding Series (2018)
15. Martinho, E., Dionísio, A.: Main geophysical techniques used for non-destructive evaluation in cultural built heritage: a review. J. Geophys. Eng. **11**(5), 053001 (2020). https://doi.org/10.1088/1742-2132/11/5/053001

Methods for Determining the Optimal Sampling Step of Signals in the Process of Device and Computer Integration

Hakimjon Zaynidinov[1] , Dhananjay Singh[2] , Sarvar Makhmudjanov[1][(✉)] ,
and Ibrohimbek Yusupov[1]

[1] Department of Artificial Intelligence, Tashkent University of Information Technologies named
after Muhammad al Khwarizmi, Tashkent, Uzbekistan
s.makhmudjanov@gmail.com
[2] ReSENSE Lab, Department of Electronics Engineering, Hankuk University of Foreign
Studies, Seoul, South Korea
dsingh@hufs.ac.kr

Abstract. In this paper, digital signal processing methods and its solution for HCI
were described. Mostly, problems are connected to taking signals or data from real
time devices. Data is often serial, stream or etc. device and computer integration in
HCI focuses to digital signal processing. Today, the use of interpolation methods
in the digital processing of biomedical signals is important, and at the same time
allows the detection and diagnosis of diseases as a result of digital processing
of biomedical signals. This paper discusses the construction of a signal model
using the spline-wavelet interpolation formula for equal intervals in the digital
processing of biomedical signals.

Keywords: Internet of things · Digital signal processing · B-spline ·
Spline-wavelets · Signal energy · Integration · Sampling steps

1 Introduction

The signals carrying IoT data are highly likely to face numerous obstacles and can be
corrupted by significant amount of noise present in the environment. Various sensors
attached to the patient's body are used to reliably receive health data, the collected data
is analyzed (using some appropriate algorithms) and sent to the server using various
transmission media (using 3G/4G or Wi-Fi connected to the Internet). All medical professionals can access and view information online, provide services remotely, and make
appropriate decisions about them [11, 16].

The types of noise which have been found to degrading the quality of IoT signals
vary from the impact noise resulting from high frequency interference and instantaneous
disturbance on the initialization of large equipment to changing connections around the
participating IoT devices or computers. Here, accuracy of IoT solutions is measured
in terms of the number of packets reporting correct information, deviation between the

© Springer Nature Switzerland AG 2022
J.-H. Kim et al. (Eds.): IHCI 2021, LNCS 13184, pp. 471–482, 2022.
https://doi.org/10.1007/978-3-030-98404-5_44

reported and actual results and the delivery to correct destination timely. Similarly, the reliability of IoT is measured using information such as failure rate of the IoT devices, average time between two consecutive failures, average repair time and probability for needing to change a component within a certain time-frame (Fig. 1).

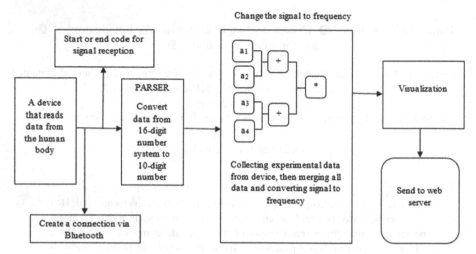

Fig. 1. Device and computer integration data structure

The sampling theorem specifies the minimum-sampling rate at which a continuous-time signal needs to be uniformly sampled so that the original signal can be completely recovered or reconstructed by these samples alone. This is usually referred to as Shannon's sampling theorem in the literature [2, 5, 6].

Digital processing of transmitted signals in IoT-based systems remains relevant today. This is because signals from experience or real life are complex and binary. It needs to be made understandable based on special algorithms. It is necessary to determine the frequency step of sampling signals received from the hardware. Many scientific works now use the Kotelnikov-Shenon theorem. But there are more effective ways. Therefore, this article discusses the development of an algorithm for determining the sampling frequency, which restores the signals to the desired accuracy by propagating one- and two-dimensional signals to splines and spline-wavelets.

2   Related Works

The famous English mathematician E. Whittaker showed that the sin-function as a general term of the cardinal series plays a central role in the theory of interpolation on a grid of discrete nodes equidistant on the abscissa axis. Subsequently, the main results of E. Whittaker were used in communication theory and information theory, when the Kotelnikov-Shannon sampling theorems proved the possibility of replacing a continuous one-dimensional signal with a finite spectrum with a sequence of discrete samples without losing information. This meant the ideal recovery of a signal that is an integral function of time, i.e. analytic function, which can be expanded into an infinite absolutely convergent series [1, 2, 5, 7, 8].

3 Methodology of Algorithm for Determining the Optimal Sampling Step Based on Spline Wavelets

Basic splines are a typical example of a function whose spectra are infinite and, moreover, $K(x, \omega) = \sin(\omega x)/\omega x$ has a lot in common with a common member of the cardinal series (in the sense of equal value of arguments) due to the duality of the core of integral transformations. There are two classes of compact basis function with compact carriers for signal selection shaping issues - basis splines (B splines) and a family of wavelet functions, for which there are fast spectral conversion algorithms. Among other wavelets, spline-wavelets are also used in such matters.

Figure 2 shows spline wavelets of the third level and order.

As mentioned in the previous sections, spline-wavelet functions are built using spline methods. In the following cases, the construction of wavelets using cubic splines is considered.

The spline-wavelet appearance of a cubic B-spline is characterized as follows:

$$B_3(x) = \frac{1}{8}B_3(2x) + \frac{1}{2}B_3(2x-1) + \frac{3}{4}B_3(2x-2) + \frac{1}{2}B_3(2x-3) + \frac{1}{8}B_3(2x-4)$$

$$(1)$$

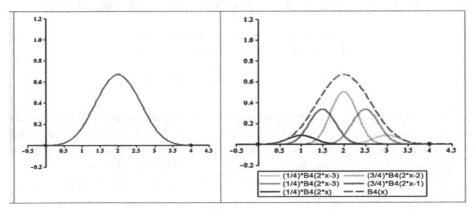

Fig. 2. Cubic base spline and spline is a graph of wavelets.

The difference $d = m - p$ is called the spline defect. Splines are divided into interpolated and polished splines. The construction of interpolation splines of the level $m \geq 2$ is associated with the need to solve systems of linear algebraic equations (SLAE), so the main role in the algorithms for calculating the coefficients is played by peripheral conditions. The results on the restoration of the experimental dependencies of the measurements on this data are only approximate. Complex data recovery algorithms and large time and resources may be required when the data size is large. Flattening splines play an important role in this. They can be constructed according to different approximation criteria, for example, by minimizing the functional capabilities of the formula:

$$J(S) = \sum_{i=0}^{n} \alpha_i (S(x_i) - f(x_i))^2 + \alpha \int_{a}^{b} (S''(x))^2 dx, \tag{2}$$

or

$$J(\alpha, S) = \alpha \int_{a}^{b} \left| \frac{d^r}{dx^r} S(x) \right|^2 dx + \sum (S(x_i) - f(x_i))^2, \tag{3}$$

if α_i, α is a positive number.

In the theory of approximation with splines, the fundamental meaning is taken by the concept of basis, as a system of basic functions. If a grid of nodes is given, then any S-spline multipliers with m-level defect $d = 1$ in the intersection [a, b] can be represented as the sum of the base splines (splines B) with b_i coefficients:

$$f(x) \cong S_m(x) = \sum_{i=-m}^{n+m+1} b_i B_{m,i}(x), \tag{4}$$

in which the $B_{m,i}$ splines themselves provide the functions defined by finite, fragment-polynomial, as well as compact carriers. They must meet the following conditions:

$$
\begin{aligned}
&B_m(x) \equiv 0, \qquad \text{when } x \notin (X_i, X_{i+m+1}) \\
&B_m(x) > 0, \qquad \text{when } x \in (X_i, X_{i+m+1}) \\
&\int_{a}^{b} B_{m,i}(\tau) d\tau = \int_{x_i}^{x_{i+m+1}} B_{m,i}(\tau) d\tau = 1.
\end{aligned}
\tag{5}
$$

The values of the lengths of the B-splines $(m + 1) h$ are not equal to 0 in the intervals and are linearly independent at [a, b]. To approximate the function f(x) with a sequence of B-splines, it is necessary to enter an additional node of number 2m (m node to the left and nodes of the same number to the right) outside the interval [a, b].

Any m ≥ 1 level B-spline is constructed using the iteration conversion formula.

$$B_{m+1}(x) = B_m(x) * B_0(x) = \int_{-\infty}^{\infty} B_m(\tau) B_0(x - \tau) d\tau. \tag{6}$$

That is, if the distance between the spline nodes in the adjacent space is the same. $x_i + 1 - x_i = h = const$, then this quantity h represents the step of the approximation (interpolation) phase for a single grid.

The analytical expressions for small odd-level (level 1 and 3) B-splines resulting in x = 0 at nodes at equal distances with step h = 1 are as follows:

- for the first level B-spline (corresponding interval $[-1, 1]$):

$$B_1(x) = \begin{cases} x - 1, & \text{when } x \in [-1, 0] \\ 1 - x, & \text{when } x \in [0, 1] \\ 0, & \text{when } x \notin [-1, 1] \end{cases} \qquad (7)$$

for the third level B-spline (corresponding interval $[-2, 2]$):

$$B_3(x) = \begin{cases} 0, & \text{when } x > 2 \\ \frac{(2-x)^3}{6} & \text{when } 1 \le x < 2 \\ \frac{1+3(1-x)+3(1-x)^2-3(1-x)^3}{6} & \text{when } 0 \le x < 1 \\ B_3(-x) & \text{when } x < 0 \end{cases} \qquad (8)$$

A graph of the given two-level B-spline sequences is shown in Fig. 3.

The matrix of the System of Linear Algebraic Equations (SLAE), which is needed to calculate the b-coefficients of the interpolation cubic spline, turns out to be a three-diagonal with a dominant diagonal. It is not unique and the calculation process in obtaining the coefficients is stable. The solution of the system of equations can be done by the method of effective progonka.

To calculate the coefficients of the grinding spline, a system of equations must be solved, and its matrix is usually five diagonals. With such a matrix, the system of equations can also be easily solved by the progonka method. In addition to such options, the theory of splines has developed algorithms called "local" grinding (close to common standards), which leads to a reduction in the processing time of the initial data arrays, without the need to solve a system of high-order algebraic equations.

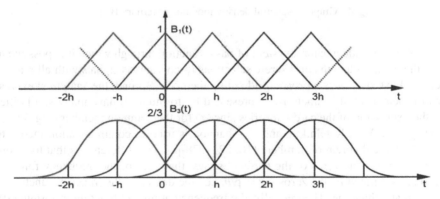

Fig. 3. 2-order (level 1) and 4-order (level 3) shifted B-splines.

The number of calculations depends less on the number of grid nodes and is mostly dependent only on the spline level. It is slightly lower than interpolation, and the results are characterized by a slight decrease in accuracy.

For example, the limit points of the three-point formula for the coefficients of cubic B-splines can be filled with the following expressions:

$$\begin{cases} b_{i-1} = 6f_i - 4b_i - b_{i+1}; & i = 0, \ 1; \\ b_{i+1} = 6f_i - 4b_i - b_{i+1}; & i = n - 1, n. \end{cases}$$

Fure variations of B-splines of any m level result in the following formulas:

$$F_m(\omega) = Ah\left(\frac{\sin(\omega h/2)}{\omega h/2}\right)^{m+1}, \tag{9}$$

where the graph of the spectral density modulus of the first and third order B-splines with amplitude A - B-spline is given in Fig. 3.

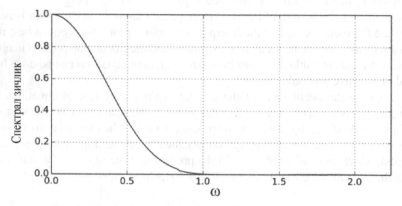

Fig. 4. Graph of spectral density modulus of tertiary B-spline.

B-splines provide a natural system of basic function through which it is possible to create the required lengths of discrete selections of continuous signals with all reasonableness. First, they have a private grid within the node. Second, the analytical expressions of their spectral characteristics presented by formula (9) have many similarities with the expression of the cardinal series sinc (x) for the common member (Fig. 4).

They were V.A. Kotelnikov and K. Shannon is used in communication theory to obtain the basic theorem of numbers [16; 221–228-p.]. The difference is that to record the selection, not the zeros of the cardinal series, the zeros of the frequency function $Fm(\omega)$ are separated by the zeros $wc = p/h$, i.e., the degree of the transient function m can be greater than one. Theoretically, the frequency argument function in formula (9) is not equal to zero along the entire abscissa axis, except for the set of points defined and calculated. With the exception of $m \geq 1$ degree, the main difference is that the frequency $\bar{o}$ can serve as a continuous variable, and the discrete values ω of step h are automatically recorded as finite-based elements, as is the important principle of spline theory, i.e. the placement of their nodes. Similarly, the function $f(x, \omega) = sinc(x, \omega)$ also has a theoretically infinite number of zeros.

When using the spectral energy formula:

$$E = \frac{1}{2\pi} \int\limits_{-\infty}^{\infty} (F(\omega))^2 d\omega, \tag{10}$$

when applying the Parseval equation for continuous signals:

$$E = \int\limits_{-T}^{T} f^2(x)dx = \frac{1}{\pi} \int\limits_{0}^{\infty} F^2(\omega)d\omega. \tag{11}$$

He also uses the term "His E energy is at the e level". It denotes the amount of energy integral for a quadratic integral function that differs by a quantity e from the total energy of the signal. As a continuous signal, the values of the function $f(x)$ are obtained as shown in Fig. 5, a graph of a closed section $[a, b]$. Interpolation and/or different levels of flattened B splines can approximate this function.

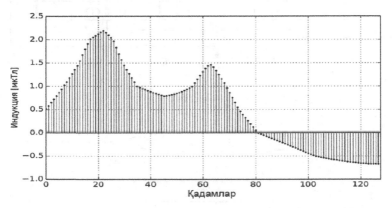

Fig. 5. Graph of a continuous signal obtained experimentally at a closed $[a, b]$ cross section.

The formula for such a sequence for the function $F_{as}(w)$ of a spectrum of uniform amplitude in shape, whose elements move a distance equal to h, has the following form:

$$F_{as}(\omega) = |F_{B0}(\omega)| \left| \sum_{i=-m}^{n+m} b_i \exp(-ji\omega h) \right|, \tag{12}$$

where F_{B0} is the amplitude (interpolation or grinding) of the initial B spline of degree m, whose coordinate head is symmetric with respect to $x = 0$, b_i - B spline coefficients, j - abstract unit.

In the frequency field, there is an approximate correlation between different types of spectral energy

$$E = \frac{1}{\pi} \int\limits_{0}^{\infty} \left(F^2(\omega)\right) d\omega \cong \frac{1}{\pi} \int\limits_{0}^{\infty} (F_{as}(\omega))^2 d\omega = E_{as}. \tag{13}$$

The graph of the spectral density sequence modulus of a cubic B spline is shown in Fig. 6.

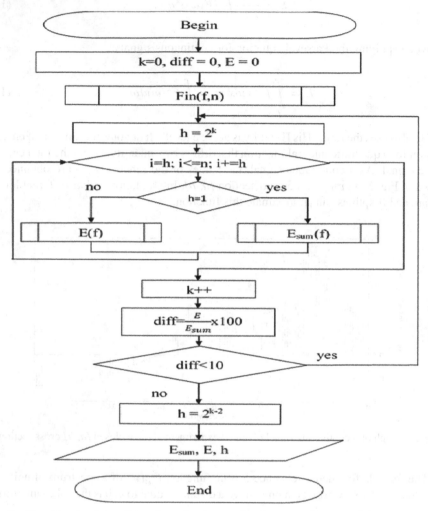

Fig. 6. Algorithm for determining the optimal step using the spectral energy of the gastroentero-logical signal.

Due to the finiteness of both the signal and the base elements, the spectra $F(\omega)$ and $F_{as}(\omega)$ are infinite. The final sequence energy of the B splines given in the compact carriers will be the last (Fig. 7).

This energy, like the function frequency, can be divided into two parts, consisting of two components - low-frequency $ELf(\omega)$ and high-frequency $Ehf(\omega)$:

$$\left(\frac{1}{\pi}\right)\int_0^\infty (F_{as}(\omega))^2 d\omega = \left(\frac{1}{\pi}\right)\int_0^{\omega_c} (F_{as}(\omega))^2 d\omega + \left(\frac{1}{\pi}\right)\int_{\omega_c}^\infty (F_{as}(\omega))^2 d\omega.$$

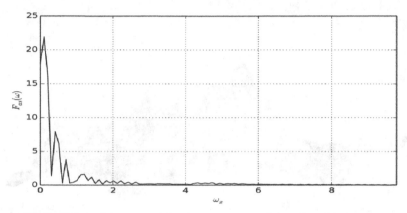

Fig. 7. Graph of the spectral density sequence modulus of a cubic B spline.

The cut-off frequency between the low-frequency and high-frequency parts of the energy spectrum can be defined as ω_c. The evaluation for high frequency energy is as follows:

$$\varepsilon E \le K_1 h^2 \int_{\omega_c}^\infty \left(\frac{2}{\omega h}\right)^{m+2} d\omega = \frac{2^{m+2} K_1}{(2m+1)\pi^{2m+1}} h. \tag{14}$$

It follows from this expression that the energy of the high-frequency part of the spectrum of the B-spline sequence, which approximates the signal, is proportional to the amount of the selection step with a multiplier depending on the spline level.

4   Experimental Results and Discussions

There is a concept of «bandwidth at level ε» and «T signal continuity at level ε» in terms of the agreement between the spectral finiteness and the signal finiteness requirements.

If the above development algorithm can be applied to digital processing of two-dimensional signals. In this case, it is necessary to carry out computational processes in the algorithm by changing the type of incoming signal.

Describes the relationship between signal/interference and anomaly, a key criterion for the effectiveness of geophysical surveys in terms of selecting the scale of the survey-assessment study within the existing physical condition.

As an example of the application of the finite basis function method to restore spatial shapes in discrete steps, including the study of anomalies, we cite the problem of measuring the magnetic properties of mountain areas and ores. The application of this type of survey depends on many factors, such as measurement accuracy, flight altitude, distances between routes, and so on. It is usually preceded by a small-scale aeromagnetic survey, e.g., 1: 200,000.

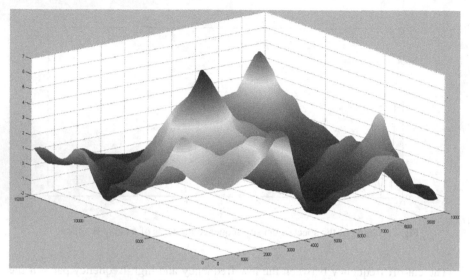

Fig. 8. Spatial graph of the magnetic field ΔTa.

Let us consider the problem of magnetic field interpolation with a sequence of two-dimensional bicubic base splines. Let us take a spatial picture of the area formed by the results of measurements at discrete points, forming a square in the size of $n_x \times n_y = 300 \times 300$ steps. This case graph is shown in Fig. 8.

The distance between adjacent steps is $h_x = h_y = 0.2$ km. Thus the area of the elementary square is $h_x \times h_y = 0.2 \times 0.2 = 0.04$ km^2. Inside the square is a square with a size of 80×80 elements. On the x-axis of the field it contains steps from 1 to 81 taken from the table, and on the y-axis - steps from 81 to 161.

Given that the field is finite in size and its energy (spatial or spectral) is finite, the spectral energy of the separated part of the field is estimated according to formula of Parseval equation. Hence, the integration boundaries of the spectral density square must be finite:

$$P_\omega = \frac{1}{\pi^2} \int\limits_{0}^{\pi/hx} \int\limits_{0}^{\pi/hy} \left| F_{\Sigma B}(\omega_x, \omega_y) \right|^2 d\omega_x d\omega_y.$$

The total value of the spectral energy of the steps in a square composed of $80 \times 80 = 1600$ node points was calculated based on Plansherel's theorem and was 1.4942415

$\times 10^3$. The results of energy calculations for consecutive selections with steps $h_x = h_y$ = 0.8 km (every 4th step), $hx = hy = 0.4$ km (every pair of steps) and $h_x = h_y = 0.2$ km are given in Fig. 9.

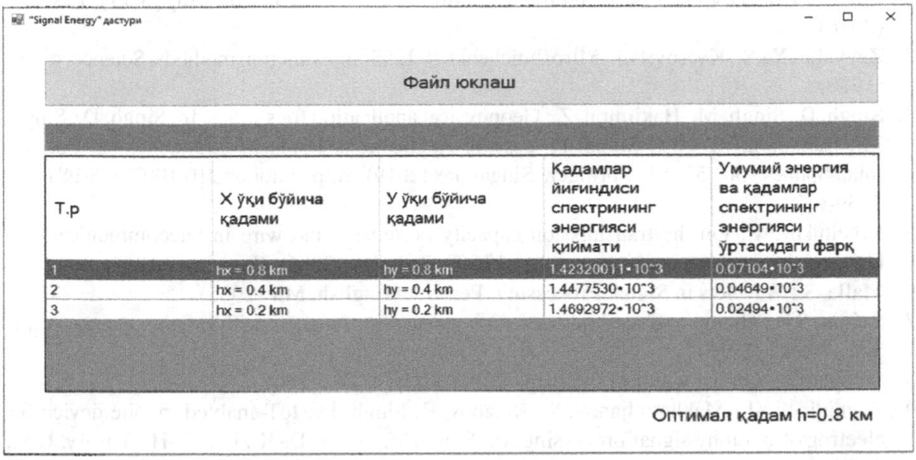

T.p	X ўқи бўйича қадами	У ўқи бўйича қадами	Қадамлар йиғиндиси спектрининг энергияси қиймати	Умумий энергия ва қадамлар спектрининг энергияси ўртасидаги фарқ
1	hx = 0.8 km	hy = 0.8 km	1.42320011·10⁻3	0.07104·10⁻3
2	hx = 0.4 km	hy = 0.4 km	1.4477530·10⁻3	0.04649·10⁻3
3	hx = 0.2 km	hy = 0.2 km	1.4692972·10⁻3	0.02494·10⁻3

Оптимал қадам h=0.8 км

Fig. 9. The result of determining the optimal measurement interval in the program "Signal Energy".

This program provides a program for determining the optimal step by calculating the energy difference by calculating the spectral energy of the signal on the basis of spline wavelets.

This is especially useful when measuring geophysical areas. That is, let a given area of a given size be used to determine if measurements are to be made every 0.2 km or 0.4 km. Measurements taken as unwanted parameter quality are uploaded to the program in the form of a file. The program calculates the initial energy based on the given data and increments the steps.

There is no existing algorithms related to this subject and only way scientists use is theorem Kotelnikov-Shannon method. In addition, it works for frequency domain, algorithms, which described in Fig. 6, is also suitable for other units of measurement.

5   Conclusion

An algorithm for determining the sampling step performed to restore the biomedical signal using spline wavelets has been developed. In this case, if we calculate the energy value of the spectral coefficients between the numbers in a sparse step h = 2 (64 counts), then it was $E_c = 136.375$. This number indicates a deviation of $\varepsilon = 0.57\%$ from total energy by itself. In a much shorter step h = 1 (128 counts) we get the amount $E_c = 136.887$. It corresponds to a deviation of $\varepsilon = 0.19\%$.

The results of the calculations show that the maximum value can be obtained if the total energy of the signal in the initial state does not differ from the energy calculated in steps of a different size. Spline-vewalet can be used not only for natural signals by computing energy based on larvae, but also for other field signals of any type.

References

1. Jerry, A.: Shannon's sampling theorem, its various generalizations and limitations. TIIER **65**(11), 53–89 (1977)
2. Zhmud, V.A.: High precision automatic control systems. Autom. Soft. Eng. **3**(17), 128–136 (2016)
3. Zavyalov, Yu.S., Kvasov, B.I., Miroshnichenko, V.L.: Spline function methods. Science, p. 352 (1980)
4. Singh, D., Singh, M., Hakimjon, Z.: Geophysical application for splines. In: Singh, D., Singh, M., Hakimjon, Z. (eds.) Signal Processing Applications Using Multidimensional Polynomial Splines, pp. 55–63. Springer, Singapore (2019). https://doi.org/10.1007/978-981-13-2239-6_7
5. Kotelnikov, V.: On the transmission capacity of "ether" and wire in telecommunications. Uspekhi fizicheskikh nauk (Appendix) **176**(7), 762–770 (2006). (Reprinted 1933)
6. Malla, S.: Wavelets in Signal Processing. Per. from English. Mir (2005)
7. Svinin, S.F.: Theory and methods of forming samples of signals with infinite spectra, p. 71. SPb., Nauka (2016)
8. Slepyan, D.: On the width of the strip. TIIER **52**(3), 4–14 (1964)
9. Zaynidinov, H., Makhmudjanov, S., Rajabov, F., Singh, D.: IoT-enabled mobile device for electrogastrography signal processing. In: Singh, M., Kang, D.-K., Lee, J.-H., Tiwary, U.S., Singh, D., Chung, W.-Y. (eds.) IHCI 2020. LNCS, vol. 12616, pp. 346–356. Springer, Cham (2021). https://doi.org/10.1007/978-3-030-68452-5_36
10. Beer, G., Marussig, B., Duenser, C.: Basis functions, B-splines. In: Beer, G., Marussig, B., Duenser, C. (eds.) The Isogeometric Boundary Element Method. LNACM, vol. 90, pp. 35–71. Springer, Cham (2020). https://doi.org/10.1007/978-3-030-23339-6_3
11. Hao, X., Lu, L., Gu, W.K., Zhou, Y.C.: A Parallel computing algorithm for geometric interpolation using uniform B-splines within GPU. Inf. Technol. J. **15**, 61–69 (2016)
12. Lara-Ramirez, J.E., Garcia-Capulin, C.H., Estudillo-Ayala, M.J., Avina-Cervantes, J.G., Sanchez-Yanez, R.E., Rostro-Gonzalez, H.: Parallel hierarchical genetic algorithm for scattered data fitting through B-splines. Appl. Sci. **9**, 2336 (2019)
13. Almotiri, S.H., Khan, M.A., Alghamdi, M.A.: Mobile health (m-health) system in the context of IoT. In: 2016 IEEE 4th International Conference on Future Internet of Things and Cloud Workshops (FiCloudW), pp. 39–42, August 2016
14. Gupta, M.S.D., Patchava, V., Menezes, V.: Healthcare based on IoT using raspberry Pi. In: 2015 International Conference on Green Computing and Internet of Things (ICGCIoT), pp. 796–799, October 2015
15. Xu, B., Xu, L.D., Cai, H., Xie, C., Hu, J., Bu, F.: Ubiquitous data accessing method in IoT-based information system for emergency medical services. IEEE Trans. Ind. Inform. **10**(2), 1578–1586 (2014). ISSN 1551-3203
16. Parkman, H.P., Hasler, W.L., Fisher, R.S.: American gastroenterological association medical position statement: diagnosis and treatment of gastroparesis. Gastroenterology **127**(5) (2004)
17. Romero, L.E., Chatterjee, P., Armentano, R.L.: An IoT approach for integration of computational intelligence and wearable sensors for Parkinson's disease diagnosis and monitoring. Heal. Technol. **6**(3), 167–172 (2016). https://doi.org/10.1007/s12553-016-0148-0

Integrated Analogical Signs Generator for Testing Mixed Integrated Circuits

José L. Simancas-García[1]($\boxtimes$), Farid A. Meléndez-Pertuz[1], Harold Combita-Niño[1], Ramón E. R. González[2], and Carlos Collazos-Morales[3]

[1] Departamento de Ciencias de la Computación y Electrónica, Universidad de la Costa, Barranquilla, Colombia
jsimanca3@cuc.edu.co
[2] Departamento de Física, Universidade Federal Rural de Pernambuco, Recife, Pernambuco, Brazil
[3] Vicerrectoria de Investigaciones, Universidad Manuela Beltrán, Bogotá, Colombia

Abstract. This paper presents the design of a functional block for testing analog and mixed-signal integrated circuits. The objective is that this functional block is embedded into an integrated circuit, IC, to generate the stimuli of the analog functional blocks. The result is a simple block with the ability to generate analog stimuli, as evidenced in the simulations carried out.

Keywords: Integrated circuit · Testing · Analog and mixed-signal systems

1 Introduction

Electronic systems tended to consist of one or more printed circuit boards, which contained a number of integrated circuits. Current design methods and manufacturing technologies make it possible to integrate all these complete systems into a single integrated circuit or chip. They are called SOC (System On Chip), and have the following advantages: high performance, low power consumption and low volume and weight [1]. They are superior when compared to traditional equivalent systems that had multiple chips. Such systems are very heterogeneous, in the sense that they contain mixed technologies, such as digital and analogue logic. It is also possible to design these systems, by integrating several re-usable building blocks called functional blocks or Cores [2, 3].

The increase in demand for consumer electronics and the increase in the packaging density of semiconductors is guiding to the embedment of more and more functional systems into a single IC. The result, among other things, is the growing need to integrate analog and mixed signal components into the same package or chip, in the same way as pure digital electronics. The development of such mixed signal systems on a single chip represents a real challenge for designers, as this type of design handles high levels of abstraction. But the difficulty is increasing because, with the increasing complexity of the systems, the parasitic effects become more critical and ways must be found to circumvent them [4].

© Springer Nature Switzerland AG 2022
J.-H. Kim et al. (Eds.): IHCI 2021, LNCS 13184, pp. 483–495, 2022.
https://doi.org/10.1007/978-3-030-98404-5_45

At the other end of the rope are the tests, which for the next generation of complete systems on a single chip represent a real challenge for designers. Such mixed-technology integrated circuits have very complex signal paths as well as very complex specifications. Automatic Test Equipment (ATE) must be used to test these systems, which are external devices that help to test the internal blocks of the integrated circuit. These ATE resources also use ad-hoc algorithms, which are nothing more than programs that carry out the management of such resources. As these tests are carried out at the production stage, the time to market for new systems is increased, and this is a risk that designers are not willing to take [5].

There is an increase in difficulty by another point of embedment at the system level, which is called integration of functional blocks. This comes when designers try to compete with the complexity of design in today's systems, and are forced to use pre-designed blocks and integrate them as part of a whole, a more complex system. These are obtained from virtual libraries that describe the operation of the blocks in the final integrated circuit [5].

In the digital domain, access mechanisms for testing, such as scanning, the use of test ports such as JTAG and design testing techniques, are very efficient. This is because the test information, which is in digital format, can be transported losslessly through the chip. For this reason, it is possible to derive a systematic procedure by which the final system integrator can access the functional blocks that make up the design [3].

Some problems arise in the analogue domain. For example, here it is difficult to explore signals inside the chip, as there may be no connections to the outside, and the difficulty of trying to transport them outside. As designs based on pre-engineered cores are now growing in popularity, analog cores have dedicated I/O ports so that their specifications can be tested by external test instruments. Recent attempts to integrate some test mechanisms have been made [3].

A single integrated circuit is a set of sufficiently complex blocks, also called Cores. Testing these blocks, whether to verify or characterize them, or to locate manufacturing defects, might seem to be testing each block independently, except for the fact that the I/O of each block is not accessible from the outside. An important effort to standardize access for testing has been evidenced, in the last couple of years. Evidence of this is the IEEE1149.4 standard for an analog test bus. This standard provides the connectivity of the blocks to the analog test bus via digitally controlled switching, i.e. your normal buses are switched by a test bus, and this switching is done digitally. The concept resembles the access structures for digital testing; however, the analog signals are being carried through the integrated circuit either from the excitation instruments or to the measuring instruments, all of which are external. Given the harsh environments generated by this type of testing, in which analogue blocks are usually integrated, the key question is whether such an approximation for block behavior measurements is feasible.

A solution to improve the measurement ability in environments rapid diagnostics are required, is to include in IC a signal generator and a digitizer, in the form of D/A and A/D converters, respectively.

This avoids the need for the analog input ports, as the D/A and A/D converters are handle using the TAP digital test port. Nevertheless, an analog test bus is used to carry the analog signals all over the chip. The difficulty presented by this solution is its high consumption of area in the integrated circuit required by the built-in data converters. In some cases, A/D and D/A converters may consume significant areas, with a typical value of around 10 mm^2 or more, in CMOS processes of fine geometry [6, 7]. Even more important is the fact that integrating such data converters requires design efforts and time, which most designers are not willing to undertake. On the other hand, the access mechanisms for the tests, which are the buses that carry the test information inside the chip, are governed by the IEEE 1149.X and IEEE 1500 standards, and the manufacturer of the integrated circuit chooses the solution that best suits him according to his criteria, the application of the circuit and its manufacturing methodology.

2 General Draft of the Proposed System

It sent stimuli into the IC. Once the stimuli have been coded, they must be sent to the inside of the integrated circuit to be tested. The communication for the entry of bit trains inside the integrated circuit is not developed in this project. That could be implemented through a test port on the IC.

Extraction of stimuli by internal hardware. This is when the internal hardware, corresponding to a functional block for testing, extracts the stimuli of interest from the bit trains that are sent to it. This block is the one developed in this work.

Figure 1 shows the block diagram of the solution in general, but taking into account that in this work we concentrate on the block corresponding to signal generation. Each part of the system is explained.

User interface. It is an application used by the user for the generation of test signals. It is in this block that the user chooses the characteristics of the stimuli he wants to generate. The interest of this work in this block is minimal, since it works with an algorithm in Matlab® that transforms the stimuli of interest to the user into a digital format. The digital format used is PDM, or Σ-Δ signals. The possibility of an interface in an integrated computer-based development environment is left open.

Communication channel. It is responsible for carrying the stimuli in digital format from the user interface to the mixed signal integrated circuit. No work was done on this article.

Signal generator. This is an internal test block that takes the digital information that the user sends from its interface, and transforms it into analog stimuli to excite the interest blocks in the integrated circuit.

Clock the system. It is a circuit in charge of generating the clock signal that will control the operation of the system.

Signal digitizer. It is the block in charge of taking the output signals of the block being excited, and sending them to the outside of the chip in a digital format. This block is presented in another article [9].

CUT. It is the block that is being excited in the integrated circuit, and which you want to test.

The following are the specifications of interest in the software implementation of the Σ-Δ modulator, due to the impact of the signal generator, as well as the technical specifications of the latter.

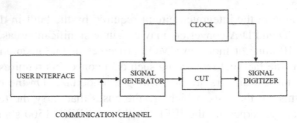

Fig. 1. Block diagram of the proposed overall solution.

2.1 PDM Signal Generator Algorithm

It is the software implementation of a 2nd order Σ-Δ modulator, which has a bandwidth of 500 kHz, as well as a theoretical SNR of 70 dB. Out-of-band noise starts in the vicinity of 5 MHz. The Σ-Δ modulation scheme has allowed the realization of high-precision data converters with resolutions between 16 and 20 bits. Sometimes a signal has been sampled and encoded to be processed digitally, in such case it is necessary to use D/A converters to recover the original signal, the signal conversion is performed by encoding a multibit digital input signal in a single bit train, with a peak-to-peak amplitude of Δ, and for this using digital signal processing and over-sampling techniques. The input sinusoidal signal in digital format, with amplitude A and frequency f_t, which has been over-sampled, is fsΔf_t. If the output of a sigma delta modulator is superimposed on its input, we can easily observe that the output switches between the high and low levels in such a way that the input analog signal is encoded in the density of the pulses of the output signal. These kinds of signals are known as PDM (Pulse Density Modulated) signals. It should be noted that the input signal is multibit, and this can be completely recovered by digital filtering of the bit train at the modulator output. The Σ-Δ encoding process guarantees that the input signal and the quantization error, occupy different spectrum frequency zones.

To convert the digital input signal into an analogue form, a filter the bit train at the modulator output with an analogue filter, with a width of W, is used. It should be pointed out that the filtering operation removes most of the quantization noise, but does not eliminate all of it. Some residual noise will remain in the band of interest. Therefore, for a second order modulator, which is the model used in this project, some noise due to quantization error appears at the output signal along with the signal of interest, and its SNR will be given by [8]:

$$SNR = 15\,log_2(OSR) + 6\,log_2\left(\frac{A}{\Delta}\right) - 8(dB) \tag{1}$$

Where OSR (OverSampling Rate) is the oversampling rate, $(\frac{fs}{2})/W$, and W is the bandwidth of the modulator. Equation (1) suggests that a very high OSR value would bring the conversion closer to the ideal. Perhaps the great advantage of PDM encoding is that only an analog filter with fixed bandwidth is required to retrieve the analog signal. That is, any signal can be placed in the modulator's pass band and obtained again with a filter tuned to that band [8].

Figure 2 shows the block diagram of the modulator Σ-Δ passes second-order casualties used in this article. Such a system is described by the following set of equations:

$$y(n) = sgn[x_2(n-1)]$$
$$x_1(n) = x_1(n-1) + u(n) - y(n) \qquad (2)$$
$$x_2(n) = x_1(n) + x_2(n-1) - y(n)$$

Where u (n) is the digital input multibit signal, and (n) is the output of a single bit, and sgn (x) represents the function sign of x. For a particular input sequence u (n) and a particular set of initial conditions x_1 (0) and x_2 (0) you can generate the PDM representation of the input, this by means of iteration through the set of ecu above and the storage of and (n). In this case, the quantization noise is eliminated in the band of interest and placed on the high frequencies.

A Σ-Δ modulator is based on a system with infinite impulsive response whose output signal converts the input analog signal into an infinitely long sequence of bits. Because of this property, with a periodic input, the output pattern of the bits does not repeat. There is no finite sequence that can be extracted from the modulator output and said to represent the periodic input signal. Fortunately, you can get approximations to the original signal from a finite bit train. To guarantee that the input signal completes an integer number of cycles in the output bit train, and repeating this infinitely, would give a close approximation to the original PDM signal. This is achieved by following the consistent sampling rules described below. For the best approximation, it must also be ensured that the N + 1 bit of the sequence of N bits being extracted is the same as the first bit of the pattern, in order to avoid the most obvious discontinuity. The following section gives a detailed description of the system and explains the method used to extract the analogue signal from periodic bit trains.

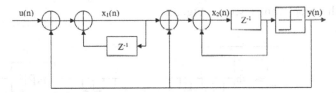

Fig. 2. Block diagram of the 2nd order Σ-Δ modulator.

This type of modulation throws the noise towards the high frequencies, which is the expected behavior as a result of the equations analyzed above [13, 14].

2.2 Specifications of the Analog Signal Generator

This is composed of a serial load displacement register, a control circuit, a deciding block, and an active analog low pass filter. The recharged serial load register has an optimal theoretical size of 512 bits, according to the calculations presented in [10]. It is built with Flip-Flops type D, the latter are fired from the negative flank, and operates at a clock frequency of 10 MHz. Due to difficulties of visualization and observability of the nodes of interest, due to their quantity, it was decided to change to a 15-bit register. This does not affect the desired objective at all, since the design has the ability to be modular, and this allows for smooth expansion. The function of this register is to host the train of bits coming from the user interface. This register also has a switch on its input, which allows it to stop the input flow from performing a feedback [3].

The deciding block consists of a conventional comparator circuit, as well as a network that generates a reference voltage. Its function is to take the logical outputs "1" and "0" which is capable of storing a record, and transforms them into the 1 and −1 of the Σ-Δ signals. The active analog filter passes low, which has the function of extracting the analog signals that are contained in the PDM bit patterns [3]. The specifications of this circuit are summarized below:

- Cut-off frequency 750 kHz.
- Transition band from 750 kHz to 1.5 MHz.
- Rice in the 1 dB step band.
- Attenuation in the suppressed band 25 dB.
- 6th order.

The main element of this block is an operational amplifier, based on the design presented in [11].

3 Detailed Draft of the Proposed System

3.1 Signal Generator

This block is divided into three sub-blocks namely; the offset register with switched input, the control circuit, the deciding block, and the analog filter passes active low. An overview of this block can be seen in Fig. 3.

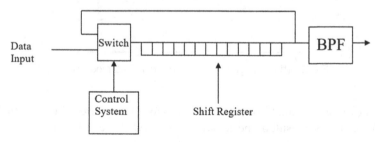

Fig. 3. Block diagram of the signal generator.

3.1.1 Displacement Record

This circuit must be 512 Flip-Flops, however, for the purposes of this article a 15-bit one is used. It has three inputs: Data Input, Reset, Data Output and CLK.

3.1.2 PDM Signal Input Control Circuit

It is the name that is made of the control and switch circuits working together. An overview of the situation described above is illustrated in Fig. 4.

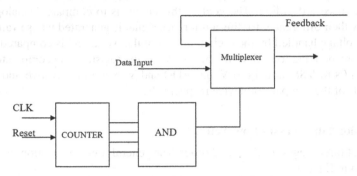

Fig. 4. PDM signal input control circuit.

To obtain a sequence of infinite length, such as that produced by a Σ-Δ modulator, all the bits of the PDM signal must be rotated indefinitely, and this is achieved by means of a feedback, as established in the previous chapter. This feedback is done by means of a control block, which basically consists of a switch and a counter.

The switch is nothing more than a multiplexer with two input streams, and also has a control signal. The purpose of this device is to process two data streams, one coming from the user with the test bit pattern, and the other coming from the feedback of the register, which helps to simulate the infinite length output typical of the Σ-Δ modulators. The control system is nothing more than a counter has the function of counting the bits that are coming to the register of displacement, this is achieved by making the counter work with the same clock of the register, but fired by the positive flank. Once your account ends, i.e. when the record is full, the block activates a control signal that causes the multiplexer to switch its status, performing the feedback of the record. The design of the meter must take into account that, the meter must preserve its final state in order to keep the control signal active, and the feedback is maintained indefinitely. The outputs of each of the constituent Flip-Flops are connected to an AND function, whose number of inputs depends on the size of the counter, and the output of this function is the one that controls the flow in the register input. It has basically 2 signals of interest to the user, CLK and Reset. CLK is that, for the record case, and this is the system clock for the operation of sequential circuits. In the case of the reset signal, the exact same thing happens. The design of the meter is then explained.

The status machine operation of the test counter and from there you can extract the Boolean equations that establish the architecture of the block of interest. The table assumes a 4-bit counter, to get the 15 accounts required by the test displacement log. As you can see, there is a peculiarity, and it is the repetition of Status 16 in the 17, this was done in order that the machine keeps its last Status indefinitely, until the user restarts the system. The resulting Boolean equations and Karnaugh diagrams are omitted for convenience, and their development is based on the technique studied in [12].

3.1.3 Block of Decision

As is known, the output of the Σ-Δ modulator is 1 bit and is given by 1s and -1s. The offset log can only store 1s and 0s, so it is necessary to use a method that helps to make the output of 1s and 0s of the log equal to 1s and -1s of the Σ-Δ modulator. To do this, the designer used a deciding. The goal of this circuit is to compare 2 analog signals and amplify their difference, for this a reference signal is generated whose value is half the power voltage handled by the digital circuits of the work, and is compared with the voltages corresponding to each of the bits stored in the register. The comparator circuit used carries 0s to VSS, and 1s to VDD. VDD and VSS are the positive and negative power levels of the comparator device respectively.

3.1.4 Analog Filter Passes Low Active

It consists of three stages, each of 2nd order. The general transfer function of each step is as written in Eq. (3).

$$\frac{V_o}{V_i}(s) = \frac{K\omega_0^2}{s^2 + s\frac{\omega_0}{Q} + \omega_0^2} \tag{3}$$

In this equation $\omega 0$ is the cut-off frequency, K is the gain in DC, and Q is the filter quality factor. The topology of each of the steps of this filter is of the Sallen Key type. The filter order required for the given specifications can be obtained. Using the specifications given in the previous section, the order of the required filter has to be 4. This translates into two stages, the first of which was designed for a cut-off frequency of 757 kHz, disregarding the quality factor. The reason for this cut-off frequency choice lies in the fact that it is difficult to equalize, and to meet both the bandwidth requirements and the quality factor requirements. Here the quality factor is neglected and the design is limited to meeting the bandwidth requirements. The resulting quality factor was Q = 0.51, and this is really low, causing the filter power spectrum to decay at a very high rate. As a result, in the vicinity of 500 kHz the signal amplitude drops to 0.7 its maximum amplitude, which is very significant.

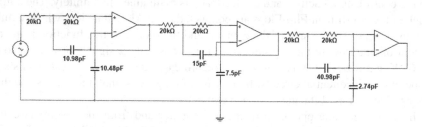

Fig. 5. 6th order low-pass filter of the Butterworth type.

In the second stage, the quality factor was slightly increased, Q = 0.707, and the cut-off frequency was taken from 750 kHz. The result was a little more satisfactory, since in the vicinity of 500 kHz the attenuation was 0.92. The total attenuation of the two stages in the vicinity of 500 kHz was 0.65, which makes the resulting signal only slightly more than half the required power. This requires the placement of a third stage, which compensates for the power losses previously obtained, of course, by making the bandwidth more flexible.

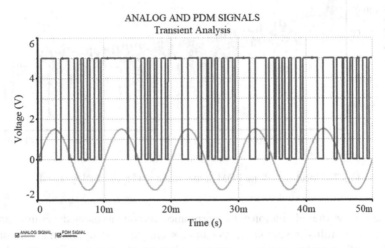

Fig. 6. Analog signal of 1.5 Vp at 100 Hz encoded in a PDM signal.

For the third second order filter, the following specifications are available: a bandwidth of 780 kHz and a quality factor of $Q = 2$. This stage provides a gain of 1.5 in the vicinity of 500 kHz, thus compensating for the drops in the previous stages. The overall result is a completely flat response up to 750 kHz and a pronounced power drop from this frequency. This iterative design process was carried out with the help of a tool called Filter Wizard, which comes with the Green Mountain Computing Systems software package, Multisim® & Electronic Workbech®. The resulting circuit is shown in Fig. 5, together with the corresponding values of each component.

4   Testing and Results

Then, tests were carried out at the electronic level of the proposed system to verify that the project was working properly, and for this the designer used a signal available in the simulators, whose spectrum, although not equal to that of the PDM signals, had similar characteristics. A PDM signal is encoded and stored in the shift register designed in this investigation. The coded analog signal is a sinusoidal of 1.5 Vp of amplitude and frequency 100 Hz. The clock frequency of the shift register is 1 kHz. In Fig. 6 you can see both signals. In Fig. 7 you can see the spectrum of the PDM signal, where you can see the in-band component of interest, and the out-of-band components corresponding to the spurious components of quantization noise that are typical of Σ-Δ modulation.. Although the encoded signal is in the 100 Hz band, a spectrum is presented up to 100 kHz because the quantization noise tends to be located in the high frequencies.

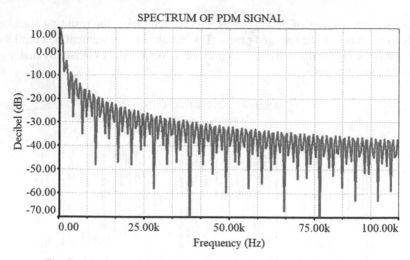

Fig. 7. Spectrum of the PDM signal that encodes the analog signal.

Figure 8 shows the calculation of the harmonic components using the Fourier analysis provided by the Multisim simulator. As can be seen, the most significant component is 1 kHz due to the clock signal at which the shift register operates. It is also observed that the 100 Hz component and the associated harmonic components stand out. For this analysis, the frequency range is extended up to 3.5 kHz to visualize part of the quantization noise components that affect the total harmonic distortion of the encoded signal.

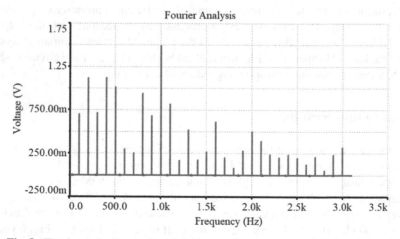

Fig. 8. Fourier analysis to estimate the harmonic components of the PDM signal.

The simulator shows that the harmonic distortion, THD, for 30 components is 455.057%. The quantization noise disperses the purity of the tone that has been encoded, but it is the price that is paid for having the information corresponding to a multi-bit

OUTPUT SIGNAL OF ANALOG FILTER
Transient Analysis

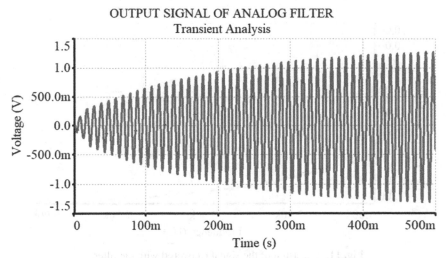

Fig. 9. Recovered signal at the filter outlet.

signal encoded in a mono-bit signal, while preserving that original resolution. Such harmonic distortion increases the demands on the filter design, which must be designed to eliminate all spurious harmonic components that mask the signal of interest.

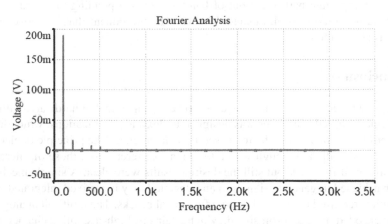

Fig. 10. Fourier analysis to estimate the harmonic components of the recovered signal.

Figure 9 shows the analog signal recovered with the filter, which was encoded in the PDM signal. The signal preserves the characteristics of the original signal, with an amplitude of approximately 1.5 Vp and a frequency close to 100 Hz. It is noteworthy the transient behavior in which it is observed how the signal starts with a reduced value and grows with the time to stability.

Figure 10 shows the Fourier analysis of the recovered signal to calculate the harmonic components of the signal that has been recovered by means of filtering. It can be seen that the predominant component is the one corresponding to 100 Hz, and it is observed that

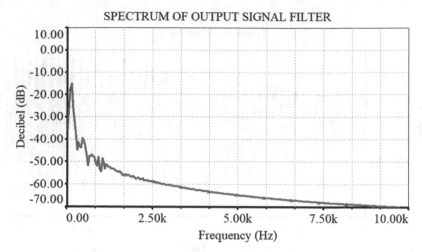

Fig. 11. Spectrum of the signal recovered with the filter.

some harmonic components close to 100 Hz are also maintained, although considerably attenuated. The simulator shows the result of the harmonic analysis of the recovered signal by filtering the PDM signal. It is evident that there is no pure recovery of the original signal, and there is a THD, for 30 components, of 10.52%. In Fig. 11 it can be seen that an important part of the out-of-band noise corresponding to the quantization of the Σ-Δ modulation is eliminated. The 100 Hz component that is recovered with filtering is also evidenced.

5   Conclusions

The integrated electronic circuit turned out to be a simple analog hardware, with some digital logic included. The filter was designed to flexible specifications, which led to a low-order filter. Which had to be increased for convenience. The principle of electronic operation was verified, although with a test signal different from those of interest due to the software difficulties, but still the desired results were clear. A simple mechanism has been achieved to generate signals in an integrated way in a mixed integrated circuit, in which it is required to test analog-type functional blocks. The multi-bit analog signal has been encoded in a mono-bit signal, which retains its high-resolution characteristics, and the hardware for its extraction is simple and easy to implement.

References

1. Simancas-García, J.L.: Diagnóstico de Circuitos Integrados Analógicos y de Comunicaciones. INGE@UAN - Tendencias en la Ingeniería **1**(2), 7–19 (2011)
2. Zorian, Y.: System-chips test strategies. In: Design Automation Conference (35th: 1998: San Francisco), San Francisco, p. 6. ACM (1998)
3. Hafed, M., Abaskharoun, N., Roberts, G.: A 4-GHz effective sample rate integrated test core for analog and mixed-signal circuits. IEEE J. Solid-State Circ. **37**(4), 499–514 (2002)

4. Rubio, A., et al.: Diseño de circuitos y sistemas integrados, p. 446. Alfaomega, Mexico (2005)
5. Kundert, K., et al.: Design of mixed-signal systems-on-a-chip. IEEE Trans. Comput.-Aided Des. Integr. Circ. Syst. **19**(12), 1561–1571 (2000)
6. Hafed, M., Roberts, G.: A stand-alone integrated excitation/extraction systems for analog BIST application. In: IEEE Costum Integrated Circuit Conference, p. 4. IEEE (200)
7. Hafed, M., Roberts, G.: Techniques for high-frequency integrated test and measurement. IEEE Trans. Instrum. Measur. **52**(16), 1780–1786 (2003)
8. Hawrysh, E., Roberts, G.: An integration of memory-based analog signal generation into current DFT architectures. IEEE Trans. Instrum. Measur. **47**(3), 748–759 (1998)
9. Simancas-García, J.L., Meléndez-Pertuz, F.A., González, R.E.R., Cárdenas, C.A., Collazos-Morales, C.A.: Digital analog converter for the extraction of test signals from mixed integrated circuits. In: Gervasi, Osvaldo, et al. (eds.) ICCSA 2021. LNCS, vol. 12949, pp. 207–223. Springer, Cham (2021). https://doi.org/10.1007/978-3-030-86653-2_15
10. Simancas-García, J.L., Caicedo-Ortiz, J.G.: Modelo computacional de un modulador $\sum$-Δ de 2° orden para la generación de señales de prueba en circuitos integrados analógicos. INGE@UAN - Tendencias en la Ingeniería **5**(9), 43–55 (2014)
11. Simancas-García, J.L.: Diseño de un Amplificador Operacional CMOS de Amplio Ancho de Banda y Alta Ganancia para Aplicaciones de Alta Velocidad. IngeCUC **9**(1) (2013)
12. Tokheim, R.: Principios digitales, 3 edn., p. 402. MacGraw-Hill, España (1995)
13. Aziz, P., Sorensen, H., van der Spiegel, J.: An overview of sigma-delta converters: how a 1-bit ADC achieves more than 16-bit resolution. IEEE Signal Process. Mag. 61–84 (1996)
14. LNCS. http://www.numerix-dsp.com/appsnotes/APR8-sigma-delta.pdf

Modeling and Metric of Intelligent Systems

Comparison of Various Deep CNN Models for Land Use and Land Cover Classification

Geetanjali S. Mahamunkar[✉] and Laxman D. Netak

Department of Computer Engineering, Dr. Babasaheb Ambedkar Technological University Lonere, Raigad 402103, India
{gsmahamunkar,ldnetak}@dbatu.ac.in

Abstract. Activities of identifying kinds of physical objects on lands from the images captured through satellite and labeling them according to their usages are referred to as Land Use and Land Cover Classification (LULC). Researchers have developed various machine learning techniques for this purpose. The effectiveness of these techniques has been individually evaluated. However, their performance needs to be compared against each other primarily when they are used for LULC. This paper compares the performance of five commonly used machine learning techniques, namely Random Forest, two variants of Residual Networks, and two variants of Visual Geometry Group Models. The performance of these techniques is compared in terms of accuracy, recall and precision using the Eurosat dataset. The performance profiling described in this paper could help researchers to select a given model over other related techniques.

Keywords: Geospatial data analysis · Deep learning · Pre-trained deep CNN models · Human centric deep learning API · Land Use and Land Cover Classification

1 Introduction

Geospatial data can be obtained through various sources like remote sensing satellites, drones, and Unmanned Aerial Vehicles (UAV). Recent breakthroughs in the field of deep learning have shown that Neural Network-based techniques provide excellent solutions for a wide range of geospatial data analysis applications, including object recognition, image classification, and scene interpretation [6].

One such geospatial data analysis application is the LULC classification. LULC classification aims to assign labels describing the represented physical land type or the way the land area is used, i.e. for industrial or residential purposes. Recently, researchers have started adopting various machine learning and deep learning techniques developed for general-purpose image processing tasks

© Springer Nature Switzerland AG 2022
J.-H. Kim et al. (Eds.): IHCI 2021, LNCS 13184, pp. 499–510, 2022.
https://doi.org/10.1007/978-3-030-98404-5_46

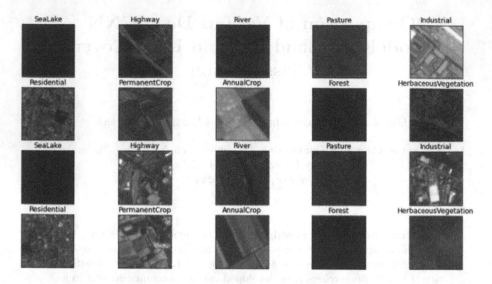

Fig. 1. Sample image patches of the 10 classes of the EuroSAT dataset

for LULC purposes. These techniques include Random Forest classifiers, Residual Networks [7] and Visual Geometry Group models [5,13]. The performance of these techniques has been evaluated using image data sets such as ImageNet [8]. However, their performance needs to be evaluated in the context of satellite images and LULC activity. In the absence of such performance profiling, selecting appropriate machine learning technique becomes a challenge. In this paper, we compare the performance of Random Forest Classifier [1,9], two variants of Residual Networks (ResNet50 and ResNet50V2), and two variants of Visual Geometry Group (VGG16 and VGG19) Models using satellite image dataset named EuroSAT [4].

This paper primarily contributes by performing the performance profiling of Random Forest Classifiers, Residual Networks and Visual Geometry Groups for the LULC classification problem. The results of the performance profiling are useful to decide upon an appropriate technique for LULC classification.

The rest of the paper is organized as follows: Sect. 2 describes various models used for LULC. Section 3 explains the methodology adopted for performance evaluation. Section 4 presents the conclusion and future scope.

2   Models for LULC Classification

We have selected Random Forest Classifier, Residual Networks and Visual Geometry Group models for LULC classification purpose. These techniques have been selected for their widespread use of image processing tasks and image data analysis. A brief description of these models is as follows:

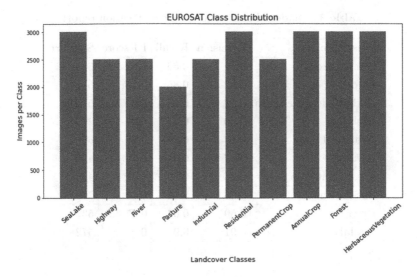

Fig. 2. Distribution of RGB images from EuroSAT dataset over various LULC classes

2.1 Random Forest Classifier

Random Forest is a machine learning technique for solving classification and regression problems. It makes use of ensemble learning, which is a technique for solving complicated problems by combining several classifiers. Many decision trees make up a Random Forest algorithm.

It is mostly used to solve classification problems. A forest is made up of trees, and more trees equals a more robust forest. Similarly, the Random Forest method constructs decision trees from data samples, extracts predictions from each, and then votes on the best option. It is an ensemble method that is superior than a single decision tree because it averages the results to reduce over-fitting.

The reason behind choosing this classifier over others is that by averaging or integrating the outputs of different decision trees, it addresses the problem of over-fitting. It performs better than a single decision tree for a wide range of data items. Its variance is lower than that of a single decision tree. Random Forests are incredibly adaptable and have a high level of accuracy. The Random Forest algorithm does not require data scaling. Even after supplying data without scaling, it maintains a high level of accuracy. Even when a major amount of the data is missing, the Random Forest algorithms maintain high accuracy.

However, the missing data is not handled by the *sklearn*[1] implementation of Random Forest. To prepare data for Random Forests in *Python* and the *sklearn* module, the dataset should be free of missing values and also convert categorical data to numerical data.

---

[1] https://scikit-learn.org/stable/index.html.

Table 1. Random Forest algorithm classification report

Class label	Precision	Recall	F1-score	Support
Annual crop	0.71	0.66	0.69	643
Forest	0.92	0.85	0.88	652
Herbaceous vegetation	0.57	0.66	0.61	522
Highway	0.30	0.53	0.39	284
Industrial	0.88	0.70	0.78	625
Pasture	0.77	0.68	0.72	450
Permanent crop	0.43	0.52	0.47	415
Residential	0.66	0.56	0.61	700
River	0.69	0.64	0.67	537
Sea lake	0.91	0.95	0.93	572

2.2 Residual Network Models

Addition of layers to a Deep Neural Network improves accuracy and performance, and is especially effective for addressing complicated issues. Also these layers gradually pick up on the features. However, it has been observed that the classic Convolutional Neural Network model has a maximum depth threshold. That is, when more layers are added to a network, its performance degrades. Hence ResNet, or Residual Networks, solves the difficulty of training incredibly deep networks. Skip connections, or shortcuts, are used by ResNet to jump past some layers. There are two key reasons to use skip connections: to avoid vanishing gradients and to avoid the degradation (accuracy saturation) problem, which arises when more layers are added to a sufficiently deep model and leads to an increase in training error. The majority of ResNet models use double or triple layer skips with non-linearities and batch normalisation in between. This innovative Neural Network was first introduced in [2].

Residual Networks have been used in various image processing applications such as pan sharpening [11], image recognition [3], image classification [10] etc.

ResNet34 was the first ResNet architecture, which required inserting shortcut connections into plain networks to convert them to their residual network equivalent. It was made up of 34 weighted layers.

ResNet50. ResNet comes in number of versions, each of which is based on the same concept but has a different number of layers. ResNet50 refers to a version of the network that can run with 50 Neural Network layers. While the ResNet50 architecture is based on the model described above in the Sect. 2.2, there is one significant difference. Due to concerns about the time required to train the layers, the building block was redesigned into a bottleneck design in this situation. Instead of the previous two layers block of ResNet34, a three-layer stack was used resulting in the ResNet50 architecture.

Table 2. Performance evaluation for ResNet

Class label	Precision	Recall	F1-score	Support
RestNet50 V1				
Annual crop	0.964527	0.951667	0.958054	600.0
Forest	0.934579	1.000000	0.966184	600.0
Herbaceous vegetation	0.962901	0.951667	0.957251	600.0
Highway	0.971074	0.940000	0.955285	500.0
Industrial	0.979960	0.978000	0.978979	500.0
Pasture	0.979167	0.940000	0.959184	400.0
Permanent crop	0.947896	0.946000	0.946947	500.0
Residential	0.970827	0.998333	0.984388	600.0
River	0.953125	0.976000	0.964427	500.0
Sea Lake	1.000000	0.963333	0.981324	600.0
RestNet50 V2				
Annual crop	0.933222	0.931667	0.932444	600.0
Forest	0.966184	1.000000	0.982801	600.0
Herbaceous vegetation	0.952462	0.935000	0.943650	600.0
Highway	0.953061	0.934000	0.943434	500.0
Industrial	0.974522	0.918000	0.945417	500.0
Pasture	0.971429	0.935000	0.952866	400.0
Permanent crop	0.908730	0.916000	0.912351	500.0
Residential	0.913110	0.998333	0.953822	600.0
River	0.957831	0.954000	0.955912	500.0
Sea lake	0.996593	0.975000	0.985678	600.0

ResNet50V2. ResNet50V2 is a modified version of ResNet50 that performs better on the ImageNet dataset than ResNet50. ResNet50V2 applies Batch Normalization and ReLU activation to the input before convolution operation while in ResNet50 convolution is performed before Batch Normalization and ReLU activation.

2.3   Visual Geometry Group models

Karen Simonyan and Andrew Zisserman proposed the Visual Geometry Group (VGG) network concept in 2013, and in the 2014 ImageNet Challenge, they submitted the actual model based on the concept [13]. In this paper, we have used model trained on ImageNet dataset so accordingly some modification has been done in the layers. The convolution stacks are followed by flattening which converts the multidimensional output to the linear output passed to the dense layer. The dense layer is followed by dropout which is a technique for reducing the amount of association between characteristics by lowering the weights (edges)

Table 3. Performance evaluation for visual geometry group models

Class label	Precision	Recall	F1-score	Support
VGG16				
Annual crop	0.970990	0.948333	0.959528	600.0
Forest	0.985197	0.998333	0.991722	600.0
Herbaceous vegetation	0.981387	0.966667	0.973971	600.0
Highway	0.981818	0.972000	0.976884	500.0
Industrial	0.989775	0.968000	0.978766	500.0
Pasture	0.970297	0.980000	0.975124	400.0
Permanent crop	0.932302	0.964000	0.947886	500.0
Residential	0.967690	0.998333	0.982773	600.0
River	0.985972	0.984000	0.984985	500.0
Sea Lake	1.000000	0.986667	0.993289	600.0
VGG19				
Annual crop	0.920339	0.905000	0.912605	600.0
Forest	0.991394	0.960000	0.975445	600.0
Herbaceous vegetation	0.931373	0.950000	0.940594	600.0
Highway	0.954635	0.968000	0.961271	500.0
Industrial	0.970646	0.992000	0.981207	500.0
Pasture	0.976623	0.940000	0.957962	400.0
Permanent crop	0.872495	0.958000	0.913251	500.0
Residential	0.990050	0.995000	0.992519	600.0
River	0.971660	0.960000	0.965795	500.0
Sea lake	1.000000	0.946667	0.972603	600.0

at a probability. The following subsections describe the general architecture of VGG16 and VGG19 models.

VGG16. In VGG16 architecture fixed-size 224×224 image with three channels − R, G, and B − is regarded as the input. Only the RGB values for each pixel are normalised as part of the pre-processing. The mean value of each pixel is subtracted to achieve this.

Following Rectified Linear Unit (ReLU) activations, the image is sent through the first stack of two convolution layers with a very small receptive area of 3×3. There are 64 filters in each of the two layers. The padding is one pixel, while the convolution stride is fixed at one pixel. The spatial resolution is preserved in this mode, and the output activation map has the same dimensions as the input image.

The activation maps are then run via spatial max pooling with a stride of 2 pixels over a 2×2-pixel window. The size of the activations is reduced by half.

Table 4. Training and validation accuracy and loss per epoch of ResNet50 and ResNet50V2

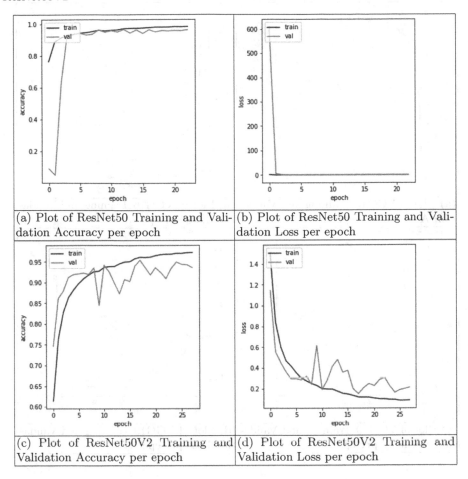

(a) Plot of ResNet50 Training and Validation Accuracy per epoch

(b) Plot of ResNet50 Training and Validation Loss per epoch

(c) Plot of ResNet50V2 Training and Validation Accuracy per epoch

(d) Plot of ResNet50V2 Training and Validation Loss per epoch

As a result, the activations at the bottom of the first stack are $112 \times 112 \times 64$ in size. The activations are then passed through a second stack, this time with 128 filters instead of 64 in the first. As a result, after the second layer, the size is $56 \times 56 \times 128$. The third stack consists of three convolutional layers and a max pool layer. The number of filters used here is 256, resulting in a stack output size of $28 \times 28 \times 256$.

After that, there are two stacks of three convolutional layers, each with 512 filters. At the end of both stacks, the result will be $7 \times 7 \times 512$. Three fully connected layers follow the stacks of convolutional layers, with a flattening layer in between. The first two layers each feature 4,096 neurons, while the final fully connected layer serves as the output layer, with 1,000 neurons corresponding to

Table 5. Training and validation accuracy and loss per epoch for VGG16 and VGG19

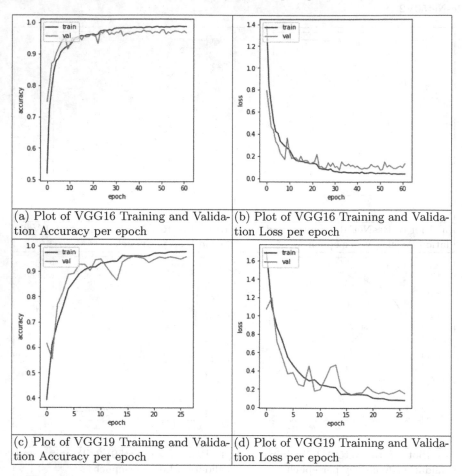

(a) Plot of VGG16 Training and Validation Accuracy per epoch

(b) Plot of VGG16 Training and Validation Loss per epoch

(c) Plot of VGG19 Training and Validation Accuracy per epoch

(d) Plot of VGG19 Training and Validation Loss per epoch

the ImageNet dataset's 1,000 possible classes. Following the output layer comes the Softmax activation layer, which is utilised for categorical classification.

VGG19. The VGG19 model is a variation of the VGG model that has 19 layers in total which includes 16 convolution layers and 3 Fully connected layer along with 5 MaxPool layers and 1 SoftMax layer. This model was given a fixed size (224×224) RGB picture as input, indicating that the matrix was of shape $(224, 224, 3)$. The only preprocessing was subtracting each pixel's mean RGB value, which was computed throughout the whole training set. It utilised kernels of size (3×3) with a stride size of 1 pixel, allowing it to cover the entire image concept. To keep the image's spatial resolution, spatial padding was applied. Max pooling was done with stride 2 over a 2×2 pixel window.

The ReLU was then used to incorporate non-linearity into the model, allowing it to classify better. Three fully connected layers were implemented, the first two of which were of size 4096, followed by a layer with 1000 channels for 1000-way ILSVRC [12] classification, and finally a softmax function.

3 Methodology

3.1 The Data Set: EuroSAT

The EuroSAT dataset consists of RGB and multi-spectral version. In this paper, we have used the RGB version of EuroSAT dataset[2] that contains 27,000 images that have been labeled with ten different land use and land cover classes. The class distribution can be plotted as in Fig. 2. Furthermore, this dataset is geo-referenced and based on publicly available Earth Observation data, allowing for a diverse set of applications.

3.2 Deep Learning API: Keras

Keras is a human-centric API, that adheres to the best practises for lowering cognitive load, such as providing uniform and simple APIs, limiting the number of user activities required for typical use cases, and providing clear and actionable error messages[3]. It comes with a lot of documentation and developer instructions. It provides ResNet V1 and ResNet V2 with 50, 101, or 152 layers. We have used the pre-trained Residual Network models ResNet50 along with ResNet50V2. Also Visual Geometry Group pre-trained models from Keras such as VGG16 and VGG19 have been used. We have also compared the Random Forest Classifier, which is a machine learning technique, to the deep CNN architectures. We have used the *sklearn* implementation of Random Forest Classifier for this purpose. *sklearn* is a machine learning library for python language.

We have also used *sklearn* to calculate the average recall, precision, and F-score which were used to assess performance of all the deep CNN models and Random Forest model. *sklearn* provides simple and efficient tools for predictive data analysis. For LULC classification, the VGG16 architecture outperforms the other CNN and Random Forest Classifiers, according to the performance analysis.

The Keras Applications library includes the ResNet and VGG models described earlier that have already been trained. The ImageNet weights are included in the pre-trained model. Transfer learning methods can be employed to train on custom images while using the pre-trained model. The pre-trained models from Keras used for LULC classification of images of the EuroSAT dataset have been described further. In this paper, we have used the *Kaggle* platform to import the various pre-trained deep CNN models using the Keras API and *sklearn* for importing Random Forest algorithm. *Kaggle* is used to search and

---

[2] https://github.com/phelber/eurosat.
[3] keras.io

publish data sets, study and construct models in a web-based data-science environment, collaborate with other data scientists and machine learning experts, and compete in data science competitions.

Initially we downloaded the EuroSAT dataset that is publicly available in the *Kaggle* platform. The dataset consists of 2 directories one containing the RGB images and the other consists of multi-spectral images taken from Sentinel-2 satellite. We have used the RGB images for LULC classification. The directory consisted of 27000 geo-referenced images of 10 classes measuring 64×64 pixels which we split into training and testing sub directories using a ratio of 80:20 respectively. The sample image patches of the geo-referenced images are shown in Fig. 1. Each class contained 2,000 to 3,000 images as shown in Fig. 2. Thus 21600 images belonging to 10 classes were used for training and 5400 images belonging to 10 classes were used for testing.

To begin with we applied a Random Forest Classifier by importing the *sklearn.ensemble* module which includes the ensemble methods for classification, regression and anomaly detection. Because of the use of *sklearn* we just need to set the parameters to implement the Random Forest Classifier. We set the number of trees in the forest by setting the $n\_estimators$ to 500, the number of jobs to run in parallel by setting the n_jobs to -1 which means using all processors, and if $bootstrap = True$, the $random\_state$ parameter controls the randomization of the bootstrapping of the samples used while building trees, as well as the sampling of the features to examine when looking for the best split at each node. We have set $random\_state$ to 7. Later the fit method validates the input data and estimate and store model attributes from the estimated parameters and provided data. Further we calculate the average, precision, recall, fscore and accuracy score using *sklearn* for performance analysis.

We then imported the ResNet50, ResNet50V2, VGG16 and VGG19 models and used different setup of dense layer for each model. Dense layer of each model was first pre-trained with 50 epochs and then end to end whole network was retrained with 100 epochs. When we have a large dataset to fit into our memory or when data augmentation is required, we call $fit\_generator$ function. To avoid overfitting a model and to improve the model's generalisation ability, we must do data augmentation. We utilised a Keras *ImageDataGenerator* object to apply data augmentation to images that were randomly translated, resized, rotated, and so on. During the training of each model, a set of callback functions was used from Keras such as *ModelCheckpoint, EarlyStopping, ReduceLROnPlateau*. We evaluate the loss and metrics for each model after end of each epoch. Finally we calculate and print the classification report in the form of the precision, recall, fscore and accuracy score for each model.

3.3 Results

Table 6 summarizes experimental results of LULC classification using Random Forest Classifier, ResNet50, ResNet50V2, VGG16 and VGG19 models. The results demonstrate that the VGG16 pre-trained model performs better on the EuroSAT RGB dataset in Keras API as compared to Random Forest and ResNet.

Table 6. Experimental results

Pre-trained model	Accuracy	F-score
Random forest	68.87%	F1-score = 0.70 (weighted average)
ResNet50	96.57%	Global F2-score = 0.96
ResNet50V2	95.16%	Global F2-score = 0.95
VGG16	97.68%	Global F2-score = 0.97
VGG19	95.72%	Global F2-score = 0.95

The classification reports of the models applied in this paper are given in Tables 1, 2 and 3. We also plot the training and validation loss and accuracy of each model as in Tables 4 and 5. The plots demonstrate the variation in the training and validation accuracy and loss per epoch.

Table 4(a) illustrates that the training and validation accuracy of ResNet50 did not improve after the 21st and 14th epochs respectively. While Table 4(b) illustrates that the least training and validation loss of ResNet50V2 was at the 13th and 21st epoch respectively. Similarly, Table 4(c) shows that the training and validation accuracy of ResNet50V2 did not enhance after the 27th and 19th epoch respectively. While Table 4(d) indicates that the least training and validation loss of ResNet50V2 was at the 18th and 27th epoch respectively.

Table 5(a) exhibits that the training and validation accuracy of VGG16 did not upgrade after the 59th and 53rd epoch respectively. While Table 5(b) displays that the least training and validation loss of VGG16 at the 59th and 51st epoch respectively. Similarly, Table 5(c) denotes that the training and validation accuracy of VGG19 did not improve and remained approximately constant after the 27th and 17th epoch respectively. While Table 5(d) reveals that the least training and validation loss of VGG19 at the 25th and 17th epoch respectively.

According to the results obtained in this paper, the VGG16 model outperformed the other models with a classification accuracy of 97.68%. According to [4] the ResNet50 model gave a classification accuracy of 96.43% for a split of 80:20 on EuroSAT RGB dataset. Thus it proves that the pre-trained model of VGG16 in Keras gave better result for the LULC classification on the dataset for the same split than the ResNet50 model in [4].

4   Conclusion and Future Scope

The paper describes the performance evaluation of three machine learning techniques for classifying land use and types of lands captured in satellite images. For this purpose, we used three machine learning models that employ Random Forest, ResNet, and VGG classifiers which are pre-trained for ImageNet dataset. These pre-trained models are evaluated against EuroSAT. We observed that: (i) the use of pre-trained models from Keras eliminated the need to implement these models from scratch. Being user-focused and easy to use, the consistent Keras API makes the Human-Computer Interaction simpler and convenient to apply for LULC. (ii) Use of *Kaggle* infrastructure simplified the process of model building and evaluation because of the availability of cloud infrastructure and open dataset. (iii) While comparing the performance of Random Forest, ResNet, and VGG, we observed that VGG16 provides better accuracy for classification. This is because the several small 3×3 size convolution filters combined in a sequence can act as larger receptive fields in VGG. If the receptive field of the network is small, it may not be able to recognize large objects so receptive field computation play a major role in image classification.

The performance evaluation described in the paper could be helpful for geospatial data analysts to select an appropriate method, especially in the absence of models trained on geospatial images. The work presented in the paper can be extended by performing model evaluation for other geospatial tasks such as object recognition and scene classification.

References

1. Breiman, L.: Random forests. Mach. Learn. **45**(1), 5–32 (2001)
2. He, K., Zhang, X., Ren, S., Sun, J.: Deep residual learning for image recognition (2015)
3. He, K., Zhang, X., Ren, S., Sun, J.: Deep residual learning for image recognition. In: 2016 IEEE Conference on Computer Vision and Pattern Recognition (CVPR), pp. 770–778 (2016)
4. Helber, P., Bischke, B., Dengel, A., Borth, D.: EuroSAT: a novel dataset and deep learning benchmark for land use and land cover classification. IEEE J. Sel. Top. Appl. Earth Observ. Remote Sens. **12**(7), 2217–2226 (2019)
5. Jangra, M., Dhull, S.K., Singh, K.K.: ECG arrhythmia classification using modified visual geometry group network (mVGGNet). J. Intell. Fuzzy Syst. **38**(3), 3151–3165 (2020)
6. Kiwelekar, A.W., Mahamunkar, G.S., Netak, L.D., Nikam, V.B.: Deep learning techniques for geospatial data analysis. In: Tsihrintzis, G.A., Jain, L.C. (eds.) Machine Learning Paradigms. LAIS, vol. 18, pp. 63–81. Springer, Cham (2020). https://doi.org/10.1007/978-3-030-49724-8_3
7. Korolev, S., Safiullin, A., Belyaev, M., Dodonova, Y.: Residual and plain convolutional neural networks for 3D brain MRI classification. In: 2017 IEEE 14th International Symposium on Biomedical Imaging (ISBI 2017), pp. 835–838. IEEE (2017)
8. Krizhevsky, A., Sutskever, I., Hinton, G.E.: ImageNet classification with deep convolutional neural networks. Adv. Neural. Inf. Process. Syst. **25**, 1097–1105 (2012)
9. Lowe, B., Kulkarni, A.: Multispectral image analysis using random forest (2015)
10. Paoletti, M.E., Haut, J.M., Fernandez-Beltran, R., Plaza, J., Plaza, A.J., Pla, F.: Deep pyramidal residual networks for spectral-spatial hyperspectral image classification. IEEE Trans. Geosci. Remote Sens. **57**(2), 740–754 (2018)
11. Rao, Y., He, L., Zhu, J.: A residual convolutional neural network for pan-shaprening. In: 2017 International Workshop on Remote Sensing with Intelligent Processing (RSIP), pp. 1–4 (2017)
12. Russakovsky, O., et al.: ImageNet large scale visual recognition challenge. Int. J. Comput. Vis. **115**(3), 211–252 (2015). https://doi.org/10.1007/s11263-015-0816-y
13. Simonyan, K., Zisserman, A.: Very deep convolutional networks for large-scale image recognition (2015)

Mathematical Modeling of the Nostational Filteration Process of Oil in the System of Oil Deposits Related to Slow Conductor Layers

Elmira Nazirova[1]([✉]) [iD], Abdug'ani Nematov[2] [iD], Rustamjon Sadikov[1] [iD], and Inomjon Nabiyev[1] [iD]

[1] Department of Multimedia Technologies, Tashkent University of Information Technologies named after Muhammad al-Khwarizmi, Tashkent, Uzbekistan
elmira_nazirova@mail.ru, magistr_uz@bk.ru
[2] Multimedia Technologies, Tashkent University of Information Technologies named after Muhammad al-Khwarizmi, Tashkent, Uzbekistan

Abstract. This paper discusses the mathematical model of the filtration process in the horizontal section of the motion of fluids in a three-layer oil system in a non-homogeneous reciprocal dynamic interaction in a porous medium, their interaction dynamics and the interaction in the layers. The mathematical model of the problem consists of three interconnected differential equations of one-dimensional parabolic type. An efficient computational algorithm for solving the boundary value problem built on a mathematical model has been developed to determine the main parameters of the filtration process. For the system of finite differences, the formula for finding the solution based on the driving method was determined and an algorithm for finding the driving method coefficients was developed. The formula for finding the values of the pressure function and the driving coefficient at the boundary is defined. Based on the developed algorithm, software was created and computational experiments were conducted, and the results were presented graphically for different situations. Computational experiments were performed on the main parameters of the filtration process of oil in porous media associated with three-layer slurry, as well as the filtration process was analyzed and studied on the basis of the obtained results.

Keywords: Multilayer oil system · Dynamic communication · Numerical methods · Disclosure scheme · Differential equation

1 Introduction

Due to the greater complexity of the natural study of the filtration processes of liquids and gases in porous media, computational experiments are carried out using mathematical and computer modeling methods to study the process. Solving such problems requires the development and widespread use of modern mathematical modeling methods. It is impossible to imagine the solution of problems arising in the study of the complex filtration process of oil and gas, especially in the operation of oil and gas fields, as well as in

© Springer Nature Switzerland AG 2022
J.-H. Kim et al. (Eds.): IHCI 2021, LNCS 13184, pp. 511–519, 2022.
https://doi.org/10.1007/978-3-030-98404-5_47

the process of their extraction in heterogeneous layers, without mathematical modeling. A lot of scientific research has been done in this regard to date. In particular, many mathematical models, computational algorithms and software have been developed for filtration problems to represent the processes that take place in non-homogeneous porous media of oils and gases. Nevertheless, the problems of analyzing the results of computational experiments that allow to study and predict complex processes in dynamically interacting multilayer non-homogeneous oil and gas fields in porous environments, as well as to create mathematical and computer models that present the results in visual graphics and animation forms are sufficient. not studied to the extent.

The article discusses an urgent problem associated with the development of oil and gas fields in order to increase gas and oil recovery of reservoir systems and determine the main indicators of the research object. The analysis of scientific works related to the problem of mathematical modeling of the process of oil filtration in porous reservoir media is presented. To conduct a comprehensive study of the process under consideration, a mathematical model was developed based on the basic laws of hydromechanics. The developed mathematical model is reduced to the joint solution of a system of differential equations of parabolic type describing filtration processes in reservoirs separated by a low-permeability bridge with appropriate initial and boundary conditions. To integrate the set, using the finite-difference method, a numerical algorithm was developed, implemented on a computer by the sweep method, and to synthesize the main parameters and their ranges of variation, computational experiments were carried out for various reservoir characteristics and production wells costs. The results of the performed numerical calculations are presented in graphical form and their analysis is given [1–4].

This paper discusses properties of mathematic modeling processes described by the Cauchy problem to the double nonlinear parabolic equation with convective transfer and damping [5].

The article considers the problem associated with the processes of filtering fluid(water, oil) in multilayer interacting pressure-sensitive porous media, predicting the groundwater levels of any region for the required period of time, taking into account the heterogeneity of the formation in plan, slope of the aquifill, infiltration feed or evaporation, and other hydrogeological, hydraulic and environmental conditions, as well as to develop the optimal layout of vertical drainage wells for the protection of the territoryand the development of oil and gas places ozhdenii. In order to make the right choice of a strategy for solving problems, the research analyzes mathematical modeling, the performance over the past 5–10 years, associated with the processes of filtering liquids in multilayer porous media. In order to solve the above problem, a mathematical model is developed, a numerical algorithm that describes a system of partial differential equations and the corresponding initial, boundary, and internal conditions. Based on the developed mathematical support of the process under consideration, computer experiments were conducted on computers, the results of which are shown in the form of graphical objects and tables. At the end of the article, a detailed analysis of the numerical calculations and conclusions related to it are presented, and the layout and capacity of vertical drainage wells for protection against flooding of irrigated and non-irrigated territories are proposed. Using the proposed mathematical tool, it is possible to obtain predicted groundwater levels of any region for the required period of time, taking into account a number of hydrogeological and hydraulic factors [6, 7].

The paper [8] used an adaptive artificial adhesion method to model the process of a one-dimensional nonlinear convection-diffusion equation. For this purpose, a scheme of second-order finite differences in the approximation of time and space has been developed. The scheme was tested using a digital solution to the problem of forming a gradient catastrophe. The two-phase filtration process was analyzed using a built-in limited difference scheme. Numerical calculations have shown that the proposed method and in this case reliably monitors the dissolution of the solution.

2   Mathematical Model

The movement of liquids in a fragmented non-homogeneous porous layer depends on the parameters of the subsurface layer: k (x, y) - the coefficient of permeability of the layer; m (x, y) - layer porosity coefficient; h (x, y) is the coefficient of layer strength (thickness). If homogeneous zones (fragments) in a layer are separated by a large size, the parameters of this non-homogeneous layer have a significant effect on the nature of the filtration flow. For this reason, all macro inequalities can be divided into the following types. Layered homogeneity, in which the layer is divided into several layers according to the thickness, and in these layers the coefficient of permeability differs from other adjacent layers (Fig. 1).

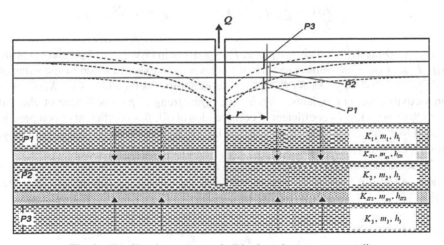

Fig. 1. The filtration process of oil in three-layer porous media

$$
\begin{cases}
\frac{\partial}{\partial x}\left[K_1(x)h_1(x)\frac{\partial P_1}{\partial x}\right] = \mu\beta h_1(x)\frac{\partial P_1}{\partial t} - \frac{K_{\Pi 1}(x)}{h_{\Pi 1}(x)}(P_2 - P_1) \\
\frac{\partial}{\partial x}\left[K_2(x)h_2(x)\frac{\partial P_2}{\partial x}\right] = \mu\beta h_2(x)\frac{\partial P_2}{\partial t} + \frac{K_{\Pi 1}(x)}{h_{\Pi 1}(x)}(P_2 - P_1) - \frac{K_{\Pi 2}(x)}{h_{\Pi 2}(x)}(P_3 - P_2) - Q(t) \\
\frac{\partial}{\partial x}\left[K_3(x)h_3(x)\frac{\partial P_3}{\partial x}\right] = \mu\beta h_3(x)\frac{\partial P_3}{\partial t} + \frac{K_{\Pi 2}(x)}{h_{\Pi 2}(x)}(P_3 - P_2)
\end{cases}
$$

$$(1)$$

$$0 < x < L; \quad t > 0.$$

The initial and boundary conditions of the matter are as follows:

$$P_1(x, t_0) = P_H(x), \quad P_2(x, t_0) = P_H(x), \quad P_3(x, t_0) = P_H(x); \tag{2}$$

$$-K_1 h_1 \frac{\partial P_1}{\partial x}\Big|_{x=0} = \alpha(P_A - P_1); \tag{3}$$

$$K_1 h_1 \frac{\partial P_1}{\partial x}\Big|_{x=L} = \alpha(P_A - P_1); \tag{4}$$

$$-K_2 h_2 \frac{\partial P_2}{\partial x}\Big|_{x=0} = \alpha(P_A - P_2); \tag{5}$$

$$K_2 h_2 \frac{\partial P_2}{\partial x}\Big|_{x=L} = \alpha(P_A - P_2); \tag{6}$$

$$-K_3 h_3 \frac{\partial P_3}{\partial x}\Big|_{x=0} = \alpha(P_A - P_3); \tag{7}$$

$$K_3 h_3 \frac{\partial P_3}{\partial x}\Big|_{x=L} = \alpha(P_A - P_3); \tag{8}$$

$$Q(t) = \sum_{i_q=1}^{N_q} q_{i_q}(t)\delta(x - x_{i_q}); \quad i_q = 1, \dots N_q \tag{9}$$

Where: δ – Dirac delta function; P_1, P_2, P_3 – pressure in layers; P_A – boundary pressure; P_{1H}, P_{2H}, P_{3H} – the initial pressure of the layers, the exact function of the value at t = 0; μ - oil viscosity; K_1, K_2, K_3 - layer permeability coefficients; $K_{\Pi 1}, K_{\Pi 2}$ - weak conductivity layer coefficients; - h_1, h_2, h_3, layer strength; β - coefficient of elasticity $\beta = (\beta_c - m\beta_H)$; β_H - coefficient of compression of oil; β_c - coefficient of compression of the layer; m - coefficient of porosity of layers; $q_{i_q} - i_q-$ well debit; L is the layer length; N_q - number of wells.

To solve the boundary value problem in a numerical way, we bring the problem to a dimensionless problem. To do this, we introduce the following definitions in the system of Eqs. (1)

$$x^* = \frac{x}{L}; \quad \tau = \frac{K_x t}{\beta \mu L^2}; \quad K_1^* = \frac{K_1}{K_x}; \quad K_2^* = \frac{K_2}{K_x}; \quad K_3^* = \frac{K_3}{K_x}; \quad K_{\Pi 1}^* = \frac{K_{\Pi 1}}{K_x}; \quad K_{\Pi 2}^* = \frac{K_{\Pi 2}}{K_x};$$

$$h_1^* = \frac{h_1}{h_x}; \quad h_2^* = \frac{h_2}{h_x}; \quad h_3^* = \frac{h_3}{h_x}; \quad h_{\Pi 1}^* = \frac{h_{\Pi 1}}{h_x}; \quad h_{\Pi 2}^* = \frac{h_{\Pi 2}}{h_x}; \quad P_1^* = \frac{P_1}{P_x}; \quad P_2^* = \frac{P_2}{P_x}; \quad P_3^* = \frac{P_3}{P_x};$$

$$Q^* = \frac{\mu L^2}{K_x h_x P_x} Q.$$

In this case, K_x, h_x, P_x are the values of layer permeability, strength and pressure of a certain magnitude, respectively:

$$K_x = \max(K_1, K_2, K_3, K_{\Pi 1}, K_{\Pi 2}), \quad h_x = \max(h_1, h_2, h_3, h_{\Pi 2}, h_{\Pi 2}), \quad P_x = \max(P_1, P_2, P_3).$$

By performing these substitutions in the system of equations, we come to the following system of dimensionless equations

$$
\begin{cases}
\frac{\partial}{\partial x}\left[K_1(x)h_1(x)\frac{\partial P_1}{\partial x}\right] = \frac{h_1 \partial P_1}{\partial \tau} - \frac{K_{\Pi 1}L^2}{h_{\Pi 1}h_x^2}(P_2 - P_1) \\
\frac{\partial}{\partial x}\left[K_2(x)h_2(x)\frac{\partial P_2}{\partial x}\right] = \frac{h_2 \partial P_2}{\partial \tau} + \frac{K_{\Pi 1}L^2}{h_{\Pi 1}h_x^2}(P_2 - P_1) - \frac{K_{\Pi 2}L^2}{h_{\Pi 2}h_x^2}(P_3 - P_2) - Q(t) \\
\frac{\partial}{\partial x}\left[K_3(x)h_3(x)\frac{\partial P_3}{\partial x}\right] = \frac{h_3 \partial P_3}{\partial \tau} + \frac{K_{\Pi 2}L^2}{h_{\Pi 2}h_x^2}(P_3 - P_2).
\end{cases}
\quad (10)
$$

$$0 < x < 1; \quad \tau > 0.$$

For convenience in the system of equations we enter the definitions $T_1 = K_1 h_1$, $T_2 = K_2 h_2$, $T_3 = K_3 h_3$.

$$
R_1 = \frac{K_{\Pi 1}L^2}{h_{\Pi 1}h_x^2}, \qquad R_2 = \frac{K_{\Pi 2}L^2}{h_{\Pi 2}h_x^2}.
$$

We solve the dimensionless boundary value problem using the finite difference method. In this we have a system of three finitely differentiated equations connected to each other.

To solve the boundary value problem (1)–(9), we develop a numerical model of it, using the method of finite subtraction. To do this, we construct the following grid on the x axis and time

$$
\omega_{x_i \tau_k} = \{x_i = i\Delta x; \ i = \overline{1, n}; \ \tau_k = k\Delta\tau; \quad k = 1, 2, ...\Delta\tau = \frac{T_0}{N_0}\}.
$$

Where is the Δx - step along the x axis; $\Delta\tau$ - step by time.

We use an explicit finite-difference scheme to solve the boundary value problem.

In this discrete field we bring the system of equations to the system of finitely differential equations

$$
\frac{T_{1i-0,5}P_{1i-1}^{k-1} - (T_{1i-0,5} + T_{1i+0,5})P_{1i}^{k-1} + T_{1i+0,5}P_{1i+1}^{k-1}}{\Delta x^2}
$$
$$
= h_{1i}\frac{P_{1i}^k - P_{1i}^{k-1}}{\Delta\tau} - R_1 P_{2i}^k + R_1 P_{1i}^k;
$$
$$
\frac{T_{2i-0,5}P_{2i-1}^{k-1} - (T_{2i-0,5} + T_{2i+0,5})P_{2i}^{k-1} + T_{2i+0,5}P_{2i+1}^{k-1}}{\Delta x^2}
$$
$$
= h_{2i}\frac{P_{2i}^k - P_{2i}^{k-1}}{\Delta\tau} + R_1 P_{2i}^k - R_1 P_{1i}^k - R_2 P_{3i}^k + R_2 P_{2i}^k;
$$
$$
\frac{T_{3i-0,5}P_{3i-1}^{k-1} - (T_{3i-0,5} + T_{3i+0,5})P_{3i}^{k-1} + T_{3i+0,5}P_{3i+1}^{k-1}}{\Delta x^2}
$$
$$
= h_{3i}\frac{P_{3i}^k - P_{3i}^{k-1}}{\Delta\tau} + R_2 P_{3i}^k - R_2 P_{2i}^k.
$$

Here

$$
R_1 = \frac{K_{\Pi 1}L^2}{h_{\Pi 1}h_x^2}; \qquad R_2 = \frac{K_{\Pi 2}L^2}{h_{\Pi 2}h_x^2}.
$$

This system of equations can be written as follows for the unknown by entering the notation (for headphones we omit the higher index k).

$$
\begin{cases}
a_{11i}P_{1i} + a_{12i}P_{2i} + a_{13i}P_{3i} = b_{1i}, \\
a_{21i}P_{1i} + a_{22i}P_{2i} + a_{23i}P_{3i} = b_{2i}, \\
a_{31i}P_{1i} + a_{32i}P_{2i} + a_{33i}P_{3i} = b_{3i}.
\end{cases}
$$

Here:

$$a_{11i} = h_{1i} + R_1\Delta\tau; \quad a_{12i} = -R_1\Delta\tau; \quad a_{13i} = 0;$$

$$b_{1i} = h_{1i}P_{1i}^{k-1} + \Delta\tau/\Delta x^2\left[T_{1i-0,5}P_{1i-1}^{k-1} - (T_{1i-0,5} + T_{1i+0,5})P_{1i}^{k-1} + T_{1i+0,5}P_{1i+1}^{k-1}\right];$$

$$a_{21i} = -R_1\Delta\tau; \quad a_{22i} = h_{2i} + R_1\Delta\tau + R_2\Delta\tau; \quad a_{23i} = -R_2\Delta\tau;$$

$$b_{2i} = h_{2i}P_{2i}^{k-1} + \Delta\tau/\Delta x^2\left[T_{2i-0,5}P_{2i-1}^{k-1} - (T_{2i-0.5} + T_{2i+0,5})P_{2i}^{k-1} + T_{2i+0,5}P_{2i+1}^{k-1}\right];$$

$$a_{31i} = 0; \quad a_{32i} = -R_2\Delta\tau; \quad a_{33i} = h_{3i} + R_2\Delta\tau;$$

$$b_{3i} = h_{3i}P_{3i}^{k-1} + \Delta\tau/\Delta x^2\left[T_{3i-0,5}P_{3i-1}^{k-1} - (T_{3i-0.5} + T_{3i+0,5})P_{3i}^{k-1} + T_{3i+0,5}P_{3i+1}^{k-1}\right].$$

This system of equations can be solved by the Kramer method with respect to P_{1i}, P_{2i}, P_{3i}. In this case, the pressure function at the internal points is defined as follows:

$$P_{1i} = \frac{\Delta P_{1i}}{\Delta_i}; \quad P_{2i} = \frac{\Delta P_{2i}}{\Delta_i}; \quad P_{3i} = \frac{\Delta P_{3i}}{\Delta_i} \quad (i = 1, 2, ..., n-1).$$

To find the values of the pressure functions at the boundary point, we write the boundary conditions in the form of finite difference equations:

$$\begin{cases} (3 - 2\Delta x\alpha)P_{10} - 4P_{11} + P_{12} = 2\Delta x\alpha P_A, \\ (3 - 2\Delta x\alpha)P_{1n} - 4P_{1n-1} + P_{1n-2} = -2\Delta x\alpha P_A. \end{cases}$$

$$\begin{cases} (3 - 2\Delta x\alpha)P_{20} - 4P_{21} + P_{22} = 2\Delta x\alpha P_A, \\ (3 - 2\Delta x\alpha)P_{2n} - 4P_{2n-1} + P_{2n-2} = -2\Delta x\alpha P_A. \end{cases}$$

$$\begin{cases} (3 - 2\Delta x\alpha)P_{30} - 4P_{31} + P_{32} = 2\Delta x\alpha P_A, \\ (3 - 2\Delta x\alpha)P_{3n} - 4P_{3n-1} + P_{3n-2} = -2\Delta x\alpha P_A. \end{cases}$$

From here

$$P_{10} = \frac{4P_{11} - P_{12} + 2\Delta x\alpha P_A}{3 - 2\Delta x\alpha}; \quad P_{1n} = \frac{4P_{1n-1} - P_{1n-2} - 2\Delta x\alpha P_A}{3 - 2\Delta x\alpha};$$

$$P_{20} = \frac{4P_{21} - P_{22} + 2\Delta x\alpha P_A}{3 - 2\Delta x\alpha}; \quad P_{2n} = \frac{4P_{2n-1} - P_{2n-2} - 2\Delta x\alpha P_A}{3 - 2\Delta x\alpha};$$

$$P_{30} = \frac{4P_{31} - P_{32} + 2\Delta x\alpha P_A}{3 - 2\Delta x\alpha}; \quad P_{3n} = \frac{4P_{3n-1} - P_{3n-2} - 2\Delta x\alpha P_A}{3 - 2\Delta x\alpha}.$$

The values of the pressure functions at the boundary point are determined at each time interval.

3   Algorithm for Solving the Problem

The computational algorithm for solving the boundary value problem given above is based on the explicit schematic form of the finite difference method and is presented in the following block diagram (Fig. 2).

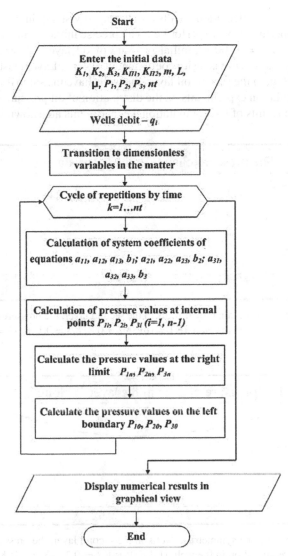

Fig. 2. Block diagram of the algorithm for solving the boundary value problem of oil filtration in a dynamically connected porous medium

4   Computational Experiments on a PC

The values of the pressure functions at the boundary point are determined at each time interval.

Based on the mathematical model and calculation algorithm, software was developed to calculate the key performance indicators of the oil field in a three-layer system that was dynamically connected using the Matlab software tool. The software consists of a block for entering initial data, a block for calculating indicators, and a block for outputting results. The calculation results are displayed visually in graphical form. The computational experiments were performed with precise initial input parameters: length of all three layers $L_x = 8000$ m, initial pressure of oil layers $P_1 = 300$ atm., $P_2 = 300$ atm., $P_3 = 300$ atm. Oil viscosity coefficient $\mu = 4$sp ., Layer elasticity coefficient $b = 0.00005$ cm^2/kg; in the second oil layer, the wells have the same flow rate, i.e., $Q = 400$ m^3/day. Calculation experiments on the distribution of oil pressure were performed for 720 days. The results of the computational experiments are shown in Figs 3 and 4.

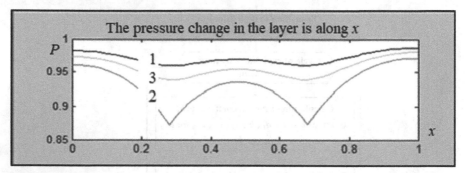

Fig. 3. When there are two symmetrical wells in the second layer, the pressure distribution in all layers and the pressure drop in the well. (K1 = 0.1; K2 = 0.3; K3 = 0.1; KΠ1 = 0.000001; KΠ2 = 0.0002)

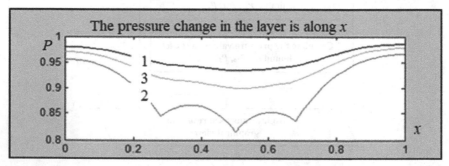

Fig. 4. When there are three symmetrical wells in the second layer, the pressure distribution in all layers and the pressure drop in the well. (K1 = 0.1; K2 = 0.3; K3 = 0.1; KΠ1 = 0.000001; KΠ2 = 0.0002)

All computational experiments show that the oil flow near the working zone of the wells occurs smoothly at high values of the permeability coefficient, as well as an increase in the values of the permeable layers, a significant decrease in pressure in the upper and lower layers in the well zones.

5   Conclusion

Carrying out computational experiments allowed to determine the main indicators of development of three-layer oil fields at different parameters of formation parameters.

The numerical results obtained are useful for analyzing the development of multilayer oil fields with a dynamic relationship.

The developed mathematical model, methods and algorithms can also be used in software process analysis and design to calculate the key performance indicators of three-layer oil fields, as well as in the development of multi-layer oil and gas fields.

References

1. Aziz, H., Sattari, E.: Mathematical Modeling of Reservoir Systems. Moscow-Izhevsk (2004)
2. Algazin, S.D.: On the calculation of the eigenvalues of the transport equations. Appl. Mech. Tech. Phys. **45**(4), 113 (2004)
3. Zakirov, S.N., Lapuk, B.B.: Design and development of gas fields. Nedra, p. 454 (1974)
4. Ravshanov, N., Nazirova, E.Sh.: Numerical algorithm and matematical models of oils extraction in two layered fluxes environment. Probl. Comput. Appl. Math. **4**(16), 33–45 (2018)
5. Aripov, M., Djabbarov, O., Sadullaeva, Sh.: Mathematic modeling of processes describing by double nonlinear parabolic equation with convective transfer and damping. In: AIP Conference Proceedings, vol. 2365, p. 060008 (2021). https://doi.org/10.1063/5.0057492
6. Ravshanov, N., Nazirova, E.Sh., Oripdjanova, U., Aminov, S.M.: On one approach to the numerical solution of elastoplastic boundary value problems. Probl. Comput. Appl. Math. **1**(25), 28–49 (2020)
7. Ravshanov, N., Shadmanov, I., Kubyashev, K., Khikmatullaev, S.: Mathematical modeling and research of heat and moisture transfer processes in porous media. In: Mathematical Modeling and Research of Heat and Moisture Transfer Processes in Porous Media. E3S Web of Conferencesthis, vol. 264, p. 01038 (2021). https://doi.org/10.1051/e3sconf/202126401038
8. Ravshanov, N., Abdullaev, Z., Aminov, S., Khafizov, O.: Numerical study of fluid filtration in three-layer interacting pressure porous formations. In: International Scientific Conference "Construction Mechanics, Hydraulics and Water Resources Engineering" (CONMECHYDRO - 2021). E3S Web Conference, vol. 264, p. 01018 (2021). https://doi.org/10.1051/e3sconf/202126401018

A Novel Metric of Continuous Situational Awareness Monitoring (CSAM) for Multi-telepresence Coordination System

Nathan Kanyok, Alfred Shaker, and Jong-Hoon Kim[✉]

Advanced Telerobotics Research Lab, Computer Science, Kent State University,
Kent, OH, USA
jkim72@kent.edu

Abstract. Humans will remain in the loop of robotic systems as the switch from semi-autonomous to autonomous decisions making. Situational awareness is key factor in how efficient a human is in a human-robot system. This study examines the role that visual presentation mediums have on situational awareness of remote robot operators. Traditional display monitors and virtual reality headsets are compared for their ability to provide a user with situational awareness of a remote environment. Additionally, a novel metric Continuous Situational Awareness Monitoring (CSAM) to capture a participants environmental awareness. Participants are asked to monitor either one or multiple robots as they navigate through a simulated environment. Results indicate that virtual reality as a medium is more efficient in keeping an operator situationally aware of a remote environment.

Keywords: Situation awareness · Human-in-loop · Virtual reality · Human-robot interaction · Human-computer interaction · Telepresence

1 Overview

This study examines the role that a visual presentation medium has in the situational awareness of robot operators. Both single-robot and multi-robot scenarios are addressed. The two visual presentation mediums utilized are traditional monitor and virtual reality headsets. The role of the operator is passive observation of scene-relevant items through autonomous robot POV. The simulated robot(s) explore an environment in a partially predetermined path (robots are given target points to navigate to) with cameras mounted. The amount of items counted is what is being observed. This study assumes that humans will remain in the loop of semi-autonomous robotic systems, such as self-driving cars. Thus is it is important to understand how to best immerse these human operators in their remote robotic environments. For example, in a search and rescue scenario, as explored in the World Robotic Summit (WRS) competitions [5], it is essential for remote workers to have sufficient knowledge of their environments. A novel metric, Continuous Situational Awareness Monitoring (CSAM) is introduced to capture a participants Situational Awareness status.

© Springer Nature Switzerland AG 2022
J.-H. Kim et al. (Eds.): IHCI 2021, LNCS 13184, pp. 520–533, 2022.
https://doi.org/10.1007/978-3-030-98404-5_48

2 Literature Review

2.1 Robotics

Robotic systems are diverse in design and illustrate several different modes and methods of control for various use-cases. Where a robot lays on the scale of autonomy often dictates the method of control and the control interface. As autonomy increase, the level of human intervention decreases, and vice-versa. Robot control is often thought of as sliding continuum ranging from teleoperation, to full scale autonomy [6]. It is important to note how the degree of human-in-the-loop changes as result of the robots placement on this scale. Humans can be directly responsible for a large degree of a robot's functionality if the robot lacks the autonomy to make up for it. A teleoperated robot relies on human input for movement and manipulation. In many ways, most of the sense-think-act cycle is handled by humans when a robot is teleoperated. Small actions can be handled by the robot where it can assist using its sensors and various components, but the human is responsible for navigation, dexterity, and manipulation tasks. Semi-autonomous robots have a variable amount of both human control and system control. One or more functionalities are performed by a robot. For example, cognitive decision making can be handled by the human operator, while localization and image detection are performed by autonomous functions of the robot's system. A large majority of robots fall into this category, with some functions being autonomous while also relying on humans for input [14]. Fully autonomous robots are able to handle the entire sense-think-act cycle on their own. The robot can act on its own, with no supervision, input or interaction from human operators. The effectiveness of operation is constrained by the design of the system, so the robot is only as smart as it is programmed to be.

Self-driving Car: Transportation of people, goods, and services encompasses large portions of human life. Not only is considerable time spent going to places, our society relies on transportation to allocate goods to areas of interest. Many professions rely on efficient transportation. The requirements of safe transportation stem from ability to react in a proper manner to different circumstances. Drivers must pay attention to not only their own vehicle, but to others and environment around them. Some parts of this process have begun to be automated. Different methods of assisted steering, cruise control, anti-lock breaks, and automatic breaking are examples. If this trend holds, as is predicted, wheel ground transportation will become increasingly automated. The car now engages in the sense-think-act cycle, through the use of its sensor suite, actuators, body, environment, and processing components.

2.2 Telepresence

Telepresence is the system when a remote operator accesses and control a robot or device that acts as their avatar. When we look at various telepresence technologies, there are various use-cases for it, such as remote tourism, and using robots for operations that are dangerous for humans, such as search and rescue.

We look at this study by Lin et al. where they talk about Telebot, a multi-modal telepresent robot, built for search and rescue [16]. It is built to be transformable and adaptable to various terrains and areas. The telebot is controlled using Robot Operating System (ROS) [2], with various control interfaces. There is a mannequin that mimics the build of the robot on a smaller scale that maps its motions 1 to 1. We also have the virtual reality operator that sees through the eyes of the robot, controlling it using a telepresent interface. The VR operator gets the information they need on their UI from the robot to monitor its status and its surroundings, being able to use the AI assistance from the robot to identify targets and process information. The robot can map the area and convey such information to the VR operator. This form of telepresent control is the core of the telebot system and allows the user to control the robot in dangerous operations from a safe distance, while being able to control the robot and exchange information effectively.

2.3 Virtual Reality

Virtual reality is one of the biggest new mediums in entertainment and research [8]. There are many applications of VR that have been explored for decades, from simple viewing of pictures and videos, to interactive experiences that take advantage of the features of VR that make it unique. VR has also been used for things beyond entertainment, such as education, therapy, and more. We look at this study by Shaker et al. where they create a VR tour with the intention of studying the therapeutic impacts it would have on individuals with developmental disabilities [18]. The tour consisted of gaze-based and controller-based control, and focused on a single setting. They set it up in a way to track where users went and how long they stayed there, and set up surveys for participants to take before and after, so that they could compare how they felt about things such as comfort and familiarity before and after. This was a multidisciplinary study, and the idea was to see if exploring somewhere and having it be familiar would allow individuals with IDD more confidence and comfort when visiting such a place, and if experiences like this were worth exploring further. They set up experiments with a few IDD individuals and found that the tour helped them want to explore a place like that and would allow them more confidence as the social anxiety aspect is lessened by the fact that they know the area and can navigate it without too much help. The control interface was suitable but they suggested changes to it that would help make it a more tailored and comfortable experience. With their responses they know that these kinds of experiences have potential in helping IDD individuals be more comfortable in the real world and that such studies should be further explored. We also look at a study by Lin et al. where they quantify the effects of music in a virtual environment on a person's mental state [15]. They constructed a virtual reality experience that included various instruments that the user could interact with. Each instrument produced a unique sound allowed the user to express themselves musically and have total freedom during the experiment. Surveys collecting data showed a positive overall angle to the experiment.

2.4 Human-in-the-Loop

In Kalyanam et al.'s study, they explore intelligence, surveillance and reconnaissance (ISR) operations where a human and machine co-operate to find and verify items on the field [11]. An unmanned aerial vehicle flies above to geolocated objects of interest which the user has to verify by observing the views streamed from each UAV. The vehicle can only revisit a location a certain number of times before it has to naturally continue its course. The goal is to classify all the items while having a low amount of false alarms (FA) and missed detections (MD). A randomized AI controller is designed that decides whether or not a revisit is necessary and also computes the altitude and angle at which the aircraft will do that. The task of detection and pattern recognition is relegated to the human operator, while the aircraft does the optimal decision making. The controller is informed of the performance of the human. Their system achieves an FA rate of 5% and MD rate of 12%. This is lower than open-loop operator-only performance metrics. They used normal GUI with windows. The operator would sit 32in in front of the 24in monitor and have to use the view from the 4 UAV to determine if the vans had a Y or V on them. They used software called MetaVR Virtual Reality Scene Generator (VRSG) to generate the video images. This program is a commercial database generation software. It had virtual worlds that the user can then deploy simulations in, which is what they are doing. They are not using real UAVs out in the field. UAV search areas did not overlap. GUI also showed UAV position and stats continuously.

2.5 Human Robot Interaction

As the term suggests, an important aspect of a successful exchange between humans and robots is the interface of interaction between them and their communication. Such interactions should be done in a user-friendly and intuitive interface with a multi-modal framework—traditional interfaces such as monitor, keyboard, and mouse, etc. are no longer acceptable as the only input modalities. The human operator should be able to communicate with robots using universal forms of human-to-human communication methods, such as speech commands, and simple motion controls. Additionally the transferred knowledge should be concise, rich, and diverse, as well as shareable with one another [19].

Furthermore, any new information produced from these interactions should be accumulated, shared, and regenerated as collaborative knowledge. Due to limitations in human knowledge acquisition capability at any given time, human needs some form of spatio-temporal knowledge review interface for visual, spatio-temporal, and contextual information accumulated from human-robot interactions and collaborative knowledge. This information can be used to understand comprehensive and complex situations and to find important clues for problem solving in various search and rescue environments [9,22].

3 Proposed Mental Model

Being able to better understand the interaction cycle between the human operator and the robot(s) will allow us to better optimize systems so that we can get the maximum performance out of the situation. In this case, we want to understand the intricacies of the interactions and the communication between the different agents in this loop. We look at various studies that describe the use and benefit of having a mental model and a shared mental model between the different agents, therefore being able to quantify the interaction and communication.

This model can account for different and varied states of being for both the human and the robot(s), such as mental an physical states, the way messages are passed, how the robot is affected by factors relating to the user and the environment around them, and how that affects the user, and so on [21]. These studies [7,13] describe various characteristics and features relating to human-robot mental models, with key elements such as trust, expecting certain outcomes, understandable actions, and adaptability. In these studies [10,20] we see some practical applications of these techniques, with models detailed and described using relevant use-cases and scenarios.

When we look at our mental model [17, 21] diagram in Fig. 1, we see the interaction loop between the user and the robot system in a way that describes their interactions based on factors from our ontology diagram in Fig. 2 that helps us understand the factors that affect each stage, such as cybersickness [12] caused by the VR robot system, fatigue from the workload and long simulation times, and so on.

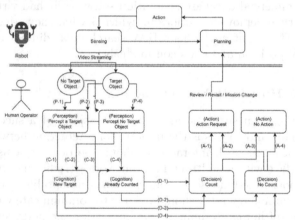

Fig. 1. Human robot interaction mental model

The four main stages on the user side of the interaction are: perception, cognition, decision, and action. Each step leads into the next, and each step is affected by the previous one, and multiple connections can occur between states, as we can see in Fig. 1. The robot system side is meant to move the robots on a path and stream to the user the video feed from each robot. Using that view, the user can start working towards their main objective of counting the various objects accurately. The result could be that they over-count or not count an object otherwise. To find this result, the user goes through the stages we mentioned.

At the perception stage the user either perceives the object being there or they do not, and that depends on different factors describes in Fig. 2. The user may accurately perceive the object being there if the quality of the feed and their mental health are good enough to be able to do that, as shown by the connection P-2. There could be instances where the user may not feel well, or the quality of the feed deteriorates for one reason or another, and the user as a result may not perceive the object correctly, shown by P-4. The user may also incorrectly perceive a target being there that doesn't exist, shown by P-1, or if their mental state is at a good enough level and the video feed is accurate, then they will not perceive anything if there is no object, shown by P-3.

After the perception stage, based on the user's cognitive state they may or may not recognize the object as a new object to count or an object that has been counted before. It is possible, in an extreme case, that the user may not have perceived the object initially but doubts themselves and thinks they

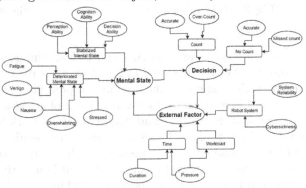

Fig. 2. Interaction system ontology

saw something that was not there and think they have a new object to count even tho previously they did not perceive it, as shown by C-2. This could be due to confusion, poor mental states, or even mistrust in the system due to it previously malfunctioning. Otherwise the user may also recognize that the object was already counted or needs to be counted, shown by C-3, or that there is no object to count, shown by C-4. If they perceived a new object that needs to be counted, the interaction labeled by C-1 happens. Which then leads to the decision phase where they decide to count the object if they perceived a new object to count, shown by D-3, or not count it if they perceived an object that was already counted or if they did not perceive anything at all, shown by D-2. This can also go both ways because of the conditions that could affect their mental state or if there is a malfunction on the robot system side. There can be occurrences where the user properly identifies a new object to be counted, but end up not counting it because of mistrust in the system or mistrust in their own cognitive abilities, shown by D-4. Or the user identifies that there is no object, but because of a bad mental state or mistrust, they count it anyway, thinking that maybe they missed a count, as shown by D-1. Finally after they count it comes the action phase. If everything went according to what they expected, there is no need to perform any further action and the user can trust that the system will proceed as normal, as shown by both A-3 and A-4. Otherwise the user may suggest a review of the system if they do not trust it or think there

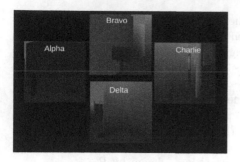

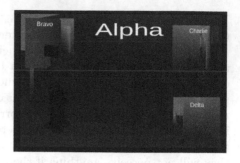

Fig. 3. Multi robot view   **Fig. 4.** Single robot view

need to be improvements on that end to help the user's end, as shown by both A-1 and A-2. With this model in Fig. 1 we want to define two possible outcomes based on various states of the human and possibly even the robot. One outcome is the object is counted correctly, as a result of a stable and healthy mental state and functional interaction and communication workflow between the user and the robot. The other result is a miscount, which could mean incorrectly counting an object a second time, or missing an object and not counting it at all. This could be from a distressed mental state that is negatively affecting the user and their perception of the scene, possibly thinking one scene is two different scenes, or not noticing an object in the scene at all. Tracking this mental state can help us understand what the condition of the user is and how they react to certain environments, conditions and control interfaces.

4   Materials and Methods

This study leverages a simulated fleet of robots to examine the role that visual mediums have in establishing situational awareness. In order to do so, two computers, a traditional display monitor and a virtual reality headset were utilized. This experiment took place in a simulated environment in which a single robot or fleet of robots autonomously explored. Two computers were used in this experiment, one for each visual presentation medium. There were two different visual presentation mediums used, a traditional 2D monitor and a virtual reality headset. During the multi-robot sessions the screen split into four panels, while the entire screen is utilized in the single robot session.

The virtual reality headset used for this study was a Vive Pro Headset. During single robot sessions, the entire visual display is used. While in the multi-robot session, the user has two presentation formats: a four panel display similar to the traditional monitor, and the ability to select a single robot's display. See Fig. 3 and Fig. 4. The selection is meant to mimic a user's ability to lean into and focus on a single robot's camera during the traditional monitor sessions.

The robot model used in this study is a Tutlebot 3 [1]. The simulated Turtlebot3 is equipped with a camera, allowing for video streaming capabilities. The live feed is broadcasted from the robot to the operator via ROS and rViz [3]. The participant is able to select between multiple views in the virtual reality portion.

Experimental systems, with their high degree of failure, can be safely verified in a simulated environment. Outside of the LIDAR/camera exchange, the simulation model does not differ from the physical model in any way. The same dimensions are used for body and wheel size. Physics surrounding wheel slippage and center of gravity are simulated identical to their real-world values. The simulation aims to be as close to real world as possible, but exact mimicry is not yet feasible. Still, simulations serve as a well-accepted paradigm to test robotic functionality in.

The simulation environment is a modified version of the open source Willow Garage Officespace [4]. Robots autonomously explore going to check points, each in one of four separate quadrants of the office. The robots never cross paths or are in view of each other. Each room a robot encounters has a variety of objects placed in it, such as fire hydrants, mailboxes, hammers, and cans.

ROS Kinetic and Gazebo were used to handle the simulation environment and information display. A Unity app was developed for display of the visual information in the virtual reality headset. This app allowed for a participant to select viewing displays. The virtual reality app utilized a 3D viewing environment, but did not allow for free head motion. The simulated robot was a Turtlebot 3, with differential drive and video streaming camera. They navigated the environment autonomously using gmapping.

During experiment sessions, participants underwent four 5-minute sessions, consisting of two different visual presentation mediums: traditional monitor (2D) and virtual reality (3D). See Fig. 5 and Fig. 6. Each visual presentation medium had both a single and multi-robot scenario. All participants had the following order of scenarios: Single-Robot 2D, Single-Robot 3D, Multi-Robot 2D, and Multi-Robot 3D. A small break between rounds would occur, with varying lengths dependent on the subject's health and preparation for the next round. As the simulated robots explored the environment, the participant was asked to

Fig. 5. Traditional monitor   Fig. 6. Virtual reality

Table 1. Symptoms checklist for health survey

Symptom	Not present	Present	Disruptive
Body discomfort	[]	[]	[]
Fatigue	[]	[]	[]
Sweating	[]	[]	[]
Stomach awareness	[]	[]	[]
Nausea	[]	[]	[]
Increased salvation	[]	[]	[]
Burping	[]	[]	[]
Heartbeat	[]	[]	[]
Headache	[]	[]	[]
Stress	[]	[]	[]
Blurred vision	[]	[]	[]
Dizzy (eyes closed)	[]	[]	[]
Dizzy (eyes open)	[]	[]	[]
Vertigo	[]	[]	[]

count the number of a specific object that either the robot or robot fleet encounters. These counts were compared to the actual number of encountered objects in the environment, giving a metric on how well the participant was spatially aware.

In addition to the count, pre and post trial health metrics were also gathered. The pre-trial metrics provided a basis on which the impacts of virtual reality could be gathered. These metrics took place as a survey, see Table 1. Additionally, the post-trial contained additional questions prompting the participant to reflect back on the experiment.

These questions prompted subjects to score immersion, resolution, mental workload, and comfort factor associated with the visual presentation mediums. Along with the ranking questions, there are some extended response questions.

1. How would you rank the immersion of the traditional/virtual reality approach? (1–7)
2. How would you rank the resolution of the traditional/virtual reality approach? (1–7)
3. What was the mental workload associated with the traditional/virtual reality approach? (1–7)
4. What was your comfort level like for the two traditional/virtual reality approach trials? (1–7)
5. Which system did you have more confidence in?
6. What were the biggest contributions to success?
7. What is the thing you dislike most about the system?
8. What would you change about the experimental design?

9. More features are planned on being added to this project, such as additional VR views and head-motion tracking. Would you be willing to come back and test this system with those improvements?

5   Results

The test population consisted of 10 computer science students at Kent State University, with current academic standings ranging from undergraduate to graduate Of the participants. Of the ten participants, 9 were male and 1 was female. Academic level and sex were not taken into account when analyzing data.

The pre-trial health survey was focused on accessing the participants current symptoms. They were asked to categorize a list of symptoms as being 1) Not Present, 2) Present, and 3) Disruptive. All participants scored low on current symptoms, with the mean symptom score being 1.1. The most common symptom was stress, with an average of 1.3.

Continuous Situational Awareness Monitoring (CSAM) was a metric developed for this study to track a user's situational awareness over time. These metrics either interrupt the trial or are taken after the fact. CSAM, on the other hand, does not suffer from these limitations. Continuous Situational Awareness Monitoring (CSAM) is measured by report disparity. The final number of objects found by a participant is compared to the actual number of objects encountered, the difference being there report disparity. A negative report disparity is known as under-reporting, a positive report disparity is over-reporting, and a report disparity of 0 is a perfect score.

The in-trial data gathered were self-reports of the participants (Table 2). For the single robot monitor trials (SRT), the mean report disparity was −2. This indicates that, on average, a participant reported two fewer objects than were actually encountered. For the single robot VR trials (SRV), the mean report disparity was −.5. For the multiple robot monitor (MRT) trials, mean report disparity was −1.8, whereas for the virtual reality (MRV) trials saw a mean report disparity of .6. The positive report disparity is a result of participants over-reporting the number of objects found. The largest under-reporting of objects, i.e. negative mean report disparity, was −5 during a multiple robot traditional monitor trial. The largest over-reporting was +7 during a multiple robot virtual reality trial. This is consistent with the trend of over-reporting being exclusive to the virtual reality trials, aside from one instance of over-reporting. Virtual reality saw both under- and over-reporting, whereas the traditional monitor trials saw only under-reporting. Overall, the virtual reality trials reported closer to perfect with .55, either over or under reported objects. Traditional monitor trials were an average of 1.9 objects away from a perfect score.

Post-Trial. Changes in health were accessed by having the participants fill out the expanded survey. Compared to the Pre-trial health survey, participants were slightly more uncomfortable with present symptoms, scoring 1.2 post-trial versus

Table 2. Results of in-trials

Report disparity	SRT	SRV	MRT	MRV
Mean	−2	−0.5	−1.8	0.6
Min (abs.val.)	0	0	1	0
Max (abs.val.)	4	5	5	4

1.1 in the pre-trial. The most reported symptom was fatigue, having impacted half of the participants in an noticeable manner.

The post-trial survey had the participants rank the immersion, resolution, mental workload, and comfort level via a series of self-rank questions (Table 3). Answers ranged from 1 (insignificant) to 7 (significant). Participants found the level of immersion between the traditional approach and virtual reality to similar. The traditional approach averaged 4.5 and virtual reality averaged 4.8. Subjectively, participants found the virtual reality to be more immersive.

The traditional method had better viewing resolution than the virtual reality displays, with the traditional scoring 6 and virtual reality only scoring 3.9. Additionally, participants were asked about the mental workload associated with both of the displays. It was found that virtual reality was harder to keep track of objects, which scored a 4.6 compared to the traditional method scoring 3.7.

Finally, subjects were asked about the comfort during the experiment. The results show that it was more comfortable using the traditional methods, which scored a 6.2, when compared to the virtual reality method, which scored 4.1. These results fit with following question, which asked users "which system did you have more confidence with?", where the majority of users answered that the traditional method was more reliable.

Table 3. Results of post-trial likert questions

Likert question	Traditional	VR
Immersion	4.5	4.8
Resolution	6	3.9
Mental workload	3.7	4.6
Comfort level	6.2	4.1

When asked what did they dislike the most, almost all participants indicated that some part of the virtual reality experience to be the main contributor. For example, many people mentioned the poor resolution as a contributing factor to their discomfort and performance. Participants varied in what they would like changed in the experiment. Increased control, whether it be manual control of the robot or head-tracking for the virtual reality portion, was frequently mentioned. Additionally, multiple users mentioned that the resolution should be better for virtual reality. Finally, participants also found the virtual environment to be a factor, either being too dark, confusing, or boring.

6   Discussion

Due virtual reality lending itself to better results in CSAM and subjective immersion, it lends itself to being a useful tool in solving the spatial awareness problem of telepresence and Human-in-the-Loop systems. Furthermore, this extends to both single and multi-robot systems. However, user confidence in virtual reality remains a problem. Participants reported less trust in the virtual reality display. This could be due to several factors, such as poor resolution and an individual's familiarity with the technology. The increased mental workload which burdens users may be mitigated in future work. By focusing on UI and human-robot-interaction principals, a more intuitive virtual reality system may be designed. Similarly, giving users more control of the system either via motion control, improved camera selection, or additional information on screen would improve immersion levels and reduce mental workload.

Since the end goal will likely be to introduce virtual reality telepresence to real-world systems, future studies should focus on using physical robotic systems. Simulations provide insight on how a system may work in a controlled environment, but they lack in authentic visual presentation. A user is aware that they are viewing a simulation, thus this may impact mental states. Participant feedback will be taken into account for future experiments, aiming to increase the immersion factions of VR. Additionally, full head-motion capabilities and additional camera angles planed to be explored. To get a firm understanding of the impact of virtual reality on situational awareness of telepresence systems, real world environments should be used.

7   Conclusion

In the case of remote monitoring of either a robot, or a robot fleet, when situational awareness is of significant importance, virtual reality lends itself to being a more efficient visual presentation medium than the traditional 2D monitor approach. Virtual reality's advantage is not without drawbacks, namely obstacles to immersion and hardware limitations. These drawbacks lead can lead to the user becoming ill or uncomfortable, thus unable to perform the task. Even though this was not seen during the experiment, it can be assumed that prolonged use of virtual reality would also lead to equivalent increases in distress of health metrics, such as vection and tiredness. However, the hardware limitations that lead to this, insufficient resolution, etc., will likely be mitigated as advances in virtual reality technology are made.

References

1. Robotis turtlebot3. https://www.robotis.us/turtlebot-3/. Accessed 12 Nov 2021

2. Ros. https://www.ros.org/. Accessed 12 Nov 2021
3. rviz. http://wiki.ros.org/rviz. Accessed 12 Nov 2021
4. Willow garage office space. http://wiki.ros.org/simulator_gazebo/Tutorials/WillowGarageWorld. Accessed 12 Nov 2021
5. World robotic summit competitions. https://wrs.nedo.go.jp/en/. Accessed 12 Nov 2021
6. Autonomy Measures for Robots, ASME International Mechanical Engineering Congress and Exposition, vol. Dynamic Systems and Control, Parts A and B, November 2004. https://doi.org/10.1115/IMECE2004-61812
7. Brooks, C., Szafir, D.: Building second-order mental models for human-robot interaction. ArXiv abs/1909.06508 (2019)
8. Burdea, G., Coiffet, P.: Virtual Reality Technology. MIT Press, Cambridge (2003)
9. Cardenas, I.S., Kim, J.H.: Design of a semi-humanoid telepresence robot for plant disaster response and prevention. In: 2019 IEEE/RSJ International Conference on Intelligent Robots and Systems (IROS), November 2019
10. Chien, S.Y., Lin, Y.L., Lee, P.J., Han, S., Lewis, M., Sycara, K.: Attention allocation for human multi-robot control: cognitive analysis based on behavior data and hidden states. Int. J. Hum Comput. Stud. **117**, 30–44 (2018). https://doi.org/10.1016/j.ijhcs.2018.03.005
11. Kalyanam, K., Pachter, M., Patzek, M., Rothwell, C., Darbha, S.: Optimal human-machine teaming for a sequential inspection operation. IEEE Trans. Hum.-Mach. Syst. **46**(4), 557–568 (2016). https://doi.org/10.1109/THMS.2016.2519603
12. Kim, H.K., Park, J., Choi, Y., Choe, M.: Virtual reality sickness questionnaire (VRSQ): motion sickness measurement index in a virtual reality environment. Appl. Ergon. **69**, 66–73 (2018). https://doi.org/10.1016/j.apergo.2017.12.016
13. Lee, S., Lau, I.Y., Kiesler, S., Chiu, C.Y.: Human mental models of humanoid robots. In: Proceedings of the 2005 IEEE International Conference on Robotics and Automation, pp. 2767–2772 (2005). https://doi.org/10.1109/ROBOT.2005.1570532
14. Lewis, M., Wang, H., Velagapudi, P., Scerri, P., Sycara, K.: Using humans as sensors in robotic search. In: 2009 12th International Conference on Information Fusion, pp. 1249–1256 (2009)
15. Lin, X., et al.: Virtual reality-based musical therapy for mental health management. In: 2020 10th Annual Computing and Communication Workshop and Conference (CCWC), pp. 0948–0952 (2020). https://doi.org/10.1109/CCWC47524.2020.9031157
16. Lin, X., et al.: Design of a novel transformable centaur robot with multilateral control interface for search and rescue missions. In: The IEEE 5th International Conference on Automation, Control and Robotics Engineering (CACRE 2020), September 2020. https://doi.org/10.1109/CACRE50138.2020.9230311
17. Nikolaidis, S., Shah, J.: Human-robot teaming using shared mental models. In: ACM/IEEE HRI Conference (2012)
18. Shaker, A., Lin, X., Kim, D.Y., Kim, J.H., Sharma, G., Devine, M.A.: Design of a virtual reality tour system for people with intellectual and developmental disabilities: a case study. Comput. Sci. Eng. **22**(3), 7–17 (2020). https://doi.org/10.1109/MCSE.2019.2961352
19. Steinfeld, A., et al.: Common metrics for human-robot interaction. In: Proceedings of the 1st ACM SIGCHI/SIGART Conference on Human-Robot Interaction, HRI 2006 (2006). https://doi.org/10.1145/1121241.1121249

20. Syrdal, D.S., Dautenhahn, K., Koay, K.L., Walters, M.L., Otero, N.R.: Exploring human mental models of robots through explicitation interviews. In: 19th International Symposium in Robot and Human Interactive Communication, pp. 638–645 (2010). https://doi.org/10.1109/ROMAN.2010.5598688
21. Tabrez, A., Luebbers, M.B., Hayes, B.: A survey of mental modeling techniques in human–robot teaming. Curr. Robot. Rep. **1**(4), 259–267 (2020). https://doi.org/10.1007/s43154-020-00019-0
22. Thrun, S.: Toward a framework for human-robot interaction. Hum.-Comput. Interact. **19**(1–2), 9–24 (2004). https://doi.org/10.1080/07370024.2004.9667338

AI-Based Syntactic Complexity Metrics and Sight Interpreting Performance

Longhui Zou[1]([⊠]) (iD), Michael Carl[1] (iD), Mehdi Mirzapour[2] (iD), Hélène Jacquenet[2] (iD), and Lucas Nunes Vieira[3] (iD)

[1] Kent State University, 475 Janik Drive, Kent, OH 44242, USA
{lzou4,mcarl6}@kent.edu
[2] R&D Department, ContentSide, 23 Jules Favre, 69006 Lyon, France
{mehdi.mirzapour,helene.jacquenet}@contentside.com
[3] University of Bristol, Beacon House, Queens Road, Bristol BS8 1QU, UK
l.nunesvieira@bristol.ac.uk

Abstract. Complex syntax may lead to increased cognitive effort during translation. However, it is unclear what kinds of syntactic complexity have a stronger impact on translation performance. In this paper, we employ several syntactic metrics which enable us to explore the impact of syntactic complexity on the quality in English-to-Chinese sight interpreting. We have operationalized syntactic complexity by six metrics, namely, Incomplete Dependency Theory metric (IDT), Dependency Locality Theory metric (DLT), Combined IDT and DLT metric (IDT+DLT), Left Embeddedness metric (LE), Nested Nouns Distancemetric (NND), and Bilingual Complexity Ratio metric (BRC). Three professional translators have manually annotated translation errors using MQM-derived error taxonomies, which includes accuracy, fluency, and style errors, each as critical or minor errors. We assessed inter-rater agreement by adopting weighted Fleiss' Kappa scores. We found that there are strong correlations between the IDT and IDT+DLT metrics and sight interpreting errors. We also found that language-specific syntactic differences between English and Chinese such as directions of branching and noun modifiers can have a strong influence on accuracy and critical errors.

Keywords: Language and speech interfaces · Cognitive interface design · AI and data · Syntactic complexity · Sight interpreting · Translation assessment

1 Introduction

AI-based translation data analytics is a multidisciplinary field that requires the integration of a variety of different domains such as symbolic/data-oriented AI, cognitive science, linguistics, psycholinguistics, and information science. In the context of translation process research (TPR), we can employ different AI-based analysis methods for measuring translators' cognitive behaviors. In this paper, we develop AI-motivated metrics and methods that help us to measure human cognitive effort during translation. The suggested metric is also useful for translation pedagogy when the available data needs

© Springer Nature Switzerland AG 2022
J.-H. Kim et al. (Eds.): IHCI 2021, LNCS 13184, pp. 534–547, 2022.
https://doi.org/10.1007/978-3-030-98404-5_49

to be analyzed to get insights about translation students' behavior and to assess their improvement.

Several scholars have researched the relationship between syntactic complexity and translation performance [1, 2, 9, 10, 18, 24, 30, 32]. For instance, Gile [18] states that grammatical and syntactic difficulties in the source text (ST) lead to higher linguistic interference in sight translation compared to other types of interpreting. Agrifoglio [1] argues that because of the difference between the nature of written and spoken STs, linguistic complexity (e.g., lexically, syntactically, stylistically, textually, etc.) in the ST of sight translation tends to be higher than other types of interpreting.

Shreve, Lacruz & Angelone [30] find that participants in a sight translation experiment spend significantly more time in syntactically more complex Areas of Interest (AOIs). The syntactic complexity in this study is operationalized informally by the density of embedded relative clauses, and the translation performance is investigated by indicators of both temporal and cognitive effort. To sum up, existing studies have investigated syntactic complexity in a variety of ways and the results and interpretations might be different due to a variation of translation modes, participant profiles, and language pairs.

Research on sight interpreting, on the other hand, is limited. Sight interpreting is a hybrid between written translation and interpreting (i.e., spoken translation). In this mode, a translator translates an oral ST with a written ST present into an oral or signed TT in real time [8]. Furthermore, most of the syntactic complexity measures adopted in previous studies tend to be subjective and qualitative. In other words, although previous research has found that complex syntax may lead to increased cognitive effort and performance decline due to the potential visual interference, it is not clear what kind of syntactic complexity in a certain language pair has more significant impact on translation performance, and how syntactic complexity impacts sight interpreting processes.

In this study, we describe a set of quantitative syntactic complexity metrics, with special concern to the English-to-Chinese language pair, to answer the following research questions about the relationship between syntactic complexity and translation performance in English-Chinese sight interpreting:

1. Do annotators of English-to-Chinese sight interpreting differ in their error identification?
2. Which syntactic complexity metrics correlate better with sight interpreting performance?
3. Do English-Chinese syntactic differences affect the performance of sight interpreting?

2   Syntactic Complexity Metrics

We introduce six syntactic complexity metrics: Incomplete Dependency Theory Metric (IDT), Dependency Locality Theory Metric (DLT), Combined IDT+DLT Metric (IDT+DLT), Bilingual Ratio Complexity (BRC), Left-Embeddedness (LE) and Nested Nouns Distance (NND). Some of them, namely IDT, DLT, IDT+DLT and (to some extent) BRC, are applications of linguistic complexity theories from Gibson's Incomplete Dependency Theory (IDT) and Dependency Locality Theory (DLT) [16, 17]. The metric LE is adopted and slightly changed from Coh-Metrix analysis [19]. NND is introduced as a new metric in this research. The metrics are chosen based on the specific syntactic difference between English and Chinese [14].

In contrast to other research [21, 25, 26, 28] that uses Categorical Proof Nets [27] for the syntactic representation of the sentences, we use universal Dependencies [13], which is a framework for consistent annotation of grammar, i.e., part of speech, morphological features, and syntactic dependencies. Also, we have adopted Blache's reformulation of IDT and DLT [4, 5] for dependency relations. In addition, we use Stanford Stanza [29] for parsing 202 already tokenized segments of the dataset IMBst18 available in CRITT TPR-DB[1] into dependency parse trees. The availability of high quality, scalable dependency parsers (such as Stanza) with wide-range language support is one of the main reasons for choosing dependency tree parsing over categorical proof nets representation. Moreover, we will show that dependency parse trees as our basic syntactic representation can lead us to acceptable results for TPR.

2.1 Incomplete Dependency Theory Metric (IDT)

Definition 1: For a given token t_i, the IDT metric counts the number of incomplete dependencies between t_i and t_{i+1}. This can be shown by Example 1.

Example 1: The reporter who the senator attacked disliked the editor.

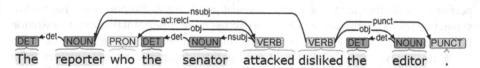

Fig. 1. Dependency parsing of Example 1 outputted from "stanza.run"

Let us calculate the IDT metric for the token *senator* in Example 1. We can observe in Fig. 1 that there are 4 dependencies, namely nsubj, obj, relcl and nsubj between the token *senator* and the next token *attacked*. Based on Definition 1, the value of IDT is 4 for the token *senator*. We can apply this token-wise IDT metric to the whole segment. We can also aggregate all IDT values for each token by different aggregation functions such as ***sum***, ***max*** and ***average***.

2.2 Dependency Locality Theory Metric (DLT)

Definition 2: A token t_i is said to be a discourse referent whenever its part-of-speech tag is a ***Proper Noun***, ***Noun*** or ***Verb***.

---

[1] See   https://sites.google.com/site/centretranslationinnovation/tpr-db/public-studies?authus er=0.

Definition 3: For a head token t_i, the DLT metric counts the number of discourse referents starting from t_i ending to its longest leftmost dependent. The boundary ending words should also be counted if they are discourse referents. For a non-head token DLT is defined as zero.

Let us calculate the DLT value for the token *disliked* in Example 1. We can see in Fig. 1 that the dependency *nsubj* is the longest leftmost dependency that starts from the head token *disliked* and ends in the dependent token *reporter*. There are three discourse referents, namely *reporter* (noun), *senator* (noun) and *attacked* (verb) under the dependency *nsubj*, so the DLT value for *disliked* is 3.

We can apply this token-wise DLT metric to the whole segment. We can also aggregate all DLT values for each token by different aggregation functions such as *sum*, *max* and *average*.

2.3 Combined IDT+DLT Metric (IDT+DLT)

Definition 4: For a given token t_i in a sentence, the combined IDT+DLT metric is the sum of IDT metric and DLT metric for token t_i.

Let us calculate the Combined IDT+DLT metric for the token *disliked* in Example 1. Based on Definition 1, the IDT value for *disliked* is 2. Also, based on Definitions 2 and 3, the DLT value for *disliked* is 3. So, the combined IDT+DLT value for the token *disliked* is the sum of the two above mentioned metrics, which is 5. We can observe in Fig. 2 the IDT values and combined IDT+DLT values for each token in Example 1.

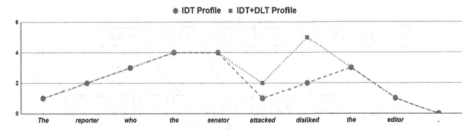

Fig. 2. IDT-based and IDT+DLT-based Complexity profiling for Example 1

2.4 Left-Embeddedness Metric (LE) Metric

Definition 5: The LE metric counts the number of tokens on the left-hand-side of the main verb which are not verbs. This can be illustrated by Example 1.

We can observe in Fig. 1 that the main verb in the sentence is *disliked*. The LE value is the number of non-verb tokens before *disliked*, which is 5.

2.5   Nested Nouns Distance (NND) Metric

Definition 6: The distance between two tokens t_i and t_j is their absolute positional distance, $|j - i|$.

Definition 7: A noun t_i is nested in another noun t_j if t_j is the ancestor of t_i in the dependency tree. In any tree structure, a node that is connected to some lower-level nodes is called an ancestor.

Definition 8: NND is the aggregation (i.e., sum, max or average) of nested noun distances.

   We can calculate the NND metric for Example 1. We can observe in Fig. 1 that the *senator* is nested in the *reporter* noun phrase. Their positions are 2 and 5, respectively. So, the NND metric is $|5–2|$ which is 3.

2.6   Bilingual Complexity Ratio Metric (BCR) Metric

Before defining the BCR metric we need to introduce the notion of word alignment. A word alignment is a correspondence between the source and target words in a translation. For instance, the English sentence "I am here" and its French translation "Je suis là" are literal word-to-word translations. We can assign the correspondence of each source and target token as a set of pairs (source, token): $\{(1, 1), (2, 2), (3, 3)\}$. A more complex example is provided in Fig. 4. We can spot a one-to-many alignment between token 6 in the source text and tokens 5, 6 and 7 in the target text. The whole alignment set is as follows: $\{(2,1), (3,2), (4,3), (5,4), (6, \{5,6,7\})\}$ (Fig. 3).

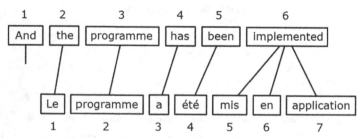

Fig. 3. Word alignments for an English-to-French translation task [source Wikipedia: Bitext_word_alignment]

Definition 9: For a group of source tokens $s_i, s_{i+1}, ..., s_n$ in a source text S, aligned with a group of target tokens $t_i, t_{i+1}, ..., t_m$ in a target text T, the BCR metric is calculated as follows:

- Given a Lx a complexity metric (IDT, DLT or IDT+DLT) calculate the complexity for each source tokens $Lx(s_i), Lx(s_{i+1}), ..., Lx(s_n)$ and aggregate them using aggregate function F_s (sum, max or average). Let us name this $S = F_s(Lx(s_i), Lx(s_{i+1}), ..., Lx(s_n))$.

- Given a Lx a complexity metric (IDT, DLT or IDT+DLT) calculate complexity for each target tokens $Lx(t_i), Lx(t_{i+1}), \ldots, Lx(t_n)$ and aggregate them using aggregate function F_s (sum, max or average). Let us name this $T = F_s(Lx(t_i), Lx(t_{i+1}), \ldots, Lx(t_n))$
- The BCR for a given alignment of source and target tokens is $\frac{T}{S}$.

Example 2: For source tokens s_1, s_2 in a source text S, aligned with t_2, t_3 and t_5 in a target text T, and the following IDT complexities, i.e., $IDT(s_1) = 1, IDT(s_2) = 2, IDT(s_3) = 3, IDT(t_1) = 4, IDT(t_2) = 5$. The BCR metric, with *sum* as the aggregation function, is *sum*(4, 5) / *sum*(1, 2, 3) = 1.5.

If we have multiple alignments, we can get the BCR value for each alignment and aggregate the whole segment with a desired aggregation function (sum, max or average).

2.7 Syntactic Complexity Analysis of the Dataset IMBst18

As mentioned above, we implemented six syntactic complexity metrics (i.e., IDT, DLT, IDT+DLT, LE, NND, and BCR), with 3 aggregation functions (i.e., Mean, Max and Sum), on both ST and TT sides, resulting in 36 syntactic complexity values (6 * 3 * 2) for each of the 202 segments in the dataset IMBst18. Six values (i.e., IDT_SUM_ST, IDT+DLT_SUM_ST, DLT_SUM_TT, BCR_SUM_SUM_SUM, LE_SUM_ST, and NND_SUM_ST) are selected as examples for each of the six metrics. Among them, IDT_SUM_ST, IDT+DLT_SUM_ST, LE_SUM_ST, and NND_SUM_ST are the sum aggregations of the IDT metric, IDT+DLT metric, LE metric and NND metric at the segment level on the ST side, respectively; DLT_SUM_TT is the sum aggregation of the DLT metric at the segment level on the TT side; and BCR is the sum aggregation of the bilingual BCR metric at the segment level.

We can see from the following Fig. 4 that the distributions of the values calculated by IDT_SUM_ST ($\mu = 97.13$, std $= 61.71$) and IDT+DLT_SUM_ST ($\mu = 102.01$, std $= 64.93$) are quite similar in this study. Additionally, different from large ranges of values by both the IDT and IDT+DLT metrics, the spectrum of BCR scores tends to be much narrower ($\mu = 3.50$, std $= 3.66$) and the mass of its distribution is concentrated between 1.02 and 2.33.

We calculated the Spearman's correlations between each pair of the two values attained by the metrics, resulting in 1296 (36 * 36) correlation coefficients. The results show that for each individual syntactic complexity value, the most correlated values are mainly aggregated by the Sum function. Therefore, we assume that the Sum aggregation function works better for segment-wise syntactic complexity measurement under this study. Table 1 shows the Spearman's correlation coefficients between the six selected syntactic complexity values with the Sum aggregation function. We can see that IDT_ST values correlate very strongly with IDT+DLT_ST, with the correlation coefficient of almost 1, which resonates with the great similarity of the distributions between these two values [11].

Furthermore, although there are generally stronger correlations between different values on the same text side (i.e., values on the ST side correlates better with values on the ST side, while values on the TT side correlates better with values on the TT side), we find that there is an overall strong correlation between values on the ST and

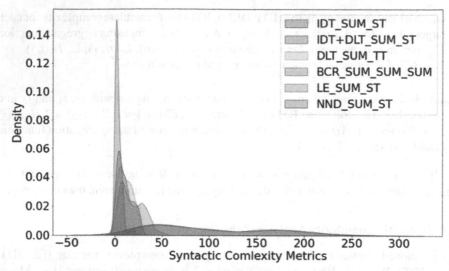

Fig. 4. Density plot for six syntactic complexity metrics

Table 1. Spearman's correlation matrix for six syntactic complexity metrics

Metric type	IDT_ST	IDT+DLT_ST	DLT_TT	BCR	LE_ST	NND_ST
IDT_ST	1	0.999**	0.728**	0.361**	0.941**	0.826**
IDT+DLT_ST	0.999**	1	0.729**	0.359**	0.946**	0.826**
DLT_TT	0.728**	0.729**	1	0.432**	0.687**	0.616**
BCR	0.361**	0.359**	0.432**	1	0.360**	0.330**
LE_ST	0.941**	0.946**	0.687**	0.360**	1	0.728**
NND_ST	0.826**	0.826**	0.616**	0.330**	0.728**	1

**Correlation at 0.01

TT. This indicates that syntactically complex ST usually corresponds to a syntactically complex TT. We also see that the two metrics we introduce for the English-to-Chinese language pair specificity (i.e., LE and NND) have very strong correlations with both IDT and IDT+DLT values on the ST sides. We therefore suggest that language-pair-specific syntactic differences can be also used as indicators of source text difficulty, which may influence cognitive effort in sight interpreting.

3   English-to-Chinese Sight Interpreting Experiment

3.1   Experimental Setting for the Dataset IMBst18

The IMBst18 dataset we use in this study was collected in April 2018 at Renmin University/China. Nine professional interpreters (2 males and 7 females) were hired to do sight interpreting with scripts of a political speech from English into Chinese. All of them were professional interpreters with formal training from one of the world's most prestigious interpreting programs at graduate level and their average length of professional practice in interpreting was 6.4 years. Their first language was Chinese, and second language English.

The participants attended the experiment individually, following the same procedure and without a time limit. The experimental design of the sight interpreting task is shown in Fig. 5. During the experiment, a participant had two input sources in parallel, that is, six consecutive sections from the beginning part of a live audio recording of a political speech (about 1 min long for each section) and the transcriptions of these six sections of audio recording (about 150 words long for each transcription) with a total of 871 words. Every participant sight-interpreted 6 texts by reading the written English ST and hearing the audio English ST and speaking the oral Chinese TT at the same time, producing altogether 202 segments. The transcriptions of the audio recording were displayed in Translog II [6] and the interpreter's eye movement data were recorded with a Tobii TX 300 eye tracker, whereas the audio input of the speech was re-played via a headset, and the audio recordings of the interpreter's sight interpreting output (i.e., their spoken translations into Chinese) were collected together with the original speech by Audacity.

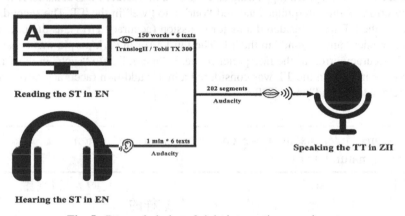

Fig. 5. Research design of sight interpreting experiment

3.2 Manual Evaluation of Translation Errors

Three professional translators were recruited to annotate the translation errors in the English-to-Chinese sight interpreting product. They were given guidelines for translation error typologies based on the harmonized Multidimensional Quality Metrics (MQM)-Dynamic Quality Framework (DFQ) of the Translation Automation User Society (TAUS).[2] Errors were mainly divided into three types, namely "Accuracy" (including the error subcategories "Addition", "Omission", "Mistranslation", "Over-translation",

---

[2] See   https://www.taus.net/academy/news/press-release/dqf-and-mqm-harmonized-to-create-an-industry-wide-quality-standard.

"Under-translation" and "Untranslated text"), "Fluency" (including error subcategories "Punctuation", "Spelling", "Grammar", "Grammatical register", and "Inconsistency"), and "Style" (including subcategories "Awkward", "Inconsistent Style", and "Unidiomatic") [23]. Depending on the severity of each error, they are further categorized by the evaluators as "Critical" and "Minor" errors.

Annotators were asked to conduct word-level alignment between the TT and their corresponding ST once an error was detected. When they came across an error which they considered an addition or omission, however, they were not required to do an alignment. In other words, there were only alignment groups for errors excluding addition or omission in this research. Different types of errors are coded by different colors, for instance, purple indicates accuracy errors, green indicates fluency errors, and pink indicates style errors. Within the same color code, the darker shade indicates major errors, while the lighter shade minor errors. Accuracy errors that are not aligned (i.e., omissions/additions) are pink if they are major and green if they are minor.

We can see in Example 2 in Fig. 6 that Annotator A annotated 3 errors on the ST side, and 3 errors on the TT side, including 1 aligned fluency error, 1 aligned accuracy error, 1 accuracy error that only occurred on the ST side, and 1 accuracy error that only occurred on the TT side. Therefore, this segment was annotated with four errors by Annotator A. The first error in dark green (appearing as yellow on this screen) was considered a major fluency error, as the interpreter rendered "our" into "we" in the TT. The second error in pink in the ST was considered a major omission (accuracy error), as the interpreter failed to render "and beyond" in the TT. The third error in dark purple was considered a major accuracy error, as the interpreter rendered "natural" into "such" in the TT. The fourth error in pink in the TT was considered a major addition (accuracy error), as the interpreter added "and" in the TT.

Our shared interests in peace and security in our region and beyond make us natural partners .

我们 在 和平 和 安全 在 这一 地区 呢 是 有 共同的 利益 的 ，
而且呢 我们 因此 呢 我们 才 成为了 这样的 伙伴 。

Gloss: We in peace and security in this region have common interests, and we therefore we have become such partners.

Fig. 6. Error annotation interface of Example 2 by Annotator A

For the purpose of this research, the total of all kinds of errors in the translations were accumulated under the label of "Any" error [7], and the occurrences of each type of error formed the following numerical relationship:

$$\textbf{Any} = \textbf{Accuracy} + \textbf{Fluency} + \textbf{Style} = \textbf{Critical} + \textbf{Minor} \qquad (1)$$

Therefore, there are overall six labels of errors in this study. We check the inter-rater agreement among the three annotators in this study by calculating weighted Fleiss' Kappa scores. Instead of taking annotations as either "True" (1) or "False" (0) for each error taxonomy, weighted Fleiss' Kappa scores take the distance between the normalized occurrences of each two error types in each segment into consideration [15]. Given that the number of errors for each type is not a categorical or factorial variable but rather a numerical value, we believe that weighted Fleiss' Kappa fits more with our research design and adopt it to measure the error annotation agreement in this study. We can see from the weighted Fleiss' Kappa scores that for all the segments in this dataset, the three annotators perfectly agree with each other on almost every error type (Any: 0.853; Accuracy: 0.915; Fluency: 0.815; Critical: 0.910; Minor: 0.866), except for style errors ($\kappa = 0.739$) [22].

3.3 Relation Between Syntactic Complexity and Translation Performance

Spearman's correlations are computed among 6 metrics and 36 different scores about syntactic complexity on 6 kinds of translation errors to examine which metrics correlate better with sight interpreting performance, and whether language-pair specific syntactic complexity affects the performance as well. Taking the same set of six values in Fig. 4 and Table 1 as an example, the results from the following Spearman's correlation matrix in Table 2 indicate an overall positive and statistically significant relationship between syntactic complexity and the number of errors annotated in the sight interpreting output. This suggests that, in general, segments with higher syntactic complexity tend to have more error occurrences.

Table 2. Spearman's correlation matrix for syntactic complexity metrics and translation errors

Metric type	Any	Accuracy	Fluency	Style	Critical	Minor
IDT_ST	0.723**	0.594**	0.304**	0.187*	0.536**	0.445**
IDT+DLT_ST	0.718**	0.590**	0.303**	0.185*	0.532**	0.443**
DLT_TT	0.559**	0.360**	0.512**	0.141*	0.357**	0.49**
BCR	0.423**	0.240*	0.421**	0.135	0.313**	0.298**
LE_ST	0.652**	0.537**	0.291**	0.141*	0.466**	0.424**
NND_ST	0.636**	0.531**	0.213*	0.235**	0.498**	0.33**

**Correlation at 0.01; *Correlation at 0.05

In terms of the 6 syntactic complexity metrics that we have introduced in this paper, we find that IDT and IDT+DLT have stronger correlations with occurrences of almost all kinds of translation errors than other metrics. We, therefore, suggest that either IDT_ST or IDT+DLT_ST be applied as the preferred metrics for calculating syntactic complexity of the ST. Take IDT_ST for instance, the Spearman's rho in the first column in Table 2 reveals that there is a very strong correlation between syntactic complexity of the ST and the accumulation of all translation errors ($rs = .723$, $p < .01$). From the data in other columns, we can see ST syntactic complexity has a strong relationship with accuracy errors ($rs = .594$, $p < .01$), critical errors ($rs = .536$, $p < .01$) and minor errors ($rs = .445$, $p < .01$), a moderate relationship with fluency errors ($rs = .304$, $p < .01$), and a negligible relationship with style errors (rs = .187, p < .05) [12]. Our data suggest that ST syntactic complexity is an important factor of translation difficulty and thus influences translation performance.

While ST syntactic complexity correlates more strongly with accuracy and critical errors, it can also be seen that the syntactic complexity metrics on the TT side, for instance, DLT_TT (rs = .512, p < .01) and BCR (rs = .421, p < .01) correlate strongly with fluency errors. This indicates that if a translator produces more complex TT than the ST, the translations tend to be more erroneous and less fluent. Our data indicates that more complicated TT syntax indicates more fluency errors, which are mostly minor errors. This can be explained by one of the commonly proposed translation universals, namely simplification, that is, that the language or message of the TT is usually simpler than that of the ST [3]. Simplification might be even more evident in sight interpreting than in written translation since the interpreters need to summarize the meaning of the ST due to time pressure.

Concerning the English-to-Chinese language pair specifically, the results show that there appears to be a strong positive correlation between left-embeddedness (LE) and translation errors (rs = .652, p < .001) especially for accuracy and critical errors. This suggests that more left-branching or head-final source segment structures imply poorer performance in English-to-Chinese sight interpreting. This can be explained by one of the opposite tendencies of word order between the grammatical structures of English and Chinese, i.e., directions of branching.

Although they are both SVO languages, English sentences tend to be more right-branching, putting modifiers to the right of the main verb to provide additional information about the subject. On the contrary, Chinese sentences tend to be more left-branching, putting modifiers to the left of the main verb [31].

By the same token, we see a strong positive correlation between Nested Noun Distance (NND) (rs = .636, p < .001) and accumulated translation errors, but also for accuracy and critical errors. This suggests that more modifiers before the head noun in a source segment make it more difficult for the translator to produce error-free interpreting output. Besides branching directions, the other major difference of word order between English and Chinese syntaxes lies in that English tends to put modifiers of a noun phrase (NP) after the head noun to provide more information, while Chinese tends to put modifiers before the head noun [20]. We assume these two opposite word order tendencies between English and Chinese affect sight interpreting performance since most of the interpreters are trained to translate the ST in a linear way with minimal change of word order [33]. Otherwise, it would require more cognitive effort in memory storage and production of sight interpreting output.

4   Conclusion

In this study, we introduced six AI-centric types of metrics for quantifying syntactic complexity, i.e., Incomplete Dependency Theory metric (IDT), Dependency Locality Theory metric (DLT), Combined IDT and DLT metric (IDT+DLT), Bilingual Complexity Ratio metric (BRC), Left Embeddedness metric (LE), and Nested Nouns Distance metric (NND). In order to make the whole experiment reproducible, the metrics including all of the related datasets and notebook experiments are made publicly available in the GitHub repository.[3]

We used these six metrics with three aggregation functions for both ST and TT sides, namely 36 scores (6 metrics times 3 aggregation functions for the source and target sides) to analyze the syntactic complexity of the 202 segments in the dataset IMBst18 available in the CRITT TPR-DB. According to the correlations between each of the 36 scores, we find that Sum aggregations work better for segment-wise syntactic complexity calculations, and that syntactically complex ST often corresponds to a syntactically complex TT.

Based on MQM-derived error taxonomies, we investigated performance in the much under-researched translation mode of sight interpreting. Three professional translators were recruited to annotate the translation errors, which were grouped under six types of errors, namely any, accuracy, fluency, style, critical and minor errors. Weighted Fleiss' Kappa scores were computed for each of the six error types. Our results show that, generally, annotators agree more on accuracy and critical errors than on fluency, style, and minor errors, and these two kinds of errors were also more frequent or more evident in our dataset.

To examine the relationship between syntactic complexity and sight interpreting performance in the English-to-Chinese dataset, we examined the correlations between each of the 36 syntactic complexity scores and the occurrences of each of the 6 translation error types. The results indicate that there is an overall positive and statistically significant relationship between syntactic complexity and the number of errors. This suggests that in general, segments with higher syntactic complexity tend to have more errors.

In addition, syntactic complexity metrics on the ST side correlate better with accuracy and critical errors, which might serve as an indicator of translation difficulty and thus a factor in translation performance. Among all 36 syntactic complexity scores, IDT_ST and IDT+DLT_ST have overall stronger correlations with the number of translation errors, and thus can be used to operationalize syntactic complexity of the ST and indicate translation difficulty. DLT_TT and BCR correlate more strongly with fluency errors, which suggests that if the TT is syntactically complex or more complex than the ST, the translations may have more fluency and minor errors. We also find that language-specific syntactic differences between English and Chinese such as directions of branching and noun modifiers can have a strong influence on accuracy and critical errors.

The research questions and analyses in this study are mostly based on segment-wise data of translation output. Further experimental research may also manipulate linguistic features at word level or textual level to investigate the relationship between translation process and translation product. Future studies might also be conducted on automatic assessment metrics (such as BLEU and Comet) to examine the correlation between automatic assessment and manual evaluation.

---

[3] See https://github.com/ContentSide/lingx.

References

1. Agrifoglio, M.: Sight translation and interpreting: a comparative analysis of constraints and failures. Interpreting **6**, 43–67 (2004)
2. Al-Jabr, A.F.: Effect of syntactic complexity on translating from/into English/Arabic. Babel **52**(3), 203–221 (2006)
3. Baker, M., Francis, G., Tognini-Bonelli, E. (eds.): Text and Technology: In Honour of John Sinclair. John Benjamins Publishing (1993)
4. Blache, P.: A computational model for linguistic complexity. In: Biology, Computation and Linguistics, pp. 155–167. IOS Press (2011)
5. Blache, P.: Evaluating language complexity in context: new parameters for a constraint-based model. In: 6th International Workshop Constraints and Language Processing, CSLP, pp. 7–20 (2011)
6. Carl, M.: Translog-II: a program for recording user activity data for empirical reading and writing research. In: LREC, vol. 12, pp. 4108–4112 (2012)
7. Carl, M., Báez, M.C.T.: Machine translation errors and the translation process: a study across different languages. J. Specialised Transl. **31**, 107–132 (2019)
8. Cenkova, I.: Sight Interpreting/translation. In: Routledge Encyclopedia of Interpreting Studies, pp. 374–375. Routledge, London/New York (2015)
9. Chen, W.: Sight translation. In: The Routledge Handbook of Interpreting, pp. 156–165. Routledge (2015)
10. Chmiel, A., Janikowski, P., Cieślewicz, A.: The eye or the ear?: source language interference in sight translation and simultaneous interpreting. Interpreting **22**, 187–210 (2020)
11. Dancey, C., Reidy, J.: Analysis of differences between two conditions: the t-test. In: Statistics without Maths for Psychology: Using SPSS for Windows, pp. 206–236 (2004)
12. Debusmann, R.: An introduction to dependency grammar. Hausarbeit fur das Hauptseminar Dependenzgrammatik SoSe **99**, 1–16 (2000)
13. de Marneffe, M.C., Manning, C.D., Nivre, J., Zeman, D.: Universal dependencies. Comput. Linguist. **47**(2), 255–308 (2021)
14. Fang, J.: Pause in sight translation: a pilot study. In: Zhao, J., Li, D., Tian, L. (eds.) Translation Education. NFTS, pp. 173–192. Springer, Singapore (2020). https://doi.org/10.1007/978-981-15-7390-3_11
15. Fleiss, J.L., Levin, B., Paik, M.C.: The measurement of interrater agreement. Stat. Methods Rates Proportions **2**(212–236), 22–23 (1981)
16. Gibson, E.: Linguistic complexity: locality of syntactic dependencies. Cognition **68**(1), 1–76 (1998)
17. Gibson, E.: The dependency locality theory: a distance-based theory of linguistic complexity. Image Lang. Brain **2000**, 95–126 (2000)
18. Gile, D.: Conference interpreting as a cognitive management problem. In: Applied Psychology, pp. 196–214. Sage, London (1997)
19. Graesser, A.C., McNamara, D.S., Kulikowich, J.M.: Coh-Metrix: providing multilevel analyses of text characteristics. In: Educational Researcher, pp. 223–234 (2011)
20. Guo, L.: An analysis of the word order pattern in the SI target language and its underlying reasons in the language combination of English and Chinese. Unpublished Ph.D. dissertation. Shanghai International Studies University (郭靓靓. 2011. 中英文同传译语语序处理方式的选择与原因研究. 上海外国语大学博士学位论文) (2011)
21. Johnson, M.E.: Proof nets and the complexity of processing center-embedded constructions. In: Retore, C. (ed.) Special Issue on Recent Advances in Logical and Algebraic Approaches' to Grammar (1998). J. Logic Lang. Inf. **7**(4), 433–447

22. Landis, J.R., Koch, G.G.: An application of hierarchical kappa-type statistics in the assessment of majority agreement among multiple observers. Biometrics 363–374 (1977)
23. Lommel, A., Uszkoreit, H., Burchardt, A.: Multidimensional quality metrics (MQM): a framework for declaring and describing translation quality metrics. Tradumàtica **12**, 455–463 (2014)
24. Mikkelson, H., Willis, J., Alvarez, N.: Introduction to sight translation. In: The Interpreter's Edge. Spreckels (1995)
25. Mirzapour, M., Prost, J.P., Retoré, C.: Categorical proof nets and dependency locality: a new metric for linguistic complexity. In: LACompLing: Logic and Algorithms in Computational Linguistics, pp. 73–86 (2018)
26. Mirzapour, M., Prost, J.-P., Retoré, C.: Measuring linguistic complexity: introducing a new categorial metric. In: Loukanova, R. (ed.) Logic and Algorithms in Computational Linguistics 2018 (LACompLing2018). SCI, vol. 860, pp. 95–123. Springer, Cham (2020). https://doi.org/10.1007/978-3-030-30077-7_5
27. Moot, R., Retoré, C.: The Logic of Categorial Grammars: a Deductive Account of Natural Language Syntax and Semantics. Springer, Heidelberg (2012)
28. Morrill, G.: Incremental processing and acceptability. Comput. Linguist. **26**(3), 319–338 (2000)
29. Qi, P., Zhang, Y., Zhang, Y., Bolton, J., Manning, C.D.: Stanza: a Python natural language processing toolkit for many human languages. arXiv preprint arXiv:2003.07082 (2020)
30. Shreve, G.M., Lacruz, I., Angelone, E.: Cognitive effort, syntactic disruption, and visual interference in a sight translation task. In: Translation and Cognition, pp. 63–84. John Benjamins Publishing Company (2010)
31. Van Riemsdijk, H.C., Williams, E.: Introduction to the Theory of Grammar, vol. 12. MIT Press (1986)
32. Vanroy, B.: Syntactic difficulties in translation. Ph.D. thesis. Ghent University (2021)
33. Zhong, W.H., Zhan, C.: A Coursebook of Simultaneous Interpreting (2009)

Gender Detection Using Voice Through Deep Learning

Vanessa Garza Enriquez[1] and Madhusudan Singh[1,2](✉)

[1] School of Technology Studies, ECIS, Woosong University, Daejeon, South Korea
msingh@wsu.ac.kr
[2] Department of AI & Big Data, ECIS, Woosong University, Daejeon, South Korea

Abstract. Particularly in an online or digital environment sometimes it is important to detect gender by other means beyond visual or facial recognition. Which is why this article is about detecting the gender of a person by their voice. With Gender Detection Using Voice, it is easier to implement it to security protocols that require gender detection with better accuracy without having people removing pieces of clothing, masks or accessories for the facial recognition. Also, it can be embedded in medical appliances as it can help detect some vocal pathologies like coughing and breathing differently which also depend on the gender as well as detecting criminals' gender through video surveillance and also in businesses, it can help with customized advertisement. The model measures the voice of males and females for optimal accuracy. Our model achieved an accuracy of 90.95% by using feature extraction upon dataset of 500 h of voice recordings.

Keywords: Gender detection using voice · Gender detection · Vocal pathologies

1 Introduction

Everywhere we go we use our voice, so with a system that uses your voice to process your gender it can make life easier for some people. Voice recognition process is seamlessly connected to detecting features of the voice such as frequency, duration, intensity, and filtering [1]. For this process, the model will need to be trained with a dataset that has a vast amount of data from two groups of people of different ages, accents, backgrounds, etc. With this software, it is possible to detect the gender of an individual through their voice by using a deep learning model that was created on the bases of other deep learning models.

2 Background Study

Many researchers created and applied their different models in order to be able to process voice and recognize the input and assign it into its labels. Various kinds of these models are: Frequency-based baseline model [2], logistic regression model [3], classification and regression tree (CART) model [4], Random Forest model [5], boosted tree model

© Springer Nature Switzerland AG 2022
J.-H. Kim et al. (Eds.): IHCI 2021, LNCS 13184, pp. 548–555, 2022.
https://doi.org/10.1007/978-3-030-98404-5_50

[6], Support vector machine (SVM) model [7], XGBoost model [8], stacked model [5] were used. According to Buyukyilmaz [9], machine learning models like random forest, boosted tree, SVM, logistic regression, among others, are less accurate than deep learning algorithms. Therefore, this article uses deep feedforward networks which are used in supervised learning problems by backpropagating in order to train the network. Becker, K. (2021). run test of different models mentioned above on dataset [10] where all records had the same value of duration (20 s) and peak frequency (0 to 280 Hz, human vocal range). Different acoustic properties were measured such as: length of signal, mean frequency (in kHz), standard deviation of frequency, median frequency etc. The results of the experiments can be seen in Table 1 which represents the accuracy of each model achieved.

Table 1. Accuracy of the models for the voice recognition

Accuracy (%)		
Model	*Train*	*Test*
Frequency-based baseline	61	59
Logistic regression	72	71
CART	81	78
Random forest	100	87
Boosted tree	91	84
SVM	96	85
XGBoost	100	87
Stacked	100	89

3   Gender Detection Using Voice in COVID-19

These days people are encouraged in some countries to wear masks at all times due to the COVID-19 pandemic which is a disease that shows acute respiratory syndrome and considered to be a highly contagious viral infection [11]. As a result, some facial recognition software is not able to work properly as people have their face covered by their mask. In these cases, it is possible to use their voice to help replace with process. Also, it is possible to detect COVID-19 by extracting features of the voice as the sound patterns during coughing and breathing differently from patients without

COVID-19. Voice detection assures that the person who being scanned does not spread to the one scanning him or to people around which creates a safe environment of COVID-19 detection [12]. Different studies have been done in such area where studies tried to apply several methods of voice recognition, feature extraction and classification. Such paper can be [13] where researchers tried to apply artificial intelligence-based methods to detect COVID-19 or where [14] they tried to categorize the process and patience in four categories which makes the classification process more accurate and with specific features.

4 Requirements Modelling

4.1 Software Requirements

In Fig. 1, our model's flowchart explaining how the system works can be seen. First, dataset collection is necessary to extract the features with the MFCC or the Mel Spectrogram methods. The purpose of this is to label the data and filter the samples into a.csv file in order to help the neural network work faster. Then building the model is essential in order to train the data and then test it. While testing the data there was a 90.95% accuracy, but as we enlarge our dataset, the accuracy will increase. To start the program, it only requires an individual's voice, and it will process it by extracting the features and the model decides if the voice inputted is male or female. After displaying the result, the program ends.

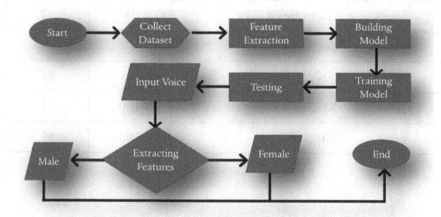

Fig. 1. Flowchart of Gender Detection Using Voice model

4.2 User Requirements

- The Gender Detection Using Voice software should provide accurate recognition of any individual's voice.
- The individual should try to speak clearly for better accuracy.

- The Gender Detection Using Voice software should generate a report stating the accuracy of the displayed result after each detection.
- The data in the database should be accurate to correctly guess the gender with the optimal accuracy.

4.3 System Requirements

- The Gender Detection Using Voice is possible by capturing the voice, processing the data, and displaying the result.
- In order for the program to work, the individual is required to speak.
- In the database, the voice files are filtered and balanced in a .csv file.
- The .csv file should be trained with the help of the deep feedforward neural network.

4.4 Functional Requirements

- Users should be able to use the software easily, which means it should have the user friendly and simple UI.
- Users should be able to add more voice recordings to the dataset in order to increase accuracy.
- Users should be able to recognize their gender in real time.
- The results should be private for the safety and privacy of the users.

4.5 Non-functional Requirements

- **Adjustability:** Application must be flexible for future changes and improvements (if any error occurs or dysfunction in the application is found) and also it should be easy to add new features not available in the initial release (if any need occurs in the future).
- **Compatibility:** The application should be able to work on all possible platforms even through web application interface (to give the users the accessibility).
- **User friendly:** The application's user interaction interface and the application itself should be simple to understand and not complicated (as the main users of the application are non-professionals and non-familiar users, they should be able to understand how to use the application from the beginning due to simple and understandable design of the application).
- **Error-free:** During the actual process of gender detection by the application, it should provide the most possible accuracy for the result.

5 Implementation Method

During the implementation process a 5-step model was used in order to build the program. Each step is essential for the program to work. A more detailed explanation will be given in the following sections and in the formula below.

$$(\theta i \rightarrow X_{\theta i})/S(m/f) \rightarrow T_{X\theta i} = S(t)$$

Expected feature extraction on the dataset
with optimal parameters.
With two sets of outputs (Male and Female)

↑

Output with
optimal
parameters

↑

Extracted
feature map

As you can see, we are expected to choose a dataset with optimal parameters divided into two presets (female and male categories), when afterwards we extract the output with optimal parameters with the help of applying the feature map "S(t)" to extract those features in our implemented classification.

5.1 Preparing the Dataset

First, the dataset collection is critical for this to work. As many data as possible is required to be collected as the amount of the dataset directly effects the accuracy of the model. Therefore, for this project a dataset containing 500 h of voice recordings was used. This dataset was downloaded from Kaggle (provides access to community published datasets, and it have become one of the biggest platforms for data scientists) called: "Common Voice". In this dataset, there are many different kinds of English accents in order to provide more variety as not everyone uses the same English accent. Also, there are many different ages of individuals as age can give different voice tone. Then, in order to make the processing faster, it is essential to extract the features of the dataset into a.csv file. This process can be done with the MFCC or Mel Spectrogram feature extraction methods. In the.csv file each voice recording will have a vector of the length 128 which will be labeled with the according gender. The.csv file will have a balanced data as well in order to help the neural network to not be biased on a certain gender. While the data that we used does not have any noise reduction methods it is possible that in real live cases in criminal's gender detection or surveillance data may have noisy data, which means some noise reduction methods might need to be applied in order to improve the accuracy of the model [15].

5.2 Installing Dependencies

In this step, all libraries need to be installed in order for the code to work. As shown in Fig. 2, the main libraries needed are Python (an object oriented, dynamic and easy to learn programming language) [16], TensorFlow (used for calculation and computation using data graphs) [17], Scikit learn (a tool for applying predictive analysis) [18], NumPy (for scientific computing with help of Python) [19], Librosa (audio analysis) [20], and PyAudio and Pandas among others. It is essential to install all libraries in one environment together.

5.3 Building the Model

In this step, building the model is needed to train the dataset afterwards. The model uses a deep feed-forward neural network with 5 hidden layers using the vector length of

Fig. 2. Dependencies

128. It uses dropout layers in order to regularize for co-adaptation prevention, and dense connection layers in order to connect all inputs and outputs. The model uses ReLU and sigmoid activation functions. The output neuron with the sigmoid activation function will output a scalar of 0 for female and 1 for male.

5.4 Training the Model

In this step, the built model will be used to train the dataset collected. The total parameters trained are 156,545 on 54,219 samples during 100 epochs (each epoch is one complete cycle through entire dataset). However, the model will stop straining after 5 epochs of not improving so it can stop at any epoch if the loss is considered low enough. After training, the model will be saved by the name of "model.h5". Now, with 0.2405 loss and 90.95% accuracy we continue to test the model.

5.5 Testing the Model

In this step, testing the model is needed to see if the model is working properly. The model works by running the "test.py" code and it will display a phrase: "Listening... please talk". This means the model is ready for the individual to start speaking. Then, after the individual starts speaking, the model will stop listening after 5 s unless the guess is not that good, then it will continue listening until the model has a good guess. After testing the model, a 5-s .wav file will be added to the folder containing the codes. Additionally, it is possible to test the model by not only a live recording, but also an already recorded .mp3 file. The file must be in the "test-samples" folder and with a simple command, it is possible to test the model with that recording.

6 Results

After testing the model with any method, we can see the part where the model is displaying the results where we input our voice and it gave the accuracy results of 94.72% which was accurate results, and here it is possible to check the accuracy of the guess as shown in Fig. 3. In this part it is possible to see how the layers in the model do their work with the parameters and below the total parameters, trainable parameters and non-trainable parameters are displayed. After that, it is shown the actual percentage of probability that the individual speaking is either a male or a female. We can see how our model is going through different stages with the dataset and the total parameters and the layers. After finishing preparing our model, we were able to feed it real time data as our voices and it was very accurate providing the results reaching accuracy as high as 94.72%.

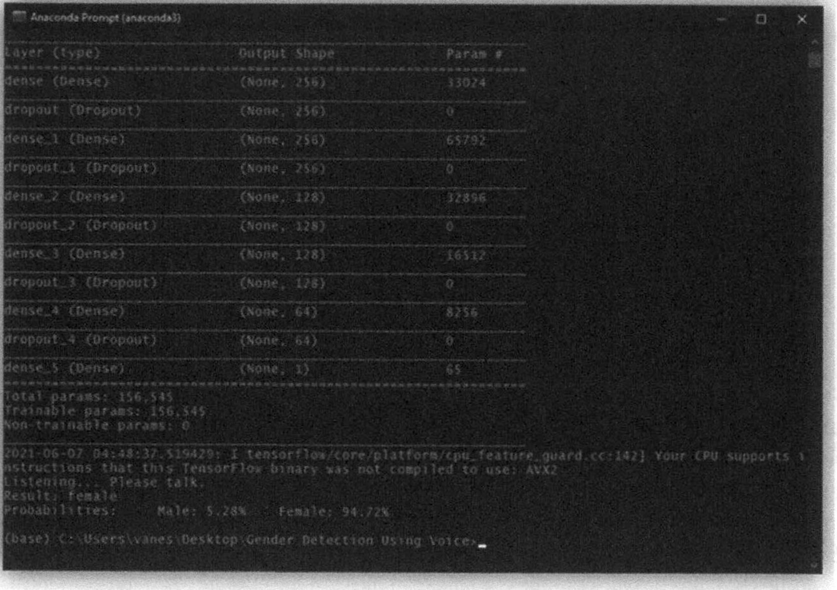

Fig. 3. Test results

7 Conclusion

This model has many advantages as it is easy and simple to use. It can provide very accurate results (94.72% in our case), which shows it is very accurate to predict the gender of the user. However, we suggest that with an even larger dataset it is possible to increase the accuracy and the model will work more efficiently. In the future, the current method could be improved as well by increasing the number of epoch loops for better accuracy even if the loss is low enough. Also, the parameters and the number of the correction and noise reduction methods can be used in the future real time dataset in order to be able to provide more accurate and reliable results.

References

1. Vogel, A., Maruff, P., Snyder, P., Mundt, J.: Standardization of pitch-range settings in voice acoustic analysis. Behav. Res. Methods **41**(2), 318–324 (2009). https://doi.org/10.3758/brm.41.2.318
2. Becker, K.: Identifying the gender of a voice using machine learning (2021). http://www.primaryobjects.com/2016/06/22/identifying-the-gender-of-a-voice-using-machine-learning/
3. Hilbe, J.: Logistic regression models (2009). https://www.routledge.com/Logistic-Regression-Models/Hilbe/p/book/9781138106710
4. Breiman, L.: Classification and regression trees (2017). https://doi.org/10.1201/9781315139470. https://www.taylorfrancis.com/books/mono/10.1201/9781315139470/classification-regression-trees-leo-breiman-jerome-friedman-richard-olshen-charles-stone
5. Breiman, L.: Mach. Learn. **45**(1), 5–32 (2001). https://doi.org/10.1023/a:1010933404324
6. Friedman, J.: Stochastic gradient boosting. Comput. Stat. Data Anal. **38**(4), 367–378 (2002). https://doi.org/10.1016/s0167-9473(01)00065-2
7. Cortes, C., Vapnik, V.: Support-vector networks. Mach. Learn. **20**(3), 273–297 (1995). https://doi.org/10.1007/bf00994018
8. Friedman, J.H.: Greedy function approximation: a gradient boosting machine. Ann. Stat. **29**(5), 1189–1232 (2001). http://www.jstor.org/stable/2699986
9. Buyukyilmaz, M., Cibikdiken, A.: Voice gender recognition using deep learning. In: Proceedings of 2016 International Conference on Modeling, Simulation and Optimization Technologies and Applications (MSOTA 2016) (2016). https://doi.org/10.2991/msota-16.2016.90
10. (2021). https://raw.githubuscrcontent.com/primaryobjects/voice-gender/master/voice.csv
11. Wu, Y., Chen, C., Chan, Y.: The outbreak of COVID-19: an overview. J. Chin. Med. Assoc. **83**(3), 217–220 (2020). https://doi.org/10.1097/jcma.0000000000000270
12. Dash, T., Mishra, S., Panda, G., Satapathy, S.: Detection of COVID-19 from speech signal using bio-inspired based cepstral features. Pattern Recogn. **117**, 107999 (2021). https://doi.org/10.1016/j.patcog.2021.107999
13. Deshpande, G., Schuller, B.W.: Audio, speech, language, & signal processing for COVID-19: a comprehensive overview. ArXiv, abs/2011.14445 (2020)
14. Han, J., et al.: An early study on intelligent analysis of speech under COVID-19: severity, sleep quality, fatigue, and anxiety. Interspeech (2020). https://doi.org/10.21437/interspeech.2020-2223
15. Shrawankar, U., Thakare, V.: Noise estimation and noise removal techniques for speech recognition in adverse environment. In: Shi, Z., Vadera, S., Aamodt, A., Leake, D. (eds.) IIP 2010. IAICT, vol. 340, pp. 336–342. Springer, Heidelberg (2010). https://doi.org/10.1007/978-3-642-16327-2_40
16. General Python FAQ—Python 3.9.7 documentation (2021). https://docs.python.org/3/faq/general.html. Accessed 15 July 2021
17. Abadi, M., et al.: TensorFlow: large-scale machine learning on heterogeneous systems (Software available from tensorflow.org) (2015)
18. Scikit-learn: machine learning in Python — scikit-learn 1.0 documentation (2021). https://scikit-learn.org/stable/. Accessed 12 July 2021
19. van der Walt, S., Colbert, S., Varoquaux, G.: The NumPy array: a structure for efficient numerical computation. Comput. Sci. Eng. **13**(2), 22–30 (2011). https://doi.org/10.1109/mcse.2011.37
20. Librosa—librosa 0.8.1 documentation (2021). https://librosa.org/doc/latest/index.html. Accessed 12 July 2021

Night Vision, Day & Night Prediction
with Object Recognition (NVDANOR) Model

Akobir Ismatov[1] and Madhusudan Singh[1,2]([✉])

[1] School of Technology Studies, ECIS, Woosong University, Daejeon, South Korea
msingh@wsu.ac.kr
[2] Department of AI & Big Data, ECIS, Woosong University, Daejeon, South Korea

Abstract. Night vision has been one of the key developments in Computer Vision system as it gave us a key point to modify an area where humans have the least ability to perform. Object detection is reliable and efficient tool to recognize objects in scenarios such as daytime images where the illumination is great. However, night pictures tend to be challenging to recognize for human being and it usually brings us less data than the images that are taken during day due to poor contrast against its background that interfere with clearly recognizing and labeling them. Different models have been proposed for night vision image processing which use denoising, deblurring and enhancing technique however, other methods can be used in order to enhance that picture and make them as usable and understandable as possible. In addition, different prediction methods and models have been developed in order to achieve different degrees of object recognition in that image, still those results and accuracy can be improved for better results. In this paper, we propose a model that can predict which time of the day it is in the picture with help of calculating average brightness on the images of different time periods with HSV. The model includes ResNet-50 and VGG-16 classifiers that can also recognize the objects and buildings in the image with good accuracy. Implementation of deep learning algorithms and image brightness enhancement tools helped us to achieve improved accuracy and better prediction. The model achieved 94% prediction results when it comes to day and night prediction and 93.75% in object detection on night images.

Keywords: Night vision · Image processing · Image classification · Object recognition · VGG-16 · ResNet-50

1 Introduction

Currently we have surveillance system all around the world working 24/7 protecting our belongings our keeping our place safe [1], autonomous cars are being tested and in process of being legal [2]. Those devices are only a few of things that require better night vision systems implementation and improvement as well as object recognition at those times. Brightness in the image is the main factor that makes difference between day and night images and as we can guess night images are the ones with less brightness and therefore challenging to process [3, 4]. We used enhancement methods to improve that brightness on the images in order to enhance the accuracy of our object detection

© Springer Nature Switzerland AG 2022
J.-H. Kim et al. (Eds.): IHCI 2021, LNCS 13184, pp. 556–567, 2022.
https://doi.org/10.1007/978-3-030-98404-5_51

and toke average brightness of the image as our main feature (does not include pictures that has been artificially brightened for object recognition training) in order to be to classify the time in those images. We used a dataset from AMOS dataset (Archive of Many Outdoor Scenes) that included 200 images of day and night images divided into two subfolder day and night and divides them into two separated folders with images that were separated for testing purposes.

Implementation of ResNet-50 was used to recognize object at Nighttime periods, and it showed a better result while used with images with brightness increase. VGG-16 classifier was also implemented in order to check and compare the results of our own model's day and night classification with VGG-16 results. In the Fig. 1, the overall model of NVDANOR can be seen.

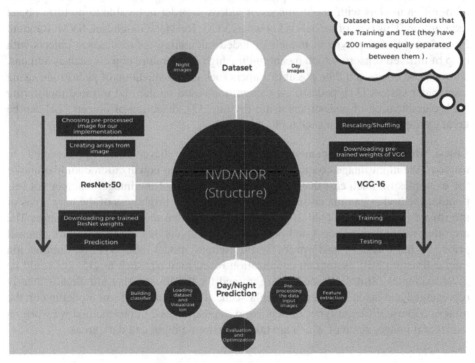

Fig. 1. Overall model of Night Vision and Night Prediction with Object Recognition Model

This article has organized as follows Sect. 2 has discussed about related works, Sect. 3 presents AMOS dataset of Day and Night images. Section 4 Proposed NVDANOR Model requirements, Sect. 5 implementation of NVDANOR, Sect. 6 has presents experimental and results discussed the results and in Sect. 7, we have concluded the article.

2   Related Work

During searching for the post existing studies in the literature, we have come across with variety of works, however we were not able to find a model that was previously build or implemented. **Night vision** is a topic that has seen a lot of improvement since its first development. It has been developed to tackle a lot of modern problems such as vehicle-pedestrian accidents that occur at night, or for surveillance system to be operating at low night conditions [2]. Many research methods were created for working with night vision devices (NVD) such as Low light amplification, thermal imaging etc. These methods are intended to work with image processing or working with images that has higher brightness tones in order to be do predictions or observations on them. Researchers have also implemented and trained their preexisting deep learning and machine learning object recognition models with Night images or videos in order to be able to perform object recognition. This type of models is known as VGG, ResNet, GoogleNet, SVM, Random Forest etc. [4]. Other type of models included calculating the distance to objects with help of infrared sensors, which meant finding high temperature objects such as humans, animals and others could be possible. Papers such as classification of pedestrians using laser radar system [11], pedestrians recognition based on thermal infrared monitoring [12], classification of pedestrians using rhythm [13], detection of objects [14] can be great examples of work on such topic.

Low-Light Image Enhancement. Many techniques have been implemented to improve the night image contrast, brightness. Histogram equalization could be one of the examples for such cast that balances the histogram of the image. Another not less popular method is gamma correction that increases the brightness of the dark areas of the image in order to be able to process it and brighten the pixels of the image. The are other methods to process and perform such analysis that are inverse dark channel prior [5], the wavelet transform [6, 7], the Retinex model [8, 9, 17–21], illumination map estimation [10], histogram equalization-based methods such as [15, 16] could be great examples. Still these models are trained for the images that are already clearly represented and taken from a good bright scene. They do not perform modelling on the images and use different types of denoising as postprocess. In our method we work on a different image, some of which are taken at extreme night and dark areas.

3   AMOS Dataset of Day and Night Images

All images included in the dataset for this work is taken from the Archive of Many Outdoor Scenes (AMOS) dataset. It contains images of a different scenes at day and nighttime period and is divided into a folder train with two subfolders for different categories (Day/Night). The day/night image dataset consist of 200 RGB color images in those two categories, you can see the example of the dataset in the Fig. 2.

Fig. 2. Examples of the image dataset with different images from different time periods.

4   Proposed NVDANOR Model Requirements

1. **User requirements**

    1. Need to provide accurate predictions (as it may result in wrong prediction).
    2. Need to be time-efficient (processes of object recognition should not take a lot of time).
    3. Easy to use (User only needs to input image, other steps are done by software)

2. **Hardware requirements**

    1. NVDANOR does not require any high-end hardware (it can be run in cloud-based IDE and pictures can be taken by phones)
    2. Does not need any further installation or purchasing additional equipment.

3. **Software requirements**

    1. Requires libraries such as OpenCV, Keras, and deep learning models (ResNet and VGG)
    2. It Can be trained on small data for day and night classification. For using in object recognition and classification can be used with pre-trained weights with help of overturning.
    3. It Could be complicated if the order of execution is not followed.

5   Proposed NVDANOR Implementation Method

The start the processes is initiated by loading our dataset and visualizing it, which represents the data for better understanding. Distinguishing characteristics need to be chosen, such as the fact that day photos are often brighter than night ones. Algorithm of the model can be seen in Fig. 3 as a step-by-step algorithm.

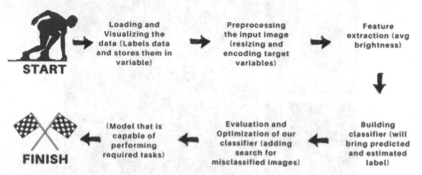

Fig. 3. Algorithm for the model

Because night photos have these extremely intense tiny areas, where the brightness of the entire image changes significantly more than it does in day photos. In the Table 1 you can clearly see the illumination difference in light level in day and night conditions.

Table 1. Common outdoor light levels in day and night conditions

Condition	Illumination	
	(ftcd)	(lux)
Sunlight	10000	107527
Full Daylight	1000	10752
Overcast Day	100	1075
Very Dark Day	10	107
Twilight	1	10.8
Deep Twilight	0.1	1.08
Full Moon	0.01	0.108
Quarter Moon	0.001	0.0108
Starlight	0.0001	0.0011
Overcast Night	0.00001	0.0001

Formula for illumination, one lux is equal to one lumen per square meter (lm/m^2), where lumen (lm) is the unit of luminous flux, that describes the quantity of light emitted by a light source or received at a surface.

Also, the color pallet in the day images is a lot grayer and bluer compared to night one Preprocessing of the data that were taken from dataset needs to be done. All the input data needs to be put in a consistent format and therefore all of them were resized, fixed to size, and encoded to the target variables. Pseudocode for NVDANOR model that goes through the whole model can be seen in the Fig. 4.

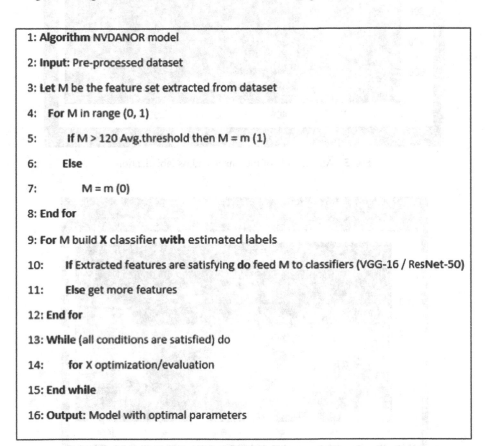

1: **Algorithm** NVDANOR model

2: **Input:** Pre-processed dataset

3: **Let M be the feature set extracted from dataset**

4:   **For M in range (0, 1)**

5:     **If M > 120 Avg.threshold then M = m (1)**

6:     **Else**

7:       M = m (0)

8: **End for**

9: **For M build X classifier with estimated labels**

10:     **If Extracted features are satisfying do feed M to classifiers (VGG-16 / ResNet-50)**

11:     **Else get more features**

12: **End for**

13: **While (all conditions are satisfied) do**

14:     for X optimization/evaluation

15: **End while**

16: **Output:** Model with optimal parameters

Fig. 4. Pseudocode for the NVDANOR model

Different approaches such as One-Hot [22] and label encoding [23] can be used for this method. In the Fig. 5 you can see the displayed standardized image and its label.

Next step is to extract the feature from the data. Average brightness of the images is calculated by using HSV color space. To be more specific the V channel (a measure of brightness), add up the pixel values in the V channel, and then divided that sum by the area of the image to get the average value of the image example of which can be seen in Fig. 6.

Fig. 5. An example of the image and its labialization

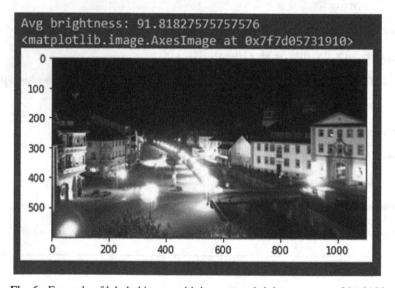

Fig. 6. Example of labeled image with its average brightness score of 91.8182

Next step will be to build the classifier. Here building a simple classifier that will set a threshold value of average brightness to separate between the two classes is done. The optimal threshold was 120 (avg. brightness) in order to separate images into two class.

6 Experiments and Results

Now the classifier needs to be evaluated and optimized if possible. In this step testing the classification algorithm using test set of data that were set aside at the beginning is done. First load in the test dataset, standardize it and then shuffle it. (Shuffling ensures that order will not play a role in testing accuracy). Feature to recognize misclassified images was implemented in order to be able to see how many images the model was not able to label to any of two classes. In Fig. 7 you can see the results of the model and its accuracy of classify images into two classes.

```
Accuracy: 0.9375
Number of misclassified images = 10 out of 160
```

Fig. 7. Results of the Day and Night classification model

As you can see, the classifier achieved the result of 94% and 10 images out of 160 testing images were misclassified which makes 16% of the training dataset.

ResNet-50 – is one of deep residual networks family member and it is a convolutional neural network (CNN) that is 50 layers deep. It is an artificial neural network (ANN) and it working principle is based on stacking residual blocks on top of one another to form a network. Most popular ResNets are ResNet-34, ResNet-50, ResNet-101, each with more layers being more accurate than other one. Residual network (ResNet) changed the way how CNN used to be trained for computer vision task. While ResNet-34 brought 34 layered network that functioned with 2-layer blocks, ResNet-50 further improved it with more layers that took use of 3-layer bottleneck blocks that improved accuracy and took less time for training [24]. ResNet-50 architecture [27] as shown in Fig. 8 includes its residual units and its filters which is the result of outputs of each convolution layer.

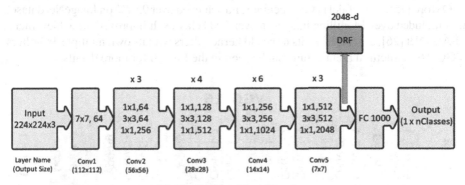

Fig. 8. ResNet-50 architecture

ResNet-50 was used in the model for object prediction on the dataset. For this part ResNet-50 network was not trained from scratch with initial dataset, instead pre-trained

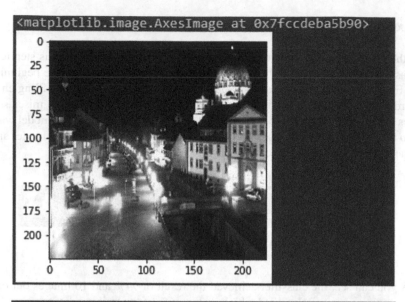

Fig. 9. Results of ResNet-50

model with its parameters and weights were implemented and fine-tuned for the model. In the Fig. 9 you can see the results of ResNet-50 prediction.

The prediction with ResNet-50 was accurate as it correctly classified the building in the image under low light conditions. However, the accuracy results were not very good. As the model was not trained on our dataset, therefore not possessed the most optimal parameters.

VGG-16 – was first introduced by K.Simonyan and A.Zisserman from the University of Oxford [25], this model is very accurate and achieved over 92.7% on ImageNet dataset, that included over 14 million images in over 1000 classes. It improved the achievements of AlexNet [26], as it replaced its large old kernel filters with its own multiple 3x3 filters. VGG-16's structural architecture can be seen in the Fig. 10 for more details.

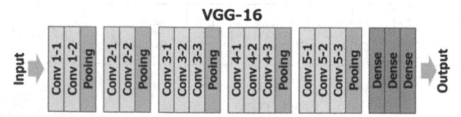

Fig. 10. VGG-16 structure

We use VGG-16 model to test it and compare it with our initial classification model. VGG was trained on all our dataset. The model was trained on 5 epochs with train_data and it achieved an accuracy of 92.79%. When tested with test_data (images that are only for testing purposes) it achieved accuracy of 93.75% that's shown in the Fig. 11.

```
5/5 [==============================] - 51s 10s/step - loss: 0.1766 - acc: 0.9375
test_loss, test accuracy [0.176627978682518, 0.9375]
```

Fig. 11. Results of VGG-16.

As seen in results VGG-16 achieves pretty good accuracy and results, performing 93.75% and over performing ResNet-50 results. Overall results off VGG-16 can be seen as a chart in the Fig. 12.

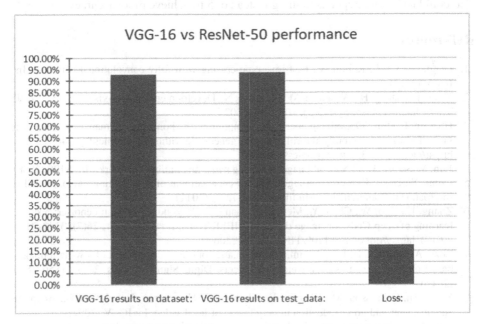

Fig. 12. VGG-16 performance on dataset and test dataset

However, it could be the results of training VGG-16 on our dataset which gave the best parameters and weights.

7 Conclusion and Future Work

In this article, we build a classifier that was capable of extracting features from the input and classify them into two labels 0 (night) and 1 (day). The feature that we took was calculation of the avg brightness of the image. As you know day pictures has more brightness compared to night images that would result into perfect classification. The threshold that was set for being night was avg of 120 (was calculated after testing avg for day and night images) and if the value was higher than that it would mean the picture is taken at daylight. During Evaluation and Optimization, we tested our proposed model with help of test data (set of images set aside for testing) and shuffled it for more accurate results (shuffling makes sure that the order of the image has no influence on results). And we added a new feature to calculate misclassified images that in process of testing were not matched with any label (label 0 and 1) For our model we used ResNet for object recognition part. It performed very well and was clearly able to recognize different structures, building etc., with our pre-processed night images that had higher brightness. With our model we achieved an accuracy of 93.75% by using only one feature extraction, i.e., the average brightness of the image. We could work more on this, for example features that involve Hue (a gradation or variety of a color spectrum) and Saturation channels could be extracted for more features which may result in more accuracy. We also could make more epochs training instead of 5 to achieve more accuracy.

References

1. Chen, Q., Xu, J., Koltun, V.: Fast image processing with fully convolutional networks. In: ICCV (2017)
2. Tsuji, T., Hattori, H., Watanabe, M., Nagaoka, N.: Development of night-vision system. IEEE Trans. Intell. Transp. Syst. 3(3), 203–209 (2002)
3. Hussain, I., et al.: Optimizing energy consumption in the home energy management system via a bio-inspired dragonfly algorithm and the genetic algorithm. Electronics 9(3), 406 (2020). https://doi.org/10.3390/electronics9030406
4. Jain, V., Seung, H.S.: Natural image denoising with convolutional networks. In: NIPS (2008)
5. Dong, X., et al.: Fast efficient algorithm for enhancement of low lighting video. In: IEEE International Conference on Multimedia and Expo (2011)
6. Zhang, K., Zuo, W., Chen, Y., Meng, D., Zhang, L.: Beyond a Gaussian denoiser: residual learning of deep CNN for image denoising. IEEE Trans. Image Process. 26(7), 3142–3155 (2017). https://doi.org/10.1109/TIP.2017.2662206
7. Łoza, A., Bull, D., Hill, P., Achim, A.: Automatic contrast enhancement of low-light images based on local statistics of wavelet coefficients. Digit. Signal Process. 23(6), 1856–1866 (2013)
8. Malm, H., Oskarsson, M., Warrant, E., Clarberg, P., Hasselgren, J., Lejdfors, C.: Adaptive enhancement and noise reduction in very low light-level video. In: ICCV (2007)
9. Park, S., Soohwan, Y., Moon, B., Ko, S., Paik, J.: Low-light image enhancement using variational optimization-based Retinex model. IEEE Trans. Consum. Electron. 63(2), 178–184 (2017)
10. Guo, X., Li, Y., Ling, H.: LIME: Low-light image enhancement via illumination map estimation. IEEE Trans. Image Process. 26(2), 982–993 (2017)
11. Adachi, T., Yoshioka, T., Morioka, S., Matsuoka, S.: Development of recognition algorithm for crossing pedestrian using laser radar system. In: Proceedings of Society Automotive Engineers Japan, pp. 363–366 (1996)
12. Hirota, M., Saito, S., Morita, S., Fukuhara, H.: Nighttime pedestrian monitoring system and thermal infrared technology. J. Soc. Auto. Eng. Jpn. 50(11), 58–63 (1996)
13. Yasutomi, S., Mori, H.: A method for discriminating of pedestrian based on rhythm. In: Proceedings of IEEE International Conference Robotics and Automation, vol. 2, pp. 988–995 (1994)

14. Kitagawa, N., Imanishi, M., Mizuno, T.: Development of foreground obstacle detection system. In: Proceedings of Society Automotive Engineers Japan, pp. 101–104 (1996)
15. Ibrahim, H., Kong, N.S.P.: Brightness preserving dynamic histogram equalization for image contrast enhancement. IEEE Trans. Consum. Electron. **53**(4), 1752–1758 (2007)
16. Abdullah-AI-Wadud, M., Kabir, M.H., Dewan, M.A.A., Chae, O.: A dynamic histogram equalization for image contrast enhancement. IEEE Trans. Consum. Electron. **53**(2), 593–600 (2007)
17. Fu, X., Liao, Y., Zeng, D., Huang, Y., Zhang, X., Ding, X.: A probabilistic method for image enhancement with simultaneous illumination and reflectance estimation. IEEE Trans. Image Process. **24**(12), 4965–4977 (2015)
18. Guo, X., Li, Y., Ling, H.: LIME: low-light image enhancement via illumination map estimation. IEEE Trans. Image Process. **26**(2), 982–993 (2016)
19. Wang, S., Zheng, J., Hu, H., Li, B.: Naturalness preserved enhancement algorithm for non-uniform illumination images. IEEE Trans. Image Process. **22**(9), 3538–3548 (2013)
20. Gu, Z., Li, F., Fang, F., Zhang, G.: A novel retinex-based fractional-order variational model for images with severely low light. IEEE Trans. Image Process. **29**, 3239–3253 (2019)
21. Hao, S., Han, X., Guo, Y., Xu, X., Wang, M.: Low-light image enhancement with semi-decoupled decomposition. IEEE Trans. Multimed. **22**(12), 3025–3038 (2020)
22. sklearn.preprocessing.OneHotEncoder (2021). https://scikit-learn.org/stable/modules/generated/sklearn.preprocessing.OneHotEncoder.html. Accessed 11 July 2021
23. sklearn.preprocessing.LabelEncoder (2021). https://scikit-learn.org/stable/modules/generated/sklearn.preprocessing.LabelEncoder.html. Accessed 11 July 2021
24. Boesch, G.: Deep Residual Networks (ResNet, ResNet50) - Guide in 2021 - viso.ai (2021). https://viso.ai/deep-learning/resnet-residual-neural-network/. Accessed 11 Aug 2021
25. Simonyan, K., Zisserman, A.: Very deep convolutional networks for large-scale image recognition. CoRR, abs/1409.1556 (2015)
26. Krizhevsky, A., Sutskever, I., Hinton, G.E.: ImageNet classification with deep convolutional neural networks. Commun. ACM **60**, 84–90 (2012)
27. Mahmood, A., et al.: Automatic hierarchical classification of kelps using deep residual features. Sensors. **20**, 447 (2020). https://doi.org/10.3390/s20020447

A Built-in Concentration Level Prediction Device for Neuro Training System Based on EEG Signal

Ha-Trung Nguyen[1], Ngoc-Dau Mai[1], Jong-Jin Kim[2], and Wan-Young Chung[1(✉)]

[1] Department of AI Convergence, Pukyong National University, Busan, South Korea
wychung@pknu.ac.kr
[2] Department of Electronic Engineering, Pukyong National University, Busan, South Korea
kimjj@pknu.ac.kr

Abstract. This study aims to develop a built-in concentration level feedback system using EEG signals. The system includes an embedded device for electroencephalography (EEG) acquisition from two electrodes mounted at designated positions on the frontal scalp for concentration level prediction. The selected EEG-based feature used in this study is the relative power spectral density (PSD) extracted from five EEG bands (Delta, Theta, Alpha, Beta, Gamma) by using the Fourier Fast Transform (FFT) method. Then, two standard machine learning models, including support vector machine (SVM) and multilayer perceptron (MLP), are trained on the personal computer (PC) with the feature of relative power spectral density (PSD) as input for concentration level prediction. After conducting the performance evaluation, MLP is adopted to deploy on the device for real-time concentration level prediction based on the evaluation. The results have demonstrated the feasibility of our EEG-based built-in concentration level prediction device in real-life applications.

Keywords: Concentration level prediction · EEG · On-chip machine learning · FFT · Relative PSD · SVM · MLP

1 Introduction

Nowadays, concentration significantly affects the result of any works. However, focusing is a challenging task for people in real life and needs to be trained for a long [1]. Furthermore, we can be unconsciously distracted by surrounding influences during studying and working. Therefore, developing an effective and real-time concentration level feedback system is necessary to show the current focus state and warn distracted users. EEG is an electrophysiological method recording electrical activity directly from the brain by using electrodes placed on the scalp [2]. Most current EEG-based concentration level detection systems are built on the computer for signal processing and prediction tasks [3, 4]. This cumbersome system can lead to inconvenience and immobility for users in real life. To overcome these limitations, we propose a wearable device with the ability to perform built-in EEG signal processing and concentration level prediction tasks. The relative

© Springer Nature Switzerland AG 2022
J.-H. Kim et al. (Eds.): IHCI 2021, LNCS 13184, pp. 568–573, 2022.
https://doi.org/10.1007/978-3-030-98404-5_52

spectral power density is extracted from five bands of EEG signals (Delta, Theta, Alpha, Beta, Gamma) for feature extraction. Two popular machine learning models, including SVM and MLP, are utilized and compared their performance to each other. The model with the best performance is deployed to the embedded device for on-chip concentration level prediction based on the evaluation result. Finally, a smartphone application is developed for receiving prediction results from the device to display and prompt an instant warning when detecting distraction.

2   Proposed System

2.1   The Embedded System for Built-In Concentration Level Prediction

Our research built a wearable embedded device to acquire the EEG signals, perform signal processing tasks for feature extraction, and run a machine learning model right on the chip to get the prediction result. Our proposed device, shown in Fig. 1(a), has 2 PCB plates. The first PCB plate collects the EEG signals using the analog front-end (AFE) integrated chip (IC) ADS1299, which is highly accurate. The second PCB plate is designed to handle signal processing and on-chip prediction tasks using a powerful microcontroller module Portenta H7. This module consists of a high-performance dual-core microcontroller IC STM32H747XI which can run at the maximum frequency of 480MHz and have 8 Mb SDRAM. Besides, the Portenta H7 module also features 5.2 Bluetooth Low Energy (BLE) communication and battery-powered ability.

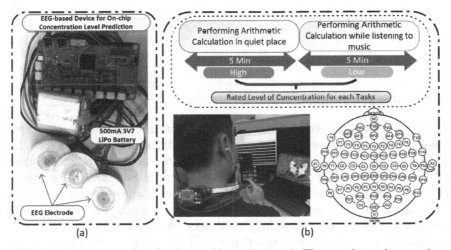

Fig. 1. (a) The proposed device for on-chip prediction, (b) The experimental protocol.

The proposed system has two operation stages: Training Stage and Implement stage. In the Training Stage, the wearable device will acquire the EEG data then transmit it to the computer. The transferred data is stored and preprocessed on the computer side, and then relative PSD is calculated to be used as the input feature for the training model. In the following step, some models are proposed for training, and we compare their performance to select the best model. The most suitable model is deployed into the embedded device for the Implement Stage by utilizing TensorFlow Lite. In the Implement Stage, after EEG acquisition, the wearable device instantly executes the task of preprocessing signal and feature extraction in the same way on the previous stage. The extracted feature data is used as input for the deployed model to predict the concentration level on the chip. Finally, the prediction result is transmitted to the Android smartphone to display and interact with the user. Figure 2 shows the whole system.

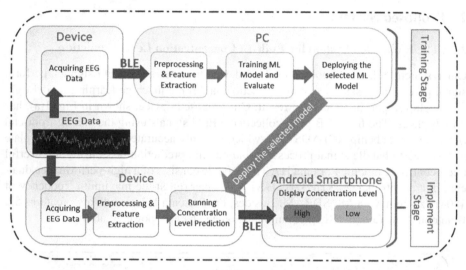

Fig. 2. The proposed system for on-chip concentration level prediction.

2.2 Experimental Protocol

Five volunteer subjects (aged 24–35), including two females and three males, participated in the experiment. They were all physically healthy and had no optical problems. Each subject was required to complete two tasks of the experiment, which lasted 5 min for each (the first 5 min as the high-level concentration, the last 5 min as the low-level one). First, they would perform arithmetic calculations in a quiet room for optimizing the concentration. Then, the second task was designed to collect the EEG data related to the low-level attention by requiring the subject to do the same previous task activity in a relaxed state while listening to a pop song. There are three electrodes, including AF7, AF8, and FPZ as a reference electrode. The permission number for the experiment is 1041386-202003-h-11-02, approved by the Institutional Review Board of Pukyong National University. Figure 1(b) shows the detailed Protocol of the experiment.

3 Methodology

3.1 Pre-processing and Feature Extraction

In the data preprocessing stage of Training stages, the data collection, which is stored with the length corresponding to the duration of 5 min for each experiment of each subject, is segmented by adopting a sliding window of 250 samples with an overlap rate of 50%. However, the discontinuity in segmented data can introduce other frequencies and distort the true spectrum by spreading the peak to surrounding frequencies. This phenomenon is known as spectrum leakage, which can negatively affect the result of FFT calculation for feature extraction. To prevent spectral leakage, the kind of sliding window we used for segmentation is the Hanning window. With the Implement stage, the raw EEG data is already in the length of 250 samples, so they only need to be multiplied with the Hanning window function for the next step. Then, we apply a notch filter to eliminate the 50 Hz power-line noise and a band-pass filter to acquire only wanted EEG data in the frequency range of 0.5–60 Hz. After normalizing the data signals of each segment, the relative PSD features are extracted from five frequencies band of EEG data according to each segmentation from the previous section. Then, these features are used as input for the classification model.

3.2 Classification

In this study, a total of two machine learning classifier models, namely SVM and MLP, have been trained on the dataset and compared the performance to each other.

SVM is a powerful machine learning model for binary classification. The goal of SVM is to find the hyperplane which separates the two classes and has the most significant margin to each class [6]. The SVM can be used with Radial Basis Function kernels to handle nonlinear datasets, which is a popular kernel function for kernelized learning algorithms. Meanwhile, MLP is one of the most frequently used feedforward neural network models, with the architecture having at least three layers: an input layer, a hidden layer, and an output layer [6]. It is trained based on the datasets using the backpropagation algorithm, a widely known and robust supervised training algorithm. The proposed MLP model is shown in Fig. 3.

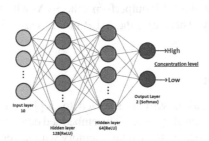

Fig. 3. The proposed MLP for on-chip concentration level prediction.

4   Result and Discussion

4.1   Classification Result

To evaluate classification models, there are two approaches used, including subject-dependent and subject-independent. In the subject-dependence approach, we consider the model on each subject dataset with 70% for training and 30% for testing. Then, we calculate the average accuracy of the model over all the subjects. Meanwhile, for the subject-independent, the training and testing data are based on the total dataset of all subjects. This approach can evaluate the generalization of the model, which is more suitable for practical application. This study has two competitive models, SVM and MLP, to select the best-performance model for concentration level prediction. Table 1 illustrates the accuracy result of classifiers.

Table 1. Classification results of the proposed models with two evaluation approaches, subject-dependent and subject-independent, across five subjects

Subjects	Accuracy (%)	
	SVM	MLP
S1	91.68	94.82
S2	88.25	93.74
S3	90.11	91.56
S4	94.41	98.12
S5	92.83	96.61
Average	91.46	**94.97**
Subject-independence	89.68	**91.43**

To be more specific, the SVM achieves the highest accuracy of 94.41% on S4, the lowest accuracy of 88.25% on S2, and the average accuracy over all subjects is 91.46%. Meanwhile, the MLP performs better with the highest accuracy of 98.12% on S4, the lowest on S3 with 91.56%, and the average accuracy of 94.97%. When it comes to the term subject-independent, the MLP outperforms the SVM with the precision of 91.43% and 89.68%, respectively. Therefore, the MLP model was selected to deploy on the device.

4.2   Model Deployment

With the higher performance, MLP is selected to deploy on our proposed on-chip machine learning microcontroller device. The embedded devices based on the microcontroller are usually constrained by their small memory with lower performance compared to the computer, and most of them are written on C/C++ for optimizing the use of hardware. These problems prevent them from utilizing the machine learning model trained on computers. Therefore, we use TensorFlow Lite [7], a toolset provided by Google for helping developers run machine learning models on mobile and embedded devices, to optimize the pre-trained model for embedded devices by lessening the model size and converting it to a C/C++ pattern. Finally, we developed an Android smartphone application to display the current user's concentration level information received from the device and prompt warning when detecting any distraction state.

5 Conclusion

This study has developed an on-chip concentration level prediction device based on EEG signals for the neuro training system. The preprocessed EEG signals are extracted with relative PSDs over five EEG frequency bands using FFT. The best-performance machine learning model selected from two models, including SVM and MLP, was deployed to the embedded EEG device for on-chip concentration level prediction. Our proposed system has proven feasible and practical for concentration level prediction in real-life applications by comparing the achieved accuracy results.

Although we do many experiments to help create a complete dataset for each subject, the number of issues is still a limitation for avoiding overfitting when training the model. Therefore, in the future, we will perform experiments on more subjects of both age and gender to increase the system's performance to suit real applications.

References

1. Rock, D.: The neuroscience of leadership. Diss. Middlesex University (2010)
2. Tong, S., Thankor, N.V.: Quantitative EEG Analysis Methods and Clinical Applications. Artech House (2009)
3. Li, Y., et al.: A real-time EEG-based BCI system for attention recognition in ubiquitous environment. In: Proceedings of 2011 International Workshop on Ubiquitous Affective Awareness and Intelligent Interaction (2011)
4. Thomas, K.P., Prasad Vinod, A., Guan, C.: Design of an online EEG based neurofeedback game for enhancing attention and memory. In: 2013 35th Annual International Conference of the IEEE Engineering in Medicine and Biology Society (EMBC). IEEE (2013)
5. Texas Instruments: Ads1299-x low-noise, 4-, 6-, 8-channel, 24-bit, analog-to-digital converter for EEG and biopotential measurements. Jul-2012 (2017)
6. Géron, A.: Hands-On Machine Learning with Scikit-Learn, Keras, and TensorFlow: Concepts, Tools, and Techniques to Build Intelligent Systems. O'Reilly Media, Boston (2019)
7. TensorFlow Lite—TensorFlow. https://www.tensorflow.org/lite

Towards Man/Machine Co-authoring of Advanced Analytics Reports Around Big Data Repositories

Amal Babour[1]([⊠]) [iD] and Javed Khan[2]

[1] Information Systems Department, Faculty of Computing and Information Technology,
King Abdulaziz University, Jeddah, Saudi Arabia
ababor@kau.edu.sa
[2] Department of Computer Science, Kent State University, Kent, OH 44240, USA
javed@kent.edu

Abstract. This paper explores the problem of generating advanced analytical report for gaining sophisticated insight from massive databases by machine assistance. This study shows a model that takes a country-specific scientometric scientific research analysis report as a template and goes into a curated source database to generate a similar insightful report for other countries. The overall process consists of three key phases. The first phase is processing the template report for identifying the generalizable data elements. The second phase is extracting the elements for the selected country from a scholarly database. The third phase is re-assembling the high-level report for the new case. A case study on big data analysis is presented for Saudi Arabia scientific research publications. The generated co-authored report was evaluated by 10 human reviewers through assessing several criteria in the report, which achieved a satisfactory evaluation.

Keywords: Azure databricks · Big data analysis · Microsoft Academic Graph · Report generation · Scientometric analysis

1 Introduction

Recently, automatic generation of reports have gained considerable attention. Automatic generations of reports can be useful for understanding massive datasets. Over the last few decades, statistical techniques have been developed for extracting specific quantitative information from large datasets. Data mining techniques find hidden patterns from massive datasets which may not be obvious to a typical human analyzer. However, understanding the patterns and making them presentable for readership is still considered a highly advanced cognitive task. Human expert authors are capable of finding very high-level relationships to reveal complex facts and figures about massive datasets and are also capable of presenting them in a comprehensible advanced text.

Several massive databases have been sources of inspiration for many data analysts. Scientometric is a discipline that analyzes scientific publications to explore the structure and growth of science. It is an important field that can measure research growth,

J.-H. Kim et al. (Eds.): IHCI 2021, LNCS 13184, pp. 574–583, 2022.
https://doi.org/10.1007/978-3-030-98404-5_53

author productivity, publication obsolescence, and collaborative research by country [1]. Scientometric research studies can be made by analysis at three perspectives: A micro perspective that involves authors analysis; a meso perspective that includes institutions analysis; and a macro perspective that includes countries analysis [2]. Together, all of these elements have been used to study research trends in the past and predict the directions of research in the future.

On the other hand, writing a scientific report that presents any single or combined level of analysis in an organized and well-written format is considered a challenging task for some researchers. The text should be very clear and interesting to the reader. Sentences should be without grammar mistakes. Claims must be supported by reliable evidence. Figures and tables should be compatible with the text and placed in the right place. Data should be clearly described. Experimental details should be reported in sufficient detail. All of these require a highly developed level of writing skills [3, 4].

Automatic report generation can be used as a tool to reduce the burden of writing reports, especially reports that have the same pattern. One such tool is SCIgen [5]. It is an automatic Computer Science research paper generator developed by MIT. However, the focus of this generated paper is not to create high value content but to create a natural language-like construct. However, very few bodies of work exist that focus on the automatic generation of reports like high value content [6–8].

What are the challenges in the process? Normally a scientific paper is driven by a sophisticated high-level quest. A significant amount of human ingenuity is needed to translate the high-level quest into a specific data query, hypotheses, and their validation/nullification by specific evidence from the data. To this effect, this study will present a template paper aimed at understanding how political epochs marked by national policy decisions translated into changes within nation-wide research productivity. A complex understanding of the domain is needed to stitch together data evidence to form the conclusions about the quest. Can this process be fully automated? Even though advanced machine learning/expert system-guided automation is conceivable in the future, the output might be prone to dramatic errors, warranting required human review.

This paper outlines a plausible approach where a case-specific data analysis of an intensive human authored paper can be replicated for other similar cases with the least amount of human effort, using assistance from computing in the domain of scientometric analysis. The goal is to explore a preliminary model to generate a semi-automatic man/machine co-authoring report without compromising the sophistication of the expert authorship. Specifically, the goal is to present a comprehensive view of research productivity by illustrating all major aspects of scientometric publications on micro, meso, and macro perspectives, including a study of period-wise research output for each study area and growth rate, collaboration pattern, major collaborative countries, and citation rates for any selected country from a massive anchor database.

The rest of the paper is organized as follows. Section 2 explains the proposed methodology. Section 3 presents an example case. Section 4 describes the evaluation results. The conclusion and future work are presented in Sect. 5.

2 Methodology

The basic approach is as follows. The model reads several features from a report requester such as the country's name, and scope of the publications study period. Using a scholarly database, the model extracts the research publication data, including affiliations belonging to a selected country, and performs an in-depth scientometric analysis about the publications. Then, it generates a high-level structured report consisting of text, figures, and tables presenting details about the research performance of the country in the given period.

The proposed method generates a report similar to the one created for the country of Vietnam [9]. The report presents information about the total number of publications in the selected country, the study areas, the number of publications in each study area, and the publication growth rate. It also presents information about the co-authorship collaboration coefficient, the publication types, the collaborative countries, and the size of the international collaboration. In addition, it reveals the number of citations from multiple aspects. In this study, the Vietnam scientific research report is called the based report, while the generated scientific research report is the stenotype report. The methodology consists of three main phases: 1) Template preparation; 2) Data extraction; and 3) Report generation. The overview of the three phases is shown in Fig. 1.

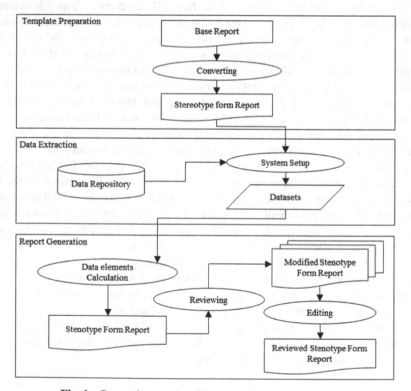

Fig. 1. Generating man/machine co-authoring report phases.

2.1 Template Preparation

In this phase, the base report is converted into a stereotype form report that can be used to present the scientific research data for any country. All the generalizable data elements related to the country of Vietnam are manually extracted and substituted with data elements variables in the based report. An example of the based report before and after converting it into a stereotype form is shown in Fig. 2.

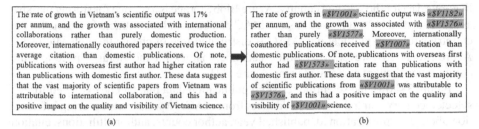

The rate of growth in Vietnam's scientific output was 17% per annum, and the growth was associated with international collaborations rather than purely domestic production. Moreover, internationally coauthored papers received twice the average citation than domestic publications. Of note, publications with overseas first author had higher citation rate than publications with domestic first author. These data suggest that the vast majority of scientific papers from Vietnam was attributable to international collaboration, and this had a positive impact on the quality and visibility of Vietnam science.	The rate of growth in «$V1001» scientific output was «$V1182» per annum, and the growth was associated with «$V1576» rather than purely «$V1577». Moreover, internationally coauthored publications received «$V1007» citation than domestic publications. Of note, publications with overseas first author had «$V1573» citation rate than publications with domestic first author. These data suggest that the vast majority of scientific publications from «$V1001» was attributable to «$V1576», and this had a positive impact on the quality and visibility of «$V1001» science.
(a)	(b)

Fig. 2. Example of the based report before (a) and after assigning the data elements (b).

The data elements assigned in the entire report are classified into three groups. Group 1 includes data elements given by the report designer such as the name of the used scholarly database and the total number of the publications in the used database. Group 2 includes data elements given by the report requester such as the name of the selected country and the starting and the ending of the study years. Group 3 includes the data elements that need to be calculated or concluded from the extracted datasets. The data elements in Group 3 are classified into six sub-groups. (1) study area data elements such as the number of publications in study area n; (2) growth rate data elements such as the study area that has the strongest growth rate; (3) coefficient collaboration data elements such as the status of the coefficient collaboration during the entire study period; (4) publication type data elements such as the percentage of single/domestic/international papers in study area n; (5) collaborative countries data elements such as the number of publications with the top ten collaborative countries; and (6) citation data elements such as the percentage of citations of single/domestic/international papers in study area n. The complete list of the data elements and their appropriate groups is shown in the Appendix.

2.2 Data Extraction

This study anchored its auto-report on a Microsoft Academic Graph (MAG) [10] which supposedly is capable of producing statistically significant analysis for almost all countries of the world. MAG is a scholarly database produced and maintained by Microsoft. It provides information about scientific papers, citations, authors, institutions, journals, conferences, and study areas [11]. Five datasets from MAG are utilized: The Affiliation dataset records institution-related information such as institution name, official page, and country. The PaperAuthorAffiliations dataset lists information about the authors of each paper and their affiliations such as author id, affiliation id, and author sequence number. The Papers dataset consists of papers information such as doi, title, and publication year. The PaperFieldsofStudy dataset contains information about the study areas for each publication such as the study area id. The FieldofStudy dataset records detail information about each study area such as the study area name and level.

For dynamic data, two Cloud services provided by Microsoft Azure were used to extract and store the publication data of the selected country: Azure Databricks and Azure Blob Storage. Azure Databricks is an Apache Spark programming platform for big data analytics [12]. It is used to process MAG database and run the code for extracting the publications data for the selected country. Azure Blob Storage is a service for storing massive amounts of data [13]. It is used to store MAG database and the extracted datasets for the country's research publications. MAG is distributed free of charge through Microsoft' Azure Storage. However, Microsoft Academic charges for the storage space and the computation that are performed using Azure [14].

Figure 3 shows the scientific research publication data that can be extracted for the selected country using the utilized datasets from MAG. New datasets covering information about each publication id, published year, author counts, author affiliations, citation count, study area, and publication type can be generated and used for further analysis.

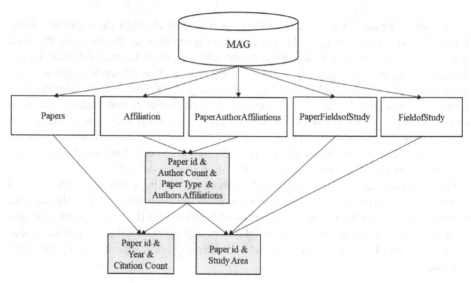

Fig. 3. MAG utilized datasets and the extracted research publication data for a selected country.

2.3   Report Generation

The data elements in Group 3 are calculated by using the extracted datasets for the selected country. The calculation of some data elements depends on the calculation of others. For example, calculating the growth rate in a study area is based on calculating the number of papers in the study area for each study periodate. The sequence of calculating the data elements in Group 3 is illustrated in Fig. 4.

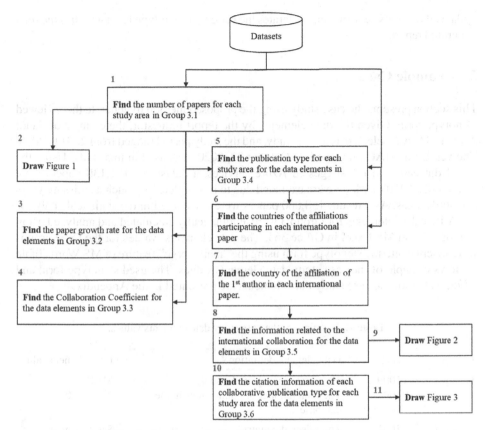

Fig. 4. Sequence of calculation group 3 data elements.

The figures are drawn using a set of the data elements calculated in Group 3. Three figures were suggested in the generated report. The first figure is a bar chart showing the percentage of publications of each study area in the selected country. This can be drawn by using a set of data elements from Group 3.1. The second figure is a star network showing the international collaborations between the selected country and other countries. This can be formed by using a set of data elements from Group 3.5. The third figure is a set of boxplots visualizing the distribution of citations per the publications type for each study area. This can be constructed by using data elements from Group 3.6.

After finding the values of the data elements, all groups' data elements and their values are saved in a.csv format. The stenotype form report is generated by substituting the data elements in the stereotype form by the assigned values in the.csv file and uploading the created figures in their right positions.

The stenotype form report is then given to three reviewers to check the report's consistency. They are asked to check each sentence in the report. If any sentence has a problem, they identify the type of the problem, and suggest a solution for each. After the reviewers complete their reviews, the editor reconciles among the suggested solutions, updates the stenotype form, and generates the reviewed stenotype form which is the final generated report.

3   Example Case

This section presents the case study using the proposed method to generate the reviewed stenotype form. Given the data elements by the report requestor, the country of Saudi Arabia (SA) was selected as a case study, and the study period ranged from 2001 to 2020. The version of MAG published on October 22, 2020, was used in this study. Using the MAG database and the suggested Azure services, a dataset of 181,130 papers were extracted, 22,270 of which were excluded due to incomplete data such as missing years and study areas. As a result, 158,860 papers were considered in the statistical analysis.

All the data elements for Group 3 were automatically calculated and analyzed using Python 3.7 and MS Excel in Office 365. The data elements' values for the three groups were inserted into the stenotype form using the "mail merge" feature of MS Word. Table 1 shows example of the case study data elements values. The used stenotype form and all the values of the case study data elements are presented in the Appendix.

Table 1. Example of the case study data elements values.

Group	Data element	Data element definition	Data element value
Group 1	$V1009 $V1004	The database used in the study The total number of publications in the database	MAG 244,000,000
Group 2	$V1001 $V1010 $V1011	The selected country Starting study year Ending study year	Saudi Arabia 2001 2020
Group 3.1	$V1013 $V1266	The study area has the highest number of papers The num. of papers in material science	Material science 28872
Group 3.2	$V1163 $V1601	% of growth rate for material science The study area has the strongest growth rate	23.18% Political Science
Group 3.4	$V1286 $V1306 $V1326	% of single authored paper in material science % of domestic paper in material science % of international paper in material science	7.32% 22.70% 69.98%
Group 3.5	$V1468 $V1488	The country has the highest num. of collaborations % of publications with United States	United States 18.76%
Group 3.6	$V1515 $V1610	% of citations of domestic paper in material science The study area has the highest citations in the international papers	23.45% Biology

The generated stenotype form was evaluated by three reviewers. They revealed five different types of problems: (1) the sentences that have information about the country of Vietnam; (2) the sentences that identify the used scholarly database; (3) the sentences that present information about the publications' category used in the analysis (journal, conference, or workshop); (4) the sentences that present complex information; and (5) the sentences that refer to the analysis tools. The reviewers suggested three types of solutions: (1) adding data elements for the piece of information related to the country; (2) rephrasing the sentences; and (3) removing the sentences. After the reviewers sent their suggested solutions to the editor, the editor reconciled among the solutions and generated the reviewed stenotype form.

4   Evaluation

A user study within a group of 10 domain experts was created to evaluate the reviewed stenotype form generated by the proposed method. An evaluation form using Qualtrics Survey API was designed and administered online. The form consists of four criteria: A. correctness; B. consistency; C. sufficiency; and D. quality. Each criterion consists of a set of questions concerning the generated report. The questions were accompanied by a five-point Likert scale ranging from "Strongly disagree" to "Strongly agree," as shown in Fig. 5. The evaluators were asked to read the reviewed stenotype report and fill out the evaluation form after reading.

It can be seen from Fig. 6 that most of the evaluators concentrated on the answer categories of "strongly agree" and "agree". However, in the first class, it can be noticed that a range from 10%–20% of the evaluators were not sure if the report consisted of

		Strongly Disagree	Disagree	Neutral	Agree	Strongly Agree
A.	**Correctness**					
	1- Sentences do not contradict each other's.	☐	☐	☐	☐	☐
	2- Sentences do not have incorrect data.	☐	☐	☐	☐	☐
	3- Sentences do not have incorrect information.	☐	☐	☐	☐	☐
	4- Sentences do not have grammatical errors	☐	☐	☐	☐	☐
B.	**Consistency**					
	1- The figures are compatible with the written description.	☐	☐	☐	☐	☐
	2- The tables are compatible with the written description.	☐	☐	☐	☐	☐
C.	**Sufficiency**					
	1- The report does not have irrelevant part.	☐	☐	☐	☐	☐
	2- The report does not have missing information.	☐	☐	☐	☐	☐
D.	**Report quality**					
	1. Overall report quality.	☐	☐	☐	☐	☐
	2. I learn something new from the report	☐	☐	☐	☐	☐

Fig. 5. Report evaluation form.

incorrect data, incorrect information, and grammatical errors. Also, in the third class, 10% of the evaluators were not sure if the report had missing information. Such responses can somewhat support the effectiveness of the generated report.

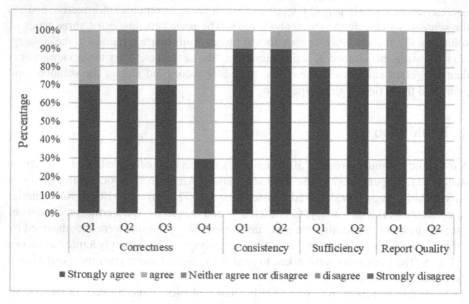

Fig. 6. Evaluation form results.

5   Conclusion

In this preliminary study, a model for generating a man/machine co-authoring report about a scientometric analysis for any selected country was introduced. To show the effectiveness of the proposed model, an experimental human/computer co-authored report for Saudi Arabia was generated, and it achieved a satisfactorily evaluation result.

The proposed model can have academic implications on scientometric researchers by providing them with the structure and the main steps that can help in generating a scientometric research analysis report. For future work, the study's researchers plan to make further improvements on assigning the data elements in the stereotype form report by using automation methods. Furthermore, conducting further statistical analysis to assess the generated report.

Appendix

Please visit the following link: http://medianet.kent.edu/techreports/TR2021-09-01-ScientometricAnalysis/TR2021-09-01-ScientometricReport.html for supporting files, including the data elements definitions, the reviewed stenotype form, and the data elements values of the case study.

References

1. Batcha, M.S., Ahmad, M.: Publication trend in an Indian journal and a Pakistan journal: a comparative analysis using scientometric approach. arXiv preprint arXiv:2102.12914 (2021)
2. Li, J., Goerlandt, F., Reniers, G.: An overview of scientometric mapping for the safety science community: Methods, tools, and framework. Saf. Sci. **134**, 105093 (2021). https://doi.org/10.1016/j.ssci.2020.105093
3. Derntl, M.: Basics of research paper writing and publishing. Int. J. Technol. Enhanced Learn. **6**(2), 105–123 (2014)
4. Astin, C., Harvey, C., Janusz, S.: Writing about science for publication. School Sci. Rev. **97**(359), 30–38 (2015)
5. Labbé, C., Labbé, D.: Duplicate and fake publications in the scientific literature: how many SCIgen papers in computer science? Scientometrics **94**(1), 379–396 (2013). https://doi.org/10.1007/s11192-012-0781-y
6. Noh, Y., et al.: WIRE: An Automated Report Generation System using Topical and Temporal Summarization. In: Proceedings of the 43rd International ACM SIGIR Conference on Research and Development in Information Retrieval (2020). https://doi.org/10.1145/3397271.3401409]
7. Gkatzia, D., Hastie, H.: An ensemble method for content selection for data-to-text systems. arXiv preprint arXiv:1506.02922 (2015)
8. Maas, L., et al.: The Care2Report system: automated medical reporting as an integrated solution to reduce administrative burden in healthcare (2020)
9. Nguyen, T.V., Ho-Le, T.P., Le, U.V.: International collaboration in scientific research in Vietnam: an analysis of patterns and impact. Scientometrics **110**(2), 1035–1051 (2016). https://doi.org/10.1007/s11192-016-2201-1
10. Ayers, M.: Quick review of Microsoft academic. Issues Sci. Technol. Librariansh. 96 (2020)
11. Salatino, A.A., Mannocci, A., Osborne, F.: Detection, analysis, and prediction of research topics with scientific knowledge graphs. In: Manolopoulos, Y., Vergoulis, T. (eds.) Predicting the Dynamics of Research Impact, pp. 225–252. Springer, Heidelberg (2021). https://doi.org/10.1007/978-3-030-86668-6_11
12. Platform, A.C., L'Esteve, R.C.: The Definitive Guide to Azure Data Engineering
13. Mazumdar, P., Agarwal, S., Banerjee, A.: Microsoft azure storage. In: Mazumdar, P., Agarwal, S., Banerjee, A. (eds.) Pro SQL Server on Microsoft Azure, pp. 35–52. Springer, Heidelberg (2016). https://doi.org/10.1007/978-1-4842-2083-2_3
14. Ropinski, T.: Combining interactive exploration and search for navigating academic citation data. Ulm University (2018)

WTM to Enhances Predictive Assessment of Systems Development Practices: A Case Study of Petroleum Drilling Project

Abdulaziz Ahmed Thawaba[1](✉), Azizul Azhar Ramli[2], and Mohd. Farhan Md. Fudzee[2]

[1] Faculty of Technology and Computer Science, University of Saba Region, Marib, Yemen
`azizth@usr.ac`
[2] Faculty of Computer Science and Information Technology, Universiti Tun Hussein Onn Malaysia, Parit Raja, 86400 Batu Pahat, Johor Darul Takzim, Malaysia
`{azizulr,farhan}@uthm.edu.my`

Abstract. Software engineering has devised several project management metrics to optimize implementation and obtain a product with high efficiency, at less time and cost. Inventors faced many challenges to find measurements that able to anticipate accurate results that help avoid errors and risks in the advanced stages of the project. The systems most affected by any errors during the development process are Safety-Critical systems (SCS), as 60% of failures during operation are due to errors during development. This paper proposes a metric that uses weight and milestones to predict implementation in advanced stages of a project. The proposed metric is called Weighted Test Metric (WTM). WTM enhance the reliability assessment and reduce failures during project development by predicting Standards Achievement (SA) in the next test. WTM results showed that faults can be reduced during the development of a petroleum drilling project to 0.67% and enhance the overall reliability to 99.16% while actual results (98.30%). This paper focuses on "How to enhance reliability assessment and reduce failures during project development activities?". This research raises the question through the application of WTM in the stages of development of the Petroleum Drilling Project.

Keywords: Safety-Critical System (SCS) · Safety-Critical System Development (SCSD) · Area: software project management metrics · Development metrics

1 Introduction

Software engineering uses metrics as an essential process throughout the system development life cycle to improve product quality [1]. There are many measurement tools that developers can use during system development. However, developers still facing huge challenges especially for the Safety-critical systems (SCS) require to measure every part of the development processes [2]. The SCS systems are used in various domains such as

J.-H. Kim et al. (Eds.): IHCI 2021, LNCS 13184, pp. 584–596, 2022.
https://doi.org/10.1007/978-3-030-98404-5_54

industrial, military, health systems, petroleum industry, spacecraft, traffic control systems etc. [3]. Developers should bear in mind that SCS systems cannot tolerate errors, and meeting SCS requirements is difficult due to the complexities of these systems [4]. For the horrible consequences of SCS systems failures, the real challenge for developers is how to reduced or terminated failures. Software companies and researchers found many solutions to minimize failures by applying new techniques, methods, standards and measurement metrics [5]. SCS systems require to measure development processes and ensures that implementation meets the standard and obtain reliability. This research will discuss project management metrics and how these metrics improve system development performance and reduce errors through weight technique and predictive evaluation. The remaining sections of this paper organized as follows; Sect. 2 is the theoretical basis for this paper, reviewing relevant research on software project management metrics, and the discussion case study (Petroleum Drilling project). Section 3 presents the Weighted Test Metric. Section 4 shows the research results and discussion. The final section is the conclusions and future directions.

2   Theoretical Background

2.1   Software Project Management Metrics

Successful project management remains a major challenge as a study showed that the performance of the 2013 projects was unsatisfactory with only 39% of projects implemented according to the required functions, within budget and on time [6]. Project management plays an important role by tracking implementation stages and ensuring that all changes applied according to budget and time [7]. Therefore, project management implemented various measurement techniques to control the development process and ensure the development of the final product following the specifications and standards [8]. Software engineering has improved the performance of project management tools by adding various metrics, such as requirements metrics, product metrics, and process metrics.

The metrics are routinely chosen to meet the requirements of project management improvement frameworks [9]. Process metrics are used to improve project development by detecting defects, determining response time to repair defects and removing defects [10]. There are some process metrics used weight to evaluate project performance, such as Weight Value (WV) or Weighted Milestone (WM). WV is the basis for calculating the overall progress used to determine the weight of each stage in the project. The project weight value is usually calculated as a percentage of the cost, meaning that the cost ratios for each task will be assigned as the project weight value. However, many factors may have a significant impact on the value of weight. Factors include size, quality, risk, and other values that can be assumed by high-level managers [11]. There are various methods for determining attribute values and weights. There are objective, subjective and complimentary weights. Good-weighting factors should only be used because weights are always subjective and influence the solution. WM is one of the Earned Value metrics that allow the management team to divide the work into small, measurable slides that each end with a milestone. The management team assigns a weighted value to each achieved milestone. WM is used as a long-term work package method, and it is best to have milestones for each month or accounting period [12]. The WM feature is measurable, objective milestones that are preferred by most clients and project managers. The disadvantage of WM is that it does not allow partial accreditation of ongoing work and requires detailed planning of milestone [13]. Some metrics use prediction techniques to improve end-product quality and reduce cost and time. The management team may also use forecasting metrics to forecast the progress of operations.

There are several prediction metrics that can use in developing SCS systems, such as Earned Value Management (EVM) and Agile Velocity. EVM is an integrated method to manage project costs and measure schedule performance. EVM analysis refers to a comparison of the project plan with implementation performance, and evaluation and forecast of future project performance [14]. EVM is generally used to measure project performance, but it can also be used to forecast of Estimated Cost at Completion and Time Estimated at Completion. Therefore, it provides project managers with information that can help at an early stage when taking corrective actions or the fate of the project [15]. The EVM control methodology was combined with an exponential prediction approach [16]. Agile offers promising solutions to overcome efficiency problems with appropriate procedures and measurements [17]. Agile Velocity measures the team's commitment to the current Sprint and also assists coordinate plans for future Sprints [18]. It is a planning tool to estimate how quickly the work is done and the time taken to complete the project. The Velocity diagram shows the average amount of work completed by a scrum team during a sprint, measured in terms of story points. The diagram is very useful for forecasts because it shows what is committed and what is delivered [19]. Also, the velocity graph shows typical highs and lows in an agile environment, given the complexity of the product and the ambiguity regarding requirements and real-life restrictions [20].

There are different types of measurements used to improve implementation performance and obtain a product that meets the standards. This paper examines two types of measurements used in project management, namely weight and prediction measures. This paper proposes a metric that uses weight technology to anticipate performance in the advanced stages of the project. The proposed measurement called Weighted Test Metric (WTM). It uses weight to predict the achievement in the stages of completion. WTM is one of the Package Metrics for Improving Software Development (PM-ISD) framework. PM-ISD is a project management measurement tool that has a set of metrics. PM-ISD can be applied to Safety-Critical System Development (SCSD) processes to support the management team through follow-up processes, verification of achievement of standards, forecasting of achievement and conformity of standards [21]. Table 1 shows comparisons between WTM and other metrics.

Table 1. Comparing WTM with other metrics

Metric	Type	Indicators	Description	Estimation Procedures
WTM	Predict (using Test weight)	Standards and Milestones	The predictive metric used to predict SA in the following test	Divide the project's milestones into several parts, create a weight for each milestone, and use the first test result to predict the results of the next tests
Weighted Value	Process (Weight)	Cost, Time, Task	To determine the cost weight of each stage in the project	Analytic Hierarchy Process, Expert judgment based on interrogation of experts, Entropy method and Integrated methods
Weighted Milestone	Process (Weight)	Time, Tasks	WM best to have milestones for accounting period	Divide the work into small, measurable slides that each end with a milestone
Velocity (Agile)	Predict (using performance)	Cost, Time, Sprint,	To estimate how quickly the work is done and the time taken	Use averages for previous projects. Monitor one or more velocities of iterations or sprints and calculate the velocity

2.2 Discussion Case Study

Petroleum systems are complex and multistage, in which the system can cover a large and applicable geographical range [22]. Industrial accidents are a threat factor in many different sectors and may cause human losses, environmental impact, or equipment damage. Different production lines contain thousands of tons of oil, which is usually flammable and toxic to humans and the environment. Therefore, any accidents that might be exposed to these lines will have serious consequences [23]. The pipeline network in this industry is very safe, but in the event of a pipeline failure, an petroleum leak can pose a major threat to the population and the environment [24]. The case study to be implemented in this research is the development of the petroleum field. The project can be divided into three sub-projects: sector development, construction of facilities, and geological and geophysical studies. Through the data obtained, the focus will be on sectors development data. The field contains four sectors, and each sector consists of a group of wells. The goal of the sector development is to drill new wells and connect them through the field pipeline network. The project's tasks are to drill 70 wells and prepare them for the petroleum extraction process. The one-year project development period started in January and ended in December. During the development period, 210 tests were performed through December 31 [25].

3   Weighted Test Metric (WTM)

Weighted Test Metric uses the test weight to predict the next results. WTM predicts achievement results for the next stages during systems development. WTM predictions are based on the first test results and project milestone weighted to predict the results of the following tests. The WTM can predict the task achievement, standards compliance and cost spending. Figure 1 shows the flow of WTM procedures. The project management team divides implementation into milestones, the division mechanism according to the type of system, project accomplishments or schedule. Then, start creating a weight for each milestone using its sub-tasks/functions divided by the sum of the subtasks for all the milestones.

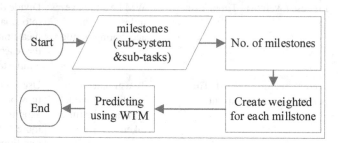

Fig. 1. WTM procedures for determining achievement weight and prediction

WTM procedures for determining achievement weight and predicting the achievement in the next tests are as follow:

1. Divide the project into several milestones (each contains several sub-tasks/functions)
2. Determine the milestone weight using the following equations:

   I.   Weighted milestone for sub-system

$$MWS = \frac{No.TAM}{No.AT} * 100 \tag{1}$$

Equation (1) calculates the milestone weight for sub-system (**MWS**) by dividing the number of sub-tasks to be accomplished at the end of the milestone (**No.TAM**) with the number of all sub-tasks (**No.AT**), then multiplying the result by 100 to obtain the weight by a percentage.

II. Weight milestone for sub-task

$$MWT = \frac{No.FAM}{No.AF} * 100 \tag{2}$$

Equation (2) calculates the milestone weight for sub-task (**MWT**) by dividing the number of functions to be accomplished at the end of the milestone (**No.FAM**) with the number of all functions (**No.AF**), then multiplying the result by 100 to obtain the weight by a percentage.

3. Use the first test result to predict the results of the following two tests (Test2 and Test3) using the following equations:

$$AW1 = \frac{MA}{TW} * MAW1 \tag{3}$$

Equation (3) calculates the achievement of the sub-tasks/functions for the first test according to the weight of milestone one (**AW1**) by dividing the results of the current milestone achievement (**MA**) of the first test with the total project tasks achievement (**TW** - 100), then multiplying the result with milestone achievement weight of the first milestone (**MAW1**).

$$ANT2 = AW1 + MAW2 \tag{4}$$

Equation (4) calculates the sub-tasks/functions that must be achieved in the next test (**ANT2**) based on the weight of the second milestone, by summing the milestone achievement weight for the first test (**AW1**) with the achievement weight of the second milestone (**MAW2**).

$$AW2 = \frac{ANT2}{TW} * MAW2 \tag{5}$$

Equation (5) calculates the achievement weight for the next test (**AW2**) by dividing the achievement for the next test (**ANT2**) with the total project tasks achievement (**TW**-100), then multiplying the result with achievement weight of the second milestone (**MAW2**).

$$PMAT2 = ANT2 + MAW2 \tag{6}$$

Equation (6) predicts the milestone achievement in the next test (**PMAT2**) by summing the sub-tasks/functions must be achieved in the next test (**ANT2**) with the milestone achievement weight for the next test (**MAW2**).

$$ANT3 = ANT2 + MAW3 \tag{7}$$

Equation (7) calculates the sub-tasks/functions that must be achieved in the next test (**ANT3**) based on the weight of the third milestone, by summing the achievement for the test two (**ANT2**) with the achievement weight of the third milestone (**AW3**).

$$AW3 = \frac{ANT3}{TW} * MAW3 - MAW3 \tag{8}$$

Equation (8) calculates the achievement weight for the next test (**AW3**) by dividing the achievement for the next test (**ANT3**) with the total project tasks achievement (**TW**-100), then multiplying the result with achievement weight of the third milestone (**MAW3**). Then MAW3 subtracts from the total to ensure that the final results will not exceed 100.

$$PMAT3 = ANT3 + MAW3 \qquad (9)$$

Equation (9) predicts the milestone achievement in the next test (**PMAT3**) by summing the prediction of sub-tasks/functions that will achieve in the third test (**ANT3**) with the milestone achievement weight for the next test (**MAW3**).

4   Research Results and Discussion

4.1   WTM Results

The petroleum (Oil & Gas well drilling) project used WTM to predict Standards Achievement (SA) in the next test. WTM depends on two factors, the result of the first test, and the weight of the milestones. Milestone Weight is the percentage of functions that must be performed at a specific time for a task/sub-task. WTM is suitable for projects with visible milestones during the development of the life cycle for each task/sub-task. The petroleum project has clear milestones. Figure 2 shows prediction results for test 2 and test 3 using the results of test 1 and milestones weight. WTM results consist of SA for the first test, SA weight for the first test, SA must be achieved in the next test (2), SA weight for the next test (2), Predicting SA in the next test (2), SA must be achieved in the next test (3), SA weight for the next test (3) and Predicting SA in the next test (3). WTM used current SA results to predict SA achievement for Test (2) and Test (3). From the petroleum project dataset, there are three milestones for each sub-task. The first weight is 50%, the second weight is 30%, and the third weight is 20%.

Development of Oil and Gas Sectors A - B - C - D
Weighted Test Metric (WTM)

ID	Task ID	Task Name	Standards Achieved	Standards Achievement Weight 1 (SAW1)	Standards Achieved Next Test (SANT2)	Standards Achievement Weight 2 (SAW2)	Predicts Standards Achievement for Next Test (PSAT2)	Standards Achieved Next Test (SANT3)	Standards Achievement Weight 3 (SAW3)	Predicts Standards Achievement for Next Test (PSAT3)
1	TPO-D-SA-W1	Sector A: Well number 1	97.9	48.95	78.95	18.685	97.64	98.95	-0.21	98.74
2	TPO-D-SA-W10	Sector A: Well number 10	94.2	47.1	77.1	18.13	95.23	97.1	-0.58	96.52
3	TPO-D-SA-W11	Sector A: Well number 11	95.4	47.7	77.7	18.31	96.01	97.7	-0.46	97.24
4	TPO-D-SA-W12	Sector A: Well number 12	95.5	47.75	77.75	18.325	96.08	97.75	-0.45	97.3
5	TPO-D-SA-W13	Sector A: Well number 13	96	48	78	18.4	96.40	98	-0.40	97.6
6	TPO-D-SA-W14	Sector A: Well number 14	95.5	47.75	77.75	18.325	96.08	97.75	-0.45	97.3
7	TPO-D-SA-W15	Sector A: Well number 15	84.2	42.1	72.1	16.63	88.73	92.1	-1.58	90.52
8	TPO-D-SA-W16	Sector A: Well number 16	96.6	48.3	78.3	18.49	96.79	98.3	-0.34	97.96
9	TPO-D-SA-W17	Sector A: Well number 17	96.2	48.1	78.1	18.43	96.53	98.1	-0.38	97.72
10	TPO-D-SA-W18	Sector A: Well number 18	86.2	43.1	73.1	16.93	90.03	93.1	-1.38	91.72

Fig. 2. SA prediction results for test 2 and test 3

WTM predicts the SA results for the following tests by using task weight and milestone weight. The following steps show how to calculate the following tests for sub-task (TP0-D-SA-W1) from the Petroleum project:

1- Standards Achievement (SA) current results of the first test
2- SA first test results for sub-task (TP0-D-SA-W1) = 97.9
3- Calculate weights using project milestones, for the Petroleum project there are three milestones for each sub-task, and the weights set as; Task total weight = 100, Task Weight (1) = 50, Task Weight (2) = 30, and Task Weight (3) = 20.
4- Calculates the achievement of the standards for the first test according to the weight of milestone one (SAW1).

$$SAW1 = \frac{Standard\ achievement}{Task\ total\ weight} * Task\ Weight(1) = 48.95$$

5- Calculates the standards that must be achieved in the next test (SANT2) based on the weight of the second part.

$$SANT2 = SAW1 + Task\ Weight(2) = 78.95$$

6- Calculates the standards achievement weight for the next test (SAW2)

$$SAW2 = \frac{SANT2}{Task\ total\ weight} * Task\ Weight(2) = 18.685$$

7- Predicts the achievement of the standards in the next test (PSAT2)

$$PSAT2 = SANT2 + SAW2 = 97.635$$

8- Calculates the standards that must be achieved in the next test (SANT3)

$$SANT3 = SANT2 + TAW3 = 98.95$$

9- Calculates the standards achievement weight for the next test (SAW3)

$$SAW3 = \left(\frac{SANT3}{Task\ total\ weight} * Task\ Weight(3)\right) - Task\ Weight(3) = -0.21$$

10- Predicts the SA in the next test (PSAT3)

$$PSAT3 = SANT3 + SAW3 = 98.74$$

The example in Fig. 3 shows the prediction result for the TP0-D-SB-W7 sub-task from the Development of Petroleum project. Actual results of Standards Achievement (SA) 77.9%. WTM SA predicted in the next two tests at 84.635% and 86.74%. The final reliability rating of TP0-D-SB-W7 is 84.04% and failure may occur but there is time available to avoid failure. WTM predicts the SA of the following tests and calculates the reliability for each test through the following:

1- Predicts the achievement of the standards in the next test
2- Calculate the failure, failure rate, fault tolerance and reliability. The acceptable standards rate used by WTM is 95 and using following:

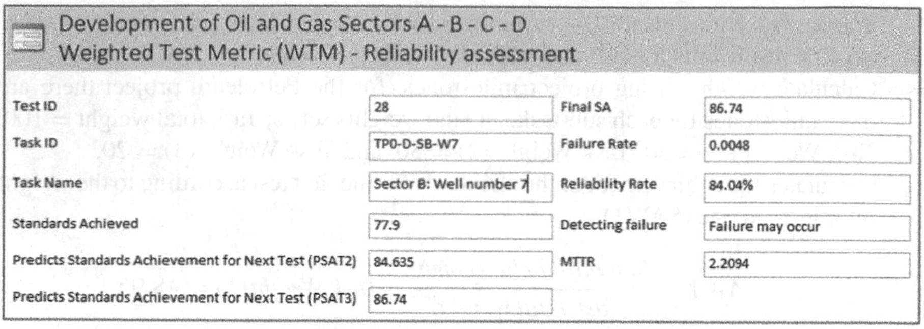

Development of Oil and Gas Sectors A - B - C - D Weighted Test Metric (WTM) - Reliability assessment			
Test ID	28	Final SA	86.74
Task ID	TP0-D-SB-W7	Failure Rate	0.0048
Task Name	Sector B: Well number 7	Reliability Rate	84.04%
Standards Achieved	77.9	Detecting failure	Failure may occur
Predicts Standards Achievement for Next Test (PSAT2)	84.635	MTTR	2.2094
Predicts Standards Achievement for Next Test (PSAT3)	86.74		

Fig. 3. WTM results for reliability assessment and failure detection

- *Number of Failures = Standards Rate Acceptance − Results of Standards*

$$Fault\ Tolerance = 100 - \left(\frac{No.\ of\ Failures}{Standards\ Rate\ Acceptance} * 100 \right)$$

$$failure\ rate = \frac{No.\ of\ Failures}{(Acceptable\ Standards\ Rate)(Time\ consumed)}$$

- Calculate the reliability rate

$$Reliability\ rate = e^{-\lambda t} = 2.71828^{-(failure\ rate)(Total\ Time)}$$

3- Detecting faults according to the following statements: If: Reliability Rate = 1, "No failure (prevention) continuous measuring", Else: "Faults may occur"

4.2 Research Discussion

WTM used current results and milestone's weight to predict the next results. The petroleum project contains three milestones for each task/sub-task. WTM used the results of the first milestone test to predict the results of the next two phases. WTM enhances reliability assessment by using two weighted techniques, which are Task Weighted Value and Weighted Milestone for predicting the completion of the next test and achieving the standards.

Table 2 shows the WTM results compared to the actual (previous) results. WTM predicted the final test result for all sub-tasks to comply with standards of 96.9% and 3.1% require action by management to avoid failures. The fault tolerance ratio for the actual results of the petroleum project was 99.27% and failure 0.69%. WTM increased the fault tolerance rate and failure decreased. WTM results showed that faults can be reduced to 0.67%. WTM enhanced the overall reliability of the following tests for 70 subtasks with 99.16%. The WTM shows an affinity with actual results in terms of reliability, demonstrating the usefulness and positive impact of this metric in enhancing the assessment of the SCS development process.

Table 2. Comparing WTM results with actual results

Comparison criteria	Actual results (Previous)		Predicting WTM	
	Completed	≥95	Meet standard	Required action
Subtasks completed and complying with standards	94.3%	95.8%	96.9%	3.1%
Failure	0.69%		0.67%	
Fault tolerance	99.27%		99.3%	
Reliability	98.30%		99.16%	

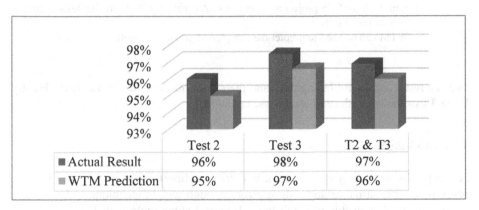

	Test 2	Test 3	T2 & T3
■ Actual Result	96%	98%	97%
■ WTM Prediction	95%	97%	96%

Fig. 4. Matching WTM results with current results for sub-tasks accomplishment

Figure 4 shows all WTM predicting results of the test (2) and test (3) for all subtasks, and the actual results from the dataset of the petroleum project. The difference between WTM prediction results and actual results is less than 2% which is an excellent forecast result. The results show a great convergence as the difference between WTM predictions and actual results was only 1%. Therefore, WTM achieved amazing results with the expectation of SA in the stage of completing all the sub-tasks of the petroleum project. WTM used weight to obtain accurate results to meet standards in the next stages using current results of SA and weighted milestone. Through a petroleum project, WTM has proven to be an excellent metric because it harmoniously uses weight and prediction techniques to improve project implementation performance. WTM predicted implementation compliance of standards in the second and third tests for each sub-task using the results of the first test. WTM used seven equations based on two indicators: the product standards and project milestones. The results of WTM showed accuracy by matching with actual results by 98.9%. Therefore, WTM is an excellent metric to help project management improve product quality and reduce cost and time.

Table 3 shows the features of the WTM metric by highlighting the type of measurement, the technique used to measure, indicators, number of equations, data required, and the classification mechanism used to classify the prediction results. It also displays the

Table 3. Features of WTM metric

Feature	Explanation
Type	Metric use to predict the SA for task/sub-task using the weighted test
Technique	Weighed-test combines the task-weight and the milestone-weight
Indicator	Standards and Milestones
Equation	Seven equations
Outcomes	Predicting SA in the next test (2), Predicting SA in the test (3) and expected reliability ratios of standards compliance for the next test
Strengths	Provides accurate results because it uses the weight of the milestone. It can implement in the development of large projects or small projects. WTM will be useful for the SCS project as it provides SA results for the following tests using the current test results WTM can be used to predict the completion of a task as well

forecast results of the following tests and their compliance with the standards. Finally, Table 3 lists the strengths and weaknesses of WTM.

5 Conclusion

This paper discussed project management metrics and how these metrics improve system development performance and reduce errors through weight technique and predictive evaluation. Studies in this research have discussed some metrics that use techniques such as weights or prediction. This research has proposed a WTM metric that combines weighing and forecasting techniques for more accurate results. The results of WTM showed high accuracy while applying to the dataset of the petroleum drilling project, as the efficiency ratio reached 98.9%. The accuracy of WTM will enable the project management team to take appropriate decisions early, which reduces errors and avoids risks during project stages. Making the right decisions will lead to obtaining a product with high efficiency in less time and cost. Project milestones are the cornerstone of WTM, so lack of clarity will lead to inaccurate results. Therefore, future research should focus on finding a mechanism for calculating project milestones, taking into account the characteristics of systems.

Acknowledgment. This research was supported by Ministry of Higher Education (MOHE) trough Fundamental Research Grant Scheme (FRGS/1/2019/ICT01/UTHM/02/2). We also want to thank to the Government of Malaysia which provide MyBrain15 programme for sponsoring this work under the self-funded research grant and L00022 from Ministry of Science, Technology and Innovation (MOSTI).

References

1. Garg, R.K., et al.: Ranking of software engineering metrics by fuzzy-based matrix method-ology. Softw. Test. Verification Reliab. **23**(2), 149–168 (2013). https://doi.org/10.1002/stv r.459
2. Thawaba, A.A., Ramli, A.A., Fudzee, M.F.M., Wadata, J.: Characteristics for performance optimization of safety-critical system development (SCSD). J. Adv. Comput. Intell. Intell. Inform. **24**(2), 232–242 (2020). https://doi.org/10.20965/jaciii.2020.p0232
3. Martins, L.E.G., Gorschek, T.: Requirements engineering for safety-critical systems: a sys-tematic literature review. Inf. Softw. Technol. **75**, 71–89 (2016). https://doi.org/10.1016/j.inf sof.2016.04.002
4. Kuchuk, G., Kharchenko, V., Kovalenko, A., Ruchkov, E.: Approaches to selection of com-binatorial algorithm for optimization in network traffic control of safety-critical systems. In: 2016 IEEE East-West Design & Test Symposium (EWDTS), Yerevan, Armenia, pp. 1–6 (2016). https://doi.org/10.1109/EWDTS.2016.7807655
5. Trivedi, P., Sharma, A.: A comparative study between iterative waterfall and incremental software development life cycle model for optimizing the resources using computer simula-tion. In: 2013 2nd International Conference on Information Management in the Knowledge Economy, pp. 188–194 (2013)
6. Liu, S.: How the user liaison's understanding of development processes moderates the effects of user-related and project management risks on IT project performance. Inf. Manag. **53**(1), 122–134 (2016). https://doi.org/10.1016/j.im.2015.09.004
7. Chen, Y.-S., Wu, C., Chu, H.-H., Lin, C.-K., Chuang, H.-M.: Analysis of performance measures in cloud-based ubiquitous SaaS CRM project systems. J. Supercomput. **74**(3), 1132–1156 (2017). https://doi.org/10.1007/s11227-017-1978-x
8. Silva, N., Vieira, M.: Towards making safety-critical systems safer: learning from mistakes. In: 2014 IEEE International Symposium on Software Reliability Engineering Workshops, Naples, Italy, pp. 162–167 (2014). https://doi.org/10.1109/ISSREW.2014.97
9. Jethani, K.: Software metrics for effective project management. Int. J. Syst. Assur. Eng. Manag. **4**(4), 335–340 (2012). https://doi.org/10.1007/s13198-012-0101-1
10. Bubevski, V.: A novel approach to software quality risk management. Softw. Test. Verif. Reliab. **24**(2), 124–154 (2014). https://doi.org/10.1002/stvr.1488
11. Zorriassatine, F., Bagherpour, M.: A new method for estimating project weight values. J. Appl. Sci. **9**(5), 917–923 (2009)
12. Hamilton, B.A.: Earned value management tutorial module 5: EVMS concepts and methods. Department of Energy, United States of America (2017). https://www.energy.gov/sites/prod/files/2017/06/f35/EVMModule5_0.pdf
13. Abd-Elkhalek, H.A., Aziz, R.F., Mohamed, M.M.: EVM Modifications To Improve Cost Control Of Construction Projects. Int. J. Eng. Sci. Res. Technol. (2016)
14. Ju, H., Xu, S.: Research status of earned value management. In: Li, X., Xu, X. (eds.) Proceed-ings of the Fourth International Forum on Decision Sciences. UOR, pp. 449–459. Springer, Singapore (2017). https://doi.org/10.1007/978-981-10-2920-2_38
15. Helmeriksen, I.S.: Enhanced earned value analysis - improving visibility and forecasts in projects by introduction of clusters, 11 S (2017). https://openarchive.usn.no/usn-xmlui/han dle/11250/2452715. Accessed 29 Dec 2019
16. Batselier, J., Vanhoucke, M.: Improving project forecast accuracy by integrating earned value management with exponential smoothing and reference class forecasting. Int. J. Proj. Manag. **35**(1), 28–43 (2017). https://doi.org/10.1016/j.ijproman.2016.10.003
17. Özcan-Top, Ö., McCaffery, F.: To what extent the medical device software regulations can be achieved with agile software development methods? XP—DSDM—Scrum. J. Supercomput. **75**(8), 5227–5260 (2019). https://doi.org/10.1007/s11227-019-02793-x

18. Damiani, E., Spanoudakis, G., Maciaszek, L.A. (eds.): Evaluation of Novel Approaches to Software Engineering. CCIS, vol. 1172. Springer, Cham (2020). https://doi.org/10.1007/978-3-319-94135-6
19. Agarwal, M., Majumdar, R.: Tracking scrum projects tools, metrics and myths about agile. Int. J. Emerg. Technol. Adv. Eng. **2**, 97–104 (2012)
20. Budacu, E.N., Pocatilu, P.: Real time agile metrics for measuring team performance. Inform. Econ. **22**(4), 70–79 (2018)
21. Thawaba, A., Ramli, A., Fudzee, M.F.Md., Wadata, J.: A mechanism to support agile frameworks enhancing reliability assessment for SCS development: a case study of medical surgery departments. In: Ghazali, R., Nawi, N.M., Deris, M.M., Abawajy, J.H. (eds.) Recent Advances on Soft Computing and Data Mining. Advances in Intelligent Systems and Computing, pp. 66–76. Springer, Cham (2020). https://doi.org/10.1007/978-3-030-36056-6_7
22. Byrne, D.J., Barry, P.H., Lawson, M., Ballentine, C.J.: Noble gases in conventional and unconventional petroleum systems. Geol. Soc. Lond. Spec. Publ. **468**(1), 127–149 (2018). https://doi.org/10.1144/SP468.5
23. Samia, C., Hamzi, R., Chebila, M.: Contribution of the lessons learned from oil refining accidents to the industrial risks assessment. Manag. Environ. Qual. Int. J. **29**(4), 643–665 (2018). https://doi.org/10.1108/MEQ-07-2017-0067
24. Mahmoodian, M., Li, C.Q.: Failure assessment and safe life prediction of corroded oil and gas pipelines. J. Pet. Sci. Eng. **151**, 434–438 (2017). https://doi.org/10.1016/j.petrol.2016.12.029
25. Najar, S., Al-Kawse, N.: The fourth stage of developing sectors A, B, C and D of the oil and gas fields - the sixth zone. Akhsat- Ma'reb/Shabwh, Report of the Department of the Development of Oil and Gas Fields- Sixth Zone 1-43A-DSOG (2018)

Face and Face Mask Detection Using Convolutional Neural Network

Muhammad Mustaqim Zainal[1], Radzi Ambar[1,2(✉)], Mohd Helmy Abd Wahab[1], Hazwaj Mhd Poad[1], Muhammad Mahadi Abd Jamil[1], and Chew Chang Choon[1]

[1] Department of Electronic Engineering, Faculty of Electrical and Electronic Engineering, Universiti Tun Hussein Onn Malaysia, 86400 Parit Raja, Batu Bahat, Johor, Malaysia
aradzi@uthm.edu.my
[2] Computational Signal, Image and Intelligence Research Focus Group, Universiti Tun Hussein Onn Malaysia, 86400 Parit Raja, Batu Bahat, Johor, Malaysia

Abstract. The COVID-19 outbreak has posed a severe healthcare concern in Malaysia. Wearing a mask is the most effective way to prevent infections. However, some Malaysians refuse to wear a face mask for a variety of reasons. This work proposes a real-time face and face mask detection method using image processing technique to promote wearing face mask. Haar Cascade is used for the face detection to extract the features of the human faces as a method of approach. On the other hand, the face mask detection utilizes convolutional neural network (CNN) to train a model using the MobileNetV2 training model designed using Python, Keras and Tensorflow. OpenCV package was used as the interface for the algorithms to be connected to a web camera. Based on the performance metric calculation of detection rate analysis of the experimental results, the face detection rate is at 90% true and 10% false detection, which shows very good detection rate. Furthermore, the training accuracy and validation accuracy for the face mask detector are efficiently near to 1.0, proving a steady accuracy over the time. Training loss and validation loss are almost near to zero and decreasing over time, reassuring the algorithm performance is accurate and efficient for a datasets of 4000 images.

Keywords: Face mask detection · Face detection · Image processing · Convolutional neural network

1 Introduction

In Malaysia, the government has declared the first standard operating procedures (SOP) to prevent COVID-19 major outbreak in the early of 2020, after the first case was reported in Malaysia of a traveler coming back from China [1]. The government has also declared a Movement Control Order (MCO) to handle and contain the spread of the virus. The move had successfully taken control of the situation in an orderly manner preventing a panic situation from happening among the people [2]. The SOP includes social distancing of 1 m between people and also mandatory face mask wearing in public places as a fine would be issued from any SOP misconduct.

© Springer Nature Switzerland AG 2022
J.-H. Kim et al. (Eds.): IHCI 2021, LNCS 13184, pp. 597–609, 2022.
https://doi.org/10.1007/978-3-030-98404-5_55

In the effort to fight against the virus outbreak, apart from issuing new laws and SOP, multiple efforts has been implemented to cope with the situation by utilizing the technology of the modern civilization. An alternative innovation to combat the spread of COVID-19 is by utilizing image processing technology that has always been part of human daily lives. Image processing technology has enabled human to achieve unthinkable task such as object detections [3], imagery editing [4] and even medicinal usage [5]. The use of image processing technology have also been applied to cope with the current pandemic situation in various stages such as detection, prevention and response stages. For instance, [6] proposed an image processing techniques to classify computed tomography (CT) chest images into normal or infected based on artificial intelligence algorithm. Recently, [7] utilized deep learning technique for computer-assisted screening tool of lung ultrasound imagery to diagnose pulmonary conditions caused by COVID-19 infection. These are examples of image processing application in detection stage. On the other hand, a study in [8] is an example of prevention stage application, where a real-time video stream-based image processing technique using YOLOv3 has been proposed to maintain social distancing in closed environment. Then, authors in [9] introduced a simulation of camera equipped drone-based network system that can capture individual images to measure social distancing and thermal images The work is an example of COVID-19 outbreak prevention stage.

It is well-informed that one of the most important preventive measure to control the outbreak of COVID-19 is by wearing face mask. Several countries have introduced rules and regulations to enforce wearing face mask in public places and closed facilities. However, it is impossible to perfectly impose these regulations because not all individuals willing to wear face mask in public places and the authority do not have enough man power to enforce the laws. Therefore, automatic system utilizing image processing techniques can be utilized to execute face mask detection in real-time. The main aim for this project is to detect human face wearing a face mask and without face mask using image processing technology and artificial intelligence (AI). The project hopefully can be a future preventive measure to warn the public to wear face mask before going to public places, thus, lowering the infection cases of COVID-19.

2   Methodology

Deep learning is an artificial intelligence (AI) function that mimics the workings of a human brain in processing data. It is also a class of deep neural networks using multiple layers of extracting features from an input [10]. In deep learning, image processing is a part of neural networks learning involving computer vision system. The capability of machine learning in computer vision can be used to assist human in object detections [3], face detections [11] and face recognition [11]. This can be implemented to counter the current pandemic by developing a system which can be used to detect and distinct face mask user and non-user.

2.1   Convolutional Neural Network (CNN)

In deep learning, CNN is utilized specifically in analysing visual imagery [4, 12]. Its algorithms are able to take an input image and assign importance such as the learnable weight and biases, and be able to differentiate one from the other. Figure 1 shows the architecture of CNN. It is made up of multiple layers of process through which the information of an input image are filtered, and the importance extracted according to the algorithms. The input takes a 2 dimensional image and process it to be classified into categories. Each layer of the process in the architecture of CNN is described in the next subchapters.

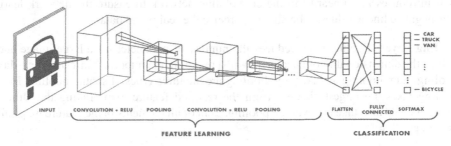

Fig. 1. Convolutional Neural Network [12].

Convolution Layer. The first layer is the convolution layer where features from an input image are extracted, whilst preserving the pixels relationships by using image data (input) from small squares. This is done to reduce the scale of the input image for simplifying the process. The process involves an arithmetic operation that uses two inputs for example an image matrix (volume) of dimension (height x width x depth) and a filter matrix (f_h x f_w x $depth$), where f_h is filter for height, f_w is filter for width, respectively.

As shown in Fig. 2, the image matrix will be multiplied with a filter through a process called Feature Mapping. The image matrix with pixels values of 0 and 1 are multiplied to fit the filter. Convolution of an image with different filters can perform operations such as edge detection, blur and sharpen by applying filters.

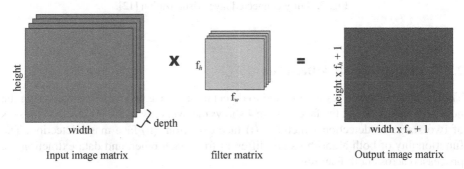

Fig. 2. Feature mapping by multiplying image matrix with a filter matrix.

Strides, Padding and Non-Linearity (ReLU). When convolution is executed, the filter (kernel) is shifted over the input matrix, which is called a stride. Depending on the stride value, the pixels is moved accordingly. In each stride, matrix multiplication operations are performed between the filter matrix and the image matrix part that the filter is hovering, until the entire image is hovered to produce convoluted output as shown in Fig. 2. Padding is done when a filter does not fit an input image perfectly by zero padding or dropping the part of unfit image. Rectified Linear Unit (ReLU) is important as it introduces non-linearity in the convolution network to ensure the network learn non-negative linear values to be able to perceive the real world data.

Pooling Layer. Pooling layer reduces the number of parameter for a large image and reduce the dimensionality of each map whilst retaining the important information. Max Pooling, Sum Pooling and Average Pooling are the three types of spatial pooling. Max pooling takes the largest element from the rectified feature map. Taking the largest element could also take the average pooling. Sum of all elements in the feature map call as sum pooling.

Fully Connected Layer. Figure 3 shows a visualization of a fully connected layer formed by flattening the matrixes into vectors and fed to the fully connected layer like a neural networks [12]. The feature map matrix will be converted to vectors (x1, x2, x3, x4) within the fully connected layer to create a model with an activation function to classify input image into categories (y1, y2, y3).

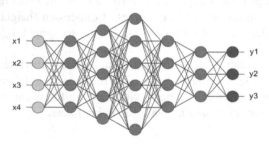

Fig. 3. Fully connected layer visualization [12].

2.2 Face and Face Mask Detection

This subchapter describes the method to detect human face and face mask covering the nose and mouth area of the face. Figure 4 shows the overview of the project that consists of two stages of detection which are (i) face detection, (ii) face mask detection. The functionality of both algorithms are different from each other, and data extraction are processed across both features.

The first stage is face detection. The algorithm starts with raw input of images and the cascade classifier extract the feature of a human face from the input and process it to be passed on to the recognizer where the human faces seen through the computer vision would be recognized and detected. The second stage is the face mask detection where the object detection algorithms are being used as a reference. The input images are preprocessed to be passed on to the CNN layers using the model trainer architecture of convolution, and the created model will be a recognizer for face mask detection through the computer vision system. The face mask detector will output two types of coloured frames on the video stream in real-time, green frames for faces with face masks, and red frame for non-face mask faces. In order to design the system using Python, a number of software packages are required which are Anaconda software, Keras application programming interface (API) with its libraries and Tensorflow. The training model used is the MobileNetV2, a small sized package that can carry the operations of CNN with a high accuracy and minimal losses. The OpenCV package was used as the interface for the algorithms to be connected to the webcam.

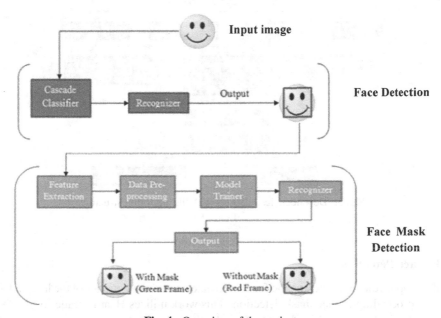

Fig. 4. Overview of the project.

Figure 5 shows the four main dependencies used to develop the algorithms which are the Keras library together with its backend Tensorflow library for deep and machine learning. This allows for construction of the algorithm possible with the wide range of programmable commands of artificial neural networks. Besides that, the training model is MobileNetV2 used for convolution layer during model training process. Lastly, OpenCV is used for its library which enables computer vision interaction and feature extraction. The dataset of people wearing face mask are obtained from Kaggle website.

The next stage is the process stage. Pre-processing is the process where datasets are augmented before being fed to the CNN layers. The image parameters are altered in the preprocessed section to enable feature extraction to be more accurate. During the CNN process, the model training began for a time period pre-set in the algorithm. The parameters for CNN layer affect the training performance of the model created. The real time video interface is the OpenCV dependencies feature to use the trained model as a recognizer and determine the detection parameter such as frame, prediction of detection and starting the interface for the program.

The interconnected arrows which moves in both ways shows the relationship of the features are interconnected and influence the performance of each feature. The algorithm uses the computer vision system, the built in web camera to begin detection and displays an output on the monitor screen. The expected output are the face detection and face mask detection.

Fig. 5. Dependencies relations with the algorithm structure.

2.3 Face Detection

In developing the face detector, the focus is to detect the characteristics of the human face before proceeding to face mask detection. This work utilizes Haar cascade for the face detector, which is a machine learning based approach where a cascade is trained with the input image data to identify the important features of a human face to be detected. OpenCV is the dependencies required for face detection, as it contains many pre-trained classifier such as the detector for eyes, nose and mouth.

Figure 6 shows the subject in the input image is seen through the web camera, then, the pre-process occurs whilst extracting feature from the subject. The classifier then examines the input data from the feature extractor to be compared with a model database for producing the output. The model database is acquired from the internet to assist in the development of the project. After a successful face detection, a frame (bounding box) is displayed around the subject face on the monitor screen and detects it in real time.

Feature Extraction and Classifier. The feature extraction utilizes the OpenCV built in libraries called Haar cascade. Haar cascade works as a cascade function that is trained

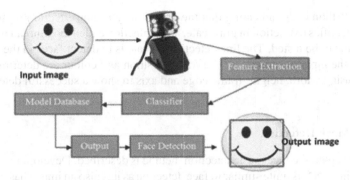

Fig. 6. Flow for face detection algorithm.

to have positive and negative images which is then used for object detection in other images. The cascade takes the input image and cascade the information in black/white squares as feature extraction. The classifier chosen for face detection is the face classifier as the algorithm is written to detect the whole human face area. Figure 7 shows a screen capture of the Python code indicating the Haar cascade function is utilized specifically to detect faces as the line face_cascade indicates. Furthermore, it is used to extract feature related to the human faces.

```
3    # Load the cascade
4    face_cascade = cv2.CascadeClassifier('haarcascade_frontalface_default.xml')
```

Fig. 7. Haar cascade function is loaded into the coding.

```
5    # Read the input image
6    img = cv2.imread('test.jpg')
7    # Convert into grayscale
8    gray = cv2.cvtColor(img, cv2.COLOR_BGR2GRAY)
9    # Detect faces
10   faces = face_cascade.detectMultiScale(gray, 1.1, 4)
11   # Draw rectangle around the faces
12   for (x, y, w, h) in faces:
13       cv2.rectangle(img, (x, y), (x+w, y+h), (255, 0, 0), 2)
14   # Display the output
15   cv2.imshow('img', img)
16   cv2.waitKey()
```

Fig. 8. Parameter setting for face detection.

Model Database and Output. The model database contains all the pre-trained classifier of the OpenCV libraries. The input image information is extracted according to the detection parameters. The output parameter is also determine in the algorithm as the wanted values needed to be set before program execution. Figure 8 shows a screen capture of Python code indicating that the input image is converted to grayscale as the classifier identifies extraction in grayscale, and a function called cv2.imread is to declare the image file to be tested. The line detectMultiScale is to detect faces in the image and converting the input to grayscale. The frame position and colour are determined in the algorithm using width, height, frame edge and axis to show a successful detection.

2.4   Face Mask Detection

In this subchapter, the face mask detection method is described. Developing a face mask detector using CNN is quite similar to face detection as it is also an image based approach method. A collection of datasets are fed to a model trainer with the exception of having two output. The first output is a face wearing a face mask and the other is a face without a face mask. The algorithm is written to predict the probability of presence of a face mask or without face mask which then will be shown in the monitor.

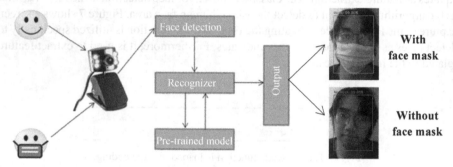

Fig. 9.   Face mask detection: without face mask and with face mask.

Figure 9 shows the overview of the proposed face mask detection algorithm. First, a still image or video streams from webcam is converted into single frame that is fed to the algorithm for face detection. From the face detection, the recognizer compares the feature extracted through the face detection with the pre-trained model of face mask detection and yield the output in a prediction values of a face mask detection percentage.

3   Experimental Results and Discussion

In this chapter, the performance of the proposed face and face mask detection algorithms are demonstrated. The obtained experimental results were tested using video and images containing a maximum of six (6) individuals in a household, as performing experiments in larger scale are restricted with the ongoing pandemic situation. The main aim is to ensure the functionality of the algorithms. Experiments were done using both real-time video stream and still images.

3.1   Face Detection Experiment

Figure 10 shows that the algorithm has successfully detected the face area and initiated blue frames around the desired faces area on a still image. The accuracy and consistency of face detection depends on the number of subject and the specification of machine used to run the program. It was found that a slight lag occurred during experiments, maybe due the specification of the laptop used in the experiment was not enough to support a smooth detection.

Figure 11 shows example images on the comparison to determine the efficiency of face detection in bright and dark surroundings. The results shown in Fig. 11(a) shows that detection in dark surrounding were difficult as the algorithm was unable to distinct between the faces and the background. For bright surrounding, it was found that an average amount of brightness is optimal, as over brightness can affect the detection of the subject faces as shown in the Fig. 11(b). Some part of the chin is laminated with bright lighting in the background, thus interrupting with the face classifier to distinguish the subject's face area.

Fig. 10. Face detection on still image.

(a) Dark surrounding   (b) Bright surrounding

Fig. 11. Comparison of dark and bright surrounding images.

3.2 Face Mask Detection Experiment

The face mask detection works by initially detecting the face area. By using the function of face detection added with another command of detecting the presence of a face mask, the result produces both output of face detection and face mask detection. The output of face mask detection is in the form of probability percentage displayed on the monitor.

Figure 12 shows the result of a face with and without a face mask. The main distinct different is the frame colour around the face detection. For a non-mask wearer, the frame will be coloured in RED, and for mask wearer it is GREEN. Red symbolizes a warning for the subject without face mask and green for approval as the presence of face mask is detected. Another displayed parameter is the probability percentage of the face mask detection. A high number of percentage indicates the accuracy of detection. A high number of percentage for a face without face mask indicates that there are higher percentage that there are no face mask detected and vice versa.

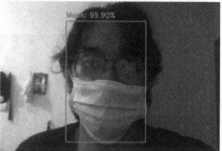

Fig. 12. Face mask detection: without face mask (left), with face mask (right).

3.3 Analysis and Discussion

The performance of an algorithm are measured using the performance matrix which includes accuracy, losses and confusion matrix calculation. Both face and face mask detection algorithms were tested with different metrics to determine the algorithm performances.

Face detection experiment were based on the face detection rate. A set of 10 images of human faces were randomly shown to the web camera and the number of times the algorithm succeeded in detecting the faces were observed and tabulated. The percentage of face detection rate can be calculated using the following formula:

$$\frac{\sum True\ Detection}{Total\ Number\ of\ Images} \times 100\% \tag{1}$$

Table 1 shows the number of True Detection and False Detection over three different testing with three different subject images. The face detection rate is at 90% true and 10% false detection based on the performance metric calculation of detection rate. The rate is considered acceptable as it is close to 100% accuracy. Other outer factors such as surrounding lightings may affect the accuracy of detection, hence the non-perfect score of detections. Besides that, the facial structure of the subject's face may be different from the dataset collection as the angle of the camera is static.

Table 1. Face detection rate.

Test no	True detection	False detection
1	8	2
2	9	1
3	10	0

The face mask detection algorithm performance were calculated using the plotted graph metric of training accuracy against losses over the time period as shown in Fig. 13. The graph were plotted directly from the algorithm model training output and saved in PNG format image. The Training_Accuracy and Validation_Accuracy is efficiently near to 1.0 proving a steady accuracy over the time whilst the Training_Loss and Valida-tion_Loss is almost near to zero and decreasing over time reassuring the algorithm performance is accurate and efficient for a datasets of 4000 images.

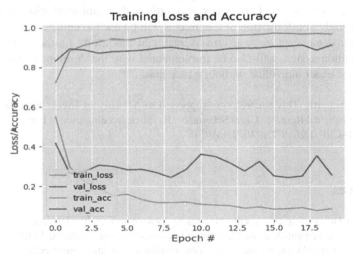

Fig. 13. Training loss and accuracy against time (Epochs).

The face mask detection algorithm performance were calculated using the plotted graph metric of training accuracy against losses over the time period as shown in Fig. 13. The graph were plotted directly from the algorithm model training output and saved in PNG format image. The Training_Accuracy and Validation_Accuracy is efficiently near to 1.0 proving a steady accuracy over the time whilst the Training_Loss and Validation_Loss is almost near to zero and decreasing over time reassuring the algorithm performance is accurate and efficient for a datasets of 4000 images.

4 Conclusions

Initially, a face shape is detected using a Haar cascade classifier which extracts the feature of a human face from the raw input images. Then, the algorithm process it to be passed on to the recognizer where the human faces seen through the computer vision would be recognized and detected. Based on the performance metric calculation of detection rate analysis of the experimental results, the face detection rate is at 90% True and 10% False detection, which shows very good detection rate. Once a face is detected, the image is processed to determine the face is with or without a face mask. The input images are preprocessed to be passed on to the CNN layers using the model trainer architecture of convolution and the created model will be a recognizer for face mask detection through the computer vision system. The training accuracy and validation accuracy are efficiently near to 1.0, proving a steady accuracy over the time. Furthermore, the training loss and validation loss are almost near to zero and decreasing over time, reassuring the algorithm performance is accurate and efficient for a datasets of 4000 images. The preliminary experimental results obtained proves the algorithm can be improvised to increase the accuracy of recognition. Through the efficiency of the proposed face mask detection algorithm which includes also face recognition algorithm, both the real time video and still images can be detected. For future works, artificially illuminated colour images based on surface gradient information of the images will be used to enhance the capability of the system to detect face mask in various backlight conditions. Furthermore, individual face recognition system will also be implemented with the developed system that can recognize the exact individual without a face mask.

Acknowledgements. This research was supported by Ministry of Higher Education (MOHE) through Fundamental Research Grant Scheme for Research Acculturation of Early Career (FRGS-RACER) (RACER/1/2019/TK04/UTHM//5).

References

1. The Star Online. https://www.thestar.com.my/news/nation/2020/03/16/malaysia-announces-restricted-movement-measure-after-spike-in-covid-19-cases. Accessed 5 Oct 2021
2. Bernama. https://www.bernama.com/en/general/news_covid-19.php?id=1890211. Accessed 5 Oct 2021
3. Dhillon, A., Verma, G.K.: Convolutional neural network: a review of models, methodologies and applications to object detection. Progr. Artif. Intell. **9**(2), 85–112 (2019). https://doi.org/10.1007/s13748-019-00203-0
4. Pak, M., Kim, S.: A review of deep learning in image recognition. In: International Conference on Computer Applications and Information Processing Technology (CAIPT), pp. 1–3 (2017)
5. Cai, L., Gao, J., Zhao, D.: A review of the application of deep learning in medical image classification and segmentation. Ann. Transl. Med. **8**(11), 713 (2020)

6. Kaheel, H., Hussein, A., Chehab, A.: AI-based image processing for COVID-19 detection in chest CT scan images. Front. Comms. Net **2**, 645040 (2021)
7. Diaz-Escobar, J., et al.: Deep-learning based detection of COVID-19 using lung ultrasound imagery. PLoS ONE **16**(8), e0255886 (2021)
8. Melenli, S., Topkaya, A.: Real-time maintaining of social distance in Covid-19 environment using image processing and big data. In: 2020 Innovations in Intelligent Systems and Applications Conference (ASYU), pp. 1–5 (2020)
9. Kumar, A., Sharma, K., Singh, H., Naugriya, S.G., Gill, S.S., Buyya, R.: A drone-based networked system and methods for combating coronavirus disease (COVID-19) pandemic. Future Gener. Comput. Syst.: FGCS **115**, 1–19 (2021)
10. Schmidhuber, J.: Deep Learning in neural networks: an overview. Neural Netw. **61**, 85–117 (2015)
11. Wu, W., Yin, Y., Wang, X.: Xu, D: face detection with different scales based on fasterR-CNN. IEEE Trans. Cybern. **49**(11), 4017–4028 (2019)
12. Medium.com Homepage. https://medium.com/@RaghavPrabhu/understanding-of-convoluti onal-neural-network-cnn-deep-learning-99760835f148. Accessed 2 Oct 2021

Evaluating the Efficiency of Several Machine Learning Algorithms for Fall Detection

Parimala Banda[1], Masoud Mohammadian[1(✉)], and Gudur Raghavendra Reddy[2]

[1] School of IT and Systems, University of Canberra, Canberra, Australia
U3197191@uni.canberra.edu.au, masoud.mohammadian@canberra.edu.au
[2] School of Design and Built Environment, University of Canberra, Canberra, Australia
raghavendra.gudur@canberra.edu.au

Abstract. Elderly falls are a growing phenomenon observed within the world. According to World Health Organization (WHO), it is the second leading cause of unintentional or accidental deaths among the elderly. Thus, the need for research regarding the development of fall detection systems is imperative. Researchers have utilized various approaches to develop fall detection systems, significant number of which have employed Machine Leaning (ML) algorithms for fall detection. In this study, we evaluated the efficiency of six ML algorithms on a public fall detection dataset. A robust deep neural network for fall detection (FD-DNN) is identified to be the current state-of-the-art, it detects falls by using a self-built sensor that consumes low power. By evaluating the efficiency of six machine learning algorithms on a publicly available joint fall detection dataset, the accuracy of the fall detection was increased from 99.17% to 99.88% by using the K-nearest Neighbor indicating that common machine learning algorithms can achieve identical or higher accuracy rendering the complex and expensive deep neural network-based fall detection systems inefficient.

Keywords: Fall detection · Elderly fall detection · Machine learning algorithms · Wearable fall detection system · SisFall dataset · MobiFall dataset · K-nearest neighbors · KNN · Support vector machines · SVM · Decision tree · Random forest · Logistic regression · Naïve Bayes

1 Introduction

An assessment undertaken by the Australian Institute of Health and Welfare stated that nearly 2 in 5 of the Australians were living alone and the likelihood of doing so increases with age [1]. Research suggests that 39% of people aged 65–74, 40% of 75–84, and 51% of aged 85 and over live independently [1]. Older people face multitude of age-related health issues, of which complications resulting from falls are the most prominent. Falls are considered a common Phenomenon among the elderly especially those aged 65 and over. World Health Organization (WHO) report notes that falls are the second leading reason behind accidental or unintentional death [2].

One of the best ways to address this problem is to either prevent falls or find a way to provide timely medical help for fall victims who are living alone. Fall detection systems

© Springer Nature Switzerland AG 2022
J.-H. Kim et al. (Eds.): IHCI 2021, LNCS 13184, pp. 610–620, 2022.
https://doi.org/10.1007/978-3-030-98404-5_56

are important as immediate medical care after a fall is essential to reduce potential damage and life-threatening injuries. Studies suggest that fall detection systems are generally accepted among the objective population as it aids their independence and reduce their fear of falling [3]. Additionally, falls impact both the physical and mental health of the user. The psychological effects include depression, anxiety, fear of falling, and restricting activities of daily living (ADL) [4]. The fear of falling has caused an estimated 60% of elderly people to restrict their ADLs [5] creating a negative cycle of not performing ADLs which impacted their gait imbalance and deteriorating muscles leading to falls.

Fall detection systems can be classified into two categories: (1) wearable-based systems and (2) context-aware systems. This paper focuses on the publicly available datasets for wearable fall detection systems. Zurbuchen et al. [7] state that approximately 50% of the falls observed in independent elderly people occur at their homes. Wearable fall detection systems offer users the portability and ease of use regardless of their location. They generally utilize a sensor/device worn by the subject to detect falls, they possess an accelerometer and a gyroscope to calculate the acceleration and angular velocity of the fall signal. There are several open-source fall detection datasets that offer raw data and/or pre-processed data. To be able to detect falls, a multitude of approaches may be used which include Machine Learning algorithms, Convolution Neural Networks (CNN) and Recurrent neural Networks (RNN), etc. This research paper aims to evaluate the efficiency of six commonly used machine learning algorithms including Decision Tree, Logistic Regression, Naïve Bayes classifier, Support Vector Machines, Random Forest, and K-nearest Neighbor on publicly available datasets for fall detection systems.

This paper is organized as follows: Sect. 2 will present a literature review of relevant papers. Section 3 will discuss the methodology of our experiments. Section 4 will present and discuss the results of the experiments and its implications. Lastly, Sect. 5 will conclude the paper.

2 Literature Review

Fall detection systems are a growing topic of interest within the research community. There is a good amount of literature discussing various open-source fall detection datasets and approaches to detect falls. This section is restricted to a few notable works in fall detection. Hussein et al. [4] discusses the occurrence of falls and the impacts they have on the physical and psychological health of the elderly. It has been identified that a multitude of fall detection systems incorrectly identify the falls as activities of daily living or vice versa. In order to fill the identified research gap, they have proposed a machine learning-based fall detection algorithm claimed to outperform the state-of-the-art techniques in terms of specificity, sensitivity, and accuracy. The most used "SisFall" [6] dataset is utilized to extract features to train and test four machine learning algorithms. The proposed algorithm is reported to possess an accuracy of 99.98% with the Support Vector Machines classifier. However, due to the utilization of the SisFall dataset it only provides comprehensive results for waist-based data.

Zurbuchen et al. [7] provide a machine learning approach for wearable fall detection systems focusing on the sampling rates selection. The falls discussed within the multi-class classification approach split the falls into pre-fall, impact, and post-fall. The paper utilizes the data from SisFall as its sampling rate is quite high, the data is pre-processed, and features are extracted. The data is then passed through five machine learning algorithms including K-nearest Neighbors, Support Vector Machines, Random Forest, Gradient Boosting created via Python libraries to perform a comparison of sampling rates using the parameters: sensitivity, specificity, accuracy, F1, and AUROC. It evaluates the sampling frequency rates' performance of Fall detection systems. The report claims that a high sampling rate improves performance, but a sampling rate of 50 Hz is sufficient to obtain an accurate detection. However, the focus area is the comparison of sampling frequency rather than the identification of optimal machine learning algorithms.

Chelli et al. [8] developed a machine learning framework to detect falls and ADLs. Similar to this research, the paper combines datasets [9, 10] and utilizes the acceleration and angular velocity to base their findings. It analyses the performance of four classification algorithms such as the artificial neural network, K-nearest Neighbor, quadratic Support Vector Machines, and Ensemble Bagged Tree (EBT). It proposes novel features (extracted from power spectral density of acceleration) to improve the classification accuracy of ADLs. Results for the acceleration data depict that EBT outperforms the rest in terms of overall accuracy being 94.1% followed by a fall detection accuracy being 99.1%. By utilizing the proposed novel features, the results are reiterated with EBT's overall accuracy equating to 97.7%, and surprisingly, the accuracy of fall detection rates for both Support Vector Machines and EBT equal to 100% without any false alarms. This research uses real-life data which are not publicly available.

Kraft et al. [11] provided a comprehensive evaluation of existing sensor-based public fall datasets from the years 2010 to 2019 whilst harmonizing the wrist-worn datasets for a robust analysis. It analyses the fall detection rate by utilizing deep learning algorithms for embedded systems and mobile. It is reported that a small-scale CNN achieves an accuracy of 97% on their harmonized fall detection dataset. The drawbacks of the paper include reduced accuracy when quantization is applied which may be optimized by calibrating the CNN based on the user's activity resulting in lower false positives and increased performance rates. These limitations are claimed to be addressed in their future work.

Liu et al. [12] research is vital to this research as the joint dataset (SisFall, MobiFall, and self-created sensor data) utilized within this paper stems from it. Their research focuses on creating an energy-efficient system based on a deep neural network for fall detection (FD-DNN). They created a sensing module-integrated energy-efficient sensor (SMIEES) with the ability to sense and cache activity data in sleep mode and an interrupt-driven algorithm is proposed to transfer data to a ZigBee integrated server where a FD-DNN detects falls accurately. A combination of CNN and long short-term memory algorithms are utilized to create the FD-DNN. The results depict that the proposed FD-DNN system achieves a fall detection accuracy of 99.17% whilst fulfilling the low power consumption requirement. The literature review aided this research immensely as it facilitated the understanding of various public datasets and techniques providing an in-depth understanding of the processes involved and the tools to proceed with our evaluation.

3 Methodology

The methodology section involves the use of machine learning algorithms to test the datasets for fall detection efficiency.

3.1 Selecting Datasets

The initial step towards successful completion of this research study is to obtain publicly available datasets for fall detection systems that contain adequate falls and ADLs. [11] aided in the selection and understanding of the publicly available datasets as it provides an excellent overview of all the available datasets, published fall detection algorithms, and shows results to help choose the most appropriate dataset/algorithm. A combination of SisFall, MobiFall, and sensing module-integrated energy-efficient sensor (SMIEES) data was used to construct a joint dataset as outlined in the [12]. The SisFall Dataset found within [6] utilizes a waist-based sensor and is one of the few datasets that contain simulations of falls and ADL performed by a range of subjects with varying age and physical features. Most importantly it contains simulations of elderly subjects. Created by Sucerquia et al., the SisFall dataset contains a bulk of 4510 files with all files containing an activity file. Although, the participants over 60 have performed a range of ADLs only one subject aged over 60 completed the fall data collection. The sensor utilizes two accelerometers ADXL345 and MMA8451Q with a range being ±16 g and ±8 g and resolution equating to 13 bits and 14 bits respectively. It also employs a gyroscope ITG3200 with a range of $\pm2000°$/s and a resolution of 16 bits.

While MobiFall Dataset available in [13], utilizes smartphone-based sensors placed in the trouser pocket of their healthy subjects in any random orientation. The data is collected via a Samsung Galaxy smartphone with the LSM330DLC inertial module which employs an accelerometer, gyroscope, and orientation data. The sensor ranges are ±2 g (A), $\pm2000°$/s (G), and $\pm360°$ (O). The sensor resolutions are noted to be 12 bits (A), and 16 bits (G). This dataset contrasts the need for the sensor to be in a specific position or have any contraptions simulating the everyday use of mobile phones. The self-developed sensor data obtained from the SMIEES is published on the author's GitHub account made available in [12]. The acceleration and angular velocity data are captured by the module that utilizes the MPU6050 integrating along with a three-axial micro-electromechanical systems (MEMS) gyroscope and an accelerometer. MPU6050's acceleration range is documented to be ±16 g, and angular velocity can measure between $\pm2000°$/s Table 1 depicts the characteristics of the subjects across the three selected datasets.

Additionally, Table 2 contains a brief analysis of the various features presented by the SisFall, MobiFall, and SMIEES datasets. An in-depth systematic analysis of the twelve most commonly available public datasets for wearable fall detection systems is undertaken in [14].

Utilizing a combination of these datasets allows for a holistic view of fall detection systems, accumulating the positive aspects from the datasets, usage of elderly movement samples, the practicality of a mobile phone-based sensor system as well as low power consumption.

Table 1. Characteristics of the subjects across the three datasets.

Parameters	SisFall	MobiFall	SMIEES
Number of subjects	38	24	20
Male	19	17	17
Female	19	7	3
Age Range (years)	[19–75]	[22–47]	[24–50]
Weight Range (Kg)	[41.5–102]	[50–103]	n/a
Height Range (cm)	[149–183]	[160–189]	n/a

Note: n/a: not applicable as it is not mentioned in the dataset documentation.

Table 2. Analysis of the features of three datasets.

Parameters	SisFall	MobiFall	SMIEES
Year	2017	2013	2020
File Types	1 text file (comma-separated values) per subject and activity	1 text file (comma-separated values) per subject, trial, and activity	2 CSV files to test and train
ADL	19	9	7
Fall	15	4	1
Number of Sensors	3	3	2
Position of Sensors	Waist (belt)	Thigh (trouser pocket)	Vest pocket
Recorded Magnitudes	A, A, G *	A, G, O	A, G**
Sampling rate (Hz)	200	87 (A) 100 (G, O)	100
Sensor Range	±16 g (A1) ±8 g (A2) ± 2000°/s (G)	±2 g (A) ±2000°/s(G) ±360° (O)	±16 g (A) ±2000°/s (G)
Sensor Resolution	13 bits (A1) 14 bits (A2) 16 bits (G)	12 bits (A) 16 bits (G)	n/a

Note: A: Accelerometer, G: Gyroscope, O: Orientation measurement, n/a: not applicable as it is not mentioned in the dataset documentation. *Sensing unit included two accelerometers obtained from varied vendors. **Designed module uses MPU6050 integrating with three-axial MEMS gyroscope and accelerometers.

3.2 Data Preprocessing

The combination of SisFall, MobiFall, and SMIEES obtained from [12] is utilized within this research. The data that is made publicly available is cleaned and feature extraction is already performed. The data obtained from SisFall and MobiFall datasets are down sampled to 100 Hz and normalized by the formula (1) as described in [12].

$$y_i = \frac{x_i - \min_{1 \leq j \leq n} \{x_j\}}{\max_{1 \leq j \leq n} \{x_j\} - \min_{1 \leq j \leq n} \{x_j\}} \tag{1}$$

Additionally, the moving average filter is used to filter noise from all three datasets as depicted in formula (2) as [15] states that it is the most efficient filter.

$$G_{filter}(n) = \frac{1}{M}(G(n) + G(n-1) + \cdots + G(n - M + 1)) \tag{2}$$

3.3 Fall Detection Simulations

Once the data is preprocessed, the activities are classified into two classes: (1) falls or (2) ADLs. The activities available within the training dataset include both ADL and fall, being, walking, jogging, jumping, going upstairs, going downstairs, standing up, sitting down, and falling. Instead of using an 80/20 split (80 for training and 20 for testing) as applied within [12], our study utilizes the 8000 samples obtained from their publicly available training data randomly sampled across the three datasets. 10-fold cross-validation is applied to the 8000 samples to obtain an optimal machine learning classifier model and mitigate bias. To successfully evaluate the efficiency of the machine learning algorithms, the six most used machine learning algorithms are simulated. The algorithms briefed below include Decision Tree (DT), Logistic Regression (LR), Naïve Bayes classifier (NB), Support Vector Machines (SVM) with Polynomial Kernel function, Random Forest (RF), and K-nearest Neighbor (KNN) with K = 1. These machine learning algorithms have been chosen as they are widely used and can be applied to most data problems.

Decision Trees are a supervised non-parametric learning method [16] that is useful when performing regression and classification. It learns simple decision rules obtained from the data features to predict the value of a target variable. It may be seen as a piecewise constant approximation [17]. The deeper the tree, the more complex the decision rules implying a fitter model. The decision trees are easy to visualize and understand and require minimal data preparation.

Logistic Regression is a transformation of a linear regression using the sigmoid function to return a probability value [18]. It is a supervised machine learning algorithm that provides a classification algorithm utilized to allocate observations to a discrete set of classes [17, 18]. When the algorithm was running to incur the results outlined in this research it was observed that building models, folds, and testing took the longest amount of time in comparison to the other machine learning algorithms.

Naïve Bayes is a supervised learning algorithm. It is a probabilistic classifier based on the application of Bayes' theorem, given the value of the class variable, a "naïve" assumption of conditional independence between every pair of features is considered [20]. It calculates the probability of an event based on prior knowledge of conditions that can trigger such an event. Naïve Bayes classifiers are typically considered extremely fast and require minimal training data to approximate the vital parameters.

Support Vector Machines abbreviated as SVM is a machine learning algorithm that consists of a set of supervised learning methods that can be applied to both regression and classification problems [21]. SVM is a two-layer recognition method based on the concept decision boundaries are defined by decision planes [22]. The kernel function used within this research is the polynomial kernel function. Mathematically, it can be represented via Eq. (3) where D sets the highest degree of this term of polynomial kernel function with the default value 3. The coefficient in the kernel function is set using C whose default value is 0 [22].

$$K(x, y) = (x \cdot y + c)^d \tag{3}$$

Random Forest is a multi-decision tree classifier. The output results of all decision trees are compared to obtain the output category. There are several advantages of using the random forest classifier include the ability to process many input variables, creation of a high-precision classifier, error balancing of the unbalanced material sets classification, and evaluation of the significance of variables [22]. It is an improved decision tree algorithm.

K-nearest Neighbor is an instance-based learning model [23] that is designed to find patterns to solve classification and regression problems. It works by dividing the data into classes based on how close data points are to each other. A larger k tends to suppress the impacts of noise but makes the boundaries of classification less distinct, implying that the k value is high dependent on it thus it dictates the most favorable choice of the value k. The k value specified for this study equates to 1 implying that the object is simply allocated to the class of that single nearest neighbor [24].

4 Results and Discussion

4.1 Results of Simulations

The simulations of the six machine learning classifiers (DT, LR, NB, SVM, RF, and KNN) are performed to obtain the confusion matrices of the classifiers as outlined in Table 3.

4.2 Analysis of Results

The confusion matrices depict that KNN outperforms the other algorithms. However, the performance of all six algorithms can be evaluated by using the three common performance metrics such as sensitivity, specificity, and accuracy. The following terms are used to define the three-performance metrics:

True Positive (TP): A fall was correctly detected
True Negative (TN): A fall was correctly not detected

Table 3. Confusion Matrices of Six ML Classifiers.

Decision Tree (DT)		Prediction result	
		Fall	ADL
Actual	Fall	923	56
	ADL	36	6985
Logistic Regression (LR)		Prediction result	
		Fall	ADL
Actual	Fall	922	57
	ADL	30	6991
Naive Bayes Classifier (NB)		Prediction result	
		Fall	ADL
Actual	Fall	941	38
	ADL	2	7019
Support Vector Machines (SVM)		Prediction result	
		Fall	ADL
Actual	Fall	971	8
	ADL	11	7010
Random Forest (RF)		Prediction result	
		Fall	ADL
Actual	Fall	972	7
	ADL	8	7013
K-nearest Neighbours (KNN)		Prediction result	
		Fall	ADL
Actual	Fall	975	4
	ADL	6	7015

False Positive (FP): A fall was incorrectly detected
False Negative (FN): A fall was not detected

   Sensitivity: Measures the system's ability to detect falls. Mathematically, it can be calculated via (4). It is simply the ratios of true positives and the total amount of falls occurred.

$$Sensitivity = \frac{TP}{TP + FN} \times 100 \tag{4}$$

Specificity: Measures the system's ability to detect falls only when they occur. Mathematically, it can be calculated via (5).

$$Specificity = \frac{TN}{FP + TN} \times 100 \tag{5}$$

Accuracy: Measures the system's ability to differentiate falls and ADLs. Mathematically, it can be calculated via (6).

$$Accuracy = \frac{TP + TN}{TP + FN + TN + FP} \times 100 \qquad (6)$$

An evaluation of the efficiency of the six machine learning algorithms on the dataset is collated within Table 4 using the three-performance metrics.

Table 4. Sensitivity, Specificity, and Accuracy of the six ML classifiers.

Classifier	Sensitivity	Specificity	Accuracy
Decision Tree (DT)	96.25%	99.20%	98.85%
Logistic Regression (LR)	96.85%	99.19%	98.91%
Naive Bayes Classifier (NB)	99.79%	99.46%	99.50%
Support Vector Machines (SVM)	98.88%	99.89%	99.76%
Random Forest (RF)	99.18%	99.90%	99.81%
K-nearest Neighbors (KNN)	99.39%	99.94%	99.88%

From Table 4, it can be observed that the accuracy rates are 98.85%, 98.91%, 99.50%, 99.76%, 99.81%, and 99.88% for Decision Tree, Logistic Regression, Naïve Bayes classifier, Support Vector Machines, Random Forest, and K-nearest Neighbor respectively. K-nearest Neighbor outperforms the other algorithms with the sensitivity, specificity, and accuracy being 99.93%, 99.94%, and 99.88% respectively. These results can be compared against the results in [12]. It can be noted that the outcomes of this research outmatch the FD-DNN's 99.17% accuracy depicted in [12] as the KNN's accuracy as observed in Table 2 is 99.88%. This depicts that a complicated deep neural network does not need to be used to create a fall detection system with near perfect accuracy.

5   Conclusion

The evaluation of the efficiency of machine learning algorithms on public fall detection datasets is performed to assess machine learning algorithms that are most suitable for fall detection. A 10-fold cross-validation technique is applied to the training data within the joint dataset obtained from [12]. Six machine learning algorithms including Decision Tree, Logistic Regression, Naïve Bayes classifier, Support Vector Machines, Random Forest, and K-nearest Neighbor are simulated and tested. K-nearest Neighbor depicts the highest accuracy rate of 99.88%. Additionally, four out of six machine learning algorithms outperform the accuracy rate of the FD-DNN (99.17%). The results provided by the evaluation depict that commonly used machine learning algorithms perform just as well to obtain near perfect fall and employment of a complicated and expensive deep neural network for fall detection is unnecessary. Finally, these results can be used for future fall detection systems to help the elderly live free from injuries caused by falls that may impede their everyday life.

Acknowledgment. The author would like to acknowledge the support provided by the Faculty of Science and Technology at the University of Canberra.

References

1. "Older Australia at a glance, Aged care assessments - Australian Institute of Health and Welfare. Australian Institute of Health and Welfare (2018). https://www.aihw.gov.au/reports/older-people/older-australia-at-a-glance/contents/health-aged-care-service-use/aged-care-assessments. Accessed 30 Sept 2021
2. WHO Global report on falls Prevention in older Age (2007)
3. Brownsell, S.J., Bradley, D.A., Bragg, R., Catlin, P., Carlier, J.: Do community alarm users want telecare? J. Telemed. Telecare **6**(4), 199–204 (2000). https://doi.org/10.1258/135763 3001935356
4. Hussain, F., Umair, M.B., Ehatisham-ul-Haq, M., Pires, I.M.: An efficient machine learning-based elderly fall detection algorithm. In: SENSORDEVICES 2018, The Ninth International Conference on Sensor Device Technologies and Applications (2018). https://www.researchgate.net/publication/327731757_An_Efficient_Machine_Learning-based_Elderly_Fall_Detection_Algorithm. Accessed 09 Sept 2021
5. Deshpande, N., Metter, E.J., Lauretani, F., Bandinelli, S., Guralnik, J., Ferrucci, L.: Activity restriction induced by fear of falling and objective and subjective measures of physical function: a prospective cohort study. J. Am. Geriatr. Soc. **56**(4), 615–620 (2008). https://doi.org/10.1111/J.1532-5415.2007.01639.X
6. Sucerquia, A., López, J., Vargas-Bonilla, J.: SisFall: a fall and movement dataset. Sensors **17**(12), 198 (2017). https://doi.org/10.3390/s17010198
7. Zurbuchen, N., Wilde, A., Bruegger, P.: A machine learning multi-class approach for fall detection systems based on wearable sensors with a study on sampling rates selection. Sensors **21**(3), 938 (2021). https://doi.org/10.3390/s21030938
8. Chelli, A., Patzold, M.: A machine learning approach for fall detection and daily living activity recognition. IEEE Access **7**, 38670–38687 (2019). https://doi.org/10.1109/ACCESS. 2019.2906693
9. Anguita, D., Ghio, A., Oneto, L., Parra, X., Reyes-Ortiz, J.L.: A public domain dataset for human activity recognition using smartphones. undefined (2013)
10. Ojetola, O., Gaura, E., Brusey, J.: Data set for fall events and daily activities from inertial sensors. In: Proceedings of the 6th ACM Multimedia Systems Conference, MMSys 2015, pp. 243–248 (2015). https://doi.org/10.1145/2713168.2713198
11. Kraft, D., Srinivasan, K., Bieber, G.: Deep learning based fall detection algorithms for embedded systems, smartwatches, and IoT devices using accelerometers. Technologies **8**(4), 72 (2020). https://doi.org/10.3390/technologies8040072
12. Liu, L., Hou, Y., He, J., Lungu, J., Dong, R.: An energy-efficient fall detection method based on FD-DNN for elderly people. Sensors (Switzerland) **20**(15), 1–16 (2020). https://doi.org/10.3390/S20154192
13. Vavoulas, G., Pediaditis, M., Spanakis, E.G., Tsiknakis, M.: The MobiFall dataset: an initial evaluation of fall detection algorithms using smartphones. In: 13th IEEE International Conference on BioInformatics and BioEngineering, IEEE BIBE 2013 (2013). https://doi.org/10.1109/BIBE.2013.6701629
14. Casilari, E., Santoyo-Ramón, José-Antonio., Cano-García, José-Manuel.: Analysis of public datasets for wearable fall detection systems. Sensors **17**(7), 1513 (2017). https://doi.org/10.3390/s17071513

15. Xiao, D., Yu, Z., Yi, F., Wang, L., Tan, C.C., Guo, B.: SmartSwim: an infrastructure-free swimmer localization system based on smartphone sensors. In: Chang, C.K., Chiari, L., Cao, Yu., Jin, H., Mokhtari, M., Aloulou, H. (eds.) ICOST 2016. LNCS, vol. 9677, pp. 222–234. Springer, Cham (2016). https://doi.org/10.1007/978-3-319-39601-9_20

16. Song, Y., Lu, Y.: Decision tree methods: applications for classification and prediction. Shanghai Arch. Psychiatry 27(2), 130 (2015). https://doi.org/10.11919/J.ISSN.1002-0829. 215044

17. Decision Trees—scikit-learn 1.0 documentation. Scikit-learn (2021). https://scikit-learn.org/stable/modules/tree.html. Accessed 07 Oct 2021

18. Sinnott, R.O., Duan, H., Sun, Y.: A case study in big data analytics: exploring twitter sentiment analysis and the weather. In: Big Data: Principles and Paradigms, pp. 357–388 (2016). https://doi.org/10.1016/B978-0-12-805394-2.00015-5

19. 1.1. Linear Models — scikit-learn 1.0 documentation, Scikit-learn (2021). https://scikit-learn.org/stable/modules/linear_model.html#logistic-regression. Accessed 07 Oct 2021

20. 1.9. Naive Bayes — scikit-learn 1.0 documentation, Scikit-learn (2021). https://scikit-learn.org/stable/modules/naive_bayes.html. Accessed 07 Oct 2021

21. 1.4. Support Vector Machines — scikit-learn 1.0 documentation, Scikit-learn (2021). https://scikit-learn.org/stable/modules/svm.html. Accessed 07 Oct 2021

22. Pan, D., Liu, H., Qu, D., Zhang, Z.: Human falling detection algorithm based on multisensor data fusion with SVM. Mob. Inf. Syst. 2020 (2020). https://doi.org/10.1155/2020/8826088

23. 1.6. Nearest Neighbors — scikit-learn 1.0 documentation, Scikit-learn (2021). https://scikit-learn.org/stable/modules/neighbors.html#classification. Accessed 07 Oct 2021

24. Altman, N.S.: An introduction to kernel and nearest neighbor nonparametric regression (1991)

Fuzzy Logic Based Explainable AI Approach for the Easy Calibration of AI Models in IoT Environments

Mohammed Alshehri$^{(\boxtimes)}$

Department of Information Technology, College of Computer and Information Sciences,
Majmaah University, Majmaah 11952, Saudi Arabia
ma.alshehri@mu.edu.sa

Abstract. The Internet of Things (IoT) permeates all aspects of human existence shortly. As a result of the IoT, it can now construct a smart world. For
this to happen, however, extracting meaningful information from raw sensory
input functioning in loud and complicated settings must be addressed to achieve
it. For example, bandwidth, processing power, and power consumption must be
addressed while building a possible IoT system. Due to the current epidemic,
the need for contactless solutions has risen. Possible solutions include a gesture-
based control system that protects user privacy and can operate several different
appliances simultaneously. When implementing such gesture-based control systems, opaque box artificial intelligence (AI) models are used. This opaque box AI
model has shown good performance metrics on in-distribution data when tested
in a lab. However, their complexity and opaqueness make them prone to failure
when exposed to real-world out-of-distribution input. In contrast to opaque box
models, explainable AI models based on fuzzy logic (EAI-FL) demonstrate comparable performance on lab data distributions. The type-2 fuzzy models, on the
other hand, are readily calibrated and modified to offer equivalent performance
to those attained on the lab in-distribution data in the real world.

Keywords: IoT · AI · Fuzzy logic · Calibration

1 Introduction to IoT Environments

The Internet of Things (IoT) technology is a state-of-the-art communication system that
integrates people, machinery, and software. Information exchange "things" devices are
connected to accessing and sharing utilizing a system identification (e.g., Internet) via
wireless means [1]. IoT's design objective is to link and connect several components
like computers, network operators, servers, environmental sensors, software, etc. That
allows the connecting users to have overall access to scattered assets on a single roof
[2].

The IoT ecosystem is integrated with service providers from various backgrounds to
satisfy customer demand, such as video, online databases, telemedicine, infrastructures,
and software applications [3]. For information dissemination and exchange between
connected devices and other services, modern, advanced technological devices are used

© Springer Nature Switzerland AG 2022
J.-H. Kim et al. (Eds.): IHCI 2021, LNCS 13184, pp. 621–633, 2022.
https://doi.org/10.1007/978-3-030-98404-5_57

by wireless media [4]. With IoT adapting several network connections and techniques, a collaboration distributes standard network processes, including transmitting data, assignment and shared prosperity, computing, and retrieving [5].

In such circumstances, the deep learning (DL) and machine learning (ML) approaches are mostly utilized as solutions in big data analysis [6–12]. To date, the use of ML and DL in advancements has produced outstanding study findings. In autonomous vehicles for lanes and object recognition, collection, mapping, scheduling, route computation, actuation, etc., ML and DL are utilized extensively. Clouds and Fog Nodes are becoming critical elements in many systems and tools. Deep learning is powered by the data of a crucial component in clouds and foggy technology. The main contributions to this article are as follows

- In this research, advanced distributed software network resources management has been designed and implemented.
- EAI-FL algorithms are built that dynamically control the scope of microservice growth of resources to fulfill its requirements for usage of goods on a timely basis.
- Comprehensive tests are conducted in six online situations in the Vehicles edges computer system to evaluate the efficacy and results of the system platforms and algorithms.
- The proposed system focused on the theoretical and distributed software managing resources.

2   Background to the IoT Systems

Microservice capacity planning has long been an important study subject in academia and industry. In this article, the background of the study for the problems to be handled in this study was presented first. Then it examined and debated two primary literature methods, the architectural style of the technology and the methodology and algorithm of management [13]. A study of taxonomies and problems associated with autoscaling implementations in edge calculation was provided by Wu et al. [14]. When variable workloads arise, they explored several kinds of network edge systems and their self-scaling problems. The main technologies linked to automatic edge computing applications: cloud frames, virtual machines, the method of surveillance, operational behavior, adjustment skills, architectural support, adaption intervals, scalable future technologies, and imaging [15]. Their findings revealed numerous research issues that must be solved to improve the efficiency of edge software packages. Ai et al. researched several techniques for microservice installation on the edge architecture [16]. They built Docker cloud applications and performed experimental studies on the efficiency of micro sim in four situations. Che et al. introduced a unique self-organizing and evolving technique widely employed throughout the IoT devices and cloud technologies network [17].

Their test findings demonstrated that microservice software systems on an edge node, like the Processor, fluctuated considerably as the application scenario varies. Their analysis indicated that the deployment of microservices in computation offloading networks confront microservice issues [18]. Edge calculation networks demanded flexible, different administration techniques to deal with changing network conditions.

3 Proposed Explainable AI Models Based on Fuzzy Logic (EAI-FL)

This section details the design and execution of the network infrastructure. The proposed framework and the systems with different diagrams are described. It demonstrates how it practically constructs and run the planned platform.

3.1 System Design

It developed and deployed the edges microservice enterprise software prototype. The framework provides different resource techniques for telecommunication companies to accomplish the sustainability of computational power. The platform consists of a fuzzy overloading mechanism for micro-services. In various microservice resource use, this system implements services such as resources tracking and installation administration. The scheduler is accountable for centralized managing resources for the whole mobile cloud distributed system in the intended platform network infrastructure. Every microservice offers the most fundamental central functions, including assignment of resources, deployment of services, and change of microservice status. The underlying layer depicts all the compute nodes of the routing layer in the platform's overall design process. Every edge node executes the cloud technology networking microservices necessary. There, the aggregator placed in each edge computing node regularly gathers the condition of each microservices and delivers them back to the higher data collectors. In this case, every microservice has an agent responsible for maintaining the data collecting. Microservices use a RESTful application programming interface (API) to interact independently with some other microservices.

3.2 Fuzzy Based Model

EAI-FL aims at optimizing the handling of requests between linked systems and cloud services. Selective problems in storing, delay in recovery, and overcrowding in specifically addressed in the administration of requests. This operation includes cloud storage planes and an Internet-of-things access plane, the descendant solution for handling requests. The hybrid model utilizing the hazy and the Artificial Intelligence optimizes the separate answer metrics used to estimate storage, latency, and congestion.

Figure 1 denotes the block diagram of the proposed EAI-FL and shows a schematic depiction of the operational Cloud application layer. It has a resource controller, fuzzy offload system, and resource monitor system for the calculation and analysis of the system. The AI-based edge computing model and local registry help to store and recollect the data. Three problems, such as storage, recovery delay, and overload, are analyzed separately in the following activities.

Storage Optimization Analysis. The supplier of cloud services manages the allocation of resources on various storage servers (S). Lack of resources is duplicated, and excess resources are moved to meet the service needs. The services request rate changes depending on the number of IoT applications generated from the accessing vehicles.

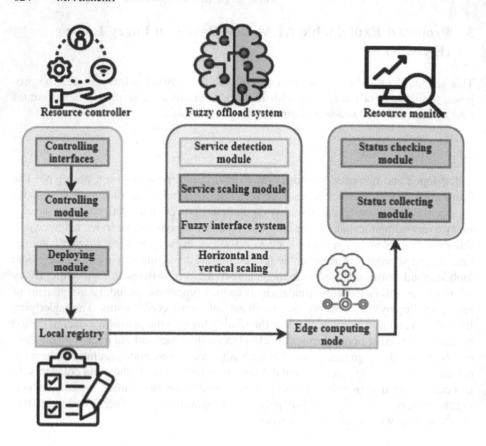

Fig. 1. The block diagram of the proposed EAI-FL

The (S_R) the factor must be reasonably high for ensuring dependable network connectivity. Reaction Factor indicates the rates of IoT queries (received) obtained from relevant telecom operators by distributing capital. Stable, efficient storage capacity is accurate in the grid for quick answers for the applications received. The storing stability depends on its expenses, which include costs of use, migration, and reaction. If P shows the inventory costs, then Eq. (1) shows the inventory cost

$$P = c_p + c_q + c_r = c_p\,(R_S, x) + c_q\,(R_S, x) + c_r\,(R_S, x) \qquad (1)$$

Where R_S are a resources demand at x and c_p, the implementation, migrating, and response costs must be c_q and c_r. R_S is based on P. Factor. $c_p\,(R_S, x)$ should be approximated to handle a R_S demand at the moment x, and it is expressed in Eq. (2)

$$c_p\,(R_S, x) = \sum_{a=0}^{M} \sum_{b=0}^{N} P_t\,(r_b, q_a) \times \frac{(r_a, q_b)}{x} \qquad (2)$$

Where $P_t\,(r_b, q_a)$ is the marked services price, $r_b \in M$ enters the marked price of the product. M and N represent here the services companies of the linked IoT systems and maximal requests. The transfer of assets is obligatory to solve the inadequate issues in a communications' response procedure. p_n is calculated using Eq. (3)

$$p_n = \frac{P_t \times r_b, q_a}{d(q_x, q_y)} \tag{3}$$

Where q_a is the fresh network operator that assigns r_b and $d(q_x, q_y)$ is the range between 'X' and 'Y' two network operators. The inventory cost is denoted P_t. The minimal migration cost is the q_a, and the cost of the service's response is evaluated for IoT equipment where demands are met via resource allocation. The received power is denoted in Eq. (4)

$$P_r\,(r_b) = \frac{1}{x}\sum_{s=0}^{x} r_s(q_x, q_y) \tag{4}$$

Where $r_s(q_x, q_y)$ is the rate of request failure across x and y delivers. Equation (5) shows the autonomous memory management aim (θ_x)

$$\theta_x = arg\left(max\left(\sum_{s=0}^{M} \frac{r_b - r_s}{r_b}\right)\right).arg\left(max\left(\sum_{s=0}^{N}\sum_{t=0}^{M} P\right)\right) \tag{5}$$

The objectives for the proper allocating resources are realized by a cumulative estimate of c_p, c_q and c_r. The request base and service price are denoted r_b and r_s. The total cost is denoted P. The hybrid approach with latency and congested measures precedes this optimizing aim.

Delay Optimization Method. As to the problem of lag time, it indicates the time that the IoT device generates r_b. Using Eq. (6) is computed the delay of service (s_t)

$$s_t = \beta_b\,(l_w + l_s + l_t) \tag{6}$$

Where β_b is the likelihood of a resource supplier's request. The awaiting, handling, and transmitting time of the demand is t, l_w, l_s and l_t. If the resources are more difficult and the amount of unattributed requests is considerable, there is a waiting time for current queries. Likewise, a demand to be made in the cloud layer from the accessible plane is subject to the network latency. The time needed for processing and allocation of services for the applicable request is called processing latency. The fluctuation is l_t. It depends on how many queries and the capability of the public cloud are processed. Consequently, l_s as in Eq. (7) is calculated.

$$l_s = \sum_{x=0}^{N} \frac{r_x}{p_r} = \sum_{x=0}^{N} \frac{r_x}{p_r \times r_y} \tag{7}$$

Where N is the maximal duration s and p_r demands are the pace of r_x. When l_s fluctuates, l_w changes. Simply put, the next arriving demand experience l_w when the clouds provider's capability is less than r_x+1. A request's l_w is indicated in Eq. (8).

$$l_w = \sum_{x=0}^{N} \left(\frac{r_x}{p_r \times r_y} \times \beta_b \right) \tag{8}$$

Where N is the maximal duration s and p_r demands are the pace of r_x. The output pace is denoted r_y. The likelihood condition of the system is denoted β_b.

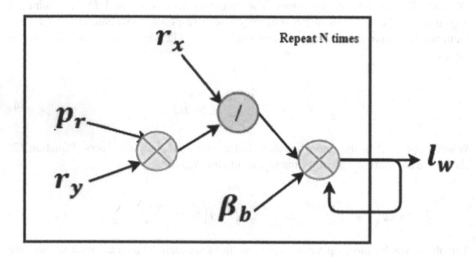

Fig. 2. Pictorial representation of l_w

The pictorial representation of l_w is depicted in Fig. 2. It uses pace, likelihood conditions to calculate the final output l_w. Where p_r is the reaction time for r_y and $(r_x - r_y) \neq 0$ for r_y. in which p r is the reply time at r_x. l_w.

Horizontal Scaling Function. The EAI-FL application scalability mechanism generates additional microservices at the same mobile-edge nodes without migrating microservices that need the extension of resources to additional network edge nodes whenever an edge computation nodes microservice has to increase computational resources. The EAI-FL verifies the number of computational infrastructures necessary by the microservice is smaller than the computational power on the network edge nodes in which the microservice is situated. Suppose the computational resources available for a computer node are lower than those accessible.

The analysis model of the proposed EAI-FL is depicted in Fig. 3. It uses a data module, and the data is extracted, normalized, and filtered for better analysis. The analyzed data is classified, and the final results using Apache and Hadoop are plotted and monitored.

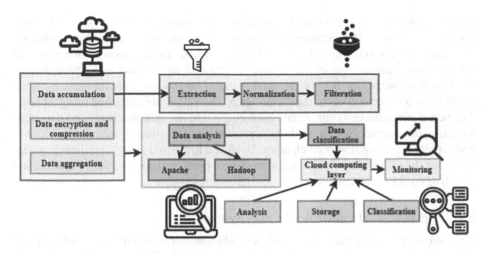

Fig. 3. The analysis model of the proposed EAI-FL

Vertical Scaling Function. Compared to the cloud-based networks, edges technology computer resources are restricted, and physical components have been increased inescapable. Unlike the horizontal scaling technique, vertical scaling migrates to new network edge endpoints microservices that demand increased computing capacity. Suppose a micro-service in the border computer node decides to increase computer resources. In that case, the microservices use the vertical scalability method to conduct resource advancement if it forecasts that the development required materials are larger than the residual information technology funds allocated in the border processor core in which the micro-service is situated.

3.3 IoT Environment Analysis

The technique presented for Massive Data IoT is investigated by establishing an effective industry surveillance system for good information handling. The process is split into three stages: judgment and executive function such as analysis, categorization, gathering, and data aggregation. IoT is frequently utilized to enhance industrial systems in several scientific disciplines. It uses applications, a data plane for data storage, gateway modules for connecting with an outside network, and an access plane and IoT layer for sensing the data. A range of sensors is generally employed for production surveillance systems that gather records and documents. Data is gathered and transmitted to the protocol stack of the Internet-of-things sensor that encrypts, collects, compresses, and aggregates data. This process of collecting data collects descriptions of the physical condition of the individual and their environment. Data is obtained through cellular connections depending on the circumstances, fabrication center, and position from sensor systems in manufacturing companies, surroundings, and neighborhoods. Data filtering is noise and unwanted element removal procedure from gathered information. A Kalman filter is used to enhance the sound-absorbing procedure in the suggested solution. It distinguishes the crucial from the non-important sounds and improves the working efficiency of the network. Research methodology is the last stage of a production application. The technique presented uses the file system provided by Hadoop to spread data packets into all devices in the network. These packets' information is divided as the main server in a fixed size of data and the efficient and effective operation in slave networks. If over one packet has to be processed by the devices in the network, it is processed using the feature map. The values are identified using Apache. The actual surveillance is enhanced based on the derived characteristics and data classification discoveries. Such a production process aims at reducing manufacturing risks and rapidly detecting abnormal changes. Using the IoT-based plant surveillance system increases the utilization of the correct processes, precise materials, fresh produce, and effective manufactured times.

3.4 Explainable AI Constrained Fuzzy Systems

This sub-section illustrates that Fuzzy's mathematics constraints are combined and defuzzification techniques to build a fuzzy logic system (FLS) to clarify each result centroid they create. In the following stages, the method is stated in brief:

1) Set the following MF index by ranking it as a lower limit of its set support.
2) Calculate its discharge intervals as the highest and lowest higher value of the feeder strengths of every set as a consequence of all the regulations when it occurs accordingly.
3) If the right endpoints of the restricted centroid have been calculated, substitute each successive MF with the right endpoints (i.e., to create the AES with the greatest centroid value); otherwise, select the leftmost AES.
4) Test all potential switching index values, from 0 to the highest index supplied for the following MFs:

   i. Utilize the greater premium of the discharge interval to compute the left endpoints to use MF with an index less than the switching index and then switch to the lesser value; alternatively, use the lower amount of the discharge intervals for the right endpoints following the initial switching index.

4   Do AES Inferences Union and Defuse the Set Produced

5) Return the maximum and minimum centroid result from the defuzzification in the preceding step as the ultimately restricted centroid.

It shows the procedure for developing a suitable embedded set to identify the restricted centroid. In addition to this, the corresponding firing intensity of the employed regulations is recognizable (i.e., the 'trunk heights'), which produces an AES that could be readily interpreted. It is easily observed that the AES is a joining of two MFs (medial and high). When each consecutive MF is substituted, one of its AESs (links or rightmost) and an inferences value is selected for each of them (i.e., one of the endings of the discharge intervals). That is why AESs that identify the restricted centroid terminals retain the same degree of readability as any fuzzy output of an FLS. That is to say, although FLSs enable uncertainties modeling of membership functions, they maintain the same accuracy quality.

5   Software Analysis and Performance Evaluation

The study conducted to create the AI facility is integrated into this part. Various situations were tested. They are built on the originally noted architecture, and a mininet emulator was used for conducting simulations and gathering information for the design process. It searches for the most comprehensive data collection using this testing ground. It needs to evaluate which features impact the quality of service (QoS) and hence the quality of experience (QoE). The proposed model investigated how various network characteristics are affected by the video quality and frames per second. The network settings are jitter, latency, and losses rate. It looked at how connection status impacts the end-user perception of visual quality.

The Table 1 show the accuracy analysis of the existing support vector machine (SVM) and proposed EAI-FL system, respectively. The simulation analysis of the proposed EAI-FL system is analyzed by varying the number of actions/requests from a minimum of 5 to a maximum of 40 with a step size of 5. As the number of actions increases, the respecting simulation outcomes of the system increasing. The proposed EAI-FL system with expandable AI and IoT environment helps the system perform well even if the high actions are required at very little time.

Table 1. Accuracy analysis of the proposed EAI-FL system

Number of actions/requests	SVM (%)	EAI-FL (%)
5	89	96
10	86	95.7
15	84	94.6
20	82	93.8
25	80	93.1
30	79	92.5
35	76	91.5
40	74	90.9

The accuracy analysis of the proposed EAI-FL system is depicted in Table 1. The simulation analysis of the given dataset is analyzed by varying the number of actions from a lower level to a higher level. As the number of actions increases, the system cant process all the incoming requests, and overall system performance reduces. The simulation outcome, such as the accuracy of the proposed EAI-FL system, shows a higher performance than the existing SVM model. The proposed EAI-FL system with expandable AI and IoT enhances the connectivity and learning to rate.

Figures 4 and 5 indicate the specificity analysis of the existing SVM model and the proposed EAI-FL system, respectively. The proposed EAI-FL system with expandable AI and IoT models produces higher results than the existing SVM model. The simulation analysis of the proposed EAI-FL system is done by changing the number of

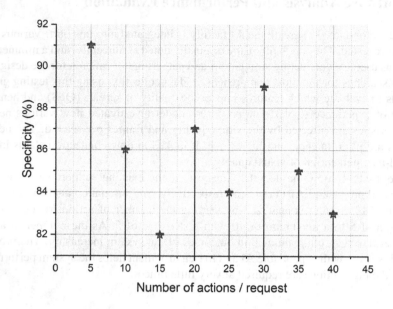

Fig. 4. Specificity analysis of the SVM model

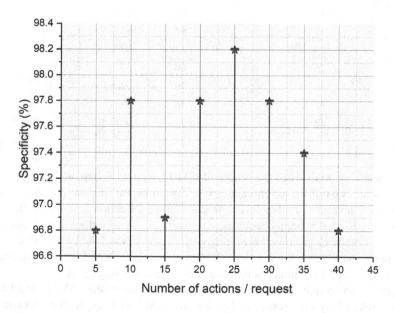

Fig. 5. Specificity analysis of the proposed EAI-FL system

requests from a minimum value to a maximum value with a step size of 5. The variations in the respective specificity of the proposed EAI-FL system are analyzed, and the results are compared with the existing models. The results indicate that the proposed EAI-FL system has higher simulation outcomes than other models. The sensitivity is calculated from the actual data and the user data required from the overall database. The simulation analysis is carried out by adopting the number of requests from 5 to 40 with a step size of 5. The simulation analysis of the proposed EAI-FL system is analyzed for one month, and the simulation outcomes are compared with the existing SVM model. The proposed EAI-FL system with an IoT environment and expandable AI enhances the system's stability and sensitivity [19–23].

The Fig. 6.

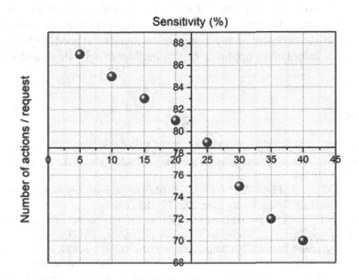

Fig. 6. Sensitivity analysis of the existing SVM model

Figure 6 shows the sensitivity analysis of the existing SVM model and the proposed EAI-FL system, respectively. The simulation outcomes of the proposed EAI-FL system are done by adopting the number of requests from a minimum of 5 requests to a maximum of 40 requests with a step size of 5 requests. The proposed EAI-FL system enhances the learning rate with the expandable AI systems, and the stability of the system is increased using an IoT environment with lesser complexity and higher computation speed. The simulation outcomes show the effectiveness of the proposed EAI-FL system over the existing SVM model [24, 25].

The proposed EAI-FL system is implemented, and the performance of the proposed EAI-FL system is evaluated using the dataset. The simulation outcomes such as accuracy, sensitivity, specificity, and other factors are analyzed. The proposed EAI-FL system with an IoT environment and expandable AI model enhances the overall system performance.

6 Conclusion and Future Scope

This research created and constructed a prototype of a resources admin panel for cutting-edge computer networks. Moreover, in line with the capacity accessible of IoT device network elements, it designed and developed horizontal plane scaled and vertically scaling methods. An explainable AI model based on fuzzy logic (EAI-FL) method for microservice development based on the idea of Fuzzy is at the heart of the platforms. The suggested method for maximizing the flushed memberships of the suggested fuzzy strategic planning algorithm is included in this paper. In this research, the efficiency of the suggested platforms and the functionality of EAI-FL algorithms have been verified in detail. The experimental findings are showed the decreased in resource adaptation reaction speed and flexibility in growing microservices. Future research on the major public cloud systems, including amazon web service (AWS), and Azure, the suggested microservice resource planning platform would be used software as a service (SaaS). In addition, it will experiment on the system to discover what needs to be strengthened further IoT edge calculations applications like intelligent agriculture and smart manufacturing.

References

1. Castañeda-Miranda, A., Castaño-Meneses, V.M.: Smart frost measurement for anti-disaster intelligent control in greenhouses via embedding IoT and hybrid AI methods. Measurement **164**, 108043 (2020)
2. Manogaran, G., et al.: FDM: fuzzy-optimized data management technique for improving big data analytics. IEEE Trans. Fuzzy Syst. **29**, 177–185 (2020)
3. Tsakiridis, N.L., et al.: Versatile internet of things for agriculture: an eXplainable AI approach. In: Maglogiannis, I., Iliadis, L., Pimenidis, E. (eds.) AIAI 2020. IAICT, vol. 584, pp. 180–191. Springer, Cham (2020). https://doi.org/10.1007/978-3-030-49186-4_16
4. Shakeel, P.M., Baskar, S.: Automatic human emotion classification in web document using fuzzy inference system (FIS): human emotion classification. Int. J. Technol. Hum. Interact. (IJTHI) **16**(1), 94–104 (2020)
5. Ding, W., Abdel-Basset, M., Eldrandaly, K.A., Abdel-Fatah, L., Albuquerque, V.H.C.D.: Smart supervision of cardiomyopathy based on fuzzy Harris Hawks optimizer and wearable sensing data optimization: a new model. IEEE Trans. Cybern. **51**, 4944–4958 (2020)
6. Amudha, G.: Dilated transaction access and retrieval: improving the information retrieval of blockchain-assimilated internet of things transactions. Wirel. Pers. Commun. (2021). https://doi.org/10.1007/s11277-021-08094-y
7. Preeth, S.K.S.L., Dhanalakshmi, R., Kumar, R., Shakeel, P.M.: An adaptive fuzzy rule based energy efficient clustering and immune-inspired routing protocol for WSN-assisted IoT system. J. Ambient Intell. Human. Comput. (2018). https://doi.org/10.1007/s12652-018-1154-z
8. Billah, M.F.R.M., Saoda, N., Gao, J., Campbell, B.: BLE can see: a reinforcement learning approach for RF-based indoor occupancy detection. In: Proceedings of the 20th International Conference on Information Processing in Sensor Networks, pp. 132–147 (2021)
9. Nguyen, C.H., Pham, T.L., Nguyen, T.N., Ho, C.H., Nguyen, T.A.: The linguistic summarization and the interpretability, scalability of fuzzy representations of multilevel semantic structures of word-domains. Microprocess. Microsyst. **81**, 103641 (2021)

10. Manogaran, G., Varatharajan, R., Priyan, M.K.: Hybrid recommendation system for heart disease diagnosis based on multiple kernel learning with adaptive neuro-fuzzy inference system. Multimed. Tools Appl. **77**, 4379–4399 (2018)
11. Ullah, I., Youn, H.Y., Han, Y.H.: Integration of type-2 fuzzy logic and dempster-shafer theory for accurate inference of IoT-based healthcare system. Future Gener. Comput. Syst. **124**, 369–380 (2021)
12. Taloba, A.I., Mohamed, I.A., Aissa, A.B., Hussein, L.F.: IoT enabled modulated residential surveillance system using fuzzy logic. Mater. Today Proc. (2021). https://doi.org/10.1016/j.matpr.2021.01.177
13. Benyezza, H., Bouhedda, M., Rebouh, S.: Zoning irrigation smart system based on fuzzy control technology and IoT for water and energy saving. J. Clean. Prod. **302**, 127001 (2021)
14. Wu, C.G., Li, W., Wang, L., Zomaya, A.Y.: A fuzzy evolutionary scheduler for multi-objective resource allocation in fog computing. Futur. Gener. Comput. Syst. **117**, 498–509 (2021)
15. Muthu, B., et al.: IoT-based wearable sensor for diseases prediction and symptom analysis in the healthcare sector. IoT-based wearable sensor for diseases prediction and symptom analysis in the healthcare sector. Peer-to-Peer Netw. Appl. **13**(6), 2123–2134 (2020)
16. Ai, C., Jia, L., Hong, M., Zhang, C.: Short-term road speed forecasting based on hybrid RBF neural network with the aid of fuzzy system-based techniques in urban traffic flow. IEEE Access **8**, 69461–69470 (2020)
17. Che, Y., Sivaparthipan, C.B., Alfred Daniel, J.: Human–computer interaction on IoT-based college physical education. Arab. J. Sci. Eng. (2021). https://doi.org/10.1007/s13369-021-05895-y
18. Shen, Y., Yu, P., Lu, H., Zhang, X., Zeng, H.: An AI-based virtual simulation experimental teaching system in space engineering education. Comput. Appl. Eng. Educ. **29**(2), 329–338 (2021)
19. Singh, R., et al.: Highway 4.0: digitalization of highways for vulnerable road safety development with intelligent IoT sensors and machine learning. Saf. Sci. **143**, 105407 (2021)
20. Srivastava, S., Pant, M., Agarwal, R.: Role of AI techniques and deep learning in analyzing critical health conditions. Int. J. Syst. Assur. Eng. Manag. **11**(2), 350–365 (2020)
21. Singh, S., Sharma, P.K., Yoon, B., Shojafar, M., Cho, G.H., Ra, I.H.: Convergence of blockchain and artificial intelligence in IoT network for the sustainable smart city. Sustain. Cities Soc. **63**, 102364 (2020)
22. Mydukuri, R.V., Kallam, S., Patan, R., Al-Turjman, F., Ramachandran, M.: Deming least square regressed feature selection and Gaussian neuro-fuzzy multi-layered data classifier for early COVID prediction. Expert Syst. e12694 (2021)
23. Kaur, M.J., Mishra, V.P., Maheshwari, P.: The convergence of digital twin, IoT, and machine learning: transforming data into action. In: Farsi, M., Daneshkhah, A., Hosseinian-Far, A., Jahankhani, H. (eds.) Digital Twin Technologies and Smart Cities. IT, pp. 3–17. Springer, Cham (2020). https://doi.org/10.1007/978-3-030-18732-3_1
24. Saini, J., Dutta, M., Marques, G.: Fuzzy inference system tree with particle swarm optimization and genetic algorithm: a novel approach for PM10 forecasting. Expert Syst. Appl. **183**, 115376 (2021)
25. Raval, M., Bhardwaj, S., Aravelli, A., Dofe, J., Gohel, H.: Smart energy optimization for massive IoT using artificial intelligence. Internet Things **13**, 100354 (2021)

AI-Inspired Solutions

Using Mask-RCNN to Identify Defective Parts of Fruits and Vegetables

Sai Raghunandan Suddapalli ⓘ and Perugu Shyam⁽✉⁾ ⓘ

National Institute of Technology, Warangal, India
shyamperugu@nitw.ac.in
https://nitw.ac.in/

Abstract. Fruits and vegetables are a major source of food for humans after cereals. Since the evolution of civilizations, they have been gathered, cultivated and modified according to our needs. During the process of modification and harvesting, there might be diseased variants that are unfit for consumption. Manual removal/segregation of the diseased fruits and vegetables is a time consuming process on a large scale, which could be automated in the near future with the help of artificial intelligence. This could be done by training a machine, using machine learning algorithms, to recognize which fruits and vegetables are fit for consumption and which ones are not, with the help of an annotated dataset. The goal of this study is to introduce a dataset that contains 11 classes of fruits and vegetables that are annotated for instance segmentation tasks and the effectiveness of the dataset in simplifying quality testing and analysis. This paper begins by explaining the usage of Mask-RCNN [5] algorithm, and then explains the properties of the dataset and further discusses the areas of application where the dataset can be used.

Keywords: Fruits · Vegetables · Instance segmentation · RCNN · Mask-RCNN

1 Introduction

At various stages of cultivation, fruits and vegetables are prone to a variety of diseases such as rust, blight, scab and wilt. These diseases can occur due to a wide variety of reasons, but can be broadly categorized into three types: non-parasitic, parasitic, and viral diseases [11]. During the time of separation/removal, it becomes cumbersome to segregate the fruits and vegetables manually, especially at a large scale. For this purpose, we can employ automation techniques, particularly machine learning algorithms, to automate this process, thereby reducing the human factor. This study proposes an annotated dataset for instance segmentation of popular fruits and vegetables. This dataset is named FV-11, as it contains 11 classes of annotated fruits and vegetables. Currently, there are 355 images with annotations, which are encouraged to be extended further by the users. Classification tasks usually require high quality images that are often fed

© Springer Nature Switzerland AG 2022
J.-H. Kim et al. (Eds.): IHCI 2021, LNCS 13184, pp. 637–646, 2022.
https://doi.org/10.1007/978-3-030-98404-5_58

to the networks as one instance of a class per image. In instance segmentation tasks, it is required to have the position of the class in the image as well, so that it can be identified by the neural network. There exists a dataset by the name Fruits-360 [9], which contains 131 fruits and vegetables that are categorized for classification purposes. Now, we attempt to propose an annotated dataset that can be used for instance segmentation as well, where the localization, and the classification task is done at the same time. This dataset could prove to have important applications in the field of agriculture, and quality testing for the food industry, where identification of defects could be made easier and faster. In this study, we have used Mask-RCNN architecture for training our model. It is a region convolutional neural network that localizes the object and also generates a bitmap for the mask that is overlaid on the object. Considering the rapid growth in the food and nutrition industries where the need for rapid categorization of raw material is of high significance, our dataset can provide a way for automation of this process. This not only saves time, but also aids in accurate categorization of usable fruits and vegetables, thereby reducing human effort for such processes. Instance segmentation [4] algorithms provide a way of identifying objects that are scattered throughout the canvas of the given/captured image at a given time. This quality of instance segmentation is very useful for quality control methods in such factories that utilize fruits and vegetables as their raw material.

2   Data Preparation

To prepare the dataset, we have chosen 200 high quality images from Unsplash [12], which is a website with images with Creative commons license. We have gathered 155 images of fruits and vegetables from a local market, where there were multiple vendors who had stalls of fruits and vegetables. The images gathered from the local market were captured using a mobile device. Since most images were in varying dimensions, we have decided to upscale the images onto a 1024×1024 canvas before sending the input to the model for training purposes. So, the input layer of the Mask-RCNN model we initialized was of the shape (1024, 1024, 3). The third dimension handles the RGB color format. All images were then annotated with an image labelling and annotating tool called Sense sixgill [1]. Here the labelling was done in a way such that we can generate masks for each instance of every class. For 11 classes on an average, we could get 60 instances that the model could be trained on. The classes are listed as follows: potato, tomato, carrot, brinjal, rotten_apple, rotten_banana, rotten_orange, apple, banana, orange, guava.

Sense sixgill is an industry standard annotation tool that can be used to generate datasets for various object detection problems. The annotations were later exported in Sense's annotation format. The data gathered should be split into training, test, and validation sets. This is done so as to prevent overfitting of the model. Overfitting is a scenario in machine learning problems where the model predicts inferences with very high accuracy on the training set data, but fails to accurately draw inferences on the test data, which the model hasn't been trained on. This leads to an erratic model, which performs well only on the data it was trained on, which is not feasible for practical reasons. So, the dataset was split into a ratio of 8:1:1 of training: validation: test data respectively.

3   Model Training

All experiments were conducted in our local workstation using tensorflow 2.0 on a Lenovo®computer; Intel®Core™i5-5200U CPU @ 2.20 GHz, 2201 MHz, 8 Core(s), 4 Logical Processor(s), with 16 Gb RAM and 1.95 Gb Cache and 8 GB NVIDIA®GeForce 840M graphics card. When we discuss about artificial intelligence and its usage in computer vision applications, one of the most common networks we come across are artificial neural networks or ANNs [9]. To put in simple terms, ANN is an imitation of the human brain, where we structure the network in the following format:

1. Input layer
2. Hidden layer, where the computation occurs. It may consist of multiple hidden layers, depending on the complexity
3. Output layer, which consists of values ranging between 0 and 1(greater than or equal to 0 and less than or equal to 1).

Computation in ANNs occurs by the virtue of the inter-connection strengths, which are known as weights. These weights are usually represented as "W", which can take positive or negative values. Negative values cause inhibition of the input signals, and positive values cause addition. Output neurons have an activation function, which yields a result in the form of 0s or 1s. For multiple instance classification problems, ANNs use an activation function called softmax, which is defined as

$$\sigma(z) = \frac{e^{zi}}{\sum_{j=1}^{K} e^{zj}} \tag{1}$$

Where σ is the softmax function, K is the number of clusters or classes, z is the input vector and e^{zi} is the standard exponential function for input vector and e^{zj} is the standard exponential function for output vector. For computer vision applications, an extension of the ANNs, called Convolutional Neural Networks, or CNNs [2] have proved to be of great importance, due to the ability of the network to extract the features of a given object. It takes this name from mathematical linear operation between matrixes called convolution. CNNs have proved to be of excellent use in natural language processing tasks, and image classification tasks. Mask-RCNN model runs on a backbone of a much complex variant of CNNs, The basic model consists of a ResNet [6] backbone, which has extended output layers that perform regression for the object's position, and classification to detect the instances of the classes the model was trained on. To create an instance segmentation model, we chose Mask-RCNN for our model's architecture. There is a choice between choosing a resnet-101 backbone and a resnet-50 backbone, which depends on the user's choice. The backbone of Mask-RCNN is usually a Feature Pyramid Network, which is usually a ResNet backbone or a VGG backbone. Formally, a Resnet building block is defined as follows

$$y = F(x, W_i) + x \tag{2}$$

As it can be observed, x and y correspond to the input and output vectors of the layers and Wi is the vector of weights. It is observed that the corresponding input vector is further connected to the final output layer in a 'shortcut'. This layer performs identity mapping on the final output layer, leading to a feed forward like behavior of the network. This leads to the layer having a less number of connected layers, and produces a competitive accuracy with much complex networks like VGG-16 [10] and Alex net [8]. The image below summarizes the working of a Mask RCNN model's working and structure [14] in a manner that is highly approachable for beginners and experts alike where we see 2 types of machine learning algorithms working. First, the classification is done to identify the type of fruit/vegetable and linear regression is performed to identify the co-ordinates of the classified objects. Figure 1 summarizes the working of a Mask RCNN model's working and structure in a manner that is highly approachable for beginners and experts alike where we see 2 types of machine learning algorithms working. First, the classification is done to identify the type of fruit/vegetable and linear regression is performed to identify the co-ordinates of the classified objects. RPN here stands for a region proposal network, which upon receiving the input image, suggests areas of interest where the objects are likely to be present. In stage 2, the 3 boxes "class", "bbox" and "mask" denote the final

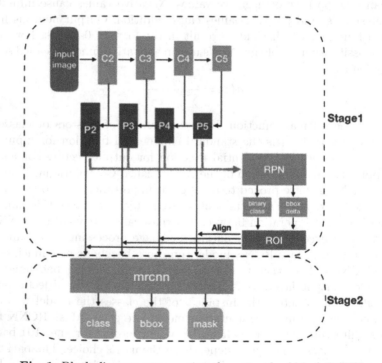

Fig. 1. Block diagram representing the network of Mask-RCNN

outputs that are presented by the model: the predicted class, the bounding box around the object of interest, and the bitmap mask generated over the object of interest. For real-time detection, other architectures like YOLACT [3] also can be used, which we will discuss in the conclusions section.

4   Results

Post training of the model, the overall accuracy was obtained to be 89% on the test dataset and 91.75% on the training dataset. Out of a 100 images for each instance that were sent for prediction, there were 10 wrongly predicted images. This gives us a practical accuracy of 90%, which can be improved by training the model further on various instances of the same classes, using more examples. This can be further improved by increasing the training time, and fine tuning the hyper parameters of the model, such as changing the learning rate, steps per epoch, no. of epochs, batch size and momentum of the optimizer. We have taken normal as well as diseased apples and were analyzed using Mask-RCNN network. The model generated a bitmap over each of the identified instances of apples. Thus localization is generated and can be seen in Fig. 2. In Fig. 4, it is shown that the model would detect guavas even when they're cut in half. We made sure the dataset contains cut fruits and vegetables as well, since some defects cannot be identified on the outer appearance. In Fig. 7, we can see the model identifies multiple instances of potatoes and carrot in the same picture. This is a key feature that can be observed in instance segmentation models, where multiple instances of different classes can be identified accurately. In Fig. 9, we see that the rotten bananas are identified here. These bananas are treated as an entirely different class, which separates them from healthy bananas. Further complexity can be added regarding the localization of the rotten part of the fruit, which is currently out of the scope of the project.

5   Discussion

Current specifications of the dataset meet a small yet significant needs of any life-scale problem. Post expansion of the dataset, we expect a significant rise in

Fig. 2. Instance segmentation of apples by the model

Fig. 3. Unlike Fig. 2, here the hand of bananas are recognized as a single unit, instead of being identified individually

Fig. 4. Instance segmentation of guavas when cut in half

Fig. 5. Here, oranges are detected by the model, both full oranges and cut oranges

the accuracy, and the usability of the dataset. As of now, the dataset contains 11 classes of fruits and vegetables that were used to train our current model. We didn't encounter any cases of overfitting in our model training phase, which indicates sufficient splitting of data. This data can be used to train automated

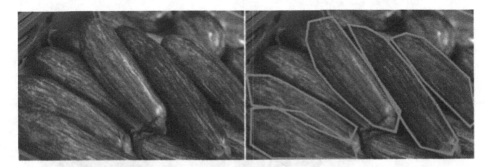

Fig. 6. Picture showing identification of Aubergines. Aubergines or Eggplants or Brinjals as they are called, are also termed as the king of vegetables in the Indian subcontinent due to its versatility in preparation of recipes

Fig. 7. Instance segmentation of multiple vegetables in a single image

systems to segregate fruits and vegetables for further processing in food and beverage industry, where fruits and vegetables are processed from their raw form into desired products such as juices, ready-made salads, etc. (Figs. 3, 5, 6, 8, 10 and 11).

We are going to train various object detection models, apart from Mask-RCNN, such as MobileNet [7], and Detectron2 [13], to obtain benchmarks of the dataset.

Fig. 8. Tomatoes being identified by the model

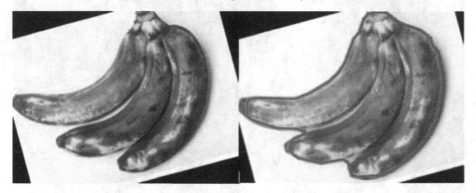

Fig. 9. Instance segmentation performed over diseased/rotten bananas

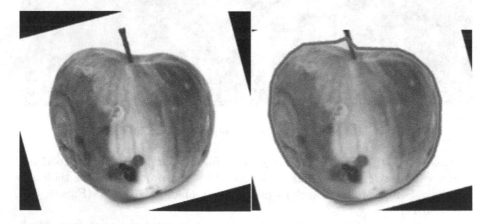

Fig. 10. Illustration showing the identification of a rotten apple by the model

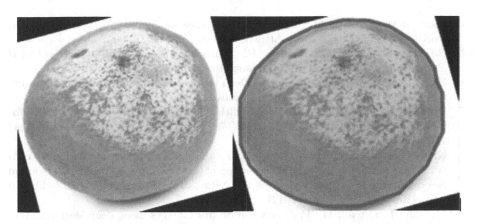

Fig. 11. Illustration showing the identification of a rotten orange by the model

6   Conclusions and Further Work

We have proposed a novel dataset for instance segmentation of diseased/rotten fruits and vegetables, and we have utilised Mask-RCNN algorithm to perform instance segmentation on our dataset.

We aim to design a standalone image sensor that can capture images and can use the model trained for instance segmentation. The entirety of this device is expected to be mobile and strong enough, so that we can carry it to places where detection of diseased fruits is key to the quality checks and analyses.

We also hope to train the model using a single shot detector model such as YOLACT which can be used in real-time video stream to identify the defects in fruits and vegetables.

We also aim to extend the dataset to identify specific diseases of fruits and vegetables, wherein timely identification of the diseases would help in implementing remedies for the crop, thereby helping boost the yield. The diseased fruits are classified purely on the basis of the presence/absence of degradation in the fruit or vegetable. This is one of our future prospects of this project where we extend the dataset to specific diseases, and not separation of healthy and diseased fruits in general. This could directly help the horticulture industry in identifying the disease on time, and implementing the remedial measures to boost the yield of the crop.

References

1. https://sense.sixgill.com/
2. Albawi, S., Mohammed, T.A., Al-Zawi, S.: Understanding of a convolutional neural network. In: 2017 International Conference on Engineering and Technology (ICET), pp. 1–6 (2017). https://doi.org/10.1109/ICEngTechnol.2017.8308186
3. Bolya, D., Zhou, C., Xiao, F., Lee, Y.J.: YOLACT: real-time instance segmentation. CoRR abs/1904.02689 (2019). http://arxiv.org/abs/1904.02689

4. Hafiz, A.M., Bhat, G.M.: A survey on instance segmentation: state of the art. CoRR abs/2007.00047 (2020). https://arxiv.org/abs/2007.00047
5. He, K., Gkioxari, G., Dollár, P., Girshick, R.B.: Mask R-CNN. CoRR abs/1703.06870 (2017). http://arxiv.org/abs/1703.06870
6. He, K., Zhang, X., Ren, S., Sun, J.: Deep residual learning for image recognition. CoRR abs/1512.03385 (2015). http://arxiv.org/abs/1512.03385
7. Howard, A.G., et al.: MobileNets: efficient convolutional neural networks for mobile vision applications. CoRR abs/1704.04861 (2017). http://arxiv.org/abs/1704.04861
8. Krizhevsky, A., Sutskever, I., Hinton, G.E.: ImageNet classification with deep convolutional neural networks. In: Proceedings of the 25th International Conference on Neural Information Processing Systems, NIPS 2012, vol. 1, pp. 1097–1105. Curran Associates Inc., Red Hook (2012)
9. Murean, H., Oltean, M.: Fruit recognition from images using deep learning. Acta Univ. Sapientiae Inform. **10**, 26–42 (2018). https://doi.org/10.2478/ausi-2018-0002
10. Simonyan, K., Zisserman, A.: Very deep convolutional networks for large-scale image recognition. CoRR abs/1409.1556 (2015)
11. Thind, S.K.: Principles of disease management in fruit crops, May 2017. https://medcraveonline.com/ICPJL/principles-of-disease-management-in-fruit-crops.html
12. Unsplash: Download free pictures & images [HD]. https://unsplash.com/images
13. Wu, Y., Kirillov, A., Massa, F., Lo, W.Y., Girshick, R.: Detectron2 (2019)
14. Zhang, X.: Simple understanding of mask RCNN, April 2018. https://alittlepain833.medium.com/simple-understanding-of-mask-rcnn-134b5b330e95

Attitude Control for Fixed-Wing Aircraft Using Q-Learning

David J. Richter[1(✉)], Lance Natonski[1], Xiaxin Shen[2], and Ricardo A. Calix[1(✉)]

[1] Purdue University Northwest, Hammond, IN 46323, USA
rcalix@pnw.edu
[2] Purdue University, West Lafayette, IN 47907, USA

Abstract. In recent years, there have been many advances in the field of Reinforcement Learning (RL). RL algorithms have achieved human master abilities in games such as Go, chess, Atari games, etc. The capabilities of RL algorithms have also now been tested in the automated transportation field for self-driving cars and aerial vehicles, where they are used to aid drivers and pilots in various situations. In this paper we apply Reinforcement Learning models to simulated airplane flight. In particular, we develop and test a Reinforcement Learning based methodology for airplane stabilization. In essence, through reward functions and Q-Learning based modeling, we analyzed and evaluated how a trained agent can learn to control a simulated Cessna 172 to stabilize itself while in flight. Our results show that, after training, the agent learns to achieve a stable attitude for the airplane. We perform the experiments using QPlane, which incorporates two flight simulators (X-Plane 11 and JSB-Sim). X-Plane 11 and JSBSim are both independently developed realistic flight simulators. The trained agent will be trained in JSBSim and tested in both simulators. Results of the analysis are presented and discussed.

Keywords: Agent based intelligent user assistance · Artificial intelligence · Reinforcement learning · Q-Learning · Aviation · Fixed-wing aircraft · Attitude control

1 Introduction

Reinforcement learning (RL) has seen a large increase in popularity in recent years, mainly due to the advances of Mnih at al. [15] and Silver et al. [23]. RL algorithms have achieved human level play in games such as go [23], chess [24], many Atari games [15], etc. The abilities of RL algorithms have also now been tested in the automated transportation field for self-driving cars [22] as well as aerial vehicles [3,13,31]. Most research in the field of RL in fixed-wing aviation focuses on using advanced Reinforcement Learning algorithms to fit the complex nature of flight. This paper explores using Q-Learning to train the agents and to adjust the state and action spaces in such a way for them to work with Q-Learning, in an effort to prove that the more simple Q-Learning algorithm can also be capable of operating in difficult, complex non-linear environments.

© Springer Nature Switzerland AG 2022
J.-H. Kim et al. (Eds.): HCI 2021, LNCS 13184, pp. 647–658, 2022.
https://doi.org/10.1007/978-3-030-98404-5_59

In this paper, we apply the Q-Learning Reinforcement Learning technique to simulated airplane flight. In particular, we develop and test a reinforcement learning methodology for airplane stabilization. Our results show that the agent is capable of controlling the airplane to keep a stable attitude after training. We perform the analysis using the QPlane [21] toolkit for Reinforcement Learning in flight simulators, which allows for training and testing on two separate flight simulators. The flight simulators used are JSBSim [2] and X-Plane 11 [14] which are both realistic flight simulators, and are developed independently, allowing the trained agents to be trained and tested in multiple separate independent environments, which further tests their robustness and generalizability.

A lot of research has been done in relation to self-driving cars and drones [13, 22]. Fixed-Wing aircraft [3, 31] have seen less work than quad-copters have. The aircraft industry for passenger aircraft, as well as automated drones for defense, has made a huge investment in remote flying and automation. Recently the airline industry showed great progress with the ATTOL project at European giant Airbus [1]. It is well known that the airline industry pursues automation quite strongly. As with all new technologies, automation can sometimes not work as originally designed. This is best evidenced by the Boeing 737 MAX and the safety problems it has experienced recently [7]. While automation here resulted in catastrophic failure, research and development has shown that eventually automated systems can achieve high levels of safety and efficiency.

Most research in RL for aviation is done for unmanned aerial vehicles (UAVs). One area where there has not been much emphasis in aircraft automation is general aviation (GA). General aviation is the classification of flying performed by private pilots. It is an area with a very high accident rate [29]. Surprisingly, many of the accidents are caused by pilot error. Therefore, general aviation could eventually improve its safety by implementing machine learning based systems that can help pilots to better fly their aircraft.

In this work, we explore the use of Reinforcement Learning (RL) techniques to develop an automated stabilization model for airplane flight. We use QPlane [14] to fly an aircraft (a Cessna 172) using a Reinforcement Learning methodology based on Q-Learning. The results that we obtain show promise for these kinds of systems. As part of the results, we provide a link to a video of the aircraft during the learning and stabilization process [20]. One of our major contributions is that we show that high dimensional, non-linear and complex tasks can also be encoded and successfully applied to algorithms like Q-Learning. The results of our experiments are presented and discussed.

2   Literature Review

Reinforcement learning (RL) techniques have started to show great progress for all types of automation and artificial intelligence. The algorithms have now been very successfully applied to games and have shown astounding results such as with AlphaGo [23] and across a set of 49 Atari games [15]. The main advantage of applying reinforcement learning to games is that games are governed by rules.

You have game states (be it screenshots of the current game state or numerical representations of the current state) and actions that lead to new states and rewards (the objective is maximize the sum of future discounted rewards). Rewards are also fairly easy to obtain from games, since most games already have a built-in scoring system, which keeps track of how well a user is doing at any given time. Because of this, no annotation is needed and instead you rely on the rules of the game for feedback (e.g., instead of annotated labels) using a trial and error like approach.

Reinforcement Learning is a subsection of Machine Learning and has seen a resurgence of interest in recent years. This is mostly due to Mnih et al. [15] and Silver et al. [23] and their successful projects, proving RL's capabilities of using neural networks to excel in highly complex environments, which was previously deemed impossible and a challenge not to complete for years to come. With these advances, other fields started applying RL for suitable tasks as well.

The application of RL techniques has for example seen extensive progress in the development of self-driving technology [8,30]. The automated flight industry has also seen progress with the research and development of RL algorithms for automated flight. Important papers in the automated flight industry include [11,17]. In [17], a remote-controlled helicopter was able to learn to hover in place and to perform several different kinds of helicopter maneuvers. The field of UAVs has also seen more and more research conducted in RL, however most of it is focused on using quad-copters, or drones [13]. These papers often times use Deep Reinforcement Learning (DRL) and policy gradient approaches (e.g. PPO) to train their agents in tasks such as attitude control [13] and landing [19], among others. There seems to be much less research done in the field of fixed-wing aircraft [3,31], but the work that does exist also mostly uses PPO and similar algorithms. The planes used are often times UAVs, with little to no focus on manned machines. General aviation as a whole has not seen as much research so far, and neither has Q-Learning for attitude control.

One possible reason to include more automation in general aviation is that it has a very high accident rate and a lot of the research [29] by the National Transportation Safety Board (NTSB) suggests that it is due to pilot error. Flight automation should eventually make its way to general aviation. Any system that could help to save a pilot's life should be desirable. In this research we propose the use of RL based Q-Learning for intelligent user assistance in the case of airplane stabilization of a simulated Cessna 172 (a common general aviation instruction aircraft). An accurate simulator is essential for good RL based research and development. In this work we use QPlane, which is a toolkit for Reinforcement Learning in fixed-wing flight using multiple flight simulators. This allows us to access and use two separate simulators to train and test on (X-Plane 11 and JSBSim). X-Plane 11 [14] is currently the standard for simulation and is sometimes even used by real pilots to practice some of their skills or at least to maintain flight awareness. Some studies that have used X-Plane for this kind of research include heading control [12], flocking [27], and collision avoidance [5], among others. The second flight simulator that will be used in this research is JSBSim. While X-Plane is a full-fledged flight simulation game that has to be bought at full price, JSBSim is an open source flight dynamics library that can be easily downloaded and installed for free and has also seen use in many research projects to this day [6,10,26].

3   Methodology

To develop the airplane stabilization model, we have used a Q-Learning architecture [4]. We performed several experiments and analyses to develop the reward functions and we measured the performance of the airplane as it tries to stabilize itself. The following sections provide a description of the main aspects of our work.

3.1   Reinforcement Learning and Q-Learning

There are many different RL algorithms. In this work we focus on the Q-Learning [28]. Q-Learning uses a lookup table like approach (see Table 1), where all Q-Values (the Q-Value represents the expected future discounted reward) are stored for all possible state-actions pairs. These Q-Values are then optimized over time in an effort to maximize the expected future discounted reward using the Bellman Equation [25] (see Eq. 1).

$$Q\left(s_t, a_t\right) = Q\left(s_t, a_t\right) + lr * \left(r + \gamma * Q\left(s_{t+1}, a_{t+1}\right)\right) \tag{1}$$

Where $Q\left(s_t, a_t\right)$ represents the Q-Value of the state s and action a at time t. lr represents the learning rate, r the reward and *gamma* represents the discount factor.

States are representations of the environment provided by the simulator. Currently, the values we picked to represent the state of the plane are pitch and roll. These values are the equivalents of reading pitch and roll from the aircraft's analog instruments (i.e., the six pack). Q-Learning only works with discrete states. Flight dynamics obviously are not only represented by discrete values, so the true state must be encoded. To calculate a state, we take an observation and extract the values for the two main flight controls (pitch and roll). These values are in the range from −180 degrees to +180°. The range for each of the two main controls is broken up into bins, and based on the observation, a bin is selected. We divided each of the two ranges into 13 bins each such as from −180 to −75, from −75 to −35, −35 to −15, −15 to −5, −5 to −2, −2 to −1 and −1 to 1 (all in degrees), where 0 is the desired position for the plane. The same is true for the positive range of both pitch and roll. Based on the value read from the six-pack instruments, we calculate the corresponding bin. This results in an binned pitch/roll range value, which is represented by a number between 0 and 12, each of which represents one of the before mentioned ranges of degrees for both pitch and roll. Since we have two axes represented by bins of size 13, we end up with a total number of states equal to 13 * 13 or 169. We use a square encoding approach to determine the state. Each binned value is used to represent the values for pitch and roll. To calculate the state, both the pitch and roll values are first put into their respective bins as shown before and are then encoded with this equation which guarantees each combination to be unique:

$$s = \theta_b * 13 + \phi_b \tag{2}$$

where s is the state, θ_b is the binned pitch value and ϕ_b is the binned roll value. The corresponding states will look like this:

Table 1. A table representing parts of the Q-Table generated with the state and action space used.

Encoded state (s)	Pitch bin θ_b (Pitch range θ)	Roll bin ϕ_b (Roll Range ϕ)
0	0 (-180 to −75)	0 (-180 to −75)
1	0 (-180 to −75)	1 (-75 to -35)
2	0 (-180 to −75)	2 (-35 to -15)
$\vdots$		
83	6 (-1 to 1)	5 (-2 to -1)
84	6 (-1 to 1)	6 (-1 to 1)
85	6 (-1 to 1)	7 (1 to 2)
$\vdots$		
166	12 (75 to 180)	10 (15 to 35)
167	12 (75 to 180)	11 (35 to 75)
168	12 (75 to 180)	12 (75 to 180)

Just like with the states, actions must be represented as discrete values for the Q-Learning algorithm to work. One way of handling this restriction would be by simply assigning each of the values you want the actions to take to a discrete value [9]. This, however, makes the action space very large. Another option would be to only allow one value to be taken for all four desired actions. But this approach limits the agent to a very small set of actions, which might either be too extreme or too minimal in their magnitude. Therefore, we decided to base the actions on the states. This allows the agent to keep a small action space of four, which are aileron left up + aileron right down, aileron right up + aileron left down, elevators up and elevators down. But it also allows the benefits of having a leveled action space, as to not resort to only one magnitude of actions.

The way this is handled is as follows: The action is chosen as if there are only four actions to choose from. Then, the selected action will be converted to a continuous value by looking at the current attitude of the plane. This results in the action being of a higher value if the plane is further from the desired state, and it being smaller if the plane is very close to the desired state (The higher the action value the stronger the action, where 0 is no action and 1 is full force).

The value conversion used was as follows: It takes the action that was picked as a one hot encoded value and changes only the picked action to a continuous value (Table 2).

Table 2. A table of the way the actions are made continuous values. α_a is the angle of the action axis in degrees and a_c is the continuous action value. The lower bound value in each of the angle columns is the upper bound value of the column to the right.

α_a	0 to -1	to -2	to -5	to -10	to -15	to -25	to -50	to -180
a_c	0.025	0.05	0.1	0.25	0.33	0.5	0.66	0.75

This same table applies to positive angles, only that the action value would then be negative. These values were found to work well during testing and parameter tuning.

3.2   Q-Learning Parameters

In this study we performed 2,000 episodes. Every epoch has 1,000 moves or steps. Each episode represents a game played. When the epoch ends, the airplane returns to a starting position. The starting positions are randomly generated within a given range. This range was set to be $[-15:15]$ for roll and $[-10:10]$ for pitch. The desired state was also randomly generated for each episode and was in the range of $[-5:5]$ for both pitch and roll (all in degrees). Testing was conducted in the JSBSim environment, with testing done in both JSBSim and X-Plane.

The parameters for our proposed model are both inspired by earlier works and their findings, as well as tests we performed to improve them to fit our task better [3,13,31]. They include a number of states equal to 169, number of actions equal to 4, gamma is equal to 0.95, learning rate is equal to 0.01, and epsilon equals to 1 with a decay of 0.00001. The actions are related to the control surfaces of the airplane, and they include pitch up, pitch down, roll right and roll left. Variations in the throttle power on the Cessna 172 as well as the yaw angle and the corresponding rudder actions were not considered for this work. The Q table was of size (states (169), actions (4)).

3.3   JSBSim Simulator

JSBSim [2] is a flight dynamics library. This means that communication with this simulator works very directly by accessing all necessary methods or variables in code. The physics loop can also be controlled and stepped by QPlane, even at a speed faster than real time. This allows for training to conclude much quicker than if all physics would be executed in real time. Besides this, JSBSim also allows to be run in headless mode, meaning that no 3D graphics need to be rendered for it to run, saving resources for the training itself. However, there is an option to have them rendered. For this the open source flight simulator FlightGear can be used [18]. This makes JSBSim the ideal simulator to be used for training purposes.

3.4   X-Plane 11 Simulator

X-Plane 11 flight simulator [14] was used for testing purposes. To communicate with X-Plane 11 we use XPlaneConnect (XPC) which is an API developed by NASA [16]. All communications are sent using UDP packages, because we do not have direct access to the games main loop, and therefore it is impossible to step the physics within QPlane itself. XPlane only runs in real time and with 3D rendering enabled, which both slows down the training tremendously. This is why X-Plane should and was only used for testing purposes. X-Plane, however, is very well suited for testing purposes, because users can interact with the controls at runtime, meaning that the user can maneuver the aircraft into any given state during testing using their mouse, controller or flight stick, allowing for human interaction with the trained agent. This allows for extended testing and allows the plane to be put in any state at any time, a feature not possible with JSBSim. Lastly, it is also a great way to test the agent for robustness and generalization to other circumstances, or even overfitting to the training environment by testing it on a secondary flight simulator.

In this paper we used the very popular general aviation aircraft Cessna 172.

3.5   Reward Functions

We implemented two distinctly different reward functions, both of which were used for training separately, and both of which performed well when testing.

The first reward function that was tested is a sparse reward function. This reward function follows the example of sparse reward functions, meaning it only gives reward if the agent is in a certain state, and otherwise the reward will be 0. In this case of attitude control, the reward is 0 for all states except when the plane is within -5 and $5°$ in both pitch and roll at the same time.

$$
\begin{aligned}
r &= 10 \mid True \; if \; |\phi| < 5 \; AND \; if \; |\theta| < 5 \\
r &= 0 \mid True \; for \; all \; other \; cases
\end{aligned}
\tag{3}
$$

Where r is the reward, ϕ is the current roll angle and θ is the current pitch angle.

The second reward function that was tested and utilized in this work is a continuous reward function, or delta reward function, which is essentially the opposite of the sparse reward function. Unlike before, in the delta reward function all states receive a reward, which is calculated by taking into account the deviation of the current state to the desired state. Using this function even bad states will receive a certain amount of reward (see Eq. 4), which they would not do in the sparse function.

$$
r = \left(\left(2 - \left(|\phi|/180 + |\theta|/180\right)\right)/2\right)^2
\tag{4}
$$

This reward function is shaped in a way that clips all rewards in the range of [0:1], where 1 is the best possible value to achieve. This reward is not yet final. More conditions are applied as follows:

$$r = r * 0.1 \mid True \; if \; |\theta| > 40 \; OR \; if \; |\phi| > 40$$
$$r = r * 0.25 \mid True \; if \; |\theta| > 20 \; OR \; if \; |\phi| > 20$$
$$r = r * 0.5 \mid True \; if \; |\theta| > 10 \; OR \; if \; |\phi| > 10 \qquad (5)$$
$$r = r * 0.75 \mid True \; if \; |\theta| > 5 \; OR \; if \; |\phi| > 5$$
$$r = r * 0.9 \mid True \; if \; |\theta| > 1 \; OR \; if \; |\phi| > 1$$

These conditions are read from top to bottom, and if one is true then the ones following will be skipped (else-if statements). The r on the right side of the equation is the r as calculated by Eq. 4. These additional condition checks help to shape the reward in a way where the difference between very bad and bad, or good and very good states becomes more apparent (unlike the sparse function). If, for example, the plane is at $-15°$ roll in the old state and $-14°$ in the new state, then a sparse reward would not characterize either state as better or worse, since both would receive a reward of 0. Only after many training iterations would Q-Values indicate certain state-action pairs as superior. When using delta reward however, the reward for -15 might be 0.45, whereas the reward of -14 might equal 0.46. This immediately represents the better state by a higher value, which makes it easier for the agent to recognize and pick up on that fact. This can also speed up the training process. When using sparse rewards, the agent needs to reach the target region at least once, but most likely multiple times, by pure randomness, for the Q-Values to trickle down. This makes success less guaranteed. In the case of attitude control for fixed-wing aircraft with Q-Learning, both functions performed well as shown in Sect. 4.

4   Analysis and Results

In this section of the paper, we present the results of the analysis. We performed multiple experiments over a period of several weeks.

Based on observation, as can be seen in the video [20], we were able to determine that the model worked and that the airplane would learn to stabilize itself. We plotted the rewards over the episodes and noticed that the plots do indeed support the claim (see Fig. 1). The reward maximizes as the training progresses and converges at an optima. This proves that the agent does in fact learn a policy that maximizes the reward and manages to stabilize the aircraft. This was true for both reward functions.

Additionally, we plotted the value deltas of the control surfaces (pitch, roll) as they change when running the agent in testing mode. The plotted testing results were gained with JSBSim while using the delta reward function, unless stated otherwise.

In Fig. 2 we can see the delta changes for pitch. Over a period of 2000 moves (i.e. steps), the pitch value levels off to the range of the desired value. We can see that in all four cases, all of which represent a different randomly spawned

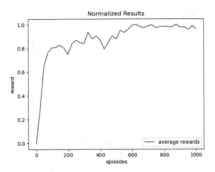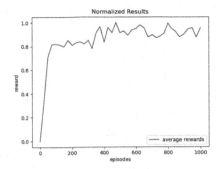

Fig. 1. Plot of total rewards per episode over time during the training phase when using the delta (left) and sparse (right) reward function for 1000 episode. The total rewards were normalized for this graph.

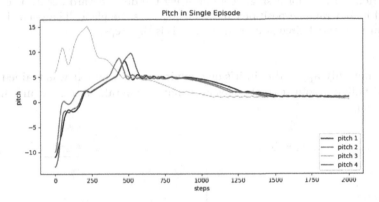

Fig. 2. Pitch per step for a single episode using the delta reward agent. The agent is spawned in four random positions and then stabilizes the plane. The y-axis is the pitch deviation from the desired state and the x-axis is the steps.

testing episode, that the agent starts off in undesirable orientations and then moves towards the desired position and stays within a very close proximity of that angle. The same can be observed in Fig. 3, where the roll in the same experiment runs was observed. Just like the pitch, the roll was also set at random, with the agent quickly stabilizing the plane.

Lastly, we also compared the trained agent in the X-Plane 11 environment and compared it to the JSBSim testing results. Note that the agent has never before interacted with X-Plane 11, and while both X-Plane and JSBSim try to simulate the same physics, they were developed completely independently from each other, therefore exposing the agent to a new unknown challenge. The results can be seen in Fig. 4. The results are not identical, which proofs that both Flight Simulators do indeed not behave the same, but it can be observed that the agent manages to stabilize the plane in both cases. This proves that the

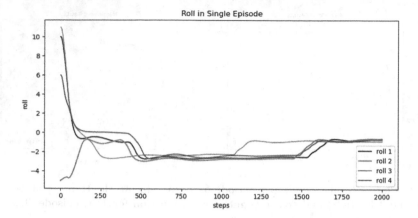

Fig. 3. Roll per step for a single episode using the delta reward agent. The agent is spawned in four random positions and then stabilizes the plane. The y-axis is the roll deviation from the desired state and the x-axis is the steps.

agent is not only applicable in it's own environment where it was trained in, but that the policy is robust to changes and that it generalizes to new and unknown environments.

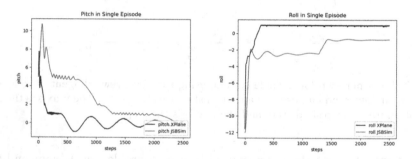

Fig. 4. Pitch and Roll per step for a single episode run in both JSBsim and X-Plane. The agent was trained exclusively in JSBSim and interacts with X-Plane for the first time.

Based on our results, we believe that the model does well for the task of airplane flight stabilization. This proves that regular Q-Learning can be successfully applied to complex, challenging environments if a supporting foundation is built. By using a state encoding system, a system that converts discrete action values to continuous values, experiment setup that supports learning and exposure to many states and reward functions that represent the problem well, the agent was able to achieve good results even in an environment that was completely unknown to it.

5   Conclusion

In this paper we have presented a methodology for aircraft stabilization while in flight. The results of our research and experimentation show promise of this type of application. We have proposed simple reward functions for airplane stabilization. Using Q-Learning, we have shown that the aircraft learns to stabilize itself in a reasonable amount of time. We have presented results for multiple reward functions, environments and also results for in testing angles and rewards. The results are very promising, as they show that Q-Learning is capable of succeeding in such a complex environment.

Future work will include creating other modules such as for flying from point A to point B, descents, ascents, and other more complicated maneuvers. Additionally, reward functions, state representations, action conversions and experiment setups could be altered to potentially achieve even better results.

References

1. Airbus: Is autonomy the future of aerial mobility? https://www.airbus.com/newsroom/stories/autonomy-aerial-mobility.html
2. Berndt, J.: JSBSim: an open source flight dynamics model in C++. In: AIAA Modeling and Simulation Technologies Conference and Exhibit, p. 4923 (2004)
3. Bøhn, E., Coates, E.M., Moe, S., Johansen, T.A.: Deep reinforcement learning attitude control of fixed-wing UAVs using proximal policy optimization. In: 2019 International Conference on Unmanned Aircraft Systems (ICUAS), pp. 523–533. IEEE (2019)
4. Calix, R.: Getting Started with Deep Learning: Programming and Methodologies using Python. CreateSpace Independent Publishing Platform (2017)
5. Cheng, Q., Wang, X., Yang, J., Shen, L.: Automated enemy avoidance of unmanned aerial vehicles based on reinforcement learning. Appl. Sci. **9**(4), 669 (2019)
6. Clarke, S.G., Hwang, I.: Deep reinforcement learning control for aerobatic maneuvering of agile fixed-wing aircraft. In: AIAA Scitech 2020 Forum, p. 0136 (2020)
7. Cruz, B.S., de Oliveira Dias, M.: Crashed boeing 737-max: fatalities or malpractice. GSJ **8**(1), 2615–2624 (2020)
8. Duan, J., Li, S.E., Guan, Y., Sun, Q., Cheng, B.: Hierarchical reinforcement learning for self-driving decision-making without reliance on labelled driving data. IET Intell. Transp. Syst. **14**(5), 297–305 (2020)
9. Huang, X., Luo, W., Liu, J.: Attitude control of fixed-wing UAV based on DDQN. In: 2019 Chinese Automation Congress (CAC), pp. 4722–4726. IEEE (2019)
10. Kim, J.P.: Evaluation of unmanned aircraft flying qualities using JSBSim (2016)
11. Kimathi, S., Kang'ethe, S., Kihato, P.: UAV heading control in windy and turbulent conditions using reinforcement learning
12. Kimathi, S.: Application of reinforcement learning in heading control of a fixed wing UAV using X-plane platform (2017)
13. Koch, W., Mancuso, R., West, R., Bestavros, A.: Reinforcement learning for UAV attitude control. ACM Trans. Cyber-Phys. Syst. **3**(2), 1–21 (2019)
14. Laminar-Research: Xplane. https://www.x-plane.com/
15. Mnih, V., et al.: Human-level control through deep reinforcement learning. Nature **518**(7540), 529–533 (2015)

16. NASA: Xplaneconnect. https://github.com/nasa/XPlaneConnect
17. Ng, A.Y., Kim, H.J., Jordan, M.I., Sastry, S., Ballianda, S.: Autonomous helicopter flight via reinforcement learning. In: NIPS, vol. 16. Citeseer (2003)
18. Perry, A.R.: The flightGear flight simulator. In: Proceedings of the USENIX Annual Technical Conference, vol. 686 (2004)
19. Polvara, R., et al.: Autonomous quadrotor landing using deep reinforcement learning. arXiv preprint arXiv:1709.03339 (2017)
20. Richter, D.J.: QPlane result video. Video (2021). https://youtu.be/Puq8paN3BKs
21. Richter, D.J., Calix, R.A.: QPlane: an open-source reinforcement learning toolkit for autonomous fixed wing aircraft simulation. In: Proceedings of the 12th ACM Multimedia Systems Conference, MMSys 2021, pp. 261–266. Association for Computing Machinery (2021)
22. Sallab, A.E., Abdou, M., Perot, E., Yogamani, S.: Deep reinforcement learning framework for autonomous driving. Electron. Imaging 2017(19), 70–76 (2017)
23. Silver, D., et al.: Mastering the game of go with deep neural networks and tree search. Nature 529(7587), 484–489 (2016)
24. Silver, D., et al.: A general reinforcement learning algorithm that masters chess, shogi, and Go through self-play. Science 362(6419), 1140–1144 (2018)
25. Sutton, R.S., Barto, A.G.: Reinforcement Learning: An Introduction. MIT Press, Cambridge (2018)
26. Vogeltanz, T., Jašek, R.: JSBSim library for flight dynamics modelling of a mini-UAV. In: AIP Conference Proceedings, vol. 1648, p. 550015. AIP Publishing LLC (2015)
27. Wang, C., Yan, C., Xiang, X., Zhou, H.: A continuous actor-critic reinforcement learning approach to flocking with fixed-wing UAVs. In: Asian Conference on Machine Learning, pp. 64–79. PMLR (2019)
28. Watkins, C.J., Dayan, P.: Q-learning. Mach. Learn. 8(3–4), 279–292 (1992)
29. Wiegmann, D., Faaborg, T., Boquet, A., Detwiler, C., Holcomb, K., Shappell, S.: Human error and general aviation accidents: a comprehensive, fine-grained analysis using HFACS. Technical report, Federal Aviation Administration Oklahoma City Ok Civil Aeromedical Inst (2005)
30. Xia, W., Li, H., Li, B.: A control strategy of autonomous vehicles based on deep reinforcement learning. In: 2016 9th International Symposium on Computational Intelligence and Design (ISCID), vol. 2, pp. 198–201. IEEE (2016)
31. Zhen, Y., Hao, M., Sun, W.: Deep reinforcement learning attitude control of fixed-wing UAVs. In: 2020 3rd International Conference on Unmanned Systems (ICUS), pp. 239–244. IEEE (2020)

Exploiting Federated Learning Technique to Recognize Human Activities in Resource-Constrained Environment

Ahmed Imteaj[1,2], Raghad Alabagi[3], and M. Hadi Amini[1,2(✉)]

[1] Knight Foundation School of Computing and Information Sciences,
Florida International University, Miami, FL 33199, USA
{aimte001,moamini}@fiu.edu
[2] Sustainability, Optimization, and Learning for InterDependent Networks
Laboratory (Solid Lab), FIU, Miami, FL 33199, USA
[3] University of Arizona, 1040 4th St, Tucson, AZ 85721, USA
ralabagi@mail.pima.edu

Abstract. The conventional machine learning (ML) and deep learning (DL) methods use large amount of data to construct desirable prediction models in a central fusion center for recognizing human activities. However, such model training encounters high communication costs and leads to privacy infringement. To address the issues of high communication overhead and privacy leakage, we employed a widely popular distributed ML technique called *Federated Learning (FL)* that generates a global model for predicting human activities by combining participated agents' local knowledge. The state-of-the-art FL model fails to maintain acceptable accuracy when there is a large number of unreliable agents who can infuse false model, or, resource-constrained agents that fails to perform an assigned computational task within a given time window. We developed an FL model for predicting human activities by monitoring agent's contributions towards model convergence and avoiding the unreliable and resource-constrained agents from training. We assign a score to each client when it joins in a network and the score is updated based on the agent's activities during training. We consider three mobile robots as FL clients that are heterogeneous in terms of their resources such as processing capability, memory, bandwidth, battery-life and data volume. We consider heterogeneous mobile robots for understanding the effects of real-world FL setting in presence of resource-constrained agents. We consider an agent unreliable if it repeatedly gives slow response or infuses incorrect models during training. By disregarding the unreliable and weak agents, we carry-out the local training of the FL process on selected agents. If somehow, a weak agent is selected and started showing straggler issues, we leverage asynchronous FL mechanism that aggregate the local models whenever it receives a model update from the agents. Asynchronous FL eliminates the issue of waiting for a long time to receive model updates from the weak agents. To the end, we simulate how we can track the behavior of the agents through a reward-punishment scheme and present the influence of unreliable and resource-constrained agents

© Springer Nature Switzerland AG 2022
J.-H. Kim et al. (Eds.): IHCI 2021, LNCS 13184, pp. 659–672, 2022.
https://doi.org/10.1007/978-3-030-98404-5_60

in the FL process. We found that FL performs slightly worse than centralized models, if there is no unreliable and resource-constrained agent. However, as the number of malicious and straggler clients increases, our proposed model performs more effectively by identifying and avoiding those agents while recognizing human activities as compared to the state-of-the-art FL and ML approaches.

Keywords: Federated learning · Human activity · Resource-limitations · Edge resources · Global model · Convergence

1   Introduction

1.1   Motivation

Human activity recognition (HAR) is one of the widely popular classification machine learning (Ml) applications that is used to identify activities (e.g., sitting, standing, walking, laying, or driving a vehicle) of a person. The HAR classifier model has immense applicability in various other applications such as surveillance system, fitness applications (e.g., counting number of steps), patient monitoring, context aware applications (e.g., automatic response to a phone call while driving) and so on. The prevailing HAR methods requires centralized server to store the collected data in order to constructing a powerful model. In such approaches, a user has no idea whether data would be leaked or modified by other entities or not once they are shared with the central server. Besides, the centralized ML approaches tends to several other issues. For example, in some cases, it is difficult to share data across various organizations due to privacy or liability concerns. Also, the amount of data collected by a human agent could be large and sending them to a central server would incur huge communication cost [3]. We present a rational conversation between an AI service provider (AI) and a customer (C) regarding data sharing and ML model generation:

C: *"We need a solution for recognizing human activities in a factory to provide early warning of unusual activities".*
AI: *"No problem. We need to collect some data from your factory to train a human activity recognition model".*
C: *"Of course. We already have sufficient amount of data which are collected from the smart devices placed in our factory".*
AI: *"Awesome! Please upload all the data in our server".*
C: *"I am afraid to say that I can not authorized to share those sensitive data with a third party!"*
AI: *"We can send our ML experts to work on-site with those data but you need to pay additional costs for that".*
C: *"Sorry, we are not able to bear additional expanses as it would exceed our current budget!"*

This is one of the situations that urges AI community to rethink inventing a new strategy of model training keeping user information private. With the same motivation, a privacy preserving distribute ML technique, Federated Learning (FL) [1] was invented that enables on-device model training and produces a global model accumulating knowledge of all the clients. FL eliminates the need of uploading dataset to a central server, reduces communication overhead, and minimizes data leakage as model are trained through model aggregation rather than data sharing. Under the FL framework, we only require to train a HAR model locally on each data owner's (i.e., FL client) side using its own computing resources, and upload the model parameters to the FL server for model aggregation. The existing FL-based HAR applications [4,5] assumed that all the FL clients have sufficient resources to perform assigned local computation and generate a local model that would be shared with the server. However, if we consider an FL-based Internet-of-Things (IoT) environment, where the small and resource-constrained IoT devices would be considered as the FL clients, then a lot of such FL clients would be incapable to perform a whole computational task. Besides, as the IoT devices are unreliable and more prone to attacks [6], it may result in ineffective model update from the clients. Hence, the client selection part is crucial in an FL setting as an unreliable and slow client (also called stragglers) can prolong the learning process. A client turns into a straggler if it is underpowered compared to the task assigned to it. Considering all these, we proposed an FL-based HAR approach by choosing proficient clients and enabling partial works based on the client resources, which is particularly suitable for resource-constrained environment. By leveraging asynchronous FL, we further reduce the straggler effect empowering immediate global model update on the FL server.

1.2   Literature Reviews

Human activity recognition (HAR) plays an important role in pervasive and ubiquitous computing. The state-of-the-art deep learning models replaced the traditional feature engineering and achieved higher accuracy [16,17]. However, all such centralized solutions for HAR rely on collected data from network clients that causes privacy issues. Federated Learning (FL) comes forward with a unique solution of preserving client's privacy and eliminates the solitary dependency on a central fusion center for model generation. As a consequence, the research domain of FL is inflating due to its unique feature of preserving data privacy, handling non-IID data, and minimizing communication overhead. Several research papers on FL [8–12] are available focusing on FL system design, components, applications, challenges, and their potential solutions. In turn, the authors in [6] presented a comprehensive survey on FL-IoT setting, where they pointed out the challenges, analyzed prospective solutions, and highlights several future directions that arise while applying FL on a resource-constrained IoT environment. The authors [7] proposed an all-inclusive FL model, FedPARL that can shrink the model size of the resource-constrained agents, selects the most proficient and trustworthy agents for training and dynamically allocate local tasks for the agents. Since the invention of FL method, it has been applied in various applications, such as recommendation system [19], keyword spotting [20], next-word prediction [18], smart robotics [21] and so on. Similar to such mobile applications and robotics systems, HAR is another vital aspect that can be benefitted from FL simplifying privacy management and providing user adequate flexibility over controlling their local data by choosing which data would be selected and how the selected data should be contributed in development of a HAR application. The authors in [13] proposed a HAR system powered by FL and they demonstrated that their proposed model performs very close to the centralized model performance that may experience privacy issues. Zhao et al. [14] designed an FL-based HAR system for human activity and health monitoring considering low cost edge devices (e.g., Raspberry Pi) and simulate the model inference time until reaching to an acceptable prediction accuracy. Besides, a locally personalized FL-based HAR system is introduced in [15] to predict human mobility. The above-mentioned proposed works adopted FL method due to the ultimate need of utility and privacy guarantee. However, the existing FL-based HAR approaches randomly select clients for training without considering their capability to perform training task that arise straggler effects. Further, all the existing FL-based HAR systems consider a uniform computational task to be assigned to all selected FL clients while in real-world scenario, it is infeasible to make sure that all clients would be able to perform equivalently. Moreover, for an FL-based HAR setting, any resource-constrained device can act as a server; hence, it is not viable to send all the human activity data to a central server and develop a HAR classifier from the collected data as like conventional ML approaches. Thus, there is a research gap in FL-based HAR application development considering a resource-constrained IoT environment.

1.3   Contributions

Our main contributions of this proposed work are listed below:

- We proposed an FL model for HAR systems that is effective for a resource-constrained environment.
- We proposed a generalization of FedAvg algorithm to develop a HAR classifier that can allocate local computational tasks to federated clients based on their available resources.
- We adapted a mechanism of selecting proficient client during training that can mitigate the straggler effects.
- We infuse asynchronous FL mechanism in HAR systems so that the FL server can perform immediate model update and accelerate the convergence.

2   System Description

2.1   Federated Learning Background

Federated Learning (FL) is a privacy-preserving distributed ML technique that leverages on-device model training of the network agents utilizing their edge-resources and learning from the accumulated knowledge of the other agents. In

FL process, the FL server initializes a global model which is shared with all the available agents within the network. Each selected agent (also called participant) generates a local model using its available data and learning from the global model. The agents apply an optimization method to solve their local objective functions which are shared with the server. The server aggregates all the received local models and generates an updated global model that holds all the latest knowledge of the network agents. The interactions between FL server and agents are continued until the global model achieves a target convergence. While applying FL for HAR within a resource-constrained environment, it is obvious that we may observe agents possessing variant system configurations and data samples. Due to resource heterogeneity, while one agent could perform an assigned task, another agent may struggle to accomplish that task and turn into a straggler. Therefore, it is not reasonable to assign a uniform computational task to all the selected FL agents. Otherwise, if a majority of the FL agents fail to share local model, then the global model quality would increase slowly and overall model convergence would be prolonged [2]. Besides, as the resource-constrained IoT devices are more prone to attacks, they may inject false model. A comprehensive survey on FL for IoT devices is presented in [6], where they pointed out such potential challenges (e.g., straggler issues, false model injection) FL process may face due to resource-constrained agents. To recognize human activities in a resource-constrained environment in a distributed fashion, it is essential to examine agent's resources, and leverage a strategy so that the learning process continues without having any effects due to stragglers or diverge model update. The state-of-the-art FedAvg algorithm [1] consider that any FL agent that shows interest to be a part of the learning process has sufficient resources for performing an assigned task. Hence, the FL server declares a uniform task for all the selected agents during training. However, in a real-world setting, such assumption is not viable that results in unsuccessful model update from the weak agents. Besides, FedAvg algorithm randomly selects agents for training that increases the risk of selecting vulnerable agents. Considering these, we focus on developing an FL model, particularly for HAR by solving the straggler issues and handling diverge model update. We propose to select proficient and honest agents tracking agents' resource status and their contributions towards model convergence. Besides, we enable partial works from the agents to solve straggler issues during recognition of human activities.

2.2 Construction of a Activity and Resource-Aware Framework

In our proposed FL-based HAR model, we integrate a mechanism that can assign trust score to the agents based on various events, and select only the proficient and trustworthy agents for the training phase. We consider several events for categorizing trust score, e.g., successful task completion, diverge model infusion, interested to be a part of the training phase, response delay, and incapable to accomplish a given task. We design the trust score table considering the significance of the events, which is presented in Table 1. At the beginning of FL process, we assign an initial trust score $T_{init} = 50$ to all the federated agents.

Any agent who shows interest to participate in training, satisfies the resource requirement to perform task but not selected for training, we assign $T_{\text{Interest}} = 1$ score to motivate that agent to participate in future tasks. Besides, any agent who successfully accomplish a task within a specified time window, we add a reward score $T_{\text{Reward}} = 8$ to that agent's existing trust score. In case, an agent has previous history of becoming straggler in <20% of its all participation in the FL process, we assign penalty score $T_{\text{Penalty}} = -2$. In turn, if an agent gives slow response for more than 20%, but less than 50% of its overall participation, then we add up the existing the trust score of that agent by $T_{\text{Blame}} = -8$. Further, any agent that becomes straggler for ≥50% of its overall activities, or sends back a diverge model, we add a ban score ($T_{\text{Blame}} = -16$).

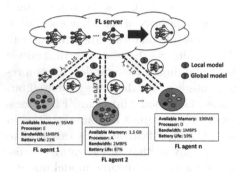

Fig. 1. Allowing partial works from the FL agents.

Table 1. Various events and corresponding trust value.

Event	Trust value
T_{init}	50
$T_{Interest}$	1
T_{Reward}	8
T_{Warn}	-2
T_{Blame}	-8
T_{Ban}	-16

2.3   Enabling Partial Works from the Agents

As we discussed in Sect. 2.1, one of the issues of the FedAvg algorithm [1] is that it does not allow partial works from the agents. As a result, any agent who fails to complete a whole task due to resource-limitations, can not share its model with the FL server. Such issue hamper the improvement of the global model quality. Considering that, we apply a strategy of generalization of FedAvg algorithm from [23] that enable each selected participant to share partial works and upgrade the global model quality by counting every little contributions from the agents. In Fig. 1, we presented a schematic overview of leveraging partial works from federated agents. It can be observed that while agent n can perform the whole task, agent 1 and 2 can only perform 15% and 37% of the whole task. The assigned task can be considered as the number of local iterations each agent needs to perform. Here, if the whole task is regarded as 100 iterations on the local data, then agent 1 and 2 can perform only 15 and 37 local epoch while the agent n successfully able to complete 100 local iterations. This strategy solves unnecessary waiting time due to straggler agents, and also reflects every little contributions from the agents on the global model quality.

2.4   Proposed FL-Based Human Activity Recognition Algorithm

We presented our FL-based human activity recognition method in Algorithm 1 considering unreliable and heterogeneous resource occupied federated agents. At the initial stage of FL process, interested agents commits registration to be a part of the FL-based HAR process (line **1**). Each agent holds a trust score. At the beginning, the FL server assigns an initial trust value to all newly registered agents, which is updated accordance to the activities of the agents, and the FL server broadcasts system requirements for performing a task to all available agents (line **2–3**). The FL server initializes the global model, w_0 and shares with the agents (line **4**). Each agent shares information about its available resources with the FL server (line **5**). At each communication round of the FL process, the FL server examines resource status of each interested agents by calling **ResourceStatus** function (line **6–7**). In **ResourceStatus** function, we consider communication round number, processing power $(\mathcal{P})$, battery-life $(\mathcal{B})$, memory $(\mathcal{M})$, and data volume $(\mathcal{V})$ as the resources of the agents, and store the resource status of agent a for communication round i into a list, $\mathcal{G}_a^i$ (line **29–30**). After that, the FL server compares the agent's resource status with the task requirements, $\mathcal{L}_{req}$ (line **31**). If the agent has sufficient resources for that task, then we store the agent's resource status information into a list, R and return the list, $\mathcal{R}$ (line **32–34**). After receiving the resource status information and checking the trust score of the agents, the FL server performs sorting and ranks the available agents, which are stored into a list $\mathcal{L}$ (line **8**). From the list, fraction of agents are selected and further, only a few agents are randomly chosen for the training round (line **9–10**). Each selected agent are requested to perform local computational tasks on their on-device data through **AgentLocalUpdate** function and the latest global model is passed as a function parameter (line **11–12**). After receiving command to perform on-device training from the FL server, each agent uses local solver determining inexact minimizer λ_a^i and performing local training to resolve local objective function (line **35–36**). Each agent splits local data points, $\mathcal{P}_a$ into batches, performs stochastic gradient descent (SGD) optimization technique considering feasible number of local epoch which is determined through local solver as well as using batches, sends back local model to the FL server (line **37–41**). After receiving model from an agent a, the FL server follows asynchronous FL strategy performs immediate aggregation to generate a latest global model without waiting for other agents (line **13–14**). The total number of data samples within FL networks is referred by n, which are distributed among the available agents, and the number of local data samples of an agent a during a communication round i is represented by n_i^a. Further, the FL server updates trust score of all participated agents based on their performance. The trust score is updated on calling **ScoreUpdate** function (line **15**). If an agent successfully sends local model update within time t, then we assign unsuccessful record during communication round i for agent a, $\mathcal{U}_a^i$ to 0 and give a reward to that agent by increasing its trust score (line **16–19**). In turn, if a client failed to send back model update within time t, we set $\mathcal{U}_a^i$ to 1 and check the agent's previous participation activities. If the $U_k^i = 1$ case occurs less than

20% of that agent's overall participation history, then we add a penalty score, $\mathcal{T}_{Penalty}$ to the agent's current trust score (line **20–23**). Likewise, if the $U_k^i = 1$ case happens $\geq 20\%$ but $< 50\%$, then we add a blame score, $\mathcal{T}_{Blame}$ (line **24–25**), and if the $U_k^i = 1$ event happen $\geq 50\%$, then a ban score is added to the agent's trust score (line **26–27**). Finally, the updated trust score, $\mathcal{T}_a$ is appended to a list (line **28**) and the score can be used during participation selection in next communication round.

3 Experimental Results

As we explained in Sect. 2.2, the trust score of participated agents in the FL process is updated based on their activities. The score is increased whenever an agent successfully accomplish a task and, decreased upon slow response, or improper model update. In Fig. 2, we visualize the activity data points that clearly shows that the dataset values are feasible to classify, and in Fig. 3, we simulate the trust score update of four FL agents corresponding to their activities in different training rounds. As per the trust score simulation of Fig. 3, we select Agent 1, Agent 2 and Agent 4 in training period $t7$.

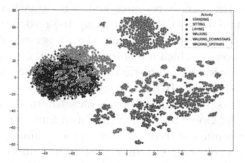

Fig. 2. Activity data point visualization of human activity recognition dataset.

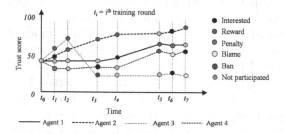

Fig. 3. Trust scores of four FL agents in various training rounds.

To evaluate our proposed FL model performance, we considered distributed mobile robots as FL agents that possess variant processing capability, battery-life, memory, and data volume. We used the UCI HAR dataset [22], which is a

---

Algorithm 1: Federated learning model for human activity recognition in a resource-constrained unreliable environment. The $\mathcal{N}$ eligible FL-based HAR agents are indexed by a; $\mathcal{F}$ = fraction of available agent, $\mathcal{B}$ = local minibatch size, E = local epoch number, η = learning rate, and t = timeout.

1 Each interested FL-based HAR agent registers in the FL network
2 Each agent a possesses a trust score, T_a. An initial trust value is assigned to registered agents, which is updated based on the agent's activities
3 System requirements are broadcasted to all interested agents
4 **FL Server executes:** initialize global model, w_0
5 Each FL-based HAR agent reveals its local resource availability
6 **for** *each communication round $i = 1, 2, \ldots$* **do**
7       $R_i = $ **ResourceStatus** $(i, \mathcal{P}_a, \mathcal{B}_a, \mathcal{M}_a, \mathcal{V}_a)$
8   Sort agents according to T_a and R_a, and keep in a list $\mathcal{L}$
9       $\mathcal{E} \leftarrow$ Top $\mathcal{L} \cdot \mathcal{F}$ agents
10     $\mathcal{A}_i \leftarrow$ (random set of $\mathcal{E}$ agents)
11   **for** *each agent $a \in \mathcal{A}_i$ execute in parallel* **do**
12         $w_{i+1}^a \leftarrow$ **AgentModelUpdate** (a, w_i)
13   **if** *Agent a respond within time t* **then**
14            $w_{i+1} \leftarrow w_{i+1} + \frac{n_i^a}{n} w_{i+1}^a$
15         $T_i = $ **ScoreUpdate** (i, a, w_a, t, γ)

16 **ScoreUpdate** (i, a, w_i, t, γ):
17   **if** *agent a sends local model w^i within t* **then**
18   set $\mathcal{U}_a^i = 0$
19   set $T_a = T_a + T_{Reward}$
20   **else**
21   set $\mathcal{U}_a^i = 1$
22   **if** $\frac{1}{i} \sum_{c=1}^i \mathcal{U}_a^c < 0.2$ **then**
23   set $T_a = T_a + T_{Penalty}$
24   **if** $\frac{1}{i} \sum_{c=1}^i \mathcal{U}_a^c < 0.5$ *and* $\frac{1}{i} \sum_{c=1}^i \mathcal{U}_a^c \geq 0.2$ **then**
25   set $T_a = T_a + T_{Blame}$
26   **else if** $\frac{1}{i} \sum_{c=1}^i \mathcal{U}_a^c \geq 0.5$ *or* G^i-$L_a^i > \gamma$ **then**
27   set $T_a = T_a + T_{Ban}$

28   Append T_a to *TrustList*
29 **ResourceStatus** $(i, \mathcal{P}_a, \mathcal{B}_a, \mathcal{M}_a, \mathcal{V}_a)$:
30   Store $(\mathcal{P}_a^i, \mathcal{B}_a^i, \mathcal{M}_a^i, \mathcal{V}_a^i)$ into a list $\mathcal{G}_a^i$
31   Compare $\mathcal{G}_a^i$ with $\mathcal{L}_{Req}^i$
32   **if** $\mathcal{G}_a^i$ *satisfies* L_{Req}^i **then**
33   Add $\mathcal{G}_a^i$ in $\mathcal{R}$

34   **return** $\mathcal{R}$
35 **AgentModelUpdate** (a, w) : // Run on agent a
36   Each FL-based HAR agent a generates a local model w_a^{i+1} which is a λ_a^i -inexact minimizer of: $w_a^{i+1} = F_a(w) + \frac{\delta}{2} \left\| w - w^i \right\|^2$ and determines optimal round of local epoch, E
37     $\mathcal{B} \leftarrow$ (split local data point of agent a, $\mathcal{P}_a$ into batch size B)
38   **for** *local epoch 1 to E* **do**
39   **for** *batch $b \in B$* **do**
40         $w \leftarrow w - \eta \nabla \ell(w; b)$
41   **return** model w to server

multivariate, time-Series dataset consisting of attributes, such as triaxial angular velocity and acceleration measured using gyroscope and accelerometer, respectively, a 561-feature vector consisting of time and frequency variables, the corresponding activity level and an identifier who collected the related data. We distribute data among agents to recognize human activities and simulate how each agent perform on-device training and generate a local model. We set up a similar transmission rate for all considered FL agents to bring simplicity of the implementation process. To simulate the straggler effects and demonstrate the effectiveness of our proposed model in HAR, we deliberately considered a number of weak agents, i.e., the agents fail to accomplish a given task due to limited resources. We assume that a global clock cycle is followed by each agent, and each chosen distributed agent can determine the number of local epoch it can perform using its resources and specified time window in training round i. Instead of using a uniform local epoch E, we apply a generalization of FedAvg algorithm that allows to execute partial works based on its available resources.

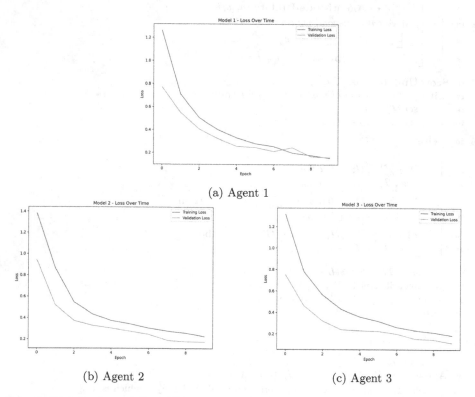

(a) Agent 1

(b) Agent 2   (c) Agent 3

Fig. 4. Training loss of three FL agents applying our proposed FL framework during recognition of human activities.

We apply our proposed FL algorithm (Algorithm 1) that enables on-device model training of the participated agents, and apply SGD optimization method

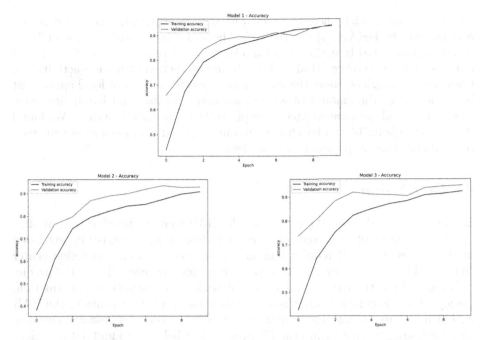

Fig. 5. Testing accuracy of three FL agents applying our proposed FL framework during recognition of human activities.

Table 2. Comparison of our proposed FL model with FedAvg model during prediction of human activities considering different local epochs and batch sizes.

Epoch	Batch size	Global model accuracy (1 out of 3 agent is straggler)		Global model accuracy (2 out of 3 agents are stragglers)	
		FedAvg	Proposed model	FedAvg	Proposed model
5	64	74.25%	76.38%	62.10%	73.45%
10	64	87.90%	90.35%	69.4%	85.7%
10	30	84.35%	87.10%	71.2%	83.4%
15	64	81.4%	84.90%	65.28%	79.8%
15	40	83.10%	85.95%	69.85%	80.5%
20	64	85.25%	88.20%	69.25%	84.10%
25	64	86.6%	89.4%	71.2%	84.9%
25	60	82.8%	86.04%	68.8%	80.4%

locally on each agent. The number local iterations on each agent side are dependent on the available resources and local data of the agents. We simulate our model for a small-scale during prediction of human activities considering three distributed agents and simulate the loss and accuracy of those three distributed agents' local models when 1 out of 3 agents are straggler (see Fig. 4 and 5). We also tested our model when 2 out of 3 agents are stragglers and compare our results with the FedAvg [1] algorithm for the same simulation settings. In Table 2, we demonstrated that the global model accuracy of our proposed FL model outperforms the FedAvg [1] algorithm during prediction of human activities in presence of stragglers. Here, the epoch resembles the number of local epoch that is considered as the amount of whole computational task and batch size refers to how the local data are splitted to apply SGD optimization method. We found that for the epoch 10 and batch size 20, our proposed FL model shows superior performance even in presence of stragglers.

4   Conclusion

In this paper, we developed an FL model for HAR that can be effectively applied in a highly unreliable resource-constrained environment. The existing prediction method based on HAR require human activity data in a central fusion center that could violate privacy and also do not consider the generation of the prediction model from the federated agents that could reveal significant information. Besides, there is currently no existing application on FL that consider the HAR within a resource-constrained environment. We integrated a resource-checking and trust score scheme within the FL process that helps us to find out proficient and trustworthy agents for the training phase. Further, we leverage a generalization of FedAvg algorithm that allows the resource-constrained agents to perform partial tasks instead of accomplishing the whole tasks that mitigates the straggler effects and helps the FL server to count every little contributions from all the participated agents. We tested the performance of our proposed FL model using HAR dataset and considering a real-word setting, and achieved a superior performance comparing to the existing HAR methods.

Acknowledgement. This material is based upon work supported by the National Science Foundation under grants CNS-1851890 and IIS-2027360. However, the authors are solely responsible for the findings presented in this study.

References

1. McMahan, B., Moore, E., Ramage, D., Hampson, S., y Arcas, B.A.: Communication-efficient learning of deep networks from decentralized data. In: Artificial Intelligence and Statistics, pp. 1273–1282. PMLR (2017)
2. Dinh, C.T., et al.: Federated learning over wireless networks: convergence analysis and resource allocation. IEEE/ACM Trans. Netw. **29**(1), 398–409 (2020)
3. Cui, L., Yang, S., Chen, F., Ming, Z., Lu, N., Qin, J.: A survey on application of machine learning for internet of things. Int. J. Mach. Learn. Cybern. **9**(8), 1399–1417 (2018). https://doi.org/10.1007/s13042-018-0834-5
4. Zhao, Y., Liu, H., Li, H., Barnaghi, P., Haddadi, H.: Semi-supervised federated learning for activity recognition. arXiv preprint arXiv:2011.00851 (2020)

5. Ouyang, X., Xie, Z., Zhou, J., Huang, J., Xing, G.: ClusterFL: a similarity-aware federated learning system for human activity recognition. In: Proceedings of the 19th Annual International Conference on Mobile Systems, Applications, and Services, pp. 54–66 (2021)
6. Imteaj, A., Thakker, U., Wang, S., Li, J., Amini, M.H.: A survey on federated learning for resource-constrained IoT devices. IEEE Internet Things J. **9**, 1–24 (2021). https://doi.org/10.1109/JIOT.2021.3095077
7. Imteaj, A., Amini, M.H.: FedPARL: client activity and resource-oriented lightweight federated learning model for resource-constrained heterogeneous IoT environment. Front. Commun. Netw. **2**, 10 (2021)
8. Tian, L., Sahu, A.K., Talwalkar, A., Smith, V.: Federated learning: challenges, methods, and future directions. IEEE Signal Process. Mag. **37**(3), 50–60 (2020)
9. Wei, Y.B.L., et al.: Federated learning in mobile edge networks: a comprehensive survey. IEEE Commun. Surv. Tutor. **22**, 2031–2063 (2020)
10. Imteaj, A., Amini, M.H.: Distributed sensing using smart end-user devices: pathway to federated learning for autonomous IoT. In: 2019 International Conference on Computational Science and Computational Intelligence (CSCI), pp. 1156–1161. IEEE (2019)
11. Li, L., Fan, Y., Tse, M., Lin, K.-Y.: A review of applications in federated learning. Comput. Ind. Eng. **149**, 106854 (2020). https://doi.org/10.1016/j.cie.2020.106854
12. Yu, T., et al.: Learning context-aware policies from multiple smart homes via federated multi-task learning. In: Proceedings of the 2020 IEEE/ACM Fifth International Conference on Internet-of-Things Design and Implementation, pp. 104–115. IEEE (2020)
13. Sozinov, K., Vlassov, V., Girdzijauskas, S.: Human activity recognition using federated learning. In: Proceedings of the 2018 IEEE International Conference on Parallel & Distributed Processing with Applications, Ubiquitous Computing & Communications, Big Data & Cloud Computing, Social Computing & Networking, Sustainable Computing & Communications, pp. 1103–1111. IEEE (2008). https://doi.org/10.1109/BDCloud.2018.00164
14. Zhao, Y., Haddadi, H., Skillman, S., Enshaeifar, S., Barnaghi, P.: Privacy-preserving activity and health monitoring on databox. In: Proceedings of the Third ACM International Workshop on Edge Systems, Analytics and Networking (Heraklion, Greece), New York, NY, USA, pp. 49–54 (2020)
15. Feng, J., Rong, C., Sun, F., Guo, D., Li, Y.: PMF: a privacy-preserving human mobility prediction framework via federated learning. Proc. ACM Interact. Mob. Wearable Ubiquit. Technol. **4**(1), 21 (2020). Article 10. https://doi.org/10.1145/3381006
16. Wang, J., Chen, Y., Hao, S., Peng, X., Lisha, H.: Deep learning for sensor-based activity recognition: a survey. Pattern Recogn. Lett. **119**(2019), 3–11 (2019)
17. Yao, S., Hu, S., Zhao, Y., Zhang, A., Abdelzaher, T.: DeepSense: a unified deep learning framework for time-series mobile sensing data processing. In: Proceedings of the 26th International Conference on World Wide Web, pp. 351–360. International World Wide Web Conferences Steering Committee (2017)
18. Hard, A., et al.: Federated learning for mobile keyboard prediction. arXiv preprint arXiv:1811.03604 (2018)
19. Chen, F., Luo, M., Dong, Z., Li, Z., He, X.: Federated meta-learning with fast convergence and efficient communication. arXiv preprint arXiv:1802.07876 (2018)
20. Leroy, D., Coucke, A., Lavril, T., Gisselbrecht, T., Dureau, J.: Federated learning for keyword spotting. In: ICASSP 2019–2019 IEEE International Conference on Acoustics, Speech and Signal Processing (ICASSP), pp. 6341–6345. IEEE (2019)

21. Imteaj, A., Amini, M.H.: FedAR: activity and resource-aware federated learning model for distributed mobile robots. In: 19th IEEE International Conference on Machine Learning and Applications (ICMLA), pp. 1153–1160. IEEE (2020)
22. Anguita, D., Ghio, A., Oneto, L., Parra, X., Reyes-Ortiz, J.L.: A public domain dataset for human activity recognition using smartphones. In: Esann, vol. 3, p. 3 (2013)
23. Li, T., Sahu, A.K., Zaheer, M., Sanjabi, M., Talwalkar, A., Smith, V.: Federated optimization in heterogeneous networks. arXiv preprint arXiv:1812.06127 (2018)

Modeling Human Decision-Making Delays and Their Impacts on Supply Chain System Performance: A Case Study

Diqian Ren[2], Diego Gallego-García[1], Salvador Pérez-García[1],
Sergio Gallego-García[1($\boxtimes$)] (ID), and Manuel García-García[1]

[1] UNED, 28040 Madrid, Spain
gallego101090@gmail.com
[2] University of Dayton, Dayton, OH 45469, USA

Abstract. The interaction between computer systems and humans is largely driven by the decision-making process of human beings. In the interaction process, delays are frequently unseen and therefore unforeseen, and their impacts are not considered as losses or as potential areas for improvement. As a result, the goal of this paper is to design a conceptual model to calculate delays impacts in decision-making interactions between humans and computerized systems. The model considers the sum of delays that occur due to various reasons; these include human delays, interface delays, and computer delays. Moreover, the conceptual model is applied in a supply chain system in which different human decisions interact with the digital planning model of an automotive manufacturer. The purpose of the simulation model is to quantify the loss and improvement potentials depending on the decision process delays in capacity measures in strategic, tactical, and operational planning horizons based on a defined target system. The results obtained show how delays significantly affect the supply chain performance. Finally, a methodological approach is presented for assessing the impacts of the delays in a sensitivity analysis.

Keywords: Decision-making processes · Human factor engineering · Human-computer interaction · Delays management · Modeling and simulation · Supply chain management · Digital twins

1 Introduction

HCI (human–computer interaction) studies the interactions and relationships between humans and computers. It is more than the analysis of user interfaces, as it is a multi-disciplinary field covering many areas. Recent HCI research goals have concerned the completion of tasks and argumentation about actions. As a result, new advances are improving the way people use computers to work, think, communicate, learn, critique, explain, argue, debate, observe, decide, calculate, simulate, and design [1].

In order to manage and control companies, an increasing number of environmental, organizational, and technological factors need to be considered in models used for decision making. This increases the level of complexity that must be handled by organizations

© Springer Nature Switzerland AG 2022
J.-H. Kim et al. (Eds.): IHCI 2021, LNCS 13184, pp. 673–688, 2022.
https://doi.org/10.1007/978-3-030-98404-5_61

[2]. In this context, the bullwhip effect is a supply chain concept that has been widely discussed in the literature, with many countermeasures taken from the side of industrial management to avoid or reduce it. However, the human factors underlying it have not yet been sufficiently explored [3]. Thus, human factors do not play the role they deserve in the design of process systems, making the systems less controllable than they could be if these human factors were properly considered. Therefore, potential improvements can be made regarding the systems' effectiveness, efficiency, reliability, and safety [4].

In the future, we expect that the human factor's role and contribution to value chains could change significantly, moving from the role of labor in the continuous search for value and existence since the first industrial revolution to a new state with a pre-industry revolution age central role [5]. Moreover, future projections state that Information and Communication Technologies (ICT) will be at the heart of new developments, where digital megatrends such e-manufacturing, e-government, entertainment on demand, virtual education, and a wide set of online services will be part of everyone's lives. As a result, new technologies together with HCI interfaces and the support of data-driven system modelling and simulation will be key factors in the near future for effective decision making for all manufacturing operations as well as the digital supply chain [2].

Moreover, Industry 4.0 cannot be considered without taking human factors and human interactions with machines as the key factors in the practical implementation of the smart factory [6]. These interactions will transform the existing workforce and change work activities in order to deal with the future market's flexibility and adaptability requirements [7]. At present, organizations can develop digital models of their production networks with current software tools. By using these tools, organizations can gain the opportunity to simulate their whole production network. These digital models together with simulation capabilities can help organizations to identify bottlenecks, capacity limitations, and workflow problems in advance [8]. By simulating different value chain scenarios in short periods of time, it is possible to define measures for dealing with possible problems before they arise, thus enhancing the decision-making capability of organizations [6]. For example, digital twins of complete value chains can improve the decision-making capability of organizations [8]. As a result, a key feature of new manufacturing systems is the ability to monitor physical processes through the use of a "digital twin" of the physical production system, thus enabling communication and cooperation between humans, machines, smart equipment, sensors, and other objects and agents [2].

Practitioners often take sub-optimal decisions due to a lack of information or delays in the decision-making process. Moreover, researchers often fail to holistically consider their dynamics over time [9]. While new technologies open up new possibilities, many managers, even in well-established companies, do not have a virtual digital twin that would enable them to analyze the expected outcomes of decisions that need to be made. In most cases, they do not have complete information and do not know all the implications of a certain decision. Therefore, the decision-making process is often delayed [9].

As a result of the arguments discussed, human behavior in supply chains has been insufficiently explored. Decision makers making the wrong decisions leads to suboptimal behavior and lower performance not only from the decision maker, but also from other stakeholders along the supply chain [3]. In order to study this complex decision situation, we developed a conceptual model for assessing human–machine decision-making delays and then applied the concept in a supply chain in which we experimentally studied the decisions made regarding different capacity options within the chain in different strategic, tactical, and operative planning horizons. Several scenarios were simulated based on the different delays and demand patterns and levels. We investigated the effects of decision-making delays on the performance of a manufacturing organization within the supply chain.

2 Theoretical Fundamentals

Human mental models for complex systems usually lead us in the wrong direction [10]. Therefore, only the study of the entire system as a feedback system will lead to correct results being obtained [11]. For this reason, system dynamics modeling is applied in this research.

Simulation models have been actively applied in the supply chain context with the goal of generating supply chain knowledge to develop and validate improvements using what-if analysis and quantification [12]. The analysis of what-if-scenarios provides the ability to make better planning decisions due to the additional information provided by the simulation. Therefore, the development of supply chain management simulation models has become a necessity [13].

Integration in Manufacturing (IiM) is the first systemic paradigm to organize humans and machines as a whole system from the managerial and corporate levels to the operator level. One of the major problems in this process concerns decisions made at the interface between the enterprise corporate level and the manufacturing shop floor level to pace production according to the life-cycle dynamics of the products, processes, and humans inside and outside the enterprise [2].

Nowadays, supply chain and manufacturing processes are supported by different systems, such as enterprise resource planning (ERP), MES (manufacturing execution systems), supply chain management (SCM), product lifecycle management (PLM), and computer-aided technology (CAx) [14]. In this regard, Industry 4.0 represents a way to achieve the real-time monitoring and synchronization of real-world activities with their digital twin model [15]. Therefore, delays occurring between processes, data analyses, and decisions can be eliminated or reduced.

Logistics systems are becoming increasingly volatile and complex, affecting the outcomes of decisions as a result. In a real-world situation in which there are complex conditions that change continuously, decisions often to be taken despite the lack of information. Therefore, it is necessary to consider the dynamic system behavior. For modelling real-world systems, mathematical modeling can support the description of deterministic processes by predicting their outcomes while reducing their complexity. On the other hand, a cybernetic approach that includes non-predictable processes in order to adapt to unforeseen disruptions quickly and robustly must be considered [6]. The purpose of this research is first to provide a mathematical model to reduce complexity while evaluating impact of delayed decision making and to develop a cybernetic system dynamics simulation model that offers the possibility of considering unexpected conditions such as various time delays and changing customer demands.

The main goals in human factors engineering are to consider any human–machine interaction as a total system with a systematic approach to ensure that the operational requirements do not exceed human abilities to arrive at practical solutions on a scientific basis [16]. Therefore, the failure to consider delays as a limitation of the whole system could lead to non-optimized systems and therefore to unstable processes. Human characteristics are often neglected in traditional decision-making models used for the design and management of production and logistics systems. Moreover, new technologies that include interactions with humans are currently being applied and developed. Thus, there is a need for the research and realization of case studies for design and management with a human-oriented approach that consider sustainable resource utilization in manufacturing and supply chains [2].

HCI has still many issues, such as delays, bad recognition abilities, and long training times [17]. Delays can take place between the instant when a person performs a gesture or motion and the instant when the computer responds [18]. Another major source of time delays is data acquisition, network, or operation system delays, which can also be significant [17].

The challenge in an world with unlimited sources of information is not only to make information available to people at any time, at any place, and in any form, but also to offer only the information that is relevant to the task at hand and to the background knowledge of the user—i.e., offering the user the "right" thing at the "right" time as a system strategy [1]. As a result, measures could be analyzed at the right time with the right information. However, the matter of how to define the right time must be determined based on the time frame and the delay between different activities in order to achieve the optimal result for the information available, the uncertainty, and planning capabilities to reach target goals. In order to obtain even better decision-making capabilities, it is very important to gain information as fast and early as possible. Even in an Industry 4.0-environment with high-speed computers, simulations take time and different situations have to be generated. Thus, delays are a major source of uncertainty that need to be considered in decision making. Moreover, to achieve the fast implementation of a virtual value chain, it is helpful to start simulating as early as possible in order to detect possible errors, which in a next step can be addressed by adequate measures. This results in better planning decisions based on preventive measures [6]. Finally, internal logistics processes need models, digital tools, and simulations if they are to face the flexibility required by the market. Currently, organizations do not have the mechanisms necessary to make the right decisions in most cases. One key reason why the majority of applications and systems reproduce this reality is the delay or lack of information, leading systems to take strategic, tactical, or operational decisions at a suboptimal time or in a suboptimal way [19].

3 Development of a Conceptual Model for Assessing Delays in Human–Computer Interactions

3.1 Modelling Decision-Making Process in the Human–Computer Interaction

First, it is necessary to mention the potential agents involved in decision making: human/s, computer/s, object/s, or decision/s based on human–computer interactions

(HCI). This latter type represents most of the cases dealt with currently. Based on the agents involved, the interactions leading to a decision can be defined as human (H), human to human (H2H), human to computer (H2C), computer to human (C2H), or computer to computer (C2C). In the model, the research focus is H2C and C2H decision processes, although these might be influenced by the interactions of H2H and H2H, as represented in Fig. 1. The model serves as basis for systems designed to assist in human decision making.

As it can be seen in Fig. 1, the HCI can be seen in terms of agents that interact with each other, providing information or inputs to one another and with certain lead times or delays occurring between actions in the decision chain. Computers have their own processing times, such as compiling times, file opening times, or simulation execution times. Meanwhile, humans have cognitive processing lead times and action lead times in the communication process. Moreover, in real organizations neither humans nor computers normally check or analyze something continuously; rather, this is carried out at discrete points of time. As a result, computer and human frequencies are considered for the analysis of the evidence that exists for taking a certain decision.

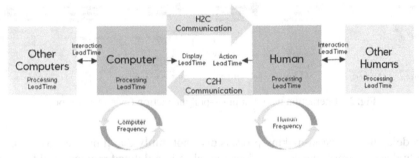

Fig. 1. The HCI modelled based on time management: interaction is defined as a function of the lead times or time delays between actions (own elaboration).

The represented model is applied not only in direct situations or operational interactions, but can also be applied for tactical and strategic planning tasks. This can be achieved by considering all the interactions, processes, frequencies, and action lead times that are required along the decision-making journey.

3.2 Interaction Nature: Drivers, Delays, and Uncertainty

The nature of an interaction can be defined according to several elements: whether the driver of the interaction is in the past (existing need) or in the future (future expectation of a need); who initiates the interaction (human, computer, both); why the interaction is initiated—i.e., what bottleneck resource need/s or parameter/s will be analyzed in the decision-making process; who is involved in the interaction—i.e., isolated HC (human–computer) interaction or multiple interactions of different types; how the interaction occurs (whether it is manual, cognitive, assisted, etc.); and how the system learns and improves from experience to gain knowledge about the system being considered.

As can be seen in Fig. 2, a HCI can be initiated by two potential drivers: an existing need such as the breakdown of a machine or an expectation of a future need such as the capacity requirements for production taking place in a certain time period. The first of these we name push nature and the second we name pull nature. A push interaction will lead to reactive planning to overcome the existing bottleneck need, while a pull interaction will lead to active planning that aims to prevent the expected bottleneck from taking place. In any case, an analysis step must first be performed to evaluate the alternative options. These can be classified as solving the bottleneck completely (full alternative solution), solving the bottleneck partially (partial alternative solution), or an alternative that does not expand the bottleneck (do nothing alternative or ineffective alternative solutions). Alternatives are compared based on given criteria. One of the options is the do nothing alternative; this is a decision where the consequences should also be considered. Then, the decision should be implemented, controlled, and monitored considering the training activities. Finally, the last step consists of comparing the expected outcome of the decision with the actual one in order to derive lessons that could help to improve the existing decision-making process.

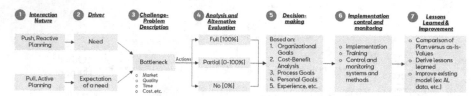

Fig. 2. Interaction nature: a push–pull interaction (own elaboration).

A delay in a decision-making process does not imply that it has negative effects. It reflects that the consequences of a decision taken in a defined moment will have other impacts than it would if the same decision was taken at another time. Therefore, the result of this statement is that after determining a method to decide whether or not to tackle a certain decision, the moment at when the decision is taken has the same or more importance.

Delays can have several causes, such as if real-time, fixed, or variable frequencies are used to evaluate the alternatives; if the lead times are known, unknown, or partially known; if information concerning the decision needs to be processed; the condition of agents involved in the HCI (human–computer interactions); the skill or training level of the agents involved; and the level of influence of other interactions.

Moreover, the risks of the decision depend on the information available up until the moment when the decision has to be taken if there is a defined deadline. Moreover, the risks depend on the accuracy of all the information considered as well as its alignment with the target goals.

3.3 Mathematical Modeling of Delay Impact on a Given Resource Need

For a resource need that is in the future or the past, there are always three areas and functions that need to be considered. The first is the actual supply capability of the given resource *C(x)*; the second is the resource need, including its future forecast *N(x)*; and the third is the alternative options for adapting the supply capability to the resource need— that is, the new *Cn(x)*. Based on this, Fig. 3 shows the different functions and areas that should be taken into consideration in the decision-making process when considering delays:

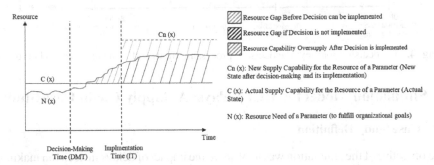

Fig. 3. Mathematical modeling of decision delays for a given resource (own elaboration).

Mathematically, these factors can be exposed with i as the different potential implementation times (*TI$_i$*) and j as the different new supply capability options (*Cn$_j$*). Moreover, the gap balance between the decision-making time (DMT) and the end of the period (EP) can be positive or negative for any defined time period—for example, "$\pm$" in the formula:

$$\text{Gap Balance DMT to EP } (x) = \pm \int_{DMT}^{ITi} N(x) - C(x)dx \pm \int_{ITi}^{EP} N(x) - Cn_j(x)dx \quad (1)$$

The "+" is defined according to whether the need is above the capability in a certain x ("+") or below the capability ("−"). The formula provides the gap; thus, if it is positive this means that there is less capacity to provide the resource need. Therefore, for each DMT one should consider what resource need gaps can be avoided for any given decision alternative versus what potential resource gaps will occur if no decision is taken. Moreover, the probability of the expected resource need and the capability dynamics should be also considered.

3.4 A Time-Oriented Model for Decisions Enabling Delays Evaluation

As can be seen in Fig. 4, decisions have several steps in their process cycle until the control and monitoring phase is reached. In each of these phases, delays in HCI can occur, causing impacts on the system that will need to be assessed and managed.

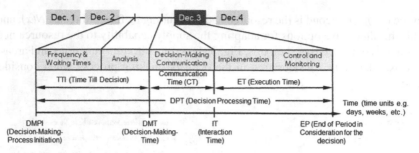

Fig. 4. The decision journey: the decision processing times and elements (own elaboration).

4 Simulation Model for HCI Delays: A Supply Chain Case Study

4.1 Case Study Definition

The objective of the simulation was to observe the impact of delays in decision making in a supply chain in the automotive industry. The hypothesis was that the simulation model without delays would present better results in terms of target indicators compared to the one that applies delays in the decision-making process with HCI. The methodology for developing the simulation model is shown in Fig. 5.

Fig. 5. Simulation model methodology (own elaboration).

First, a series of assumptions are defined to simplify the model to allow us to focus on the objectives of the simulation, such as non-variable manufacturing times, non-variable transportation times, the distribution of finished products, and the procurement of raw materials. The simulation also considers two different car models without variants. Moreover, a comparison can be made between the simulation models as the conditions are the same—i.e., they have the same demand, the same demand patterns, replicas with the same production capacities for each facility, the same investments, the capacity expansion over the simulation period, the same processing times, and the same staff capacity.

The case study presents a model of an automotive producer within a supply chain. The case study considers the relevant factor of production capacity as one of the key elements of the planning horizon in supply chains. An assessment of the necessary capacitive resources is an important task that must be undertaken in every planning period. System constraints are influenced by delays in HCI. There are four procedures, from short to long term, that are used to adapt supply capacity to demand requirements: variations in the working hours, additional or reduced numbers of shifts, external production, and investments in new capacities.

If a constraint condition persists over time, customer satisfaction decreases, and companies lose their market share and sales potential. Moreover, investments are not immediate [20]. Therefore, a delay between the time when a decision is made and when it is implemented must be considered.

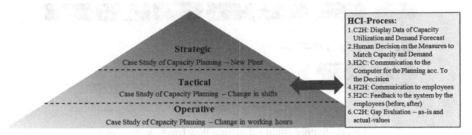

Fig. 6. HCI for capacity planning in the different planning horizons (own elaboration).

4.2 Development of a System Dynamics Model for the Case Study

For the development of the system dynamics model, the simulation models and their delay characteristics are first defined as shown in Fig. 6. Secondly, as shown in Fig. 7, the simulation flow is considered (Fig. 8):

Fig. 7. Simulation models and delays per planning horizon (own elaboration).

One car model is in its mature stage with a stable demand, providing a 1000 USD/car margin. The new model is in its launching process and provides 2000 USD/car. The simulation model considers volume loss when the customer order lead time is greater than 60 days. If this occurs, it is assumed that the new model will experience a loss in volume. Operational adjustments enable us to change the shift model, with a maximum of three shifts. Moreover, the number of employees per shift can change, providing a flexibility of 5% to the existing production capacities.

Furthermore, the following key performance indicators (KPIs) were calculated from the simulation over the 1000 working days: demand (units): sum of market demand

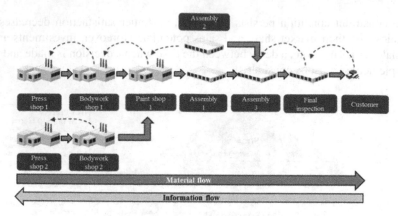

Fig. 8. Supply chain simulation flow (own elaboration).

for the car models; real demand (units): demand minus the demand loss due to long customer order lead times; production (units); capacity utilization (%); maximum production capacity (units/day); customer order lead time (days); service level (%): the quantity of units delivered on time divided by the demand per planning week; service level adjusted (%): the quantity of units delivered on time divide by the real demand per planning week; operational savings (million USD); investment (million USD): the amount of the investment made to increase capacities (the value is 30 million USD for an increase of up to 700 units per day for all models and scenarios); profits (in millions USD).

4.3 Model Validation

Before the results were extracted and interpreted, a validation was performed. The extreme value test method was used in this paper. Its application proved that the response is plausible when taking extreme values for different input parameters. These input variables were nominal capacity and customer demand. For a lower nominal capacity (units per day), the volume loss, customer order lead time, and capacity utilization must be higher, and the total number of units delivered to customers must be lower.

		Demand Pattern		
		Stationary	Trend	Seasonal
Demand Level	High	High-Stationary (HS-1)	High-Trend (HT)	High-Seasonal (HS-2)
	Low	Low-Stationary (LS-1)	Low-Trend (LT)	Low-Seasonal (LS-2)

Fig. 9. Definitions of scenarios as a function of demand level and pattern (own elaboration).

4.4 Scenarios Definition

Six demand scenarios based on different demand levels and patterns were simulated. In all scenarios, there were two products or car models. The demand was calculated in Excel so that the replication would have exactly the same demand in all models. This data generation method allowed us to create customized demand patterns to be read by Vensim (Fig. 9):

4.5 Simulation Results for the Case Study

The six scenarios presented the same trend between the delayed model and non-delayed model, with better results always being shown for the model in which the decision-making process and its implementation had no delays. Moreover, as can be seen in Table 1, Table 2 and Table 3, the differences were larger if the demand level was higher.

Table 1. Simulation results for demand scenario 1, stationary scenario.

Nr.	Key performance indicator (KPI)	High level with stationary pattern (HS-1)		Low level with stationary pattern (LS-1)	
		Non-delayed model	Delayed model	Non-delayed model	Delayed model
1	Demand (units)	780,017	780,017	683,046	683,046
2	Demand real (units)	734,533	703,201	683,044	671,855
3	Production (units)	689,445	657,582	670,587	648,456
4	Capacity utilization (%)	98.5	94.0	95.8	92.7
5	Max. prod. capacity (units/day)	700	700	700	700
6	Customer order lead time (days)	71.2	87.5	40.2	64.6
7	Service level (%)	89.3	84.0	93.9	92.3
8	Service level adjusted (%)	88.4	84.3	98.2	94.9
9	Operational savings (Mill. USD)	1.048 M	0.165 M	1.242 M	0.132 M
10	Investment (Mill. USD)	30 M	30 M	30 M	30 M
11	Profits (Mill. USD)	1,168 M	1,106 M	1,065 M	1,043 M

Therefore, we can state that the demand level is a relevant criterion that increases the risks when delaying the implementation of the decision-making process in capacity planning. Furthermore, it can be also observed how, for low demand levels, the difference in delaying the capacity adaptation measures has a lower influence on the results obtained for the LS-1 scenario and almost no influence in the LT scenario, which is the scenario with the lowest average demand per day. Moreover, when considering only the economic indicator, an investment of thirty million is worthwhile for HS-1 and HS-2, as the difference between the profit levels of the non-delayed and delayed models is lower than the investment value. However, when considering service indicators, such as customer order lead times and service levels, the investment also has a significant impact on the other scenarios—for instance, LS-2 has only a ten million profit difference but more than twenty days in order lead time and an almost three percent difference in service level.

Table 2. Simulation results for demand scenario 2, trend scenario.

Nr.	Key performance indicator (KPI)	High level with trend pattern (HT)		Low level with trend pattern (LT)	
		Non-delayed model	Delayed model	Non-delayed model	Delayed model
1	Demand (units)	697,016	697,016	598,240	598,240
2	Demand real (units)	688,994	680,149	598,238	598,143
3	Production (units)	657,016	645,384	593,786	591,756
4	Capacity utilization (%)	93.9	92.2	84.9	84.6
5	Max. prod. capacity (units/day)	700	700	700	700
6	Customer order lead time (days)	49.5	62.8	37.4	44.5
7	Service level (%)	91.4	90.7	95.9	95.2
8	Service level adjusted (%)	94.3	92.6	99.3	98.9
9	Operational savings (Mill. USD)	5.302 M	2.740 M	11.850 M	10.370 M
10	Investment (Mill. USD)	30 M	30 M	30 M	30 M
11	Profits (Mill. USD)	1,077 M	1,060 M	896 M	896 M

Table 3. Simulation results for demand scenario 3, seasonal scenario.

Nr.	Key performance indicator (KPI)	High level with seasonal pattern (HS-2)		Low level with seasonal pattern (LS-2)	
		Non-delayed model	Delayed model	Non-delayed model	Delayed model
1	Demand (units)	727,749	727,749	629,136	629,136
2	Demand real (units)	710,934	685,389	629,135	624,305
3	Production (units)	676,695	649,234	623,442	606,752
4	Capacity utilization (%)	96.7	92.8	89.1	86.7
5	Max. prod. capacity (units/day)	700	700	700	700
6	Customer order lead time (days)	59.8	76.6	38.5	61.3
7	Service level (%)	90.9	90.6	95.6	93.4
8	Service level adjusted (%)	93.0	89.2	99.1	96.4
9	Operational savings (Mill. USD)	4.288 M	2.978 M	15.570 M	12.570
10	Investment (Mill. USD)	30 M	30 M	30 M	30 M
11	Profits (Mill. USD)	1,121 B	1,070 B	958	948

5 Discussion

Managers need to deal with uncertainty and delays from multiple sources. In today's organizational environments, humans and computers interacting in almost all decision-making processes. Therefore, for the successful realization of managerial positions, a methodological approach is key in order to consider the impact of delays in the target criteria of the supply chain or production system according to the strategic, tactical, and operational levels. For that purpose, Fig. 10 provides a methodology that consists of eight steps in order to guide managers and planning employees. This methodology starts from the relevant factor that must be considered from a process perspective, followed by the mapping of the processes related to it. Then, the interrelationships can be described, and the different tasks carried out within the process can be classified attending to the nature of the interaction between the elements involved. As a result, the HCI points, the tasks in which there is a HCI, the interrelationships of the tasks with other elements, and their place in the process are identified. From an in-depth analysis of the HCI tasks, the potential bottlenecks and related measures and decisions can be determined. Based on this analysis, models based on mathematical formulation, simulation, and AI can be designed to assess the impacts of delays on the system's performance. Moreover, a sensitivity analysis can be performed to show, for example, what would happen if we checked the capacity level of this production step each month instead of every year when there is a high seasonal demand. The methodology supports the determination of priorities and increases the frequency with which certain decisions are considered in the global system, as well as enabling the use of lessons learned, such as by planning actual deviations to develop AI models and creating recommender systems for future planning periods.

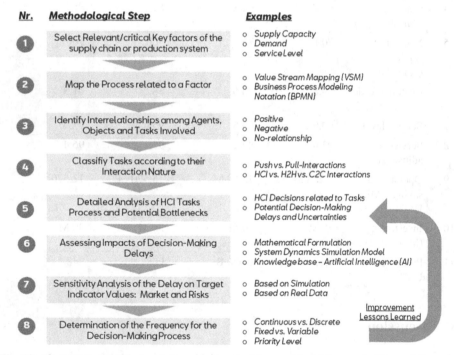

Fig. 10. Methodological approach for assessing decision-making delays: priorities and frequencies (own elaboration).

6   Conclusions and Future Outlook

In this research work, challenges in supply chain systems, decision-making processes and delays, as well as the human factor in the HCI in the fourth industrial revolution were discussed. Moreover, a mathematical formulation was defined to help managers to analyze decision-making alternatives and their implications. Furthermore, we created a definition of the decision-making process with different phases and lead times, which could provide a useful framework for the monitoring of decision-making processes. As a result, delays in HCI can be properly considered, leading to a higher system performance being obtained.

To prove the value of our concept, a system dynamics simulation model was successfully developed to complement the mathematical formulation. This simulation was used as part of a case study that considers capacity planning when making decisions concerning reducing or increasing production capacity at the strategic, tactical, and operational levels. The simulation shows how delays in the decision-making process have a significant influence on the system performance. A higher influence can be seen for higher demand levels and non-stationary demand patterns. As a result, the simulation carried out as part of a specific case study proved the usefulness of this methodology for gaining insights into the influence of delays on system performance. Thus, this methodology can help to enhance the adaptability of the system to future unexpected disruptions.

Our final goal is to transfer this research method to real planning systems as a tool to assist managers in the simulation of delays within what-if scenarios, thereby speeding up the methodological process used for assessing decision-making delays as a unique selling proposition (USP) of an organization. The results show the benefits of the use of a digital twin approach in which top management can determine the optimum time to analyze which measures should be used for which factors of a global system. This can be achieved by knowing all the potential implications of this decision and considering the alignment with the organizational goals. The conceptual model includes limitations, as it can consider other HCI theories and models. In addition, the simulation model does not represent the real complexity of the supply chain in detail, as it does not monitor the different decision-making steps or HCI and does not consider decision-making alternatives other than doing nothing or making an investment. As a result, the question of how to implement this approach in large organizations with multiple plants and departments remains to be answered.

Future research could aim to develop AI and recommender models to support planning activities by considering the risks of decision-making process delays, improving the viability of a company over time. As a result, there is evidently a need for such a system as a standard element in future digital twin tools for managers in order to increase the efficiency and adaptability of organizations.

References

1. Fischer, G.: User modeling in human–computer interaction. User Model. User-Adap. Inter. **11**(1), 65–86 (2001)
2. Panetto, H., Iung, B., Ivanov, D., Weichhart, G., Wang, X.: Challenges for the cyber-physical manufacturing enterprises of the future. Annu. Rev. Control. **47**, 200–213 (2019)
3. Brauner, P., Runge, S., Groten, M., Schuh, G., Ziefle, M.: Human factors in supply chain management. In: Yamamoto, S. (ed.) HIMI 2013. LNCS, vol. 8018, pp. 423–432. Springer, Heidelberg (2013). https://doi.org/10.1007/978-3-642-39226-9_46
4. Nachreiner, F., Nickel, P., Meyer, I.: Human factors in process control systems: the design of human–machine interfaces. Saf. Sci. **44**(1), 5–26 (2006)
5. Huy, D.T.N., Van, P.N., Ha, N.T.T.: Education and computer skill enhancing for Vietnam laborers under industry 4.0 and EVFTA agreement. Ilkogretim Online **20**(4) (2021)

6. Brecher, C.: Advances in Production Technology, p. 211. Springer, Heidelberg (2015). https://doi.org/10.1007/978-3-319-12304-2

7. Romero, D., Bernus, P., Noran, O., Stahre, J., Fast-Berglund, Å.: The operator 4.0: human cyber-physical systems & adaptive automation towards human-automation symbiosis work systems. In: Nääs, I., et al. (eds.) APMS 2016. IFIP Advances in Information and Communication Technology, vol. 488, pp. 677–686. Springer, Cham (2016). https://doi.org/10.1007/978-3-319-51133-7_80

8. Schuh, G., Potente, T., Wesch-Potente, C., Weber, A.R., Prote, J.-P.: Collaboration mechanisms to increase productivity in the context of industrie 4.0. In: 2nd CIRP Robust Manufacturing Conference (RoMac 2014), pp. 51–56 (2014)

9. Gallego-García, S., Reschke, J., García-García, M.: Design and simulation of a capacity management model using a digital twin approach based on the viable system model: case study of an automotive plant. Appl. Sci. 9(24), 5567 (2019)

10. Ford, A.: Modeling the Environment: An Introduction to System Dynamics Modeling of Environmental Systems. Island Press, Washington, DC (1999)

11. Márquez, A.C.: Dynamic Modelling for Supply Chain Management: Dealing with Front-End, Back-End and Integration Issues. Springer, Heidelberg (2010). https://doi.org/10.1007/978-1-84882-681-6

12. Campuzano, F., Bru, J.M.: Supply Chain Simulation: A System Dynamics Approach for Improving Performance. Springer, Heidelberg (2011). https://doi.org/10.1007/978-0-85729-719-8

13. Chang, Y., Makatsoris, H.: Supply chain modeling using simulation. Int. J. Simul. 2(1), 24–30 (2001)

14. Rouhani, A., Fazelhashemi, S.: Forget About TPM, 1st edn. Rasa Cultural Services Institute, Tehran (2009)

15. Amershi, S., et al.: Guidelines for human-AI interaction. In: Proceedings of the 2019 CHI Conference on Human Factors in Computing Systems, pp. 1–13, May 2019

16. Licht, D.M., Polzella, D.J., Boff, K.R.: Human factors, ergonomics and human factors engineering: an analysis of definitions. Crew System Ergonomics Information Analysis Center, Dayton (1993)

17. Zander, T.O., Kothe, C., Jatzev, S., Gaertner, M.: Enhancing human-computer interaction with input from active and passive brain-computer interfaces. In: Tan, D., Nijholt, A. (eds.) Brain-Computer Interfaces: Applying our Minds to Human-Computer Interaction, pp. 181–199. Springer, London (2010). https://doi.org/10.1007/978-1-84996-272-8_11

18. Manresa, C., Varona, J., Mas, R., Perales, F.J.: Hand tracking and gesture recog-nition for human-computer interaction. ELCVIA Electron. Lett. Comput. Vis. Image Anal. 96–104 (2005)

19. Gallego García, S., García García, M.: Design and simulation of production and maintenance management applying the viable system model: the case of an OEM plant. Materials 11(8), 1346 (2018)

20. Beschaffungsmanagement Revue De L'acheteur; Verein procure.ch: Aarau, Switzerland, vol. 10/10, pp. 16–17 (2010)

reSenseNet: Ensemble Early Fusion Deep Learning Architecture for Multimodal Sentiment Analysis

Shankhanil Ghosh[1], Chhanda Saha[1], Nagamani Molakathala[1], Souvik Ghosh[2], and Dhananjay Singh[3]([✉])(iD)

[1] School of Computer and Information Sciences, University of Hyderabad, Hyderabad, India
{20mcmb04,20mcmb01,nagamanics}@uohyd.ac.in
[2] Applied Electronics and Instrumentation Engineering, Heritage Institute of Technology, Kolkata, India
[3] Department of Electronics Engineering, Hankuk University of Foreign Studies, Seoul, South Korea
dsingh@hufs.ac.kr

Abstract. Multimodal sentiment analysis is an actively emerging field of research in deep learning that deals with understanding human sentiments based on more than one sensory input. In this paper, we propose reSenseNet, an ensemble of early fusion architecture of deep convolutional neural network (CNN) and Long Short term Memory (LSTM) for multimodal sentiment analysis of audio, visual, and text data. ReSenseNet consists of feature extraction, feature fusion, and fully connected layers stacked together as a three-layer architecture. Instances of the generalized reSenseNet architecture have been experimented on several variants of modalities combined together to form different variations in the test data. Such a combination has produced results in predicting average arousal and valence up to an F1 score of 50.91% and 35.74% respectively.

Keywords: Multimodal deep learning · Sentiment analysis · Feature fusion · Long short term memory · Arousal · Valence · Deep learning

1 Introduction

Diagnosis of mental health issues is a big challenge in Human-Computer Interaction research. This research is focused this problem and attempts to find technological solutions towards the same by developing novel multi-modal deep learning methods for sentiment analysis tasks. It is inspired by the proposition by World

This research was supported under the India-Korea Joint Programme of Cooperation in Science & Technology by the National Research Foundation (NRF) Korea (2020K1A3A1A68093469), the Ministry of Science and ICT (MSIT) Korea and by the Department of Biotechnology (India) (DBT/IC-12031(22)-ICD-DBT).

© Springer Nature Switzerland AG 2022
J.-H. Kim et al. (Eds.): IHCI 2021, LNCS 13184, pp. 689–702, 2022.
https://doi.org/10.1007/978-3-030-98404-5_62

Health Organization (WHO) saying "no health without mental health", which clearly mentions the importance of mental health in people's lives. Approximately 792 million people worldwide suffered from a mental health disorder, according to Hannah Ritchie and Max Roser[1] (2017). It is slightly more than one in ten people globally, and that number is increasing with time. Researchers worldwide are trying to develop solutions towards various problems associated with mental health problems. On the other side, a massive volume of opinionated data recorded in digital form available for analysis in today's world.

The authors Soleymani et al. [1] have discussed the various challenges and opportunities in the domain of multimodal sentiment analysis. Using sentiment analysis techniques, it is possible to automate the extraction or classification of sentiments from opinionated data or reviews. Sentiment analysis techniques can analyze the reviews and opinions and classify them according to different classes of sentiment. To quantify the emotions while someone is reviewing, two variables called arousal and valence can be used. Arousal represents the state of excitement of the speaker, and valence represents the pleasantness of the sentiment. It helps us in identifying the speaker's emotions and sentiments. Since a significant portion of today's data is available in multiple modalities, recent research attempts to combine different modalities where it results in better accuracy.

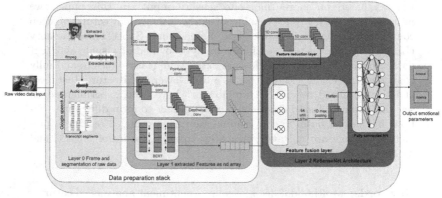

Fig. 1. Integrated deep learning stack for multi-modal sentiment analysis from raw video input. Our proposed reSenseNet is a part of this integrated stack

1.1 Research Contribution

This work predicts advanced intensity classed of emotional parameters. These parameters are arousal and valence. The work uses segmented audio-visual-textual data. An integrated deep learning stack has been developed as shown in

---

[1] https://ourworldindata.org/mental-health.

Fig. 1. The novelty of the proposal lies in the deep convolution neural networks (CNN) and Long Short term Memory (LSTM) based Early fusion architecture. This architecture is called reSenseNet.

1. ReSenseNet architecture to perform multimodal sentiment analysis on segmented audio-visual-textual data.
2. Empirical experiments are performed on different instances of the architecture to predict emotional variables arousal and valence have been done. Performance measuring metric is F1 score.
3. Finally, two instances to predict arousal and valence is proposed. They have an F1 score of 50.91% and 35.74% respectively across three modalities.

2 State of Art in Sentiment Analysis

This research motivation is inspired by Kaur et al. [2], who propose a search-based stacking model that collectively exploits multiple base learners for human-activity analysis. Further exploration of sentiment analysis methods in context of deep learning application and multimodal feature fusion have been performed. Soleymani et al. [1] comprehensively presented "sentiment" and "sentiment analysis" in context of multimodal sentiment analysis is well summarized. Zhang et al. in [3] also proposed a brief survey about the application of deep learning in this context. Morency et al. [4] addresses opinion harvesting from large-scale multimodal raw data, proof-of-concept from joint model which integrates audio, visual, textual features to identify sentiments from web resources.

2.1 Deep Learning Research in Sentiment Analysis

Rosas et al. in [5] have applied deep learning techniques to perform sentiment analysis on Spanish online videos, also have shown that deep multimodal features provide better accuracy than the singular features. Yadav et al. [6] have reviewed different deep learning techniques applied in sentiment analysis and solved different difficulties faced during this task. Another application can be seen in [7] where a deep learning-based framework for the multimodal sentiment analysis has been proposed, which gets a better result. [7] have also stated that by combining the audio, visual, and text feature, they got 10% improvement. Poria et al. [8] have proposed a decision level fusion framework used in deep learning techniques for a multimodal sentiment analysis task with a margin of 10–13% and 3–5% accuracy on polarity detection and emotion recognition, respectively.

2.2 Multimodal Deep Learning in Sentiment Analysis

The Multimodal Sentiment Analysis in Real-life Media Challenge (MuSe) 2020 [9] focused on the task of sentiment recognition, topic engagement, and trust-worthiness detection. Three sub-challenge named MuSe-Wild, MuSe-Topic, and MuSe-Trust were proposed for teams to participate. Similarly, the 2nd Multimodal Sentiment Analysis Challenge (MuSe 2021) [10] focused on multimodal sentiment recognition of user-generated content and in stress-induced situations. This challenge compared multimedia processing and deep learning methods for automatic audio-visual, biological, and textual-based sentiment and emotion-sensing under a standard experimental condition set. Four sub-challenges named MuSe-Wilder, MuSe-Sent, MuSe-Stress, and MuSe-Physio were proposed under MuSe 2021 challenge. The data for the challenge was provided by [11], which was collected from YouTube and manually annotated. Ghosh et al. [12] have proposed one data acquisition tool[2] which can be used to collect multimodal data for such tasks.

One significant task by Stappen et al. [13] have described about unifying a wide range of fusion methods and proposed the novel Rater Aligned Annotation Weighting (RAAW), which aligns the annotations in a translation-invariant way before weighting and fusing them based on the inter-rater agreements between the annotations. Strappen et al. [14] have also proposed a topic extractor on video transcripts, which uses neural word embeddings through graph-based clustering. This research also uses the MuSe-CaR dataset [11].

2.3 Multi-modal Feature Fusion Methods

One primary technological method needed in this research is multimodal feature fusion methods, which allows us to fuse features across different sources and modalities into one single feature vector. Our inspiration came from some of the recent research papers on feature fusion methods. [15] have proposed a model which starts its task by eliminating the noise interference in textual data and extracting more essential image features, after which the feature-fusion part based on attention mechanism learns internal features from the text and images data through symmetry. The model then applies the fusion features to the sentiment classification tasks. Majumder et al. in [16] have proposed a novel feature fusion strategy, which proceeds hierarchically, first fusing the modalities two in two and then fusing all three modalities. Zadeh et al. in [17] solve the problem of multimodal sentiment analysis as an instance of modeling intra-modality and inter-modality dynamics and propose Tensor Fusion Network, which learns both such dynamics end-to-end. The proposed approach has been designed to make it worthwhile for the volatile nature of spoken language in online videos, voice, and gestures.

3 The ReSenseNet Architecture

The reSenseNet architecture for multi-modal feature fusion for sentiment analysis task is a part of a three-layered integrated deep learning stack for multimodal sentiment analysis. The architecture uses an Early fusion mechanism to fuse various features across various modalities. ReSenseNet is made of three significant layers: the feature reduction layer, the Early Fusion Layer, and the Fully connected neural network. The detailed description of the ReSenseNet architecture is shown in Fig. 2.

---

[2] https://intellispeechscis.web.app/.

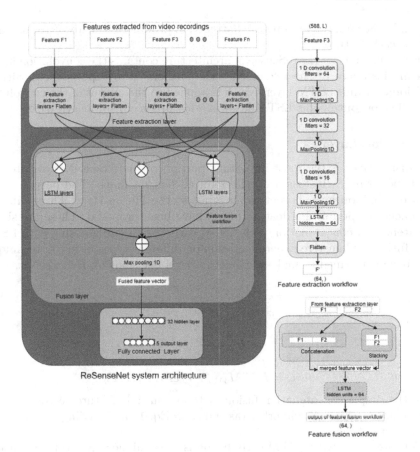

Fig. 2. A detailed description of a deep-learning stack that integrates reSenseNet to predict arousal and valence (left). The resenseNet architecture is to the right. The figure also includes description of the feature reduction workflow and the feature fusion workflow. The optional layers are denoted in dotted boxes.

3.1 Feature Reduction Layer

The intial layer of the reSenseNet layer is the feature reduction layer. Out of various methods of feature reduction, two techniques have been considered: consecutive convolution layers (followed by a max-pooling layer), and Long-short-term memory, or LSTM layers.

The model initially performs an 1D convolution on all the modal features. The intuition behind this is to build reduced feature maps for timestamped data. As mentioned previously, each audio, video, and text feature matrices are of size $(588, F_s)$, where the first dimension of the feature vectors represents the timestamp dimension (after zero padding). The convolution layers are followed by 1D Max pooling layers along the feature-length. The model applies these layers repeatedly over the features until it achieves a feature vector of sufficient length. In the end, the features are flattened to produce a feature vector of length 160 for each feature.

Every instance of the reSenseNet architecture contains the convolution layers. In some instances of the reSenseNet, the authors have experimented with an additional 64-unit LSTM layer, which is applied to the output of the convolution layer. The output of this LSTM layer is a feature vector of length 64.

3.2   Fusion Layer

The fusion layer is the most important portion of the reSenseNet architecture which performs early fusion on the reduced feature maps. The output of the feature reduction layer is sent as an input to the Fusion layer. Three different approaches to performing feature fusion have been proposed. These are simple concatenation, concatenation with LSTM early fusion and stacking with LSTM early fusion. Exhaustive experimentation on different types of fusion techniques have been performed to make architecture level decisions on ReSenseNet.

$$F_k'^{(2n,1)} = F_i^{(n,1)} || F_j^{(n,1)} \tag{1a}$$

$$F_k'^{(n,2)} = F_i^{(n,1)} || F_j^{(n,1)} \tag{1b}$$

$$\forall F_i \epsilon F_1, F_2, \ldots F_n$$

$$lstm_i = LSTM_{64}(f), \forall f \epsilon F_1, F_2 \ldots F_n \tag{2}$$

1. In the simple concatenation fusion method, multiple feature vectors are concatenated against one another (as shown in Eq. 1a and feeding it to the fully connected layer.
2. Concatenation with LSTM early fusion is a technique where certain features are concatenated (Eq. 1a) and then passed through 64-unit LSTM layer, as shown in as described in Eq. 2.
   Furthermore, the output of the LSTM layers is again passed to a stacking sub-layer and then passed into a pooling layer. The output is flattened and sent into the final fully connected layer.
3. In the Stacking with LSTM early fusion technique, the first level of feature fusion is performed by stacking feature pairs (F_i, F_j) on top of one another, to produce features $F_1', F_2', \ldots F_N'$, which are of size $(L, 2)$ each. Stacking is mathematically defined in Eq. 1b. Each of these stacked feature matrices are then passed into N separate 64-unit LSTM layers. The output of the LSTM layers are passed through a stacking layer and max-pooling layer after which it is sent to the fully connected.

3.3   Fully Connected Layer

The final layer of the reSenseNet architecture is where the feature fusion layer's output is passed into a fully connected neural network, with one hidden layer containing 32 hidden units and five output units. Specific details of the fully connected neural network in the later sections.

4   Dataset and Data Preparation

4.1   The Dataset and the Multi-modal Features

The dataset used in this research the MuSe-CaR dataset [11] which is a collection of 40+ hours of YouTube videos of car reviews. Data annotation of continuous values like arousal, valence for this dataset have been done by human annotators. This research uses the pre-extracted features that are provided by the MuSe-CaR dataset. In the audio features, eGeMAPS [18] and VGGish [19] have been considered for the experimentation. EGeMAPS and VGGish are feature vectors of lengths 88 and 128 for a specific timestamp for each audio segment. In the visual/facial modality, Xception [20], Facial Action Units and VGGface [21] have been considered. Xception, FAU, and VGGface have feature vectors of length 2048, 35, and 512, respectively, for each audio segment at a certain timestamp. For the text modality, BERT [22] feature is used which has a feature vector of length 768.

In future mentions VGGish will be used as v'_f, eGeMaps as eGe, Xception as X, VGGFace as v_f, FAU as au_f and BERT as B_T.

4.2   Data Preprocessing

The data was available to us in the form of raw audio-visual data and pre-extracted feature vectors. The features that are being used for this study are pre-extracted from the audio, video, and text data in the MuSe-Car dataset. Each audiovisual-textual sample from the dataset is divided into smaller segments of variable length. Each segment is several timestamps long. The valence and arousal are annotated against each segment, meaning that each segment has one annotation of valence and arousal. Hence, one unit of data is made of multiple feature vectors, thus forming a feature matrix. However, these feature matrices are of variable dimension because of the variable-length segments. Thus, the feature matrices are preprocessed to make them uniform length. For all samples that have segment length lesser than 588, zero paddings have been applied to the right of the feature matrix, and for those samples whose segment length is greater than 588, the feature matrix have been truncated. Hence, at the end of preprocessing, the feature matrix of each segment is of size $(588, L_f)$, where L_f is the feature-length. L_f is 35, 4096, 2046, 88, 512, 128, 2048 for Facial Action Units, DeepSpectrum, BERT, eGeMaps, VGGFace, VGGish and Xception respectively. All these features were padded and stored in separate h5 files for further usage. The model reads the feature matrices from the disk in small batches and sends them to the model for training and evaluation. The preprocessing procedure is described in Algorithm 1.

Algorithm 1. Given a feature matrix file of ith video data, generate the pre-processed feature matrix

---

1: **procedure** PREPROCESS(F_i, featureName)
2:     outputFile ← $OPEN(featureName.H5)$
3:     totalSegments ← total number of segments in that feature matrix file.
4:     $F' ← emptymatrixwithshape(totalSegments, 588, L_F)$
5:     **for** s in range(0, totalSegments) **do**
6:         $S ← F_i[s]$ ▷ $|S| = (L_S, L_F)$, where L_S is the length of the segment, and L_f
    is the feature length.
7:         **if** $L_S < 588$ **then**
8:             $S' ← zeroPadding(S, extraWidth = (588 - L_S))$
9:         **else if** $L_S > 588$ **then**
10:             $S' ← truncate(S)$ ▷ Making $|S'| = (588, L_F)$ by padding or truncating
11:         $F'.append(S')$
12:     outputFile.write(F')

---

5   Performance Analysis

5.1   Experimental Setup

The models have been trained using the Keras functional API, set for a maximum of 20 epochs with a batch size of 32. An early stopping mechanism has been set in place with a patience of 15 epochs, and the metric used in this case is the training validation F1 score. The model was compiled using Adam optimizer with Categorical cross-entropy as the loss function. The entire dataset was split with an 80-20 ratio, with 20% of the data (randomly chosen) was used for validation. The fully connected neural network has one hidden layer of 32 units and an output layer of 5 units (for five levels of arousal/valence). Dropout layers (with dropout rate = 0.2) and L1 and L2 regularizers have been deployed to prevent overfitting. L1 and L2 regularization factor is 0.000001 and 0.00001.

5.2   Evaluation on reSenseNet Architecture

The proposed architecture have been used to build models to predict the sentiment variables, namely arousal, and valence. And for that purpose, a set of experiments have been designed, based on which two separate fine-tuned models have been proposed for each variable. The reSenseNet architecture have been evaluated with various combinations of modalities and fusion methods, along with an extensive hyperparameter search. The following set of evaluation experiments have been performed on the reSenseNet architecture

1. Modality search: To study which combination of modalities work best. Various combinations of features, keeping the hyperparameters and fusion method the same, were tested. The symbols A, V and T indicate audio, visual and text modalities respectively. Only concatenation was used as the fusion method. Learning rate $\alpha = 0.001$, Dropout frequency = 0.2, Regularizer parameter

$L_1 = 10^{-5}$ & $L_2 = 10^{-6}$, were kept constant through the experiments. Given in Table 1.

2. Fusion method search: To study which specific combination of features work the best. Various fusions of features within the fusion layer were evaluated, keeping the features and hyperparameters the same. Three different fusion mechanisms (as described early in the paper) have been tested out in these set of experiments: Concatenation, Concatenation + LSTM, Stacking + LSTM. The various combinations of features in the A+V and A+V+T modality have been tested here. In the *Feature* column, the brackets indicate the way stacking/concatenation was performed. Learning rate $\alpha = 0.001$, Dropout frequency $= 0.2$, Regularizer parameter $L_1 = 10^{-5}$ & $L_2 = 10^{-6}$, were kept constant through the experiments. Given in Table 2.

3. An extensive hyper-parameter search against the features and fusion method. Various hyperparameters for the model have been tested. The experiments were conducted against the A+V+T modality only because it gave better results in the past experiments, (Table 1. Two different fused features are used as model input, which are $(eGe + B_T) + (v_f + B_T) + (X + B_T)$ and $(eGe+B_T)+(v_f+B_T)+(eGe+au_f)+(X+au_f)$. The regularizer parameters have been kept constant, as $L1 = 10^{-5}$ & $L2 = 10^{-4}$. Given in Table 3.

For evaluation, the entire annotated dataset is split into separate training and testing sub-dataset. 1641 data samples are used for training and 572 data samples for testing the models in the experiments as mentioned above. While splitting the datasets, it is ensured that there is no overlap between the train and test dataset, meaning that the test dataset is entirely unseen by the model. This ensures that the results provided by the model are entirely accurate.

Table 1. Evaluation table for modality search.

Modality	Feature	Arousal	Valence
		Train/Test	Train/Test
A	v_f'	45.21/31.23	20.26/9.14
A	eGe	46.32/33.15	22.13/15.23
V	au_f	46.55/36.71	38.11/16.32
V	$au_f + v_f$	50.45/44.97	50.00/29.08
T	B_T	**86.82/46.20**	**85.12/33.92**
A+V	$(au_f + v_f) + eGe$	**50.15/44.93**	51.11/29.12
A+V+T	$au_f + eGe + v_f'$	43.21/28.12	95.21/27.40
A+V+T	$(v_f + au_f) + (eGe + X) + B_T$	**68.08/46.88**	**62.08/32.12**

Table 2. Evaluation table for fusion method search

Fusion method	Modality	Feature	Arousal	Valence
			Train/Test	Train/Test
Concatenation	A+V	$(au_f + v_f) + eGe$	46.67/42.12	50.00/29.08
	A+V+T	$au_f + eGe + v'_f$	43.21/28.12	45.67/27.40
	A+V+T	$(v_f + au_f) + (eGe + X) + B_T$	68.08/46.88	62.08/32.12
Concatenation + LSTM	A+V	$(au_f + v_f) + eGe$	50.45/44.97	50.11/29.08
	A+V+T	$au_f + eGe + v'_f$	47.11/32.98	50.67/30.18
	A+V+T	$(v_f + au_f) + (eGe + X) + B_T$	65.18/46.10	65.12/33.21
Stacking + LSTM with Early fusion	A+V	$(au_f + v_f) + eGe$	50.45/44.97	49.22/29.18
	A+V+T	$au_f + eGe + v'_f$	46.18/42.12	45.12/37.36
	A+V+T	$(v_f + au_f) + (eGe + X) + B_T$	59.18/47.67	52.58/33.11
	A+V+T	$(eGe + B_T) + (v_f + B_T) + (X + B_T)$	52.77/50.91	54.78/35.74
	A+V+T	$(eGe + B_T) + (v_f + B_T) + (eGe + au_f) + (X + au_f)$	52.77/49.24	54.78/35.88

Table 3. Evaluation table for hyperparameter searching.

Input fused feature	Learning rate	Dropout	Arousal	Valence
			Train/Test	Train/Test
$(eGe + B_T) + (v_f + B_T) + (X + B_T)$	**0.001**	**0.2**	**52.77/50.91**	54.78/35.74
	0.002	0.2	52.42/49.11	54.72/35.32
	0.001	0.4	53.21/49.21	55.11/35.04
	0.002	0.4	53.25/49.56	55.18/34.98
$(eGe + B_T) + (v_f + B_T) + (eGe + au_f) + (X + au_f)$	**0.001**	**0.2**	52.77/49.24	**54.78/35.74**
	0.002	0.2	54.42/48.03	54.11/35.14
	0.001	0.4	53.98/48.74	53.18/35.01
	0.002	0.4	54.18/48.04	54.05/35.23

5.3   Results and Discussion

The results of the experiment shows that the best results comes out when all the three modalities (audio, video, and text) are fused to predict the variables. From Table 1 there could be observed a significant increase in F1 scores in training and testing scenarios. For example, from Table 1, it can be seen that using modalities audio + video, there is jump in test F1 score from 33.15% to 44.97%. It must also be noticed that the text modality itself is potent for predicting arousal and valence because it scored an F1 score of 46.20% and 33.92% respectively for test datasets.

From Table 2 in the fusion method search, the Early fusion Stacking + LSTM is outperforming all the other methods of feature fusion. In the concatenation

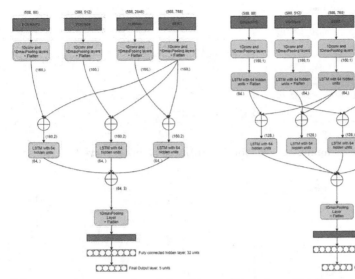

(a) reSenseNet-Arousal model archi-   (b) reSenseNet-Valence model architecture   tecture

Fig. 3. reSenseNet-Arousal and Valence model architecture

feature, reSenseNet model achieved a highest F1 score of 46.88% and 32.12% on test dataset, for arousal and valence respectively. In that experiment, feature fusion has been performed as $(au_f + v_f) + eGe$. Using Concatenation + LSTM early fusion method, the highest F1 score was obtained as 46.10% and 33.21% for feature sets as $(v_f + au_f) + (eGe + X) + B_T$. However, some of the highest F1 scores were achieved by using stacking + LSTM early fusion. In that method, feature set $(eGe + B_T) + (v_f + B_T) + (X + B_T)$ achieved an F1 score of 50.91% for arousal and feature set $(eGe + B_T) + (v_f + B_T) + (eGe + au_f) + (X + au_f)$ achieved an F1 score of 35.88%, indicating that these feature sets, used with stacking + LSTM produce the best result.

In Table 3, the best feature sets from the previous experiments have been considered. These are $(eGe + B_T) + (v_f + B_T) + (X + B_T)$ and $(eGe + B_T) + (v_f + B_T) + (eGe + au_f) + (X + au_f)$ and perform a hyperparameter search for Dropout frequency and learning rate. The best results came out with learning rate $\alpha = 0.001$ and Dropout frequency = 0.2. Hence, considering the best result from the experiments, a training F1 score of 52.77% and test score of 50.91% for arousal, and a training F1 score of 54.74% and a test F1 score of 35.88% for valence have been achieved.

Based on the above experiment results, the authors propose that the best model for predicting arousal is where the reSenseNet architecture uses the $(eGe + B_T) + (v_f + B_T) + (X + B_T)$ feature set with Stacking + LSTM early fusion method. It uses a 0.2 dropout frequency on the fully connected layer, with regularizer parameters $L_1 = 10^{-5}$ & $L_2 = 10^{-6}$, and learning rate of 0.001. The model needs to be trained for 20 epochs (which can early-stopped with patience

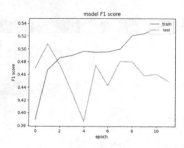

(a) F1 score training curve for Arousal

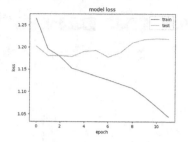

(b) Loss training curve for Arousal

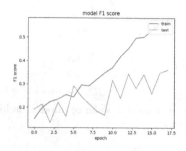

(c) F1 score training curve for Valence

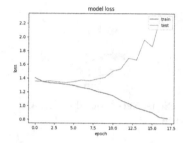

(d) Loss training curve for Valence

Fig. 4. reSenseNet-Arousal and Valence training curves

Table 4. Final table describing results and specifications of ReSenseNet-Arousal and ReSenseNet-Valence

Modality	Arousal	Valence
	A+V+T	A+V+T
Feature maps	$(eGe + B_T) + (v_f + B_T) + (X + B_T)$	$(eGe + B_T) + (v_f + B_T) + (eGe + au_f) + (X + au_f)$
Extraction method	CNN	CNN + LSTM
Dropout frequency	0.2	0.2
Learning rate	0.001	0.001
Regularziers L1/L2	10^{-5} & 10^{-4}	10^{-5} & 10^{-4}
Train/Test	52.77/50.91	54.78/35.88

of 15 epochs). This model is called reSenseNet-Arousal. Similarly, for predicting valence, the usage of feature map $(eGe + B_T) + (v_f + B_T) + (X + B_T)$ and $(eGe + B_T) + (v_f + B_T) + (eGe + au_f) + (X + au_f)$ with Stacking +

LSTM early fusion, with a dropout frequency $= 0.2$, regularizer parameters $L_1 = 10^{-5}$ & $L_2 = 10^{-6}$ andlearning rate $= 0.001$ is suggested. The model is trained for maximum of 20 epochs with early stopping mechanism in place, for 15 epoch patience. This model is called reSenseNet-Valence. The structure of the models are given in and the structure is visualized in Fig. 3, and the training curves for F1 score and loss are given in Fig. 4. The details of the models are documented in Table 4. As it can be seen, the test F1 score for valence never reaches the same level as arousal, indicating that predicting valence in this case might be difficult. The authors assume that this might be due to nature of the dataset MuSe-Car, where the YouTubers (subject of the video dataset) maintain a certain level of valence (or pleasantness of voice) for their own audience. Also, the videos are about car reviews, where it is not expected to have a very big difference in valence. However, there are other datasets to train the models to predict valence in a better way.

6   Final Discussion

In this paper, the authors have proposed the reSenseNet architecture, which is a novel deep learning based architecture for predicting emotional parameters (arousal and valence) in an sentiment analysis task across various modalities. Extensive tests are performed on the architecture and finally proposed 2 models based on the reSenseNet architecture, namely reSenseNet-Arousal and reSenseNet-Valence for predicting arousal and valence respectively. These models have scored an F1 score of 50.91% and 35.74% on test datasets.

Acknowledgement. This research was supported by the National Research Foundation (NRF), Korea (2020K1A3A1A68093469) funded by the Ministry of Science and ICT (MSIT), RESENSE Lab HUFS.

References

1. Soleymani, M., Garcia, D., Jou, B., Schuller, B., Chang, S.-F., Pantic, M.: A survey of multimodal sentiment analysis. Image Vis. Comput. **65**, 3–14 (2017). Multimodal Sentiment Analysis and Mining in the Wild Image and Vision Computing
2. Kaur, M., Kaur, G., Sharma, P.K., Jolfaei, A., Singh, D.: Binary cuckoo search metaheuristic-based supercomputing framework for human behavior analysis in smart home. J. Supercomput. **76**(4), 2479–2502 (2019). https://doi.org/10.1007/s11227-019-02998-0
3. Zhang, L., Wang, S., Liu, B.: Deep learning for sentiment analysis: a survey. Wiley Interdisc. Rev.: Data Min. Knowl. Discov. **8**(4), e1253 (2018)
4. Morency, L.-P., Mihalcea, R., Doshi, P.: Towards multimodal sentiment analysis: harvesting opinions from the web. In: Proceedings of the 13th International Conference on Multimodal Interfaces, ICMI 2011, pp. 169–176. Association for Computing Machinery, New York (2011)
5. Rosas, V.P., Mihalcea, R., Morency, L.-P.: Multimodal sentiment analysis of Spanish online videos. IEEE Intell. Syst. **28**(3), 38–45 (2013)

6. Yadav, A., Vishwakarma, D.K.: Sentiment analysis using deep learning architectures: a review. Artif. Intell. Rev. **53**(6), 4335–4385 (2019). https://doi.org/10.1007/s10462-019-09794-5

7. Cambria, E., Hazarika, D., Poria, S., Hussain, A., Subramanyam, R.B.V.: Benchmarking multimodal sentiment analysis. In: Gelbukh, A. (ed.) CICLing 2017. LNCS, vol. 10762, pp. 166–179. Springer, Cham (2018). https://doi.org/10.1007/978-3-319-77116-8_13

8. Poria, S., Peng, H., Hussain, A., Howard, N., Cambria, E.: Ensemble application of convolutional neural networks and multiple kernel learning for multimodal sentiment analysis. Neurocomputing **261**, 217–230 (2017). Advances in Extreme Learning Machines (ELM 2015)

9. Stappen, L., et al.: MuSe 2020 - the first international multimodal sentiment analysis in real-life media challenge and workshop (2020)

10. Stappen, L., et al.: The MuSe 2021 multimodal sentiment analysis challenge: sentiment, emotion, physiological-emotion, and stress, April 2021

11. Stappen, L., Baird, A., Schumann, L., Schuller, B.: The multimodal sentiment analysis in car reviews (MuSe-CaR) dataset: collection, insights and improvements. IEEE Trans. Affect. Comput. (2021)

12. Ghosh, S., Molakathaala, N., Saha, C., Das, R., Ghosh, S.: Speech@SCIS: annotated Indian video dataset for speech-face cross modal research (draft)

13. Stappen, L., et al.: MuSe-toolbox: the multimodal sentiment analysis continuous annotation fusion and discrete class transformation toolbox (2021)

14. Stappen, L., Thies, J., Hagerer, G., Schuller, B.W., Groh, G.: GraphTMT: unsupervised graph-based topic modeling from video transcripts (2021)

15. Zhang, K., Geng, Y., Zhao, J., Liu, J., Li, W.: Sentiment analysis of social media via multimodal feature fusion. Symmetry **12**(12), 2010 (2020)

16. Majumder, N., Hazarika, D., Gelbukh, A., Cambria, E., Poria, S.: Multimodal sentiment analysis using hierarchical fusion with context modeling. Knowl.-Based Syst. **161**, 124–133 (2018)

17. Zadeh, A., Chen, M., Poria, S., Cambria, E., Morency, L.-P.: Tensor fusion network for multimodal sentiment analysis (2017)

18. Eyben, F., et al.: The Geneva minimalistic acoustic parameter set (GeMAPS) for voice research and affective computing. IEEE Trans. Affect. Comput. **7**, 1 (2015)

19. Hershey, S., et al.: CNN architectures for large-scale audio classification. In: International Conference on Acoustics, Speech and Signal Processing (ICASSP) (2017)

20. Chollet, F.: Xception: deep learning with depthwise separable convolutions. CoRR, abs/1610.02357 (2016)

21. Parkhi, O.M., Vedaldi, A., Zisserman, A.: Deep face recognition. In: British Machine Vision Conference (2015)

22. Devlin, J., Chang, M.-W., Lee, K., Toutanova, K.: BERT: pre-training of deep bidirectional transformers for language understanding. CoRR, abs/1810.04805 (2018)

Analysis of User Interaction to Mental Health Application Using Topic Modeling Approach

Ajit Kumar, Ankit Kumar Singh, and Bong Jun Choi$^{(\boxtimes)}$

Soongsil University, Seoul, South Korea
kumar@ssu.ac.kr , davidchoi@soongsil.ac.kr

Abstract. Mental health-related illnesses like depression and anxiety have become a major concern for society. Due to social stigma and unawareness, many such patients lack proper doctors' consultancy, diagnosis, and treatments. Many of such problems arise due to the urban living style, social and family disconnect. Nonetheless, various health-related mobile applications offer ways to minimize the risks by providing an option for remote doctor consultations, connecting to family and friends, or sharing thoughts. To investigate the effectiveness and discover the key issues of such apps, we analyze the user's interaction, discussion, and responses to mental health apps through topic modeling approaches. The experimental results show that many users found many applications helpful and complained mostly about technical issues and business practices. We also evaluated topics and keywords from feedbacks to further improve the application interface and functionalities.

Keywords: Mental health · Depression · Mobile application · Depression · User interaction · Topic modeling

1 Introduction

The use of smartphones has grown significantly due to ICT development and the availability of low-cost hardware [24]. The high growth of smartphone hardware directly impacts the rate of mobile application (Apps) development [13, 30]. Today, one or more apps is available for almost every aspect of human life: entertainment (e.g., games, music, and video), business (e.g., communication, and office word related apps), utility (e.g., multi-purpose remote and photography apps), and personal care (e.g., exercise guide and activity tracer). There are also a large number of mobile apps related to healthcare considered as mHealth [22]. All these apps are available and distributed by OS-affiliated app stores (Google Play for Android and Apple store for iOS) or third parties. Recently, mental

This research was supported under the India-Korea Joint Programme of Cooperation in Science & Technology by the National Research Foundation (NRF) Korea (2020K1A3A1A68093469).

J.-H. Kim et al. (Eds.): IHCI 2021, LNCS 13184, pp. 703–717, 2022.
https://doi.org/10.1007/978-3-030-98404-5_63

health-related illnesses like depression, stress, and anxiety have become a major concern for society. Such problems arise due to the urban living style, social, and family disconnect [26].

Recently, the smartphone's usability, ubiquity, and features (e.g., various sensors and HD cameras) provide a way to address various mental health-related issues like depression, stress, and anxiety. So, there are many apps available primarily to support and help mental health issues. In addition to other growth factors of mental health, social stigma, fear of discrimination, and hesitation to share personal details with doctors pushed users to unintrusive mental health mobile apps that provide protection. Before the availability of such apps, many such patients were not receiving doctors' consultancy, diagnosis, and treatments. Now, various mental health-related apps can assist in minimizing the risks by providing an option for remote doctor consultations, connecting to family and friends, or sharing thoughts, even using chatbots. The use of mental health apps has increased by up to 10–30% in the recent COVID-19 pandemic [28].

Although there has been a rapid growth in the use of mental health-related apps, there are concerns and questions on the benefits of these apps [6]. There is a lack of research on measuring the effectiveness of apps, and only a few (5%) are considered for measuring effectiveness and performance [14]. The knowledge about the effectiveness of mental health is seldomly available [19]. The limited inclusion of apps for study and shortage of performance results can be attributed to the time-consuming and complex manual process. Therefore, the proposed work analyzes users' interaction, discussion, and responses to mental health apps using topic modeling approaches. We collected user reviews from *Google Play Store*[1] for selected mental health mobile applications and performed topic modeling to discover the app users' topics or themes of discussion. The topic modeling methods can help to understand the topics that emerged through the user's reviews. Our analysis results show that many users found the application helpful, and there were only complaints about technical issues and business practices. We also look for topics and keywords in terms of feedback that can further help to improve the application interface and functionalities. In general, the proposed work aims to find the answer to the following questions:

1. How effectively do mental health apps can help treat depression, stress, and anxiety?
2. What are the key issues reported by users?
3. How important technical robustness and user interface (UI)?
4. What are vital directions or suggestions for developing mental health apps?

2   Related Work

With the rapid development in Internet and computer technologies, there has been exponential growth in digital platforms like mobile and web applications for various tasks from online shopping to personal health care [9]. The ubiquity,

---

[1] Official platform for sharing and maintaining all the Android applications.

accessibility, and ease of use have attracted users to smartphones rather than traditional desktop computers. Hence, the popularity and acceptability of mobile applications (or apps) have risen daily. Such rapid growth has also brought competition and challenges to maintain customer satisfaction. The mobile app markets (Google Play, App Store, etc.) provide a mechanism to collect customer responses in textual reviews and other quantitative methods like star rating. Processing, understanding, and making meaning for this feedback is complex and challenging due to the scale and diversity of user interaction [15,29].

The manual analysis of customer feedback is time-consuming, error-prone, and impossible to keep up with an immense amount of data. Machine learning has recently provided automated methods like sentiment analysis, text summarization, text clustering, and topic modeling to analyze and understand textual reviews and other feedback. Fuad and Al-Yahya [10] used topic modeling to study the Arabic apps in the Google play store. The study used Latent Dirichlet Allocation (LDA) to study the features and apps classification. Authors suggested that topics from textual reviews effectively suggest new categories for apps while the current pre-defined categories are incorrect and unable to group new Arabic apps [10]. Another study used the LDA-based topic modeling approach and users' reviews for recommending Android apps to users [21]. Ghosh and Pamela, 2016 [11] used apps reviews and topic modeling to understand the low adoption rate and effectiveness of adolescent mobile safety apps. Their result shows that there is a gap between users' needs and the design of safety apps. Mankad et al. [17] used supervised topic modeling to study apps reviews, and the outcome can be used to provide feedback on the app's quality and other testing aspects to the developer. Authors used matrix factorization and ordinal regression to understand a single app's performance and enable systematic comparison of different apps over time to guide the developers [17].

Similar to this work, Liu et al. [16] used the app's description to gets a high-level feature and then get the user's sentiments from reviews. The study establishes a relationship between the app's features and user sentiments. It builds a classifier that can classify review to the app features and experiment result achieved an F measure 86.13% [16]. Another work in [27] uses topic modeling to understand the mapping between app functionalities and the requested permissions using user's reviews and various android API documents. It helps the user to understand the gap between the functionalities and the actual behaviors of an app. Recently, work in [31] identified the key topics and issues reported by diet-tracking app users using topic modeling on reviews available on the Google Play store. The authors suggested further improvements for such apps based on their findings. Similar to the proposed work, Oyebode and Rita Orji [20] used LDA topic modeling to find persuasive strategies implemented in 100 selected mental health-related apps using reviews. Their experiment found self-monitoring as the most used persuasive strategy. In recent work, Dantu et al. [7] explored the topic modeling for studying research patterns in IoT for healthcare using abstract and keywords from published literature between 2010–2018 in healthcare IoT. The experimental results can help understand the trend in the focused research area and dominant research topics over the years.

Table 1. Related works on topic modeling with review of mobile application.

Works	Topic modeling	Application	Dataset	Method and optimum topics
Tianhao Pan et al., 2016 [21]	LDA	App recommendation	App review	Perplexity (10)
Ghosh and Pamela, 2016 [11]	LDA	Understanding adolescent online safety apps	App review	3+3 (top and low rated reviews)
Mankad et al., 2018 [17]	Supervised TM	Prediction	App review (+ iTunes)	Coherence 4)
Liu et al., 2018 [16]	TBTM[a]	Guiding Software development	App description and review	N/A (7)
Wang et al., 2020 [27]	BTM[b]	App functionalities and permission mapping	App review and description	Permission (10)
Oyebode and Orji, 2020 [20]	LDA	Finding persuasive strategies	App review (2018) + Apple Store)	Perplexity (50)
Zecevic et al., 2021 [31]	N/A[c]	Topic and issues identification in diet-tracking app	App review	Coherence (11)
Dantu et al., 2021 [7]	LDA	Research trend	Manuscript abstract	Coherence (27)
Fuad and Al-Yahya, 2021 [10]	LDA	Features understanding and categorization	App review	User given (10)

[a] Topic Based Topic Modeling
[b] Biterm Topic Model (BTM)
[c] Not available

The literature review indicates a usable application of topic modeling on apps reviews for different tasks, from understanding the technical issues for guiding development to finding permissions implications over the functionalities. Table 1 provides a summary of related work on apps review and topic modeling. Based on the discussion mentioned above, the proposed work applies topic modeling to understand user interaction about mental health apps specifically. Unlike previous similar study [20], which are close and limited to finding persuasive strategies only from positive reviews, the proposed work aims to understand the comprehensive discussion evolving within the users of mental health apps.

3   Mobile Application for Mental Health

A mobile application or app is software that runs on a smartphone with the help of a mobile operating system (OS). Android and iOS are two popular mobile

OSs with 73% and 27% global market share[2]. Mobile apps are being developed for many tasks, from office use to game, and most of these apps are designed and developed for both OS platforms to service more users. Recently, there has been a rise in healthcare-related mobile applications that can be used individually by the doctor, patient, or other parties involved in the healthcare process. Mental health-related apps are one of the main subsets of these healthcare applications. These apps aim to provide education, diagnosis, support, and treatment of mental health illnesses like depression and anxiety [18]. People suppress the early symptoms of mental illness and avoid doctor consultation due to social stigma and discrimination. Such existing restrictions gave rise to mental health apps that provide consultation in a non-physical manner; hence users' privacy can be guarded [14]. The COVID-19 pandemic that caused year month-long indoor stay, isolated living, and restrictive physical gathering is another factor in this mental health applications [28].

Fig. 1. Classification of healthcare mobile application and mental health apps.

Healthcare mobile applications can have a wide range of apps that can be group into different categories. Fig. 1 shows the three major such categories and their placement in mental health apps. The development of mental health apps needs unique guidance from clinical psychology and includes features from fitness and self-care, diet tracking, and doctor-patient applications [6]. NIMH classifies mental health apps into six categories based on functionality: self-management, cognition improvement, skills-training, social support, symptom tracking, and passive data collection[3]. Clinical psychology provides comprehensive guidance

[2] https://gs.statcounter.com/os-market-share/mobile/worldwide.

[3] Technology and Future of Mental Health Treatment. National Institute of Mental Health 2017. Available online: https://www.nimh.nih.gov/health/topics/technology-and-the-future-of-mental-health-treatment/index.shtml

about mental and behavioral health. The four main characteristics of a highly effective mental app are high patient engagement, simple user interface and experience, transdiagnostic capabilities, and self-monitoring features [6]. The mental health apps can be in all three stages of treatment, namely (1) identification and monitoring symptoms, (2) clinical psychological treatment, and (3) intervention. However, these apps are being used in two ways, it either substitutes some treatment methods completely or supplements a method as an additional tool.

Recently, mental health apps are using techniques from artificial intelligence for evaluation, monitoring, and intervention tasks [1]. For example, machine learning and deep learning-based classifiers help evaluate and diagnose depression or anxiety from user's symptoms derived from collected metadata, text, audio, or video interaction [23]. Intelligent medical chatbots are being used to engage the patient and provide support and intervention [2].

Although the growth of mental health mobile applications is exponential, there is a challenge in its acceptance and success. There is deficient awareness about the existence and clinical effectiveness of mental health apps [3]. Furthermore, the privacy of users' information, validation, and certification of the treatment process are critical issues that must be addressed to promote and increase the acceptability of mental health applications. The cost or usage model of using services (premium) concerns young students and non-earning adults. In the case of artificial intelligence-based solutions, the data requirement, processing, and performance (accuracy) of algorithms are critical challenges and need to be addressed. The proposed work aims to understand users' responses to the abovementioned issues and challenges through topic modeling on submitted reviews.

4   Topic Modeling Methods

The broad area of Natural Language Processing (NLP) has many techniques to understand the meaning and semantic from text like sentiment analysis, summarization, clustering, and classification. Under NLP, topic modeling is a method of creating probabilistic models from the text for uncovering the underlying semantic structure using hierarchical Bayesian analysis [4]. The process works by finding and mapping patterns of words to documents. Over the years, topic modeling has been applied and tested in various domains having unstructured text and has proved very useful in finding topics and themes. Some of the applications are understanding email, scientific abstracts, newspapers, reviews, and social media posts. There are many different approaches of topic modelling, such as Latent Dirichlet allocation (LDA) [4,5], Structural Topic Model (STM) [25], Latent Semantic Analysis (LSA) [8], and Non-negative Matrix Factorization (NMF) [12]. Among all these, the LDA is a simple, first, and the most used technique among various available topic modeling approaches. The LDA method is based on Latent Semantic Indexing (LSI) and probabilistic LSI. LDA assumes and model documents as the output of multiple topics, and a topic has defined a distribution over the fixed vocabulary of terms. The algorithm assumes a K number of topics associated with a text collection and that each document exhibits these topics with varying proportions. LDA is unsupervised and uses a generative approach, i.e., it makes a random assignment of a topic to each word in each document. After the initial assignment, LDA assigns weights based on the probability of the word for a topic. Then, via iterations, two distributions are created: (1) the proportion of topics for each document and (2) the probability distribution of topics across the words in the corpus. The proposed work uses LDA for topic modeling.

4.1 Number of Optimum Topics

As mentioned earlier, LDA assumes K number of topics for the collection, random initial assignment, and a probabilistic model. It varies with different executions. So, finding the best value of K is significant for the performance, and there are two main scoring methods: coherence and perplexity scores.

1. **Perplexity Score:** It measures the log-likelihood of the held-out test set. The document collection is split into two parts: one part is used to build the topic model (training set) and the other (test set) is used for testing [4]. The perplexity of test set w is defined as:

$$perplexity(w) = exp\left\{-\frac{L(w)}{\text{count of tokens}}\right\},\tag{1}$$

where $L(w)$ is log-likelihood of test document w. The lower perplexity score indicates a better model. We obtained the perplexity score -7.154[4] for the corpus used in the proposed work and it acceptable and can be improve further by hyper-parameter tuning.

2. **Coherence Score:** It measures the degree of semantic similarity between high scoring words in the topics. The coherence score can be calculated using Eq. 2, where w_i, w_j are the top words of the topic. In the proposed work, we used C_v coherence measure that uses Normalized Pointwise Mutual Information (NPMI) to calculate the $score(w_i, w_j)$ as:

$$CoherenceScore = \sum_{i<j} score(w_i, w_j).\tag{2}$$

The higher coherence score indicates a better model. Figure 2 shows the coherence score for varying number of topics (2–10), and it is evident that total topic 6 has the highest values (0.45). So, in the subsequent section, we extracted 6 topics from the LDA model for analysis and reporting. The optimum coherence score for a given number of topics can be searched and found by a testing model with different values of α and β.

---

[4] The negative sign is because perplexity score is calculated as logarithm of a number.

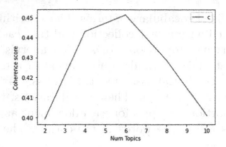

Fig. 2. Coherence score with different number of topics.

5   Experiment and Result

The proposed work is carried out in four stages: (1) data collection, (2) data cleaning and pre-processing, (3) LDA topic modeling, and (4) result analysis. Figure 3 shows all four stages carried out in the proposed work. Each stage is explained in detail in further sections.

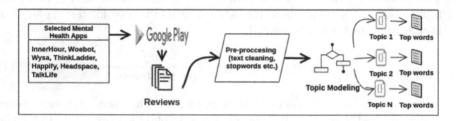

Fig. 3. Process diagram of performing topic modeling

5.1   Experimental System

The tasks and experiments were carried on a desktop computer with a Ubuntu 20.04 LTS, 64-bit OS, and Intel i5 CPU. The system has 16 GB primary and 1 TB secondary memory. Custom-made scripts and methods from various Python frameworks were used for data collection to model training. The key modules used in the proposed work are the google-play-scraper, NLTK, spacy, gensim, matplotlib, and pandas.

5.2   Data Preparation: Collection and Pre-processing

App Selection: We selected seven apps (*innerhour, woebot, wysa, thinkladder, happify, headspace,* and *talklife*) based on the following criteria: it is a free version, it contains relevant keywords (depression, anxiety, stress), and it has a good reputation (number of downloads and review score). Table 2 list and provide description of the selected apps.

Table 2. Description of selected apps for the topic modeling. Note: Apps indicate by *
are free to download and use with limited features. Users need to pay to buy premium
features for these apps.

App name	Techniques	Disorder	Payment	Download	Total reviews	Review score
wysa[a]	Chatbot, CPT, DBT, meditation	Depression, stress, anxiety, sleep disorder	free*	1,000k+	101k	4.8
woebot[b]	AI-coach CBT, self-guidance	Pragmatic thinking	free*	100k	10.8k	4.7
happify[c]	AI-coach interactive activities (games)	Stress, adherence	free*	500k	2866	3.5
innerhour[d]	CBT, positive psychology	Anxiety, depression, self-care, stress	free*	100k	16k	4.5
thinkladder[e]	Guided instructions	Self discovery, anxiety	free	10k	105	4.2
headspace[f]	Guided meditations	Stress, anxiety, sleep	free*	10,000k	247k	4.5
talklife[g]	In-person talk	Anxiety, depression, stress	free*	1,000k	33k	4.2

[a] https://play.google.com/store/apps/details?id=bot.touchkin
[b] https://play.google.com/store/apps/details?id=com.woebot
[c] https://play.google.com/store/apps/details?id=com.happify.happifyinc
[d] https://play.google.com/store/apps/details?id=com.theinnerhour.b2b
[e] https://play.google.com/store/apps/details?id=com.thinkladder.android.thinkladder
[f] https://play.google.com/store/apps/details?id=com.getsomeheadspace.android
[g] https://play.google.com/store/apps/details?id=com.bearpty.talklife

Collecting Reviews: After selecting the apps for the study, we collected the
app_id (*package name*) for each application. These app_ids were used to collect
reviews for each application using a custom-written python script. We collected
the detailed information of each app and then collected reviews by providing filtering criteria. Some of the key information, i.e., ratings, installs, score, reviews,
and descriptions collected about each app, is mentioned in Table 2. Other information about each review was collected during the app's review collection, such
as *userName, score, reviewId*, and *review time*. A total of 6788 reviews and other
attributes' values were collected and stored as CSV[5] files for further experiments.
Table 3 shows the count of total reviews for each given score where the score is
the number (5 is best and 1 is worst) of stars given to the app by users. It can
be learned from Table 3 that the collected dataset is balanced, i.e. the *number
of reviews* for each score is nearly equal except for score value 3. The reviews
in such distribution were collected by applying a filter for all apps, such as the
number of reviews (200 for score 3 and 100 for the rest) for each score, relevant[6],
and newest.

Pre-processing: The review collected for each app is user-given data in a free
flow text input box. We restricted the review to English, yet such input text
can have many noises (typing mistakes, slang, and user-specific word shorten).
Fig. 4 shows an example review from the dataset, and one can notice that the

---

[5] A file format that stores data as rows and columns and values in each row is separated
by a comma.
[6] Review relevance is based on Google Play method.

Table 3. Number of review for as per ranking (best to worst [5-1])

Score	5	4	3	2	1
Count	1236	1176	1994	1178	1204

first mention (yellow highlight) of "fraud" is either a typing mistake or a user's shorten form. Such noise is difficult to correct and often appears in the result of model output. We performed the first pre-processing by replacing the punctuation symbols with whitespace. For example, "it's" will be changed to "it s" and "money(coz" will become "money coz" (refer to the yellow highlights in Fig. 5).

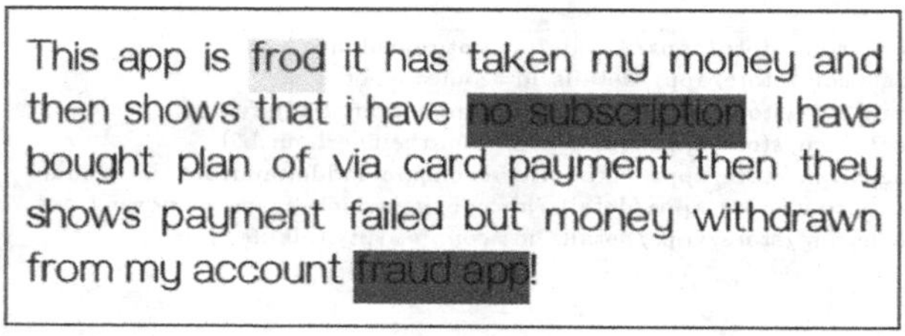

This app is frod it has taken my money and then shows that i have no subscription I have bought plan of via card payment then they shows payment failed but money withdrawn from my account fraud app!

Fig. 4. Example review 1: user complaining about the payment method.

For further pre-processing, the text needs to be converted into words from the sentence. Then, all the stopwords were removed from the dataset using the extended NLTK[7] stopwords list by adding apps names as stopwords. Then we performed parts-of-speech (PoS) tagging and only kept the noun, adjective, verb, and adverb terms in the dataset. In the selected genism python framework for topic modeling, the dataset or corpus must be converted to a python dictionary object by assigning each term a number as a unique id. The corpus is then converted to the term-document frequency representation for the topic modeling method.

5.3   Result and Analysis

Creating LDA Model: The term-document frequency representation of corpus, i.e., the output of the pre-processing stage, is used to train and create a topic model using the LDA algorithm. We mentioned in the Sect. 4.1 finding the optimum number of topics (K) for a corpus is challenging and often discovered by building and evaluating models with different values of K and coherence or perplexity score. We trained models for $K = 2$ to up to $K = 10$. The result is

---

[7] Natural Language Toolkit (NLTK) is a python framework for natural language processing.

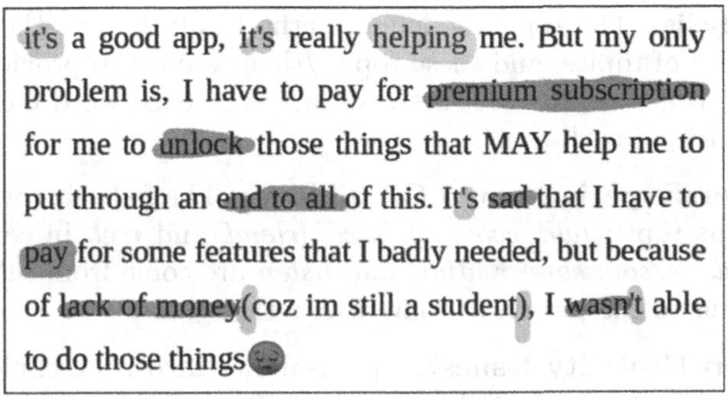

> it's a good app, it's really helping me. But my only problem is, I have to pay for premium subscription for me to unlock those things that MAY help me to put through an end to all of this. It's sad that I have to pay for some features that I badly needed, but because of lack of money(coz im still a student), I wasn't able to do those things😔

Fig. 5. Example review 2: user mentioning paid premium features as a challenge.

Table 4. Topics and top 20 words in each topic with weight score.

Topic 1 user experience and credibility	Topic 2 app usability issues	Topic 3 cost and purchase	Topic 4 mental health issues	Topic 5 impersonal involvement/diagnostic	Topic 6 effectiveness
people: 0.0789	app: 0.117	app: 0.0781	time: 0.0772	feel: 0.0932	great: 0.0696
talk: 0.0559	work: 0.0643	pay: 0.0722	day: 0.0375	make: 0.0804	app: 0.0643
good: 0.0407	start: 0.0286	free: 0.0617	anxiety: 0.028	good: 0.0719	helpful: 0.0558
lot: 0.0355	activity: 0.0197	money: 0.0295	issue: 0.0265	thing: 0.0557	love: 0.0456
problem: 0.0349	fix: 0.0195	subscription: 0.0253	sleep: 0.0264	give: 0.0556	meditation: 0.0318
nice: 0.0282	download: 0.0191	premium: 0.0224	stress: 0.0208	bad: 0.0301	find: 0.0283
friend: 0.0184	open: 0.0178	content: 0.0195	message: 0.0188	option: 0.0299	feature: 0.0234
therapist: 0.0179	account: 0.0168	year: 0.0189	check: 0.0163	response: 0.0224	life: 0.0214
exercise: 0.0168	phone: 0.0162	month: 0.016	depression: 0.0162	understand: 0.0177	recommend: 0.0194
experience: 0.0167	update: 0.0144	access: 0.0138	change: 0.016	positive: 0.015	bit: 0.0171
real: 0.0163	stop: 0.0139	happy: 0.0129	minute: 0.0152	question: 0.0149	amazing: 0.0163
person: 0.0152	sign: 0.0111	stuff: 0.0122	calm: 0.0152	answer: 0.0142	tool: 0.0151
conversation: 0.0148	send: 0.011	version: 0.0116	mind: 0.0136	bot: 0.0137	easy: 0.0151
find: 0.0147	game: 0.0107	enjoy: 0.0111	hope: 0.0133	support: 0.013	long: 0.0141
post: 0.0147	back: 0.0105	trial: 0.0105	daily: 0.0133	write: 0.0113	idea: 0.014
listen: 0.0131	play: 0.0105	buy: 0.0103	week: 0.013	word: 0.0112	add: 0.0124
therapy: 0.0125	notification: 0.0104	plan: 0.0097	learn: 0.0129	put: 0.0106	star: 0.0119
user: 0.0122	load: 0.0098	offer: 0.0093	hard: 0.0107	end: 0.0106	session: 0.0118
comment: 0.0111	show: 0.0097	cost: 0.0093	set: 0.0105	type: 0.0103	worth: 0.011
mood: 0.0106	crash: 0.0096	track: 0.0091	read: 0.009	point: 0.0087	thought: 0.0108

shown in Fig. 2, and we found out that the $K = 6$ has the best coherence score (0.45). Hence, we kept our final LDA model for a total of six topics. Table 4 shows the top 20 terms with for each of those six topics.

Result Analysis: The topic modeling method only groups the words into a selected number of topics, and these topics/themes need to provide a title after going through the word list. So, first, we analyzed each word cluster and then provided the title to each topic.

Topic 1 (User Experience and Credibility): The following words are associated with this topic: *talk*, *good*, *lot*, *nice*, *friend*, and *real*. In comparison, the words like *real*, *person*, *conversation*, and *listen* are come from *talklife* app that provides talking to the person to share user's thoughts.

Topic 2 (App Usability Issues): App usability involves technical difficulties to use and other software-related bugs. The following words are associated with this topic: *start*, *fix*, *download*, *update*, *stop*, *sign*, *notification*, *load*, and *crash*. The words like *crash*, *sign*, *load*, and *fix* are related to negative user experience. The example review shown in Fig. 4 clearly indicates that a technical problem with mental health apps has a more adverse effect on the user. So, the user with unsuccessful app access even after making payment seems angry and calls the app fraud.

Topic 3 (Cost and Purchase): The following words are associated with this topic: *pay*, *free*, *money*, *subscription*, *premium*, *year*, *month*, *trial*, *offer*, and *cost*. In Table 2, we can see that except for *thinkladder* all the other apps have free and paid features. Although, all apps can be downloaded and use for free with limited features. From the example review shown in Fig. 5, we can understand that price for premium features can be an obstacle for low-income users or unemployed users such as a student. The cost of features in mental health app is one of the keys and prime considerations for the developer. The high cost and inability to access required features can harm the user due to their vulnerable state. This underlying theme is evident from the sentence "it's **sad** that I have to pay for some **features** that I **badly needed**, but because of **lack of money**... , I **wasnt'** ..." in the example review (refer Fig. 5). Topic 2 and 3 are related to Value Sensitive Design (VSD), which explains the theoretical background of technology design and emphasizes keeping the accounts of human values principled and comprehensive throughout the development.

Topic 4 (Mental Health Issues): The following words are associated with this topic: *anxiety*, *issue*, *sleep*, *stress*, *depression*, *calm*, *mind*, and *hope*.

Topic 5 (Impersonal Involvement and Diagnostic): The following words are associated with this topic: *feel*, *good*, *bad*, *understand*, *positive*, *bot*, and *support*. Most of the mental health apps aim to promote self-discovery through user's action monitoring and participation. In such a case, user participation, trusting the technology and accepting the diagnosis is essential. The word cluster in topic 5 signifies a similar trend.

Topic 6 (Effectiveness): The effectiveness of the mental health apps provides a sense of feedback on the apps' features and services. Almost all the terms have a positive sentiment. Especially, words like, *great*, *helpful*, *love*, *recommend*, *amazing*, *easy*, and *worth* validate that the apps are helpful for many users and find the solution to their problem.

After performing a primary analysis of the result, as additional analysis, we also performed the persuasive strategies mapping as mentioned by Oyebode and Orji [20] on our topics and terms. The Persuasive strategies match only came for topics 2, 3, and 4 for two, two, and three words, respectively. Table 5 shows the mapping of persuasive strategies. Although the proposed work and Oyebode and Orji [20] used the same method of topic modeling, the dataset preparation and result representation are different. The proposed work has all positive (review score > 3), neutral (review score = 3) and negative (review score < 3) reviews and mixed for all the seven apps, while Oyebode and Orji [20] used only the positive reviews and results are represented per application.

Table 5. Persuasive strategies mapping on topics based on words (Oyebode and Orji [20]).

Topic	Persuasive strategies match
Topic 2	Activity: Self monitoring Game: Simulation and Rehearsal
Topic 3	Plan: Tunneling Track: Self monitoring
Topic 4	Time: Self monitoring Change: Personalization and Tailoring Learn: Simulation and Rehearsal

6   Conclusion and Future Scope

The proposed work studied the user interaction related to mental health-mobile apps using LDA topic modeling and reviews from Google Play for seven selected apps. Six topics were chosen as optimum based on the coherence score and built the topic model. Using the top 20 words from each topic, as a result, we answered our research question.

1. Do mental health applications work and help to treat the issues like depression, stress, and anxiety? Topic 1 and Topic 6 indicate the credibility and effectiveness of mental health app.

2. What are the key issues being reported by the users? Based on topics 2 and 3, the derived key issues are app download and update, freezing and crashing, and notification and loading time. Few apps are AI-powered chatbots, so that they may create lots of notifications. The cost of premium functions is a significant issue, as evident from topic 3 and the example review shown in Fig. 5.

3. How important technical robustness and user interface (UI) is for mental health applications? Due to the vulnerable state of the user, robustness and accessible UI for mental health app is essential. Topic 2 highlight this aspect of the user's review.

4. What are vital directions or suggestions for developing a mental health application? The three significant trends that emerge from the result are: (1) reducing the cost of required features, (2) making the app's execution robust, and (3) reducing the load and response time. These directions also apply to other mobile apps but are vital for the success of mental health apps because users are already in a low psychological state, so this can drive them away.

We will expand the dataset by adding more apps and performing an inter-group comparison of topic models in future work. More experiments will be carried out to understand the relation of topics based on review score (1–5) and developer reply. The result will also guide our future work to design and develop a mobile health app for diagnosing, detecting, and treating depression using machine learning.

References

1. Aguilera, A., et al.: mHealth app using machine learning to increase physical activity in diabetes and depression: clinical trial protocol for the diamante study. BMJ Open **10**(8) (2020)
2. Ahmed, A., et al.: A review of mobile chatbot apps for anxiety and depression and their self-care features. Comput. Methods Program. Biomed. Update 100012 (2021)
3. Becker, D.: Acceptance of mobile mental health treatment applications. Proc. Comput. Sci. **98**, 220–227 (2016)
4. Blei, D.M., Jordan, M.I.: Modeling annotated data. In: Proceedings of the 26th Annual International ACM SIGIR Conference on Research and Development in Information Retrieval, pp. 127–134 (2003)
5. Blei, D.M., Jordan, M.I.: Variational inference for Dirichlet process mixtures. Bayesian Anal. **1**(1), 121–143 (2006)
6. Chandrashekar, P.: Do mental health mobile apps work: evidence and recommendations for designing high-efficacy mental health mobile apps. Mhealth **4** (2018)
7. Dantu, R., Dissanayake, I., Nerur, S.: Exploratory analysis of internet of things (IoT) in healthcare: a topic modelling & co-citation approaches. Inf. Syst. Manag. **38**(1), 62–78 (2021)
8. Dumais, S.T.: Latent semantic analysis. Ann. Rev. Inf. Sci. Technol. **38**(1), 188–230 (2004)
9. Einav, L., Levin, J., Popov, I., Sundaresan, N.: Growth, adoption, and use of mobile e-commerce. Am. Econ. Rev. **104**(5), 489–94 (2014)
10. Fuad, A., Al-Yahya, M.: Analysis and classification of mobile apps using topic modeling: a case study on google play Arabic apps. Complexity **2021** (2021)
11. Ghosh, A.K., Wisniewski, P.: Understanding user reviews of adolescent mobile safety apps: a thematic analysis. In: Proceedings of the 19th International Conference on Supporting Group Work, pp. 417–420 (2016)
12. Hoyer, P.O.: Non-negative matrix factorization with sparseness constraints. J. Mach. Learn. Res. **5**(9) (2004)
13. Islam, R., Islam, R., Mazumder, T.: Mobile application and its global impact. Int. J. Eng. Technol. (IJEST) **10**(6), 72–78 (2010)

14. Lecomte, T., et al.: Mobile apps for mental health issues: meta-review of meta-analyses. JMIR Mhealth Uhealth **8**(5), e17458 (2020)
15. Lin, C.C.: A critical appraisal of customer satisfaction and e-commerce. Manage. Audit. J. (2003)
16. Liu, Y., Liu, L., Liu, H., Wang, X.: Analyzing reviews guided by app descriptions for the software development and evolution. J. Softw. Evol. Process **30**(12), e2112 (2018)
17. Mankad, S., Hu, S., Gopal, A.: Single stage prediction with embedded topic modeling of online reviews for mobile app management. Ann. Appl. Stat. **12**(4), 2279–2311 (2018)
18. Marley, J., Farooq, S.: Mobile telephone apps in mental health practice: uses, opportunities and challenges. BJPsych Bull. **39**(6), 288–290 (2015)
19. Marshall, J.M., Dunstan, D.A., Bartik, W.: Effectiveness of using mental health mobile apps as digital antidepressants for reducing anxiety and depression: protocol for a multiple baseline across-individuals design. JMIR Res. Protocols **9**(7), e17159 (2020)
20. Oyebode, O., Orji, R.: Deconstructing persuasive strategies in mental health apps based on user reviews using natural language processing. In: BCSS@ PERSUASIVE (2020)
21. Pan, T., Zhang, W., Wang, Z., Xu, L.: Recommendations based on LDA topic model in android applications. In: 2016 IEEE International Conference on Software Quality, Reliability and Security Companion (QRS-C), pp. 151–158. IEEE (2016)
22. Pires, I.M., Marques, G., Garcia, N.M., Flórez-Revuelta, F., Ponciano, V., Oniani, S.: A research on the classification and applicability of the mobile health applications. J. Personal. Med. **10**(1), 11 (2020)
23. Razavi, R., Gharipour, A., Gharipour, M.: Depression screening using mobile phone usage metadata: a machine learning approach. J. Am. Med. Inform. Assoc. **27**(4), 522–530 (2020)
24. Rennhoff, A.D., Routon, P.W.: Can you hear me now? The rise of smartphones and their welfare effects. Telecommun. Policy **40**(1), 39–51 (2016)
25. Roberts, M.E., Stewart, B.M., Tingley, D., Airoldi, E.M., et al.: The structural topic model and applied social science. In: Advances in Neural Information Processing Systems Workshop on Topic Models: Computation, Application, and Evaluation, vol. 4, pp. 1–20. Harrahs and Harveys, Lake Tahoe (2013)
26. Srivastava, K.: Urbanization and mental health. Ind. Psychiatry J. **18**(2), 75 (2009)
27. Wang, R., Wang, Z., Tang, B., Zhao, L., Wang, L.: SmartPI: understanding permission implications of android apps from user reviews. IEEE Trans. Mob. Comput. **19**(12), 2933–2945 (2019)
28. Wang, X., Markert, C., Sasangohar, F.: Investigating popular mental health mobile application downloads and activity during the COVID-19 pandemic. Hum. Factors 0018720821998110 (2021)
29. Xu, C., Peak, D., Prybutok, V.: A customer value, satisfaction, and loyalty perspective of mobile application recommendations. Decis. Support Syst. **79**, 171–183 (2015)
30. Zamfiroiu, A., Despa, M.L.: Reasons, circumstances and innovative trends in mobile environments. Inform. Econ. **17**(2) (2013)
31. Zečević, M., Mijatović, D., Koklič, M.K., Žabkar, V., Gidaković, P.: User perspectives of diet-tracking apps: reviews content analysis and topic modeling. J. Med. Internet Res. **23**(4), e25160 (2021)

Alzheimer's Dementia Recognition Using Multimodal Fusion of Speech and Text Embeddings

Sandeep Kumar Pandey[1]([✉])(ID), Hanumant Singh Shekhawat[1](ID),
Shalendar Bhasin[2], Ravi Jasuja[2,3], and S. R. M. Prasanna[4]

[1] Indian Institute of Technology Guwahati, Guwahati, Assam, India
{sandeep.pandey,h.s.shekhawat}@iitg.ac.in
[2] Brigham and Womens Hospital, Harvard Medical School, Boston, MA, USA
{Sbhasin,rjasuja}@bwh.harvard.edu
[3] Function Promoting Therapies, Waltham, MA, USA
[4] Indian Institute of Technology Dharwad, Dharwad, Karnataka, India
prasanna@iitdh.ac.in

Abstract. Alzheimer's disease related Dementia (ADRD) compromises the memory, thinking and speech. This neurodegenerative disease severely impacts the cognitive capability and motor skills of affected individuals. ADRD is accompanied by progressive degeneration of the brain tissue, which leads to impairments in the memory formation, and loss of verbal fluency among other adverse physiological manifestations. Cognitive impairment becomes particular evident over time since it overtly alters the communication with repetitive utterances, confusion, filler words, and inability to speak at a normal pace. Most prevailing methodologies for ADRD recognition focus on mental health scores given by clinicians through in-person interviews, which can potentially be influenced by subjective bias of the evaluation. Accordingly, use of alterations in speech as a robust, quantitative indicator of Alzheimer's progression presents an exciting non-invasive prognostic framework. Recent studies utilizing statistical and deep learning approaches have shown that assessment of ADRD can be effectively done algorithmically, which can serve as an objective companion diagnostic to the clinical assessment. However, the sensitivity and specificity of extant approaches are suboptimal. To this end, we present a multimodal fusion-based framework to leverage discriminative information from both speech and text transcripts. Text transcripts are extracted from speech utterances using the wav2vec2 model. Two fusion approaches are evaluated - score-level fusion and late feature fusion for classifying subjects into AD/Non-AD categories. Experimental appraisal of the fusion approaches on the Interspeech 2021 ADDreSSo Challenge dataset yields promising recognition

This research was supported under the India-Korea joint program cooperation of science and technology by the National Research Foundation (NRF) Korea (2020K1A3A1A68093469), the Ministry of Science and ICT (MSIT) Korea and by the Department of Biotechnology (India) (DBT/IC-12031(22)-ICD-DBT).

J.-H. Kim et al. (Eds.): IHCI 2021, LNCS 13184, pp. 718–728, 2022.
https://doi.org/10.1007/978-3-030-98404-5_64

performance with the added advantage of a simpler architecture, reduced compute load and complexity.

Keywords: Speech recognition · Human-computer interaction · Computational para-linguistics · Alzheimer's dementia · Multimodal · Score fusion

1   Introduction

Speech is the most preferred form of communication between individuals, and it contains a multitude of information ranging from speaker identity to the emotional state of the individuals [20]. The paralinguistic information underlying a speech utterance can be exploited for numerous use, such as improving Human-Computer Interaction by incorporating emotional information, automatic diagnosis and assessment of mental health status of individuals for issues such as clinical depression [1], Dementia [11], schizophrenia [8], etc. Speech signal becomes the apt choice for monitoring and diagnosing mental health issues because of the easy availability of speech data and less manual effort as smart wearable devices and smartphones can record speech from patients without disturbing them.

Alzheimer's Dementia (AD) is a mental health issue that falls under the category of neurodegenerative disease [16], thereby impacting the cognitive capability and motor skills of the affected individuals and thus affect speech. Since age constitutes a significant risk factor, older people are at high risk as AD is a significant cause of disability and dependency for older individuals [10]. As there is no cure for AD currently, early detection is crucial for effective intervention by healthcare specialists to slow the progression of the disease. Most of the clinical methods for detecting AD in individuals are invasive and costly such as PET imaging and analysis of cerebrospinal fluid to measure the concentration level of amyloid plaques in the brain [18]. Another non-invasive clinical method is clinical interviews by psychologists, which constitutes lengthy questionnaires and picture descriptions, etc. [28]. However, the drawback of such clinical interviews is that it is biased towards the psychologist's interpretation and scoring. A more cost-effective, non-invasive, and automatic diagnosis and assessment tool is the need of the hour to help clinicians combat AD.

Many research works have explored the use of speech signals in the automatic detection of mental health issues such as depression, AD, etc. Dementia is marked by a change in speech and language, faulty reasoning, impaired vocabulary, etc. This makes methodologies based on speech signals suitable for the early detection of AD. The work in [25] explores various standard acoustic feature sets such as IS09, IS10, IS11 etc., for the task of AD vs. healthy control classification. Moreover, with the advancement in the deep learning field, the reliance on hand-crafted features have decreased considerably with the usage of speech representations such as MFCC, mel-spectrograms as well as raw speech directly in combination with deep learning architectures such as CNN+LSTM, Attention-based architecture, etc. for extraction of high-level deep features and classification in an end-to-end framework [19,20]. In this direction, the works in [9] a bi-modal network is proposed leveraging both acoustic as well as linguistic modality to improve the recognition performance on ADReSS Dataset, gaining an overall improvement of 18.75% over the baseline on ADReSS Dataset provided by INTERSPEECH 2020. In [6] proposed an automatic assessment model for cognitive decline using recurrent neural network and feature sequence representation, showing appreciable performance using 120 speech samples. Also, the work in [27] used a multimodal approach by fusing perplexity scores generated from transcripts using an n-gram model along with x-vectors and i-vectors generated from speech signals and using an SVM for AD versus Non-AD classification. On similar lines, the work in [5] explores several acoustic features such as speech-based statistical functionals, rhythmic features, x-vector, etc., and text-based features such as Glove embeddings. The conclusion derived was that multimodal fusion helped generalize the model over test set compared to uni-modal approaches. One major challenge associated with Dementia classification is data imbalance in earlier existing datasets in terms of age, gender, etc., which hugely impacts system performance. To address this issue, ADDreSSo Challenge provides a dataset that is balanced in terms of the aspects mentioned above.

Motivated by the success of multimodal fusion of acoustic and linguistic modalities, we propose a multimodal fusion system based on a simplistic architecture that employs CNN and robust BERT-based features for text modality. Despite the considerable success of BERT and its variants in text processing applications such as sentiment analysis [26], keyword spotting [22], text summarizing [17], its application in the mental health field has been limited to few works [3]. Also, most of the earlier works utilize hand-crafted feature sets such as ComPARe, IS09/IS13 feature set, etc. In contrast, this work explores mel-spectrogram representations for acoustic modality, as mel-spectrograms have shown to contain substantial paralinguistic information [29].

The remainder of the paper is organized as follows. The methodology for transcript generation and text embedding extraction and architecture for audio modality along with the fusion approaches explored is described in Sect. 2. Section 3 describes the implementation details and dataset description. Results are discussed in Sect. 4, and Sect. 5 concludes the paper.

2 Methodology

We propose the multimodal fusion of information from both text and audio modality based on previous research in this field [14]. To this end, a CNN-based audio embeddings model is employed to extract AD-related features from speakers' speech utterances. A pre-trained BERT model is used to extract text embeddings for the corresponding utterances. Finally, we employ two fusion strategies - late feature fusion and decision level fusion, which are discussed in detail below.

2.1   Transcript Generation

Since Alzheimer's dementia affects speech production and motor skills, linguistic information plays an essential role in effectively diagnosing AD subjects from healthy controls. To this end, we employ the state-of-the-art wav2vec2 [2] by Facebook to extract transcripts from the speech utterances. Wav2vec2 is based on self-supervised learning from unlabelled training data, thus making it easy to adapt for multiple languages and dialects. Wav2Vec2 accepts raw speech signal as input and masks it to latent space and solves a contrastive task over the quantization of latent representations jointly learned.

Wav2Vec2 consists of a multi-layer feature encoder comprising of 1d Convolution, which takes raw speech signal as input. Given a speech signal $\mathcal{X}_t$ where $t \in 1, 2, \cdots, T$ is the time steps, the convolution layers transform it into hidden space representations $\ddagger_t$ which serves as an input to a transformer. The transformer encodes these encoded hidden space representations to incorporate temporal dependency. The feature encoder finally yields c_t encoded time sequence. The feature encoder outputs are quantized to II_t using a quantization module as in a VQ-VAE, where the latent representations are matched with a codebook to select the most appropriate representation of the data.

The inputs to the transformer from the feature encoder are masked partially and matched with the quantized outputs II_t using a contrastive loss function. The model is pre-trained on unlabelled data and then is fine-tuned using labeled data and CTC loss for downstream tasks such as speech recognition. In our work, we have used the pre-trained Wav2vec2 model from HuggingFace transformers library[1].

2.2   Text Modality

To extract linguistic information from the transcripts generated from speech signals using the Wav2vec2 model, we employ BERT based on its success in similar AD recognition tasks [3]. We have used DistillBert [23], a distilled variant of Bert base model but with 40% fewer parameters, retaining its language understanding capability by 97% and making it faster by 40%. For the generation of text embeddings, we utilize a pre-trained DistillBert on the transcripts of the participants. The sentences in the transcripts are first tokenized, and a task-specific special token CLS is appended to the beginning of the sentence tokens, which collects sentence-level information for classification tasks. The embeddings from the DistillBert embedding layer are extracted corresponding to the CLS token, which serves as the sentence level feature corresponding to the speaker utterance segment.

2.3   Audio Modality

Most of the earlier works which explored audio modality for AD detection have utilized hand-crafted feature sets such as eGeMaPs, ComPare, etc., as inputs to

---

[1] https://huggingface.co/transformers/model_doc/wav2vec2.html.

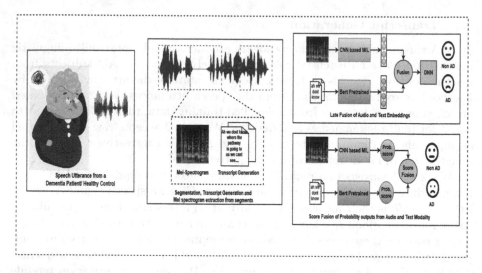

Fig. 1. Proposed AD recognition methodology using two fusion approaches - fusion of embeddings and score level fusion

their deep learning architecture. However, mel-spectrograms have shown appreciable performance in paralinguistic tasks such as speech emotion recognition (SER). Motivated with this, we employ a simple CNN-based architecture to extract discriminative features corresponding to Ad/Non-AD classes from mel-spectrograms extracted from speech utterances. The audio-based architecture consists of three feature learning blocks, with each block comprising of a 2D convolution layer, a Batch Normalization layer in order to force the learned features to have zero mean and unit variance, an activation layer consisting of elu activations, and a max-pooling layer to reduce the size of feature maps produced and remove noise. The feature learning block is followed by Dense layers and a Softmax output layer as per the requirement of the fusion methods discussed below (Fig. 1).

2.4 Fusion Methods

Previous works on AD detection have shown that multimodal systems using both audio and text information perform better than single modality systems [5]. We explored two fusion techniques for leveraging information from both audio and text modality - feature fusion and score fusion. A brief description of the two proposed methods is given below-

Decision Level Fusion. For decision level fusion, the average of the prediction probabilities generated from each modality - text, and audio- is accumulated for all the utterance groups of a subject, as a subject will have many utterance groups as discussed in the next section. Then the average of probabilities for the utterance groups of a particular subject is the final prediction probability for that subject. For example, a speaker having 100 utterances (segmented from one long interview) will have 20 segment groups with five utterances in each group. The average probability for the 20 segment groups is the probability for the speaker level. This is done for both audio and text modality. Finally, an average over the probabilities obtained from the two modalities is taken as the final multimodal probability, used to generate binary classification label (AD/Non-AD)

Late Feature Fusion. We also explored feature-level fusion to train a smaller DNN model on the fused features from both modalities to extract higher-level information leveraging audio and text cues. To this end, the features from Audio-based CNN architecture and the bert embeddings are fused together to form a feature vector. This feature vector is further passed through a multi-layered DNN with a sigmoid layer, in the end, to generate a single class probability for an utterance segment. Like the decision level fusion, the probability scores are averaged for all the utterance groups, giving the final probability at the speaker level.

3 Experimental Evaluation

In this section, we discuss the dataset details and the parameter details, and implementation of Multimodal architecture.

3.1 Dataset Description

The dataset used in this study is provided by ADDreSSo Challenge of Interspeech'21 [12]. It consists of two parts intended for two tasks- diagnosis and progression. We have used only the diagnosis pat of the dataset as we attempt only AD/Non-AD Classification Task. The Diagnosis subset is further divided into train and test splits consisting of speech data from 166 speakers recorded using the cookie-theft picture description method of the Boston Diagnostic Aphasia exam. Those recordings have been acoustically enhanced (noise reduction through spectral subtraction) and normalized. The diagnosis task dataset has been balanced with respect to age and gender in order to eliminate potential confounding and bias. The number of speakers belonging to the AD category of train set is 87, and that of CN (Healthy Control) is 79. The number of speakers for the test set of diagnosis task is 71.

3.2 Implementation Details

The speech utterances provided for each speaker are first segmented according to the duration details provided, resulting in many utterances of variable length per speaker. CNN requires fixed-sized inputs; therefore, the speech utterances are either zero-padded or spliced to make them of equal length. As an input to CNN,

Table 1. Recognition performance in terms of Precision, Recall, Accuracy and F1-scores for 5 fold Cross Validation for Audio, Text and Audio+Text feature and score fusion using ADDreSSo Challenge Dataset

Modality	Class	Precision	Recall	F1-score	Accuracy
Audio	AD	72.56	80.99	75.94	73.67
	Non-AD	61.46	60.47	60.63	
Text	AD	74.01	68.73	68.60	70.88
	Non-AD	72.55	65.36	63.89	
Audio+Text (Late Feature Fusion)	AD	74.29	82.81	78.14	76.70
	Non-AD	79.88	66.52	71.73	
Audio+Text (Score Fusion)	AD	78.80	86.92	82.55	**81.01**
	Non-AD	82.61	73.00	77.31	

log mel spectrograms are extracted from the speech utterances. For extracting the log mel spectrograms, the speech signal is first windowed using hamming window and a frame-size of 2048 samples and frame-shift of 512 samples. Then Short-Time Fourier Transform (STFT) is calculated for the windowed frames. The magnitude spectrogram obtained from STFT is passed through a mel filter bank to get the filter bank energies. Finally, a log operator is used on the filter bank coefficients to obtain the log mel spectrogram.

The number of speech segments selected from each speaker for utterance group formation is 5, based on performance for group sizes in the range 2,20. If a speaker has more than five speech segments, then more sets of 5 utterances are created. The last set is completed with repeated utterances, randomly chosen from the original utterance segments for that speaker. This helps to reduce the wastage of information that could be levied from additional utterances of a speaker.

The mel spectrograms are calculated using the python library Librosa [15]. The CNN architecture is implemented using Keras Library. Bayesian Optimization [24] is used to select the values of the hyperparameters such as batch size, optimizer, etc. For the training set, utterance groups consisting of 5 utterances per group are constructed, and each utterance group is treated as a separate speaker while training. For validation, the validation data for speakers are divided similarly to the train set. However, the final label for a speaker in the validation set is generated by taking the average of the probabilities of the multiple utterance groups of 5 utterances for that speaker and then comparing it with the threshold.

Table 2. Recognition performance in terms of Precision, Recall, Accuracy and F1-scores for test data for Audio+Text feature and score fusion using ADDreSSo challenge dataset

Classes	Feature fusion				Score fusion			
	Precision	Recall	F1 Score	Accuracy	Precision	Recall	F1 Score	Accuracy
AD	54.83	60.71	57.62	56.14	69.69	82.14	75.40	73.68
Non AD	57.69	51.72	54.54		79.16	65.51	71.69	

Table 3. Comparison of performance with state-of-the-art methods in terms of Accuracy on the test partition of ADDreSSo challenge dataset

Research work	Accuracy
Luz et al. [13]	78.87
Perez et al. [21]	80.28
Gauder et al. [7]	78.87
Balagopalan et al. [4]	67.61
Proposed	**73.68**

4   Results

The AD/Non-AD classification task is a binary classification problem and thus the metrics used for evaluation of recognition performance are - precision, recall, F1 score and accuracy. The proposed Multimodal architecture is trained using the ADDreSSo Challenge Dataset. The training part of the dataset is split into two parts -training and validation comprising of 80% and 20% of the speakers, respectively. The splits are performed using five random seeds, and thus, each of the training and validation partitions is speaker-independent to remove any biasedness towards a particular speaker. Table 1 shows the recognition performance of the proposed system in terms of Precision, Recall, F1 score, and Accuracy for the individual modalities - audio and text as well as the two fusion approaches for multimodal scenario - Late feature fusion and Decision level fusion. For the validation set, the recognition performance is the mean of the performances for the five folds. From the table, it can be observed that Score Fusion approach performs better compared to the Late feature fusion approach for multimodal scenario. This can be attributed to the individual modality's robustness in capturing dementia related cues which in turn helped boost recognition performance when score-fusion is done. Moreover, in case of individual modality, the audio part performs slightly better compared to the text in terms of accuracy. However, the F1 scores reveals that the model trained using text is more balanced as compared to the model trained with audio modality. Also, the low performance of text modality compared to the audio modality can be attributed to the Automatic Speech Recognition (ASR) error from the Wav2Vec model. As no ground truth for transcriptions are provided, the assessment of generated transcriptions is difficult.

For the test partition, Table 2 shows the comparison of recognition performances for both Feature fusion and Score fusion techniques. Similar to the validation data scenario, the score fusion approach performs better in comparison to the late feature fusion. The performance of late feature fusion degrades in the unseen test set scenario. Moreover, the F1 scores for the score-fusion approach demonstrates that the trained model is balanced and not biased towards a particular class. Also, Fig. 2 shows the confusion matrices for the test data in the Feature Fusion and Score Fusion scenario. From both matrices Figs. 2(a) and 2(b), it can be seen that maximum confusion occurs while modeling Non-AD speakers.

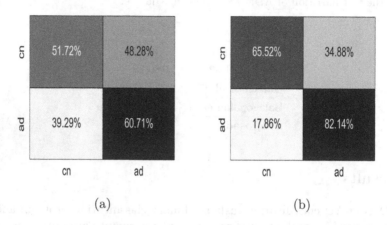

(a)   (b)

Fig. 2. Confusion matrices for the two fusion approaches using Test Dataset of ADDreSSo Challenge. (a) Feature fusion. (b) Score fusion

4.1   Comparison with State-of-the-Art

Table 3 presents comparison of recognition performance with state-of-the-art techniques published in recent times on the same dataset. The proposed system performs appreciably good when compared to [4] which uses a combination of acoustic features and pre-trained embeddings for AD/Non-AD classification from speech. The results are also comparable to other techniques such as [7, 21] which uses acoustic features, word embeddings and emotional embeddings for the task of AD classification from speech and text. The proposed system provides a trade-of between model complexity and model performance. The CNN based MIL architecture with BERT embeddings provide a light weight alternative to complex architectures thereby reducing model inference time. This becomes significant when such systems have to be deployed on wearable smart devices where continuous monitoring of patient is performed in the background and the inference time should be less.

5   Conclusions

Automatic diagnosis of Alzheimer's Dementia (AD) is a challenging research direction and need of the hour to provide easy and non-invasive techniques for early AD detection. To this end, we proposed a Multimodal fusion-based framework, which learns from multiple utterances of a speaker by utilizing the common information shared across the utterances in a group with leveraging the linguistic information from text transcripts as well. Experimental evaluation on the ADDreSSo Challenge 2021 Dataset shows that the proposed technique is effective in classifying AD vs Non AD based on speech and text only, thereby suggesting that speech can be further explored to aid diagnosis of mental health issues such as Dementia. However, the proposed method faces limitations with respect to transcript generation as the speech data is of spontaneous nature and the ASR systems such as Wav2vec2 introduces significant recognition error during speech-to-text conversion. As such, a more robust ASR, trained on domain matched speech, can mitigate these issues.

References

1. Alghowinem, S., Goecke, R., Wagner, M., Epps, J., Breakspear, M., Parker, G.: Detecting depression: a comparison between spontaneous and read speech. In: 2013 IEEE International Conference on Acoustics, Speech and Signal Processing, pp. 7547–7551. IEEE (2013)
2. Baevski, A., Zhou, H., Mohamed, A., Auli, M.: Wav2Vec 2.0: a framework for self-supervised learning of speech representations. arXiv preprint arXiv:2006.11477 (2020)
3. Balagopalan, A., Eyre, B., Rudzicz, F., Novikova, J.: To BERT or not to BERT: comparing speech and language-based approaches for Alzheimer's disease detection. arXiv preprint arXiv:2008.01551 (2020)
4. Balagopalan, A., Novikova, J.: Comparing acoustic-based approaches for Alzheimer's disease detection. arXiv preprint arXiv:2106.01555 (2021)
5. Campbell, E.L., Docío-Fernández, L., Raboso, J.J., García-Mateo, C.: Alzheimer's dementia detection from audio and text modalities. arXiv preprint arXiv:2008.04617 (2020)
6. Chien, Y.W., Hong, S.Y., Cheah, W.T., Yao, L.H., Chang, Y.L., Fu, L.C.: An automatic assessment system for Alzheimer's disease based on speech using feature sequence generator and recurrent neural network. Sci. Rep. **9**(1), 1–10 (2019)
7. Gauder, L., Pepino, L., Ferrer, L., Riera, P.: Alzheimer disease recognition using speech-based embeddings from pre-trained models. In: Proceedings of Interspeech 2021, pp. 3795–3799 (2021)
8. Kerr, S.L., Neale, J.M.: Emotion perception in schizophrenia: specific deficit or further evidence of generalized poor performance? J. Abnorm. Psychol. **102**(2), 312 (1993)
9. Koo, J., Lee, J.H., Pyo, J., Jo, Y., Lee, K.: Exploiting multi-modal features from pre-trained networks for Alzheimer's dementia recognition. arXiv preprint arXiv:2009.04070 (2020)
10. Lisko, I., Kulmala, J., Annetorp, M., Ngandu, T., Mangialasche, F., Kivipelto, M.: How can dementia and disability be prevented in older adults: where are we today and where are we going? J. Intern. Med. (2020)
11. Luz, S., Haider, F., de la Fuente, S., Fromm, D., MacWhinney, B.: Alzheimer's dementia recognition through spontaneous speech: the ADReSS challenge. arXiv preprint arXiv:2004.06833 (2020)

12. Luz, S., Haider, F., de la Fuente, S., Fromm, D., MacWhinney, B.: Detecting cognitive decline using speech only: the ADReSSo challenge. medRxiv (2021). https://doi.org/10.1101/2021.03.24.21254263, https://www.medrxiv.org/content/early/2021/03/27/2021.03.24.21254263
13. Luz, S., Haider, F., de la Fuente, S., Fromm, D., MacWhinney, B.: Detecting cognitive decline using speech only: the ADReSSo challenge. arXiv preprint arXiv:2104.09356 (2021)
14. Martinc, M., Pollak, S.: Tackling the ADReSS challenge: a multimodal approach to the automated recognition of Alzheimer's dementia. In: INTERSPEECH, pp. 2157–2161 (2020)
15. McFee, B., et al.: librosa: Audio and music signal analysis in Python. In: Proceedings of the 14th Python in Science Conference, vol. 8, pp. 18–25. Citeseer (2015)
16. McKhann, G.M., et al.: The diagnosis of dementia due to Alzheimer's disease: recommendations from the national institute on aging-Alzheimer's association workgroups on diagnostic guidelines for Alzheimer's disease. Alzheimer's Dement. **7**(3), 263–269 (2011)
17. Miller, D.: Leveraging BERT for extractive text summarization on lectures. arXiv preprint arXiv:1906.04165 (2019)
18. Nordberg, A.: Pet imaging of amyloid in Alzheimer's disease. Lancet Neurol. **3**(9), 519–527 (2004)
19. Pandey, S.K., Shekhawat, H.S., Prasanna, S.: Emotion recognition from raw speech using wavenet. In: TENCON 2019–2019 IEEE Region 10 Conference (TENCON), pp. 1292–1297. IEEE (2019)
20. Pandey, S.K., Shekhawat, H., Prasanna, S.: Deep learning techniques for speech emotion recognition: a review. In: 2019 29th International Conference Radioelektronika (RADIOELEKTRONIKA), pp. 1–6. IEEE (2019)
21. Pérez-Toro, P., et al.: Influence of the interviewer on the automatic assessment of Alzheimer's disease in the context of the ADReSSo challenge. In: Proceedings of Interspeech 2021, pp. 3785–3789 (2021)
22. Qian, Y., Jia, C., Liu, Y.: BERT-based text keyword extraction. In: Journal of Physics: Conference Series, vol. 1992, p. 042077. IOP Publishing (2021)
23. Sanh, V., Debut, L., Chaumond, J., Wolf, T.: DistilBERT, a distilled version of BERT: smaller, faster, cheaper and lighter. arXiv preprint arXiv:1910.01108 (2019)
24. Snoek, J., Larochelle, H., Adams, R.P.: Practical Bayesian optimization of machine learning algorithms. Adv. Neural Inf. Process. Syst. **25** (2012)
25. Warnita, T., Inoue, N., Shinoda, K.: Detecting Alzheimer's disease using gated convolutional neural network from audio data. arXiv preprint arXiv:1803.11344 (2018)
26. Xu, H., Liu, B., Shu, L., Yu, P.S.: BERT post-training for review reading comprehension and aspect-based sentiment analysis. arXiv preprint arXiv:1904.02232 (2019)
27. Zargarbashi, S., Babaali, B.: A multi-modal feature embedding approach to diagnose Alzheimer disease from spoken language. arXiv preprint arXiv:1910.00330 (2019)
28. Zaudig, M., et al.: SIDAM-a structured interview for the diagnosis of dementia of the Alzheimer type, multi-infarct dementia and dementias of other aetiology according to ICD-10 and DSM-III-R. Psychol. Med. **21**(1), 225–236 (1991)
29. Zhang, S., Zhang, S., Huang, T., Gao, W.: Multimodal deep convolutional neural network for audio-visual emotion recognition. In: Proceedings of the 2016 ACM on International Conference on Multimedia Retrieval, pp. 281–284 (2016)

Exploring Multimodal Features and Fusion for Time-Continuous Prediction of Emotional Valence and Arousal

Ajit Kumar[1], Bong Jun Choi[1(✉)], Sandeep Kumar Pandey[2], Sanghyeon Park[3], SeongIk Choi[3], Hanumant Singh Shekhawat[2], Wesley De Neve[3], Mukesh Saini[4], S. R. M. Prasanna[5], and Dhananjay Singh[6]

[1] Soongsil University, Seoul, South Korea
davidchoi@soongsil.ac.kr
[2] IIT Guwahati, Guwahati, Assam, India
[3] Ghent University Global Campus, Incheon, South Korea
[4] IIT Ropar, Rupnagar, Punjab, India
[5] IIT Dharwad, Dharwad, Karnataka, India
[6] ReSENSE Lab, HUFS, Seoul, South Korea

Abstract. Advances in machine learning and deep learning make it possible to detect and analyse emotion and sentiment using textual and audio-visual information at increasing levels of effectiveness. Recently, an interest has emerged to also apply these techniques for the assessment of mental health, including the detection of stress and depression. In this paper, we introduce an approach that predicts stress (emotional valence and arousal) in a time-continuous manner from audio-visual recordings, testing the effectiveness of different deep learning techniques and various features. Specifically, apart from adopting popular features (e.g., BERT, BPM, ECG, and VGGFace), we explore the use of new features, both engineered and learned, along different modalities to improve the effectiveness of time-continuous stress prediction: for video, we study the use of ResNet-50 features and the use of body and pose features through OpenPose, whereas for audio, we primarily investigate the use of Integrated Linear Prediction Residual (ILPR) features. The best result we achieved was a combined CCC value of 0.7595 and 0.3379 for the development set and the test set of MuSe-Stress 2021, respectively.

Keywords: Emotion detection · Excitation source features · Human pose · LP analysis · Multimodal fusion · Multimodal sentiment analysis

1 Introduction

Understanding emotion from different types of media content like text, audio, and video is a critical development for the early detection of mental health issues

This research was supported under the India-Korea Joint Programme of Cooperation in Science & Technology by the National Research Foundation (NRF) Korea (2020K1A3A1A68093469), the Ministry of Science and ICT (MSIT) Korea and by the Department of Biotechnology (India) (DBT/IC-12031(22)-ICD-DBT).

J.-H. Kim et al. (Eds.): IHCI 2021, LNCS 13184, pp. 729–744, 2022.
https://doi.org/10.1007/978-3-030-98404-5_65

such as depression and anxiety. The recent growth in deep learning methods has helped to improve the automated understanding of different types of media content. The research effort outlined in this paper was conducted within the context of the Multimodal Sentiment Analysis in Real-life Media (MuSe) 2021 challenge. This challenge consists of four sub-challenges, namely MuSe-Wilder, MuSe-Sent, MuSe-Stress, and MuSe-Physio [1], with these sub-challenges relying on two datasets: MuSe-CaR and U_{LM}-TSST [2]. The work proposed in this paper addressed the Multimodal Emotional Stress (MuSe-Stress) 2021 sub-challenge, targeting the prediction of the level of emotional arousal and valence in a time-continuous manner from audio-visual recordings. The MuSe-Stress 2021 dataset (i.e., U_{LM}-TSST) was distributed in two versions: (1) extracted features and (2) raw audio-visual recordings, along with a text version of the speech. We studied the results obtained by the provided baseline, leading to the observation that the extracted features had already been experimented with in different setups. Hence, we focused on engineering new features, with the goal of improving the effectiveness of emotional stress prediction.

For the video modality, we explored and experimented with various pre-trained vision models and found ResNet-50 [3] to obtain the best performance for the development test. Further, to explore novel features, we extracted new features related to human pose. In particular, we exploited the emotional attributes encoded in human body language like hand gestures, shoulder movement, neck movement, and full-body position. Extracting features from human pose was challenging due to the following reasons: (1) hand gesture identification: all participants have a sensor in one hand, which makes it difficult for a model to identify both hands (often only one hand was detected), (2) foot gesture identification: the video was recorded at a certain distance, with many frames having missing lower body parts, and (3) natural movement: all participants were equipped with sensors, with these sensors restricting the natural movement of body parts, thus limiting the availability of pose and associated emotional information. Some of these challenges were resolved through the use of OpenPose [4], YOLO [5], and pre-processing (e.g., resizing of the bounding box of a hand). We observed that human pose is able to provide good features for detecting human emotions. Still, to solve the aforementioned challenges in a more effective way, other approaches can be leveraged to obtain better features from human gestures.

For the audio modality, we experimented with the provided features and also investigated new features, namely Integrated Linear Prediction Residual (ILPR) features [6]. Our final audio predictions were based on the combination of eGeMAPS [7] and ILPR features. For the text modality, we experimented with BERT [8] features. Still, from the baseline and based on our experiments, we learned that text features generally degrade the performance when combining them with other features. We largely used the model and code given as the baseline to implement our deep learning approach, tuning various parameters like the network size and the learning rate. Since early fusion (concatenation of features before model training) was not resulting in a good performance, we adopted the late fusion approach used by the baseline.

Our best performing combination achieved CCC values of (0.7549, 0.7640), outperforming the baseline result (0.5043, 0.6966) for the development set (for arousal and valence, respectively). However, our best performing combination (0.2297, 0.4158) did not do well on the internal test set of MuSe-Stress 2021, compared to the baseline test result (0.4562, 0.5614). We plan to further mitigate this performance gap in future work.

The remainder of this paper is organized as follows. Section 2 discusses the features and the model used by our approach. Section 3 describes our experiments and the results obtained. Finally, Sect. 4 concludes the paper.

2   Features and Model

2.1   Audio

Speech, which is the preferred form of communication between individuals, carries a substantial amount of primary information (e.g., the intended message) and secondary information (e.g., emotion, speaker identity, and gender). Speech production characteristics are different for neutral speech and emotionally charged speech. This difference in speech production characteristics under different emotion scenarios is reflected in terms of changes in the vocal tract system and the excitation source [6]. This motivated us to explore information about both the excitation source and the vocal tract for feature extraction for the purpose of time-continuous prediction of emotional valence and arousal.

Excitation Source Features for Audio. The task of separation of the vocal tract and excitation source information from a given speech signal has been explored in the literature [9–11]. Researchers have suggested the use of Linear Prediction (LP) analysis, with proper order selection [12] to model the vocal tract and excitation source information. The LP Coefficients obtained from LP analysis represent the vocal tract information, and the LP residual signal obtained using the inverse filter represents the excitation source information. For a detailed overview of the Integrated Linear Prediction Residual (ILPR) signal extraction process, please refer to [13]. A brief description regarding the extraction of the ILPR signal is given below.

Given a speech signal $s[n]$, where n represents the sample index and $n = 0, 1, \ldots$, the first stage involved is using a pre-emphasis filtering to enhance the high-frequency components of the speech signal. The filtered signal $s_e[n]$ is then used for further LP analysis. The LP analysis works by predicting the present speech sample $\hat{s}_e[n]$ based on a combination of p past speech samples ($s[n-1], \ldots, s[n-p]$). This combination of p past samples can be mathematically represented as

$$\hat{s}_e[n] = -\sum_{k=1}^{p} c_k s_e[n-k], \tag{1}$$

where c_k represents the Linear Prediction Coefficients (LPCs). The LP residual (LPR) signal $e[n]$ can then be computed as follows:

$$e[n] = s_e[n] + \sum_{k=1}^{p} c_k s_e[n-k].$$

(2)

The LPCs are computed using the Levinson-Durbin Algorithm [14]. An inverse filter $I_{lp}(z)$ is realized using the computed LPCs. The transfer function of the inverse filter in the z-domain is given as follows:

$$I_{lp}(z) = 1 + \sum_{k=1}^{p} c_k z^{-k}.$$

(3)

Finally, the ILPR signal is obtained by passing the original speech signal $s[n]$ through the inverse filter $I_{lp}(z)$. The resulting ILPR signal can then be further used to compute speech features.

eGeMAPS Features. eGeMAPS features for the audio modality are part of the baseline feature set. In accordance with the time step defined in the baseline, eGeMAPS features of 88 dimensions are computed from the ILPR signal at a time step of 500 ms. The ILPR eGeMAP and the Speech signal eGeMAPS are concatenated to form a combined feature vector of dimensionality 164. The ILPR eGeMAP represents information from the excitation source, whereas the speech eGeMAP represents vocal tract characteristics. This combined feature vector is used in our work to model the emotional information from the audio modality.

2.2 Video

ResNet. Computer vision applications such as object detection and object recognition are actively exploring the use of Convolutional Neural Networks (CNNs), given the ability of these artificial neural networks to identify features of interest without human intervention. Moreover, multi-layered CNNs like VGG can obtain a high effectiveness for a multitude of prediction tasks, including the task of face recognition [15].

In general, CNNs perform better as the number of layers increases [16]. Indeed, a higher number of layers allows a neural network to learn more complex features, eventually enabling the neural network to solve more complex tasks. However, one drawback of deep neural networks is the occurrence of vanishing gradients during backpropagation, making it difficult to train multi-layered neural networks. The issue of vanishing gradients refers to the phenomenon where the gradients of the loss function get smaller as they are propagated towards the initial network layers, given the application of the chain rule.

Residual Networks (ResNets) [3] were proposed in 2016 to mitigate the vanishing gradient problem. A ResNet is composed of a series of convolutional layers with residual blocks. These blocks have skip connections that allow gradients to flow directly from the later convolutional layers to the initial convolutional layers. For the MuSe-Stress 2021 sub-challenge, we leveraged ResNet-50 to extract features from the video modality, obtaining these features from the last convolutional layer present in this network architecture. Note that ResNet-50 is a network deeper than VGG-16 [15], where the latter is used as a baseline architecture by the organizers of the Muse-Stress 2021 sub-challenge. Furthermore, ResNet-50 outputs 2048-D features, whereas VGG-16 produces 512-D features.

The inputs used for feature extraction are the facial images cropped directly from the raw video using MTCNN [17]. Due to variations in size, all facial images were re-sized to a resolution of 224×224 before being fed into a ResNet-50 pre-trained on VGGFace2 (no fine-tuning was used). VGGFace2 [18], a further development of VGGFace [19], is a large-scale dataset for recognizing faces, consisting of 3.31 million images of 9,131 identities. In what follows, the features (activation vectors) extracted through ResNet-50, pre-trained on VGGFace2, will be referred to as *RN50*.

OpenPose. To extract additional features from the video modality, we made use of OpenPose, an open-source system for multi-person 2-D pose detection in real time [4]. The OpenPose approach, which relies on the use of stacked CNNs, consists of two major parts: while one part predicts 2-D confidence maps for keypoints of interest (e.g., body, foot, hand, and facial keypoints), the other part predicts so-called Part Affinity Fields (PAFs), with a PAF referring to a set of 2-D vector fields that encode the location and orientation of limbs over the image domain [4,20].

Among the different kinds of features that can be extracted by OpenPose, we decided to work with facial features and body&foot features. Throughout the remainder of this paper, these features will be further referred to as *OFF* and *OBF*, respectively. For *OFF*, 70 2-D keypoints were extracted, whereas for *OBF*, 25 2-D keypoints were extracted[1]. The 70 *OFF* and 25 *OBF* keypoints are shown in Fig. 1.

As *OFF* and *OBF* aim at representing different types of visual information, the inputs used to extract the aforementioned features are different. In particular, the inputs used for facial feature extraction are the same facial images used for ResNet-50 feature extraction. Furthermore, unlike the cropped facial images used for obtaining *OFF*, *OBF* is created using the corresponding full-resolution images. Given these different inputs, we made use of two different pre-trained models. First, for OBF, we made use of the body25 model, which has been pre-trained on a combination of the MPII dataset and a subset of foot instances taken from the COCO dataset [21], and where the latter was labeled using the Clickwork platform [21]. Second, for OFF, we made use of a face model that has been pre-trained on facial keypoints taken from the COCO dataset [4].

---

[1] The 25 *OBF* keypoints are Nose, Neck, R/L Shoulders, R/L Elbows, R/L Wrists, MidHip, R/L Hips, R/L Knees, R/L Ankles, R/L Eyes, R/L Ears, R/L BigToes, R/L SmallToes, R/L Heels, and Background (R/L stands for Right/Left).

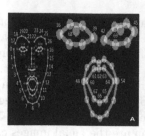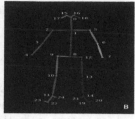

Fig. 1. Image A shows the 70 facial keypoints extracted by OpenPose. Image B shows the 25 body&foot keypoints identified by OpenPose.

Besides the use of facial features and body&foot features, we also investigated the extraction of hand features. The U_{LM}-TSST dataset is composed of videos that feature free-talking participants in a stressful situation, and with these participants making use of minimal body movements. However, while talking, the participants are still freely moving their hands around. As such, we hypothesize that these hand gestures are representative of the emotional state of the participants (i.e., we hypothesize that these hand movements convey emotional information).

OpenPose can identify 21 hand keypoints, making available a model that has been pre-trained on the COCO dataset. However, the extraction of hand features using OpenPose is still a work in progress due to the limitations discussed below.

- OpenPose is unable to identify keypoints from full-resolution images properly. This is for instance illustrated in Fig. 2, where most of the keypoints are wrongly identified. Hence, we decided to crop hands before doing keypoint recognition using You Only Look Once version 3 (YOLOv3) [5].
- Using the cropped hand images as input for feature extraction purposes also comes with limitations. Indeed, OpenPose can only identify keypoints from one hand at a time, as depicted in Fig. 3B. Furthermore, difficulties are also encountered when an object (e.g., a sensor) is attached to a hand, as illustrated in Fig. 3C.

YOLOv3, which is pre-trained on the CMU Hand DB dataset [22], was used to detect and crop hands from full-resolution images. However, it is still necessary to choose a proper bounding box size to avoid having cropped images that contain both hands. In addition, we believe the detection problems that arise due to a hand holding an object can be addressed through the use of skin masking for removing this object [23] (alternatively, a future version of the U_{LM}-TSST dataset may avoid the presence of hands with sensors attached altogether). Once the above-mentioned limitations are overcome, it should be possible to leverage the extracted hand gesture information to better predict valence and arousal values in a time-continuous manner.

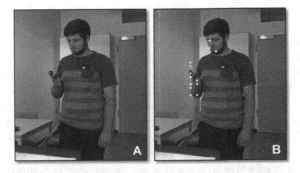

Fig. 2. Image B shows the hand keypoints recognized by OpenPose in the full-resolution Image A.

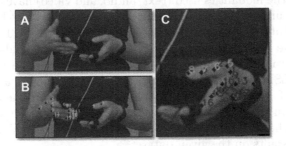

Fig. 3. Image A shows a hand image cropped from a full-resolution image. Image B shows the keypoints identified in Image A using OpenPose. Image C visualizes the keypoints found when an object is attached to a hand.

2.3 Text

The Bidirectional Encoder Representations from Transformers (BERT) [8] features were provided for the text modality. We observed from the baseline results that these features do not perform well in a standalone setting, even degrading the performance when used in conjunction with other modalities (i.e., audio and video). We explored the possible causes for the low performance of BERT features. The first cause is related to the breaking of text based on segment length rather than the end of a sentence, with the new model SentenceBERT [24] also having this problem. From the literature, one can learn that BERT features work well with full sentences, with full sentences helping to capture the context in which a word is used. The second cause is related to human psychology: in a stressful setting, humans are less likely to speak, resulting in lots of blank segments. We believe that these segments must have emotional information but we could not verify this using the other modalities as we aimed at improving the performance. We can take this as another direction for future research.

2.4 Fusion

Humans are essentially complex multimedia systems. They have multiple senses and express their behavior in terms of multiple modalities, such as voice, facial appearance, activity, and text. With the rapid development of sensing technologies, it is easy to capture these modalities automatically. There are two main techniques for fusing multimodal information: early fusion and late fusion [25]. In early fusion, we combine the features from multiple modalities at an early stage and train a classifier on top of it. Various early-fusion techniques have been explored for early fusion, particularly for image analysis. It has been observed that early fusion is effective in scenarios where the spatio-temporal organization of the data is similar (e.g., RGB images and thermal images) [26]. This is probably because, at the initial stage, the feature maps still contain local structure.

In our case, the modalities used (text, audio, and video) have different spatio-temporal structures. In addition, a single classifier would not be able to learn the class distributions of the individual modalities effectively. Therefore, we are inclined to make use of late fusion. Yet, instead of using hand-crafted weights to fuse the decisions from individual modalities, we feed the late multimodal features to an LSTM-RNN and let it learn the fusion weights automatically by looking at the data [20]. The LSTM does not only exploit the complementary information from multiple modalities, but it also implements a self-attention mechanism in the given time-series data. We find that such mid-level fusion gives the best results on the given dataset.

3 Experiments and Results

3.1 Experimental Setup

Video. All experiments with features extracted from the video modality (i.e., *RN50*, *OBF*, and *OFF*) were performed using the baseline LSTM-RNN model[2]. In particular, a bi-directional LSTM-RNN was used and trained for 100 epochs, relying on early stopping with a patience of 15 epochs. The number of seeds was set to 10, saving the predictions made by the best-performing model. The features and labels were segmented as stated in [1], using a window size and a hop size of 300 steps (150 s) and 50 steps (25 s), respectively.

A grid search was performed to investigate the optimum combination of different hyperparameter settings, taking into account the normalization of input features (n), the hidden state dimension (h), the number of LSTM-RNN layers (r), and the learning rate (lr). The values tested for each hyperparameter are as follows: $n = \{$True, False$\}$, $h = \{8, 32, 64, 128\}$, $r = \{1, 4, 5, 9\}$, and $lr = \{2e{-}5, 5e{-}5, 0.002, 0.2\}$.

To mitigate issues in terms of overfitting, three different methods were investigated in a later stage of our experimentation: dropout, L_2 regularisation, and data augmentation. Similar to the previously described hyperparameter tuning

---

[2] https://github.com/lstappen/MuSe2021.

Table 1. Valence and arousal results obtained for hyperparameter tuning when making use of the *RN50* features and $lr = 0.002$.

Hyperparameter tuning											
Valence						Arousal					
h	r	n	d	$L2$	CCC	h	r	n	d	$L2$	CCC
64	4	False	0.0	0.0	0.3310	64	4	False	0.0	0.0	0.2022
128	5	False	0.0	0.0	0.6108	64	4	True	0.0	0.1	0.0036
128	5	False	0.5	0.0	0.6056	64	4	True	0.0	1e−6	0.2954
128	5	False	0.7	0.0	0.5078	64	4	True	0.0	1e−8	0.3339
128	5	False	0.5	1e−4	0.5687	64	4	True	0.5	1e−8	0.3397
128	5	False	0.7	1e−4	0.5875	64	4	True	0.7	1e−8	0.3955
128	5	False	0.5	1e−6	0.6198	16	4	True	0.0	0.0	0.4088
128	5	False	0.7	1e−6	0.5725	16	4	True	0.7	1e−8	0.3295
128	5	False	0.5	1e−8	0.6249	64	4	True	0.2	0.0	0.3320
128	5	False	0.7	1e−8	0.5802	64	2	True	0.0	0.0	0.2241
128	5	False	0.3	1e−8	**0.6337**	64	4	True	0.0	0.0	**0.4368**

approach, the impact of different values for dropout $(d) = \{0.2, 0.3, 0.5, 0.6, 0.7\}$ and L_2 regularisation $(L2) - \{0, 1e-8, 1e-6, 1e-4, 0.1\}$ was investigated. Data augmentation was applied to the facial images through random horizontal flipping (flipping probability used: 0.5), leading to an increase in dataset size. For each type of visual feature used, the best predictions obtained for the valence and arousal dimensions were then passed onto the late fusion stage of the proposed approach.

Late Fusion. All experiments with late fusion made use of an LSTM-RNN model with the following default hyperparameter values: $\{h, r, lr\} = \{32, 2, 0.001\}$. The exception is the late fusion of *OFF* and other modalities (third submission), for which $h = 64$.

3.2 Results and Discussion

Video. Table 1 shows the CCC values obtained when predicting continuous arousal and valence values using the *RN50* features for the development set and for different hyperparameter settings. The best results achieved are indicated in bold. Given the different hyperparameter settings, we were able to obtain the best results for valence when making use of 128-D hidden states, a learning rate of 0.00005, a dropout value of 0.3, and an L_2 penalty of 1e−8. In addition, we obtained the best results for arousal when using 64-D hidden states, a learning rate of 0.002, and feature normalization, not using dropout and not using L_2 regularisation. In summary, the highest CCC value achieved for the development set is 0.6337 for valence and 0.4368 for arousal.

Table 2. Impact of data augmentation on valence and arousal when making use of the *RN50* features. CCC_i and CCC_f refer to the CCC values obtained, without and with data augmentation, respectively.

Data augmentation															
Valence								Arousal							
lr	h	r	n	d	$L2$	CCC_i	CCC_f	lr	h	r	n	d	$L2$	CCC_i	CCC_f
0.00200	64	4	False	0.0	0.0	**0.3310**	**0.5089**	0.002	64	4	False	0.0	0.0	0.2459	0.3203
0.00005	128	5	False	0.0	0.0	0.6108	0.5027	0.002	64	4	True	0.0	0.0	**0.4193**	**0.3413**
0.00005	128	5	False	0.3	0.0	0.6253	0.5583	0.002	64	4	True	0.5	0.0	0.3187	0.3468
0.00005	128	5	False	0.5	0.0	0.5904	0.5919	0.002	64	4	True	0.0	1e−4	0.1794	0.3094
0.00005	128	5	False	0.7	0.0	0.5717	0.5682	0.002	64	4	True	0.5	1e−4	0.2517	0.2926
–	–	–	–	–	–	–	–	0.002	64	4	True	0.7	1e−4	0.3200	0.3277
–	–	–	–	–	–	–	–	0.002	16	1	True	0.5	0.0	0.1429	0.1830
–	–	–	–	–	–	–	–	0.002	16	4	True	0.0	0.0	0.1387	0.1083

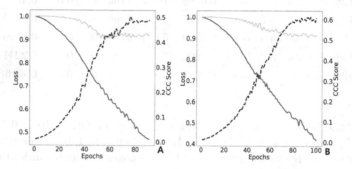

Fig. 4. Valence learning curves: (A) after data augmentation and (B) before data augmentation. The blue, red, and black dotted lines represent train loss, validation loss, and development CCC score, respectively. (Color figure online)

Additionally, Table 2 shows how data augmentation affects the predictions made. Given the valence results presented in Table 2, we can observe that data augmentation often helps in getting better predictions along this dimension when not making use of hyperparameter tuning (row 1); however, the CCC values obtained after data augmentation and hyperparameter tuning are lower than the CCC values obtained before data augmentation but after hyperparameter tuning (rows 2–5). Furthermore, the arousal results presented in Table 2 also show that data augmentation often helps in getting better predictions along this dimension; however, the highest CCC value obtained after data augmentation is still lower than the highest CCC value obtained before data augmentation.

Furthermore, Fig. 4 shows how the training and validation loss change as a function of model training, depicting the training loss using a blue line and the validation loss using a red line. We can observe that the validation loss in Fig. 4(A) follows the training loss more closely than in Fig. 4(B). However, the highest CCC value obtained is much higher in Fig. 4(B). For arousal, we can observe trends similar to the trends observed for valence, as illustrated by Fig. 5.

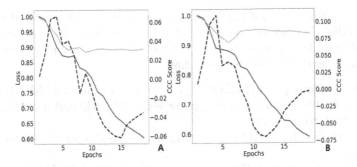

Fig. 5. Arousal learning curves: (A) after data augmentation and (B) before data augmentation. The blue, red, and black dotted lines represent train loss, validation loss, and development CCC score, respectively. (Color figure online)

Table 3. Valence and arousal results obtained for our five submissions, levering late fusion of different modalities (A for audio, V for video, and T for text). The best CCC values obtained for the development set and the test set are highlighted in bold.

Submission	Features	Valence	Arousal	Combined
		dev/test	dev/test	dev/test
1	Best A + Best V	–/–	0.6324/0.1798	0.6620/0.2669
	Best A + Best V + Best T	0.6916/0.354	–/–	
2	*OFF*	0.6024/0.2953	0.5203/0.0403	0.5613/0.1678
3	Best A + Best V + *OFF*	–/–	**0.7553**/0.1330	0.7456/0.2896
	Best A + Best V + Best T + *OFF*	0.7366/**0.4461**	–/–	
4	Best A + Best V + *OBF*	–/–	0.7017/0.2159	0.7205/0.3146
	Best A + Best V + Best T + *OBF*	0.7393/0.4113	–/–	
5	Best A + Best V + *OFF* + *OBF*	**0.7640**/0.4158	0.7549/**0.2297**	**0.7595/0.3228**

In particular, we can again observe that the validation loss follows the training loss more closely in Fig. 5(A) than in Fig. 5(B). However, the highest CCC value in Fig. 5(A) is still lower than the highest CCC value that can be found in Fig. 5(B).

Given the experimental results obtained, we can conclude that data augmentation can help in preventing overfitting. Nevertheless, for the MuSe-Stress 2021 sub-challenge, we decided not to make use of data augmentation. Indeed, when hyperparameter tuning is in place, most CCC values obtained after data augmentation are then lower than the corresponding CCC values obtained before data augmentation, for both valence and arousal. Furthermore, since we only paid a limited amount of attention to the use of data augmentation for mitigating the risk of overfitting, we believe future work could still explore the use of other types of data augmentation, such as random vertical flipping and random cropping, as well as an optimization strategy that makes it possible to effectively combine hyperparameter tuning and data augmentation.

Submission Results. Table 3 shows the results obtained for our five submissions. All submissions leveraged late fusion, except for the second submission, which obtained the predictions when only making use of *OFF*. The best A (audio), V (video), and T (text) values represent the best development scores obtained for each modality, for which the feature and hyperparameter combinations used are summarized below.

- Best A: Combining *ILPR eGeMAPS* features with an LSTM-RNN ($[h, r, lr]$ = $[64, 4, 0.002]$) yielded a development score of 0.5632 and 0.4841 for valence and arousal, respectively.
- Best V: The models used for predicting valence and arousal adopted different settings.
  - Valence: Combining *RN50* features with an LSTM-RNN ($[h, r, lr] = [128, 5, 5e-5]$) yielded a development score of 0.6253.
  - Arousal: Combining normalized *RN50* features with an LSTM-RNN ($[h, r, lr] = [128, 9, 0.002]$) yielded a development score of 0.4399.
- Best T: Combining *BERT* features with an LSTM-RNN ($[h, r, lr] = [64, 4, 0.002]$) yielded a development score of 0.3626 and 0.2308 for valence and arousal, respectively.

For each submission, the combination of features submitted for valence and arousal typically differed as it is not necessary to use identical modalities to predict valence and arousal. Our third submission obtained the highest test score for valence, namely 0.4461. Furthermore, our fifth submission obtained the highest test score for arousal, namely 0.2297, and the highest combined score, namely 0.3228.

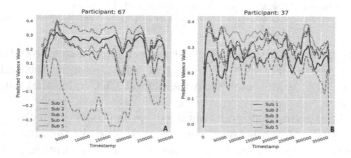

Fig. 6. Late fusion results for valence: (A) Participant 67 and (B) Participant 37.

Discussion of Submission Results. Figure 6 and Fig. 7 show the valence and arousal values obtained for a number of participants of interest (i.e., participants showing a clear contradicting result) when leveraging late fusion, combining the speech, text, and video modalities. The labels Sub 1 to Sub 5 refer to the corresponding submissions listed in Table 3.

For Fig. 6(A), we can observe that all of the curves follow a similar trend, except for Sub 2. Different from Fig. 6(A), we can observe that all of the curves in Fig. 6(B) follow a similar trend. Also, using Table 3 to examine Sub 2 in more

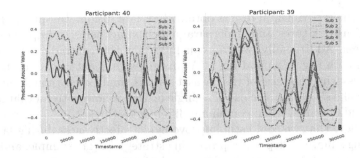

Fig. 7. Late fusion results for arousal: (A) Participant 40 and (B) Participant 39.

detail, which is the submission that only made use of *OFF*, we can see that this submission achieved the lowest development and test score for valence. This leads to the assumption that the use of a single feature for predicting emotional valence and arousal tends to come with limited effectiveness and that leveraging other features (e.g., from a different modality) helps in producing better predictions. For Participant 67, we can observe particularly contradictory valence predictions in Fig. 6(A), and where this observation can most likely be attributed to different participant behavior. Indeed, most of the participants freely talk for five minutes without any aid, whereas Participant 67 talks while using written notes. Taking the position of the camera into consideration, the entire face of Participant 67 is hardly visible, and her eyes are focused on the document she has with her. This makes it difficult to extract meaningful facial information (70 keypoints).

For arousal, we can observe two curves with a deviating trend in Fig. 7(A), namely Sub 2 and Sub 3. Specifically, for Sub 3, we can observe that the values obtained are not close to the values obtained by the other submissions, although Sub 3 and the other curves fluctuate similarly (except for Sub 2). For Fig. 7(B), we can observe that all of the curves, including Sub 2, follow a similar trend. Also, looking into the results presented in Table 3, we can again conclude that better arousal predictions can be obtained when making use of multiple features from different modalities. Indeed, when examining Sub 2 and Sub 3 in more detail, we can see that these submissions obtain the lowest arousal development and test scores, with both submissions making use of *OFF* for predicting valence and arousal. In addition, making the comparison to Sub 1, we can observe that the use of *OFF* lowers model effectiveness. Furthermore, given that the curves for Participant 40 and Participant 67 show a similar trend, it is of interest to look at the commonality between these participants in order to achieve a better understanding of the effectiveness of *OFF*. Doing a manual inspection of the audio-visual recordings of these two participants, we notice that the camera angle used is not frontal in nature but rather tilted towards the left. As a result, the face of these participants is not entirely visible in the corresponding recordings, hampering the extraction of all essential features. In this respect, it is also worth noting that in 65 out of the 69 videos available (94.2% of the dataset), the entire face of the participant is visible.

Given the experimental results obtained for late fusion, we can conclude that using multiple features and hyperparameter tuning helps in improving model effectiveness. Additionally, we can conclude that the contradictory results, as present in both Fig. 6(A) and Fig. 7(A), have a significant impact on the model effectiveness when the size of the dataset used is small, even though our experimental results show that the use of a single feature follows a trend that is similar to the trend obtained when combining different features.

We believe that we could still improve model effectiveness during late fusion by applying a more in-depth pre-processing strategy. As an example, and as mentioned in Sect. 2.2, we made use of full-resolution images to extract 25 body key points. Since these full-resolution images contain information unrelated to body key points, the extracted features might contain wrong information. This wrong information may have a negative impact on the model effectiveness obtained during late fusion. As a result, by performing tight cropping so that the images used only contain relevant subjects, we believe the features extracted from these cropped images can help in improving the effectiveness of late fusion.

4   Conclusions and Future Work

In this paper, we explored the simultaneous use of multimodal features, both engineered and learned, to improve human emotion detection for the MuSe-Stress 2021 sub-challenge. Specifically, by applying an LSTM-RNN-based late fusion approach using ResNet-50 and OpenPose features for video, ILPR and eGeMAPS features for audio, and BERT features for text, we achieved a combined CCC value of 0.7595 and 0.3379 for the development set and the test set of MuSe-Stress 2021, respectively. An experimental investigation of the degradation in effectiveness obtained for the test set points to the need for incorporating different strategies to further improve the effectiveness of late fusion, such as data pre-processing and data augmentation.

References

1. Stappen, L., et al.: The MuSe 2021 multimodal sentiment analysis challenge: sentiment, emotion, physiological-emotion, and stress. In: Proceedings of the 2nd International on Multimodal Sentiment Analysis Challenge and Workshop. Association for Computing Machinery, New York (2021)
2. Stappen, L., Baird, A., Schumann, L., Schuller, B.: The multimodal sentiment analysis in car reviews (MuSe-car) dataset: collection, insights and improvements. IEEE Trans. Affect. Comput. (2021)
3. He, K., Zhang, X., Ren, S., Sun, J.: Deep residual learning for image recognition. In: 2016 IEEE Conference on Computer Vision and Pattern Recognition (CVPR) (2016)
4. Cao, Z., Hidalgo, G., Simon, T., Wei, S.-E., Sheikh, Y.: OpenPose: realtime multi-person 2D pose estimation using part affinity fields. IEEE Trans. Pattern Anal. Mach. Intell. 43(1), 172–186 (2019)
5. Redmon, J., Farhadi, A.: YOLOV3: an incremental improvement (2018)

6. Baghel, S., Prasanna, S.R.M., Guha, P.: Classification of multi speaker shouted speech and single speaker normal speech. In: TENCON 2017–2017 IEEE Region 10 Conference, pp. 2388–2392. IEEE (2017)

7. Eyben, F., et al.: The Geneva minimalistic acoustic parameter set (GeMAPS) for voice research and affective computing. IEEE Trans. Affect. Comput. **7**(2), 190–202 (2015)

8. Devlin, J., Chang, M.-W., Lee, K., Toutanova, K.: BERT: pre-training of deep bidirectional transformers for language understanding. arXiv preprint arXiv:1810.04805 (2018)

9. Degottex, G.: Glottal source and vocal-tract separation. Ph.D. thesis, Université Pierre et Marie Curie-Paris VI (2010)

10. Rothenberg, M.: Acoustic interaction between the glottal source and the vocal tract. Vocal Fold Physiol. **1**, 305–323 (1981)

11. Loweimi, E., Barker, J., Saz-Torralba, O., Hain, T.: Robust source-filter separation of speech signal in the phase domain. In: Interspeech, pp. 414–418 (2017)

12. Prasanna, S.R.M., Gupta, C.S., Yegnanarayana, B.: Extraction of speaker-specific excitation information from linear prediction residual of speech. Speech Commun. **48**(10), 1243–1261 (2006)

13. Baghel, S., Prasanna, S.R.M., Guha, P.: Exploration of excitation source information for shouted and normal speech classification. J. Acoust. Soc. Am. **147**(2), 1250–1261 (2020)

14. Makhoul, J.: Linear prediction: a tutorial review. Proc. IEEE **63**(4), 561–580 (1975)

15. Simonyan, K., Zisserman, A.: Very deep convolutional networks for large-scale image recognition (2015)

16. Krizhevsky, A., Sutskever, I., Hinton, G.E.: ImageNet classification with deep convolutional neural networks. Commun. ACM **60**(6), 84–90 (2017)

17. Zhang, K., Zhang, Z., Li, Z., Qiao, Y.: Joint face detection and alignment using multitask cascaded convolutional networks. IEEE Signal Process. Lett. **23**(10), 1499–1503 (2016)

18. Cao, Q., Shen, L., Xie, W., Parkhi, O.M., Zisserman, A.: VGGFace2: a dataset for recognising faces across pose and age. In: 2018 13th IEEE International Conference on Automatic Face & Gesture Recognition (FG 2018) (2018)

19. Parkhi, O.M., Vedaldi, A., Zisserman, A.: Deep face recognition, pp. 1–12. British Machine Vision Association (2015)

20. Stappen, L., et al.: MuSe 2020 challenge and workshop: multimodal sentiment analysis, emotion-target engagement and trustworthiness detection in real-life media: emotional car reviews in-the-wild. In: Proceedings of the 1st International on Multimodal Sentiment Analysis in Real-life Media Challenge and Workshop, pp. 35–44 (2020)

21. Cao, Z., Hidalgo, G., Simon, T., Wei, S.-E., Sheikh, Y.: OpenPose: real-time multi-person 2D pose estimation using part affinity fields. arXiv preprint arXiv:1812.08008 (2018)

22. Simon, T., Joo, H., Matthews, I., Sheikh, Y.: Hand keypoint detection in single images using multiview bootstrapping. In: 2017 IEEE Conference on Computer Vision and Pattern Recognition (CVPR), pp. 4645–4653 (2017)

23. Qin, S., Kim, S., Manduchi, R.: Automatic skin and hair masking using fully convolutional networks. In: 2017 IEEE International Conference on Multimedia and Expo (ICME) (2017)

24. Reimers, N., Gurevych, I.: Sentence-BERT: sentence embeddings using Siamese BERT-networks. arXiv preprint arXiv:1908.10084 (2019)

25. Atrey, P.K., Hossain, M.A., El Saddik, A., Kankanhalli, M.S.: Multimodal fusion for multimedia analysis: a survey. Multimed. Syst. **16**(6), 345–379 (2010)
26. Zhang, Q., Xiao, T., Huang, N., Zhang, D., Han, J.: Revisiting feature fusion for RGB-T salient object detection. IEEE Trans. Circ. Syst. Video Technol. **31**(5), 1804–1818 (2020)

Simulation Model of a Spare Parts Distribution Network in the Airline Industry for Reducing Delays and Improving Service Levels: A Design of Experiments Study

Javier Gejo-García, Diego Gallego-García, Sergio Gallego-García$^{(\boxtimes)}$ (ID),
and Manuel García-García

UNED, 28040 Madrid, Spain
gallego101090@gmail.com

Abstract. Currently, delays are the most common cause of airline disputes. One of the factors leading to these situations is the distribution of spare parts. The efficient management of the spare parts distribution can reduce the volume of delays and the number of problems encountered and therefore maximize the consumer satisfaction levels. Moreover, airlines are under pressure due to their tight competition, a problem that is expected to grow worse due to the COVID-19 pandemic. By carrying out efficient maintenance and distribution management along the supply chain, authorities, airlines, aircraft manufacturers, and consumers can obtain various benefits. Thus, the aim of this research is to perform a design of experiments study on a spare parts distribution network simulation model for the aviation industry. Based on this model, the effect of the input parameters and their interactions can be derived. Moreover, the findings are converted to a combined methodology based on simulation and design of experiments for the design and optimization of distribution networks. This research study thereby provides an approach to identify significant factors that could lead to a better system performance. In conclusion, this proposed approach enables aircraft maintenance systems to improve their service by minimizing delays and claims, reducing processing costs, and reducing the impact of maintenance on customer unsatisfaction.

Keywords: Distribution network design · Spare parts distribution management · Operational excellence · Simulation · Design of experiments · Airline industry · Aircraft maintenance

1 Introduction

Currently, delays are the most common source of airline disputes. These can include delays in the arrival or departure of commercial flights. In this context, the management of spare parts distribution is very important in airline business. The efficient management of related maintenance and distribution activities is necessary in order to reduce the number of claims. Therefore, a methodological approach must be implemented to

© Springer Nature Switzerland AG 2022
J.-H. Kim et al. (Eds.): IHCI 2021, LNCS 13184, pp. 745–760, 2022.
https://doi.org/10.1007/978-3-030-98404-5_66

minimize the risks of delays and other related problems. To achieve this, collaboration between the different entities involved is required. Along the supply chain, authorities, airlines, aircraft manufacturers, and consumers can obtain various benefits, such as lower budgets being allocated for claims; better customer satisfaction; more potential new customers due to the airline receiving better ratings on social media; improvements in the manufacture of aircraft due to there being more information about the reliability of aircraft components; better service for customers; customers experiencing less uncertainty about delays and the processing of claims.

Many consumers do not make claims due to the lack of assistance available to consumers, among other issues [1]. Although many consumers do not make claims, they are likely to avoid flying with the same airline again after having a bad experience. Therefore, customer unsatisfaction leads to lower numbers of future consumers and lower profits. In addition, airlines are under pressure due to their tight competition; this problem is expected to become worse due to the COVID-19 pandemic. In this context, delays cause consumers to be dissatisfied. Therefore, the challenge for airlines is to remain competitive while improving their level of customer service. For both purposes, maintenance represents an opportunity to increase plane availability and reduce the number of departure and arrival delays. In this context, the efficient internal management of the distribution of spare parts can improve maintenance management and the condition of airplanes, leading to a better service and providing a USP (Unique Selling Proposition) in the airline market. Therefore, this paper discusses how optimizing management can lead to shorter lead-times, higher customer satisfaction, lower costs, and fewer lost customers.

Thus, the aim of this study is to perform a design of experiments study on a spare parts distribution network simulation model for the aviation industry. For that purpose, a simulation model of an airline operating in different countries was developed. The simulation model and its parameters were used to perform the design of experiments by defining the minimum and maximum levels for each of the factors. Based on this, the effects of the input parameters and their interactions were derived. The results of the model demonstrated the effect of each parameter on the other indicators and target values. In this way, the global system used for supplying the required parts for the maintenance activities could be optimized and the knowledge gained could be used for designing new distribution networks and managing them more efficiently, as the interactions and their significance level are known. This process provides more information about the system in order to allow for better decision making. This research study provides an approach that can identify significant factors that if improved could lead to better system performance. In conclusion, this proposed approach enables aircraft maintenance systems to have internal mechanisms to secure their levels of service by minimizing delays and claims, reducing processing costs, and reducing the impact of maintenance on customer unsatisfaction.

2 Theoretical Fundamentals: Distribution for Maintenance

Industrial maintenance essentially has the task of ensuring and/or restoring the operation of a maintenance object during its useful life [2]. In recent decades, there has been some general rethinking in the philosophy of industrial maintenance. This change came from focusing on maintaining functions to moving to a philosophy of value creation. Logistics can be described as an interdisciplinary strategy. This means that all business areas are affected by the interdisciplinary logistics strategy. Some types of logistics, such as purchasing logistics, distribution logistics, reverse logistics, transportation logistics, information logistics, plant logistics, and maintenance logistics, allow us to achieve maintenance objectives. Availability is, therefore, the central concern of logistics, which in turn is the link between logistics and industrial maintenance [3].

Distribution logistics includes all storage and transport activities carried out during the distribution of goods to the customer and the related information, control, and inspection activities [4]. It represents the link between entrepreneurial production logistics and customer procurement logistics [5]. Distribution logistics is a key driver of the overall profitability of a firm because it directly affects both supply chain cost and customer service [6]. The goal of distribution logistics is to ensure the physical availability of the products and the associated flow of information [7] in order to achieve a highly efficient delivery service while minimizing distribution costs and trying to acquire new customers.

The design of a distribution network determines the potential performance and cost structure of the logistics network in the long term. Design principles of logistics networks include [7]:

- Cost efficiency vs. responsiveness;
- Centralized vs. decentralized;
- "Push" vs. "pull".

Design of experiments (DOE) is an optimized methodology used for analyzing selected variables and determining whether they have a statistically significant effect on a selected response. DOE determines the influence of each factor and their interactions on the system response [8]. The potential applications of DOE include manufacturing processes, such as improving process stability, and service processes, such as identifying the key system variables that influence the process performance [9].

3 Methodology and Model Development

3.1 Methodology

The methodology used consists of a combination of simulations and design of experiments. For the first part, Vensim was used; for the second, data from the simulation were analyzed with the Minitab software. There are three basic steps that must be taken when performing a simulation: preparation, execution, and evaluation [10]. The method used to reach a goal must first consider the challenges of the airline industry and the potential of distribution management with regard to maintenance management to develop the conceptual model. For this purpose, system dynamics was chosen as a framework to determine which policies should be used to control the behavior over time and how these policies should be designed and implemented in order to give a robust response to change [11]. System dynamics is increasingly being used to design more success-ful policies for companies and in public policy settings [12]. Consequently, Vensim—a software package enabling system dynamics modelling—was selected for this project.

For this study, the design of experiments (DOE) methodology was realized using the Minitab and Vensim programs in five steps:

1. A factorial design was created in Minitab by selecting the factors and defining their levels. In this case, fifteen factors with two levels per factor (low and high levels) were chosen. At the end, the factorial design was copied into a text file.
2. The simulation of the experiments was carried out in Vensim by introducing constant values with the option Montecarlo Simulation and exporting these results on Minitab 14. For each scenario analyzed, 128 randomized experiments were performed.
3. The results were exported from Vensim to a text file and then copied into Minitab.
4. The factors and results were analyzed using Minitab's tools, such as: normal plots of the effects, Pareto charts of the effects, residual plots, p-values in Minitab (factorial fit analysis), main effects plots, and interaction plots.
5. The results were interpreted, and the conclusions were extracted.

After having explained the steps performed, the DOE Scenarios will be defined. After performing the DOE for many others scenarios, it was chosen the following scenarios to be shown as overview for the DOE analysis The selection of these scenarios was done attending to the high cases for each demand pattern type and for the more demanding mixed demand patterns:

- Scenario 1: Stationary demand pattern with high demand level
- Scenario 2: Trend demand pattern with high demand level
- Scenario 3: Sporadic demand pattern with high demand level
- Scenario 4: Seasonal demand pattern with high demand level
- Scenario 5: Mixed demand pattern with high demand level
- Scenario 6: Mixed demand pattern with often demand changes in all airports.

3.2 Simulation Model Development in Vensim

In the case of study, the goal of the project is to design a simulation model of a spare parts distribution network to improve the maintenance activities performed in the airports to provide a better service to consumers. To reach and exemplify the goal of the model the following distribution network was elected based on literature [13]. The production facility follows a make-to-stock strategy in order to satisfy spare parts maintenance orders from stock. Consequently, inaccurate forecasts could lead to an excessive inventory or stock-outs [14]. The distribution network consists of a three stages distribution for a single product. The production facility (PF) represents the first distribution stage. It is made the hypothesis that the second distribution stage is the central warehouse (CW) that should take care of the deliveries for a certain distribution area of an airline such as a continent. Moreover, every single warehouse of the third stage, regional warehouse (RW), is in different regions of the distribution area such as in different countries. The CW receives all the goods produced by the production facility and storages them. Moreover, the RWs store and deliver the spare parts to the airport that requires it at their appropriate time, which is when the airport places a maintenance order. Figure 1 shows the simulation models in the same representation order as it is reproduced in the software Vensim. Initially the model has fifteen airports assigned to three RWs. Moreover, the model has the capability to open two new RWs with a new grouping of airports. Depending on the number of regional warehouses opened there are four different types of distribution network structures.

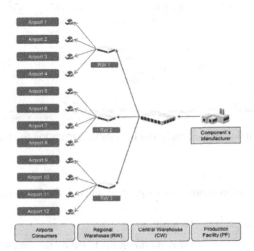

Fig. 1. Spare parts distribution network structure of the simulation model (own elaboration).

For the simulation model, the logistics targets should be defined in order to assess the alternatives for the different scenarios [7]. The objective is to analyze how these models respond to different input demands and different settings of parameters. The response is then evaluated according to the following key performance indicators (KPI):

- On time delivery (OTD) (% of quantity).
- Service level (% of days).
- Customer backlog (products); customer backlog t = 1000 days (products); customer backlog (days); customer backlog with 1, 2, and 3 or more days (products); customer backlog due to there not being enough employees in RW (products).
- Stock in central warehouse (products), stock in regional warehouses (products), stock total in CW and RW (products).
- WIP (work in progress) between CW and RW (products); WIP between production facility and CW (products).
- Utilization ratio of employees (%).
- MAD (mean absolute deviation) of production forecast (products).

After the problem has been defined, modelers have to start generating assumptions, standard values, and the logic that defines the models, as shown in Fig. 2 and Table 1. These provide the basis for the model behavior and how the research question arose.

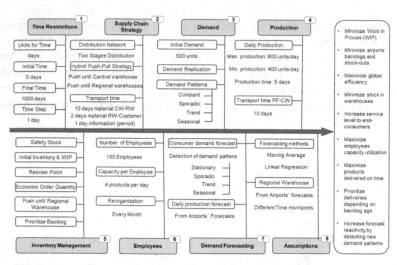

Fig. 2. Simulation model: logic and hypothesis generation (own elaboration).

Table 1. Simulation areas: description of functions and interrelationships.

No.	Simulation area	Description
1	Production	Daily production is based on the forecast demand make to stock. Production compares airport demand to control products moving to airports
2	Operative distribution	Considers the distribution operational activities and their relationships
3	Shipping coordination	Contains the causal relationships that influence the coordination of shipments in two situations: when satisfying airport orders and when satisfying RW requests
4	Procurement planning	Represents the relationships between the three material transportation initiation methods (push until RW, reorder point (ROP), and economic order quantity (EOQ)) between the CW and the RWs
5	Employees planning	After each cycle of redeployment of employees, whether the allocation of employees to RWs is correct for the future demand in the next cycle is tested and, if necessary, the employees are reorganized
6	Demand planning	Indicates the adjustment loop of the forecast method or the parameters of the forecast method to increase the level of precision of the forecast
7	Logistics management	Develops the consequences of the decoupling point of the "push-pull" strategy as well as the opening of new regional warehouses

4   Design of Experiments of a Spare Parts Distribution Network Simulation Model

4.1   Design of Experiments Using Minitab

Factors of the DOE. The purpose of the DOE is to understand the effect of the input parameters and their interactions on the results of the simulation model. The results in this case are the key performance indicators (KPIs) for the distribution network. Out of all the KPIs, only some will be analyzed in detail (those with bold type in Fig. 3).

No.	Factors	Results
1	Variant coefficient limit	**Service Level (%)**
2	Backlog limit	**Quantity delivered on time (%)**
3	Safety factor, k	**∑ Customer backlog (products)**
4	Total number of employees	Backlog customers t=1000 days (products)
5	Factor redistribution employees	**∑ Customer backlog (days)**
6	Delay Material Central Warehouse - RW	∑ Backlog caused by missing manpower (products)
7	Delay Production	∑ Backlog = 1 days (products)
8	Smooth time	∑ Backlog = 2 days (products)
9	Minimum Quantity delivered	∑ Backlog ≥ 3 days (products)
10	Demand reactivity	**Utilization ratio of employees (%)**
11	Limit to open new warehouse	∑ Stocks regional warehouses (products)
12	Backlog limit to make push strategy RW	∑ Stocks central warehouse (products)
13	Stock Initial	**∑ Total stocks (products)**
14	Max. Production	∑ WIP (stocks CW + shipments PF-CW) (products)
15	Min. Production	∑ WIP (stocks RWs + shipments CW-RW) (products)
16		MAD Total demand - forecast

Fig. 3. DOE factors and results (own elaboration).

Definition and Levels of the Factors. The factors are the input parameters of the model that influence the global behavior of the system. The value of these input factors should always be specified in order to run the model. Then, every exogenous variable can be selected as a factor and therefore the most relevant exogenous variables can be chosen as factors for the DOE. The selection of factor levels is one of the most important steps in the DOE. For this case of study, a low and a high level should be chosen for each factor, as the DOE is a 2K factorial that is performed to evaluate the model validation, determine policies, and optimize the values of the input parameters in order to obtain a better overall distribution network performance. The definition of the factor levels has certain limitations. These restrictions can be subject to equipment, physical, statistical, or compatibility limitations. With the factors described, the design of experiments is performed for six different demand scenarios for the simulation model. As seen in Fig. 4, letters are used as a notation for the factors in order to simplify the following analysis.

DOE Results. The DOE results will be focused on five of the fifteen key performance indicators. These were selected according to their importance for the distribution performance and included service level (%), quantity delivered on time (%), customer backlogs (products/days), stock total (products), utilization rate of employees (%), and MAD forecast production for all customers (products). A level of significance of 0.05 was used for all the analyses for the different DOE scenarios.

Factor letter	Factors	Description	Unit	Minimum	Maximum
A	Backlog limit	When this quantity of units backlogged is reached, the model changes from EOQ to RP	Products	0	2000
B	Backlog limit to make push strategy RW	Units backlogged until the push strategy until RWs is considered	Products	500	5000
C	Delay Material Central Warehouse - RW	Transport time between the CW and the RW	Days	5	20
D	Delay Production	Transport time between the PF and the CW	Days	5	20
E	Demand reactivity	Quickness of the reaction against demand pattern changes	-	0.25	5
F	Factor redistribution employees	Time between reallocation of employees between the RW	Months	1	12
G	Limit to open new warehouse	Number of airports with backlog until a new RW is opened	Customers	1	4
H	Max. Production	Maximum Production	Products	600	700
J	Min. Production	Minimum Production	Products	400	500
K	Minimum Quantity delivered	Minimum delivery quantity between CW and RW	Products	0	500
L	Safety factor, k	Safety factor to calculate the SS of the RWs	-	1.28	3.09
M	Smooth time	Production time	Days	5	20
N	Stock initial	Initial stock in the RWs	Products	1000	2000
O	Total number of employees	Employees that are performing the warehouse activities in the RWs	Employees	145	155
P	Variant coefficient limit	When this variant coefficient is reached, the model changes from EOQ to RP	-	0.02	0.2

Fig. 4. Factors used in the DOE: descriptions, units. and levels (own elaboration).

4.2   DOE for Stationary Demand: High Case (Scenario 1)

The analysis of the DOE started by calculating the effects of the factors and their interactions on the results. From these effects, which factors significantly effect the result were determined. The results for scenario 1 and the KPI service level (%) are explained step by step. The same analysis process was carried out for all the KPIs in all the scenarios. Later, the complete results, including for the other scenarios and KPIs, are shown with the overview tables. The service level (%) in this case is the output variable analyzed. The following two graphs in Fig. 5 are called effects plots and allow the visualization of the most important effects at a glance.

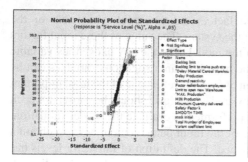
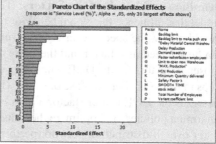

Fig. 5. DOE scenario 1: normal probability plot and Pareto chart for service level (%).

Minitab marks the border at which the effects are considered significant using an estimation of the standard deviation of the effects [15]. For Fig. 5 it is the line 2.04. From the case that has been chosen as an example, it is possible to observe that the most important significant factors regarding the service level (%) are EO/G/O/F/E. The next step is to fit a new model using only the terms identified as important by the results of fitting the full model—that is, screening out the unimportant effects. Figure 6 generates four different residual plots together in one graph window to visualize the effect displays. The residual plots in the graph include:

- Normal probability plot: this verifies the normality assumption because the residuals follow a straight line.
- Histogram of residuals: to be in line with the assumption, the histogram should be bell-shaped.
- Residual vs. fitted values: the residuals should be dispersed randomly around the zero line.
- Residuals vs. the order of the data: the residuals are depicted in the order of the corresponding observations. This plot can be helpful in a DOE in which the runs are not randomized. To validate this assumption, the residuals should fluctuate in a random pattern around the central line.

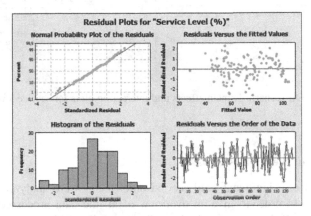

Fig. 6. DOE scenario 1: residual plots.

The influences of the factors and their interactions on the output variables are analyzed by evaluating to the p-values. For the analysis, a level of significance of 0.05 was chosen. The p-values demonstrate which of the factors and interactions are significant. The p-value for each term in the model is less than 0.05, indicating that the factor is significant for the corresponding output. The null hypothesis is that the factor does not influence the result, while the alternative hypothesis indicates a significant influence in the output variable. Two graphs are presented in Fig. 7 these allow the main effects plot and the interaction effects plot to be visualized. The main effects plot isolates each of the factors and shows how the response variable changes due to changes in the factor being studied. The steeper the line is, the greater the effect of the change will be [8]. The main effects plot enables the factors that have more influence on the service level to be recognized and defines whether the influence is positive or negative when changing from the low to the high level of the factor. For instance, it is possible to observe how the "Factor redistribution employees" has a strong influence on the service level (%) and it is evident that the service level (%) diminishes when the factor increases. Three extreme cases can be distinguished in interaction plots. A single dominant main effect will appear near-parallel, essentially horizontal lines when plotted against the minor factor. When both factors are important but do not interact strongly, the lines remain approximately parallel but are no longer simply horizontal. A dominant interaction shows markedly non-parallel lines that often cross. Combinations of effects generate intermediate plots, which show approximately equal individual factor effects combined with a strong interaction term. The lines are not parallel, but consistently higher or lower responses may be visible for one or more levels [16]. The DOE results for other scenarios and KPIs under consideration followed this same methodology.

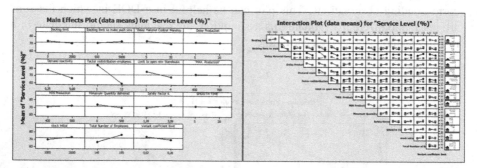

Fig. 7. DOE scenario 1: main effects and interaction plots for service level (%).

4.3 Overview of the DOE Results

The factors that are significant until second-order terms were analyzed for the most important KPIs. In order to give an overview of all the data processed in the DOE without showing all the graphs and tables, four overview tables were created. These tables contain the standardized effects of the factors, the classification of the importance of the effects, the influence of the factors on the KPIs (if the effect is positive or negative when increasing the factor), and a final overview of the one-factor significant effects for all the DOE scenarios. The classification of the effects tries to summarize the relative effect weights of the different factors using the following formula:

$$\frac{x - reference\ value}{maximum\ value - reference\ value} * 100 = [\%] \tag{1}$$

The different chromatic values were determined as shown in Fig. 8.

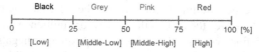

Fig. 8. Classification colors for the significant effects.

The summarized results for the KPI service level are the following: first, the values for the standardized effects are obtained. Using their absolute values, the classification of the significant effects Fig. 8 can be carried out according to the chromatic classification.

Moreover, using the sign of the standardized effects, the influences on the service level can be determined as shown in the right part of Fig. 9. Figure 9 shows how the most important factors for the service level are F, G, O, and E. Moreover, the relative importance of these factors varies depending on the scenario. For example, factor G concerns limit on opening a new warehouse: it has a low importance in scenario 1 because the customer demand is stationary and does not require a new warehouse to be opened in most of the experiments, while in scenario 3 (sporadic demand), scenario 4 (seasonal demand), and scenario 5 (high demand forces the opening of new warehouses) factor G has a high importance.

Furthermore, it can be observed not many factors are present in all the scenarios as significant factors. These are F, E, O, G, BK, and L. As final evidence, we can state they are all one-factor significant effects with the exception of BK. Figure 9 shows the effect of increasing the value of the factor on the KPI—in this case, the service level. For instance, when increasing factor F, the redistribution of employees, the service level decreases. This table also shows how some factors have a positive influence in some scenarios but a negative influence in others. This is the case of factor E, demand reactivity, and it happens because in scenarios 3 and 4 the increase in the changes between forecasting methods or in the forecasting parameters (when the demand reactivity is higher, the control limits needed to modify the forecasting are extended, meaning that adjustments in the forecasting procedure need to be made less frequently) do not contribute to an increase in the service level. This is logical because when dealing with sporadic and seasonal demand patterns. The variance of the demand should be compensated for by maintaining a longer time horizon forecast due to their uncertain natures.

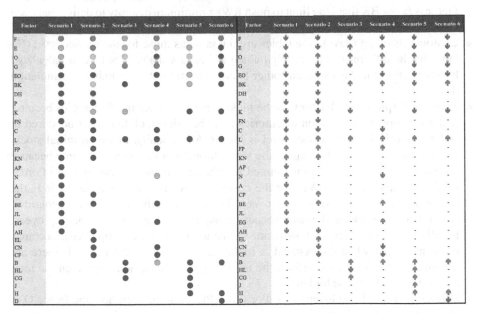

Fig. 9. Classification of the significant effects for service level (%) and the influences of the significant effects in service level (%) (own elaboration).

Figure 10 shows the effects that are significant for one factor in order to demonstrate for which factors a detailed analysis should be carried out and which of them should be screened out.

Service Level (%)						
Factor	Scenario 1	Scenario 2	Scenario 3	Scenario 4	Scenario 5	Scenario 6
A	●					
B			●	○	●	●
C	●	●		●		
D						●
E	○	○	○	○	○	●
F	○	○	○	●	○	●
G	●	○	●	●	●	●
H					●	●
J					●	
K	●	○	○		●	●
L	●	●	●	●	●	●
M						
N	●			●		
O	○	○	○	●	○	●
P	●	●				

Fig. 10. Overview of the first-term significant factors for the service level (%).

An overview of the DOE results for the other KPIs is as follows:

- Quantity delivered on time (%), OTD (%): The same overview tables were created for OTD (%). Factors F, E, C, O, and G are the most important factors.
- Customer backlog (products): Factor F is the most important factor in all scenarios except in scenario 5, where the limitation of employees, factor O, is the most important. Another relevant factor is the demand reactivity, factor E. An important second-term factor is factor BK (backlog limit to push RWs x minimum quantity to deliver between CW and the RWs).
- Customer backlog (days): The tables are the same as those for the service level (%) but with the influences with the sign changed because the service level is calculated by subtracting the days with customer backlog from the total number of simulation days.
- Total stock (products): Factor C is the most important factor in all scenarios because if the transport time between inventories is higher, the stock that must be stored in order to reach the goal service level is higher. Additionally, factor N, initial stock, is important because it determines the stock throughout the simulation time because the simulation models are programmed to balance demand and production in order to always have the same WIP for the customers. A third important factor is F, the frequency of redistribution of employees. This is especially important in scenario 3, which features seasonal demand, because it requires a high flexibility of employees. Finally, it can be observed how factor O, the total number of employees, becomes more important when the demand is higher, as happens in scenario 5. If there are not enough employees to perform the necessary warehouse activities, then the total amount of stock will be higher.
- Utilization rate of employees (%): For this KPI, it can be seen how the factor O is clearly the most significant factor for all the scenarios. This is logical because it refers to the number of employees performing the warehouse activities, which has a direct influence on the utilization rate (%).

- MAD (products): The only factor influencing the MAD is factor E, demand reactivity. The reason behind this is the fact that demand reactivity is the only factor that influences the demand forecast; therefore, the error varies in comparison with the current demand.

Screening out of factors: after the analysis of the factors that are important for the different scenarios and variables, it is possible to conclude what the most important factors are and which of them can be excluded in order to conduct a detailed analysis of the remaining factors.

1. Most important factors: factor E (demand reactivity), factor F (redistribution of employees), factor G (limit on opening new warehouses), factor O (total number of employees), and factor C (transportation lead time between the CW and the RWs).
2. Moderately important factors: factor L (safety factor k), factor N (initial stock), factor P (variance coefficient limit), factor B (backlog limit to make push strategy until RW), and factor K (minimum quantity that needs to be delivered between the CW and the RWs).
3. Less important factors: factor J (min. production), factor H (max. production), factor M (smooth time), factor D (delay production), and factor A (backlog limit to make ROP).

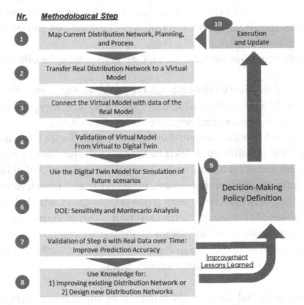

Fig. 11. Methodological approach for improving and designing distribution networks based on digital twins, simulations, and DOE (own elaboration).

5   Discussion

Based on the simulation model and the design of experiments performed, a combined methodology for improving existing distribution networks as well as for influencing new distribution network designs can be derived. As a result, Fig. 11 shows 10 steps that, if followed, will enhance the decision-making capabilities of managers, thereby providing a competitive advantage as for the airline industry and consumer satisfaction due to fewer delays occurring.

6   Conclusions and Future Outlook

In this research work, the importance of the design and management of spare parts distribution networks was proven. Moreover, the challenges faced by the aviation industry were successfully analyzed and an efficient spare parts distribution management system was created in order to improve maintenance management, as this is a relevant factor for improving airline competitiveness. Moreover, the system dynamics were improved to provide the necessary notation and functionality in order to design distribution-related models using the Vensim commercial software. Furthermore, the use of simulation and DOE as a combined methodology was successfully applied for optimizing existing maintenance and spare parts operations as well as for the future design of spare parts distribution networks. DOE was applied to validate the model with a sensitivity analysis and DOE was applied as a tool for evaluating the factors in the simulation model. In addition, from the analysis of the DOE results, the following conclusions can be extracted:

- In general, the effects from singular factors are higher than the effects from multiple factors.
- The importance of the factors depends on the scenario and therefore on the demand that must be met. Moreover, the influence of the factor can vary, making one strategy positive for a certain demand and negative for another one.
- The most important factors in the distribution network are factor E (demand reactivity), which indicates how to define the rules how to change the forecasting methods; factor F (factor for the redistribution of employees), which defines the level of flexibility of the workforce of the company (for this reason, most companies have temporary workers); factor G (which imposes limits on opening new warehouses), which determines how to increase the number of customers; factor O (total number of employees), which relates to performing warehouse activities; factor C (the transportation lead time between the CW and RWs), which increases the uncertainty along the distribution network as well as the stock needed to reach the same service level.

DOE provides the potential for the optimization of input parameters by performing a Monte Carlo analysis. As result, input parameters can be managed, controlled, and changed in order to find a better response to the KPIs of a model. Below, we list some other methods of investigation or possible ways to improve the project.

- A detailed analysis of the factors of the DOE as an input for artificial intelligence systems, expert systems, and data analytics models.

- The extension of the functionality of the simulation model, including through promotions, price fluctuations, the economic situation, the costs of the activities (controlling department), more than one product, the improvement of demand forecasting methods, increasing the flexibility of the distribution network by allowing different routes to be followed, the use of a different number of customers, the use of different distances between stages, and the consideration of the product cycle.
- The application of the simulation model to a real-case distribution network.

The final goal is to transfer this research method to real systems where it could be applied in particular cases as a tool to assist managers by centralizing all data related to the spare parts distribution network in a short period of time, thus enabling the simulation of what-if scenarios, speeding up the methodological process used for designing new distribution networks, or improving existing distribution networks as a unique selling proposition (USP) of an organization. The results show the benefits of the use of a digital-twin approach combined with simulations and a design of experiments methodology, in which top management can determine the goal for the global system by tracking all the potential implications and considering a given target system. Future research could develop AI and expert systems to support planning activities by considering the risks of decision process delays and thus improvingthe viability of a company over time. As a result, there is evidently a need for such a system as a standard element in future digital twin tools for managers in order to increase the efficiency and adaptability of organizations.

References

1. ECC-Net: European Small Claims Procedure Report, September 2012
2. Biedermann, H.: Ersatzteilmanagement: Effiziente ersatzteillogistik für industrieunternehmen. Springer, Heidelberg (2008)
3. Matyas, K. (ed.): Instandhaltungslogistik: Qualität und produktivität steigern, 5th edn. Carl Hanser Verlag, München, Wien (2013)
4. Wannenwetsch, H.: Integrierte Materialwirtschaft, Logistik und Beschaffung. Springer, Heidelberg (2014). https://doi.org/10.1007/978-3-642-45023-5
5. Pfohl, H.-C.: Logistiksysteme. Betriebswirtschaftliche Grundlagen, 8 edn. Springer, Heidelberg (2010). https://doi.org/10.1007/978-3-642-04162-4
6. Chopra, S., Meindl, P.: Supply chain management. Strategy, planning & operation. In: Das Summa Summarum des Management, pp. 265–275. Gabler (2007)
7. Schuh, G., Stich, V.: Logistikmanagement. 2., vollständig neu bearbeitete und erw. Auflage (2013)
8. Khan, R.M.: Problem Solving and Data Analysis Using Minitab: A Clear and Easy Guide to Six Sigma Methodology. Wiley, Hoboken (2013)
9. Antony, J.: Design of Experiments for Engineers and Scientists. Elsevier, Amsterdam (2014)
10. Feldmann, K., Schmuck, T.M.: Distributionsprozesse elektronischer konsumgüter: Modellierung unter verwendung von referenzbausteinen für die ablaufsimulation. ZWF Zeitschrift Wirtschaftlichen Fabrikbetrieb **102**(12), 869–874 (2007)
11. Coyle, R.G.: System Dynamics Modelling: A Practical Approach. Chapman & Hall, London (2008)
12. Sterman, J.D.: Business Dynamics: Systems Thinking And Modeling for a Complex World (2000)

13. Schulte, C.: Logistik: Wege zur Optimierung der Supply Chain. Vahlen (2013)
14. Thaler, K.: Supply Chain Management: Prozessoptimierung in der Logistischen Kette. Fortis-Verlag (2001)
15. Cintas, P.G., Almagro, L.M., Llabres, X.T.M.: Industrial Statistics with Minitab. Wiley, Hoboken (2012)
16. Ellison, S.L., Barwick, V.J., Farrant, T.J.D.: Practical statistics for the analytical scientist: a bench guide. R. Soc. Chem. (2009)

KeyNet: Enhancing Cybersecurity with Deep Learning-Based LSTM on Keystroke Dynamics for Authentication

Jayesh Soni[✉] and Nagarajan Prabakar

Knight Foundation School of Computing and Information Sciences, Florida International University, Miami, FL, USA
jsoni@fiu.edu, prabakar@cis.fiu.edu

Abstract. Currently, everyone accumulates, stores, and processes their sensitive data on computers which makes it essential to protect computers from intrusion. Several approaches employ biometric data such as voice, retinal scan, fingerprints, etc., to enhance user authentication. There is an added overhead of sensors needed to implement these biometric approaches. Instead, an improved and strong password authentication would be cost-effective and straightforward. Keystroke dynamics is the analysis of temporal patterns to validate user authenticity. It is a behavioral biometric that makes use of the typing style of an individual and can be used to enhance the current authentication security procedures efficiently and economically. Such a behavioral biometric system is fairly unexplored compared to other behavioral verifications models. In this study, we focus on applying and training deep learning approach based Long Short Term Memory (LSTM) algorithm in an optimized way to validate temporal keystroke patterns of users for improved password authentication. Our research shows an enhanced authentication rate for the keystroke dynamic benchmark dataset.

Keywords: Keystroke dynamics · Long short term memory · Password authentication

1 Introduction

Workstations have become an integral part of our society. In 2011, cyberattacks on corporations led to the closure of their systems and disrupted the private data of lots of users. As we rely heavily on computers to accumulate and process subtle data, keeping it secure from intruders has turned out to be increasingly important. Low-cost devices are required for user authentication and identification in several computer-based applications. A user can be defined as someone trying to access data on a digital device or through the internet using typical devices like a keyboard. The use of biometric devices such as facial recognition, finger impressions, and signatures, needs extra equipment to obtain biometric with add-on costs. Behavioral biometric applications using a human typing pattern can be attained using prevailing devices such as ordinary keyboards, creating it an affordable technology and can be used to further enhance existing cyber security systems.

© Springer Nature Switzerland AG 2022
J.-H. Kim et al. (Eds.): IHCI 2021, LNCS 13184, pp. 761–771, 2022.
https://doi.org/10.1007/978-3-030-98404-5_67

Authenticity is the procedure of determining who a person is. This authentication process is usually divided into several factors [1] that include: 1) password, 2) Tokens, certificates, etc., and 3) Fingerprint, retina scan. Typing pattern of the user is a behavioral trait that is cultivated over some time and thus cannot be lost. Any active biometric system can be expected to see a significant change in characteristics for different users. Yet, they provide enough information that can be used to identify and validate. However, to use such structures, added sensors are required as an input, and the rate of those sensors differs by the marketplace. We use keystroke typing characteristics for the authentication. Keystroke typing behavior can be well-defined as a unique feature where a user types keys on a keyboard. Simply extracting features from each user's typing pattern can be done as a promising validation system that costs less than biometric because the system is exempt from additional sensors and allows the users to do so quickly. This study focuses on using a deep learning based Long Short Term Memory (LSTM) algorithm with multiple hyperparameter optimization to differentiate the keystroke characteristics of each user.

The outline of the rest of the sections is as follows. Section 2 provides the literature survey on keystroke dynamics. Section 3 explains the dataset in detail. Section 4 describes the in-depth overview of the proposed framework. Results and experiments are discussed in Sect. 5; we conclude in Sect. 6 with future work discussion.

2 Related Work

Dynamic keystrokes have been studied for many years. In 2002, Bergadano et al. led a study on flexible keystrokes for user authentication using personal data collected from a volunteer (not a benchmark dataset), resulting in only 0.01% fraud [2]. Yu and Cho conducted an experimental study in 2003 for feature selection on validation of keystroke dynamics using GA-SVM that brings decent precision and speed [3]. In 2007, Revett et al. surveyed user validation and began examination with a powerful authentication keystroke [4]. The author projected that biometric is vital, especially fingerprints; however, it can be deceived easily. In 2009, Zahid et al. researched an effective mobile keystroke to target users [5]. At the front end, they used particle swarm optimization and genetic optimization algorithm in the backend. They found three diverse characteristics that can identify a user: 1) key capture time, the key Time difference between press and release. 2) Diagraph time, the time variance between releasing and pressing one key to the succeeding key. 3) Error rate, counting the use of backspace key. Furthermore, the authors used those three features and trained five different classifiers. This study aims to provide access to whether the user has the right to access the bank account as per the Personal Identification Number entered by the user.

Epp et al. experimented with categorizing the user's emotional state by using their press on the keyboard [6]. Their study aims to differentiate the following emotions: confidence, doubt, fear, comfort, sadness, and fatigue, with a promising accuracy rate ranging from 77% to 88%. Furthermore, with 84% accuracy, the effect of anger and excitement was enormous. The data was compiled by themselves. Participants were asked to log their actions in real-time over some time rather than synthetically generating fake emotional information in the laboratory. The task consists of 15 elements, after which they are trained using tree-based algorithms. A study of classifying age groups using typing patterns was conducted in 2018 [7]. The study was conducted with machine learning algorithms such as nearest neighbors and support vector machines to separate minors from Internet users using benchmark data, resulting in 91.2% accuracy. Bai et al. detect eavesdroppers based on acoustic signals [8]. Yu et al. [9] and Zhang et al. [10] researched field event detection in the information security and network security areas. Guruprakash et al. applied genetic algorithms in the IoT domain [11]. Most of the proposed standard machine learning algorithms in the literature work well [12], yet the results can be improved. Therefore, in this study, we proposed a deep learning-based algorithm. Our research indicates that using deep learning algorithms is more significant than the standard machine learning algorithms.

3   Keystroke Dynamic Dataset

A powerful keystroke analysis system has many benefits, such as low cost, transparency, non-invasion to its users, and continuous monitoring of the system. Keystroke dynamic is a research area that learns the unique pattern of typing of each individual. Information such as when the keys on the keyboard are pressed or raised and switch movement from one key to another can be extracted. Dynamic Keystroke refers to a person's keyboard typing pattern that reflects their unique writing style and signatures. In this study, we used the Keystroke dynamic dataset [13]. The dataset is in a tabular format with 31 columns as shown in Table 1.

Table 1. Dataset description

# of Samples	# of Features	# of Classes	# of TrainingData	# of TestingData
20400	31	51	14280	6120

Each row in the dataset represents the time taken by the individual subject to enter the password. A sample row with all fields is listed in Table 2. The subject value in the first column is an unique identifier. The dataset comprises 51 subjects (classes), but not each subject contributed to every session. SessionIndex ranging from 1 to 8 is the feature representing the session in which the password was entered. Rep column ranging from 1 to 50 is another feature representing the password repetition in the corresponding session. The remaining features represent the timing info for the typed password. Feature name of the type H.key indicates the time difference between pressing and releasing the key (i.e. hold time). Feature name of the type DD.key1.key2 marks the time taken between pressing down key 1 to pressing down key 2. Feature name of the type UD.key1.key2 indicates the time from releasing key1 to pressing down key2.

The sample row shown in Table 2 represent feature vector for subject 7, with session 5 and repetition 8. All subjects (users) entered the same password (".tie5Roanl" followed by Return key) for all sessions and repetitions. In this sample row, the subject (user) held down time for the period key was *0.1732*s, the time taken between pressing down '.'

Table 2. Sample dataset

Subject	SessionIndex	Rep	H.period	DD.period.t	UD.period.t	...
S007	5	8	0.1732	0.3861	0.2377	...

key and 't' key was *0.3861*s, and the time elapsed between the release of '.' key to the pressing of 't' key was *0.2377*s and so on.

4   Proposed Framework

The proposed framework is described in Fig. 1. It has mainly four stages: Dataset Collection, Data Pre-Processing, Detection Algorithm Training, and Deployment. Below we provide details for each of the stages in brief.

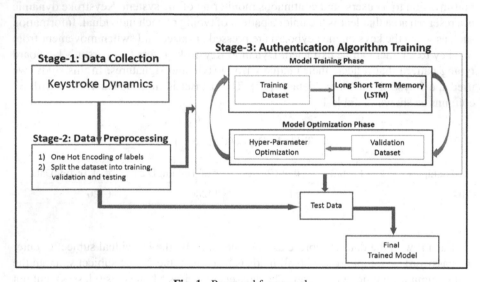

Fig. 1. Proposed framework

Stage-1: Data Collection
We use the keystroke dynamic dataset collected from [1] as described in the previous section.

Stage-2: Data Preprocessing
In this stage, we perform the following data preprocessing task:

1) One Hot encoding of the labels
2) Split the dataset for training, validation, and testing using stratified sampling.

Stage-3: Authentication Algorithm Training
This is the main stage of the whole framework where we train the authentication algorithm in two sub-phases as below:

3.1) Model Training Phase
    Here we train a deep learning-based Long short term memory algorithm using the training dataset [14].
    LSTM is one of the types of recurrent neural networks (RNN). In addition to RNN [15], LSTM has memory cells [16]. To overcome the inaccuracies of the RNN, gates have been attached to the LSTM system. These gates act as a memory. The memory is updated when the cell reads an input. LSTMs have the following gates.

Forget gate: It controls the volume of info to be removed.
Memory gate: It is used to create a new memory.
Input gate: It regulates the total of new memory info that needs to be updated.
Output gate: The output gate decides the amount of the memory cell info that needs to be extracted and updates the new hidden state.

    With the presence of such internal memory, the long term dependency problem of RNN is overcome.
    Given a sample dataset in the form of a $= (a_1, a_2, a_3, a_{N-1}, a_N)$ as input to network, it learns the output variable by updating the values of the above four gates in hidden layer. It is updated as follows:

$$(a_t, d_{t-1}, s_{t-1}) \rightarrow (d_t, s_t) \tag{1}$$

$$i_t = \sigma(p_{ai}a_t + p_{di}d_{t-1} + p_{si}z_{t-1} + k_i) \tag{2}$$

$$f_t = \sigma(p_{af}a_t + p_{df}d_{t-1} + p_{zf}z_{t-1} + k_f) \tag{3}$$

$$z_t = f_t * z_{t-1} + i_t * \tanh(p_{az}a_t + p_{dz}d_{t-1} + k_z) \tag{4}$$

$$y_t = \sigma(p_{ay}a_t + p_{dy}d_{t-1} + p_{zy}z_t + k_y) \tag{5}$$

$$d_t = y_t * \tanh(z_t) \tag{6}$$

where k_i, k_f, k_y, k_z denotes the bias units for the input gate, forget gate, output gate, and memory cell, respectively. Furthermore, the weight matrix is denoted by p, memory state as z, and hidden layer output as d. We also have tanh and sigmoid activation functions.
    We developed and trained the LSTM model architecture shown in Fig. 2. The dataset is divided into training and testing with 70% and 30%, respectively. Additionally, we use K-fold cross-validation approach with K = 10 to get the optimal hyper-parameters value. The proposed architecture has four LSTM layers and four dropout layers. We used the dropout layer to avoid overfitting. Each LSTM layer has 96 neurons. Finally, we have the dense layer at the end used to classify the subjects.

We used the following metrics to evaluate the model.

$$Recall = TP/(TP + FN) \tag{7}$$

$$Precision = TP/(TP + FP) \tag{8}$$

$$Specificity = TN/(TN + FP) \tag{9}$$

$$Accuracy = (TP + TN)/(TP + FP + FN + TN) \tag{10}$$

$$False\ Negative\ Rate\ (FNR) = FN/(TP + FN) \tag{11}$$

$$False\ Positive\ Rate\ (FPR) = FP/(FP + TN) \tag{12}$$

Where TP: True positive, FN: False Negative, TN: True Negative, and FP: False Positive.

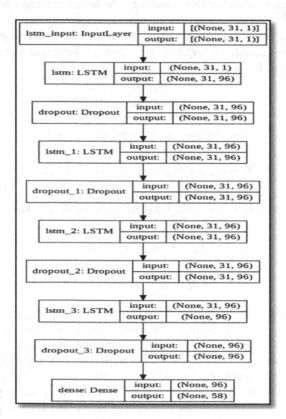

Fig. 2. LSTM model

3.2) Model Optimization Phase

We used the validation dataset to perform the hyper-parameters optimization of our LSTM learning model [17]. The following hyper-parameters are tuned:

- Epochs: Number of times a model is trained on the entire dataset.
- Batch-size: Number of data points used to train the LSTM model before each weight update of the model.

Once we train our LSTM model with fine-tune optimization, we evaluate it with our test data and generate the final testing accuracy. This final trained model can be used for actual user authentication.

5   Experimental Results

We trained the LSTM model with ReLu (Rectifier Linear Unit) as an activation function in hidden layers and SoftMax activation in the dense output layer. Furthermore, we use Adam optimizer to update the gradients to get the optimal weights and calculate the loss using categorical cross-entropy metrics. A Batch-size of 64 gives the optimal accuracy rate.

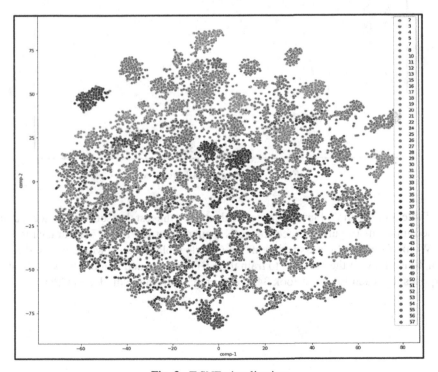

Fig. 3. T-SNE visualization

Figure 3 shows the two-dimensional view of the dataset. These two principal dimensions are extracted using T-SNE (T-distributed stochastic neighbor embedding) algorithm [18]. From this figure, we can observe that each subject has his/her typing behavior. Since there is a distinct cluster for each subject with a unique color as in the right palette, this dataset can be used for authentication classification purposes.

BatchSize is one of the hyper-parameter that needs to be tuned while training the deep neural network. There are three variants of setting the batch size values. They are batch gradient descent, stochastic batch gradient descent, and mini-batch gradient descent. In batch gradient descent, we update the weights at the end of the training data. Next, in stochastic gradient descent, we update the weights at every data point. Lastly, in mini-batch gradient descent, we update the weights at the end of every batch of data.

We used the mini-batch gradient descent algorithm and trained the LSTM network with batch sizes of {16, 32, 64, and 128}. Figure 4 shows the accuracy value for batch size. We found out that batch size 32 gives the highest accuracy of 0.989.

Figure 5 shows the accuracy value at each Epoch, whereas Fig. 6 shows the loss at each Epoch. Our trained model gives 98% accuracy rate with a loss of 0.05%.

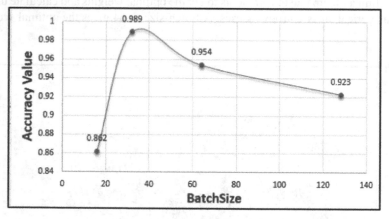

Fig. 4. Accuracy w.r.t BatchSize

Table 3 shows the achieved metrics evaluated on the test dataset. We can see that the trained model distinguished each subject's typing patterns with 98% accuracy rate.

We performed all our experiments on Google Colaboratory, where we used Keras with TensorFlow at the backend to train the LSTM model and seaborn for visualization purposes. For each Epoch, it took 34 s on average to train the model on CPU.

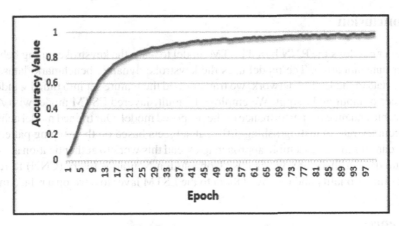

Fig. 5. Accuracy w.r.t epoch

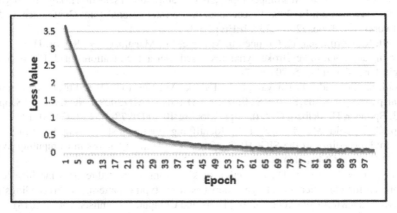

Fig. 6. Loss w.r.t epoch

Table 3. Evaluated metrics

Recall	Specificity	Precision	FPR	FNR	Accuracy
0.896	0.987	0.899	0.002	0.103	0.989

6   Conclusion

This paper employs the RNN based LSTM model to learn the keystroke typing behavior for user authentication. The model uses the keystroke dynamic benchmark dataset. To feed the data to the LSTM network, we transformed the feature set into timed windowed sequences of input and output. We employed a multi-layered LSTM model with Adam optimizer to enhance the performance of the proposed model. Our trained model achieved 98% accuracy rate in distinguishing different subjects based on their typing patterns.

We can employ an ensemble approach to extend this work to authentication accuracy of the model. Furthermore, we can use Convolution Neural Network (CNN) to reduce feature dimensionality and then feed them to the LSTM layer to develop a robust model.

References

1. Jain, A.K., Ross, A., Prabhakar, S.: An introduction to biometric recognition. IEEE Trans. Circ. Syst. Video Technol. Spec. Issue Image Video-Based Biometr. **14**(1), 4–20 (2004)
2. Bergadano, F., Gunetti, D., Picardi, C.: User authentication through keystroke dynamics. ACM Trans. Inf. Syst. Secur. (TISSEC) **5**(4), 367–397 (2002)
3. Yu, E., Cho, S.: GA-SVM wrapper approach for feature subset selection in keystroke dynamics identity verification. In: 2003 Proceedings of the International Joint Conference on Neural Networks, vol. 3, pp. 2253–2257. IEEE (2003)
4. Revett, K., Gorunescu, F., Gorunescu, M., Ene, M., Magalhaes, S., Santos, H.: A machine learning approach to keystroke dynamics based user authentication. Int. J. Electron. Secur. Digit. Forensics **1**(1), 55–70 (2007)
5. Zahid, S., Shahzad, M., Khayam, S.A., Farooq, M.: Keystroke-based user identification on smartphones. In: Kirda, E., Jha, S., Balzarotti, D. (eds.) RAID 2009. LNCS, vol. 5758, pp. 224–243. Springer, Heidelberg (2009). https://doi.org/10.1007/978-3-642-04342-0_12
6. Epp, C., Lippold, M., Mandryk, R.L.: Identifying emotional states using keystroke dynamics. In: Proceedings of the SIGCHI Conference on Human Factors in Computing Systems, pp. 715–724. ACM (2011)
7. Roy, S., Roy, U., Sinha, D.: Protection of kids from internet threats: a machine learning approach for classification of age-group based on typing pattern. In: Proceedings of the International MultiConference of Engineers and Computer Scientists, vol. 1 (2018)
8. Bai, J.-X., Liu, B., Song, L.: I Know your keyboard input: a robust keystroke eavesdropper based-on acoustic signals. In: Proceedings of the 29th ACM International Conference on Multimedia, pp. 1239–1247 (2021)
9. Yu, W., Huang, X., Yuan, Q., Yi, M., An, S., Li, X.: Information security field event detection technology based on SAtt-LSTM. Secur. Commun. Netw. **2021** (2021)
10. Zhang, H., Kang, C., Xiao, Y.: Research on network security situation awareness based on the LSTM-DT model. Sensors **21**(14), 4788 (2021)
11. Guruprakash, J., Koppu, S.: EC-ElGamal and Genetic algorithm-based enhancement for lightweight scalable blockchain in IoT domain. IEEE Access **8**, 141269–141281 (2020)
12. Soni, J., Prabakar, N., Upadhyay, H.: Feature extraction through deepwalk on weighted graph. In: Proceedings of the 15th International Conference on Data Science (ICDATA 2019), Las Vegas, NV (2019)
13. Killourhy, K.S., Maxion, R.A.: Comparing anomaly-detection algorithms for keystroke dynamics. In: Proceedings of the International Conference on Dependable Systems and Networks, pp. 125–134 (2009). https://doi.org/10.1109/DSN.2009.5270346

14. Lecun, Y., Bengio, Y., Hinton, G.: Deep learning. Nature **521**, 436–444 (2015). https://doi. org/10.1038/nature14539
15. Zaremba, W., Sutskever, I., Vinyals, O.: Recurrent neural network regularization. arXiv preprint arXiv:1409.2329, 8 September 2014
16. Greff, K., Srivastava, R.K., Koutník, J., Steunebrink, B.R., Schmidhuber, J.: LSTM: a search space odyssey. IEEE Trans. Neural Netw. Learn. Syst. **28**(10), 2222–2232 (2016)
17. Soni, J., Prabakar, N., Upadhyay, H.: Behavioral analysis of system call sequences using LSTM Seq-Seq, cosine similarity and jaccard similarity for real-time anomaly detection. In: 2019 International Conference on Computational Science and Computational Intelligence (CSCI), pp. 214–219 (2019). https://doi.org/10.1109/CSCI49370.2019.00043
18. Soni, J., Prabakar, N., Upadhyay, H.: Visualizing high-dimensional data using t-distributed stochastic neighbor embedding algorithm. In: Arabnia, H.R., Daimi, K., Stahlbock, R., Soviany, C., Heilig, L., Brüssau, K. (eds.) Principles of Data Science. TCSCI, pp. 189–206. Springer, Cham (2020). https://doi.org/10.1007/978-3-030-43981-1_9

Emotion Recognition from Brain Signals While Subjected to Music Videos

Puneeth Yashasvi Kashyap Apparasu and S. R. Sreeja[✉]

Department of Computer Science and Engineering, Indian Institute of Information Technology Sri City, Chittoor, Andhra Pradesh, India
{puneethyashasvi.a18,sreeja.sr}@iiits.in

Abstract. Emotions are simple, yet complex windows to the brain. Music and emotions are associated closely together. There are few things that stimulate the brain the way music does. It can be used as a powerful tool to regulate one's emotions. In recent years, emotion detection using brain waves has become an active topic of research. Various researchers are implementing different feature extraction techniques and machine learning models to classify the emotion by predicting the measurement of the electroencephalography signals. Many researchers are working on improving the accuracy of this problem and employing different techniques. In our study, we looked into achieving good scores by trying to predict the actual 4 emotional quadrants of the 2 dimensional Valence-Arousal plane. We evaluated and looked into various feature extraction approaches, modeling approaches and tried to combine best practices in our approach. We used the publicly available DEAP dataset for this study. Features from multiple domains were extracted from the EEG data and various statistical metrics and measures were extracted per channel. In our proposed approach, a one-dimensional convolutional neural network and a two-dimensional convolution neural network model were combined and fed through a neural network to classify the four quadrants of emotions. We did extensive and systematic experiments on the proposed approach over the benchmark dataset. The research findings that may be of significant interest to the user adaptation and personalization are presented in this study.

Keywords: Electroencephalography (EEG) · Emotion recognition · Music · Feature extraction · Classification

1 Introduction

Emotions are the purest forms of communication. They transcend all languages. What exactly is emotion? According to Merriam-Webster dictionary [1], emotion is a conscious mental reaction (such as anger or fear) subjectively experienced as a strong feeling usually directed toward a specific object and typically accompanied by physiological and behavioral changes in the body. It is a state of mind and a response to a particular stimulus. There are six primary emotions namely

J.-H. Kim et al. (Eds.): IHCI 2021, LNCS 13184, pp. 772–782, 2022.
https://doi.org/10.1007/978-3-030-98404-5_68

happy, sad, fear, anger, surprise, and disgust. There are many secondary and tertiary emotions. To understand them we can use the colour analogy where we can consider the primary emotions as the primary colours which when mixed forms secondary colours and tertiary colours. An emotion wheel is a good representation of all the different emotions.

Music has a high impact on the brain. Music can change one's ability to perceive time, improve mood, evoke memories, assist in repairing brain damage and much more. Music has the ability to evoke and change emotions. Basic human emotion can be expressed through facial expressions [18], eyes or body movement but it is difficult for an untrained eye to decide what the emotions are and how strong they are. Primarily, emotions and behaviors are nothing but communication between neurons in our brains. Apart from analysing brain waves, emotions can also be detected using pupillometry, facial expressions, heart rate. Discrete emotions like happiness and anger can also be detected by speech patterns and handwriting. In this work, our main focus is to identify the emotions using Electroencephalogram (EEG) brain signals.

There are billions of cells in our brain. Half of them are neurons, while the rest help and ease the activity of neurons. Synapses are gaps that separate two neurons. Neurons communicate by releasing chemicals that travel across these gaps. Activity in the synapses generates a faint electrical impulse known as the post-synaptic potential. When a large number of neurons activate at once, an electric field that is strong enough to spread through tissue and skull is generated [5]. Eventually, it can be measured on the scalp. This electrical impulse is then captured by the BCI devices. Apart from EEG, there are various BCI noninvasive devices like positron emission tomography or PET, functional near infrared or fNIR, Magnetoencephalography or MEG, functional resonance imaging or fMRI have been accepted and employed to measure the brain signals in both medical and non-medical contexts. Although there are many ways of identifying emotions, methods like EEG have shown potential in recent times [5]. EEG is an effective tool to record the electrical impulses our brain cells produce to communicate with each other. It has small metal disks or electrodes that are attached to the subjects head where each electrode records the electrical impulse of the corresponding part of the brain they are located at.

Generally, Emotions can be described in a two-dimensional space of valence and arousal. Valence is a positive or negative effect whereas arousal indicates how exciting or calming the stimulation is. Arousal arises from the reptilian part of our brain. It stimulates a fight or flight response that helps in our survival [7]. The objective of this study is to detect human emotions by inspecting and analyzing the brainwaves, which are generated by synchronised electrical pulses from a bunch of neurons communicating with each other. The data points collected from analyzing the brainwaves would then be used to classify the emotions using various techniques in our arsenal.

2   Literature Survey

Emotions have a key role in determining the stress level and they can interpret the positive emotional effect on an individual as per the study on the emotional effect of music therapy on palliative care cancer patients [15]. Various researchers are implementing different feature extraction techniques and machine learning models to classify the emotion by predicting the measurement of the psychological metrics. Many research works have been conducted recently on emotion recognition using EEG signals. Many studies tried constructing models by using different forms and aspects of the electrical signals represented by EEG and observed the results and reported the efficiency of their experiments.

From the literature, it is observed that some works used the time domain features of the EEG signal. Some works used other features from the frequency domain, wavelet domain, etc. There are also approaches that used features from multiple domains and fused them. In another work [18], the author used power spectral density (PSD) extracted from theta, alpha, beta and gamma bands as features and used them to train LSTM. In [22], the author used Gabor filter to extract the spatial and frequency domain features to train the SVM classifier. In [6], human emotion related features were extracted using multi-wavelet transformation. Normalized Renyi entropy, ratio of norms based measure and Shannon entropy were also used to measure the multi-wavelet decomposition of EEG signals. However, it is still a research problem, whether the extracted features are optimal features or not.

There are a good number of research papers available where human emotions were classified using different machine learning and deep learning algorithms [2,3,11,12,19–21]. In [3], to classify human emotions from EEG signals, the author used deep neural network and achieved an accuracy of 66.6% for valence, 66.4% for arousal classification. A recent work on EEG-based emotion detection system [2], used a Neucube-based SNN as a classifier, with an EEG dataset of fewer than 100 samples. They achieved an accuracy of 66.67% for valence classification and 69.23% for arousal classification. Even though, many researchers have made significant contributions and improvements in this field of research, most of the reported works used the classifiers for binary emotion classification problem.

3   Data and Method

This section will describe the EEG-based emotion dataset used in this research and then the proposed model for emotion classification.

3.1   Dataset Description

DEAP Dataset [13] is a multimodal dataset for the analysis of human affective states. The EEG and peripheral physiological signals of 32 participants were recorded as each watched 40 one-minute long excerpts of music videos. Participants rated each video in terms of the levels of arousal, valence, like/dislike, dominance and familiarity. For 22 of the 32 participants, frontal face video was also recorded. There are two parts in the DEAP dataset: the ratings rated by 14–16 volunteers based on arousal, valence and dominance when subjected to 120 one-minute music video extracts in an online self-assessment and the physiological recordings and face video of an experiment where 32 volunteers watched a subset of 40 music videos. The actual duration of each EEG signal is of 63 s, which includes the preparation time of 3 s. After pre-processing, the sampling frequency is down-sampled to 128 Hz (Table 1). The 2D valence-arousal emotional space is given in Fig. 1.

Table 1. Characterization of the dataset.

No. of stimuli	40
Stimuli duration	60 s each
Rating scale	Valence, arousal, liking, familiarity
Number of participants	32
Recorded signal properties	32 channel 512 Hz EEG
Total data points	1280 data points

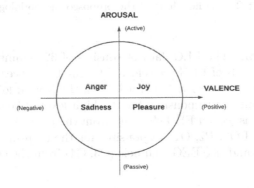

Fig. 1. The valence-arousal emotional plane.

3.2 Methodology

In this study, only the channels indicating EEG data were considered. A deep learning approach was used for emotion classification. The features from time domain, frequency domain, wavelet domain and statistical measures are extracted from EEG channels. For the target, the valence and arousal were separated into four emotions, namely *anger, joy, sadness* and *pleasure* as shown in Fig. 1. Both the multi-dimensional features and the statistical features are passed through two networks, a one-dimensional convolutional neural network and a two-dimensional convolutional neural network which are later merged together with the help of a merge layer and output results were observed. The methodology followed is outlined in Fig. 2.

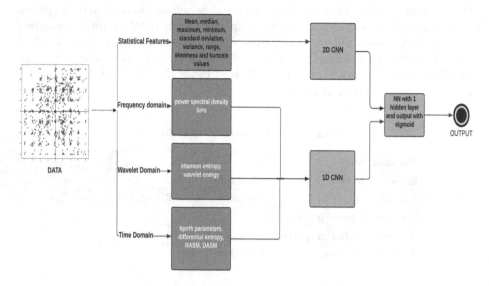

Fig. 2. The flowchart of the proposed methodology.

Channel Selection: The EEG dataset consists of 32 channels. Out of 32, the mandatory 16-channels of EEG are selected for further processing. The selected channels includes the *seven* EEG channels from the frontal lobe (Fp1, Fp2, F3, F4, F7, F8, Fz) that are responsible for the high level of cognitive, emotional, and mental functions; *seven* EEG channels from the parietal and occipital lobes (CP2, P3, P7, P8, PO3, Pz, O1) responsible for the auditory and visual information processing; and *two* EEG channels (C3, C4) from the central region were selected [8, 12].

Feature Extraction

Frequency Domain: As EEG data is a time-series data, which proves to be difficult for an in-depth analysis. Frequency domain is helpful in doing much deeper analysis as it captures the changes in the EEG data. Hence, Short-Time Fourier Transform (STFT) was used as it returns a time-frequency distribution that specifies complex amplitude versus time and frequency for any signal [16]. STFT is a Fourier-related transform used to determine the sinusoidal frequency and phase content of local sections of a signal as it changes over time [17]. In STFT, the signal is divided into shorter segments of equal lengths and fourier transform is performed on each segment. In our experiment, an STFT with a hanning window and a segment length of 64 with 50% overlap was performed per channel of the EEG data and the power spectrum features were extracted. The power spectrum is divided into 5 bands: Delta (0–4 Hz), Theta (4–8 Hz), Alpha (8–12 Hz), Beta (12–30 Hz), Gamma (30–45 Hz).

Time Domain: According to some researches, there is evidence that the asymmetry ratios between the left and right hemisphere of the brain affects the emotions [9]. Hence the differential asymmetry (DASM) and rational asymmetry (RASM) feature was calculated from the electrodes Fp1–Fp2 [12]. Hjorth parameters of activity, complexity and mobility and differential entropy of the signal were also calculated in the time domain.

Wavelet Domain: A wavelet is an oscillation, similar to a wave, which has an amplitude that starts at zero, rises, and comes back to zero. It is like a short oscillation similar to the recordings of a heart monitor or a seismograph. In general, wavelets are designed to have particular properties that make them beneficial for signal processing. As a mathematical tool, they can aid in extraction of information from a variety of data. Sets of wavelets are needed to inspect a data completely. A set of harmonious wavelets will decompose data in a stretch, making the decomposition process mathematically reversible [17]. Daubechies (*db1* and *db6*) wavelets which are usually used to decompose EEG signals, were used to transform the EEG data in our experiment. Daubechies wavelet with order 1 gave a better result in this use case. After performing discrete wavelet transform, the wavelet energy and Shannon entropy were extracted from the transformed data.

Statistical: Analogous to the methods in [20], *nine* statistical features, such as mean, median, maximum, minimum, standard deviation, variance, range, skewness and kurtosis were calculated for each channel data. Each EEG channel of 63 seconds has $63 * 128 = 8064$ data points, which was divided into 10 batches and then compressed to $(10 * 9)$ 90 data points.

Therefore, for 32 users and 40 stimuli ($32 * 40 = 1280$), *three* Hjorth parameters, *sixteen* differential entropies, *one* wavelet energy, *one* wavelet entropy, RASM, DASM and *five* bands of power spectrum features and statistical features $(1280, 90)$ were calculated.

Classification
As the dimensions of the statistical features and the multi-domain features are different, they cannot be passed through the same model without embedding or reshaping one of them. We did an experiment by reducing the dimensions using auto-encoder compression techniques and concatenating both the features, but the results were slightly on the lower end.

Hence, both the multi-domain features and the statistical features were taken as input to a one-dimensional convolutional neural network and a two-dimensional convolutional neural network and the outputs of these CNNs were flattened and merged together by passing it through a layer that concatenates both the outputs. The steps followed by the classification model is shown in Fig. 3. The combined output is then passed through a two layer neural network that is analogous with logistic regression (LR), *i.e.,* one hidden layer and an output layer with sigmoid activation function which predicts if it is the said emotion or not. We did experiment with creating a single neural network that classified all the four emotions with a help of a softmax activation function, but the accuracy achieved was very less.

In order to improve the performance of the model, a stochastic gradient descent (SGD) with learning rate of 0.00001 with decay of $1e-6$ and momentum of 0.9 was used to reduce the binary cross entropy loss of the model. The hyper-parameters of the models were tuned with help of keras-tuner [14], where a search space was created for each hyper-parameter, like number of filters in a convolutional layer, kernel shape, number of dense units and different values. The obtained optimal values were substituted to the model and the best model was taken by comparing the validation accuracies.

4   Experimental Results

From the selected 16 channels, multi-domain features and statistical features have been extracted and it is fed as input to two-dimensional CNN and one-dimensional CNN, respectively. From the extracted data, 33% of data was used for validation and the rest for training. With an early stopping call back, the models were trained with the data corresponding to the emotion it has to predict. The hyper-parameters for the classification model are tuned with keras-tuner [14]. For each emotion, the obtained optimized hyper-parameter are listed in Table 2.

The best classification model was selected based on the validation accuracies. The best accuracy obtained are noted and it is listed in Table 3. Except Joy (high arousal-positive valence), other emotions achieved an accuracy above 75% and we got the maximum accuracy for the emotion - pleasure (low arousal-positive valence), which achieved an accuracy of ≈81%.

Most of the existing works on emotion prediction concentrate on different signal transformation methods or different machine learning techniques. As most of the work on this DEAP standard dataset is on binary classification problem. Hence, in the following, we have listed some of the works where they achieved good accuracy on classifying multi-class emotions. The work by T. B. Alakus *et al.* [4] gave accuracies of 75.00% for High Arousal Positive Valence; 96.00% for High Arousal Negative Valence; 71.00% for Low Arousal Positive Valence; 79.00% for Low Arousal Negative Valence, respectively. Another work by Y. Huang *et al.* [10] which gave 74.84% Anger; 71.91% Boredom; 66.32% Fear; 63.38% Joy; 69.98% Neutral; 72.68% Sadness. Our proposed approach was also able to produce better results in most of the emotions.

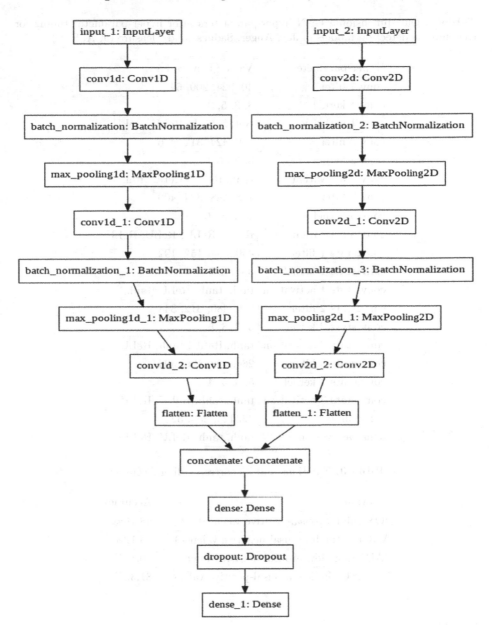

Fig. 3. The steps followed by the classification model.

Table 2. One dimensional CNN hyper-parameters after hyper-parameter tuning for the emotion detection models of Joy, Anger, Sadness and Pleasure (J, A, S, P)

Hyper-parameter	Value (J, A, S, P)
conv 1 filter	40, 224, 200, 64
conv 1 kernel	3, 3, 5, 3
conv 1 activation	ReLU, tanh, ReLU, ReLU
conv 2 filter	280, 424, 312, 416
conv 2 kernel	3, 3, 5, 3
conv 2 activation	tanh, ReLU, ReLU, ReLU
conv 3 filter	168, 488, 384, 400
conv 3 kernel	5, 3, 5, 3
conv 3 activation	ReLU, ReLU, ReLU, ReLU
conv_stats 1 filter	440, 384, 152, 192
conv_stats 1 kernel	3, 5, 3, 5
conv_stats 1 activation	tanh, tanh, ReLU, tanh
conv_stats 2 filter	240, 480, 312, 344
conv_stats 2 kernel	5, 3, 3, 5
conv_stats 2 activation	tanh, ReLU, tanh, ReLU
conv_stats 3 filter	264, 488, 176, 304
conv_stats 3 kernel	5, 3, 5, 4
conv_stats 3 activation	tanh, tanh, ReLU, ReLU
dense units	32, 128, 256, 32
dense activation	tanh, tanh, ReLU, ReLU

Table 3. Emotions and its corresponding Accuracy

Emotion	Accuracy
JOY (high arousal-positive valence)	68.79%
ANGER (high arousal-negative valence)	76.12%
SADNESS (low arousal-negative valence)	80.14%
PLEASURE (low arousal-positive valence)	81.32%

5   Conclusion

Unlike many approaches, in this work statistical features and the features extracted from time, frequency and wavelet domain were combined and used as inputs to a set one-dimensional convolution and two-dimensional convolution models which were combined in a later layer to give an output. From the output, we can see that the model was able to give better accuracy for pleasure compared to other emotions. Future work includes experiment to broaden the emotion spectrum and improve the accuracies of the current emotions along with creating a *Music Recommendation system* that recommends music according to the emotions of a user.

References

1. Merriam-webster (n.d.). Emotion, in merriam-webster.com dictionary (2021). https://www.merriam-webster.com/dictionary/emotion
2. Al-Nafjan, A., Alharthi, K., Kurdi, H.: Lightweight building of an electroencephalogram-based emotion detection system. Brain Sci. **10**(11), 781 (2020)
3. Al-Nafjan, A., Hosny, M., Al-Wabil, A., Al-Ohali, Y.: Classification of human emotions from electroencephalogram (EEG) signal using deep neural network. Int. J. Adv. Comput. Sci. Appl. **8**(9), 419–425 (2017)
4. Alakus, T.B., Gonen, M., Turkoglu, I.: Database for an emotion recognition system based on EEG signals and various computer games-GAMEEMO. Biomed. Signal Process. Control **60**, 101951 (2020)
5. Arvaneh, M., Tanaka, T.: Brain-computer interfaces and electroencephalogram: basics and practical issues. Signal Process. Mach. Learn. Brain-Mach. Interfaces (2018)
6. Bajaj, V., Pachori, R.B.: Detection of human emotions using features based on the multiwavelet transform of EEG signals. In: Hassanien, A.E., Azar, A.T. (eds.) Brain-Computer Interfaces. ISRL, vol. 74, pp. 215–240. Springer, Cham (2015). https://doi.org/10.1007/978-3-319-10978-7_8
7. Birkett, A.: Valence, arousal, and how to kindle an emotional fire (2020). https://cxl.com/blog/valence-arousal-and-how-to-kindle-an-emotional-fire/
8. Choi, E.J., Kim, D.K.: Arousal and valence classification model based on long short-term memory and DEAP data for mental healthcare management. Healthc. Inform. Res. **24**(4), 309–316 (2018)
9. Davidson, R.J.: Anterior cerebral asymmetry and the nature of emotion. Brain Cogn. **20**(1), 125–151 (1992)
10. Huang, Y., Tian, K., Wu, A., Zhang, G.: Feature fusion methods research based on deep belief networks for speech emotion recognition under noise condition. J. Ambient. Intell. Humaniz. Comput. **10**(5), 1787–1798 (2017). https://doi.org/10.1007/s12652-017-0644-8
11. Islam, M.R., et al.: Emotion recognition from EEG signal focusing on deep learning and shallow learning techniques. IEEE Access **9**, 94601–94624 (2021)
12. Khateeb, M., Anwar, S.M., Alnowami, M.: Multi-domain feature fusion for emotion classification using DEAP dataset. IEEE Access **9**, 12134–12142 (2021)
13. Koelstra, S., et al.: DEAP: a database for emotion analysis; using physiological signals. IEEE Trans. Affect. Comput. **3**(1), 18–31 (2011)
14. O'Malley, T., et al.: Kerastuner (2019). https://github.com/keras-team/keras-tuner
15. Ramirez, R., Planas, J., Escude, N., Mercade, J., Farriols, C.: EEG-based analysis of the emotional effect of music therapy on palliative care cancer patients. Front. Psychol. **9**, 254 (2018)
16. DSP Related: The short-time fourier transform. https://www.dsprelated.com/freebooks/sasp/Short_Time_Fourier_Transform.html

17. Sejdić, E., Djurović, I., Jiang, J.: Time-frequency feature representation using energy concentration: an overview of recent advances. Digit. Signal Process. **19**(1), 153–183 (2009)
18. Soleymani, M., Asghari-Esfeden, S., Fu, Y., Pantic, M.: Analysis of EEG signals and facial expressions for continuous emotion detection. IEEE Trans. Affect. Comput. **7**(1), 17–28 (2015)
19. Teo, J., Hou, C.L., Mountstephens, J.: Deep learning for EEG-based preference classification. In: AIP Conference Proceedings, vol. 1891, p. 020141. AIP Publishing LLC (2017)
20. Tripathi, S., Acharya, S., Sharma, R.D., Mittal, S., Bhattacharya, S.: Using deep and convolutional neural networks for accurate emotion classification on DEAP dataset. In: Twenty-Ninth IAAI Conference (2017)
21. Yin, Y., Zheng, X., Hu, B., Zhang, Y., Cui, X.: EEG emotion recognition using fusion model of graph convolutional neural networks and LSTM. Appl. Soft Comput. **100**, 106954 (2021)
22. Zamanian, H., Farsi, H.: A new feature extraction method to improve emotion detection using EEG signals. ELCVIA: Electron. Lett. Comput. Vis. Image Anal. **17**(1), 29–44 (2018)

Author Index

Printed in the United States
by Baker & Taylor Publisher Services